963
H528

LAYERS OF TIME

PAUL B. HENZE first visited Ethiopia in 1962, as an officer of the U.S. Foreign Service. He was designated Political Counsellor of the American Embassy in Addis Ababa in 1968, and served there till August 1972. In 1977 he was appointed as a senior staff member of the National Security Council under Zbigniew Brzezinski in the Carter administration and was involved firsthand in the dramatic events of 1977-80 in the Horn of Africa, undertaking three official missions. On retiring from government service at the end of 1980, Henze became a Wilson Fellow at the Smithsonian Institution. He joined the RAND Corporation as a Resident Consultant in 1982.

PAUL B. HENZE

Layers of Time

A History of Ethiopia

ST. MARTIN'S PRESS, NEW YORK

LAYERS OF TIME

Copyright © 2000 by Paul B. Henze

All rights reserved. No part of this book may be used or reproduced in any manner whatsoever without written permission except in the case of brief quotations embodied in critical articles   or reviews. For information, address:

St. Martin's Press, Scholarly and Reference Division,
175 Fifth Avenue, New York, N.Y. 10010

First published in the United States of America in 2000

Printed in Malaysia

ISBN 0-312-22719-1

Library of Congress Catologing-in-Publication Data

Henze, Paul B., 1924-
    Layers of time : a history of Ethiopia / by Paul B. Henze.
        p. cm.
    Includes bibliographical references (p.) and index.
    ISBN   0-312-22719-1
    1. Ethiopia–History. I. Title
DT381.H465   2000
963–dc21   99-33311
                                                          CIP

CONTENTS

Preface and Acknowledgements	*page*	xi
Note on Dates and Names		xv
Glossary		xvi
Acronyms		xviii

Chapters

1. Layers of Time: The Geological and Human
   Foundations of Ethiopia: 1
   - *The Rift Valley and the Mediterranean* 1
   - *Early man in Ethiopia* 4
   - *The beginnings of civilization* 10
   - *Trade and travel from the Mediterranean world* 15
   - *South Arabia and Ethiopia* 19

2. The Aksumite Empire: Ethiopia as a World Power 22
   - *The rediscovery of Aksum* 22
   - *From city states to Empire* 26
   - *Coinage and Christianity* 30
   - *Architecture and artifacts* 34
   - *Language, writing, and evangelization* 37
   - *The final flowering of Aksum* 39
   - *The rise of Islam* 42

3. Medieval Ethiopia: Isolation and Expansion 44
   - *The decline of Aksum* 44
   - *The Zagwe Dynasty* 49
   - *The Beta Israel (Falashas) and the Kebra Negast* 53
   - *The Solomonic restoration* 56
   - *Iyasus Mo'a and Tekle Haymanot* 60
   - *From Amde Tseyon to Zara Yakob* 63
   - *The Christianization of Lake Tana and Gojjam* 72
   - *Language, art, and culture* 76

4. Ordeal, Recovery, Decline: Ethiopia and the World
   around it on the Threshold of Modern Times 83
   - *The growth of Muslim power in the Horn of Africa* 83
   - *Turks and Portuguese* 85
   - *Ahmad Gragn's assault on the Christian kingdom* 86

The advance of the Oromo   90
Portuguese success and failure   92
The Gondarine era   100
Europeans and Ethiopia   107
Regions and borderlands   110

5.   The Empire from Atrophy to Revival: The Era of the
     Princes and Tewodros II   119

The era of the Princes   119
Missionaries   125
The rise of Shoa   127
Tewodros II: from victory to disaster   133

6.   Yohannes IV and Menelik II: The Empire Restored,
     Expanded, and Defended   144

Menelik, King of Shoa   144
Menelik and Yohannes IV: competition and accommodation   146
The challenge of Italy   154
The end of Yohannes IV   159
Emperor Menelik II and the Powers   160
The prelude and the Battle of Adwa   167
Menelik's triumphal decade   171
Trade and diplomatic relations with America   176
The significance of Adwa   180
Menelik's final years   185

7.   The Rise of Haile Selassie: Time of Troubles, Regent,
     Emperor, Exile   188

Tafari's early years   189
Time of troubles   191
Ras Tafari and Empress Zewditu   198
Tafari and the outside world   199
Reform and opposition   202
Emperor Haile Selassie I   205
Economic development   209
Eritrea under Italy   210
Mussolini prepares to absorb Ethiopia   214
The Italian invasion   216
Europe, America, and the Ethiopian crisis   220
Africa Orientale Italiana (AOI)   223
Resistance   227

8. Ethiopia in the Modern World: Haile Selassie from
    Triumph to Tragedy   229

    Liberation   229
    Ethiopia, Britain and the United States   235
    Imperial consolidation   237
    The "disposal" of Eritrea   240
    Formalization of the American relationship   245
    The Weyane rebellion   248
    The Constitution of 1955   252
    The Bodyguard Coup of 1960   253
    Aftermath of the coup: education   256
    Aftermath of the coup: government and foreign affairs 258
    The legacy of the coup   259
    Insurgency in Bale   260
    Intellectual life, literature and art in the 1960s   265
    A quarter century of economic development   269
    The end of the Eritrean Federation   273
    *Ethiopia's international position at the beginning of
    the 1970s*   279

9. Revolution, War, and "Socialism": The First Decade
    of the Derg   282

    Prelude to revolution   282
    Ferment turns into revolution   284
    The Derg and Eritrea   287
    The proclamation of Ethiopian "Socialism"   290
    Moscow's dilemma   295
    The United States and the Derg   297
    The Ethio-Somali war and Soviet intervention   300
    The struggle in Eritrea   303
    Consolidation of the Soviet relationship   304

10. The End of the Derg: The Victory of the Northern
    Guerrilla Movements   308

    The Great Famine and its consequences   308
    The revolution unravelling   311
    A surprising Israeli initiative   315
    Reform and aftermath - too little too late   316
    Relations among guerrilla groups - positioning for victory 320
    United States involvement becomes decisive   323

Contents

The dog days of the Derg 327
The Derg disintegrates and EPRDF forces enter the capital 329
The rebel movements become governments 330

11. Ethiopia Resurgent: on the Threshold of the 21st Century 334

From the TGE to the FDRE and independent Eritrea 334
Looking backward 338
Looking forward 341

Bibliographic Guide to Further Reading 344

Index 361

ILLUSTRATIONS

between pages 46 and 47

The High Semien, the "Roof of Africa"
Rock carvings near Kersa, Arsi
Sabaean temple at Yeha, Tigray, 7th century BC
Stela Park, Aksum
Fallen monolithic Aksum stela
Church of Abba Libanos, Lalibela
6th-century monastery atop Debre Damo, Tigray
16th-century mosque, Massawa
New mosque at Negash, Tigray
Pages from Tullu Gudo Book of Saints (14th century)
Castles at Gondar
Peasant farmer plowing

between pages 146 and 147

Sahle Selassie, King of Shoa, receiving gifts from the Harris expedition, Ankober, 1841
Slaves being led to the coast, 19th century
Church of St Michael, Ankober
Magdala burning, 17th April 1868
Emperor Yohannes IV
Emperor Menelik II
Empress Taitu Betul
Church of Enda Giyorgis, Adwa
Ras Tafari and Princess Menen Asfaw at the time of their marriage, 3 August 1911
Emperor Haile Selassie, Bath, 1937

between pages 288 and 289

Haile Selassie with Mao Zedong, Beijing, October 1971
Painting of Mengistu Haile Mariam
Revolution Square, Addis Ababa, 1980
Kiros and Ali, Kishe resettlement site, 1987–an example of the Derg's policy of ethnic mixing
Derg soldiers expelled from Eritrea, Adwa, July 1991
Lenin's statue: in place; painting of it being pulled down by the crowd; fallen and dumped at the edge of the city
Bullet-ridden portrait of Mengistu, June 1991
Classical Arab street architecture, Massawa
Oromo farmer in Arsi with his 12 children, 1989

MAPS

Ancient Ethiopia   xx
Medieval Ethiopia   xxi
Modern Ethiopia   xxii
Provinces, 1946-1980   xxiii
Federal Ethiopia (since 1994)   xxiv

PREFACE AND ACKNOWLEDGEMENTS

Since the fall of the Derg in 1991, Ethiopia has once again become open to the world. Officials, businessmen, scholars, students and tourists visit it in increasing numbers. Exhibitions, new archaeological discoveries, reports and articles in journals and even newspapers (many of them available on the Internet) now draw attention to the country's long history, its culture, its art, and the immense variety of peoples and ways of life that exist there. How did it all happen? Time and again I have been asked to recommend a comprehensive history of the country, one extending from very ancient times to the modern era. I decided three years ago to write one myself.

Like many Americans, I became aware of Ethiopia as a boy of eleven when news of Mussolini's invasion shocked the world. As a young adult I read several of the classic travel accounts – Nesbitt's *Desert and Forest*, e.g. – well before I had an opportunity to set foot in the country in 1962 when I spent a week there at the end of a long official visit to Africa. I resolved to go back as soon as I had the opportunity. In 1968 I requested assignment to the American Embassy in Addis Ababa and had the good fortune to be selected. These were the last years of the imperial era when the whole country was open. It was easy to make friends with Ethiopians at all levels of society. Compared to the developed world, Ethiopia was still backward, but it was enjoying a level of peace and prosperity it had never attained before in its long history. It was also beginning to outstrip the capacity of the last Lion of Judah to lead it onward, but when I said good-bye to him in August 1972, I found him alert and abreast of developments in the world.

I described impressions of some of the people and places I encountered in travels during those years in *Ethiopian Journeys, 1969-1972*,[1] a book written in 1973 but not published until four years later when the military junta that seized power in 1974 had plunged the country into chaos.

In 1977, when I joined Zbigniew Brzezinski as a senior staff officer of the US National Security Council, I found myself in the thick of Ethiopian affairs again and was officially involved in Ethiopia and the Horn of Africa for the next four years. When President Carter sent me to Ethiopia in September 1977 to find out whether the country was falling apart, I met Mengistu Haile Mariam in Haile Selassie's palace. He and the country had fallen into a deep crisis. But on the streets and in the countryside I sensed that

[1] Ernest Benn, London, 1977.

the country was rallying to defeat the invading Somalis. On return to Washington I advised the President that the United States should not give up on Ethiopia – it would somehow survive its travails. The Soviets, whom Mengistu admired, drove the Somalis back, but in the following years did little else to help. When famine struck in the mid-1980s, Americans and Europeans led the world in coming to the rescue. As Mengistu worked himself ever deeper into difficulties, the United States again took the lead in facilitating his departure and a peaceful transition to a new government.

I made nine visits to Ethiopia during the Derg era, the first two official, the other seven after I left US Government service at the end of 1980. Most of these visits lasted several weeks. I traveled throughout most of the country. First as a Fellow of the Wilson Center for Scholars at the Smithsonian Institution and afterwards as a Resident Consultant at RAND's Washington office I was continually involved in research, writing and lecturing on Ethiopia and neighboring countries. I came to know all the leading exiles who escaped or defected from Mengistu's regime, as well as the major guerrilla leaders who defeated the Derg from the inside. On 28 May 1991, the day the Derg finally collapsed, Meles Zenawi telephoned from London and asked me to come to observe the transition. I spent most of June and July 1991 in Ethiopia and, as of early 1999, I have made nine visits to the country since totalling almost three-quarters of a year. I was an observer in the 1993 referendum in Eritrea and have visited it on four other occasions. I have traveled to all parts of Ethiopia to see the process of recovery under way and have spent many weeks in remote regions in the northern countryside in historical and cultural research.

I have published more articles on Ethiopia than I can count during the past quarter century. I have also published three books and several monographs on Ethiopia and the Horn. I have always regarded myself more as a participant in history than as an academic historian. I was persuaded three years ago that I should capitalize on my firsthand experience, my reading, and all my other contacts and involvements with Ethiopia by writing a comprehensive history of the country. This book is the result.

I hope it will be read with pleasure and benefit by a wide audience – ranging from travellers to the country, journalists and diplomats in need of background and reference material, to Ethiopian intellectuals and Ethiopians in all walks of life, not in the least students who have had precious little to read about their own history during the past two decades. I have tried to reflect as much of the latest and best research as possible. Ethiopia's long history still has many shadowy and blank spots. There is controversy about facts and dates, let alone interpretations of events and motives of leaders. I have tried to avoid arcane and pedantic detail, but I have had to point out areas and issues of uncertainty. I have not hesitated to offer judgments and opinions. I have tried to enliven all the chapters with quotations from participants in the history I recount. I have also included recollections of my own experiences where they make personalities and events alive.

I have made a continual effort to put Ethiopia's history into perspective. Ethiopia has been an important part of my life, but by the time I became involved with it, I had already studied and worked in, and on, several other parts of the world: Germany, Eastern Europe, Russia and her colonies, especially the Caucasus and Central Asia, and Turkey. I gained my first intense experience of the world as an eighteen-year-old soldier in World War II and crossed into Germany in September 1944. I have had the good fortune to be close to many of the other great events of the twentieth century ever since. Experience and knowledge of old countries undergoing change and development and recovering from the effects of authoritarian abuse and totalitarian zeal have deepened my understanding of Ethiopia. The late Hugh Seton-Watson, who was my good friend, wrote nearly forty years ago:

Of all my travels I think the most enlightening were in the Balkans, whose combination of intellectual subtlety and crudity, of tortuous intrigue and honest courage revealed more truths about the political animal man than are to be found in most textbooks of political science.[2]

I can say the same about my travels in Ethiopia and my excursions through its history. I have no sympathy with the naive deconstructionists who denigrate Ethiopia's historical experience and claim that the country is an artificial, even mythical construct. Its people have always known that it is one of the oldest political entities in the world. Ethiopia is a country where history is always alive. The landscape reflects it, as do the faces of the people. Ethiopia's history is worth telling.

I have been fortunate in having many Ethiopians and foreign scholars of Ethiopia read the eleven chapters which follow. All have been helpful. Some have provided additional facts and kept me from making errors. Nevertheless I am sure there are imperfections and omissions. Some of my conclusions may be debatable. I am eager to hear them debated and to participate in the process.

---

[2] *Neither War nor Peace*, Methuen, London, 1960, p. 15.

Acknowledgements

I owe gratitude to many people who have aided and supported me in producing this book. As important as any are the hundreds – perhaps thousands – of Ethiopians who have offered hospitality, information and insights into their country in my travels through most parts of it over three decades. I am grateful to the US Government for the opportunities it gave me to live in Ethiopia, revisit the country again and again, and become involved in relations with it at critical periods in its history. Over the years a succession of American ambassadors and their staffs, both Americans and Ethiopians, have provided me with hospitality on the beautiful embassy "campus" in Addis Ababa. I am thankful to them.

It is obvious that a book as comprehensive as this rests on the work of generations of travellers, archaeologists, scholars, diplomats and others who have explored Ethiopia, lived and worked there, and studied the country and its peoples. I have drawn on much of this literature and provided references for those who wish to read more deeply. In the course of writing these chapters I have enjoyed the good will and direct support of several dozen Ethiopian and *ferenji* scholars. I will list only those who provided specific information or suggestions, reviewed drafts, or served directly as sources of fact and interpretation: Asfa Wossen Asserate, Bahru Zewde, Kathryn Bard, Stanislaw Chojnacki, Christopher Clapham, Haggai Erlich, Thomas Kane, Richard Pankhurst, Shifferaw Bekele, Taddesse Tamrat, Teshome Gebre Mariam and Wudu Tafete. Judgments and conclusions, of course, are mine, not theirs. They share no responsibility for errors and omissions I may have made.

No one has been more supportive and helpful than my wife Martha whose knowledge and understanding of Ethiopia extends my own. Over thirty years she has been a lively and perceptive companion on my travels. She has been invaluable as a reviewer and critic of everything I have written.

Finally I would like to express my deep appreciation to Michael Dwyer who persuaded me to write this book. He and Christopher Hurst have led me through the process of editing and publication with keen interest and professional skill.

Washington, DC   PAUL B. HENZE
August 1999

NOTE ON DATES AND NAMES

There is no universally recognized system for transliterating Ethiopian languages into the Latin alphabet. To avoid adding to the confusion I have refrained from inventing my own or from using diacritical marks for words and phrases in Amharic or other Ethiopian languages. In reproducing names of places and people I have used forms which are simple and familiar in current international usage and which approximate local pronunciation. In citations the spelling or transliteration of the original source is used; therefore the reader will notice inconsistencies from time to time. The glossary includes terms in Amharic or other languages used in the text.

The Ethiopian calendar runs from September to September and is thus seven or eight years behind the Gregorian calendar. Ethiopian months do not match ours, but overlap. All years and specific dates have been transposed into the Gregorian calendar. In the rare instance where an Ethiopian date is cited, it is preceded by "EC".

Ethiopians do not use surnames. The same system is used by both Christians and Muslims. An individual's name consists of his proper name followed by his father's name. Individuals are, therefore, normally referred to by their proper (i.e. first) name. Both the proper name and the father's name may have two components; thus a name may consist of three or four words. In addition secular or religious titles may be added to one or both names. I have tried to include all titles used in the text in the glossary. Many Ethiopian names are, in effect, phrases. I have translated many in brackets. Wives do not take their husbands' names. Three courtesy titles are used in Ethiopia: *Ato* (Mr), *Woizero* (Mrs), and *Woizerit* (Miss).

GLOSSARY

ABBREVIATIONS

Amh. = Amharic; bot. = botanical; Gz. = Ge'ez; rel. = religious

abba	father (rel.)
Abbay	Blue Nile
Abun(a)	bishop, patriarch
amba	flat-topped mountain, mesa
amole	salt bar
arbanya	partisan, Patriot
atse	emperor, king (title)
bahr, bahir	sea, lake
bet	house
birr	silver, basic unit of currency
bisi	"man of" (Gz.)
Bitwoded	"Beloved", privy counsellor (title)
buna	coffee
chat	Catha edulis, shrub whose leaves are chewed as a narcotic (bot.)
Dejazmach	"Guardian of the Gate", count, general (title)
Derg	committee, common term for the communist regime, 1974-91.
echege	archbishop, traditional head of the Monastery of Debre Libanos
Enderassie	Viceroy (title)
enset(e)	*Ensete edulis*, false banana (bot.)
eqabet	treasury
gadla	chronicle
genet	paradise
Germawi	Imperial, exalted (title)
gesho	*Rhamnus prinoides*, leaf used as a fermenting agent (bot.)
gra, gragn	left
habesh	Abyssinian
hizb	people
Itege	Empress (title)
Ityopya Tikdem	"Ethiopia First", Derg slogan
ketema	fortified camp, town

kosso	tree whose blossoms are used as a vermifuge
Leul	Prince (title)
Liquamaquas	personal aide, alter ego (title)
lisan	language, tongue
Meridazmach	"Reserve Commander", "Chief of Staff " (title)
merikani	white cotton cloth
neftanya	rifleman, settler
negarit	ceremonial drum
negash	ruler
negus	king
Negusa negast	King of Kings, Emperor (title)
nug	*Guizotia abyssinica,* Niger flower, safflower (bot.)
Orit	Old Testament (rel.)
quanqua	language
Ras	Duke, literally head (title)
samena worq	wax and gold
Shaleqa	Major (title)
shengo	assembly, parliament
shifta	outlaw, bandit
shumshir	shifting of officials, shuffle
tabot	sacred tablet of a church, ark
talla	home-brewed beer
tarik	history
tezkar	commemorative feast forty days after a death
timqat	baptism
tsadkan	"Righteous Ones" (Gz.)
worq	gold
zemecha	campaign

ACRONYMS

AAU	Addis Ababa University
AOI	Africa Orientale Italiana
BIEA	British Institute in Eastern Africa (Nairobi)
CELU	Confederation of Ethiopian Labor Unions
COPWE	Committee to Organize the Workers' Party of Ethiopia
DUPE	Democratic Unity Party of Ethiopia
EDU	Ethiopian Democratic Union
ELF	Eritrean Liberation Front
ELM	Eritrean Liberation Movement
EOC	Ethiopian Orthodox Church
EPDM	Ethiopian People's Democratic Movement
EPLF	Eritrean Popular Liberation Front
EPRDF	Ethiopian Popular Revolutionary Democratic Front
EPRP	Ethiopian Popular Revolutionary Party
ESUNA	Ethiopian Students' Association of North America
FDRE	Federal Democratic Republic of Ethiopia
HSI	Haile Selassie I
HSIU	Haile Selassie I University (AAU after 1975)
IEG	Imperial Ethiopian Government
IES	Institute of Ethiopian Studies
IMF	International Monetary Fund
JIES	Journal of the Institute of Ethiopian Studies
MEISON	All-Ethiopia Socialist Movement (Amh.)
OLF	Oromo Liberation Front
OPDO	Oromo People's Democratic Organization
PDFJ	Popular Front for Democracy and Justice (Eritrea)
PDRE	People's Democratic Republic of Ethiopia (third phase of the Derg)
PGE	Provisional Government of Eritrea
PMAC	Provisional Military Administrative Committee (first phase of the Derg)
PMGSE	Provisional Military Government of Socialist Ethiopia (second phase of the Derg)
TPLF	Tigray Popular Liberation Front
TGE	Transitional Government of Ethiopia
WPE	Workers' Party of Ethiopia (Amh. ESP)

MAPS

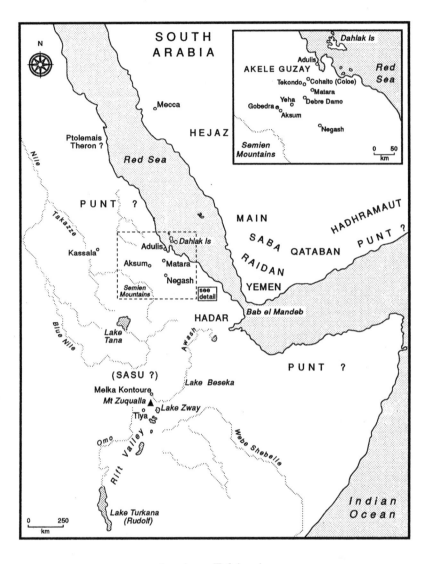

Ancient Ethiopia

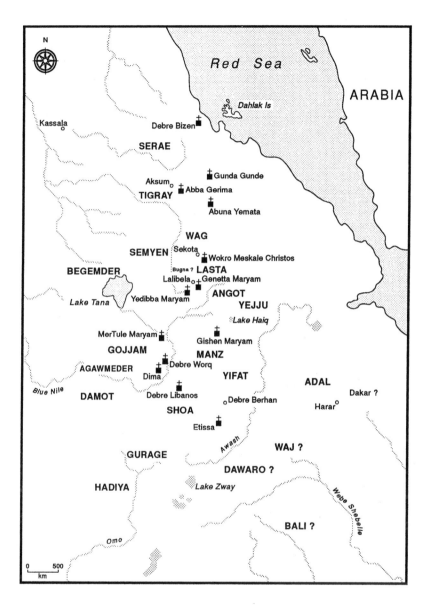

Medieval Ethiopia

Modern Ethiopia

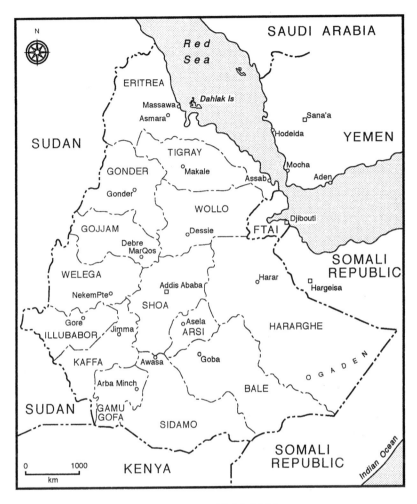

Provinces, 1946-1980

xxiii

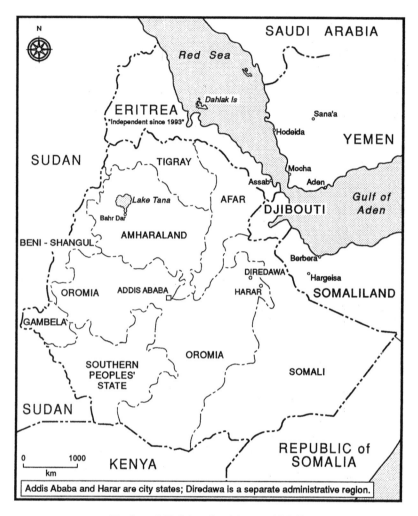

Federal Ethiopia (since 1994)

1

LAYERS OF TIME

THE GEOLOGICAL AND HUMAN
FOUNDATIONS OF ETHIOPIA

Ethiopia has a strong claim to being the oldest country in the world. Written and pictorial records reveal aspects of its history extending back well beyond 4,000 years. Petroglyphs take it back at least another 5,000 years. Archaeology and paleontology bring the country's history back millions of years. Ever since the American paleontologist Donald Johanson discovered the skeleton of a twenty-year-old hominid female on 30 November 1974 in a dried up lake bed at Hadar in the Afar Triangle 100 miles northeast of Addis Ababa, Ethiopia has come into the forefront of regions where mankind is believed to have first evolved. This famous young ape lady whom Johanson called Lucy and gave the scientific name *Australopithecus Afarensis* ("Afar Ape-man"), lived more than 3 million years ago.[1] Evidence of early human ancestors had already been found in other parts of Ethiopia. The search for hominid origins came almost to a halt during the seventeen years of Derg communist rule. It resumed soon after the Derg collapsed in 1991 and trained Ethiopian scientists have now joined foreigners in it. New discoveries are being made every year. Bones of at least seventeen individuals who appear to be more than a million years older than Lucy were recently found at Aramis on the left bank of the Awash. What is now a desolate region was a rich woodland full of wildlife several million years ago. The earliest chipped stone artifacts yet known were found on the banks of the Gona river in the Afar depression in 1996. They push back the date of tool-making at least 200,000 years earlier than finds in Kenya and Tanzania. Discoveries are still continuing in the Afar depression.

Ethiopian history has largely been determined by the country's geography which reflects the working of dramatic geological forces, most of them still operative. Much new light has been shed on these processes during the past quarter century. Study of the geology and history of Ethiopia is a continuous adventure in discovery.

The Rift Valley and the Mediterranean

Ethiopia has always been part of Africa and Africa is considered by geologists as being one of the most ancient of continents. Ethiopia

---

[1] Donald C. Johanson and Maitland A. Edey, *Lucy, the Beginnings of Humankind*, New York, Simon & Schuster, 1981.

contains Africa's most extensive high regions. Its Semien Mountains are rightly called "The Roof of Africa". But Ethiopia's civilization as far back as it can be traced has also been linked to the Middle East and, above all, to the Mediterranean world. So has its geology. Scientists in the 1970s discovered that its relationship to the Mediterranean was much older than anyone had realized. Ethiopia has two major links to the Mediterranean: the great Rift Valley and the valley of the Nile. The Rift Valley is, in effect, a crack in the earth's surface that extends from Syria to Mozambique. The Red Sea occupies a major portion of the northern Rift. Midway along the Eritrean coast the Rift turns inland and divides the Ethiopian highlands in two, with portions of its floor occupied by lakes. The same pattern extends through Kenya and all the way to Malawi.

Geologically the Rift Valley is a comparatively new feature of the earth's surface. Some geologists attribute it to an asteroid impact, perhaps the same one which ended the age of the dinosaurs about 65 million years ago. Others believe it was merely the result of movement of the great plates that form the continents and date its beginnings to perhaps fifty million years ago, about as long as mammals have been the dominant life form on earth. Intense volcanic activity raised highlands on both sides of the Rift and at times spilled into the valley, leaving layers of deposits which help date fossil finds. In parts of the Rift volcanoes broke through the valley floor. In the region where Ethiopia, Eritrea and Djibouti meet some are still active. Everywhere along the Rift (even at the bottom of the Red Sea) hot springs still bubble up from the depths, evidence of continuing vulcanism below. Though the Rift Valley floor sinks below sea level in the Danakil Depression along the Ethiopian-Eritrean border, it rises in its mid-section to more than 1,600 m. around Lake Zway, and then gradually slopes downward into southern Ethiopia and Kenya.

More will undoubtedly be learned in years to come about the geology of Northeast Africa. What seems clear is the fact that the Rift Valley has always formed an environment particularly favorable to life: a complex strip "of valley, hill, grassland, swamp, woodland, and forest,"[2] where a great variety of plant and animal life could flourish and interact. Thus it seems to have served as a Garden of Eden, where mankind evolved.

The Rift Valley may still be widening, though at a slower rate than in earlier geological periods. Scientists calculate the Red Sea to be spreading at the rate of about 2.5 cm. a year, which adds up to

---

[2] Chris Johns, *Valley of Life, Africa's Great Rift*, Thomason-Grant, Charlottesville, VA, 1991, p. 27.

an increase of 25 km. in a million years. Some scientists predict that
100 million years from now the whole eastern section of the Horn
of Africa will have broken away to form an island or a new mini-
continent. Ethiopians who worry about the potential fragmentation
of the country as a result of the ethnic–based policies of the post-
Derg government need not, however, become too aroused about
this possibility, for Ethiopia as it exists today is likely to retain its
basic geography for thousands, if not millions, of years to come.[3]

Twenty million years ago the Red Sea and the Mediterranean
linked the Indian Ocean with the Atlantic and separated Africa completely from Asia and Europe. As the great African continental plate
shifted northward and eastward, the Mediterranean was cut off at
both ends about fifteen million years ago. The Sinai isthmus rose and
the Straits of Gibraltar closed. During the next 10 million years the
Mediterranean shrank to a series of salty lakes occupying its deepest
sections while the greater part of the floor of this great sea turned into
a desert. The peninsulas and beautiful islands of historic times –
Sardinia, Malta, Crete, Italy, Greece, Cyprus – became mountains rising to great heights from a hot dry desert floor, which in some places
reached a depth of more than 3,000 meters below sea level–far lower
than any such area known on earth today. African fauna migrated
northward across the exposed seabed, horses and apes to Spain,
rodents to Europe, and hippopotami from the Nile to Cyprus and
Anatolia. Many years ago I was surprised to find an array of hippo-
potamus teeth on display in the museum at Kara-In, a Neolithic cave
in southwestern Turkey. They had been excavated from the cave and
nearby swamps. Lions managed to survive in many regions of the
Middle East until a century ago.

Most of the water that flowed from the south into the dry Mediterranean basin was supplied by the Nile, for the Ethiopian and other
East African highlands caught the monsoon rains, as they do today,
and enormous floods flowed down the Nile tributaries into the
main channel of the river.[4] So much, in fact, that the force of the river
carved a deep canyon through Egypt. Russian engineers probing to
make the foundations of the Aswan Dam in the 1950s discovered that
the modern river was underlain by a narrow gorge cut through solid

[3] In addition to Johns, cited above, another recent book provides a good general
account of the geology of the Rift, the evolution of its animal and human inhabitants, and its current life: Anthony Smith, *The Great Rift, Africa's Changing Valley*, BBC
Books, London, 1988.

[4] Ethiopia's Blue Nile and its tributaries normally supply up to 80 per cent of the
Nile water reaching Egypt. Much of the flow of the White Nile is lost through evapo-
ration and seepage in the vast Sudd swamp in Sudan. The pattern of flow was probably much the same several million years ago.

granite over 300 m. below the present level. Aswan is 1,200 km. from the coast. The river deepened its canyon steadily as it rushed northward. In the 1970s petroleum geophysicists verified the existence of a 2,500 metre-deep canyon under the Nile at Cairo. It continues on under the Delta and far out into today's Mediterranean. There is now no mystery where all the earth and rock went that was carved out of the immense gorges and canyons that the Nile and its tributaries cut through the Ethiopian highlands. Buried gorges and long underwater extensions have been found at many other places around the edge of the Mediterranean.

How did the Mediterranean again become filled? About five million years ago the Atlantic rose and began to erode the land bridge between Spain and Morocco. As the process gained momentum, a gigantic waterfall developed, perhaps the greatest the world has ever known. With the volume of a thousand Niagaras it poured 40,000 cubic kilometers of water each year into the Mediterranean basin, refilling the sea in perhaps 100 years.[5] The waters of the Nile continued to flow, gradually filling its gorge with rock and silt to the present level of the riverbed. The fertile portions of present-day Egypt, above all the Delta, were formed from silt, sand, and rock brought down from Ethiopia. Egypt is not only the "Gift of the Nile". It is a gift brought from Ethiopia. The intertwining of the history of the two countries which has continued throughout history has deep geological roots.

The refilling of the Mediterranean caused immense changes in the climate of both Africa and Europe: in rainfall, plant life, and in distribution and evolution of living creatures. These effects are still being studied. It is tempting to speculate that some of these changes may have caused the acceleration of primate evolution that led to the emergence about five million years ago of the forerunners of humankind and the increasingly human successors that culminated in the emergence of modern human beings. Ethiopia will remain a key area for the study of all these questions for decades to come.[6]

Early Man in Ethiopia

Lucy and her family were not the first Ethiopian proto-humans. They were a late stage in the long evolution of primates, starting perhaps as much as sixty-five million years before. Around thirty-two million years ago apes diverged from monkeys. Both spread through all of

---

[5] The Mediterranean continues to be a "deficit sea". Rainfall and rivers that flow into it do not provide enough water to maintain its level, which depends on inflow from the Atlantic through the Strait of Gibraltar.

[6] The above account of the dramatic changes in the Mediterranean during the past

Africa and eventually into Asia and Europe, where monkey and ape fossils dated up to 15 million years old have been found. The most productive course of primate evolution seems, nevertheless, to have continued in eastern Africa. It goes without saying that modern state boundaries had no meaning in this process. What happened in Ethiopia was part of a larger scene encompassing the Rift Valley to the south and the Nile Valley to the east. The Olduvai Gorge in Tanzania, the scene of the famous discoveries of Louis and Mary Leakey, was the first intensively studied area. Hominid fossils found there and nearby in Kenya at a site called Laetoli are similar to Lucy. Fossils dated from 2.5 to 1.5 million years old, given names such as *Australopithecus Africanus* and *Australopithecus Robustus* have been found in the Omo valley in southwestern Ethiopia as well as in Olduvai and South Africa. Recent discoveries in Ethiopia have resulted in the designation of a new line of hominid ancestors, *Australopithecus Ramidus.*

The use and making of tools is regarded as the most important evidence of emergence of the genus *homo – genuine* humans – and a regular progression has been accepted by most paleontologists from *homo habilis,* a tool-maker who first appears a little over two million years ago, through *homo erectus,* who spread throughout the old world about 1 million years go, to *homo sapiens* who, it is believed, originated in Africa perhaps 150,000 years ago and, according to current theories, is thought to have eventually replaced all other forms of humankind throughout the world, including Neanderthals. Human paleontology as a field of study is evolving rapidly as the twentieth century comes to a close. Work on these topics is likely to accelerate during the next several decades as field research becomes easier and more fossil discoveries are made. The application of new scientific techniques to the study of fossils, especially DNA analysis, as well as the study of the geology, fauna and flora of ancient sites, is opening vast new horizons. Many current assumptions and hypotheses are bound to be revised in years to come.[7]

---

20 million years is drawn largely from the Epilogue and Postscript of Kenneth J. Hsu, *The Mediterranean was a Desert, a Voyage of the Glomar Challenger,* Princeton University Press, 1983, pp. 170-84.

[7] Richard Leakey, son of the famous couple who contributed so energetically to African hominid research and who himself has a distinguished record as a palaeontological explorer, recently published a thoughtful review of what is now known and its significance: Richard Leakey and Roger Lewin, *Origins Reconsidered, in Search of What Makes us Human,* New York, Doubleday, 1992; and with his co-author followed it with a palaeontological perspective on the current wave of popular concern about mankind's heritage and the future of life on earth: *The Sixth Extinction, Patterns of Life and the Future of Humankind,* New York, Doubleday, 1995.

Tool-making is only one of three characteristics considered essential in defining human beings. The second, bipedalism – walking on
two feet – may have begun to evolve before the widespread making
and use of tools; the other, the use of language, remains a mystery.
Some of the problems in determination of the early development
of all these basic human characteristics were well stated more than
two decades ago by scientists involved in the study of the Omo Valley in Ethiopia and Lake Turkana to the south:

Human origins are distinguished more by changes in behavior than by
change in gross anatomy, so that archaeological traces of characteristic
human activities are a crucial complement to the fossils in reconstructing
the trajectory of evolution. [...] Most hominid-find spots do not have artifacts,
and most archeological sites do not have hominids–and when they do ... it
is questionable whether the particular fossilized hominid "owned" the site.
Until we find a number of hominids preserved with their tools in their hands,
our response to these questions will remain largely subjective or speculative.[8]

The most heated current controversies about human origins relate
to the relatively recent period as modern man spread first throughout the Old World and then into the New World. They are the result of DNA studies. Geneticists studying modern populations and
their interrelationships have concluded that modern humans must
have originated in Africa 100,000 to 200,000 years ago. Some have
dramatized this theory by hypothesizing a *"Mitochondrial Eve"*, a
woman who may have lived in Ethiopia and contributed some of
her genes to all human beings born since. Eve is a simplification of
complex scientific reckoning, but the conclusions are persuasive: a
small original African population, no more than 100,000 individuals, spread out into Asia, then into Europe, and eventually penetrated
into Australasia and the Americas. A recent examination of the
concept and review of the evidence judges that

The conclusion warranted by the DNA analysis is that Mitochondrial Eve is
the ancestor of modern humans in the maternal line ... [and that] the rest
of the DNA was inherited from other contemporaries of Mitochondrial Eve.[9]

So all human beings are descendants of Africans! The concept will
no doubt continue to be debated, and refined, for many years to
come. It is obvious that there is much still to learn.[10] I will mention

[8] F.C. Howell and G.L. Isaac in Yves Coppens et al. (eds), *Earliest Man and Environ-
ments in the Lake Rudolf Basin*, University of Chicago Press, 1976, pp. 474-5.

[9] Francisco J. Ayala, "The Myth of Eve: Molecular Biology and Human Origins",
Science, 22 December 1995, p. 1934.

[10] For one of the most recent efforts to put available information on the develop-
ment and spread of human beings in Africa into a coherent framework, see James
L. Newman, *The Peopling of Africa, a Geographic Interpretation*, Yale University Press,
New Haven, CT, 1995.

a few of the Ethiopian regions where important finds of ancient man have been, and continue to be, made.

The first area to be systematically investigated was the lower Omo Valley in the southwest, starting at the beginning of the twentieth century.[11] The investigations there in the 1930s under the leadership of the French scholar, Camille Arambourg, laid the basis for work that has continued in this region to the present. These investigations mesh closely with the work around Lake Turkana in Kenya in which Richard Leaky was pioneer.[12] Work at these sites is important not only for the information on hominid development that has resulted, but equally so for information gained about the development of large East African mammals.

The richest palaeontological area of all has been the valley of the Awash river, which rises on the western Ethiopian plateau about 50 km. southwest of Addis Ababa, flows down into the Rift Valley and continues northeastward along the floor of the widening Rift. During the spring and summer rains this river carries an enormous flow of water which is now partly held back to irrigate sugar and cotton plantations. Johansen and his team discovered Lucy, and they and others have continued to make discoveries in the lower Awash Valley. This river eventually loses itself in swamps and salt flats of the Danakil depression northwest of Djibouti and never reaches the sea.

The richest single site in Ethiopia is located along the upper Awash, just above the point where it tumbles over a ledge and enters a deep gorge.[13] Here, at Melka Kontouré, human beings have been active for the better part of 2 million years, from the early Palaeolithic through the Neolithic to the Christian era. I have watched Oromo herdsmen bringing great herds of cattle, goats and sheep to the Awash for watering during the dry times of the year and jumping into the water themselves to splash each other. In the early 1970s boys from the nearby village were selling passing motorists splendid handaxes and finely shaped scrapers for a few birr. After rains the gullies leading into the river are thick with stone artifacts left from hundreds of thousands of years of occupation by bands of *homo habilis* and *homo erectus*. Strolling through this

[11] Zelalem Assefa, "History of Paleoanthropological Research in the Southern Omo, Ethiopia", *Proceedings of the 11th IESC, 1991*, Vol. I, pp.71-85.

[12] Richard Leakey and Roger Lewin, *People of the Lake*, Doubleday, New York, 1978, and Richard Leakey, *The Making of Mankind*, Simon & Schuster, New York, 1981.

[13] The sides of the gorge are honeycombed with caves, some of which appear to have served as primitive sites of worship. Christians later turned some of them into rock churches.

landscape, one can easily get the feeling of going back a million years in time.[14]

French archaeologists sponsored by the Mission Archéologique Française en Éthiopie worked at Melka Kontouré for two decades, starting in the 1960s. They uncovered more than thirty separate occupation sites spread for several miles across the savannas above the broad river valley. Over hundreds of thousands of years the area experienced episodes of volcanic deposition from the great volcano to the southeast, Zuqualla, now extinct with a crater lake on its summit.[15] Layers of volcanic ash make dating easy and accurate, but the basic shape of the terrain seems to have changed very little since hominids first found it an attractive area to settle.

The early inhabitants of Melka Kontouré were hunter-gatherers who established camps and worksites near the water. The location was ideal for hunting as animals came to the river to drink. Meat formed a major component of the diet. Great quantities of large animal bones, teeth and tusks have been found, along with occasional hominid fossils. Many small and some larger stone-edged circles appear to mark out living and work areas and perhaps the foundation lines of shelters made of branches and thatch. Hearths with scorched pebbles reveal that the use of fire became common about 400,000 years ago. There are many parallels between findings at Melka Kontouré and those in the Olduvai Gorge and at Kenyan sites.[16]

[14] The terms Old Stone Age (Palaeolithic) and New Stone Age (Neolithic) are often loosely applied. The time boundaries are difficult to establish because developments, which continued over hundreds of thousands of years, occurred at different tempos in different areas. I have not tried to be consistent in use of these terms. In general the Old Stone Age is believed to have extended from the time people first began making stone tools to about 200,000 years ago. An intervening period often termed Epipaleolithic may stretch between 200,000 and 25,000 years ago; the New Stone Age may begin 50,000 years ago and extend almost to the present. Some Neolithic cultures, including a few in remote parts of Ethiopia, have come to an end only in the last generation or two.

[15] The popular Ethiopian medieval saint, Abuna Gebre Manfas Qiddus, of Egyptian origin, is alleged to have lived on this mountain for 700 years. Zuqualla is held sacred not only by Christians but also by the originally pagan Oromo who came into the region in the late 16th century. On 15 March each year two days of colorful ceremonies commemorate the saint and attract pilgrims, monks, and holy men from all over central and southern Ethiopia. From what we know of volcano worship in other parts of the world – e.g. the inhabitants of Çatal Höyük pictured the now extinct Hasan Dağ in Central Anatolia in one of their murals 9,000 years ago – we can speculate that early humans who lived at Melka Kontouré may also have regarded Zuqualla as the abode of gods.

[16] Unfortunately a comprehensive popular account of the results at Melka Kontouré is not yet available, though the French archaeologists who worked there published a series of reports and scientific papers. The best summary is Jean Chevaillon, "Le

Not far away, on the other side of Zuqualla, a Polish and American team worked in the area west of Lake Zway during the early 1970s and discovered a series of Neolithic sites above the ancient lakeshore rich in stone artifacts.[17] During the same period 100 km. to the northeast, in a lower part of the Rift Valley, another American, Steven Brandt, excavated at Beseka, not far from Metahara, uncovering occupation sites with stone artifacts giving dates ranging from 3500 BC almost to the present. Meanwhile J. Desmond Clark of the University of California, who had also excavated in the region of Harar, examined a Palaeolithic site at Gadeb in Bale on the eastern plateau along the upper reaches of the Webe Shebelle river in the mid-1970s.[18]

Excavations of Bronze Age settlement sites by the Italian Rodolfo Fattovich near Kassala in Sudan, immediately west of the Eritrean border, have provided important information about pottery, cattle, and the development of agriculture. They shed light on the last 5,000 years BC. So does excavation of the rock shelter at Gobedra, not far from Aksum, by David Phillipson, of the British Institute in Eastern Africa. Occupation here is thought to go back at least 7,000 years. All the archaeological surveys and excavations in northern Ethiopia and Eritrea raise important questions about the introduction of domesticated livestock, the evolution of agriculture, the development of indigenous crops, and the use of pottery and metals. Before discussing some of these developments further, however, let us look at another related aspect of late prehistory in Ethiopia.

During the early 1920s an ambitious French undertaking shed an enormous amount of light on the past of eastern and southern Ethiopia. Father Azais, a Capuchin missionary who had served as an army chaplain during World War I,[19] was persuaded to make a comprehensive survey of both ancient remains and current life in the eastern and southern provinces of Ethiopia. He had the support of the French government and several prestigious scientific bodies.

Gisement paléolithique de Melka-Kunture, Evolution et Culture", *Proceedings of the 8th IESC, 1984,* Vol. I, pp. 47-54.

[17] F. Wendorf and R. Schild, *A Middle Stone Age Sequence from the Central Rift Valley, Ethiopia,* Polish Academy of Sciences, Warsaw, 1974. A period of heavy precipitation 10-15,000 years ago created a much larger lake which encompassed Lake Zway and the three Rift Valley lakes immediately to the south.

[18] Kassaye Begashaw, "Archaeological Research in Ethiopia, Progress and Current Situation" in Claude LePage (ed.), *Etudes Ethiopiennes* (Proceedings of the 10th IESC), Societé Française pour les Études Éthiopiennes, Paris, 1994.

[19] At the end of his military service, he had undertaken archaeological explorations in Thrace and Asia Minor.

He was assigned a young linguist, Roger Chambard, as assistant.
Regent Ras Tafari welcomed this initiative and facilitated the work
in many ways. These Frenchmen spent five years (1921-6) measur-
ing and photographing stone structures, megalithic monuments
of many kinds, and gathering ethnographic data. At that time travel
conditions in these regions had improved little over those prevailing in the medieval era. The richly illustrated report of their findings has never been equalled for the variety and thoroughness
of the work done.[20] The decision of the French to concentrate on
parts of Ethiopia that were not part of classic northern – Aksumite –
civilization was deliberate. After World War II, specialists working
under the auspices of the Mission Française Archéologique undertook extensive new work in the east and south, and at the same
time, working in the north, contributed substantially to understanding of the period before the rise of Aksum and connections, both
early and late, with South Arabia.[21]

From the 1920s onward Italians did a great deal of archaeological exploring in Eritrea and Tigray, identifying many locations of
rock art as well as sites of pre-Aksumite and Aksumite activity and
settlement (1000 BC to AD 1000), which often have both stone
artifacts and pottery. Frenchmen in Djibouti and Britons in
Somaliland also discovered examples of rock art. What are believed
to be the earliest examples of rock art in the Horn of Africa are
scenes of hunting, often depicting men with spears and other weapons attacking wild animals. The advent of herding of cattle and
smaller livestock gave rise to a proliferation of representations of
domestic animals and activities connected with them.[22] Thus, at last,
we reach the beginnings of agriculture and settled life – the first
stages of civilization.

The beginnings of civilization

When did human beings in Ethiopia begin to establish permanent
villages and shift from gathering wild foods to cultivating them?
When did early Ethiopians begin domesticating the unique crops

[20] R.P. Azais & R. Chambard, *Cinq Années de Recherches Archéologiques en Éthiopie,
Province du Harar et Éthiopie Méridionale*, 2 vols, Geuthner, Paris, 1931. In his
introduction to this work, Edmond Pottier of the Louvre stated:

These processes are still under way in Ethiopia and will continue indefinitely.

[21] Some of the highlights of their work are reported in an impressive recent volume,
Roger Joussaume (ed.), *Tiya, l'Éthiopie des Mégalithes, du Biface a l'Art Rupestre dans la
Corne d'Afrique*, UNESCO/CNRS, Paris, 1995.

[22] Joussaume's *Tiya* volume cited above contains numerous illustrations on pp.
38-60.

they still grow? What was the climate like four, five, or six thousand years ago? What was the original natural vegetation of the are as where these developments occurred – how much forest cover was there? When and how did early farmers acquire grains (wheat and barley) that we know were domesticated in the Middle East? When did they begin to keep domestic animals? Who were the people who made these decisive advances toward settled life? What languages did they speak? What was their religion? To what extent were these developments the result of migrations of people from the outside?

None of these questions can be answered completely or with certainty. A great deal of information that bears on them has accumulated, but archaeologists need a great deal more and are now busy gathering it. Naturally there is a good deal of debate and controversy. I will try here only to speculate and summarize the most important things now thought known.[23]

What is said here applies almost exclusively to the north – Eritrea, Tigray, parts of Wollo perhaps, and to a limited extent to areas along the Red Sea to the east, including present-day Djibouti and neighboring Somaliland. Processes that began in the north several thousand years ago gradually spread southward and in remote regions around the edge of the country continued into modern times, as later chapters will demonstrate. One of the most interesting underlying questions in this field is the extent to which developments in the Fertile Crescent and Anatolia – from Egypt to Mesopotamia – influenced the Horn of Africa and through which channels : up the Nile Valley, down the Red Sea, across the Red Sea from Yemen? Later influences through all these regions are well attested historically, but when did they start? Wheat and barley, domesticated in Asia Minor and Iran, began to be cultivated in Egypt during the 6th millennium BC. There is evidence of their spread to southern Egypt by 4500 BC. From there they could have been brought up the Nile Valley and into the Ethiopian highlands, where climate and soil conditions would have favored their cultivation. Archaeological techniques such as palynology (study of pollen) and dendrochronology (study of tree rings) that are proving rewarding in other parts of the world have only begun to be applied

[23] For evaluation of some of the most recent Ethiopian evidence see Kathryn A. Bard (ed.), *The Environmental History and Human Ecology of Northern Ethiopia in the Late Holocene, Preliminary Results of a Multidisciplinary Project*, Istituto Universitario Orientale, Naples, 1997. Archaeology in Yemen is providing evidence that high civilization developed there earlier than had heretofore been assumed. It may have had connections with and impact on the Ethiopian side of the Red Sea. See C. Edens and T.J. Wilkinson, "Southwest Arabia During the Holocene: Recent Archaeological Developments", *Journal of World Prehistory*, 12/1, March 1998, pp. 55-119; also "Yemen's Stonehenge Suggests Bronze Age Red Sea Culture", *Science*, 6 March 1998.

in Ethiopia. DNA studies of both animal and human remains now promise to open up new vistas.

The most logical route for the introduction of domestic livestock would have been via the Nile Valley from Sudan. The excavations around Kassala have provided some substantiation of this hypothesis. Livestock herding probably preceded both agriculture and settlement, for nomadic pastoralism appears to have a long earlier history in the Sahara and the Sahel when these regions were still green and well watered. The camel seems more likely to have come across the Red Sea from Arabia. Camels have been attested in northern Ethiopia from about 1000 BC onward.

An especially interesting aspect of agriculture in Ethiopia concerns the crops that seem to have originated there. Most of them remain important in Ethiopian life today. Teff (*Eragrostis tef*), the most characteristic Ethiopian grain, is widely cultivated throughout the highlands and used primarily for the griddle-baked flatbread, *injera*. It has high food value and mineral content. Another highly nourishing grain, finger-millet or *Dagusa (Eleusine coracana)* is thought to have been domesticated in the Ethiopian highlands too, though some attribute it to Uganda.[24] It continues to be used in Ethiopia as a source of food as well as the basis of a strong fermented beer. Enset (*Ensete edulis, Ensete ventricosum*), popularly called the false banana, is a staple source of food (*kocho*) among western and southwestern Ethiopian peoples. Its cultivation is complex, requiring advanced propagation techniques and diligent gardening skills. Its preparation as food entails skill and patience in fermenting the stem and root. The bright yellow-flowering plant, sometimes mistakenly called the Niger flower, *nug* in Ethiopia (*Guizotia abyssinica*), produces a rich oilseed. It is now a commercially valuable crop.[25]

No product of Ethiopian origin is as well known worldwide as coffee.[26] Long simply picked wild in the southwest, where in the form of bushes and small trees it forms a major element in the

[24] *Lost Crops of Africa, I, Grains,* National Academy Press, Washington, DC, 1996, pp. 39-57.

[25] The Christian church's prohibition of all animal foods during fasting periods gave Ethiopians incentive to develop sources of vegetable oil. The most important sources today, in addition to *nug,* are sesame and safflower (*suf*).

[26] Kaffa, the native region of coffee, is often assumed to be the origin of the name. Curiously, however, the plant, the bean and the brew are all known as *buna* throughout Ethiopia, from which the Arabic *bunn* for the bean seems to have been derived. The Arabic term for the brew is *qahwa,* and the Turkish *kahve,* from which the name in various European languages was derived.

undergrowth of middle-altitude forests, it is now also grown commercially in several other parts of the country (as far north as Eritrea, in fact) as well as in home gardens. It may have been taken across the Red Sea to Yemen for large-scale planting earlier than it was domestically cultivated in Ethiopia. It was introduced into Europe from Arabia by the Ottoman Turks and thus acquired the scientific name *Coffee Arabica.*

Ethiopia's unusual variety of micro-climates and altitudes has resulted in an extraordinarily rich flora, parts of which are still being discovered and classified.[27] Hundreds of plants are used for traditional medical purposes. Such uses undoubtedly go back to ancient times.[28] Nevertheless remarkably little is firmly known about the development of cultivation of either major food crops or medicinal plants. J.D. Clark, one of the most diligent students of early Ethiopia, has observed: "We know appreciably more about the behavior of early hominids in Ethiopia than we do about the origins of its traditional agricultural systems."[29]

More is known and can be systematically deduced from neighboring areas about the spread of herding and livestock raising into Ethiopia. Cattle were independently domesticated in Europe, North Africa, the Sahara and India. Cattle-herding appears to have entered Ethiopia from the north and west, i.e. from the Nile Valley around the beginning of the second millennium BC. The humped Indian-type of cattle common in Ethiopia today appear to be later arrivals and did not prevail widely until they spread into North Africa after the Arab conquests, though some might have been brought by sea to Ethiopia directly from India or South Arabia. Sheep and goats did not originate in Africa. They were domesticated in the Middle East. When sheep and goat bones appear in archaeological sites in Ethiopia, it is reasonable to assume that they were already being herded either by nomadic pastoralists, settled farmers, or people who combined both forms of activity. Sheep and goats

---

[27] An Ethio-Swedish project is currently resulting in publishing a series of authoritative volumes by the Swedish Science Press, Uppsala.

[28] Other unique Ethiopian cultivated plants include *gesho (Rhamnus prinoides),* a shrub whose dried leaves are used as a fermenting agent, and *chat/qat (catha edulis),* a shrub whose leaves when chewed have a mild narcotic effect. *Chat* growing, originally concentrated in the eastern plateau around Harar, has expanded during recent years and become a major export to Djibouti and Yemen. It is now also grown in the southern Ethiopian highlands where it is popular among Muslims. Use of *chat* has recently become a fad among Ethiopian youth of all denominations.

[29] John Desmond Clark, "A Review of the Archaeological Evidence for the Origins of Food Production in Ethiopia", *Proceedings of the 8th IESC,* Vol. I, 1988, pp. 55-69.

probably arrived in Ethiopia both via the Nile Valley and the Red
Sea coast.[30] Horses, so much a part of Ethiopian life during the past
1,000 years, were probably introduced from the Nile Valley, coming
originally from North Africa and the Sahara during the second half
of the second millennium BC. The donkey, on the other hand, was
common in the wild in desert regions of the Horn all the way up to
Egypt, and may have been domesticated independently in both Egypt
and Ethiopia. Small numbers of wild asses still survive in eastern
Ethiopian deserts.[31]

Definite answers to all the questions about the development of
settled life in Ethiopia cannot yet be given, but new information is
accumulating rapidly. The study of seeds in archaeological deposits
and the development of Ethiopian pollen studies will provide more
authoritative data on plants and crops. Glottochronology – the
projection of linguistic data backward in time, another technique
only in its infancy – can provide evidence on movement of peoples
and comparisons of words for agricultural techniques, animals and
crops.[32] Comparative study of pottery and application of the most
advanced dating techniques will enable much firmer chronologies
of archaeological sites to be established.

There has long been debate about highland forests in northern
Ethiopia. The highlands must have been well forested as agricultural settlement expanded from the fourth and third millennium
BC onward and population increased as food production and animal husbandry replaced hunting and gathering as a way of life. The
most obvious evidence for earlier extensive forestation is the continued existence of old-growth forests in inaccessible locations
and the survival of large trees – cedar, podocarpus, wild olive, and
species of large fig, among others – in sacred groves around churches
and monasteries throughout Eritrea, Tigray and Wollo. Accounts
of Egyptian travel and trade down the Red Sea for the purpose of
acquiring ivory and skins and the hunting of elephants for war
purposes confirm that large African animals existed in abundance
throughout present-day Eritrea and northeastern Ethiopia in
pre-Christian times. They could not have flourished on the sparse
vegetation that is characteristic of much of the countryside in
these regions today. As recently as the early nineteenth century,

[30] Andrew B. Smith, *Pastoralism in Africa: Origins and Development Ecology*, Hurst, London, 1992.

[31] J.D. Clark (ed.), *The Cambridge History of Africa*, vol. I, Cambridge University Press, 1982, pp. 420ff, 494.

[32] Christopher Ehret and Merrick Posnansky, *The Archaeological and Linguistic Reconstruction of African History*, University of California Press, 1982.

Europeans who came to Tigray described vast herds of wild animals and frequent hunting expeditions by local chiefs.[33]

Trade and travel from the Mediterranean world

To the ancient Egyptians the lands to the south were a source of curiosity and mystery and they were sometimes called "the Gods' Land". The Egyptians might have known no more than Europeans did until recent times about the sources of the Nile, but the annual floods of the great river were essential to their way of life. When Nile floods were late or sparse, Egyptian priests concluded that the Gods had been offended. There are references to the Land of Punt in Old Kingdom times – third millennium BC – in Egypt, but the best - known report comes from the New Kingdom period, the 15th century BC, when Queen Hatshepsut sent a trading expedition to Punt and commemorated it on the walls of her funerary temple at Deir el-Bahri across the Nile from her capital, Thebes:

Here we see the flotilla of five large ships sailing from their Red Sea port, the arrival at Punt where the inhabitants lived in grass huts built on piles, the Egyptians offering the trade-goods of all such African adventurers ever since – strings of beads, axes, and weapons – and the triumphant return with gold, ivory, apes, and precious myrrh-trees, their root-balls carefully protected by baskets for transplanting in Thebes.[34]

Where was Punt? Somewhere along the Red Sea, perhaps even beyond the Straits of Bab el Mandeb on the coast of Somalia or in southern Arabia. The name actually may have included the whole Horn of Africa and South Arabian region, a general term the way we now use "The Horn of Africa" or "the Middle East". Or, since it was used for thousands of years, it may have referred to different regions on either side of the Red Sea at different times. Punt was important for the Egyptians as a source of incense, a necessity in religious rituals and in embalming the dead, and as a source of ivory, spices, hides and exotic animals.[35] Slaves, too, became an object of trade. All these commodities could have been obtained on the Ethiopian coast, so Ethiopia was almost certainly part of Punt. Occasional finds of Egyptian goods – pottery, glass, scarabs, metal – in northern Ethiopia confirm that Egypt's southward trade included Ethiopia.

[33] E.g., Nathaniel Pearce, *Life and Adventures in Abyssinia,* London, 1831, reissued by SASOR, London, 1980, 2 vols.

[34] Cyril Aldred, *The Egyptians,* Thames & Hudson, London, 1961.

[35] Incense was and continues to be collected on both sides of the Red Sea, in Eritrea and northern Ethiopia, in coastal regions extending into Somalia, and in southern Arabia as well. Ivory would only have been obtainable on the Ethiopian side of the

Trade developed along the Nile Valley too. Early Egyptians traded with Nubia, the area which straddles the present Egyptian-Sudanese border, and established relations with developing states in the northern part of Sudan: Kush, Napata and Meroe.[36] Egyptian records provide information about military expeditions to these southern regions as early as the mid-2nd millennium BC. They must also have obtained information about the lands to the east, i.e. northern Ethiopia.

However, our most comprehensive information about Ethiopia's trade with Egypt, and eventually other parts of the eastern Mediterranean world, comes from later times, though trade seems to have developed steadily from the second millennium onward. Phoenicians, long the most adventuresome seamen of the Mediterranean, were involved. South Arabians and the inhabitants of Northern Ethiopia evidently developed the ability to navigate in the Red Sea, and perhaps, quite early, penetrated beyond the Straits of Bab el Mandeb.[37] By the time of the Ptolemys in Egypt (the last three centuries BC), Red Sea trade was highly developed. Egypt's Ptolemaic rulers were eager to obtain elephants for military purposes and encouraged the peoples in the Red Sea hinterland to hunt them. They built a special port somewhere near Suakin[38] called Ptolemais Theron "Ptolemais of the Animals" to load them for shipment north.

Red Sea. Most exotic animals, and probably hides, skins, and gold would also have been primarily African products.

[36] Some scholars believe that Egyptian civilization arose when peoples from the south came down the Nile Valley as the Sahara dried up. And some maintain that the Semitic languages developed in Africa and spread across the Red Sea to the Arabian Peninsula and the Near East 8-10,000 thousand years ago. See Grover Hudson, "Language Classification and the Semitic Prehistory of Ethiopia", *Folia Orientalia*, XVIII, 1977. Kush flourished in the early second millennium BC. From it the term "Cushite" is derived and is still applied to non-Semitic peoples of Ethiopia such as the Agau and the Oromo. Napata, a successor state, flourished at the beginning of the first millennium. It was superseded by Meroe, where, along the Nile north of Khartoum, imposing pyramids can still be seen. Meroe's period of maximum expansion coincided with the Ptolemaic period in Egypt. The Roman emperor Nero considered conquering Meroe and sent an expedition to reconnoiter the region about AD 65. It reported a queen named Candace reigning at Meroe but concluded the country was too poor to be worth invading. P.L. Shinnie, *Meroe, a Civilization of the Sudan*, Thames & Hudson, London, 1967; W.V. Davies (ed.), *Egypt and Africa, Nubia from Prehistory to Islam*, British Museum, 1991.

[37] George F. Hourani, *Arab Seafaring* (expanded edition), Princeton University Press, 1995.

[38] Its exact location is still a matter of debate among scholars. It was apparently founded between 270 and 264 BC and was "a full-scale colonial venture involving the cultivation of the surrounding fields and the raising of flocks" (Lionel Casson, *Periplus Maris Erythraei*, Princeton University Press, 1989, pp. 100-1).

Greeks from Egypt as well as from mainland Greece and Asia Minor played a major role in Red Sea navigation during this time. Two wrote guidebooks to the region which even today make entertaining and informative reading, for they not only describe ports, trading conditions and geographical features, with distances and sailing times, but give lists of products traded and information about the peoples living in the region and their political status. The name of only one of these authors is known, Agatharchides of Cnidus, who lived in Egypt in the late second century BC.[39] The second author whose name has not been preserved was a Greek sea captain who lived two centuries later. He produced a handbook for merchants, *The Periplus of the Erythraean Sea,* which covers not only the Red Sea, but ports in the Indian Ocean all the way to India and Ceylon as well as the African coastal regions of modern Kenya and Tanzania.[40]

These accounts supply a good deal of information on coastal and inland Ethiopia during the period of the rise of the Aksumite Empire. The entire country directly south of Egypt – i.e. present-day Sudan, Eritrea and the lowlands to the south – was called Barbaria. Most of the inhabitants were apparently herders, but some were described as fish eaters, *ichthyophagoi,* others as wild animal eaters, *agriophagoi,* or eaters of roots and stalks, *moschophagoi.* Greek geographers of the time lumped them all together as Troglodytes, "a backward race, utterly remote from the Greek world".[41] They were probably ancestors of the Hamitic pastoral peoples who still predominate in the desert lowlands of the Horn. By the time of the *Periplus* elephant hunting for military purposes had declined and hunting for ivory had severely depleted the herds of small forest elephants around Ptolemais Theron. Here the principal export was now tortoise shell, an important commodity at all Red Sea ports. Carved into combs and other such items, it served as the plastic of the ancient world.

The anonymous author of the *Periplus* describes the ivory trade out of Ethiopia at this period:

[39] Stanley M. Burstein (ed.), *Agatharchides of Cnidus on the Erythraean Sea,* Hakluyt Society, London, 1989.

[40] The Erythraean Sea of this period included not only the Red Sea (its literal meaning) but the entire western section of the Indian Ocean, i.e. the Arabian Sea as far as India, with the Gulf of Hormuz and the Persian Gulf as well. Several editions of the *Periplus* have appeared in modern times. The most recent and thoroughly annotated is that edited by Lionel Casson cited in n.38 above. It incorporates the results of more recent research than the edition edited by G.W.B. Huntingford published by the Hakluyt Society in London, 1980.

[41] Casson, *op.cit.,* p. 99.

Beyond Ptolemais ... is Adulis. It is on a deep bay extending due south, in front of which lies an island called Oreine ["hilly"] ... that lies parallel to the coast. Here at the present time arriving vessels moor because of raids from the mainland. On this part of the coast opposite Oreine...is Adulis, a fair-sized village. From Adulis it is a journey of three days to Koloe, an inland city that is the first trading post for ivory, and from there another five days to the metropolis itself, which is called Aksum. Into it is brought all the ivory from beyond the Nile through what is called Kyeneion, and from there down to Adulis. The mass of elephants and rhinoceroses that are slaughtered all inhabit the upland regions, although on rare occasions they are also seen along the shore around Adulis itself.[42]

The author of the *Periplus* reported a relatively organized political system in Ethiopia. We know from other sources that in the coastal region Greek influence was growing. He describes its ruler as Zoskales, "a stickler about his possessions and always holding out for getting more, but in other respects a fine person and well versed in reading and writing Greek".[43] Because of the similarity of the names, some scholars have equated Zoskales with the Za-Haqale of a much later Ethiopian king list, but others believe he was only a local ruler, for it is not clear from either the *Periplus* or other available information to what extent Aksum had already consolidated political dominion over the coast.[44]

The objects traded included as exports: elephant tusks and tortoise shell, as already mentioned, plus rhinoceros horn, hides and skins, various kinds of incense and fragrant gums, dyes, aromatic woods, spices of many kinds, precious stones and pearls, live exotic animals and slaves. In return traders offered cloth and several kinds of clothing, olive oil and wine, axes, adzes and other tools of iron, copper, and bronze, pottery, drinking cups, gold and silver objects (made for the king "in the shapes of the country") and glassware (perhaps beads).

Agatharchides had earlier provided a vivid description of the Troglodytes of the coastal region who do not seem to have changed greatly by the time of the *Periplus* and were already following some

---

[42] Ibid. pp. 51-3. The deep bay is the Bay of Zula (a name which is obviously related to Adulis, the Greek form of an early Ethiopian name which has not been firmly established). Oreine appears to be the Red Sea island of Dissei south of the site of Adulis; Koloe is Cohaito. The length of time required for the land journey to Koloe and Aksum is unusually short. Casson believes Kyeneion may be the district now known as Wolkayt.

[43] Ibid, pp. 53, 109-10.

[44] Assuming that Zoskales would have paid a portion of the customs dues at Adulis to the ruler of Aksum, Huntingford sees Zoskales as the forerunner of the *Bahrnegash* of later times, the Ethiopian emperors' viceroy in the coastal region. Huntingford (ed.), *Periplus*, p. 148.

of the customs that have continued among the Afar and other peoples of the lowlands into modern times:

[They] lead a pastoral life. They have many despotic chiefs; their women and children are common property, except those of the chief; and those who lie with a chief's wife are fined a sheep. The women carefully paint their eyebrows with antimony, and they wear shells hung round their necks as amulets against the evil eye. The men fight over grazing grounds, first with fists, then with stones, and then wounds are inflicted with arrows and swords.[...] They live on meat and bone broken up together, wrapped in skin and then cooked ... They drink blood mixed with milk. The ordinary people drink water in which the *paliuris* plant has been soaked; the chiefs drink honey and water, the honey being pressed from some kind of flower. They have a winter, when the monsoon blows and rain falls; the rest of the year is summer. They go naked or clad in skins, and carry clubs. They not only mutilate their bodies, but some are circumcised like the Egyptians. [...] Some of the Troglodytes bury their dead, binding the neck to the feet with cords of *paliuris* fiber; then they cover the body with stones, laughing and joking till the face is hidden; then they put a goat's horn on top of the cairn and depart. They travel by night and fasten bells to the necks of the male stock so that the noise may scare wild beasts.[45]

South Arabia and Ethiopia

Ancient South Arabian peoples may, according to some theories, have originally migrated out of Africa across the Straits of Bab el Mandeb when sea level was much lower than at present, but ancient South Arabian civilization appears to have been ultimately derived from cultures that arose from the 4th millennium BC onward in Mesopotamia and along the shores of the Persian Gulf. South Arabia also had early and close links with the high Semitic cultures that developed at the eastern end of the Mediterranean. The distinctive South Arabian script is thought to be derived from an early Canaanite alphabet which developed in Syria/Palestine during the 2nd millennium BC. It seems to have evolved parallel with the Hebrew and Phoenician alphabets – though the exact lines of evolution have not yet been clarified. By 500 BC, perhaps even earlier, it was already widely used.

Ancient South Arabians made good use of writing, creating a vast number of inscriptions on stone which record the history of several rival, long-lasting kingdoms: Qataban and Saba (the Biblical Sheba), Himyar, Hadhramaut, Ma'in and others. American-led expeditions to this region in the early 1950's collected a large body of inscriptions and artifacts which have subsequently been

[45] Burstein, *Agatharchides*, pp. 108-12; the paraphrased translation cited is from Appendix 3 to Huntingford, *Periplus*, p. 144.

published.[46] The inscriptions provide information not only on the South Arabian kingdoms, but also on early Ethiopian history, with mention of Aksum and Aksumite rulers. They mesh well with knowledge gained in northern Ethiopia.

The South Arabian kingdoms were commercially active and politically expansionist. Domination of trade routes provided a motive for extending their power. South Arabians were probably crossing the Red Sea and in contact with people in northern Ethiopia before 1000 BC but the archaeological record has so far given evidence of sustained South Arabian influence and permanent settlement only during the second half of the first millennium BC. New excavations in both Yemen and northern Ethiopia may eventually produce evidence of substantial earlier contact. Some traditions go back earlier, among them including the Ethiopian national epic, the *Kebra Nagast,* which recounts a visit of the Queen of Sheba to King Solomon in Jerusalem and depicts her as an Aksumite ruler, which would have had to be about the middle of the ninth century BC, long before Aksum developed into an important political center. The son she allegedly conceived by Solomon who returned to Ethiopia as a young man, Menelik I, is regarded as the founder of the Solomonic Dynasty which officially came to an end only with the deposition of Emperor Haile Selassie in 1974.

What did the South Arabians encounter when they entered the north Ethiopian highlands? It used to be thought that they arrived among primitive African hunter-gatherers, with whom they had no more in common than the first Europeans had with most Native Americans. This may well have been the case along the coast. The highlands were different, for in these areas of temperate climate and higher rainfall, farming and herding of domesticated animals were probably already well established. As archaeologists expand their work in Yemen, Eritrea and northern Ethiopia, much more will be learned.[47] Cattle of the long-horned humpless type, which may have originated in the Sahara and spread outward as the desertification process accelerated, have been present in northern Ethiopia since very ancient times and may have been brought from there to South Arabia.

The South Arabians who came across the Red Sea encountered people practicing a more varied agriculture than they knew them-

[46] Wendell Phillips, *Qataban and Sheba, Exploring Ancient Kingdoms on the Biblical Spice Route of Arabia,* Gollancz, London, 1955; Gus W. Van Beek, *Hajar bin Humeid, Investigations at a Pre-Islamic Site in South Arabia,* Johns Hopkins Press, Baltimore, MD, 1969.

[47] Rodolfo Fattovich, "The Peopling of the Tigrean Plateau in Ancient and Medieval Times: Evidence and Synthesis" in Bard, *op.cit.,* pp. 81-105.

selves, but of the indigenously domesticated Ethiopian crops only coffee became significant as a transplant across the Red Sea. It seems probable that the use of copper and iron had already penetrated to northern Ethiopia before the South Arabians arrived. Iron smelting was highly developed in the northern Sudanese kingdoms. Metals probably came into Ethiopia from the west as well as through Red Sea trade.

South Arabians were building dams for irrigation and water supply at the beginning of the first millennium. Their settlements developed around reservoirs. Some of the immigrants to Ethiopia probably brought sophisticated concepts of irrigation with them. Dams forming reservoirs are a common feature of ancient urban sites in Tigray and Eritrea, the best known being Mai Shum, the so-called "Queen of Sheba's Bath" in Aksum.

Several urban sites developed along the most practical route from the coast inland to Aksum. The port of Adulis may have been the main entry point to the highlands for South Arabians before it became a major center of trade with Egypt. Eritrean towns that retained prominence in the Aksumite Empire show distinct South Arabian influence: Tekondo with stone monuments similar to those at Marib, and Cohaito (Koloe) with its intact South Arabian type dam. Farther south, not far from the present Eritrean-Ethiopian border near Senafe, is Matara, an immense city extensively studied by the French Archaeologist, Francois Anfray, in the 1960s.

2

THE AKSUMITE EMPIRE
ETHIOPIA AS A WORLD POWER

The Rediscovery of Aksum

The Persian prophet Mani, who lived in the third century AD, wrote:

There are four great kingdoms on earth: the first is the Kingdom of Babylon and Persia; the second is the Kingdom of Rome; the third is the Kingdom of the Aksumites: the fourth is the kingdom of the Chinese.[1]

The Aksumite Empire was well known to the Greek and Roman worlds,[2] to the Byzantines, the Arabs, and the Persians. Vague knowledge of it extended as far as ancient China.[3] But in Medieval Europe it was forgotten. All that persisted was the legend of Prester John who ruled a mysterious Christian empire somewhere beyond the boundaries of the known world. Some placed it in Africa, others in Asia. Aksum itself declined but never ceased to exist. In Ethiopia it remained a political and religious symbol. But there are no records of visits to it by Europeans until the fifteenth century. The first extensive description was given by the great Portuguese traveler, Father Francisco Alvares, who spent six years in Ethiopia in the 1520s. In his still highly readable account of this experience, *The Prester John of the Indies,* he described it at length:

...the whole region is cultivated and full of domestic animals among which is a very good town named Aquaxumo. [...] We stayed in it for eight months, by order of the Prester John. This town was the city, court, and residence of the Queen of Saba ... who took the camels laden with gold to Solomon, when he was building the temple of Jerusalem. There is in this town a very noble church, in which we found a very long chronicle written in the language of the country. [...] This church is very large; it has five aisles of good width and of great length, vaulted above, and all the vaults closed, the ceiling and sides all painted. [...] The church has a large enclosure, and it is also surrounded by another larger enclosure, like the enclosing wall of a large town or city. [...] In the large enclosure, at the gate nearest to the church, there is a large ruin, built in a square, which in other times was

[1] As cited in Yuri M. Kobishchanov, *Axum,* Pennsylvania State University Press, 1979, p. 59.

[2] Frank M. Snowden, Jr., *Blacks in Antiquity : Ethiopians in the Greco-Roman Experience,* Harvard University Press, 1970.

[3] Philip Snow, *The Star Raft, China's Encounter with Africa,* Weidenfeld & Nicolson, London, 1988, pp. 1-8.

a house, and it has at each corner a big stone pillar, squared and worked, very tall with various carvings. Letters can be seen cut in them, but they are not understood, and it is not known in what language they are.

The town is situated at the head of a beautiful plain, and almost between two hills, and the rest of this plain is almost all full of these old buildings, and among them many of these chairs, and high pillars with inscriptions. Above the town there are many stones standing up and others on the ground, very large and beautiful and worked with beautiful designs, among which is one raised on another, and worked like an altar stone. [...] The raised stone ... is very straight and well worked, made with arcades below, as far as a head made like a half moon. [...] This very long stone ... has, at the height of a man, the form of a portal carved in the stone itself, with a bolt and a lock, as if it were shut up. [...] There are more than thirty of these stones and they have patterns on them; most of them have large inscriptions, which the people of the country cannot read, neither could we read them; according to their appearance, these characters must be Hebrew...

Above the town, on a hill which overlooks much distant country, and ... about a mile ... from the town, there are two houses under the ground into which men do not enter without a lamp ... There were in our company Genoese and Catalans who had been prisoners of the Turks, and they affirmed and swore that they had seen [buildings] in Troy ... and Egypt ... but that these ... were ... altogether much larger, and it seemed to us that the Prester John had sent us here, in order that we should see these buildings, and we had rejoiced at seeing them, as they are much greater than what I write. [...] In this town and in its countryside which is all sown in their season with all kinds of seed, when there come thunderstorms, and ... they are over, there are no women or men, boys or children, who are old enough, left in the town who do not come out to look for gold among the tillage, for they say the rains lay it bare, and that they find a good deal.[4]

Alvares produced an extensive description in words but copied no inscriptions and made no drawings. It was not until 250 years later that the extraordinary monuments of Aksum became widely known to Europe through the writings and drawings of travellers such as the Scot James Bruce and three decades later, Henry Salt, who visited Ethiopia in the first years of the 19th century and left a travel account illustrated with a series of beautiful etchings that still capture the feel of the north Ethiopian landscape better than most photographs. Bruce was familiar with the ancient monuments of Egypt and so impressed by them that he convinced himself that the monuments at Aksum had been Egyptian, probably from the time of the Ptolemys. He regarded the great stelae as a variation on Egyptian obelisks and imagined avenues of sphinxes and statues of the jackal-headed god, Anubis. He even recorded a remarkable stone

[4] C.F.Beckingham and G.W.B. Huntingford (eds), *The Prester John of the Indies*, Hakluyt Society, Cambridge, 1961, pp. 145-60.

carved with Egyptian hieroglyphics, apparently genuine, which has only recently been rediscovered in Edinburgh, no doubt brought back by Bruce.[5] Salt was affected differently by Aksum:

The first impression on beholding the Aksum church is its great resemblance to the Gothic seats of noblemen in England. As we came nearer, we passed the fallen ruins of a great number of obelisks, some of which present no appearance of having been ever decorated with sculpture, while others seem to have had much attention paid to them in this respect; at length, after passing a large reservoir of water on our left, we were much gratified with a view of an obelisk still erect.[...] It is about eighty feet high and formed out of a single block of granite, curiously carved and in excellent proportion. My attention was for a long time riveted on this beautiful and extraordinary monument. [...] It is difficult to conceive the method by which such a solid mass of granite was raised ... after passing through a country now reduced to so rude a state as Abyssinia.[6]

European visitors became more frequent in the nineteenth century. A French mission surveyed Adulis in 1840 and the famous Napier expedition to Magdala, which landed nearby, did some excavation there in 1868. Another Englishman, J. Theodore Bent, visited northern Ethiopia in 1893, concentrating on Yeha and Aksum. He collected inscriptions and published several in a richly illustrated account of his investigations, which also included sites in the then new Italian colony of Eritrea.[7]

The first systematic excavation at Aksum was undertaken by the German Professor Enno Littmann. A philologist who specialized in ancient Semitic languages, Littmann was invited to Princeton University in 1901. He secured the university's support for an expedition which worked at Aksum during the years 1905-6. These excavations were unusually fruitful and the four-volume report of them which was published in Berlin on the eve of World War I remains a basic source of information on Aksum and northern Ethiopia to this day.[8]

[5] The stone is illustrated in David W. Phillipson, *Ancient Ethiopia*, British Museum Press, London, 1998, p. 25.

[6] "Mr. Salt's Narrative" in George, Viscount Valentia, *Voyages and Travels to India, Ceylon, the Red Sea, Abyssinia, and Egypt in 1802...1806*, London, 1809, vol. III, p. 87.

[7] J. Theodore Bent, *The Sacred City of the Ethiopians*, Longmans, Green, London, 1893. By this time South Arabian connections with Ethiopian civilization had been recognized and the inscriptions which Father Alvares thought must be Hebrew were known to be in the ancient South Arabian script, but for another half century South Arabia was to remain less explored than Ethiopia.

[8] A 200-page summary with illustrations, diagrams, references, and commentary has been prepared by the director of the current excavations at Aksum of the British Institute of Archaeology in Eastern Africa, David Phillipson, *The Monuments of Aksum*, Addis Ababa University Press/BIEA, 1997.

Italians identified a number of archaeological sites in Eritrea during the colonial period and in 1939 an Italian archaeologist, Puglisi, did some work at Aksum. With the founding of the Ethiopian Institute of Archaeology in 1952 and generous French support for its work, Italian and French archaeologists began surveys and excavations at many sites in Tigray and Eritrea, notably at Yeha and Matara. Not until 1973, however, did a new concentrated archaeological effort begin at Aksum by a team from the British Institute in Eastern Africa in Nairobi headed by the late Neville Chittick. The team's extremely promising work had to be halted in 1974 because of the revolution which brought the Derg to power. Chittick died in 1984. In spite of these strokes of bad luck, Stuart Munro-Hay, a member of the British team, undertook the formidable task of publishing all the significant findings and followed his detailed technical report[9] with an attempt at reconstructing the history of Aksum. It was the first of its kind by an archaeologist intimately familiar with both the site and the written sources.[10]

In the sections which follow, I will draw extensively on Munro-Hay's and Phillipson's information and judgments because they are the most comprehensive available even though they may be subject to revision in light of ongoing and future discoveries. My discussion will also reflect my own familiarity with the region and visits to most of the known sites. In many respects the study of Ethiopian archaeology and history is at the same stage of development as Middle Eastern archaeology was at the end of the nineteenth century. Only with the fall of the Derg in 1991, and the end of the civil war that had made research in Tigray and Eritrea impossible for the better part of two decades, was it possible for survey work and excavation to resume. The British Institute in Eastern Africa under Phillipson resumed work at Aksum in 1993. He found, fortunately, that the Institute's unfinished excavations in the stela park around the famous stelae of Aksum had remained undisturbed during the civil

[9] S.C. Munro-Hay *et al., Excavations at Aksum, an account of research at the ancient Ethiopian capital directed in 1972-4 by the late Dr. Neville Chittick,* British Institute in Eastern Africa, London, 1989.

[10] Stuart Munro-Hay, *Aksum, an African Civilisation of Late Antiquity,* Edinburgh University Press, 1991. A Soviet scholar, Yuri Kobishchanov, who, when I last saw him in Paris in 1988, told me he had never had the good fortune to visit Aksum (the province of Tigray was inaccessible to the Russians during most of the period of their support of the Derg), published a remarkable history of Aksum in 1966 in Moscow based on meticulous study of inscriptions, scholarly articles, and excavation reports. Kobishchanov's work was translated and published by Pennsylvania State University Press in 1979, edited with an introduction by Joseph W. Michels, Professor of Anthropology at that University. Michels himself made an extensive survey of north Ethiopian sites in the early 1970s.

war. In 1993 Kathryn Bard of Boston University, an Egyptologist, joined Rodolfo Fattovich of the University of Naples in annual excavations that have already resulted in significant new finds in and around the city. French archaeologists are resuming work at Yeha. Other nationalities will be joining in and Ethiopians themselves are developing a corps of archaeologists and historians to take part in this important work.

The first decade of the twenty-first century is bound to bring new understanding of many aspects of Aksumite civilization. New monuments, inscriptions, and artifacts will be uncovered in unprecedented quantity. More attention will be directed toward learning about the daily life of the people. New techniques of dating, archaeoclimatology, study of pollen and tree rings, and other advanced scientific methods will produce knowledge far more rapidly than was possible a few decades ago. The early twenty-first century is likely to bring clarification of many of the obscure and controversial aspects of the history of the Aksumite Empire and its relations with surrounding areas. New controversies will no doubt also arise. The recent rapid expansion of archaeological research in South Arabia will extend knowledge of Ethiopian connections and developments.

From city states to Empire

Trade was crucial for the development of Aksum. Indeed, it may have been the key factor in evolution of the city into the capital of an empire, and the empire's subsequent expansion. Red Sea trade increased steadily in the late first millennium BC and the first centuries of the Christian era. Demand grew for African goods that could only be supplied in quantity from the interior. Elephants were overhunted near the coast and became scarce. They were plentiful in the highlands and westward toward the Nile Valley. In the countries around the Mediterranean, in the Levant, and in Persia and Central Asia, the market for ivory expanded. So traders had strong incentive to go farther west to procure tusks. Transport in the highlands had to be by caravan. Aksum was situated at a logical crossroads for caravan traffic and well positioned to control caravans coming from the west.

The area around Aksum appears to have gone through a long period of increased settlement and spread of intensive agriculture during the second and first millennia BC. It originally had substantial forest cover and was fairly well watered. Thus it was able to support a growing population to provide labor for public works and manpower for military purposes as well as enough agricultural produce to feed craftsmen, soldiers, and officials. The original focus of South Arabian settlement and political influence was farther to the east, around sites such as Koloe, Matara, Atsbi and Yeha. Situated on the western edge of this region, Aksum was the logical site for consolidation of a civilization that was an amalgam of South Arabian and indigenous characteristics. The first centuries AD seem to have been a period of particularly favorable climate, with dependable rainfall. The areas around Aksum would, therefore, have provided food for a continually expanding urban population during the period of maximum expansion of the Empire.

There is not much evidence that Aksum itself became a significant urban center until the early first century AD. Archaeologists and historians have established many schemes for dividing Aksumite history into periods based on pottery, coins, military expeditions, and evidence of development of the governmental system. For a brief historical summary it is most convenient to divide it into three periods, as Fattovich and Bard do: (i) Proto-Aksumite – the last four centuries BC; (ii) Pre-Christian – from the late first century BC to the mid-4th century AD; and (iii) Christian – from the mid-fourth century AD to the decline of the city in the eighth or ninth century.

During the Proto-Aksumite period South Arabian influences blended with indigenous elements. Agriculture and trade expanded, but techniques of food production seem to have developed mostly on the basis of indigenous north Ethiopian practices. Domestic animals and important crops such as wheat and barley had probably already come in from Egypt via the Nile Valley and contacts with these regions continued. Traditions of kingship and administration owed a great deal to South Arabian models, but north Ethiopian features blended with them. The same is true of architecture. South Arabian cut stone buildings gave way to a distinctive Aksumite style, in all likelihood because of the greater availability of wood. Direct South Arabian influence in temples, tombs, inscriptions, altars, statuary and pottery lessened. Styles of worship and gods on both sides of the Red Sea remained similar. The Ge'ez language evolved, though epigraphic South Arabian continued to be used for inscriptions. On the coast, at least, Greek influence increased concurrently with expansion of trade with Egypt and the Mediterranean.

Discovery and interpretation of further inscriptions may clarify the problem of state formation and, in particular, the kingdom of Damot/Diamat. Was it a direct precursor of the Aksumite state? What was its territorial extent? Was it a centralized state or a league of city-states? We do not yet know.

During the first century AD, apparently relatively rapidly, Aksum, which may have been only a cluster of villages up till that time, seems to have taken urban form and gained in political importance. Yeha was still significant, but Aksum soon overshadowed it. Zoskales, referred to in the *Periplus of the Erythraean Sea* in the first century AD (see Chapter I, p 17) may have been an early emperor. Even if he were only viceroy of the coastal region, the fact that he spoke Greek demonstrates the importance of trade and contact with the Mediterranean world to the evolving Aksumite state. There is evidence that the Romans already knew of Aksum as an expanding economic and military power. In and around the city large structures began to be built and elaborate funerary monuments – rock tombs and stelae – began to be cut and erected.

Until coins began to be issued (about AD 270), most names of Aksumite rulers come from South Arabian inscriptions. Since the South Arabian alphabet did not indicate vowels, these names are clusters of consonants and subject to varying readings. King GDRT (usually transcribed Gadarat) who ruled around AD 200, headed a state vigorous enough to undertake expeditions to South Arabia and take sides in struggles between kingdoms there. Inscriptions at the great temple of the moon god, Ilmuqah, at Marib in Yemen, identify not only GDRT, but also ADBH, ZQRNS, and DTWNS as "*nagashi* of Habashat [Abyssinia] and Aksum". Other inscriptions refer to BYGT and GRMT. The Marib inscriptions commemorate victories by the rulers of the kingdoms of Saba and Himyar, which at various times vied for Aksumite help in wars against each other. South Arabian politics in this period are still not well understood, but Munro-Hay speculates that Aksumite rulers may have begun intervening there for purposes of gaining more influence over Red Sea commerce.[11] Trade with the Levant and Persia which followed caravan routes on the east side of the Red Sea and perhaps maritime commerce into the Indian Ocean may also have been factors.

One of these Aksumite rulers may be identical with Sembrouthes, who is known only from a Greek inscription found at Decamere, southeast of Asmara. It declares the "King of Kings of Aksum, the great Sembrouthes came and dedicated [this inscription] in [his] 24th year." Sembrouthes is thought to have reigned about the middle of the third century AD. The location of this inscription indicates that Aksumite power had by this time extended far to the northeast. It is possible that Sembrouthes could be the same ruler who erected one of the most famous Aksumite monuments, the *Monumentum Adulitanum*, on which he had a long inscription carved in Greek. It was on a stone throne erected near a broken third century BC inscription of King Ptolemy III of Egypt on the road leading inland from Adulis.[12] Both inscriptions were copied by an Egyptian

[11] *Aksum*, pp. 71-5.

[12] For the text of Ptolemy's inscription, which deals primarily with elephant

Greek merchant known as Kosmas Indicopleustes, in the sixth
century AD and are preserved in his *Christian Topography*, a work
particularly significant for the information it provides on Roman
trade with India and China and for evidence of Ethiopian and Arab
participation in it.[13] The throne itself has not been rediscovered in
modern times. Kosmas, unfortunately, did not copy the ruler's name
or titles.

This anonymous ruler boasts of conquests that included some
identifiable regions of northern Ethiopia and extended "beyond
the Nile in inaccessible mountains covered with snow" where "the
Samene people" dwelled. By Nile he probably means the Takazze, a
major Blue Nile tributary, and the Samene are very likely to be the
inhabitants of the Semien mountains beyond. This spectacular
region, the highest part of Ethiopia, still occasionally receives snow.
He continues:

Having defeated the Taggaiton who dwell up to the frontiers of Egypt, I
had a road constructed going from the lands of my empire to Egypt.[...] I
defeated also the barbarian people of Rauso who live by the aromatics
[incense] trade, in immense plains without water, and the Solate, whom I
also defeated, imposing on them the task of guarding the sea-lanes.[...] I
sent an expedition by sea and land against the peoples living on the other
side of the Erythraean Sea ... and after subjugating their kings, I commanded
them to pay me tribute and charged them with guaranteeing the security of
communications on land and sea. I conducted war from Leuke Kome to the
land of the Sabaeans. I am the first and only of the kings my predecessors
to have subdued all these peoples by the grace given me by my mighty god
Ares, who also engendered me. It is through him that I have submitted to
my power all the peoples neighbouring my empire, in the east to the Land
of the Aromatics, to the west to the land of Ethiopia and the Sasou.[...]
When I had reestablished peace in the world which is subject to me, I came
to Adulis to sacrifice for the safety of those who navigate on the sea, to Zeus,
Ares, and Poseidon. After uniting and reassembling my armies, I set up
here this throne and consecrated it to Ares, in the 27th year of my reign.[14]

Like Sembrouthes this ruler enjoyed a long reign. Mention of his
twenty-seventh year, the fact the inscription is in Greek, and the reference to major military expeditions to the west, the north, and across
the Red Sea, all add to the impression that the two inscriptions may
be the work of the same man. The "Land of the Aromatics" must refer

hunting, see Huntingford, *Periplus*, pp. 166-7; the text of the *Monumentum Adulitanum*
is given in Munro-Hay, *Aksum*, pp. 222-3.

[13] Vimala Begley and Richard Daniel de Puma (eds), *Rome and India: The Ancient Sea
Trade*, University of Wisconsin Press, Madison, 1991.

[14] Munro-Hay, *Aksum*, pp. 222-3.

to the dry coastal region, a major source of incense extending from
the Ethio-Sudanese lowlands to Somaliland. It could also have included parts of South Arabia. "Ethiopia" in Greek often referred to the
entire region south of Egypt, i.e. Sudan and Abyssinia. The exact site
of Leuke Kome has not been identified, but it appears to have been
on the Arabian coast well to the north of Jeddah.[15] According to
another passage in the work of Kosmas, Sasou was a major source of
gold. It took caravans six months to make a round trip there. This
region was in the west, perhaps as distant as Wollega, or in Sudan.
The references to pagan gods make it clear that this ruler, though
strongly influenced by Mediterranean culture, had not adopted
Christianity.

The *Monumentum Adulitanum* permits no doubt that Aksum's
imperial reach had by this time – probably the late third century
AD – expanded to control the trade of the whole Red Sea region.
The emperors had developed military power to protect their trading interests. Rome and Persia valued these trading connections
and respected Aksum's power and influence. The Persian prophet's
inclusion of Aksum among the four great empires of the world, cited
at the beginning of this chapter, was justified. Munro-Hay sums it
up well:

As far as the history of civilisation in Africa is concerned ... Aksum ...,
Pharaonic and Ptolemaic Egypt, and Meroe [– each of them –] was before
its eclipse, the only internationally recognized independent African
monarchy of important power status in its age. Aksumite Ethiopia, however, differs from the previous two in many ways. Its economy was not based
on the agricultural wealth of the Nile Valley, but on the exploitation of the
Ethiopian highland environment and the Red Sea trade; unlike Egypt and
Meroe, Aksumite Ethiopia depended for its communications not on ... a
great river, but on the maintenance of considerably more arduous routes
across the highlands and steep river valleys. For its international trade, it
depended on sea lanes which required vigilant policing. Most important,
Aksum was sufficiently remote never to have come into open conflict with
either Rome or Persia, and was neither conquered by these contemporary
powers, nor suffered from punitive expeditions.[16]

Coinage and Christianity

Both the inauguration of coinage and the introduction of Christianity were the consequence of Aksum's expanding interrelationships with the Mediterranean world. Coins were first issued by
Emperor Endubis about AD 270, more than half a century before

[15] See Casson, *Periplus*, pp. 141-2.

[16] Munro-Hay, *Aksum*, p. 3.

the adoption of Christianity by Emperor Ezana. Aksumite coins, which continue to be found in large quantities, have been an enormous boon to historians, for they provide names and related information and make compilation of a fairly reliable chronology possible.[17] The three emperors who followed Endubis: Aphilas, Wazeba, and Ousanas, continued to issue coins in gold, silver, and bronze. The coinage was based on the Roman monetary system. The coins of these pre-Christian rulers all included the disc and crescent symbol of the South Arabian-derived religion. They provide other information that adds to our understanding of Aksumite rule. Many contain the word *bisi*, which means "man of", and a place or tribal name after the emperor's name, which gives clues to the emperors' origins and clan or regional ties that may become more significant as additional inscriptions and coins are found. The emperor is usually shown wearing a crown on one side of the coin and bare-headed or with a smooth cap on the other. The emperor's portrait is surrounded by ears of wheat or barley. Cultivation of these important grains had apparently provided Aksum with a major source of agricultural wealth by this time. The early coins bore legends in Greek. Wazeba began to use the native Ge'ez.

Coinage was needed for purposes of trade. It placed Aksum on a par with other coin-issuing states of the time and was probably profitable to the government. It also served to underscore the empire's status among other major powers. The emperors took full advantage of their coins to advertise their power. The coinage was used both for international and domestic trade and continued for the next several centuries. Coins continue to be found in all parts of Aksumite territory, but we do not yet know where they were minted. Until recently Aksumite coins were only rarely found outside Ethiopia and Eritrea, however, large numbers of Aksumite gold coins have come to light in India.[18] More such finds can be expected. Foreign coins were also known and used in Ethiopia, probably well before the emperors began issuing their own coinage. A major hoard

[17] 153 types of Aksumite coins are now known, plus many die variants. More may come to light. The most recent and thorough discussion of the subject is Stuart Munro-Hay and Bengt Juel-Jensen, *Aksumite Coinage*, Spink, London, 1995.

[18] The recent Indian discoveries, which also include large numbers of late Roman gold coins, were described and illustrated by Dr Wolfgang Hahn in a conference of the German cultural organization *Orbis Aethiopicus* in Cologne in October 1998 and subsequently published in "Spätantikes Handelsgold in Südindien" in *Moneytrend* (Vienna), November 1998, pp. 54-7. The Roman coins date from the mid-4th to the mid-5th century; the Aksumite coins are all from the reigns of Ousanas and Ezana (AD 320-c.350), evidence that they may have been in circulation for some time before being brought to India. Phillipson, *Ancient Ethiopia*, offers additional recent information and speculation on Aksumite coinage: pp. 71-4.

of Roman coins was found at Matara. The most dramatic find is a large collection of Central Asian Kushan coins dated to the early third century AD that came to light at the monastery of Debre Damo.

Ousanas may have been the same king whose throne name was Ella Amida, who according to tradition was the father of Ezana, the emperor who adopted Christianity in the third decade of the fourth century AD. Ezana left many inscriptions which provide a good deal of information about his long reign. His coins, as well as the inscriptions, confirm his abandonment of the claim of being the son of the war god Mahrem and adoption of Christianity. Ezana's earlier coins feature the South Arabian disk and crescent symbol used by his predecessors. His later coinage bears the cross, sometimes multiple crosses.

The Roman church historian Rufinus gave a direct report at the end of the fourth century of the colorful circumstances of Ezana's conversion:

[...]Meropius, a philosopher of Tyre, wished to visit India ... taking with him two small boys who were related to him and whom he was educating.[...] The younger of these was called Aedesius, the other Frumentius. [On return] the ship on which he travelled put in for water ... at a port. It is the custom of the barbarians of these parts that, if ever the neighbouring tribes should report that their treaty with the Romans is broken, all Romans found among them should be massacred. The ship was boarded; all ... were put to the sword. The boys were found studying under a tree ... and taken to the king. He made ... Aedesius his cupbearer. Frumentius, whom he had perceived to be sagacious and prudent, he made his treasurer and secretary...

The king died, leaving his wife with an infant son as heir of the bereaved kingdom. He gave the young men liberty to do what they pleased but the queen besought them ... to share with her the cares of governing the kingdom until her son should grow up, especially Frumentius whose ability was equal to guiding the kingdom ... While they lived there and Frumentius held the reigns of government in his hands, God stirred up his heart and he began to search out ... Roman merchants who were Christians and to give them great influence and to urge them to establish [prayer sites], in every way promoting the seed of Christianity in the country.

When the prince for whom they exercised the regency had grown up, they ... faithfully delivered over their trust and...returned to the Roman Empire. Aedesius hastened to Tyre.[...] Frumentius went to Alexandria. [...] He laid the whole affair before the bishop [Athanasius] and urged him to look for some worthy man to send as bishop over the many Christians already congregated and the churches built on barbarian soil.[...] Athanasius ... declared: "What other man shall we find in whom the Spirit of God is as in thee, who can accomplish these things?" And he consecrated him and bade him return in the grace of God whence he had come. [...] These facts I know ... from the mouth of Aedesius himself, who had been Frumentius' companion and was later made a priest in Tyre.[19]

Frumentius, who in Ethiopian church tradition has acquired the name Abuna Selama Kesate Berhan (Father of Peace, Revealer of Light), thus became the first bishop of Ethiopia, consecrated by the Patriarch of Alexandria.[20] The relationship with what became the Coptic Church of Egypt continued until the mid-twentieth century. Rufinus's account reveals that the two Christian boys must have come to the royal court during the reign of Ousanas and provides reason to believe that Ousanas may have been Ezana's father. Ezana's titles as used on inscriptions (which have been found in all three languages used at this time: Greek, South Arabian, and vocalized Ge'ez) include claims to extensive territories in South Arabia[21], but there is little evidence from there that the Aksumites any longer maintained anything but nominal suzerainty over the major kingdoms and perhaps a foothold on the coast. Ezana's major military expeditions were all in Africa, along the edges of his empire, where he subdued rebellious tribes and gathered booty, In a campaign, for example, against the Tsarane of Afan (unidentified):

503 men of Afan and 202 women were put to death, in all 705. Men and their women were made prisoner, 40 men and 165 women, total 205. The booty comprised 31,900 head of cattle and 827 beasts of burden.[22]

A major campaign against peoples in Sudan, the Noba and Kasu, is also attested by inscriptions found at Meroe and seems to have taken place after Ezana's conversion. A vocalized Ge'ez inscription begins, "By the might of the Lord of Heaven who in the sky and on earth holds power over all beings" and continues:

[19] As cited in Munro-Hay, *Aksum*, pp. 202-4.

[20] Ethiopian traditional accounts of the conversion have Emperor Ella Alada (*sic*) succeeded by two brothers, Abreha and Atsbeha, the country's first Christian kings. Throne (and coin) names and popular names may have been confused. Ezana may have had a brother Sazana, but the traditional legend may also refer to the most prominent emperor of the 5th century, Kaleb, whose throne name was Ella Atsbeha. He crusaded in Yemen. Abreha was the name of the rebellious Axumite general who built a great cathedral at Sana'a. Undiscovered inscriptions and coins may eventually enable legends and reality to be sorted out. See Munro-Hay, *Aksum*, pp. 205-6; also J. Spencer Trimingham, *Christianity among the Arabs in Pre-Islamic Times*, p. 196 ff.

[21] The frequently repeated formula is "King of Aksum and Himyar and Raydan and Saba and Salhen and Habashat and Siamo and Beja and Kasu." Four of these territories are in South Arabia. The distinction between the territory of Aksum and Habashat – the Arabic equivalent of Abyssinia – is unclear. Perhaps Habashat originally referred to territory east of Aksum.

[22] Deutsche Axum-Expedition inscription no.10 as cited in Munro-Hay, *Aksum*, p. 227.

"They will not dare to cross the Takazze", said the Noba people.[...] I set forth by the might of the Lord of the Land and I fought at the Takazze and the ford Kemalke. Here I put them to flight, and, not resting, I followed those who fled for 23 days during which I killed some everywhere they halted.[...] I burnt their villages, both those with walls of stone and those of straw. My people took their cereals, bronze, iron and copper and over-threw their idols in their dwellings, as well as their corn and cotton, and threw them into the [Blue Nile]. Many lost their lives in the river... At the same time my people pierced and sank their boats which carried a crowd of men and women.[...] I erected a throne at the confluence of the [Blue Nile] and Takazze opposite the town with walls of stone which rises on this peninsula...[23]

An inscription in Greek with a South Arabian version on the reverse is much more specific about Christ's help in overcoming the Noba:

In the faith of God and the power of the Father, Son and Holy Spirit who saved for me the kingdom, by the faith of his Son, Jesus Christ, who has helped me and will always help me ... I went out to fight the Noba [because other tribes said] "the Noba have ground us down; help us because they have troubled us by killing".[24]

Architecture and artifacts

The six great granite, multi-storeyed stelae – obelisks – are the best known feature of Aksum and the most impressive for visitors in mod-ern times. They are the largest examples of monolithic stone cutting known from the ancient world. We have no clues to the technology required to quarry and transport them, raise them to the vertical, and stabilize them in place. The largest of all, over 33 m. in height, apparently fell when, or soon after, it was erected. It is carved on all sides and has twelve stories. As it fell it partly crushed a tomb complex near its base capped by an enormous rectangular flat stone, in itself a technological wonder.

Unornamented stelae of moderate size may have been a feature of north Ethiopian religious symbolism long before Aksum emerged as the center of an Empire. They are found in many places through-out the region: at major sites like Yeha and at many smaller sites, e.g. in the cemetery of a modern church built on Aksumite founda-tions, Maryam Tehot, south of Edaga Hamus in eastern Tigray. They are notoriously hard to date. The same must be said of the huge ornamented stelae that are the hallmark of the city. No Christian symbolism has been found on any of them. Their erection is now believed to have begun as early as the third century BC and to have

[23] Deutsche Axum-Expedition inscription no.11, as cited in *ibid.*, pp. 227-8.

[24] As cited in *ibid.*, *Aksum*, p. 229.

ceased after the adoption of Christianity. The excavations of the British Institute in Eastern Africa in 1973-4 settled the fact that they were funerary monuments with tombs at their bases. But whose? No king's name or artifacts have been found to identify the rulers commemorated. Metal or wooden plates attached to the top of the stelae (the holes are still visible) may have identified them. None has been found. Tombs so far opened were robbed in antiquity, though significant objects have still been found in them.

Early travellers related the stelae to Egyptian obelisks, but there is no affinity. They have been related to South Arabian architectural styles – e.g. the great mud-brick buildings of the Hadhramawt which rise to eight and ten stories – but there is little real similarity and high mud-brick buildings were not constructed in northern Ethiopia. Stone was too plentiful. The carved stelae are unique. They duplicate classic Aksumite architectural characteristics in stone – the visible round "monkey-headed" cross-beams, and the doors and windows framed in square-cut interlocking wooden beams – that developed in Ethiopia. Wood had to be plentiful for this style of building.

There are more general South Arabian features which some Aksumite architecture shares. Square corners and rectangular alignments prevail. There is a preoccupation with symmetry. Ornamentation is lean. Major buildings all rise from a massive stone podium and most have monumental entrances with well designed symmetrical staircases. Rock-cut tombs are sometimes approached by similar well designed stairs. Large buildings whose foundations have been excavated at Aksum and at Agula were immense in size with many separate rooms. The great palace of Ta'akha Maryam at Aksum, 120 x 80 m. in extent, was far larger than Roman and Byzantine palaces of the time. It may have risen to a height of several stories with the ceilings of its large rooms supported by columns. Wooden columns on stone bases may have been used as well as stone. Roofs must have been supported by wooden beams which have long since disappeared. Walls were often constructed of layers of small stones separated and reinforced by wooden beams. The beams would eventually have rotted and caused the walls to crumble into piles of stones. There is evidence of columned porticoes and internal stairwells in some buildings. Kosmas Indicopleustes refers to "the four-towered palace of the king of Ethiopia". This could have referred to one of several structures whose foundations have been excavated within Aksum.

Though excavations have revealed evidence of one or two stories, none survives beyond this level, but a good example of what these buildings may have looked like is provided by some of the rock-cut churches of Lalibela, especially Bet Amanuel and Bet Giyorgis, the latter essentially a tower in a deep pit. In these, stone-cut windows and doorways duplicate construction in wood. Wall surfaces alternate between projections and indentations formed by massive interlocking beams of wood. This style permitted construction with relatively small and sometimes even irregular pieces of stone fill. The main church on Debre Damo, Enda Abuna Aregawi, Ethiopia's oldest monastery, attributed to the sixth century, has been rebuilt several times (most recently under the supervision of David Buxton[25] after World War II), but is probably still close to the original of Aksumite times. The elaborate gate structures to the compound of St. Mary's Orthodox Church in the center of Asmara, as well as the huge square church itself, are impressive modern re-creations of the main features of Aksumite style. Aksumite characteristics, particularly the massive wooden door-and window-frames, have persisted in all parts of Ethiopia into modern times.

What were these buildings like inside? The Debre Damo church has wooden columns and an elaborate coffered ceiling with representations in beautifully carved wood of wild and domestic animals. Animal and geometric ceiling patterns in both wood and stone can be found in many Tigrayan rock churches. The oldest rock churches may give us the best impression of the feel of Aksumite buildings, with columns "supporting" the roof and coffered ceilings with ornamentation cut into the rock. Many of the two or three hundred rock churches and chapels still in use in Eritrea, Tigray, Wag, and Lasta may originally have been pre-Christian sanctuaries for the worship of nature spirits, but the prevalence of Aksumite architectural features is evidence that they are likely to have taken their permanent form only after the spread of Christianity.

No significant example of Aksumite painting has come to light but one of the Prophet Mohammed's later wives, Umm Habiba, is reported to have returned from exile in Ethiopia during the decade following 620 praising the walls covered with paintings in the cathedral at Aksum.[26] A good deal of stone sculpture in the round has been uncovered at various sites in North Ethiopia. Bulls and female deities carved in stone probably date from the pre-Aksumite period, for they are much the same as similar figures found in Yemen. Clay representations of animals are fairly common. Small ceramic

[25] Chapter 4 of Buxton's *The Abyssinians*, Thames & Hudson, London, 1970, remains one of the best brief discussions of pre-Aksumite and Aksumite architecture available and includes excellent drawings of the main features of Aksumite construction.

[26] Sergew Hable Selassie, *Ancient and Medieval Ethiopian History to 1270*, Addis Ababa University Press, 1972, p. 186.

human heads, many of them with a good deal of individuality and often with the tightly braided women's hair style common in North Ethiopia today, are also often found. Great quantities of pottery have been found at all excavated Aksumite sites. Some common ancient styles of pottery are still made and can be bought in Tigrayan markets.

Language, writing and evangelization

From the third century onward, though Greek was used for commercial and monumental purposes and on coins, the use of Ge'ez spread. It became the *lingua franca* of the empire. The origins of Ge'ez are unclear. It is a rich, highly evolved Semitic language still used in Ethiopia for church liturgy, like Latin in Europe, and also like Latin, the source of new terms in Amharic and Tigrinya. Where does the name come from? It is probably related to that of the southernmost Eritrean province, Akele Guzay, and that may derive from a group mentioned in Aksumite inscriptions, the Agazain, who are thought by some historians to have been one of the original groups of immigrants from South Arabia.[27]

Ge'ez was first written in the South Arabian script. Like all Semitic alphabets, this script has a peculiar disadvantage: only consonants are indicated. Vowels were not shown. Ge'ez, like the modern Ethiopian languages derived from it, has seven vowels and several diphthongs which must be indicated in writing if the meaning is to be clear. By the fourth century Aksumites were using an ingenious vowel system involving appendages or changes in the form of the consonants. This system has continued in Ethiopia to this day for all the Semitic languages. The Ge'ez vowel system was either an original invention or may have been inspired by Indian examples. Indian alphabets, which also ultimately derive from Syro-Palestinian originals, had by this time developed systems for noting vowels. The possibility of Indian alphabetic influence is credible, for Red Sea navigators had learned how to exploit the monsoons and opened water routes to Persia, India and Ceylon. Indian traders may also have come to Ethiopian ports. Aksumite traders even made contact with traders from China.[28]

[27] See *ibid.*, pp. 27, 63, 85, for the hypothesis that the term Agazain eventually came to be applied to all of the early Aksumites.

[28] The chronicles of the Chinese Han dynasty refer to a country inhabited by a people called Huang-Chi, which was a twelve-month journey and 30,000 li (15,000 km.) from China. It produced rhinoceros horn, tortoise-shell, and ivory. Some Chinese ships are reported to have come into the Red Sea: Sergew Hable Selassie, *op.cit.*, pp. 84-5. The port of Mantai in Ceylon was a transfer point for trade between the Red Sea area and China, with merchants from both regions meeting there: John Carswell, "The Port of Mantai, Sri Lanka" in Begley and De Puma, *Rome and India*, pp. 197-203.

Aksumites may have written on wood, and in all likelihood on parchment, for parchment continued in use during medieval and into modern times, though neither wood nor parchment has been recovered during excavations. Traditional scribes in Ethiopia still produce beautiful manuscripts on parchment and churches prefer it for religious books because it is much more durable than paper.

Christianity was probably known in Ethiopia, brought by Jews and Greeks, well before Frumentius and Aedesius arrived and Ezana officially adopted it, but no evidence of organized early Christian communities or buildings used for Christian worship has yet been found. Following the official conversion, several Christians are said to have come from the Roman Empire to help spread the Gospel. They have gone down in Ethiopian tradition as the *Tsadkan*, the Righteous Ones, but little is known about them. The most important development for the spread of Christianity throughout the country was the arrival of the Nine Syrian Saints in the latter half of the fifth century. They have been glorified in Ethiopian tradition and commemorations of them remain important in the Ethiopian Orthodox Church calendar, but it is not easy to sift fact from legend. They are thought to have been monks and priests expelled from the East Roman Empire after the Council of Chalcedon in AD 451. This council rejected the Monophysite doctrine, which affirmed the single nature of Christ, and alienated many eastern Christians.

Only two or three of the saints actually came from Syria. Others have been traced to Constantinople, Cilicia, Cappadocia, and even Rome. They were warmly received by Emperor Ella Amida II and were active during the next three reigns establishing churches and monasteries, translating the Bible and organizing Christian communities. Several important churches and monasteries are attributed to them. Abba Pantelewon is said to have established a church on a steep hill on the northeast edge of Aksum, originally the site of a pre-Christian temple, where his cell can still be seen by visitors. Abba Gerima founded a large monastery in the mountains south of Adwa. The most famous and reputedly the oldest Ethiopian religious establishment is the monastery atop the *amba* of Debre Damo, sacred to the memory of Abuna Aregawi, who is said to have been pulled up to this inaccessible site by a huge snake. It can still be reached only by climbing a long leather rope.

The traditions of the Nine Saints in chronicles and church histories combine tales of determination and courage with accounts of extraordinary asceticism and self-denial. Most of them cannot have led isolated lives as hermits, as later alleged, and yet accomplished the building of churches, the standardization of ritual, and the creation of the impressive body of doctrine and religious literature that formed the foundations of the Ethiopian Orthodox Church and which has persisted with little change to modern times. The hardy traveller who climbs several hundred feet up the almost sheer cliffs of the mountain of Guh in the Tigrayan Geralta to the church of Abuna Yemata[29] where Christian history and the deeds of the Nine Saints are commemorated in magnificent wall and ceiling paintings, will find it impossible to believe that the good father accomplished his work by sitting and meditating in this inaccessible site, though he may have retired there in his old age and then worked on translations.[30]

Coins of the time of the activity of the Nine Saints include Christian mottoes. The cross, often skillfully gilded, is used on them. Pure gold Aksumite coins of this period are often found in South Arabia. But some have no rulers' names at all. One ruler, known only as MHDYS [Mehadeyis?] issued copper and bronze coins with a Ge'ez legend identical to Emperor Constantine's motto, *"In hoc signo vinces"* ("In this sign [of the cross] you will conquer"). There is no evidence of backsliding into the old South Arabian faith. The Ge'ez translations of the Old and New Testaments show affinities with Syriac in religious terms and phraseology. The same is true of church liturgy. Monasticism in Ethiopia, which became firmly rooted, was based primarily on the Rule of Pachomius from Egypt. Church buildings in northern Ethiopia and Eritrea are still mostly rectangular, like the Near Eastern basilica, and divided lengthwise into three sections.[31] The round church that later became characteristic of most of the rest of the country must be an adaptation of African building styles. The Ethiopian church has remained Monophysite. It continued to depend on the Coptic Church of Egypt to supply its patriarch until after the Second World War.

The final flowering of Aksum

The reign of Emperor Kaleb in the sixth century marked the final period of Aksumite expansion under the banner of Christianity and in the context of association with, though not subordination to, the

[29] Celebrated and illustrated by Georg Gerster in *Churches in Rock*, Phaidon Press, London, 1970, pp. 135ff.

[30] The most remarkable activity of the early church fathers is the translation of so much Christian literature into Ge'ez. Enormous erudition was required for this task. Some parts of the Apocrypha are only completely known in their Ethiopic versions. Getachew Haile, "Ethiopic Literature" in Roderick Grierson (ed.), *African Zion, the Sacred Art of Ethiopia*, Yale University Press, 1993, provides an excellent introduction to the subject.

[31] Sergew, *op. cit.*, pp. 115-21.

East Roman (i.e. Byzantine) Empire. In contrast to earlier periods, a large group of sources in Greek, Latin, Syriac, Arabic and Ge'ez report on events of this time, so there is a wealth of information, though sources are not consistent with each other. Kaleb, who was probably the son of Tazena and grandson of Ella Amida II, used the throne name Ella Atsbeha.[32] He invaded Yemen to oust a Jewish Himyarite ruler who was persecuting the Christian population. Trade as well as political considerations and Christian enthusiasm must have motivated this action.

Judaism had become well established in the Hejaz, with traditions going back to the time of the legendary visit of the Queen of Sheba to King Solomon. It appears to have been adopted by Dhu Nuwas, the Himyarite king, as a state religion in opposition to the Christianity of the Byzantines and Aksumites. On the South Arabian coast, Christian communities maintained ties to Aksum. The Monophysite faith had become firmly established in Najran during the previous century. This town, today in Saudi Arabia, lies in a fertile valley where the caravan routes from Marib and more southerly centers led north ward to the Hejaz while others branched off across the desert to the Persian Gulf.

The Byzantine Emperor Justin I had written his "brother" in Aksum urging assistance to the Christians of Yemen. Power politics of the day played a role in this appeal. While Kaleb prepared an expedition, the King of Himyar, Dhu Nuwas, ordered a massacre of the Christians of Najran, which aroused the whole Christian world. The Aksumite expedition set out in 525, overthrew and killed Dhu Nuwas. Kaleb recognized an indigenous Christian king by the name of Sumyafa Ashwa as "governor on behalf of the *negus*". Byzantine Emperor Justin I was eager to enlist the South Arabians[33] as allies against the Persians, for Persia and Rome were rivals for dominance in the Near East at this period. Internal dissension in the region was too great for this aim to be achieved.

Aksumite rule in Yemen was beset by problems. After four years Sumyafa was overthrown in a rebellion and an Aksumite general, Abreha, took over, consolidated power as an almost independent sovereign first over Himyar and Saba, then over Hadhramawt. There is evidence of rivalry between Abreha and other Aksumite commanders. Though Abreha initially acknowledged subordination to Aksum, Kaleb soon considered him rebellious and sent troops against him. Though he was engaged in continual military operations, Abreha

[32] The name Atsbeha takes other forms in foreign reports and chronicles of the time, e.g. Ellesbaas, Hellesthaeos.

[33] The Himyarites are referred to as Homeritae and Sumyafa Ashwa as Esimiphaios in the *De Bello Persico* of the Byzantine historian Procopius.

was able to extend the range of his authority. In a long inscription at Marib he recorded measures he took following the disaster caused by the bursting of the great dam there. He is reported to have built a cathedral at Sana'a and restored churches in many locations. The Egyptian church dispatched a bishop and priests to assist in consolidating Christianity in Yemen. In later years Abreha used the title "King of Saba, Himyar, Hadhramawt, Yamanat, and all the Arabs of the Coastal Plain and the Highlands". He undertook an expedition to subdue the tribes controlling Mecca about 547, which may have had more to do with trade than Christianity. Whether Abreha reached some degree of *modus vivendi* with Kaleb is unclear, but the period of his domination in South Arabia and that of his two sons, Yaksum and Masruk – over a quarter of a century – was considered Ethiopian rule by the local inhabitants and was less to their liking than the period of Persian rule which followed in the 570s.

Though forced to withdraw from active involvement in South Arabia, Kaleb, like earlier Aksumite emperors, continued to use the same titles as Abreha, claiming lordship over the entire region, but his son Wazeb (Ella Gabaz), claimed to be ruler only over Saba and Himyar. As Munro-Hay observes:

Glorious though Kaleb's re-establishment of the Christian faith in the Yemen seemed to contemporary (and later) ecclesiastical historians, it was Aksum's swan song as a great power in the region. The real result may well have been quite the opposite, a weakening of Aksumite authority, over-expenditure in money and man-power, and a loss of prestige. The venture was, it seems, too ambitious for the times, and did Aksum nothing but harm in the long run.[34]

According to Ethiopian tradition, Kaleb abdicated, sent his crown to Jerusalem to be placed in the Holy Sepulchre and isolated himself in a cell at the monastery of Abba Pantelewon. A large rock-cut tomb north of Aksum, one of a pair, has been traditionally regarded as Kaleb's. The other is said to be that of his son, Gebre Maskal "Slave of the Cross", who is not attested by coins but about whom a great many traditions arose.[35] Under Kaleb's successors the Empire continued to play a role in international commerce and diplomacy, trading via the Nile Valley as well as on the Red Sea. Coins give evidence of eight rulers following Kaleb, but the quality of the coinage deteriorated. The last coins were issued by Emperors Gersem and Armah. Armah is sometimes identified with the *Najashi* Ashama ibn Abjar of Muslim sources, whose throne name could have been Ella Sahem. He was reported as ruler of Aksum at the time of the rise of Mohammed.

---

[34] Munro-Hay, *Aksum,* p. 88.

[35] E.g., as summarized by Sergew, *op.cit.,* pp. 161-4.

The rise of Islam

By the middle of the seventh century the city of Aksum seems to have been in decline. There is evidence that the once fertile agricultural lands around the city were becoming exhausted. Forests had been cut for fuel and construction. The climate seems to have worsened. Information on Nile levels in Egypt from this period provides evidence of erratic rainfall. Persian dominance in Yemen affected Red Sea trade. Meanwhile a new turning point in world history was developing: the rise of Islam. The rise of Islam did not contribute immediately to the decline of the Aksumite Empire. Quite the contrary. Mohammed, who was born about 570, had favorable associations with Ethiopia from childhood. According to some traditions, Mohammed when a child had an Ethiopian nurse. There was an Ethiopian Christian community in Mecca consisting of traders, artisans, and soldiers with whom Mohammed is likely to have had contact. He probably gained a favorable impression of Ethiopians from knowledge of Aksumite opposition to Jews and Persians in South Arabia. The Koran provides evidence of Mohammed's knowledge of Ethiopia and contains over 200 words which appear to be derived from Ge'ez.[36]

As Mohammed developed his mission, he fell into difficulties with the Quraish clan who controlled Mecca's holiest shrine, the Kaaba. Some of his followers felt endangered and decided to flee. He advised them, according to an oft-recounted tradition: "If you were to go to Abyssinia, it would be better for you until such time as Allah shall relieve you from your distress, for the king there will not tolerate injustice and it is a friendly country."[37] The first group of twelve men and five women fled across the Red Sea and reached Aksum in 616. Mohammed's daughter Rakiya and her husband were among them. A second group followed the next year, led by a cousin of the Prophet. Envoys sent by the Quraish to Aksum to persuade the *Najashi* Ashama ibn Abjar to send the Muslims back to Arabia were unsuccessful. One of these Muslims is reported to have accompanied the *Najashi* on a military expedition to the Nile from which the emperor returned victorious. A later Islamic tradition alleges that the *Najashi* was so impressed by the refugees that he himself became a secret convert to the new faith.[38]

In the sixth year after the Hejira (628) Mohammed himself, now in authority, sent an emissary to Ethiopia to request the return of

[36] Ibid., p. 181.

[37] Ibn Hisham, *Sira*, Cairo, 1937, as cited in J. Spencer Trimingham, *Islam in Ethiopia*, Frank Cass, London, 1965, p. 44.

[38] No evidence of a conversion has come to light in Ethiopia from written sources or traditions, but the allegation has continued to be repeated by Muslim writers into

his followers. The *Najashi* placed two ships at their disposal but only sixteen chose to return. The rest, according to Ethiopian tradition, settled at Negash in eastern Tigray where a substantial Muslim community has survived ever since that time.[39] When the *Najashi* died in 630, the Prophet is reported to have prayed for the repose of his soul. "Leave the Abyssinians in peace," he is reported to have said, "as long as they do not take the offensive." No jihad was ever declared against the Aksumite empire by the early Muslims. Trade continued, but as Islam gained strength, the Aksumites gradually lost control of much of the Red Sea during the following two centuries and Islam spread into the coastal regions where it has remained dominant ever since.

---

modern times. For a discussion of the allegations in the framework of early Islamic relationships see Haggai Erlich, *Ethiopia and the Middle East,* Lynne Rienner, Boulder, CO, 1994, pp. 3-19.

[39]Tombs at Negash attributed to these refugees are revered as a place of pilgrimage by Ethiopian Muslims. In recent years a large mosque has been built at the site and the tombs have been refurbished.

3

MEDIEVAL ETHIOPIA

ISOLATION AND EXPANSION

The slow decline of the Aksumite Empire after the reign of Emperor Kaleb brought a shift in Ethiopia's orientation. During medieval times the highlands from Wag and Lasta southward through Shoa, along the Rift Valley, and on to the southernmost regions of modern Ethiopia were politically, culturally and economically incorporated into the Ethiopian cultural region and, for the most part, into the Ethiopian state. This happened during the thousand years when Gibbon held that the Ethiopians were sleeping. They were doing nothing of the kind, but they had changed their priorities from the north to the south.[1] They never forgot the Mediterranean world, for Christianity flourished and spread and Jerusalem remained a living concept among the people with a contingent of Ethiopian monks maintaining a church there where pilgrims could gather. Heads of the church came from Egypt and there was contact with the Patriarch of Alexandria through correspondence[2] and occasional embassies; but the bulk of the political, economic and religious energy which Ethiopians expended during the medieval period was concentrated on southward expansion. While Ezana had conquered the Noba to the west and Kaleb had defeated and occupied Himyar and Saba across the Red Sea, Amda Tseyon's glorious victories and Zara Yakob's campaigns brought new southern lands into the realm of Ethiopian civilization – conquests that proved more lasting than those of the rulers of Aksumite times.

The decline of Aksum

Though the exact course of developments remains obscure, many factors have been adduced as contributing to the decline of Aksum. Emperor Kaleb's South Arabian campaigns must have been costly in men and resources and frustrating because of the lack of lasting political success. His abdication and retirement to a monk's cell led to a crisis over the succession. The problem was eventually overcome and eight successive rulers issued coins from the mid-sixth century

---

[1] Sergew Hable Selassie, *Ancient and Medieval Ethiopian History to 1270*, Addis Ababa University Press, 1972, pp. 215-92.

[2] Stuart Munro-Hay, *Ethiopia and Alexandria: The Metropolitan Episcopacy of Ethiopia*, Nubica/Polish Academy of Sciences, Wiesbaden/Warsaw, 1997.

through the first decade of the seventh.[3] The fact that rulers' titles are often replaced on their coins by exhortations such as "Mercy and Peace to the Peoples" may be evidence of troubled times. Rulers' names on coins, however, seldom correspond to names from other sources, because given names, throne names and titles are often confused and Arab, Persian, Greek and other sources use varying forms. Outlying regions of the empire experienced revolts. The Beja tribes in the northeast established separate kingdoms under their own rulers. Persian conquest of South Arabia put an end to Aksumite involvement there, but Persian hegemony was brief and was followed by Islamic conquest in the next century. The expansion of Islam eventually had far-reaching consequences for Ethiopia. Meanwhile erratic rainfall and depletion of soils and forests seem to have affected the prosperity of the area around the capital; 600 years of intensive exploitation of the land had taken its toll.

Trade with Egypt and the Mediterranean world continued, but Aksum lost control of Red Sea navigation after the middle of the 8th century. Aksumite products continued to be in demand, nevertheless: incense, ivory, skins, tortoise shell, animals and slaves. There is some evidence that Adulis suffered a destructive attack in the middle of the seventh century, but Massawa, the Dahlak Islands and Zeila (much farther south), were active as trading ports during the succeeding centuries.[4] Trade also continued through the Nile Valley, though Aksum no longer exercised predominance over the northern Sudanese states. Nubia was Christianized from Egypt in the latter half of the 6th century. Common religious faith in a period when Islam was expanding provided a basis for friendly relations with Ethiopia. Little evidence has come to light, however, of close Nubian political and cultural relations with the Ethiopian highlands.[5]

[3] Identifications are controversial. As more coins come to light and are more intensively studied, this judgment is subject to change. Stuart Munro-Hay comments: "After Kaleb I usually situate Alla Amida, Wazena, Ella Gabaz, Ioel, Hataz, Israel, Gersem, and Armah. Some ... have proposed cross identifications. I wonder, for example, if Ella Gabaz, only known from gold [coins], might be the issuer of the mysterious 'Za-ya abiyo la-Madkhen' coins." (Private communication, November 1998)

[4] A cache of Arab coins with dates up to the equivalent of AD 865 has been found at Debre Damo. Egyptian textiles from the same period have been found both at Debre Damo and Abba Pantelewon near Aksum; Sergew Hable Selassie, *op.cit.*, pp. 206, 219. These finds provide evidence of trade with Egypt and other Arab countries at least to the end of the ninth century.

[5] Polish excavations at the Sudanese sites of Faras and Old Dongola during the past quarter century have brought to light the remains of a brilliant Nubian Christian civilization which produced impressive art: Stefan Jakobielski (ed.), *Nubia Christiana*, Akademia Teologii Katolickiej, Warsaw, 1982. Christianity survived

Some scholars believe Aksum ceased to be the capital as early as the mid-seventh century.[6] Archaeology provides evidence of dilapidation of the large buildings of the capital and decline in its population, but whatever its condition, the city retained symbolic and religious importance – as it has ever since – in Ethiopian life. The two preeminent Ethiopian historians who have gathered all available traditions and combed Ethiopian chronicles, studied Byzantine and Arab historians, and examined sources such as the *History of the Patriarchs of Alexandria*[7] for references to this period – Sergew Hable Selassie and Taddesse Tamrat – have not yet been able to combine this information into a systematic narrative of Aksum's final centuries. However, traditions of several personalities active during these Ethiopian "Dark Ages" provide some impression of what was going on during the early medieval centuries.[8]

The Hatsani Danael has been identified from two late vocalized Ge'ez inscriptions at Aksum in which the *Hatsani* described a campaign against the Barya, a people living in what is today western Eritrea whose territory extended as far as Kassala, from whom he took booty and slaves back to Aksum. He also repulsed an attack on Aksum by people from Wolqayt, across the Takazze, who had attacked a region called Hasla on their way to the capital. Danael appears to have been a general who in the course of these campaigns may have usurped the role of an ineffective emperor, or even deposed him. The dates of his activity have not been determined. He did not assume the imperial designation *Najashi/Negus*. The title which he used, *Hatsani*, became familiar later as *Hatse* or *Atse*, a term for emperor used in Ethiopia into modern times. It may be derived from the Agaw word *asena*, meaning king. If Danael was an Agaw, he may have been a precursor of the Zagwe dynasty that came to power in the early eleventh century and finally moved the Ethiopian political center

---

in Nubia until the beginning of the sixteenth century. Only tenuous evidence of Ethiopian associations, however, has been found: Bogdan Zurawski, "Nubia and Ethiopia in the Christian Period - Some Affinities" in Paul B. Henze (ed.), *Aspects of Ethiopian Art from Ancient Axum to the Twentieth Century*, JED Press, London, 1993, pp. 33-41.

[6] E.g. Munro-Hay, *Aksum*, p. 93.

[7] Sergew Hable Selassie, *op.cit.*, pp. 159-79, 205-37; Taddesse Tamrat, *Church and State in Ethiopia*, Clarendon Press, Oxford, 1972, pp. 21-68; Munro-Hay, *Ethiopia and Alexandria*.

[8] Entries in *The Dictionary of Ethiopian Biography*, vol. I (from early times to the end of the Zagwe Dynasty), IES, AAU, 1975, are useful as summaries of information on prominent figures in early Ethiopian history. I have drawn on them in the discussions which follow but have not referenced them separately. See also Phillipson, *Ancient Ethiopia*, Chapter 6.

Above The High Semien, the "Roof of Africa", viewed from Adi Arkay.
Left Rock monoliths such as Ethiopians have carved since prehistoric times. These, from the early 20th century, stand near Kersa in Arsi.

Above The Stela Park in Aksum in July 1991, having survived the civil war in the north unscathed. *Below* The Sabaean temple at Yeha in Tigray from the 7th century BC – the oldest standing building in Ethiopia.

Above The largest Aksum stela is a monolith over 33 m. high. It apparently fell and broke while being erected and has lain undisturbed ever since. A tomb was recently discovered beneath its base. Each of the eleven rock-cut churches of Lalibela is different. The Church of Abba Libanos, *left*, is cut into a high cliff-face.

ISLAM IN ETHIOPIA. *Above* The oldest mosque in Massawa, dating from the 16th century. *Below* The new mosque at Negash, Tigray, where a group of the Prophet Mohamed's followers fled from Arabia for safety and were welcomed by the Aksumite emperor. Their tombs are near the mosque.

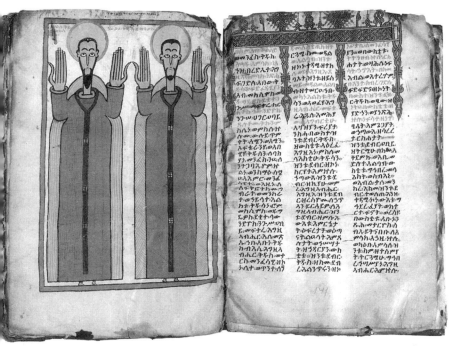

Above Pages from the Tullu Gudo Book of Saints, late 14th century, Lake Zway. *Below* Ethiopia's oldest monastery, founded in the 6th century, is on the top of Debre Damo, a flat mountain near the Eritrean border in Tigray. To reach it visitors must climb an 80-foot leather rope.

Above After Gondar became the capital in the 17th century each successive emperor built a castle. Most reveal Portuguese influence.

Below A skin-clad Amhara farmer using a wooden plow drawn by oxen in Lasta in 1991. Peasant agriculture in Ethiopia has continued unchanged for millennia.

of gravity from Tigray southward to Wag and Lasta.[9] Arab sources in the ninth and tenth centuries describe the Abyssinian *Najashis* or *Hadanis* as ruling from a capital called Ku'bar or Kobar. Al-Mas'udi wrote in the mid-tenth century:

The capital of Abyssinia is Ku'bar. It is a great city and the seat of the kingdom of the Najashi. The country has many towns and extensive territories stretching as far as the Abyssinian Sea. To it belongs the coastal plain opposite Yaman where there are many cities, such as Zaila, Dahlak, and Nasi, in which are Muslims tributary to the Abyssinians.[10]

The period of Aksum's decline was a time of continual expansion of the Orthodox Church and consolidation of its doctrine, ritual and organizational structure. Yared, the founder of Ethiopian church music and composer of the traditional hymnary, the *Deggwa*, was active during the reign of Emperor Gebre Maskal, a son of Kaleb.[11] Yared is credited with laying the groundwork for the entire system of Ethiopian religious education, systematizing Ge'ez grammar and establishing the rules for composition of *Qene*, Ge'ez poetry. Some of the accomplishments traditionally ascribed to him are undoubtedly in part the work of his pupils and successors over the next centuries. These developments created deepened understanding of Christian dogma and lore and served as inspiration for the energetic priests and lay leaders who planted Christianity and established imperial authority firmly among the Amhara, the Agaw, and other peoples of the south.

A ninth-century ruler called Dagna-Jan is described in chronicles as an ardent evangelizer of the southern provinces:

During his reign he took 150 priests from Aksum to Amhara and named them Debteras. After he left Tigray he made his capital city Weyna Dega. There were 60 *tabots* accompanying him to the battlefield. His soldiers drank the water of Fik from the Lake of Misrae Derginda, right of the Takazze from Tahiya Girai, Rib. It was astonishing that none of his men knew the region. Then he returned from Rib and when he counted his army he found 180,500 who were equipped

---

[9] Sergew, *op.cit.,* pp. 207-9; Munro-Hay, *Aksum,* pp. 262-3.

[10] Sergew, *op.cit.,* p. 223. Ku'bar has yet to be found. Since both churchmen and military leaders were giving priority to expansion southward, it would not be surprising if its site should eventually be found in Wag, the ancient principality directly to the south of Tigray. Wag, whose population is still basically Agaw, was a target of Christian evangelization as early as the 6th century. The high pass leading from southern Tigray into Wag is to this day named for Abba Mata, who appears to be identical with Abba Yemata, one of the Nine Syrian Saints. Old churches in Wag have traditions linking them to the earliest period of Christianization. Munro-Hay has offered the speculation that Ku'bar might be "an early stage of Lalibela" (personal communication, December 1998).

[11] There is little specific evidence of Gebre Maskal's reign, but it is likely to have encompassed part of the second quarter of the 6th century.

with battle helmets. He made them to follow him and went to his father [who]
left his son Dil-Na'od here. [...] From him the kingdom was taken and given
to others who were not Israelites and ruled 137 years.[12]

Except for Weyna Dega, in Begemder, the places are unidentified, but the fact that Dagna-Jan shifted his capital as he undertook
military campaigns is evidence of a practice that probably set in two
or three centuries earlier with the decline of Aksum as an active
administrative center.[13] The huge figure for Dagna-Jan's army is
fanciful, but is evidence of the chronicler's desire to make him seem
powerful and important. The final reference is to the replacement of
the Solomonic line by the Zagwe dynasty not long after Dagna-Jan's
time.

Emperor Dil Na'od, the last of the Solomonic line in many Ethiopian king lists, is associated with the founding of the famous mon
astery of Debre Egziabeher on a mountain overlooking Lake Hayq
in Wollo, which is believed to have occurred around the end of the
ninth century. Lake Hayq later became a base for evangelization of
the center and southern part of the country. It reached its apogee as
the seat of the great thirteenth century monastic activist, Iyasus Mo'a
(see below).

The most dramatic personality of this era is a mysterious woman,
the wicked Queen Judith or Gudit, who attacked Aksum toward the
end of the tenth century. She has variously been characterized as a
pagan, a lapsed Christian, a Jew, an Agaw or a Beja, and as a subordinate of the Emperor who rebelled to lead a pagan resurgence against
Christianity. She is credited with a lust to destroy by fire and sword
churches, monasteries, buildings and everything that symbolized
Christian and imperial power, and is often called Esato in Amharic,
a name derived from the word for fire. She is said to have killed the
emperor, ascended the throne herself, and reigned for forty years.
Accounts of her violent misdeeds are still related among peasants
in the north Ethiopian countryside.[14] A letter from an unidentified
Ethiopian emperor to King Girgis II of Nubia preserved in the *History
of the Patriarchs of Alexandria* reports he has been attacked by the

[12] As cited from a manuscript in the National Library, Addis Ababa, by Sergew
Hable Selassie, *op.cit.,* p. 203. Dagna-Jan is nineteenth on the list of emperors
between AD 623 and 915 cited by Sergew, the immediate predecessor of Dil
Na'od, and assigned dates 885-905. Taddesse Tamrat dates his reign nearly half a
century earlier, *op.cit.,* p. 36.

[13] This practice persisted for the next seven centuries until Gondar became a
permanent capital in the seventeenth century.

[14] On my first visit to the rock church of Abreha and Atsbeha in eastern Tigray in
1970, I noticed that its intricately carved ceiling was blackened by soot. The
priest explained it as the work of Gudit, who had piled the church full of hay and
set it ablaze nine centuries before.

"Queen of the Bani al-Hamwiyya" and "bemoans his fate, attributing his distress to a rift between the monarchy and the patriarchate, and begs the Nubian king to intercede for him with the Alexandrian patriarch".[15]

Gudit's fame was widespread. The Arab writer Ibn Haukal wrote:

The country of the *Habasha* was been ruled by a woman for many years now; she has killed the king ... who was called *Hadani*. Until today she reigns with complete independence in her own country and the frontier areas of the territory of the *Hadani*, in the southern part of the country of the *Habasha*.[16]

The reference to the "southern part" of Abyssinia is significant in light of the speculation of some scholars that Bani al-Hamwiyya ("Sons of the Ḥamwiyya") should actually be read Bani al-Haghwiyya, "Sons of the Agaw". One tradition identifies Gudit as daughter of the King of Lasta who resided in Bugna. On the other hand, the hypothesis of the great Italian Ethiopianist, Conti Rossini, that Gudit's people were the al-Damutah, is appealing. This Sidama people, distinct from the Agaw, lived in a region which was adjacent to (or may even have formed part of) the area called Sasu, probably south of the Blue Nile, where Aksumite rulers sent caravans to obtain gold and slaves. These Aksumite expeditions may have contributed to resentments which were eventually expressed in Gudit's depredations and conquest of Aksum when it had already declined and retained only the symbolism of a capital. The modern version of the name al-Damutah may survive as the district of Damot in the rich highland province of Gojjam, which still has a significant Agaw population and did not begin to undergo conversion to Christianity until the twelfth century.[17]

There is no confirmation that Gudit actually ruled from Aksum. She is credited by both Ethiopian tradition and scholarly opinion with weakening what remained of the Aksumite state and undermining the Solomonic imperial line to the point where a new dynasty took its place and completely abandoned the old capital.

The Zagwe Dynasty

Gudit is said to have been succeeded by Dagna-Jan, whose throne name was Anbasa Wudem. He temporarily restored peace and order and was succeeded by his son, Dil Na'od. But the condition of the

[15] As cited by Munro-Hay, *Aksum*, p. 15, and discussed in the same author's *Ethiopia and Alexandria*, pp. 133-8. Sergew, *op.cit.*, devotes seven pages to summarizing references and traditions about Gudit (pp. 225-32) but concludes that it is impossible to reach firm judgments about her origin or her activities.

[16] As cited by Taddesse, *op.cit.*, p. 39.

[17] Taddesse, *op.cit.*, pp. 38-41.

50 *Layers of Time*

dynasty had been so weakened that Dil Na'od, though credited with rebuilding churches and undertaking military expeditions to the south, was unable to reestablish Aksumite authority. There were strains with Egypt over the appointment of a new patriarch. Chronicles record several legends explaining the change of dynasties. One of the most entertaining recounts that

Dil Na'od had a daughter named Mesobe Worq whom he loved much among his children. A learned old man told him that whosoever will marry your daughter will deprive you of your kingdom. To avoid this, the emperor kept her alone in the palace and forbade anyone to visit her. [...] There was a man from the Agaw of Lasta, Merara Tekle Haymanot, who finally succeeded in becoming good friends with the Emperor. The man was brave and distinguished himself on the battlefield against people in all parts of the Empire. He fell in love with the princess at first sight and the same happened to Mesobe Worq. She told him how he could take her as his wife. [...] [The two collaborated in deceiving the emperor.] The officer took the princess to his country. When the emperor learned what had taken place, he sent a messenger to Merara Tekle Haymanot telling him to return his daughter. Merara knew the intention of the emperor and refused to return Mesobe Worq. The emperor had no other choice than to use military means to regain his lost daughter. Even this failed and the sovereignty passed into the hands of Merara Tekle Haymanot.[18]

The tradition is noteworthy for the way it links the new, "non-Israelite" dynasty to its Solomonic predecessor. Though the Zagwe rulers did not claim Solomonic blood, they did not represent or desire a sharp break with Aksumite traditions. In at least three key respects, in fact, the new dynasty represented a reaffirmation and revival of previous traditions: the concept of divine kingship; devotion to Christianity; and architecture. The Agaw language did not replace Ge'ez for religious and literary purposes, though it may have been used in administration and in the army. Amharic seems by this time to have evolved into a language of wide use.

The name Zagwe is probably derived from the term Agaw. It was indeed an Agaw dynasty. Merara was from a princely family of Bugna in Lasta. The date of his accession to the throne may have been in the first half of the twelfth century. King lists vary wildly[19] as do traditions of the length of Zagwe predominance. Succession among the Zagwe

[18] Abbreviated from Sergew's translation of the *Gadla Iyasus Mo'a, op.cit.*, pp. 236-7.

[19] Merara's patronymic, Tekle Haymanot, may have been added later by chroniclers to underscore the fact he was Christian. In some traditions, a man named Tekle Haymanot is cited as the first Zagwe ruler. Some kinglists contain as few as five and others as many as sixteen Zagwe rulers. Some may have been brothers or sons who did not ascend the throne, for there is little evidence that some of those in the lists ruled at all; Sergew, *op.cit.*, pp. 239-42.

seems to have more often passed from one brother to another and then from uncle to nephew than from father to son. Later chronicles were compiled for four of the most active Zagwe emperors: Yimrahana-Christos, Lalibela, Na'akuto-La'ab, and Yitbarek. Taddesse Tamrat thinks it probable that Yimrahana-Christos was the third ruler of the dynasty and that he was succeeded by Harbe, brother of Lalibela. Lalibela was followed by Na'akuto-La'ab and Yitbarek.[20]

Yimrahana-Christos, is credited with reviving close cultural contacts with Egypt and asked the Egyptian ruler to send him building material. He is considered to have inaugurated the tradition of hewing rock churches. A splendid cave church in the countryside north of Lalibela bears his name. About the same time another outstanding example of Aksumite architecture in rock was cut south of Sekota, the capital of Wag, Wokro Meskale Christos. These and the two Bilbala churches, also north of Lalibela, may all be antecedents of the great churches at Lalibela, all attributed to the king of that name, the most famous and revered of all the Zagwe rulers.

An enormous amount of legend developed around Lalibela, much of which was incorporated into the lengthy chronicle of his reign compiled about a century later, early enough to have drawn on live traditions. He was born in Roha, also called Adefa, the Zagwe capital which since his death has borne his name. As he emerged from his mother a dense cloud of bees enveloped her and she gave him the name Lalibela, which means "the bee recognizes his sovereignty." He grew up to be an unusually handsome and healthy young man but his brother, the reigning king Harbe, became jealous and tried to poison him. He did not succumb on this or on a second attempt, when he miraculously survived drinking a bowl of poisoned beer that immediately killed a dog.

Angels came to him and gave him God's command to build ten monolithic churches. After a period in the wilderness, God gave him a wife but he was accused of stealing her from another man and flogged at the order of his brother. An angel rescued him and arranged for him to be carried to Jerusalem, where he saw all its wonders and then returned to Ethiopia. God ordered his brother Harbe to go on foot to meet him and beg forgiveness. Harbe abdicated and crowned Lalibela king. The new king put all his energy into cutting the churches, joining workmen by day and letting angels continue the work at night. This work accomplished, he is said to have endowed his churches handsomely and given all his worldly goods to the poor. He fell ill at the age of 70 and died on 22 June 1220.[21]

[20] Taddese, *op.cit.*, p. 56.

[21] Summarized, probably somewhat imaginatively, by Budge, *op.cit.*, pp. 279-83.

The Lalibela churches are indeed a wonder of the world, as the Portuguese Jesuit Father Francisco Alvares declared on seeing them in the 1520s. Though Lalibela has survived in tradition as a benign, saintly figure, he must in reality have been an energetic politician and effective organizer. The cutting of the eleven rock churches was a project of major proportions, said to have taken twenty-four years. Saladin captured Jerusalem in 1189 and is said to have shown favor to the Ethiopians there. Nevertheless pilgrimage to the Holy City, which had become popular among Ethiopians by this time, seems to have been interrupted by the Muslim advance into the Holy Land. Lalibela is believed to have aspired to create a second Jerusalem as a place of pilgrimage. The stream flowing through the area was named the Jordan and a tomb of Adam was built at the entrance to Bet Golgotha-Mikael.

Alvares was told that Egyptian stonecutters were hired.[22] Modern scholars have speculated that Indians may also have had a role in creation of the churches. Whoever did the work, it was a project that must have required massive mobilization of labor, highly professional supervision of the rock-cutting, and substantial resources to provide for the maintenance of the large workforce. Like the great stelae at Aksum, the cutting of these churches in the remote mountain fastnesses of central Ethiopia remains a technological wonder. It has been estimated that the amount of stone removed equalled at least five times the quantity taken out in the carving of the great Egyptian temple at Abu Simbel. The churches faithfully reproduce Aksumite construction in detail. There is no evidence of mistakes in the carving. There had to be models and careful planning. The most remarkable feature is the carefully executed interior carving and ornamentation, all of which would have had to be done by the light of torches.[23]

Envoys of the Patriarch of Alexandria reported in 1210 that Lalibela had two sons, Yitbarek and Na'akuto-La'ab. According to the latter's

[22] There is evidence that skilled Egyptian workmen emigrated to Ethiopia at the time of the great famine of 1200-1. See Munro-Hay, *Ethiopia and Alexandria*, p. 180. "One, perhaps a supervisor, left his name cut on the great column in Bet Maryam, but the priests at Lalibela do not show it to visitors and keep the column wrapped in cloth. I have a photograph of it." (Personal communication from Prof. Stanislaw Chojnacki). In 1971 priests in this church told me that the wrapped column contains the history of the world – both past and future – but it cannot be revealed to mortals; *Ethiopian Journeys*, p. 55.

[23] Alvares was astounded by the Lalibela churches, described them at length, but finally declared: 'I weary of writing more about these buildings because it seems to me that I shall not be believed if I wrote more because regarding what I have already written they may blame me for untruth.[...] No other Portuguese went to see these buildings except myself, and I went twice to see and describe them because of what I had heard said about them'.

chronicle, he was actually a nephew of Lalibela (perhaps the son of his predecessor, Harbe) whom he initially chose as his successor. Rivalry and competition, common among Ethiopian princes, seems to have developed with Na'akuto La'ab being displaced from the throne by Yitbarek after a short reign. Dissension among the Zagwe princes appears to have inspired political movements against them and encouraged assertiveness among the Amhara and Tigrayans. These circumstances brought about the end of the Zagwe dynasty.

The period of the Zagwe emperors marked an important stage in the process of Christianization of Ethiopia. But before recounting the next stage – the replacement of the Zagwe emperors by new rulers claiming to be rightful descendants of Solomon and Sheba — let us summarize the conclusions of serious scholars about the Ethiopian Jews, the Falashas or, as they call themselves, the *Beta Israel.* The legends of Queen Gudit attribute significant political importance to this group. Their origin is both mysterious and controversial.

The Beta Israel (Falashas) and the Kebra Negast

The traditional Ethiopian historian is a writer or reciter of history without academic training or background who bases it on traditions preserved orally or in chronicles. Aleqa Taye Gebre Maryam, writing in *Y'ityop'ya Hizb Tarik,* originally published in 1922, repeats traditions of the origin of these people that have survived to modern times and provided a basis for romantic speculation about them by interested Europeans since the nineteenth century, with Americans joining them in the twentieth:

The three accounts about the Falashas which we said may be believed are as follows. The roots and origin of the Falashas who are in Ethiopia are without doubt in the lineage of Israel. However, it is at three different times that they entered Ethiopia from Palestine and Israel. First are those who came together with ... Menelik I. They stayed together up to New Testament times. The people, kings, and the entire kingdom of Ethiopia believed in the Gospel and were converted to Christianity by Abba Salama Kesate Berhan. The Falashas, however, were separated from their brothers and countrymen and refused to give up the Laws of Orit and to believe the word of the Gospel and be converted to Christianity. They remained apart.

Second, at the time that King Asbyanos and T'it'os of Rome sacked Jerusalem, burned its temple and decimated the people of Israel, those who survived were scattered to various parts of Israel, and one group migrated from Palestine and entered Ethiopia.

For his text and commentary see C.F. Beckingham and G.W.B. Huntingford (eds), *The Prester John of the Indies...being the narrative of the Portuguese Embassy to Ethiopia in 1520,* 2 vols, Hakluyt Society, Cambridge, 1961, pp. 205-28, 526-42.

Third, there are those who during the era of Gudit fled from the King of
Egypt, entered Ethiopia with Gudit, overthrew and destroyed the Christian
kingdom, burned the churches of Aksum and reviled Christianity. The earlier
Falasha united with those of the later period and because they helped Gudit
overthrow the kingdom, persecuted Christians and reviled the faith of the
Gospel, and when Gudit died and King Anbasa Weddem was crowned, he
decimated the Falashas and took revenge for the blood of the Christians...[24]

Since 1975 the official Israeli view has been that the Ethiopian
Beta Israel are direct ethnic descendants of original Jewish emigrants
to Ethiopia, thereby justifying their immigration to Israel under the
Law of Return. According to this theory the first emigrants would
indeed have accompanied the son of King Solomon and the Queen
of Sheba, Menelik I, others would have followed, and a major wave
would probably have come at the time of the Roman conquest of
Palestine. Scholarly effort has produced no evidence whatsoever to
support these hypotheses.

Romantic pseudo-scholars have long resorted to entertaining
speculation about conversions of Ethiopians to Judaism by Jews from
Egypt and Yemen. These writers have allotted the Jewish military
community that Herodotus reported in the fifth century BC on the
island of Elephantine near Aswan a major role in carrying Judaism to
Ethiopia. Jewish captives allegedly brought to Ethiopia after the
South Arabian campaign of Emperor Kaleb have been claimed
as ancestors of Beta Israel adherents.[25] Evidence to support these
theories has also had to be invented or "rediscovered" under questionable circumstances. There is no reference to Jews in Aksumite
inscriptions. There is no evidence of use of Hebrew in Ethiopia until
modern times. No Falashas knew it until taught by Israelis in the
1950s. There is no mention of Beta Israel in Ethiopian chronicles
before the fourteenth century. Beta Israel music and ritual have been
shown to be derived from Ethiopian Christian tradition,[26] while the

[24] *History of the People of Ethiopia by Alaqa Tayya Gabra Maryam*, translated by
Grover Hudson and Tekeste Negash, Uppsala University, 1987, p. 53.

[25] For an entertaining recent American recitation of all these legends see Louis
Rapoport, *The Lost Jews*, Stein & Day, New York, 1981. By far the most elaborately
embroidered compilation of all the mythology that has accumulated through the
years about both Ethiopian Jews and the origins of Christianity in the country is
a massive piece of fiction masquerading as historical research by the Englishman
Graham Hancock, *The Sign and the Seal*, Heinemann, London, 1991. Reprinted
and translated several times and purveyed to tourists who go to Ethiopia, it out-
does the most improbable legends Ethiopians themselves relate about their past.
Christopher Clapham in his review "A far-fetched treasure" in the *Times Literary
Supplement* of 15 May 1992, employs both humor and logic to expose the flimsy
foundations on which Hancock's theses rest.

[26] Kay Kaufmann Shelemay, *Music, Ritual and Falasha History*, Michigan State
University Press, East Lansing, MI, 1986.

manuscripts and art of this group are also patterned directly on Christian models.[27]

Evidence that Queen Gudit was actually a Jewish adherent is tenuous, to say the least. Evidence that she represented a pagan reaction against Christianization is more logical. The kind of reaction that Gudit represents seems to have been associated with the resentment and resistance of the Agaw and other more southerly peoples to Christian proselytizing, conquest and rule from the north. These groups came into conflict with the military colonies and Christian missions which were the main instruments of the extension southward of the power of the Ethiopian state. They may have been joined by dissident or rebelling northern Christians who felt their interpretations of ritual, sacred texts and traditions of art represented a more ancient Israelite connection than Orthodox Monophysite Christianity itself. The Beta Israel can thus be understood as a manifestation of the kind of rebellious archaism that has often come to the surface in Christianity – e.g. Russian Old Believers and German Old Lutherans. Assertion of Jewish derivation, they felt, provided them with a stronger claim to legitimacy than their Christian enemies.

It was not irrational in the Ethiopian context for opponents of north Ethiopian Christian expansion to claim to be Jews, for in spite of the absence of evidence of an ethnic Jewish element in the Ethiopian population, there is clearly a body of Jewish-related lore and tradition that extends back to pre-Aksumite times. This was a major part of the general body of East Mediterranean religious and intellectual tradition that began to penetrate Ethiopia through both the Nile Valley and over Red Sea/South Arabian routes early in the 1st millennium BC. Ezana's official adoption of Christianity was not a new departure, but a continuation – evolution – of this tradition. The evangelizing of the *Tsadkan* and the Nine Syrian Saints reinforced Old Testament (*Orit*) awareness. Ethiopian Christianity thus retained and nurtured early Christian traditions and practices, as a visitor to an Ethiopian country church can see today by examining the wall paintings and listening to the priest's explanation of them. The Bible with its many references to Cush and Ethiopia provides affirmation of the mutual awareness of East Mediterranean Christians (and Jews) and Ethiopians.[28] Over two millennia these traditions had become so well anchored in Ethiopian awareness that "pagan" resistance to the southward expansion of the Christian empire was justified within an Israelite context.[29]

[27] Richard Pankhurst, "Falasha-Christian or Christian-Falasha Art?" in Henze (ed.), *Aspects*, pp. 42-52.

[28] Edward Ullendorff, *Ethiopia and the Bible*, Oxford University Press for the British Academy, London, 1968.

[29] By far the most definitive analysis of the origins of the Beta Israel and their role

When the Zagwe dynasty came to an end with the restoration of the Solomonic dynasty in 1270, the contest continued in the same Judeo-Christian context. The *Kebra Negast* ("The Glory of Kings"), the Ethiopian national epic, was committed to writing early in the fourteenth century by Nebure-id Yeshaq of Aksum. It is primarily a compilation and interpretation of material long known: the legend of the Queen of Sheba and King Solomon, excerpts from the Old and New Testaments and the Apocrypha, and material from Greek, Coptic, Syriac and Arabic religious writings. References to the Old Testament and parallel Jewish writings are the most frequent, though "the manner in which the *Kebra Negast* uses Old Testament quotations is apt to be rather cavalier at times ... the meaning of a passage may be stretched to fit any subject the wording will bear."[30] This book rapidly attained the status of a sacred text, revered, copied in monasteries throughout the late Middle Ages, and still cited in the two constitutions of Haile Selassie's reign as the foundation of the Ethiopian state and authority for the origin of the Solomonic dynasty.[31] Though modern Ethiopians no longer take the Queen of Sheba legend literally, it commands wide belief among traditional elements of the population and continues to inspire both popular and serious art.[32]

The Solomonic restoration

What has been called the Solomonic restoration in Ethiopian history seems to have been only a change of dynasties, but the fact that the members of the new dynasty claimed Solomonic ancestry extending

---

in later Ethiopian history is James Quirin, *The Evolution of the Ethiopian Jews: A History of the Beta Israel (Falasha) to 1920,* University of Pennsylvania Press, Philadelphia, 1992.

[30] Ullendorff, *op.cit.,* pp. 77-8. The eminent Ethiopian scholar, Getachew Haile, judges the *Kebra Negast* primarily in religious terms: "[It] is a legendary history which claims that Ethiopia, through the union of the Queen of the South (i.e. Ethiopia) and King Solomon of Israel, has replaced the old Israel and become the African Zion" – "Ethiopic Literature" in Roderick Grierson (ed.), *African Zion,* Yale University Press, 1993, p. 49.

[31] Two copies of the *Kebra Negast* were among the cache of manuscripts captured at Magdala by the Napier Expedition and presented to the British Museum. Emperor Yohannes IV wrote to Queen Victoria and the Foreign Secretary in1872 requesting their return: "There is a book called *Kebra Negast* which contains the Law of the whole of Ethiopia; and the names of the chiefs, churches, and provinces are in this book. I pray you will find out who has got this book and send it to me, for in my country my people will not obey my orders without it" (as cited by Ullendorff, *op.cit.,* p. 75).

[32] A new translation of the *Kebra Negast,* with comment by editor Miguel F. Brooks, was issued by Red Sea Press, Lawrenceville, NJ, in 1996.

back to the rulers of Aksum and the fact that their claim has been widely accepted ever since gives the change the effect of a restoration. It demonstrates the enormous importance of historical continuity in Ethiopia and the deep sense of history that has always permeated Ethiopian life. Deep as this sense of history was in the medieval centuries, it did not result in much concern for the accuracy of historical records. As we have seen, the entire period from the fall of Aksum through the Zagwe dynasty is extremely difficult to sort out. The same is true of the events connected with the end of the Zagwe dynasty and the rise of the next. Sources are skimpy and contradictory. Traditions have been embroidered *ex post facto* to justify later views of events which probably have little relationship to reality as well as the power relationships of later times. About the general course of events, however, there is little disagreement. A man who took the throne named Yekuno Amlak ("He Shall Rule") conquered the last Zagwe king, killed him, and

founded a new Christian dynasty. [...] Common resentment of Lasta domination probably brought him much support in Tigre, where the Amhara
tradition of Tigre origin strengthened his position as against the Zagwe.
The predominantly Agaw rulers of the Christian kingdom were deposed,
and the throne was once again occupied by a Semitic-speaking monarch.
Only in this sense was the advent of Yikunno-Amlak a *restoration.*[33]

As early as the 8th century the political center of the country had begun to move southward from the Tigrayan heartland which by that time had been mostly Christianized. The advent of the Zagwe dynasty brought the political center firmly into Agaw country in Wag and Lasta. The Agaw, in spite of the exertions of pious rulers such as Lalibela, were difficult to convert completely to Christianity. Large pockets of people adhered to traditional beliefs intermingled with Judaic practices and resisted Christian domination. They seem to have become the Falasha. Meanwhile Christian colonists kept mov-ing southward through Angot and the region that became known as Amhara and reached Shoa. While Muslim principalities grew up along the western edge of the Rift Valley, Muslims did not penetrate far into the highlands. Christians established themselves in this attrac-tive region among pagan populations, probably of Sidama stock. Good land was plentiful. Religion probably had less to do with the expan-sion and consolidation of a prosperous Semitic-speaking peasantry than did the spread of ox-plow cultivation, introduction of more pro-ductive crops long known in the north, and expansion of improved practices in animal husbandry and poultry raising.[34] Muslims were

---

[33] Taddesse Tamrat, *op.cit.,* p. 68.

[34] The two introductory chapters in James C. McCann, *People of the Plow, an*

active in trading with the coast. Through their Muslim neighbors, who supplied trade goods, highland Shoa became tenuously linked to the wider world.[35]

Yekuno Amlak, whose baptismal name may have been Tesfa Yesus ("Hope of Jesus"), was allegedly descended through his father from the last Aksumite ruler, Dil Na'od.[36] The connection remains tenuous and may have been invented only after his accession to power. His mother is said to have been the servant of a rich Amhara chief. Connection with this family may have given him the opportunity to gain military and political experience. During fighting against the Zagwe he is said to have been caught and imprisoned by Yitbarek. According to tradition he escaped and made a pact with Iyasus Mo'a of Debre Hayq, organized a widespread revolt against Yitbarek, and established an independent kingdom in Amhara and Shoa.[37] It is possible that Yekuno Amlak was allied for a time with the Muslim Sultanate of Shoa. The date of his killing of Yitbarek may have been as early as 1268, but 1270 has become accepted as the date of the change of dynasties since it is believed to have been the date of the death of Na'akuto La'ab who was in a struggle with Yitbarek for primacy.[38]

It is difficult to take issue with Budge's judgment of the Zagwe period:

There was little to show ... for the rule of the Zagwe kings, for they conducted no wars of importance, they made no conquests, and they added no

---

Agricultural History of Ethiopia, 1800-1990, University of Wisconsin Press, Madison, 1995, pp. 23-83, provide perspective on these developments.

[35] Archaeological excavation at medieval sites (none has been undertaken in Ethiopia to date) offers promise of extending understanding of politics and movements of people during this period. Coins, metal objects, remains of textiles and pottery would all provide evidence of trade connections. Pollen analysis would provide information on crops. I discuss this at length in a privately circulated essay, "Archaeology in Ethiopia - the Importance of the Medieval Period", 1997.

[36] Dil Na'od is supposed to have escaped to Shoa where his descendants for eight generations kept the memory of their Solomonic origin alive. See Sergew, *op.cit.,* p. 289.

[37] There is a tradition that Yekuno Amlak studied at Hayq and there developed a close friendship with Iyasus Mo'a, who, convinced of his Aksumite lineage, supported him in his revolt against the Zagwe. After defeating Yitbarek, Yekuno Amlak conferred the title of *Aqabe Sa'at* ("Guardian of the Hours") on the Abbot with the understanding that all of his successors as abbots of Hayk would also have it. The practice continued until the invasion of Ahmad Gragn.

[38] Taddesse Tamrat, *op.cit.,* pp. 64-8. Budge recounts traditions of two Zagwe kings who are supposed to have ruled after Yitbarek, but at best they appear to have been pretenders who had only small territories. Sergew Hable Selassie's version of the rise of the new dynasty differs in several respects from Taddesse's, *op.cit.,* pp. 289-92.

territory to the kingdom. Their principal monuments are the rock-hewn churches.[...] During their reigns the Arabs consolidated their rule in the countries they had conquered and [to the west] Islam ... made its way as far south ... as Meroe. In fact Abyssinia was shut in on both the east and the west sides by Arabs...[39]

Yekuno Amlak originally had friendly relations not only with the Muslims of Ifat, but also made contact with the rulers of Yemen and Egypt. In 1273, in a letter sent through Yemen to Mamluke Sultan Baybars requesting a new *Abun*, he declared his friendly sentiments toward Muslims. But the Egyptians sent no bishop during his reign and he eventually blamed the Yemeni ruler for interfering with his relations with Cairo. Yekuno Amlak's major military undertaking was a campaign against pagan Damot to the southwest, though he did not succeed in completely subjecting the region. Devoted to Christianity, he caused the church of Genneta Maryam to be cut in the base of a mountain east of Lalibela, had it richly painted, and commemorated his work with an inscription which begins: "By the Grace of God I King Yekuno Amlak, after I had come to the throne by the will of God, built this church".

The frescos which cover the walls and ceiling of this skillfully carved church are the earliest datable wall paintings so far discovered in Ethiopia. They include not only representations of human beings, saints, and angels, but birds, and domestic and wild animals, including two elephants. The paintings contain extensive inscriptions. In this respect they differ markedly from the rock churches of Lalibela, which, except for identifications of a few of the saints in Bet Golgotha Mikael, are devoid of inscriptions.[40]

Yekuno Amlak was succeeded in 1285 by his son Solomon who took the throne name Yigba Tseyon ("Let Zion Enter"), who immediately attempted to repair strained relations with neighboring Muslim principalities and again wrote to Egypt asking the Sultan to have the Patriarch of Alexandria send an *abun*. The Egyptians, unsure of what was happening in Ethiopia, held off.[41] Toward the end of his brief reign,

[39] *History of Ethiopia*, p. 284.

[40] Most of the frescoes of Genneta Maryam have withstood the ravages of time for well over 700 years, but they urgently need the attention of specialists who could clean accumulations of dust, bring out the color of figures, clarify inscriptions where there has been fading and flaking, and stabilize plaster that has begun to loosen. These paintings have yet to be fully published and analyzed. The most recent work done on them is a lengthy analysis by Ewa Balicka-Witakowska presented at the XIXth International Congress on Byzantine Studies in Copenhagen in August 1996, to be published in its *Proceedings*.

[41] Munro-Hay, *Ethiopia and Alexandria*, pp. 199-206. Both Tadesse Tamrat and Munro-Hay believe that the absence of an Egyptian patriarch during this period may have generated the popular legend that ascribes to St. Tekle Haymanot a

Yigba Tseyon refused to choose one of his five sons as successor and instead decreed that each should rule for a year. Surprisingly, the arrangement seems to have worked for a few years after 1294, but it broke down completely in 1299 and a younger son of Yekuno Amlak, Wudem Ar'ad, took the throne. During his fifteen-year reign, he had difficulties with the aggressive Muslims of Ifat who were trying to expand onto the eastern edges of the plateau, but he seems to have been successful in holding them back and leaving a favorable situation to his son and successor, perhaps the greatest of the medieval emperors, Amde Tseyon.[42] Before recounting the principal events of his long reign, however, let us go back to look at two of the greatest religious leaders of the era, for the expansion of Ethiopia southward was as much the result of the efforts of energetic clerics as of warrior emperors.

Iyasus Mo'a and Tekle Haymanot

Born to a Christian family in Dahana in Wag, Iyasus Mo'a travelled to Tigray about 1241 and entered the monastery of Debre Damo, where he served under Abba Yohanni, said to have been the seventh abbot after its founder, Abuna Aregawi, one of the Nine Syrian Saints.[43] The young Iyasus Mo'a showed a talent for writing, copying the four Gospels while at Debre Damo, and was sent out on missionary journeys, which became his main vocation. About 1248 he travelled to Lake Hayq in Wollo.[44] There he turned the church of St. Stephen on an island off the north shore into a major monastic establishment, Hayq Istifanos. According to tradition, this church was founded in Aksumite times. Iyasus Mo'a had a strong commitment to Aksumite traditions. He attracted young men from Christian communities to the south and west of Hayq. These he trained to go out and establish new monasteries themselves.[45] This was a marked change from the widespread

---

major role in establishing the new dynasty. Iyasus Mo'a's role may have been more important.

[42] Taddesse Tamrat, *op.cit.*, pp. 128-32.

[43] If Debre Damo was actually founded in the sixth century, all its abbots must have been very long-lived! Anomalies of this sort are common in most Ethiopian chronicles and in oral traditions. They recall similar disparities in treatment of time in the Old Testament.

[44] Taddesse Tamrat, *op.cit.*, pp. 36-7, 158-64.

[45] They included the founder of Daga Istifanos in Lake Tana, Abba Hiruta Amlak; several others who founded monastic communities in Amhara, notably Abba Anorewos, who founded Debre Gol and was then joined by another of Iyasus Mo'a's pupils, Beselote-Mikael, who later travelled to Tigray, while Anorewos went to an island in Lake Zway. At least three evangelists of the name Anorewos figure in the religious literature of the time; however, it is not always possible to distinguish one from another.

practice of Christian hermits who dwelt in caves in isolated locations, prayed, told fortunes and gave advice to the sick, but did little to spread Christianity actively.

The secular clergy, who function in the world, living among and serving the population in contrast to the monastic clergy, consisted of married priests, deacons and other church functionaries who had little formal education and who often farmed, traded or served as local officials – (as they have in Ethiopia ever since). Iyasus Mo'a believed that Christianity needed solid monastic foundations to spread and survive. He admired learning and instilled respect for it in his disciples who carried it to the monasteries they founded. A manuscript at Hayq contains a personal note which states, "I, Iyasus Mo'a sinner and unworthy ... gave this book of the Four Gospels to Hayq Istifanos" and is followed by a list of eighty-nine further books he left to the monastery on his death in 1292.[46]

The most famous of Iyasus Mo'a's missionary pupils was Tekle Haymanot, who was born about 1215 in Shoa. His father is said to have been a priest. At Etissa in the district of Salalish near the head of the Kassem Gorge, now a popular pilgrimage site, the stone on which his mother is said to have borne him is still shown to visitors. Large monumental tombs have been built over the graves of his mother and father nearby.[47] When I visited Etissa in the April 1997, I was also shown a cave where Tekle Haymanot is reputed to have sheltered. A short distance beyond it a young monk from a nearby parish had begun to carve a new rock church in the tufa cliffside. He proudly led us through its passageways, still dusty from his rock-cutting, to the chamber that would soon receive the *tabot* which would sanctify the church. In spite of Mengistu Haile Mariam's efforts to discourage religious observance, the religious impulse remained very much alive in Ethiopia during the Derg period and, in fact, as in so many other countries dominated by communism, gained strength.[48]

Traditions of Tekle Haymanot's ancestry take it back ten generations when settlers from Tigray first came to Shoa, but there seems to have been relatively little evangelization until the thirteenth century, for Christian settlers lived side by side with pagans and the region was dominated by the strong pagan Kingdom of Damot, whose legendary

---

[46] Taddesse Tamrat, "The Abbots of Dabra-Hayq, 1248-1535", JES VIII/1, January 1970, p. 90.

[47] Etissa may, however, be a late nineteenth-century "discovery", for no evidence of its being identified as Tekle Haymanot's birthplace has come to light in chronicles.

[48] One manifestation of it is the revival of the practice of cutting rock churches, examples of which I describe in "Three New Rock-hewn Churches" in the *Proceedings of the 3rd International Conference on the History of Ethiopian Art,* forthcoming. I have since found four more in the process of being cut.

king, Motalami (who may actually have been several successive rulers) tolerated them. As both secular chiefs and Christian proselytizers became active in the thirteenth century, Motalami is reported to have struck out against Christian communities, burning churches and settlements.

Tekle Haymanot must have been well into his thirties by the time he joined Iyasus Mo'a. He is reported to have stayed nine years at Hayq, deepening his knowledge of Christian traditions, before going to Tigray to visit early Christian sites. He settled at Debre Damo and gathered a following of monastic disciples, some of whom went out to found monasteries in that region. Returning to Hayq, he was urged by Iyasus Mo'a to go back to Shoa where he launched a religious revival and in 1284 decided to set up a new monastery in a pagan area along the gorge of the Jama river, a tributary of the Blue Nile. It was strategically well chosen for evangelising efforts throughout the region. It was first called Debre Asbo and later renamed Debre Libanos, becoming the center of Shoan Christianity. He attracted many followers who went out to establish monasteries and convert pagan communities to the south and west.[49] These activities complemented the activities of the restored Solomonic rulers. Tekle Haymanot lived for twenty-nine years after the monastery's founding and died shortly before Emperor Wudem Ar'ad did. His accomplishments prepared the way for the expansionist policies of Emperor Amde Tseyon.[50]

[49] The activities of the Tigrayan monastic evangelist Ewostatewos (1273-1352), who lived half a century later than Tekle Haymanot, resulted in a somewhat parallel revival and spread of monasticism in the northern part of the country. Reportedly a nephew of Abba Daniel of Geralta, Ewostatewos established a vigorous community in Serae. He fell into controversy over the observance of the Sabbath as well as Sunday and left the country about 1338, going to Egypt, Jerusalem, Cyprus and Armenia, where he died. His disciples returned to Ethiopia but found themselves at odds with the main body of the church, so went out to remote border areas to establish monasteries. One of their most successful foundations was Debre Bizen in Hamasien on the Eritrean escarpment, founded by Abba Filipos in 1390. Another was Gunda Gunde in the northeasternmost corner of Tigray. See Taddesse Tamrat, *op.cit.,* pp. 206-22; also the same author's "Notes on the Fifteenth Century Stephanite 'Heresy' in the Ethiopian Church", *Rassegna di Studi Etiopici,* XXII/1968, pp. 102-15; and Antonio Mordini, 'Il Convento di Gunde Gundie", *Rassegna di Studi Etiopici* (1954), pp. 29-48.

[50] The widespread tradition that Tekle Haymanot played a direct role in the advent to the throne of Yekuno Amlak appears to be a later appropriation of the role of Iyasus Mo'a. See Munro-Hay, *Ethiopia and Alexandria,* pp. 205-6. The absence of an *abun* of Egyptian origin during much of this period may have resulted in the practice of making the abbot of the Monastery of Debre Libanos the *Echege,* i.e. the senior Ethiopian bishop. The extensive and often contradictory religious chronicles of this period contain many later misrepresentations designed to bolster the supremacy of Debre Libanos over Hayq. Taddesse Tamrat

The popular image of Tekle Haymanot shown in hundreds of modern paintings is of an old man with wings on his back praying on one leg, while a severed leg is shown in the lower left corner discreetly wrapped in a cloth. He may well have lost a leg in old age, for he allegedly died at the age of ninty-eight. For most of his life he must have been an extraordinarily vigorous, enterprising man as one might expect from a description of him as a youth:

> He learnt riding horses, hunting wild animals and using arrows and other implements. [...] And his arrow never missed, and was always smeared with blood.[51]

Like the early Christian missionaries in Europe who went from Ireland and England to convert Germans and Slavs, medieval Ethiopian evangelists needed more than piety and persuasion to accomplish their mission. Many took risks and tolerated rough practices by local rulers, though they sometimes tried to discourage them. A description from the *Gadla Anorewos* of the actions of one Beragban, a pagan chief who took the name of Zekaryas on becoming a Christian, provides a striking example:

> Beragban took his arrow and went to the woods. He found there three sorcerers sitting at the foot of an oak tree. He shot at one of them who fell and died; the second fled, and he captured the third, tied his hands behind him, and took him to Abuna Anorewos. When Anorewos saw him he said, "After all a man of magic is a human being!" [Beragban] took a knife and slew [his captive] at the Abuna's feet. After some time Anorewos built a small church on the site.[52]

From Amde Tseyon to Zara Yakob

"Amde Tseyon was one of the most outstanding Ethiopian kings of any age and a singular figure dominating the Horn of Africa in the fourteenth century."[53] This assessment of Amde Tseyon ("Pillar of Zion") (1314-44) by the British Ethiopianist Edward Ullendorff is surpassed only by his even more enthusiastic judgment of the ruler's

---

attempts to sort out the main lines of development and identify the most important religious activists in *op.cit.*, pp. 160-89. Controversy aside, the essence of these developments is that Christianity spread, became solidly established, and served as a major factor in consolidation of the control of the Ethiopian state over the center and south of the country.

[51] Taddesse Tamrat, *op. cit.*, p. 157.

[52] As cited in Taddesse Tamrat, *op.cit.*, p. 181.

[53] Edward Ullendorff's review of G.W.B. Huntingford's translation and commentary on the chronicle, *The Glorious Victories of Amda Tseyon, King of Ethiopia* (Brit. Mus. Orient. 821), Clarendon Press, Oxford, 1965, in *Bulletin of the School of Oriental and African Studies*, 1966/3.

great grandson, the most outstanding ruler of the next century, Zara
Yakob ("Seed of Jacob") (1434-68): "He was unquestionably the
greatest ruler Ethiopia had seen since Ezana, during the heyday of
Aksumite power, and none of his successors on the throne–excepted
only the Emperors Menelik II and Haile Selassie–can be compared
to him."[54]

The century and a half that includes the lengthy reigns of both
these rulers and equally the intervening reigns of three other strong
emperors: Sayfa-Ar'ad (1344-72), Dawit I (1382-1413) and Yeshaq
(1414-29), was the crowning era of medieval Ethiopia. It was a time of
both the spread and consolidation of Orthodox Christianity and of
expansion of the power of the state. "The name Ethiopia itself was
given a meaning which raised it from a mere designation of a country
to the level of a religious concept."[55] It meant a melding of the authority of church and state. The legends and traditions of the Solomonic
dynasty became so firmly anchored in the mentality of the population
that the country was able to withstand and survive the gruesome trials
it had to undergo in the century and a half which followed this series
of energetic emperors.

Amde Tseyon took the throne name Gebre Maskal ("Slave of the
Cross"). For a man so devoted to Christian symbolism and dedicated
to expanding the Christian Empire, he had a bad beginning with the
church. Habits of a boisterous youth apparently persisted into the
first years of his reign and he was accused by several prominent religious leaders of fornicating with his father's concubine and two of his
sisters and later chastised for marrying three wives. Successors to
Tekle Haymanot were trying to enforce higher standards of morality
among the elite. Amde Tseyon had the monks who berated him first
upbraided and then excommunicated and beaten. He exiled *Echege*
Filipos of Debre Libanos to an island in Lake Zway. Others fled to
Dembea, Begemder and islands in Lake Tana.[56] Many churchmen
seem, however, to have avoided a rupture with the monarch who, as
he grew more mature, may have moderated his behavior. The most
important chronicle of his reign, *The Glorious Victories,* makes no
mention of his troubles with the clergy.[57] Amde Tseyon's military
exploits and his dedication to Christian expansion completely overshadowed issues of immorality.

[54] Ullendorff, *The Ethiopians,* p. 69.

[55] Shifferaw Bekele, *loc.cit.,* in *Kasa and Kasa,* p. 320.

[56] Budge, *op.cit.,* p. 288-89; Huntingford, *Glorious Victories,* pp. 6-9.

[57] Both native churchmen and Egyptian *Abuns* who attempted to persuade
Ethiopian princes to improve their promiscuous habits, multiple marriages, and
keeping of concubines, seldom had much success. Patterns of behavior prevalent
in ancient and medieval times persisted into the twentieth century.

Amde Tseyon's first successful campaigns were in Hadiya, Damot, and Gojjam, where he established his authority in 1316-17. By 1320 he appears to have had control of the entire Tana region. He then turned to Tigray. During the fall of the Zagwe dynasty many Semitic Christians from Lasta had migrated northward and established themselves in the northeastern Tigrayan highlands. These people welcomed Amde Tseyon's army and supported his efforts to subdue the recalcitrant rulers of Enderta and Tembien. During the Zagwe period a power vacuum had developed in the Eritrean highlands and coastal region which Muslims from the Dahlak Islands and the settlements on the coast tended to fill. Egypt had lost control of Yemen, but was trying to regain it and Red Sea trade was affected. The still substantial Christian communities of the region welcomed the reassertion of imperial power, for it ensured a smoother flow of trade.

Trade was important to Amde Tseyon. A prime purpose of his conquests was control of trade routes which connected Massawa and Zeila with Tigray, Wollo, Shoa and the southern highlands. Slaves were a valuable commodity, procured in the southwest by Muslim traders from their local partners, and marched to the coast. Captives taken in military campaigns were also commonly enslaved. Though slaves were not unusual in Christian families and gifts of slaves were sometimes made even to prominent churchmen, the slave trade was considered primarily a Muslim activity about which the church had at least theoretical reservations. The *Gadla Zena Marqos* cites a group of recently converted Muslims saying, "We no longer sell slaves [like the Muslims] after being baptized in the name of Christ."[58] Ivory and other animal products from western and southwestern border regions were also commodities in demand by merchants on the coast. Food products of many kinds were exported from the highlands to the eastern lowlands and coastal ports. References in chronicles to trade are comparatively rare, but a few provide evidence of its importance and extent:

The Muslim traders did business in India, Egypt, and among the people of Greece with the money of the king. He gave them ivory, and excellent horses from Shoa and red, pure gold from Enarya ... and these Muslims ... went to Egypt, Greece, and Rome and exchanged them for very rich damasks adorned with green and scarlet stones and with the leaves of red gold, which they brought to the king.[59]

[58] Taddesse Tamrat, *op.cit.,* p. 87.

[59] As cited from the *Gadla Samu'el* in Taddesse Tamrat, *op.cit.,* p. 88. The references to Greece are undoubtedly to the Byzantine Empire. Occasional finds of coins, textiles, and other objects in the treasuries of Ethiopian churches and monasteries provide material evidence of medieval trade. Archaeological excavation at medieval sites will eventually produce more concrete information.

Amde Tseyon's most important victories were against the Muslim states to the east of the Christian highlands which shifted the balance of power in favor of the Christians for the next two centuries. He conquered Ifat and continued offensives into the region east of the Awash, but the Muslim ruler, Sabr-ad-Din, rallied the Muslims and began a counteroffensive in early 1332. Amde Tseyon defeated him and again sacked Ifat. Concerned above all with maintaining open trade routes through the area for both Muslims and Christians, Amde Tseyon led his army into Dawaro, Bali and smaller states in the region and inspired his troops with a crusading spirit:

Behold, the kingdom of the Muslims has come to an end. In former times you used to fight for the sake of your transitory kingdom, and for the sake of gold, silver, and precious clothes. But today, rise and fight for the sake of Christ.[60]

The Muslim states were divided in their interests and often failed to coordinate their defense. Their military forces consisted mostly of pasto-ralists who were difficult to discipline. They were no match for Amde Tseyon's well organized army. Many Muslim traders favored Ethiopia and after Amde Tseyon's continual successes, so did their rulers:

...When one of these [Muslim] kings dies, and if he has any male issues, all of them go to the King of the Amhara and they employ all possible means to gain his favours because it is he who chooses the one on whom he confers power.[...] In front of him they are only his lieutenants.[61]

Amde Tseyon's conquests more than doubled the size of the Christian Empire. His chroniclers glorified him as a pious crusader who could overcome all obstacles, rising from his sickbed and defeating the enemy singlehanded:

The king was thus fortified by the Lord; he forgot his illness and his weakness, girded the sword with two cutting edges, namely prayer and supplication, and dressed himself in his victorious armour, that is to say confidence and faith; then he cried out: "Come to my help, God of Moses and Aaron!" and addressed himself to the priests: "Intercede for me with God," he said, "and do not forget me in your prayers!" [His frightened soldiers had fled and he found himself alone.] Then the army of the unbelievers advanced, bows extended, swords in hand. [...] They were as numerous as locusts, as the stars of the sky, or the grains of sand on the edge of the sea ... [With a few loyal followers] the King attacked the enemy on their left flank, which was the weakest; he attacked without looking behind him and without turning back, despite the spears and arrows which fell like hail around him... He threw himself into the ranks [of the unbelievers] with such force that, by the

---

[60] As cited in Taddesse Tamrat, *op.cit.*, pp. 140-1.

[61] The Arab writer Al-'Umari on the situation in the 1330s as cited by Taddesse Tamrat, *op.cit.*, p. 144.

power of God, he killed two of his enemies simultaneously with his spear. Then the unbelievers scattered and gave way to flight...[62]

Amde Tseyon's eldest son, Sayfa Ar'ad (throne name: Newaya Kristos, "Vessel of Christ"), succeeded him and reigned twenty-eight years, following his father's policies toward the Muslims on the east, most of whom continued to be tributaries of the Christian Empire. The Muslim merchants were eager for peace. A divide-and-rule approach resulted in splitting the ruling Walasma family. The more militant elements moved east and eventually founded what became the Sultanate of Adal with its center in the region of Harar. Ifat was effectively eliminated as a threat, but Adal would eventually grow to become a greater menace. Toward the end of his reign Sayfa-Ar'ad took strong measures against Egyptian merchants in retaliation for the Egyptian Sultan's efforts to extort tribute from the Patriarch of Alexandria. The Sultan backed down.

During the ten-year reign of Sayfa-Ar'ad's eldest son, Wudem Asfare (throne name: Newaya Mariam, "Vessel of Mary") (1372-82), Haq-ad-Din, Sultan of Adal, was killed in battle with the Ethiopians and succeeded by his brother, Sa'ad-ad-Din, who became a major challenger to Sayfa-Ar'ad's second son, Emperor Dawit I (1382-1411). He had to cope with continual attacks against the eastern border regions where the Muslims raided for cattle and slaves and then retired across the desert. He invaded Adal several times and succeeded in pursuing Sa'ad-ad-Din all the way to Zeila in 1403, captured and killed him, and sacked the town. Muslim power was at its lowest ebb, but Sa'ad-ad-Din's six sons escaped to Arabia and soon returned to pose new challenges.

Dawit was an enthusiastic Christian. He shifted his attention to the Falashas. Amde Tseyon's campaign against them in 1332 had failed to achieve a complete annexation of their territory in Semien. They rebelled, led by a renegade monk, and attacked both officials and Christian clergy. Dawit called on the governor of Tigray to help suppress them. He then applied the same divide-and-rule tactics that had been effective against Ifat, drawing cooperative Falasha chiefs to his side and building churches in Falasha regions, but many Falashas remained unreconciled to defeat and conversion. Dawit was more successful encouraging Christian expansion in Gojjam and supporting establishment of more monastic establishments on the shores and islands of Lake Tana. Like most rulers of the time, he was a great

---

[62] Pankhurst, *Chronicles*, pp. 23-4. The British scholar of both Egypt and Ethiopia, E. Wallis Budge, considered Amde Tseyon's style of fighting similar to that of the Pharaohs of the XIIth Dynasty and compares the incident cited above with a similar episode in the Battle of Kadesh when Rameses II found himself surrounded by Hittites; Budge, *op.cit.*, p. 298.

horseman. He died when a spirited horse struck him in the head. His body was taken to Daga Istifanos on Tana. He had four sons from two wives, all of whom succeeded to the throne in the next three decades.

Dawit's eldest son Tewodros I reigned only nine months in 1413-14 but for reasons that remain obscure his brief time on the throne later became legendary as a golden age of peace and plenty (see Chapter 5 below). He was apparently killed fighting Muslims beyond the Awash. He was followed by the second son, Yeshaq (1414-29) who took the throne name Gebre Maskal. He continued his father's efforts to bring the Falashas under control during his first years, seems to have penetrated the Shankalla region beyond Agawmeder in Gojjam, and then had to devote most of his energy to the Muslims in the east, for Sa'ad-ad-Din's sons had come back from Arabia and were again harassing Christian-held areas and interfering with trade. Yeshaq employed a Mamluke refugee to drill his soldiers and another Egyptian to teach them how to make Greek fire, but these advances were still not enough to enable the Christian armies to keep the Muslims at bay. Battles were won by both sides and the Christians finally came out ahead, though it appears that Yeshaq may have been killed in the fighting.[63]

Yeshaq's death was followed by five years of dynastic confusion during which his son Indiryas, his brother Tekle Mariam, and two sons of Tekle Maryam briefly occupied the throne. Finally Dawit I's youngest son, Zara Yakob, was brought out of isolation and declared emperor in 1434. He had been born in 1399 at Tilq in Fatagar while his father was campaigning there. According to legend, monks foretold a great future for him while he was still a child which made his oldest brother, Tewodros, jealous. For his safety his mother entrusted him to a monk who took him to Tigray where he received religious training in Aksum and then entered the Monastery of Debre Abbay in Shire. He remained in obscurity until the confusion following the death of Yeshaq. He relates in one of his works, *Mitshafa Berhan* (The Book of Light), that he came down from the royal prison on Amba Gishen only shortly before he was proclaimed emperor, but he must have been in contact with key men of the church and the aristocracy during his final years of seclusion.[64] He took the throne name

[63] Taddesse Tamrat believes that both Tewodros I and Yeshaq were killed in fighting against the Muslim armies but their deaths were misrepresented by chroniclers reluctant to admit that Christian kings could so perish: "In the royal chronicles and other traditions of the period, one can detect a deliberate attempt to suppress the violent ends of Ethiopian kings at the hands of their enemies"; *op.cit.*, p. 153, n. 5.

[64] As with so many prominent religious and secular personalities in Ethiopia, later traditions and embroidering by writers of chronicles make it difficult to establishhard

Kwestantinos, as a mark of his admiration for the Roman Emperor Constantine.

His time in Tigray must explain his relative tolerance toward the followers of Ewostatewos, which helped him create greater unity and dynamism in the church. Over the preceding century intense conflict had developed over observance of the Sabbath. The Tigrayans favored observance of both Saturday and Sunday while the Alexandrian Patriarch and his representative in Ethiopia, Abuna Bartolomewos, as well as the clergy of Debre Libanos, were opposed to Saturday. Monasteries in newly conquered regions were often confused about where their loyalties should lie and much of the argumentation went over the heads of the poorly educated village priests, itinerant monks and hermits. Arcane doctrinal issues acquired political significance and members of the royal family were deeply involved in these controversies when Zara Yakob became emperor. He travelled to Aksum in 1436 for his coronation and remained in Tigray for three years. While there, he was successful in persuading the two newly arrived Egyptian bishops, Mikael and Gabriel, to support his program for restoring church unity on the basis of Old Testament principles. They continued to collaborate closely with him until their deaths late in his reign.[65]

During his first years on the throne Zara Yakob launched a strong campaign against survivals of pagan worship and irregular practices in the church. He also took measures to centralize the administration of the country, bringing outlying regions under much tighter imperial control. The common denominator in his approach to both secular and religious matters was to strengthen the power and authority of the monarchy. His campaigns against the Falashas were less than totally successful. They defended themselves in their mountain fastnesses around Gondar. He accomplished much more in his efforts against the Muslims to the east and toward Egypt.

When he received news in 1441 of the demolition of the Egyptian monastery of Debre Mitmaq, sacred to the Virgin Mary, he ordered a period of mourning and built a church of the same name at Aguba in Tegulet. An appearance of the Virgin at the monastery in Egypt had caused great popular excitement and provoked Muslim wrath against the Copts. Sultan al–Zahir Jaqmaq ordered its destruction. Zara Yakob sent envoys to Cairo with a strong letter of protest against persecution of the Copts and reminded the Sultan that he had Muslim subjects whom he treated fairly. He also warned the Sultan that he had the

---

facts about Zara Yakob's early years. This account is based primarily on Taddesse Tamrat, *op.cit.*, pp. 216-48; Pankhurst, *Chronicles*, pp. 29-40; and Budge, *op.cit.*, pp. 304-12.

[65] Abuna Bartolomewos died in 1437. The new bishops arrived in 1438.

power to divert the Nile but said he refrained from doing so to avoid the human suffering it would cause.[66] These admonishments are remarkable for what they reveal of the sense of power and confidence that prevailed in Ethiopia at the time. Jaqmaq sent an envoy to Ethiopia with gifts but rejected Zara Yakob's demand for restoration of churches in Egypt. The emperor was angered and ordered the envoy imprisoned.[67]

Zara Yakob gained further in self-confidence and prestige from his defeat of the Adal ruler Badlay-ad-Din at the battle of Gomit in Dawaro in 1445. Badlay had invaded Dawaro two years before with Egyptian blessing. In retaliation the Egyptian sultan had the Patriarch of Alexandria, Yohannes, severely beaten and threatened to execute him. Zara Yakob finally agreed to release the Egyptian envoy. News of these victories reached Europe. In a letter dated 3 July 1448 the Grand Master of Rhodes wrote Charles VII of France: "Indian priests here in Rhodes [have reported] that Prester John of the Indies has greatly demonstrated [his powers] over the Saracens ... and has killed many of them, above all those who claim descent from Muhammad."[68]

The Grand Master went on to predict that Prester John would soon devastate Egypt, Arabia and Syria, a prediction most Europeans were happy to hear. Such reporting ensured a good reception for the mission Zara Yakob sent to Europe in 1450 led by Pietro Rombulo of Messina in Sicily. Rombulo had come to Ethiopia in the last years of the reign of Dawit I and had already undertaken a mission to India for Zara Yakob. The Rombulo mission had an audience with Pope Nicholas V and was received by Alfonso of Aragon, King of Naples and Sicily. Dawit and Yeshaq had sent to Europe for technicians. Rombulo's mission may have had the same purpose, for he is said to have taken artisans back to Ethiopia. It is difficult to gain anything approaching a complete picture of Ethiopian contacts with Europe in the late medieval period, though further bits of information can be expected to keep coming to light in Europe and in Ethiopia. Objects of European origin have been found in many Ethiopian monasteries and churches. European artisans – and artists (see the concluding section of this chapter) – who came to Ethiopia were usually welcomed and given useful employment. Many stayed for the rest of their lives.[69]

---

[66] Egyptian fears and Ethiopian threats of blocking the Nile have a long history and go back at least to the time of Lalibela. See Haggai Erlich, *Ethiopia and the Middle East*, Lynne Rienner, Boulder, CO, 1994, pp. 23-5.

[67] Taddesse Tamrat, *op.cit.*, pp. 261-3.

[68] Ibid., *op.cit.*, pp. 263-4.

[69] A volume of the Hakluyt Society, O.G.S. Crawford (ed.), *Ethiopian Itineraries, circa 1400-1524*, Cambridge University Press, 1958, gathered most of the infor-

Zara Yakob's experience of Tigray during his years of early maturity must have heightened his interest in the northernmost parts of
the country. He was eager to extend Ethiopia's control over the coastal
region and to challenge Muslim predominance in Massawa and
the Dahlak islands. He established military colonies on the Eritrean
plateau in the late 1440s and placed large parts of Tigray, including
Hamasien, under the administration of his *Bahir–Negash* whose
authority he extended by building a port at Grar on the mainland
opposite the island of Massawa. He later attacked Massawa and the
Dahlak sultanate.

He capped off his efforts to produce harmony in the church in
1450 by convening a council of the clergy which he presided over
at his new Church of Debre Mitmaq in Tegulet. This brought to an
end several decades of strife within the church, officially reconcil-
ing Ewostathians with Debre Libanos and Alexandria and also got the
clergy to agree that both Saturday and Sunday could be observed as
holy days, a practice which has continued in the Ethiopian Orthodox
Church ever since.

Military campaigns and foreign affairs never diverted Zara Yakob
for long periods from his preoccupation with strengthening the
church as an adjunct of the state and improving its quality. He drew
all the major monasteries of the country into a program for training
more clergy and sending newly ordained monks and priests out to
deepen religious understanding among both pagans and newly
Christianized populations who still adhered to pagan customs. He
ordered expansion of production of religious books and parapher-
nalia. He encouraged the building of new churches and monasteries, often on the very sites where pagan religious rites were conducted.
His zeal led to excesses. Abbots of monasteries were sent on inspec-
tion tours accompanied by soldiers who punished people not
conforming to the practices the emperor prescribed: strict observance of fasting days, mass attendance at Saturday and Sunday
religious services, placing the sign of the cross on all belongings of
Christians, including weapons and plows. Large land grants were
made to successful monasteries and churches. On the other hand,
persons who persisted in consulting soothsayers, participating in
or even watching pagan rites were flogged, sometimes killed, and
their houses burned and property confiscated.

---

mation then known. It includes analyses of two maps that appeared in Europe in
the 15th century: *Egyptus Novello,* c. 1454, and Fra Mauro's *Mappamundo* of 1460,
which are filled with Ethiopian place names and other geographical information,
little of which is fanciful; Appendix III also contains an analysis of an abstract
of a Bergamese chronicle that reports an Ethiopian mission to Europe in 1306,
pp. 212-15.

Total regimentation of the population with the aim of enforcing religious conformity naturally provoked resistance, even among the clergy. Abba Tekle Hawariat of Debre Libanos is cited chastising the emperor for "the futile deaths of men, the arrests and the beatings which take place". Zara Yakob had him beaten and imprisoned and he died a few months later.[70] In his *Matshafa Berhan* Zara Yakob describes a plot which aimed at deposing him which seems to have occurred around 1453.

Zara Yakob's favorite residence was Debre Berhan in north eastern Shoa where he had a church built to celebrate "a wonderful light that appeared in the sky and remained there for several days".[71] He wrote several of his commentaries on the early Christian church there.[72] His son and successor, B'aeda Mariam, was born there about 1448. Despite his zealous piety, Zara Yakob was polygamous. He had at least four wives. The most famous was Eleni, daughter of the King of Hadiya, and originally a Muslim. He also had a preoccupation with sorcery and attributed adverse events to demons. During his declining years he became obsessed with the notion that his wives and children were plotting against him and had several of them beaten.

Tseyon Mogasa, mother of Ba'eda Maryam, died of mistreatment about 1462 and the son severely castigated his father, leading to a complete break. The two appear eventually to have become reconciled and Zara Yakob reportedly designated Ba'eda Maryam his successor before his death in 1468. Having no mother himself, Ba'eda Maryam gave Eleni the title of Queen Mother. Though Ba'eda Maryam died at the early age of thirty in 1878, Eleni outlived Zara Yakob by a half a century and became one of the most influential women of Ethiopian history.

The Christianization of Lake Tana and Gojjam

To judge by the legends linked to it, Ethiopian history has revolved around Lane Tana, the great heart-shaped lake through which the Blue Nile flows. Gathering countless tributaries, the Blue Nile (called Abbay in Ethiopia) supplies more than three-quarters of the water that reaches Egypt. Emperor Menelik I, son of King Solomon and the Queen of Sheba, is said to have come to Lake Tana's eastern shore

[70] When the next emperor, Ba'eda Maryam, succeeded his father, he had Tekle Hawariat's remains removed to a monastery where they became the object of pilgrimage – Taddesse Tamrat, *op.cit.*, p. 242.

[71] Budge, *op.cit.*, p. 309.

[72] Zara Yakob stands out as a major contributor to Ethiopian religious literature. See Getachew Haile, "Ethiopic Literature".

when he arrived in Ethiopia from Jerusalem bringing the country's first *tabot*. This *tabot* was allegedly kept for 600 years on the island of Tana Cherqos before being transferred to Aksum. When I visited this island on the eastern shore of the great lake a few years ago, the monks led me to a large boulder where the Virgin Mary was said to have rested on her way back to the Holy Land from Egypt. More than 300 years later, Frumentius, who brought Christianity to Ethiopia, is supposed to have found his way to the lake where he established a church where Jewish rites had previously been observed. When he died he was allegedly buried on Tana Cherqos.

When did this lake and the region around it really become Christianized? There is no evidence to substantiate all these entertaining legends. The process seems to have started rather late in comparison with most of northern Ethiopia. The body of Emperor Yekuno-Amlak, now cased in a glass-fronted coffin which Emperor Haile Selassie provided, is kept in the *eqabet* (treasury) of the monastery of St Stephen on the island of Daga along with those of four later emperors.[73] The monastery was founded by a disciple of Iyasus Mo'a, Abba Hirute Amlak, in the latter half of the twelfth century.[74]

In Aksumite times and during the still little understood period following the collapse of the great north Ethiopian empire, the entire region around Lake Tana and the upper Blue Nile was in all likelihood inhabited by the ancestors of the Wayto, who still live by fishing and hunting from their reed boats on the lake; by the Agaw; and by the Gumuz, who live in the lower Metekel country to the east, extending all the way to the Sudan lowlands. Agaw traditions cite Wag and Lasta as their region of origin. The pagan kings of Gojjam whom Ethiopian emperors fought from the late thirteenth century to the beginning of the fifteenth were Agaw. A substantial Agaw population has survived into modern times in central Gojjam in the district called Agawmeder.

Traders from the north must have reached Tana and penetrated the country to the south in Aksumite times. From this period onward, vague knowledge of Judaism and Christianity must have filtered in. Systematic Christian settlement seems to have begun only in the thirteenth century. Christianization accelerated in the fourteenth century during the reign of Amde-Tseyon. The islands of the lake were probably originally attractive to monks because of the safety

---

[73] Dawit I (1382-1413), Zara Yakob (1434-68), Za Dengel (1603-4), and Fasilidas (1632-67).

[74] Major R.E. Cheesman's *Lake Tana and the Blue Nile: An Abyssinian Quest*, 1936, repr. Frank Cass, London, 1968, remains the best available description of Lake Tana and northeast Gojjam and can still serve as a useful guide for exploration of the region.

they offered. There are traditions that Amde Tseyon favored the Monastery of Debre Maryam on a low island at the outflow of the Nile, while one of his sons is said to have become abbot at Mandaba on the north shore of the lake. Monks at the still flourishing monasteries on the eastern edge of the Gojjam plateau within the great bend of the Blue Nile – Dima, Debre Worq, Mertule Maryam, Wafa Yesus and Getisemani – tell stories of their founding in the time of Abreha and Atsbeha, (i.e. fourth century); serious traditions and chronicles indicate that they were actually established during the reign of Dawit I around 1400. They were probably expanded in Zara Yakob's time. Daga Istifanos on Tana, is among those that possess icons and manuscripts painted by artists known to have worked during his reign.

Because of its imposing ruins Mertule Maryam is the most impressive of these monasteries, though probably not the oldest. All compete with each other in claiming seniority. Since I have visited it several times, I will summarize my research as an example of both what is known and what remains to be discovered.

We know that medieval Christian missionaries often chose pagan forest glades where sacred trees, rocks and sometimes springs were centers of worship, for churches in order to maintain an aura of sacredness while depriving their converts of the opportunity to use their former sites for pagan rites. The pagan beliefs they aimed to supplant centered around nature, spirit worship and animistic practices. For example, pagans of a district were described as worshipping:

the rocks, trees, or rivers. They did not know God except very few [among them]. They lived by eating, drinking, and committing adultery all their lives.[75]

Another chronicle describes an episode in one of Tekle Haymanot's evangelistic journeys to a pagan area:

Tekle Haymanot came to a hill called Bilat. This was the headquarters of the sorcerers and here they sacrificed the blood of cows and goats. [...] There lived their king and the witch-doctors, the diviners, and all the men of magic worshipped him.[76]

Mertule Maryam is located on a prominent hill in a grove of old cedars and olives. It is the kind of site early Christian missionaries could easily have chosen for a first church. Archaeological excavation – of which there has been none at any of these sites – could determine the earliest occupation. Empress Eleni is now said to have been the founder of the present church which must have been raised to the status of monastery soon if the site did not already have that status

---

[75] *Gadla Filipos*, p. 175, as cited in Taddesse Tamrat, *op. cit.*, p. 179.

[76] As cited in E.A.W. Budge, *The Life and Miracles of Takla Haymanot*, *op. cit.*

when she chose it. If there had been an earlier founder of a church on the site, Eleni's fame may well have eclipsed him. A chronicler of Zara Yakob's reign says of her:

... she was accomplished in everything: in front of God, by practicing righteousness and having strong faith; by praying and receiving Holy Communion; as regards worldly matters she was accomplished in the preparation of food, in her familiarity with books, in her knowledge of the law, and in her understanding of the affairs of state.[77]

Eleni was practically co-monarch during the reign of Ba'eda Maryam (1468-78). During the confused period following Ba'eda Maryam's death, she was for a time eclipsed, but soon reasserted herself. She served as regent during the minority of Emperor Lebna Dengel (1508-40) and appears to have lived into the early 1520s. The Portuguese Jesuit, Father Francisco Alvares, who arrived in Ethiopia in 1520, reported that the Kingdom of Gojjam belonged to her and that when she decided to build a church at Mertule Maryam she ordered Pero de Covilhao (see Chapter 4) to come to advise on the construction of its altar. Alvares says she was buried there. He gives no dates, but recounts:

There was great rumour and talk at the Court about the death of Queen Elena. They said that since she had died all of them had died great and small, and that while she lived, all lived and were defended and protected; and she was father and mother of all.[78]

Probably born no later than 1430, for she was married to Zara Yakob in 1445, this remarkable woman appears to have lived to the age of 90. She apparently ordered her church built at Mertule Maryam during the last decade of the fifteenth century.

The huge ruin, some of whose stone walls still stand to a height of almost 10 metres, has many features that resemble a palace more than a church. The stone must have been brought from some distance and the quality of the stone cutting, carving and fitting is very high. Wooden joists to separate floors partly survive. There is a great deal of mostly floral ornamentation but no inscriptions of any kind have been detected. Many stones from the main building appear to have been removed to construct two other churches within the compound as well as houses where monks and nuns live outside the compound walls. There is evidence within the compound walls of old foundations now buried. Outside the walls of the monastery compound on the south, commanding a splendid view over rich lands belonging to the monastery to the Nile Gorge and the heights of Amhara Saynt beyond, there is an area of ruined walls and buildings. There appears to have been a substantial settlement here in earlier times.

[77] Ibid., p. 288.
[78] Alvares, *The Prester John of the Indies,* Cambridge University Press for the Hakluyt Society, 1961, vol. II, pp. 434, 459.

Eleni's original building is said to have been sacked by Ahmad
Gragn (see Chapter 4) a few years after her death and may also have
suffered earthquake damage, but the site was obviously regarded
as important and rebuilding took place at least twice during the next
100 years. This culminated in a major renovation by Emperor
Susenyos (1607-32), probably because he was first offered the crown
at Mertule Maryam in 1604. His renovation was apparently followed
by a brief occupation by Catholic monks converted by the Portuguese
Jesuits Susenyos favored, but with his abdication the monastery
reverted to the Orthodox, for whom it has ever since remained a
significant monastic institution. Mertule Maryam's treasury contains
dozens of crosses, icons, manuscripts, vestments, and crowns. The
monastery is dedicated to the Virgin Mary and the most credible
explanation of its name is "Home of Mary". On the annual Feast of the
Virgin at the end of January hundreds of priests, monks, nuns, and
hermits, and tens of thousands of Christians from all over Gojjam
make the pilgrimage to attend the ceremonies.

We still know much too little about the extension and consolidation of Aksumite rule over the center and south of the country and
the related process of Christianization. Too little is known of the
influence of outsiders on Ethiopian life during this and earlier periods, not only Europeans and people from the eastern Mediterranean,
but influences from as far away as Persia and India. Who carved the
spectacular churches of Lalibela? The rock-hewn churches there
show a remarkable ornamental, though non-functional, adherence
to the most important features of Aksumite architecture, but there is
also evidence (and traditions) of foreign influence, cited above. The
churches of Lalibela are at least four centuries earlier than the ruins
of the great building at Mertule Maryam. The ruins at Mertule
Maryam, however, exhibit no Aksumite architectural features. Instead
they reveal a curious combination of European and Middle Eastern
style and ornamentation that does not readily relate to any known
buildings in the Mediterranean region. Only serious archaeological
investigation can begin to shed more light on this impressive site.

Language, art, and culture

The oldest surviving Ethiopian manuscripts, with the exception
of the Abba Gerima Gospels, date from the thirteenth century.[79] During succeeding centuries manuscript production flourished,

---

[79] The Abba Gerima Gospels are kept at the monastery of the same name in the
mountains south of Adwa. Its founder was one of the Nine Syrian Saints. These
Gospels are believed to date from the eleventh century, but are regarded by some
scholars as earlier.

reaching its peak in the fifteenth century. All these manuscripts are written on parchment in Ge'ez, the principal language spoken in the Aksumite Empire (see Chapter 2). How did Ge'ez evolve into its successor languages? Did related languages from South Arabia also accompany immigrants from across the Red Sea? Were several dialects of Ge'ez spoken in Aksumite times? These are open questions. Thousands of Ge'ez inscriptions on stone, metal (especially coins), and pottery have been found and more continue to come to light. Use of the language was relatively uniform. This fact argues against the possibility that Tigrinya, Amharic and the other Semitic languages of Ethiopia evolved from different dialects of Ge'ez, but it does not rule it out.

From the time of the decline of Aksum to the end of the Zagwe Dynasty evidence for the evolution of spoken languages is lacking. The fact that the spoken languages exist, however, proves that it occurred. What about other languages spoken in the lands south of the northern highlands? Did Zagwe rulers speak Agaw and use it in their armies? We do not know. There is no evidence that they wrote it. Language evolution in Ethiopia appears to have been much as it was in southern Europe with Latin. Vernaculars in the former Roman Empire developed as spoken languages but were not written and did not replace Latin for religious and administrative purposes until comparatively late. The vernaculars were influenced by other languages spoken before and around them, especially in vocabulary, less so in structure and grammar, though complex forms often became simplified. Patterns of development in the Ethiopian Semitic languages are parallel to those of the Romance languages and they are mutually intelligible to much the same extent that modern Romance languages are.

There are nevertheless curious differences among them. The vocabulary of Amharic is about 70 per cent Semitic, that of Tigrinya, which is closer to Ge'ez, even more so. Amharic is remarkably uniform, with dialects that are mutually intelligible. Dialects in Tigrinya, on the other hand, often differ sharply from each other. Richest in dialect variation is the language of the Gurage, the southernmost Semitic speakers in Ethiopia. Some Gurage dialects cannot be understood by speakers of others.[80]

[80] Perhaps because of the challenge of its richness, Gurage is the most studied minor Ethiopian Semitic language. The leading scholar of Gurage, Harari, Gafat and many non-Semitic languages is the American Wolf Leslau, a major portion of whose life work went into his monumental *Etymological Dictionary of Gurage (Ethiopic)*, Harrassowitz, Wiesbaden, 1979, whose three volumes total nearly 3,000 pages. The great German ethnographer, Eike Haberland, reviewing it in 1983, called it "The Compendium of a Culture". Leslau's *Concise Dictionary of Amharic,*

Amharic and Gurage absorbed many words from Cushitic and Sidama languages. Harari, the language of the city state, has retained many basic Semitic features, but seems never to have been spoken by large numbers of people. It has been influenced by Arabic and alone among Semitic languages was written in the Arabic script.[81] Just how the Semitic languages of Harar and the many Gurage dialects came southward is still unclear. The same is true of two other Semitic languages: Gafat and Argobba. Gafat, which was spoken in southern Gojjam until the nineteenth century, has died out. Argobba communities still survive along the escarpment in the area of Antsiokia and in Harar. Many speakers of Argobba were traders who operated caravans across the desert.

Amharic has been called *lisane negus* or *yenegus qwanqwa*, "the language of the king" since medieval times and was used as a court and administrative language from the time of Yekuno Amlak. It was probably also in military use.[82] It was rarely written, however, until several centuries later. Ge'ez continued as the normal medium for writing until the seventeenth century. The Portuguese Jesuits printed religious tracts in Amharic and used it for teaching. It has been similarly used by missionaries since the nineteenth century. Tewodros was the first Ethiopian monarch to have royal chronicles written in Amharic, thus confirming that it had become the national language.[83] It was also widely used in Tigray as the language of administration. Since most village priests had only an elementary knowledge of Ge'ez, they contributed to the spread of Amharic as new territories were added to the Empire from late medieval times onward.

Amharic and Tigrinya are both rich languages with varied modes of expression, traditions of folk poetry, and given to puns and other forms of humor and double meaning (samena worq–"wax and gold"). Tigrinya, however, remained almost entirely in oral use until the end of the nineteenth century, when it came to be used in Eritrea for local administrative and religious purposes. Tigrinya came into its own as

University of California Press, 1976, is the most useful single-volume Amharic-English/English-Amharic dictionary available. It has been exceeded in scope by Thomas Kane's comprehensive *Amharic-English Dictionary*, Harrassowitz, Wiesbaden, 1990, in two volumes totalling over 2,350 pages. As of this writing, Kane is completing a comparable Tigrinya dictionary.

[81] The thick symposium volume edited by M.L. Bender and others, *Language in Ethiopia*, Oxford University Press, 1976, is a rich source of information on languages. The proceedings of the triennial International Ethiopian Studies Conferences regularly contain numerous reports of recent research.

[82] Among the earliest extant examples of Amharic secular literature is a group of soldiers' songs from the time of Amda Tseyon. See Huntingford, *Glorious Victories*, pp. 129-34.

[83] Robert L. Cooper, "The Spread of Amharic" in Bender *et al.; op.cit.,* pp. 289-301,

a written language only during the British occupation of Eritrea after 1941. The languages of the Oromo, which include many dialects, and of other peoples of the south and southwest continued, of course, to be used for trade and everyday purposes, but were never written until foreign missionaries became active in the nineteenth century. Among Muslim populations and those converted to Islam, as well as among Muslim traders, Arabic was sometimes used as a *lingua franca,* but few, except in Harar and on the coast, knew it well or were able to write it.

Though thousands of manuscripts and icons were reported destroyed during the invasion of Ahmad Gragn in the 1530s, a surprisingly large number of religious books and illuminated manuscripts survived, some of them of very high quality. The same is true of icons. The oldest dated wall paintings in churches also go back to the thirteenth century. The unusually rich fourteenth century paintings on the walls and ceiling of the rock church of Abuna Yemata in the Tigrayan Geralta and those of the rock church of Yedibba Maryam in Daunt are among the most remarkable, but there are many others. Most rock-hewn churches are difficult to date. Some may contain paintings earlier than the thirteenth century. The oldest icons in the form of diptychs and triptychs are from the fifteenth century. On present evidence, it appears that their production in Ethiopia did not start much earlier. European influences became increasingly important and varied. Examples of Christian art and craftsmanship probably began to be brought to Ethiopia from Europe and the Near East in the thirteenth century. In the next three centuries Italian, Spanish, Portuguese, Greek, Armenian, Coptic, and perhaps Persian and Indian, artists and artisans lived in Ethiopia for long periods, were employed by princes and churchmen, instructed indigenous artists and craftsmen, and created paintings and constructed buildings which Ethiopians admired and imitated.[84]

Many of these foreigners are unknown by name. Three, however, have been identified in written records and by some of their works: Nicolo Brancaleon, Gregorio Bicini and Lazaro de Andrade.[85] The first two were Italian, the third Portuguese. Brancaleon, the first to arrive, is the best known both from written references (he is mentioned four times by Father Alvares) and from his works. He was a

[84] The most comprehensive work on Ethiopian religious art, the study of which is still in its infancy, is Stanislaw Chojnacki, *Major Themes in Ethiopian Painting...from the 13th to the 19th Century,* Steiner, Wiesbaden, 1983. See also Roderick Grierson (ed.), *African Zion, the Sacred Art of Ethiopia,* Yale University Press, New Haven, CT, 1993; and the introductory essay by Prof. Chojnacki and myself, "A Rich Heritage - Still Inadequately Explored" in Henze (ed.), *Aspects of Ethiopian Art from Ancient Axum to the Twentieth Century,* JED Press, London, 1993, pp. 9-16.

[85] See Chojnacki, *op.cit.,* pp. 376-408.

Venetian who came to Ethiopia in 1480. Since no records of him have been found in Venice, he was probably quite young and of modest origin. He was over sixty when Alvares met him in the 1520s, wealthy and widely respected. He must have died in Ethiopia, probably in the late 1520s or early 1530s. Brancaleon was a painter of great skill and highly productive. He was popular at court and had a close association with important monasteries in Gojjam and nearby areas. He signed his work in both his own name ("Opus Meus Nicolasu Bracaleo Venetus") and with the Ethiopian pseudonym Marqorewos.

In 1973 the intrepid English lady traveller, Diana Spencer, discovered a pattern book of miniatures signed by him at Wafa Yesus and a large triptych depicting the Dormition of the Virgin as well as the Apostles at the nearby monastery of Getisamani in the Goncha Gorge. In 1995 Professor Chojnacki and I confirmed that these had survived the vicissitudes of the Derg era when the monks stored them in caves. We photographed them in detail. On a visit to Mertule Maryam two years before we had found a large twelve-panel icon which appeared to be by Brancaleone but after study of the inscriptions on its back proved to be the work of one of his Ethiopian students, Afnin, hitherto unknown. Many unsigned paintings are attributed to the Venetian. No doubt more will be confirmed and discovered. Though much has been learned about Ethiopian religious art in recent decades, it is still a challenging field where important new discoveries are likely to be made.

Painting in Ethiopia in all its forms–icons, illuminated manuscripts, wall paintings–remained, with a few exceptions, exclusively religious in inspiration until the late ninteenth century. Religious painting nevertheless provides a great deal of information about secular life and customs as well as political data on rulers, their associates and their activities. Donors who paid for the picture are often shown prostrate at the bottom of paintings and are often identified. They were prominent people, sometimes rulers and other royal personages, often prominent local citizens of whom no other record survives. Donor portraits become increasingly common after the seventeenth century. Manuscript and wall paintings in churches supply details of clothing and style of dress, furnishings, items of daily use such as basketry, pots, utensils and tools, horse trappings, weapons carried by soldiers and warrior saints, writing materials, textiles, architecture, and both wild and domestic animals and birds.

Painting, chronicles and saints' lives, reports of foreign travellers, correspondence between Ethiopian rulers and church and secular authorities in Egypt, Arabia, Europe, and Jerusalem, all reveal cultural patterns which took shape in medieval times that have survived until the present. Most Ethiopian Christians were subsistence farmers who, when weather was good and, in the absence of war, produced a modest surplus of food which they brought to markets to sell. The same style of life was common to the Agaw and the Falasha as well as the non-Christian peoples of the south. People lived simply, but those who gained wealth and influence also had a taste for luxuries like fine clothes, jewelry, weapons, horse trappings, carpets, furniture which came from the Mediterranean world or areas to the east of the Red Sea extending as far as India. Such goods were paid for by ivory, skins, civet, gold and other natural products. Ethiopians manufactured almost nothing but simple cotton cloth, baskets, pottery, simple weaponry, and elementary items of leather and furniture. All but the clergy were illiterate, but a few of the elite learned to read, Zara Yakob and Queen Eleni among them.

There is no way of calculating the population of Ethiopia during medieval times but, like Europe, total numbers were probably surprisingly small in comparison to modern times. Plagues and famine took a heavy toll from time to time, but population losses seem to have been made up rapidly. In spite of serial marriages, polygamy, and concubinage, family ties were strong and awareness of lineage important. Infant mortality must have been high and average longevity was probably not above thirty-five. Since life was short, people married early and produced offspring as rapidly as nature allowed. Large numbers of young men lost their lives in warfare, but there is little evidence that many tried to avoid service as soldiers. The opportunity to plunder when victorious had great appeal, but when armies were defeated, soldiers disappeared into the landscape to avoid capture and enslavement.

The church recognized the desirability of higher standards of morality and behavior and enunciated them, but not many rulers or churchmen consistently observed the standards themselves. Nevertheless, over the four centuries after Yekuno Amlak the quality of life probably slowly improved for most Ethiopians, though the notion of progress, as such, remained foreign to the Ethiopian mentality. Ethiopians gradually became more aware of the outer world, though understanding and knowledge of its extent was still extremely limited. Old Testament stories depicted on church walls and recited during religious services were real to people because their own lives followed the same patterns and confronted them with the same kind of problems. Life in medieval Ethiopia was much like life in medieval Europe only a century or two before. Change came slowly for ordinary people. Medieval Ethiopia had no permanent cities or even villages of much size.

In the early 1990s, after travelling in the back reaches of Tigray, Wollo, and Gojjam I came home and read Barbara Hanawalt's reconstruction of life in medieval England based on meticulous study of church and court records of the time: *The Ties that Bound: Peasant Families in Medieval England.*[86] I was astonished at the extent to which the patterns and customs she described corresponded to those I had just experienced in the contemporary north Ethiopian countryside where I slept with the livestock in peasant homes, attended joyous weddings of girls of ten to boys of fourteen, and drank *talla* at thatched houses where a horn cup on a stick in front of the door told passers-by that there was fresh homebrew for sale.[87]

[86] Oxford University Press, 1988.

[87] Summing up all these observations and comparisons, I wrote a short essay, "Traditional Ethiopia and Medieval England", forthcoming in Roderick Grierson (ed.), *Festschrift for Richard Pankhurst.*

4

ORDEAL, RECOVERY, DECLINE

ETHIOPIA AND THE WORLD AROUND IT ON
THE THRESHOLD OF MODERN TIMES

The growth of Muslim power in the Horn of Africa

As we have seen in the previous chapter, the Muslim principalities that arose between the Rift Valley and the coast from the late ninth century onward were a constant worry for Ethiopian rulers as they expanded southward.[1] Many of these small Muslim states were originally tributary to Ethiopia, but competition among them for trade and territory led to a complex process of interactions with the Christian rulers of the plateau: alliances, betrayals, wars, cooperation. The Makhzumi sultanate of Shòa, founded in the late tenth century lasted for almost 300 years but fell into decay and was conquered in 1285 by Wali Asma. His successors, who claimed distinguished Arab ancestry, were called the Walasma dynasty. As they expanded their realm, it became known as the Sultanate of Ifat, a name which survives in modern Ethiopia in the district of Yifat in northeast Shoa. The continual hostilities between the Christian kingdom and Ifat during the reigns of Amde Tseyon and his successors, as described in the previous chapter, led to a decisive defeat of Ifat's Muslim rulers. But their sons succeeded them and established a successor state, the Sultanate of Adal, with its capital at Dakar, near Harar.

The Adal Sultanate prospered from trade with the highlands through Zeila and Berbera but was soon ready to challenge the highlanders again. After Emperor Zara Yakob defeated Sultan Badlay-ud-din in 1445, the Adalites retreated and regrouped. Defeat had few lasting consequences for them because of their extensive trading relationships with the Muslim world. Trade and other contacts with the highlands did not stop but the Ethiopian monarchy was weakened by a series of succession crises. Sultan Badlay's son and successor, Muhammad, proposed amicable relations with Ba'eda Maryam (1468-78), but when Muhammad died, conflict flared up again. Ba'eda Maryam moved his court to the Gurage country and undertook campaigns in Dawaro and Bale, as did his successor, Iskinder (1478-94).[2]

---

[1] "The Challenge of the Muslim Sultanates" in Erlich, *Ethiopia and the Middle East*, pp. 25-8.

[2] Dakar was badly damaged when Iskinder's forces captured it about 1480 but it recovered and served as the Adal capital until 1520 when Sultan Abu Bakr Muhammad

Ba'eda Maryam's son Iskinder came to the throne as a six-year-old, and Queen Mother Eleni was first pushed aside by jealous nobles, but this clever woman quickly recovered her role and continued to be influential during Iskinder's reign and that of the next ruler, second son of Ba'eda Maryam, Na'od (1494-1508).[3] From her childhood in Hadiya, Eleni retained awareness of the wider Muslim world and sought to achieve a degree of reconciliation and good commercial relations between the Christian kingdom and Adal. Sultan Muhammad, who reigned there for thirty years (1488-1518), reciprocated her positive intentions, but was unable to keep the emir of Harar, Mahfuz, from periodically attacking Christian territory. Na'od's reign was troubled by internal dissension. He was killed in Ifat in a campaign against the Muslims when his son Lebna Dengel was only seven years old. For the third time Queen Mother Eleni became regent for a young boy.[4]

Eleni was probably well into her seventies by this time, 1508. She was nevertheless remarkably active and foresighted. Eager to match the sympathy and aid the Muslims received from Arabia and the Levant with support from Christian states, she dispatched an Armenian named Mateus to Portugal to ask for help for Ethiopia in resisting Muslim pressure. In her effort to seek Portuguese help she was in all likelihood advised by Pero da Covilhão, by that time resident at the court for more than a decade. Mateus proceeded to Europe by way of India, had a series of misadventures, but finally reached the court of King Manoel I in Lisbon in 1514, where he was well received. Even so, the Portuguese waited until 1520 to send an exploratory mission to Ethiopia.

The intervening years were eventful. Emir Mahfuz of Harar invaded the highlands in 1516. Lebna Dengel, now exercising the

---

abandoned it for Harar. I have attempted to give only a relatively schematic summary of a very complex sequence of historical developments which the Italian historian Enrico Cerulli summarized on the basis of research in Harar in the late 1920s: *Studi Etiopici,* I: *La Lingua e la Storia di Harar,* Istituto per l'Oriente, 1936. Many aspects of this history remain obscure. The most useful secondary sources, which are based primarily on Ethiopian royal chronicles and Arab writings, are Trimingham's *Islam in Ethiopia* and Taddesse Tamrat's *Church and State,* both cited frequently in the preceding chapter. Budge's *History of Ethiopia: Nubia and Abyssinia* is also useful. The works of these authors often do not agree on details or on interpretations of contradictory information.

[3] Na'od's mother was a second wife of Ba'eda Maryam, thus he was a half-brother of Iskinder. Iskinder died at twenty-two, leaving an infant son as heir. As a child this son, Amde Tseyon II, was the object of intrigue which ended with his death and the accession of Na'od.

[4] C.F. Rey, *The Romance of the Portuguese in Abyssinia,* originally published in London in 1929, reissued by Negro Universities Press, New York, 1969, pp. 28-35.

authority of emperor, was eager to demonstrate his prowess. He led his army to a successful ambush of Mahfuz's forces in a gorge, slew him and pursued the Adalites back into their own territory, where he destroyed one of the sultan's castles at Zankar. At the same time a Portuguese fleet attacked Zeila and burned it. Lebna Dengel returned to the highlands a hero and chroniclers declared the Muslim menace at an end. They were mistaken.

Turks and Portuguese

Since the fall of the Roman Empire, Ethiopia had enjoyed immunity from political and military pressure from Mediterranean powers. This comfortable situation changed at the beginning of the 16th century. The vigorous, expanding Ottoman Empire, successor to the Byzantines, defeated the Egyptian Mamlukes in 1517 and quickly expanded its reach into the Red Sea in pursuit of trade and slaves. The Ottomans offered support to the Muslim principalities along the coast, and conquered Yemen in the 1530s. Their advance encouraged the Adal rulers with whom they were in close contact.[5]

The most remarkable feature of the period is the role which Portugal, a small country on the fringe of Europe, came to play in world affairs. Fourteenth-century maps reveal that its seamen had been accumulating knowledge of the Atlantic islands and west African coast long before Bartolomeu Dias rounded the Cape of Good Hope at the turn of the year 1487-8 and Vasco da Gama opened up navigation of the Indian Ocean ten years later. King Joao II in Lisbon set about collecting information on the distant lands the Portuguese aimed to reach: India and the mysterious kingdom of Prester John. In the same year that Dias rounded the Cape, João sent Pero da Covilhão overland to reconnoiter the East. He took the disguise of a Muslim merchant and travelled via Cairo to India. He then made his way to Ormuz, the trading center at the mouth of the Persian Gulf.[6] He finally reached Ethiopia in 1493 and never left it, becoming an influential advisor in the imperial household. When the Portuguese mission Queen Eleni had requested finally arrived in Ethiopia in 1520, Covilhão, an old man, was its most valuable source of information and advice about the country.[7]

[5] "The Ottomans and the Habesh *Eyaleti*" in Erlich, *Ethiopia and the Middle East*, pp. 33-40.

[6] The port has disappeared but the name survives in the Straits of Hormuz.

[7] Covilhão was the first of a long line of European advisors to Ethiopian monarchs, including the Swiss Alfred Ilg who worked for Menelik II and two Americans: A.E. Colson, who served Haile Selassie before the Italian invasion and John Spencer, who advised him from the 1940s to the 1960s.

There are remarkable historical coincidences in the Ethiopian-Portuguese relationship. Christian Portugal experienced an extraordinary burst of vigor as the Muslims were being expelled from the Iberian Peninsula. Within a decade of Vasco da Gama's voyage, Portugal became a major sea power in the Indian Ocean, challenging centuries of Arab supremacy in these seas. Its ambitious rulers hoped to dominate Asian trade with Europe. Ethiopia had lost most of its coast and interest in the sea after the rise of Islam. Suddenly Ethiopian and Portuguese interests coincided. The Portuguese sought allies against the Muslims who controlled Indian Ocean trade. Ethiopia needed help against Muslim threats to its own territory.

Queen Mother Eleni understood this, but Lebna Dengel did not. When the Portuguese mission led by Rodrigo da Lima arrived in Massawa in 1520 to negotiate a permanent alliance, Lebna Dengel dawdled:

> ... it met a king flushed with success and suspicious of Portuguese motives. The old Queen Eleni had retired to her domain in Gojjam[8] and the king [i.e. Lebna Dengel] denied that the Armenian Mateus had received any official sanction to solicit an alliance. The mission remained in Abyssinia six years and it sailed away in 1526 shortly after a youth of 19 named Ahmad ibn Ibrahim had won a notable victory over an Abyssinian expedition at a time when Adal had relapsed into a state of anarchy.[9]

Ahmad Gragn's assault on the Christian kingdom

After Lebna Dengel's initial victory the internal weaknesses in the kingdom of Adal soon showed themselves. The older generation ... headed by the Walasma, living in settlements and towns, interested in commerce, indifferent in religion, and ready to come to terms with Abyssinia, were opposed by newly converted Afar and Somali tribes, moved by motives both religious and migrational and led by warlike, fanatical emirs. Sultan Muhammad was murdered in 1518 on his return from the campaign against [the Ethiopians] and Adal was torn by intestinal struggles during which five sultans succeeded in two years.[10]

Internal strife in Adal left young Ahmad ibn Ibrahim free to plan new attacks from Harar after he killed Sultan Abu Bakr in 1520. Nicknamed *Gragn*, the left-handed, Ahmad had both vision and vigor. His goal was nothing less than complete conquest of the Ethiopian Christian kingdom and conversion of the population to Islam. He attacked first in 1529 and inflicted a heavy defeat on Lebna Dengel, then withdrew. Two years later he launched a well planned invasion of the

[8] She apparently died soon after. Alvares refers to her death but gives no date.

[9] Trimingham, *Islam in Ethiopia*, p. 84.

[10] *Ibid.*

highlands, burning churches and monasteries and forcibly converting Christians. He reached Lake Hayq in Wollo, looted its famous
island monastery, and made his way across to Lake Tana, where he
failed to reach the most important islands. Confronted by the stone
churches of Lalibela, he looted objects made of precious metals,
burned manuscripts and everything of wood, but did relatively little
damage to the churches themselves. He led his army on through Wag
and into Tigray. Here two Turks who had become Christians helped
the Ethiopians acquire muskets and cannons. Axum's defenders
put up stiff resistance, but Gragn overcame them and destroyed the
old church of St Mary of Zion. He moved northward into Hamasien[11],
but stopped before reaching the country's northernmost monastery,
Debre Bizen, located atop a steep mountain above Nefasit, below
Asmara. When I visited this still active religious establishment in
1995, the monks recounted how Gragn had been frustrated by God
because, they said, He made the monastery invisible to him and he
was unable to find it.[12]

Gragn's armies destroyed much of Ethiopia's literary, architectural and cultural heritage. Chroniclers recorded the horror the
population experienced, perhaps with some dramatic exaggeration:

... In every place where they had triumphed they laid waste and destroyed
and burned and turned the country into a desert. They carried off from the
churches the gold and silver vessels, the precious Indian stuffs, which were
sewn with gems, and everything of value, and then they set fire to them and
razed the walls to the ground. They slew every adult Christian they found, and
carried off the youths and the maidens and sold them as slaves. The remnant
of the Christian population were terrified at the ruin which was overtaking
their country, and with the view of staying the attacks ... nine men out of ten
renounced the Christian religion and accepted Islam. A mighty famine
came on the country. [...] Lebna Dengel and his family were driven from
their house and city, and for some years they wandered about the country
hopeless, and suffered hunger and thirst and hardships of every kind.
Under these privations he was smitten with grievous sickness and died, and
Claudius [Galawdewos], one of his younger sons, became king in his stead.[13]

[11] The central province of Eritrea in which Asmara, which was then only a small
village, is located.

[12] God was still being helpful during the monastery's recent difficulties, the
monks said, for during the 1980s the area in which it is located was between Derg
and EPLF positions. God rendered Derg artillery incapable of firing into it, they
explained, so it came through the war undamaged.

[13] Cited from Budge, *op.cit.*, p. 337. If the devastation were as complete as this
summary states, it is difficult to believe Ethiopia could have recovered. Material
damage was indeed great and can still be seen today, but there is little evidence
that people forcibly converted to Islam by Gragn remained Muslims after he was
defeated. Highland culture was firmly established in secluded valleys and on
ambas Gragn did not reach and revived comparatively rapidly.

Emperor Galawdewos, who succeeded to the throne in 1540 at the age of eighteen, faced a desperate situation but had the strength to begin to rally his soldiers and his people. He had already dealt Gragn's armies several defeats when 400 Portuguese, well-armed musketeers under Christovão da Gama, son of Vasco, landed in Massawa on 10 February 1541. They brought great quantities of arms, including cannons, gunpowder, and other supplies and were accompanied by nearly 150 craftsmen, gunsmiths and slaves. It took them several arduous months to move into the highlands of Tigray. There they met the Queen Mother, Sebla Wangel ("Harvest of the Gospel"), and were joined by small groups of Ethiopian warriors. This modest force made its way across Tigray, engaging much larger contingents of Gragn's troops but using their European weaponry to good effect. Alarmed at the performance of the Portuguese, Gragn appealed to the Turks in Yemen and received 900 well-armed reinforcements from Zabid. Somewhere beyond the Takazze, da Gama maneuvered his force into a situation where Gragn, who had moved up from Lake Tana, was able to besiege the expedition.[14] When the Muslims attacked, da Gama and all but 120 of the Portuguese were captured or killed. Da Gama's head was sent to the Pasha of Zabid along with twelve Portuguese prisoners.

Galawdewos, having brought his army from Tegulet in Shoa, reached the area soon after the catastrophe. Arms which the Portuguese had stored at Debre Damo were brought up while new supplies of gunpowder were manufactured locally. The emperor built up his own forces around the remaining Portuguese and their weaponry. On 6 February 1543 Galawdewos set out for Lake Tana. He took Gragn's army by surprise when he attacked on 21 February.[15] Galawdewos's chronicle says Gragn's troops were "as thick as locusts" an estimated 15,000 against an Ethiopian-Portuguese force of no more than 9,000. The Portuguese were determined to avenge the disaster da Gama had experienced and fought furiously. A musketeer dashed almost singlehandedly into the midst of the Muslims, found Gragn, and shot him through the breast, then fell mortally wounded himself. Gragn's troops panicked and dispersed. His son was captured, though

[14] The encounter occurred south of the Takazze on an *amba* called "The Mountain of the Jews". Neither it, nor the exact route the party followed across northern Ethiopia, has been firmly identified. Two of the Portuguese in the expedition survived to write accounts of it: Miguel de Castanhoso and Joao Bermudez. Both were published in a volume edited by R.S. Whiteway, *The Portuguese Expedition to Abyssinia, 1541-3*, Hakluyt Society, London, 1902. C.F. Rey, *op.cit.*, pp. 127-98, provides a recapitulation of Castanhoso's narrative.

[15] Considering the great distances and difficult terrain which had to be traversed, the scene of da Gama's defeat and Galawdewos's regrouping would seem to have been in Gaynt, a considerable distance south of the Takazze.

his wife, Bati Del Wambara, escaped with a remnant of the Turks fighting with his forces. The Ethiopians severed Gragn's head and displayed it in the surrounding countryside.[16]

The forces of Galawdewos pursued the retreating Muslims and fought several successful battles. In 1545 Galawdewos reached Bale and ejected the Muslims, but the Ethiopian hold there was tenuous, for most of the indigenous inhabitants had only been lightly Christianized and the Ethiopians soon had to retreat before the advancing Oromo. Gragn's widow Bati Del Wambara returned to Harar to rally his lieutenants to continue attacking the Ethiopians. She agreed to marry Gragn's nephew, Nur ibn Mujahid, on condition that he would avenge Gragn's defeat. Nur strengthened the city's defenses by surrounding it with the walls that still stand today. In 1550 he became emir, but his initial sorties against the Ethiopians were unsuccessful and provoked an Ethiopian counteroffensive in the course of which the city itself was sacked. But Nur's forces recovered quickly and continued raids on Ethiopian-held territory.

These were not the only misfortunes the Ethiopians experienced in the wake of Gragn's defeat. The Ottoman Turks under Özdemir Pasha seized Massawa and Arkiko in 1557 and fought their way up into Hamasien where they built a fortress at Debarwa, south of Asmara. This provoked strong Tigrayan resistance. The Tigrayans drove the Turks back toward the coast but could not dislodge them from Suakin, Massawa and Arkiko, and the Turks made repeated incursions into northern Ethiopia during the remainder of the century, at times gaining the support of rivals of the emperors.[17] Urged on by Gragn's wife, Nur mounted a major offensive against Ethiopian territory which drew Galawdewos away from Gojjam, where he had been fighting the Agaw. Though the advancing Ethiopian army succeeded in taking Harar and killing Sultan Barakat of Adal, the last of the Walasma line, Galawdewos went on to attack Nur, who fought back vigorously, defeated the Ethiopians and killed Galawdewos himself on Good Friday 1559. Nur lived on until 1567 and had to repulse an Oromo

---

[16] An outsize blue velvet robe with enormous sleeves said to have belonged to Gragn is kept in the treasury of the monastery of Mertule Maryam in Gojjam and still shown to visitors. Gragn's son was eventually exchanged against Galawdewos's brother Minas (who succeeded him in 1559) who had earlier been captured by Gragn's troops and taken to Zabid in Yemen.

[17] The northern coastal region remained under Ottoman rule for 300 years and was called the Province of Habesh. Egypt, still nominally an Ottoman vassal state, assumed control of the coast in the mid-19th century. This period of Ottoman/Muslim domination in Eritrean history has attracted very little attention, though a modern Turkish scholar produced a detailed study of it in the early 1970s, drawing on documents from Ottoman archives: Cengiz Orhonlu, *Habes Eyaleti*, Istanbul University Press, 1974.

advance into his own territory. He became a legend in Harar and his tomb a place of pilgrimage, but both the Adal sultanate and the Christian kingdom were weakened by their violent encounters in the mid-sixteenth century and both experienced subsequent times of troubles.

In Ethiopia the damage which Gragn did has never been forgotten. British emissary Harris who spent a year and a half in Shoa in 1842, reported:

The most preposterous legends are to this day believed with reference to the personal prowess of [Gragn], his gigantic stature, and the colossal size of his steed. Gragn is said to have wielded a brand twenty feet in length; and, although it is a matter of notoriety that he was shot in the manner already narrated by a Portuguese soldier, he is represented to have received four thousand musket bullets before yielding up the ghost. The supernatural achievements of this conqueror are handed down in an extant Amharic volume; and his inroads gave birth in the mind of the people of Shoa to a superstitious dread of the Adal, such as was long entertained of the Turks in Northern Europe...[18]

Every Christian highlander still hears tales of Gragn in his childhood. Haile Selassie referred to him in his memoirs. I have often had villagers in northern Ethiopia point out sites of towns, forts, churches and monasteries damaged or destroyed by Gragn as if these catastrophes had occurred only yesterday. Though some modern Somali nationalists have attempted to make him a national hero, the case is unconvincing. Somali tribes had not developed a sense of common identity in his time. They were still in the process of expanding into the territories they eventually occupied. Gragn's forces were composed of Afars, Hararis, Ṣomalis and Arabs and were augmented by a few Turks. Their common language was Arabic and their sense of purpose lay in their loyalty to Islam.[19]

The advance of the Oromo

Gragn's invasion and the fighting which followed between the Christians and Muslims opened the way for the great migrations of the Oromo. This people, largely pastoral at the time of their advance northward, speak a Cushitic language like the Somalis. They most probably originated in the far southern highlands of Ethiopia and may have been an element of the population of medieval Muslim

---

[18] Major W. Cornwallis Harris, *The Highlands of Ethiopia*, Longmans, London, 1844, vol. II, pp. 255-6.

[19] A Harari chronicler, Shihab-ad-Din compiled a history called *Futuh al-Habasha* (The Abyssinian Victories) which describes Gragn's campaigns to the year 1535 from the Muslim point of view. It was translated into French by René Basset, *Histoire de la conquête de l'Abyssinie,* Paris, 1897-1901.

kingdoms against which Amde Tseyon fought: Ifat, Waj, Dawaro, Fatajar and Bali. The extent to which the Oromo engaged in agriculture and the manner in which cultural influences from the north and east may have reached them are still matters of controversy among scholars, as is the origin of the Somali.[20] The Oromo who began to move northward in the latter part of the 16th century were mostly nomadic pastoralists without a written language. They espoused neither Christianity nor Islam. They had a remarkably egalitarian culture with a complex age-class system, through which all men rotated in their lifetime. They seem also to have been extraordinarily prolific, for even if Christian chroniclers exaggerated their numbers and painted them as the essence of evil, it is clear that a vast population was involved in their movements. The monk Bahrey who wrote a history of this people in 1593 explained his purpose:

... to make known the number of their tribes, their readiness to kill people and the brutality of their manners. If anyone should say. [...] "Why has he written a history of bad people?" I would answer by saying, "Search in the books and you will find that the history of Mohammed and the Moslem kings has been written and they are our enemies in religion."[21]

"How is it that the Galla defeat us, though we are numerous and well supplied with arms?" Bahrey went on to ask. He concluded that it was because all their men were trained as warriors while among Ethiopian Christians only the warriors fought, while monks, priests, craftsmen, farmers, traders and servants did not. The Ethiopians fell back before the Oromo onrush, which also affected Adal, the region around Harar coming to be occupied entirely by Oromo, who remain the basic population of the area today. Oromo pastoralists learned to use horses and kept moving into the center and northern parts of the country for the next century and a half. Gradually, many settled, adapted to agriculture, and adopted Christianity. Oromo leaders became a major element in regional politics, but it was rare for the Oromo who were intermixed among the Amhara to act together politically as Oromos above the family and clan level. After they settled and became Christianized, they often intermarried with Amhara and other Semitic peoples, and became assimilated. In the southern part of the country, especially in Bale, Arsi and the outer

[20] The origins of both of these peoples and their early history require a great deal of further study, as stressed by Mohammed Hassen in his important pioneering work, *The Oromo of Ethiopia: a History, 1570-1860*, Cambridge University Press, 1990.

[21] *Ye-Galla Tarih*, translated in C.F. Beckingham and G.W.B. Huntingford, *Some Records of Ethiopia, 1593-1646*, Hakluyt Society, Cambridge, 1954; termed Galla until 1974 (see p. 111, n.2 for the possible origin of the term), these people have since insisted on being called by the name they have long used for themselves, Oromo.

fringes of the southwest, Oromos remained the dominant element in the population. Some continued a pastoral life into modern times (e.g. the Borana) and many eventually converted to Islam.

Several Oromo kingdoms in western and southwestern Ethiopia gained dominance over the Sidama and Omotic peoples indigenous to the area and remained essentially independent of imperial authority, especially in the Gibe region and in Wollega, till the late 19th century. Strong hereditary leaders emerged who did not recognize subservience to Ethiopian central authority until the time of Menelik II, after conquest (which was particularly cruel in the case of Kaffa),[22] and as a result of trade and political penetration and alliances (as in Wollega).[23]

Portuguese success and failure

Participation in the defeat of Gragn was only the beginning of the Portuguese adventure in Ethiopia which continued for another century. A couple of hundred soldiers and supporters survived the campaign against the armies of Adal. While a few eventually found their way back to Portugal, most remained, marrying and siring families, becoming absorbed into the local population. They were in demand as craftsmen and builders. Bridges, fortifications, churches and other buildings can still be found all over north-central Ethiopia that were built by Portuguese craftsmen and their descendants. Only a few can be exactly dated, but the affinity to late medieval architecture in Portugal is readily apparent in the castles of Gondar and in churches, bridges and fortifications in other parts of the northern highlands.

The Portuguese were not content with rescuing the Ethiopians from the Muslims; some aspired to political influence. They hoped to transform the country into a bastion of Roman Catholicism. When the first Portuguese mission left Ethiopia in 1526, one of their group, João Bermudez, stayed behind. He is an enigmatic figure. When he finally returned to Portugal thirty years later, he published a detailed memoir in which he claimed to have been appointed head of the Ethiopian church, a claim for which no confirmation in Ethiopia has ever been found. In 1536 he journeyed to Rome, where he claimed to have been confirmed as a bishop by Pope Paul III. He went on to

---

[22] Herbert S. Lewis published a study of one of the most significant, *A Galla Monarchy: Jimma Abba Jifar, 1830-1932*, University of Wisconsin Press, Madison, 1965.

[23] The paucity of information on the history of this important part of modern Ethiopia has begun to be rectified in recent years by a number of works based on detailed research, notably Donald Donham and Wendy James (eds), *The Southern Marches of Imperial Ethiopia*, Cambridge University Press, 1986.

Portugal, where he was instrumental in getting the Portuguese king to organize the expedition which arrived in 1541 to help defeat Gragn. He fought in this campaign but, according to his countryman Castanhoso, was often a source of dissension and made exaggerated claims about his performance.

Bermudez, apparently for trying to press Galawdewos to acknowledge submission to the Pope, fell out of favor and was exiled from the court in spite of support from the Queen Mother. He was sent to Tigray where he provoked further trouble. He left Massawa in 1556 on a Portuguese vessel that brought in two more priests while he made his way back to Portugal via Goa. Thus began more than 70 years of determined efforts, dominated by Jesuits, to persuade the Ethiopian church to sever its connection with Alexandria and accept submission to Rome. There were misconceptions on all sides. Galawdewos and his next three successors gave the Portuguese no reason to believe that they were susceptible to abandoning monophysite Christianity and their traditional religious practices. The Ottomans feared the Portuguese as rivals and assumed they were ready to back their religious efforts with military strength. The Portuguese kings were unwilling, however, to overextend themselves militarily in Ethiopia or in the Red Sea.

The Portuguese Jesuits were persistent. No sooner was Bermudez gone than Jesuit Bishop Andre da Oviedo accompanied by five priests and a small party of servants landed at Arkiko in March 1557 and designated himself Archbishop of Ethiopia, moving up into Tigray and on to the Emperor's camp. Galawdewos, who had just founded and dedicated an important church in Wollo, Tedbaba Maryam, made no concessions in discussions with Oviedo, who accused the Ethiopians of practicing a false form of Christianity contaminated with Judaism.[24] Galawdewos composed an impressive document defending monophysite orthodoxy which became known as his Confession.

Minas, the brother who succeeded Galawdewos in 1559, immediately undertook a campaign against the Falasha of Semien and was unsuccessful. He then became entangled in the politics of Tigray, where Bahr Negash Yishaq, bearer of the title of ruler of the region along the sea, allied himself with the Ottomans and crowned a nephew of Minas as a rival emperor. The Turks pushed Minas's forces back and Minas died of fever in 1562. The Shoan commanders of the army,

---

[24] *Inter alia*, the Jesuits objected to the observance of the Jewish Sabbath, the practice of circumcision, temporary marriage, the commemoration of Epiphany (*Timqat*) as repeated baptism, and Old Testament dietary restrictions. Most fundamentally they condemned the Orthodox Church's adherence to the doctrine of monophysitism.

supported by the Queen Mother, elected Minas's young son, Sarsa Dengel ("Sprout of the Virgin"), emperor. He was barely fourteen years old, but he was supported by the Amhara aristocracy who feared Tigrayan influence. By the time the young emperor reached his majority, Yishaq came to the royal camp and swore allegiance, turning against the Turks. But he reversed course in 1575 and allied himself with them again. Sarsa Dengel, who meanwhile was involved in constant fighting with the Oromo, Adal and the Falasha, marched into Tigray in 1576. He defeated the Turks and both Yishaq and Ozdemir Pasha were killed. Sarsa Dengel's reorganization of the army contributed to his success in defending the Christian kingdom from enemies on all sides. He died in 1597 after a reign of thirty-four years.

During Minas's short reign, the Jesuits had been banished to a site between Aksum and Adwa originally called Maigoga ("Noisy Water") which they renamed Fremona to commemorate Frumentius, who had converted Emperor Ezana. They led an isolated and harsh life there, being allowed to venture out only to serve other Portuguese and look after children of Portuguese liaisons with local women. Sarsa Dengel forbade them to proselytize among Ethiopians. Oviedo schemed with Yishaq against the emperor and made repeated appeals to Rome and Lisbon for military support, but the Portuguese regent, Prince Henry, refused and advised Pope Pius V to relieve Oviedo of his Ethiopian bishopric and send him into Asia. Oviedo nevertheless managed to stay on until his death at Fremona in 1577. Of the five priests who came with him, two were murdered; three survived him, all of whom died at Fremona, the last at the age of 80 in 1597. Nevertheless the Jesuits persisted.

Next to arrive in Ethiopia was the Spanish-origin Father Pero Pais (Pedro Paez). Born in 1564, he was still in his thirties. He had to endure a series of acute misfortunes, including capture by the Turks and imprisonment in Dhofar and Yemen, on his first attempt to reach the country. But he profited from these experiences by studying Arabic and learning about the history of the region. He finally succeeded in landing at Massawa in 1603 disguised as an Armenian merchant and proceeded to Fremona by way of Debarwa. Sarsa Dengel had died and the country had fallen into a ten-year period of confusion over the succession. Several claimants to the throne reigned for short periods. After waiting at Fremona for several months during which he studied Amharic and Ge'ez, Pais was summoned by the young emperor then on the throne, Za Dengel, a nephew of Sarsa Dengel, to come to Dankaz[25] near Lake Tana, where he had returned from fighting against the Oromo in Damot.

[25] For a summary of the history of Dankaz as a royal campsite and eventually a royal residence, see Richard Pankhurst, *History of Ethiopian Towns from the Middle Ages*

Pais was a very different kind of man from Oviedo: gentle, learned, considerate of the feelings of others. He quickly mastered Ge'ez and Amharic and so impressed Za Dengel with his knowledge of Ethiopian customs and his careful explanations of Catholic belief and practice that the young emperor decided to convert, as did some members of his retinue, though Pais cautioned him against declaring himself openly too quickly. Za Dengel decreed changes in the observance of the Sabbath which provoked a rebellion. The Abuna excommunicated him. In spite of the aid of a contingent of 200 Portuguese, Za Dengel was killed in the subsequent turmoil. Pais, however, had returned to Fremona to avoid direct involvement in these events.

This foresight left Pais free to develop a relationship with Emperor Susenyos who captured the throne in 1607.[26] Susenyos invited Pais to his camp and a friendship developed. Pais accompanied the emperor to Aksum, where he was crowned in March 1609. His description of this occasion provides a good example of the pomp and luxury Ethiopian emperors liked to display:

> The ground was covered with large and rich carpets, the great men drew up on both sides. The Maidens of Sion stopped the way crossing it with a silk line up to which the Emperor went three times and being asked by the Maidens who he was, the first and second time answered, "I am King of Israel." Being asked the third time who he was, he answered, "I am King of Zion," and drawing the sword he wore cut the line, the maids then saying, "You are truly our King of Zion." And then the air resounded with acclamations of joy, volleys of small shot, and the voice of trumpets, kettledrums. . .and other musical instruments... The Emperor had on a fine vest of crimson damask, and over it a Turkish robe of brocade like the ancient Roman gowns, the sleeves straight but so long that they hung down to the ground...girt with a broad girdle all of pieces of gold curiously wrought, and on his neck a thick chain of gold which went several times about hanging down on his breast and the ends of it falling deep behind, all which, he being a handsome man, became him very well.[27]

Susenyos was crowned by Abuna Simon, recently arrived from Egypt. Since Gragn's attack, Aksum had degenerated into a shabby village, but the ceremonies in the recently rebuilt Church of St. Mary of Zion

---

to the Early Nineteenth Century, Steiner Verlag, Wiesbaden, 1982, pp. 107-10.

[26] Susenyos' Solomonic descent came from Emperor Dawit. When he was nine years old, he was captured by the Oromo and remained with them for a year and a half. He was rescued in the course of a successful Ethiopian campaign in Damot and came under the care of Sarsa Dengel's mother, Admas Mogasa, living in Gojjam. He thus gained substantial knowledge of a region which was still in some degree a frontier area.

[27] Cited from Rey, *op.cit.*, p. 238.

among the ancient ruins underscored the continuity of the Solomonic
line. Though properly launched into the reign in traditional Orthodox ritual, Susenyos found a closer relationship with the Portuguese
appealing. There can be little question that an important aspect of
the motivation of both Za Dengel and Susenyos was the desire to gain
military support from the Portuguese and other Catholic Europeans
to eject the Turks from the north and overcome the Falasha, Agau
and Oromo who were still challenging Ethiopian rulers. In 1613
Susenyos dispatched a mission led by the priest Antonio Fernandes
which was to travel via southern Ethiopia to Malindi on the coast of
Kenya and then make its way to Europe to seek support from Portugal, Spain and the Pope. After a series of setbacks and clashes with
the Oromo, it had to return. During this same period Susenyos fought
repeatedly against rivals and conspirators in several parts of the country. Pais often accompanied him on his campaigns. Pais used these
opportunities to engage in theological discussions and won the
Emperor's brother, Sela Christos, and some of his lieutenants as
open converts. In the course of these travels he became the first
European to visit the source of the Nile at Gish Abbay in Sakala in
central Gojjam.[28]

Susenyos gave Pais land to establish a Jesuit center on the peninsula of Gorgora which juts out from the north shore of Lake Tana. Pais
first built a large stone church there. He had a particular love of
architecture. He then developed a grand plan for a palace for Susenyos,
for which he organized workmen and had tools manufactured. Built
of massive cut stones on a height with a splendid view over the lake, its
ruins are still imposing. Nobles and officials established residences
in the neighborhood. During this period Pais also found time to
compose a long history of Ethiopia with the aim of educating Europeans about the country.[29] Pais's last building, a large European-style
stone church built for Susenyos at Azezo west of Dankaz, was dedicated in January 1622 and called Genneta Yesus ("Paradise of Jesus").
Returning from a campaign where he had won a decisive victory,
Susenyos decided to become a full convert to Catholicism. His relations with Abuna Simon had become severely strained. To show his
sincerity he rejected all his wives and concubines except the first and
solemnly received the sacraments. Pais's patience and perseverance

[28] James Bruce's later claim to be the discoverer is unjustified.

[29] His aim was not achieved until modern times, for the work remained unpublished. It was issued by C. Beccari as part of a 15-volume series in Rome during the
years 1905-17: *Rerum aethiopicarum scriptores occidentales inediti.* A 3-volume Portuguese edition appeared in the series *Biblioteca Historica de Portugal e Brasil* in
Oporto in 1946: Pero Pais, *Historia da Etiopia.* Unlike the other major Portuguese
works on Ethiopia, it has never been translated into English.

had been rewarded; but he lived only a few weeks to enjoy the triumph, dying of fever on 3 May 1622.[30]

Susenyos wrote to Rome requesting more priests before Pais died. There were only five Jesuits in Ethiopia at that time and one of them died later that year. Jesuit headquarters in Rome ordered twelve priests to be sent from Goa. On 22 November 1622, the first of them, Manoel da Almeida and two others, departed. After an arduous voyage they reached Massawa on 24 January 1624, eluded the Turks, and made their way inland. Now that Ethiopia had become a Catholic country, Alfonso Mendes, a senior Jesuit, was chosen as patriarch, consecrated at Lisbon, and sent off with two bishops in March 1623. There had been disagreement about his appointment, however, which seems not to have been approved by the Pope. Two years earlier the young Jesuit, Jeronimo Lobo, still in his twenties, had left for Ethiopia. He spent three years in India and made an abortive effort to enter Ethiopia via the Juba river before joining Mendes and his party and entering through the tiny Red Sea port of Beilul, crossing the Danakil country, and reaching Fremona in June 1625.

In anticipation of Mendes' arrival, Susenyos had taken his brother Sela Christos, his first wife and his two sons by her, Fasilidas and Marqos, to Aksum in 1624 and issued a proclamation stating his reasons for having become a Roman Catholic. He explained that the edifying character of the Jesuits – in contrast to the depravity of the Orthodox Abuns – had been the major factor in his conversion. The newly arrived Jesuits found the atmosphere in Tigray hospitable and set to work amending the Orthodox liturgy and teaching the Ethiopian clergy their way of saying mass. Very early, however, the contrast in behavior between the haughty Mendes and the humble Lobo and others of the simple Jesuits became apparent:

... had the successors of Pais confined themselves to work on his lines, there seems to be no doubt that the whole nation would have embraced the Roman Faith. [...] Mendes was a brave and a bold man, but rigid, uncompromising, narrow-minded and intolerant, and in his dealings with the Abyssinians preferred violent to peaceful and tactful measures.[31]

[30] Pais' activities in Ethiopia constitute the major portion of Philip Caraman's *Lost Empire: The Story of the Jesuits in Ethiopia,* University of Notre Dame Press, 1985. This book, detailed and entertaining, unfortunately suffers from the author's apparent lack of firsthand knowledge of Ethiopia and is chronologically inconsistent.

[31] The quotation is from Budge, *op.cit.,* pp. 389-90. Lobo's remarkable memoirs show him to have been more like Pais. Known as the *Itinerario,* these memoirs were long thought to have been lost but were found in the public library at Braga in Portugal in 1947. A translation by Donald M. Lockhart with Introduction and Notes by C.F. Beckingham was issued by the Hakluyt Society in 1984. They are one of the most valuable firsthand sources of information on Ethiopia of this period.

Mendes did not meet Susenyos until early February 1626. He was given a pompous welcome at the emperor's camp:

Half a league from the camp he was met by 15,000 armed horsemen [who] took him between their lines, the air resounding with the sound of kettle-drums, pipes, and shouts. [...] He donned a cope and white mitre, mounted a pied horse which was cloaked in white damask, and rode to the church under a canopy carried by six governors of provinces. [...] At the entrance to the church he was received by a discharge of all the cannon in the emperor's armory and some small shot. The *Benedictus* was then sung as he proceeded up the chancel where Susenyos, with a gold crown on his head, rose to embrace him.[32]

Mendes' erudite address to the assembled dignitaries lasted most of the day. He argued the primacy of Rome and condemned the waywardness of the eastern churches. A day or two later a mass cere-mony was held for clergy and laity to swear obedience to Rome. It began as Susenyos, holding the Gospels, knelt before Mendes, and took an oath of allegiance to the Pope. The multitude of Ethiopians who followed misled Mendes into believing that all that remained for him to do was to impose Catholic practice on the country as rapidly as possible. He proclaimed a series of onerous restrictions on continuation of any Orthodox practices and decreed their imme-diate imposition throughout the provinces. This grandiose occasion was the beginning of a troubled period. Almost all the common people rejected the changes. Rebellions broke out everywhere: rebels seized converts and hanged them; the Agaw rose against the emperor; Oromos invaded Gojjam; the Viceroy of Tigray abandoned Catholi-cism. In 1630 the Viceroy of Begemder, Sarsa Christos, a nephew of Susenyos, proclaimed Fasilidas emperor, but was captured and brought before the emperor, who ordered him hanged. Mendes praised Susenyos' use of force.

Force did not dampen rebellion, but Susenyos was dismayed by the disorder the change of religion had provoked. In 1631, while Mendes was away from court, he issued a proclamation to the effect that Ethiopians "might follow their ancient customs provided they were not repugnant to faith", i.e. abandon Catholic practices. A furi-ous Mendes persuaded him to reverse the proclamation. This caused the emperor's brother, Malka Christos, to assemble a large army in Lasta to march against him in June 1632. Susenyos defeated it at the cost of 8,000 killed. The day after the battle his son Fasilidas is reported to have said to him as they walked on the battlefield:

The men you see lying dead here were neither pagans nor Muslims over whose deaths we could rejoice, but Christians, your subjects and fellow-countrymen, and some of them were your kin. It is not victory that we have

<hr />

[32] Caraman, *op.cit.*, p. 141.

gained, for we have driven our swords into our own bodies. [...] Through carrying on this war and abandoning the Faith of our ancestors, we have become a byword among the pagans and Arabs...[33]

Susenyos, now seriously ill and depressed, returned to Dankaz and issued a proclamation over Mendes' objections which ended Jesuit ambitions in Ethiopia. He granted his subjects freedom of religion, in effect restoring Orthodoxy. He then brought his 25-year reign to an end, abdicating in favor of his son Fasilidas. Susenyos died on 7 September 1632, having been given Catholic last rites by a Portuguese priest, and was buried in the church of Genneta Yesus.

Fasilidas lost no time making his religious stance clear. He refused to allow the Jesuits to remain at Dankaz, took away property that had been given to them as well as their firearms. He ordered them all to Fremona. Nearly two dozen gathered there. Experiencing hostility from the population along the way, Mendes and his party reached Fremona at the end of April 1633. From Fremona Mendes dispatched Manoel de Almeida and three priests to India to ask for troops. They had to be smuggled out through Arkiko, were captured and imprisoned for six months at Aden, ransomed, and reached India almost a year and a half later. No troops came, but when Fasilidas received word that a Portuguese fleet had bombarded Mombasa, he assumed Mendes had instigated an attack from the south and ordered him and all the Jesuits to leave Ethiopia immediately. Mendes and nine priests made their way to Massawa only to be imprisoned by the Turks who demanded gold. But they had none, for the party had already been robbed several times on the way. So they were sent on to Suakin where the Pasha put them in irons and demanded ransom. They were released only after borrowing a large sum from Indian merchants. On his accession Fasilidas had sent to Egypt for a new Orthodox *abun.*

While Mendes was held at Suakin the new *abun* passed through on his way to Ethiopia. Mendes found he was extremely anti-Catholic and, to make matters worse, he was accompanied by a young German Lutheran, Peter Heyling, who hoped to spread Protestantism in Ethiopia![34] Mendes finally reached India at the end of May 1635. He lived to a ripe old age there, dying in Goa in 1656. Of seven other

[33] Budge, *op.cit.*, p. 393.

[34] Heyling was a scholar who had studied under the great Dutch polymath, Hugo Grotius. He was well received by Emperor Fasilidas in Gondar where he taught languages and practiced medicine, married an Ethiopian and remained until 1652. Practically everything known about him is summarized in Gustav Aren, *Evangelical Pioneers in Ethiopia: Origins of the Evangelical Church Mekane Yesus*, EFS Forlaget, Stockholm, 1978, pp. 34-8, 409-10.

Jesuits who chose to remain in Ethiopia, two were assassinated and five hanged on Fasilidas's orders.

The Portuguese adventure had come to a miserable end, but the failure had little effect on Portugal itself. Lay Portuguese who had come to Ethiopia in considerable numbers remained and were absorbed into the population.

During the 1980s many Ethiopians saw parallels between Susenyos's attempt to force an alien faith on a reluctant population and Mengistu Haile Mariam's stubborn effort to force the country to accept Stalinist communism. Both provoked multiple rebellions. Both failed utterly. While in the case of the Portuguese, Alfonso Mendes emerges clearly as a principal partner and prime mover in pressing Susenyos to extremes, no single Soviet figure has been identified as playing the same role with Mengistu. In the end, in fact, and in contrast to Susenyos, Mengistu refused repeated opportunities to modify his extremism and brought calamity upon himself and his closest associates.

The Gondarine Era

The establishment of Gondar as permanent capital, which it was to remain for more than two centuries, marked an important change in Ethiopian imperial practice. Without carrying the comparison with Europe too far, in a cultural sense it marked the beginning of an Ethiopian Renaissance. From the time of the decline of Aksum, with the possible exception of the still unidentified Kubar, Ethiopian rulers did not establish permanent capitals but ruled from encampments which were sometimes enormous in extent. The encampments usually depleted the firewood and other natural resources in their immediate area and had to be moved. From the time of Lebna Dengel the political center of gravity in Ethiopia shifted to Dembea – the area northeast of Lake Tana. This is not surprising, for the region is rich in natural resources, moderate in elevation by Ethiopian standards (averaging around 2,000 m.), and has easy access from several directions. The camps which Sarsa Dengel, Za Dengel, and Susenyos established in the area and where the Portuguese, with the help of Indian and Egyptian masons and carpenters, oversaw the building of palaces, churches and other structures of stone and wood, began to acquire some of the characteristics of towns. It was quite natural, therefore, for Fasilidas, who came to the throne a mature and experienced man, to carry this process to completion with the establishment of a capital at Gondar.

Fasilidas moved to Gondar, 30 km. north of Dankaz, in 1636 and had a castle built. It is not clear that he originally envisioned founding a city here, but the site was well suited to evolve into an attractive urban center: it was on a flat volcanic ridge above a basin surrounded by wooded hills and more distant mountains on all sides but the south. Two rivers, the Angareb and the Qeha, flow past the city and across the Dembea plain to Lake Tana. The region has dependable rainfall. The area had been long settled by Christian Amhara peasant cultivators. Fasilidas's huge stone castle still dominates an Imperial Compound where his successors added their own castles during the next 150 years. Administrative buildings and churches followed. Fasilidas still spent long periods of time campaigning against the Oromo, who continued their northward advance, and against recalcitrant regional chiefs. But on return he invariably gave new impetus to the development of the city. Gondar rapidly became a thriving commercial center, with Jews and Muslims settling there as craftsmen and traders. By the time Fasilidas died in 1667 the city was firmly established and had gained perhaps 25,000 inhabitants.[35]

Fasilidas's successor, Yohannes I, was the fourth of his father's many sons, but was judged the ablest by a council of elders who arranged for all his brothers to be imprisoned on Wehni.[36] He, like Fasilidas, went out on military expeditions each year and on return to Gondar took up more building projects. He was a strong supporter of Orthodoxy and interested in doctrinal matters. He established a library for religious manuscripts. When half a dozen Franciscans disguised as Armenian merchants succeeded in entering the country and were discovered, he had them killed.[37] He ordered all Catholic converts expelled if they did not return to Orthodoxy. He had the Catholic religious books that the Portuguese had had translated collected and burned. He convened a religious council in 1668 which ordered Muslims and Jews to reside in quarters separate from

---

[35] Practically all available information from chronicles and travellers' reports on the founding and development of Gondar is summarized in the several sections on the city in Pankhurst's *History of Ethiopian Towns*.

[36] Where rulers are polygamous or have concubines as well as a legal wife (as was usually the case in Ethiopia), the problem of multiple, competing heirs has to be faced. The Ottoman dynasty developed the practice of having all the new sultan's brothers strangled on his accession. Ethiopia developed a less drastic solution, keeping all or most of an emperor's sons imprisoned in a remote place, often including the crown prince. The flat-topped mountain of Wehni in Belesa, southeast of Gondar, served as a "royal prison" during the Gondarine period. Thomas Pakenham, *The Mountains of Rasselas*, Weidenfeld & Nicholson, London, 1959, described a visit to it in the late 1950s. In 1998 he retraced this journey and published a beautifully illustrated account of it, Weidenfeld & Nicolson, London, 1998.

[37] They had been sent by Pope Alexander VII in hope that they might succeed where the Jesuits had failed.

Christians and forbade them to employ Christians. But he was not
opposed to all foreigners. In fact, he favored Armenians. Armenian
traders represented an important link with the Mediterranean world
and an Armenian archbishop paid a visit to Gondar. Yohannes was
pleased by the archbishop's exposition of monophysite doctrine, for
he followed the theological disputes of the time. Near the end of his
comparatively short reign Yohannes called his son Iyasu back from
the governorship of Gojjam and assigned him to nearby Semien to
ensure a smooth succession.

Iyasu the Great reigned from 1682 to 1706. Aged about twenty
when he succeeded his father, he was the greatest of the Gondarine
emperors, noted for his mildness and generosity and his success at
managing the intrigues which always arose around the imperial court.
One of his earliest acts was to visit his brothers on Wehni, where he
gave orders to improve their circumstances. But he also exemplified
the Amhara ideal of a warrior king. He undertook campaigns to
extend Ethiopian control in the south and campaigned repeatedly
against the Shankalla, the tribes of the western lowlands. He brought
Oromos into imperial service and made one Oromo leader *dejazmach*.
He was a legendary hunter of wild animals. Each rainy season he
returned to Gondar, where he had a castle built which is second in
size only to that of Fasilidas. He continued to have other buildings
constructed and the city acquired an attractive urban character. The
first Iyasu had two churches built, the most distinctive being Debre
Berhan Selassie in a shaded compound on an outer ridge facing the
center of the city. The original appears to have been a round church.
It was later replaced by a rectangular one whose interior walls and
ceiling were covered with paintings that are still admired by modern
visitors. Iyasu invited outstanding priests and scholars from all over
Ethiopia to settle in Gondar and encouraged the refinement of
several branches of religious studies: *zema* (chant), *qene* (poetry), and
tergum [interpretation].

Iyasu delayed his crowning until 1693 when he travelled to Tigray
for an elaborate ceremony in the rebuilt cathedral at Aksum. He gave
this church a new charter restoring all its ancient lands. Soon after he
found himself in a dispute with the Turkish Naib of Massawa over
confiscation of trade goods. He took quick action:

[The Naib] learned that on the King's orders food was cut off and the King
was soon to attack him. He was terrified and trembled, not knowing what to
do. He was seized with pains like those of a woman about to give birth. He
reflected and realized that there was nothing he could do to save himself
except make peace with the King and return his property ... Naib Musa
hastened to take the King's goods, added to them others a thousand times
more numerous ... met him at Aksum, bowed down before him and said,

"Have pity on me, O King, my master, and forgive me everything I have done and should not have done to a King!" The King's dignitaries begged him to have pity on Naib Musa because clemency was his custom. The King reprimanded and reproached [him]. [...] He appeared to him in all his royal majesty and had pity on him.[38]

Iyasu called a conference to revise the tax system on salt brought from Tigray. Given his proclivity to regularize and codify administrative procedures, this was a logical preoccupation, for Gondar had become a major trading center. Caravan connections were maintained with Massawa via Adwa, with Sudan, and through Gojjam to the southwest. Salt bars, called *amole*, had served as currency throughout Ethiopia for many centuries and some are reported to have found their way even to central Africa. All the salt was cut from the vast surface deposits in the northern Danakil desert and carried by camel across highland Tigray.[39] *Amole* became standardized by size and weight. Their value varied primarily according to the distance required to transport them. Most trade was by barter well into the 18th century, though in addition to salt several other materials served as media of exchange: gold (cut into small wedges), iron in flat bars, cowrie shells, and lengths of cotton cloth. On the coast many kinds of European and Middle Eastern coins were also used and some found their way inland.[40]

Iyasu's successful reign came to a sad end. A severe earthquake damaged Gondar in 1704. A plot against Iyasu's life was uncovered. The Oromo beyond the Blue Nile threatened to advance and the emperor took his army southward across Gojjam to rebuff them. He was successful and pushed all the way to Enarya in the southwest.

---

[38] Pankhurst, *Chronicles*, p. 111.

[39] Cutting and transport of salt in the northern Danakil continues in Ethiopia to this day. Though most of it is brought up by truck, I have seen traditional caravans of salt-hauling camels in Tigray as recently as 1998.

[40] Highland Ethiopia had no indigenous coinage after the decline of the Aksumite Empire. Even in Aksumite times most trade probably entailed barter. Harar may have developed its own coinage as early at the seventeenth century, though the subject needs further study (see Ahmed Zakaria, "Harari Coins: A Preliminary Survey", *JES* XXIV (1991), pp. 23-46). At the end of the eighteenth century the Maria Teresa dollar was introduced and rapidly became standard in Ethiopia and many neighboring countries in the region around the Red Sea. It continued as legal tender until the mid-20th century. For detailed discussion of currency in Ethiopia from the late Middle Ages into modern times, see Richard Pankhurst, *An Introduction to the Economic History of Ethiopia*, Sidgwick & Jackson, London, 1961, pp. 260-8, and Pankhurst, *Economic History of Ethiopia, 1800-1935*, HSIU Press, Addis Ababa, 1968, pp. 460-503. For a comprehensive survey of the coinage of Ethiopia and contiguous areas into modern times see *The Coinage of Ethiopia, Eritrea, and Italian Somalia*, privately published by Dennis Gill, PO Box 175, Garden City, NY 11530, in 1991.

There he received news that his favorite concubine, mother of three of his sons including the later Dawit III, had died. He returned grief-stricken and withdrew to an island in Lake Tana. Courtiers argued that, like Aksumite Emperor Kaleb, Iyasu had in effect abdicated, and crowned in his absence his first son by Queen Malakotawit, Tekle Haymanot. More than a year of infighting and confusion followed at the end of which Tekle Haymanot arranged to have his father assassinated. Iyasu died on 13 October 1706 and was buried in a huge tomb on the Tana island of Mitraha.[41]

During the next fifteen years four emperors had short and troubled reigns. Tekle Haymanot was stabbed to death. Tewoflos was probably poisoned. Yostos, a non-Solomonic intruder, was forcibly deposed. Iyasu's son Dawit III managed to reign during a hectic five years and was remembered for patronage of popular Amharic minstrels, but also ended up poisoned. Oromo advances caused a fall in revenues available to the crown. The country needed respite and finally Bakaffa, another of Iyasu's sons who had spent his childhood on Wehni and who had fled to the Oromo when Dawit became emperor, was chosen. He had gained a reputation for piety and decency on Wehni, but courtiers and nobles had developed the habit of interfering in the succession process. There was controversy about his selection and during his first years on the throne he had to stay constantly on the alert to protect himself from pretenders and rivals. Nevertheless, his nine-year reign was a time of better government than the country had known for almost two decades:

[Bakaffa] saved the country from drifting into anarchy. [...] He realized that the power of the throne was waning, and that there was only one way of arresting the general decay of the nation: namely to break the power of the old feudal chiefs. His attack on their privileges was systematic and persistent and whatever popularity he enjoyed among the lower classes was due to this policy. [...] He spared no one whom he suspected of treasonable sentiments. [...] The poorer classes found him severe but just. [After he died] many believed that he was not dead, but would return again and protect them from the feudal lords who oppressed them.[42]

Bakaffa was interested in architecture and added an attractive castle to those of his predecessors in Gondar, but his most valuable contribution to his capital and his country was his wife, Mentuab ("How Beautiful!"), and the young son who succeeded as Emperor Iyasu II when he died in 1730. Queen Mentuab was said to be a descendant

---

[41] Major Cheesman, the intrepid explorer of Tana, visited it in the late 1920s and concluded that the tomb must have been built by Europeans: R.E. Cheesman, *Lake Tana and the Blue Nile: An Abyssinian Quest*, 1936, repr. Frank Cass, London, 1968, pp. 190-3.

[42] Budge, *op.cit.*, pp. 445-6.

of Emperor Minas and also to have had Portuguese ancestors. She was allegedly discovered by courtiers sent out to search for the most beautiful girl in the region as wife for Bakaffa after he became emperor. The chronicle recounts how the future Empress's mother, Princess Yolyana

... selected clothes of silk from among her treasures and dressed her daughter with them; she anointed her with perfumes, put a ring of gold on her finger and sent her off with great pomp. Mentuab entered into the chamber of the king, and when the King of Kings Bakaffa saw her he was very happy because she was so completely beautiful; he said to her, "You have no fault at all!" Then he made her sit beside him on his right hand and had delicious foods brought and they ate and drank together. That day he knew her as Adam knew Eve ... and she conceived that day.[43]

A more romantic legend relates that Emperor Bakaffa became ill while travelling in a remote area and was nursed back to health by a farmer's beautiful daughter. The maiden – Mentuab – not only restored his health but won his heart and was later summoned to become his partner on the throne. It is probable that neither story is true and the descent from Minas may be a later invention, but both illustrate the Ethiopian penchant for entertaining tales which persists to this day. What cannot be contested is the fact that like Queen Eleni, Mentuab, whatever her origins, rapidly became one of the dominant personalities of her time.

Bakaffa died after only a nine-year reign. The energetic Queen Mother, politically and culturally active until late in life, played a major role during Iyasu II's twenty-five years on the throne and outlived him. Nobles mounted a rebellion during the second year of her regency and charged Mentuab with secretly favoring Catholics. In the fighting great damage was done to several public buildings, but this determined lady mustered loyalists who defeated the rebels and left her firmly in charge.

Mentuab built a palace in the Imperial Compound near Bakaffa's castle but later had a new castle built on a low rounded hill south west of the capital next to her favorite church, Debre Tsehay ("Mountain of the Sun"). Its ruins are still one of the most attractive sites of Gondar. Mentuab called it Qusquam, after the place where the Virgin Mary was believed to have resided in Egypt. The great hall of this castle recalls many of those of medieval times in Europe and other features of the building, e.g. huge red tufa crosses and reliefs of saints and animals, bear out Mentuab's reputation as a devout Christian and humane patron of the arts with a keen eye for detail. Her richly illustrated prayerbook, now in the Museum of the Institute of Ethiopian

---

[43] Pankhurst, *Chronicles*, p. 123.

Studies in Addis Ababa, is a good example of the high quality of art produced in Gondar at this period. Iyasu II, as he reached maturity, shared his mother's taste for good architecture and employed many foreign craftsmen to add new buildings, including two churches, to the city, as well as buildings outside it, such as a villa at Azezo. Mindful of the growing power of the Oromo, Mentuab arranged for Iyasu to marry an Oromo princess, Wobit.[44]

Iyasu II's final years were even more troubled than those of his predecessor of the same name. He came under criticism for devoting too much time to pleasure (he loved hunting) and for spending too many resources on embellishing the capital, paying foreign workmen, and importing luxury goods, ornaments, and mirrors from Europe. He was derisively called "Iyasu the Little". To deflect criticism he embarked on a campaign against the Funj Kingdom of Sennar which turned out to be a disaster. An icon of Christ and a piece of the True Cross which the army carried into battle were captured and had to be bought back with 8,000 ounces of gold. The region fell victim to two locust plagues and an epidemic took hundreds of lives. Abuna Christodoulos died and, with an almost empty treasury, Iyasu lacked money to finance the procurement of a new *abun* from Egypt. Imperial authority extended little farther than Gojjam and Lasta. In Tigray Prince Mikael Sehul was consolidating his power.

Iyasu II fell seriously ill in May 1754 and died in June 1755. The succession fell to his infant son Iyo'as. When Mentuab ordered gold to be brought from the treasury to pay the churches and monasteries for her son's funeral commemorations, only a few dinars could be collected. Desolate, she resolved to go to a convent and finish her days as a nun. The nobility insisted she again serve as regent for her grandson, who had a troubled reign until 1769, when he was murdered.[45] Bakaffa's brother Yohannes II succeeded him but reigned only from May to October of 1769, when he may have been poisoned. His son Tekle Haymanot II, then fifteen years old, was put on the throne but was deposed in 1777.

Politically the great days of Gondar were unquestionably past at the end of Iyasu II's reign. For the better part of the century that followed, which became known as the Era of the Princes or Judges,

[44] Their son, Iyo'as, became the country's first emperor with Oromo blood and grew up speaking Oromifa as well as Amharic.

[45] Mentuab remained a power to reckon with in Gondar until her death in 1772, marrying one of her daughters to Mikael Sehul and one to his son. She fled to Gojjam after an abortive coup against Mikael in 1770 but returned at the pleading of Tekle Haymanot II when Mikael guaranteed her safety. From this time onward the Tigrayan Mikael Sehul was the real power behind the throne in Ethiopia.

the Christian Empire ceased to exist as a centrally administered entity. It can be argued that the establishment of a permanent capital undermined the classic Ethiopian imperial state by confining political life to a narrow area and permitting regional leaders to consolidate their power. It is difficult to demonstrate, however, that a continuation of the medieval pattern of ceaselessly campaigning rulers moving from one part of the country to another, would necessarily have produced a different result.

The rise of regional centers of power had many causes. The Gondarine era left a positive legacy in at least four important respects. First, it completed the evolution of the Amhara as the primary rulers of the country. Secondly, it furthered the evolution of the Orthodox Church as a national institution. Thirdly, for all the vicissitudes Gondarine emperors experienced, the concept of the Solomonic monarchy emerged unscathed and survived the disorder and deterioration of the Era of the Princes. And, last but not least, the cultural and economic renaissance that occurred during the Gondarine era, only in part inspired by European contacts and examples, continued well beyond the decline of the city as a political capital. Art continued to flourish in Gondar as did religious scholarship, chronicle-writing, music and poetry. Seven more churches were built in the reign of Tekle Haymanot II. The city remained a crossroads for commerce and a center of crafts.[46]

Europeans and Ethiopia

Writing of the fifteenth century, Taddesse Tamrat concluded:

Although the advent of Europeans in Ethiopia in this period has left very little trace in Ethiopian documents, there can be no doubt that in the first half of the 15th century, precarious, but none the less continuous, relations were established between Europe and Ethiopia. The most authentic pieces of evidence for this are the map known as *Egyptus Novelo* (c. 1454) and Fra Mauro's *Mappamondo* of 1460, which could only have been the outcome of many years of geographical knowledge about the Ethiopian highlands.[47]

Traces of Ethiopia in Europe are also few until the advent of the Portuguese.[48] The most valuable contribution to posterity of the Portuguese who came to Ethiopia from the late fifteenth century to the seventeenth is the great body of memoirs, letters and travel

---

[46] Donald N. Levine's classic *Wax and Gold, Tradition and Innovation in Ethiopian Culture*, University of Chicago Press, 1965, celebrates and analyses the importance of Gondarine traditions in the evolution of modern Ethiopia.

[47] *Church and State*, p. 267.

[48] The Hakluyt Society has published a collection of the earliest references: Crawford (ed.), *Ethiopian Itineraries circa 1400-1524*.

accounts they produced. *The Prester John of the Indies* of Father Francisco Alvares, an account of the Portuguese mission of 1520-6 which also includes information supplied by Covilhão, can still serve as a guide for visitors to many parts of Ethiopia, so accurate are its descriptions of places and customs.[49] First printed in Lisbon in 1540, it was translated into many languages and republished in subsequent centuries. Most of the other major Portuguese memoirs have been referred to above, though more may still be discovered in Portugal. Europeans from other countries soon followed with accounts of their travels and impressions. The French physician Charles Poncet arrived in Gondar in 1699 to treat Iyasu I, having come by way of Sennar, and stayed for nearly a year. He returned to Europe via Tigray and Massawa. He published an account of his experiences in Paris in 1704.[50]

The next significant European visitor was a Czech Franciscan stationed in Cairo, Remedius Prutky, who led a three-man mission consisting of another Czech and a Syrian Christian to Ethiopia in the early 1750s at the invitation of Iyasu II. They entered through Massawa and reached Gondar on 19 March 1752. They had extensive discussions, mostly on religion, but also on European politics in which the emperor was interested, with both Iyasu and Mentuab. They had a particularly favorable impression of Mentuab. These missionaries became popular because of their medical skills and collected an immense amount of information on all aspects of Ethiopian life. Their very presence aroused the opposition of the clergy and the emperor asked the two Czechs to depart at the end of the year, but requested that the Syrian stay for nine months to translate the Pentateuch into Arabic. The first two finally departed from Massawa at the end of April 1753 and reached Rome in 1754.[51]

The great Scottish traveller, James Bruce, arrived at Massawa in 1769 and visited much of northern Ethiopia as well as the region south of Lake Tana. His descriptions of Gondar provide vivid detail on life in the city during the first years of the reign of Tekle Haymanot II and the final days of Empress Mentuab. He also recorded much information

[49] *The Prester John of the Indies, a True Relation of the Lands of the Prester John...,* translated by Lord Stanley of Alderley (1881) revised and edited by C.F. Beckingham and G.W.B. Huntingford, 2 vols, Cambridge University Press for the Hakluyt Society, 1961.

[50] A modern English translation is included in William Foster (ed.), *The Red Sea and Adjacent Countries at the Close of the 17th Century,* Hakluyt Society, London, 1949.

[51] Prutky sent his voluminous Latin Manuscript to Prague where it remained until it came to the attention of Richard Pankhurst in the 1980s who arranged for translation into English and publication of the sections dealing with Ethiopia and neighboring countries: J.H. Arrowsmith Brown (translator and editor), *Prutky's Travels in Ethiopia and Other countries,* Hakluyt Society, London, 1991.

about earlier periods in Gondar. He took scientific measurements and was interested in flora and fauna, making many fine drawings. When he returned to Britain he took a collection of Ethiopian manuscripts valuable to scholars. He spent the better part of two decades preparing his monumental account of his travels for publication.[52]

A quarter-century later another Briton, George Annesley, Viscount Valentia, was sent to survey the Red Sea. A man of broad interests, he took along his secretary, Henry Salt, and on arriving in Massawa in 1804 sent him and three other Englishmen to visit Ras Wolde Selassie, ruler of Tigray, and explore the interior of the country. These explorations, along with some of Salt's splendid etchings, were subsequently published in a lavish account of his travels.[53] In 1809 Salt went back to Ethiopia on a mission for the British Government. At Massawa he was met by Nathaniel Pearce, who had stayed behind after the original Valentia mission left. In 1814 in London Salt published his *Voyage to Abyssinia*, an extensive account of these travels along with vocabularies of the major Ethiopian languages. Meanwhile Pearce, a remarkable young Englishman, remained at Ras Wolde Selassie's court, married a Tigrayan lady, and kept a diary which provides enormous detail about day-to-day Ethiopian life as well as accounts of campaigns on which he accompanied the Ras. He left in 1819 and died in Cairo. His diary was published in 1831.[54]

From this time onward a steady stream of Europeans came to Ethiopia: Britons, Frenchmen, Germans, Italians, Scandinavians and eventually Americans. Many wrote accounts of their experiences. I will refer to them as appropriate in the chapters which follow.

Though from late Aksumite times Ethiopians began to go to Jerusalem and a religious colony formed there, serious scholarly interest in Ethiopia began in Rome. Two Ethiopian delegates came to the Council of Florence in 1441 and occasional pilgrims followed. In 1539 the Vatican bought a house for them behind St. Peter's attached to the Church of San Stefano. Germans, in particular, took an interest from the viewpoint of philology in Ethiopians who had gathered there and several came to study.[55] More than a century later this casual

---

[52] A first edition of *Travels to Discover the Source of the Nile in the Years 1768, 1769, 1770, 1771, 1772, and 1773* was published in 5 volumes in Edinburgh in 1790. A second edition in 8 volumes followed in 1804, followed by another in 1813. Several shortened editions were later published. See J.M. Reid, *Traveller Extraordinary: The Life of James Bruce of Kinnaird*, W.W. Norton, New York, 1968.

[53] George, Viscount Valentia, *Voyages and Travels to India, Ceylon, the Red Sea, Abyssinia, and Egypt in the Years 1802...1806*, 3 vols, London, 1809.

[54] *Life and Adventures in Abyssinia, 1810-1819*, 2 vols, London, 1831, reprinted by SASOR, London, 1980.

[55] Ullendorff, *Ethiopians*, pp. 7-11.

beginning led to production of the most important book on Ethiopia
in early modern times: Job Ludolf's *Historia Aethiopica*, which appeared
in Latin in Frankfurt in 1681 and was immediately translated into
English by John Philips, nephew and secretary of John Milton, and
published in London in 1682.

Ludolf, born in Erfurt in 1624, was a brilliant student of languages.
Arriving in Rome in 1649, he met four resident Ethiopians and
began to study Ge'ez. Abba Grigorewos, then about 50, became his
regular tutor and with him Ludolf learned not only Ge'ez and Amharic
but an enormous amount of Ethiopian history and lore. Grigorewos
was drowned off the coast of Syria in 1658 but Ludolf continued his
study of Ethiopian languages and history, publishing a Ge'ez grammar in 1661 and devoting himself to gathering every relevant scrap of
information on the country to utilize for his history. The history was
an immediate publishing success, with two English reprintings in
1684, a French translation in the same year and a Dutch translation
in 1687.[56] In 1691 Ludolf published a huge collection of all the
documentation he had used in his history with a portrait of Abba
Grigorewos, whom he regarded as co-author. In 1698 he published
an Amharic grammar and dictionary, and in 1701 a Ge'ez-Latin edition of the Psalms of David. He died in 1704.[57]

Regions and borderlands

From its very beginnings, as previous chapters have made apparent,
Ethiopia was a multi-ethnic country. Furthermore, its spectacular
geography predisposed the country toward regionalism. It is surprising, in fact, considering its division into natural regions sharply
defined by mountain barriers and deep gorges, that Ethiopia evolved
into a large unified polity at all. Other less geographically fragmented
parts of Africa failed to reach this stage of political and cultural
development. The foremost task in relating Ethiopia's history is to
recount the manner in which rulers expanded their authority,
extended their reach, and caused their religion and language to
spread. The history of Ethiopia is incomplete, however, if we simply
recount what rulers did or tried to do from the center. As has been
the case with many ancient polities, political and cultural processes
in Ethiopia have been broadly cyclical: the center gains power, is
challenged from the periphery, weakens, and regions become
focal points of authority. A particular region then gains strength and

[56] The Philips translation of Ludolf's history was republished in London by
SASOR in 1982.

[57] He was appropriately celebrated as the father of Ethiopian studies at a conference in Halle of the German-Ethiopian association *Orbis Aethiopicus* in September 1996.

eventually extends its dominance over the entire country. We have just seen how the Solomonic Dynasty, beset by inroads of Muslims and Oromos, experienced a steady decline from the end of the seventeenth century onward. The effective territorial authority of the imperial government contracted and regional rulers took more power into their own hands. Meanwhile various factors combined – in some cases ethnicity, in others religion, in still others a combination of circumstances less easy to define – to cause particular ethnic and religious groups and regions to maintain a high degree of separate identity. Some of these merit separate historical treatment. Let us look briefly at a few of the most important or interesting.

The Agaw. All available evidence indicates that these Cushitic-speaking people formed the basic population of northern and central Ethiopia over which Semitic-speaking peoples gained domination during the last millennium BC. As Aksumite rulers extended their authority southward and westward, they progressively subjected and absorbed Agaws. When Christianization began in earnest in the 5th and 6th centuries, Agaws became the target of early missionaries, for their areas had already been penetrated by Aksumite traders. The process of Christianization and absorption into the mainstream of Semitic culture continued through the Middle Ages and into modern times. Some Agaws who resisted appear to have adopted Judaism to stress their separate identity and resist imposition of imperial political and religious authority. Some of these groups retained their language into modern times. On the other hand, other Agaws became fervent mainstream Christians and entered the primary current of Ethiopian political and religious development, as the rise of the Zagwe Dynasty and subsequent evolution during medieval and early modern times demonstrate.[58] The largely Agaw population of Semien, Wag and Lasta joined the imperial mainstream, not always of their own volition, between the thirteenth and the sixteenth centuries. During the seventeenth and eighteenth centuries the Agaw south and east of Lake Tana, whose territory spread southwestward through Gojjam, were absorbed through a combination of military and missionary effort. Nevertheless a large community of Agaw remained unassimilated in central Gojjam in a region still called Agawmeder and the same is true of substantial Agaw-speaking communities in Wag and Lasta. In central Eritrea, around the ancient city of Keren, the Bilen, a closely related Agaw subgroup, have maintained separate identity since ancient times.

[58] Taddesse Tamrat combined evidence from chronicles, traditions and field research in a fundamental paper, "Ethnic Interaction and Integration...the Case of the Agau", *Proceedings of the 9th IESC,* Moscow, 1988, V, pp. 192-206.

Tigray and Eritrea. The old Aksumite heartland, Tigray, which
included the northern highland provinces of Serae, Akele Guzay
and Hamasien, remained culturally distinct and fervently Christian
from medieval into modern times, a core component of the Ethiopian polity. Furthermore, no Ethiopian ruler acknowledged loss of
authority over the lowlands or the coast before or after Ottoman
occupation of Massawa in 1557. Even during Turkish rule the role of
the *Bahr Negash*, the emperor's viceroy for the coastal region, retained
importance. The western and northern regions of Eritrea, however,
were much more tenuously connected with the highlands. In terms
of religion, trade and politics, they were often drawn toward Sudanese
kingdoms. A substantial body of mythology developed during the
long Eritrean insurgency and struggle for independence between
1960 and 1990 to the effect that Eritrea had had a distinct identity
and independent political and cultural evolution since ancient times.
There is no historical basis for the claim. It is likely to atrophy when
Eritreans develop a capacity to examine their history honestly.
Unlike Aksumite rulers, no Zagwe or restored Solomonic emperor
gave priority to campaigning against the Beja or, with the exception
of Iyasu II's ill-fated expedition toward Sennar, undertaking major
campaigns against Sudan.[59]

As the Gondarine state weakened during the seventeenth and
eighteenth centuries, local Tigrayan rulers extended their influence.
Mikael Sehul became a power broker in Gondar, curbing Oromo
influence, and deposing Iyo'as. Ras Wolde Selassie of Cheleqot was
more powerful during the first quarter of the nineteenth century
than any emperor in Gondar. Later in the century, Tigray became the
scene of some of the most important developments affecting the
Ethiopian state.

The Gurage. This southernmost Ethiopian Semitic group may have
originated from a southward Semitic movement in medieval times for
which practically no written evidence has been found. Traditions of
military expeditions to the south from late Aksumite times which left
isolated colonies of Semitic speakers seem a logical explanation of
all the southern Semitic languages: Gurage, Harari, Argobba and the
extinct Gafat. That there was a substantial migration is obvious because
a few soldiers are unlikely to have been able to implant their language
so effectively, but how this process proceeded remains a mystery. The
traditional Ethiopian historian, Aleqa Taye Gebre Maryam, wrote:

[59] No modern historian of Ethiopia has made a more perceptive analysis of Tigray's
attitudes and role in Ethiopian history than Haggai Erlich. The references to this
region in two of his most important books are too numerous to list separately, but
see *Ethiopia and the Middle East* and *Ethiopia and the Challenge of Independence*,
Lynne Rienner, Boulder, CO, 1986.

In the time of Emperor Amde Tseyon an army which had left Gura in ... Akele Guzay came ... and camped in Aymallal. Therefore that people and country are called Gurage. Additionally they say that because they camped to the left of the camp of the king, they were called *Girage* [People of the Left]. With long passage of time *Girage* changed and they were called Gurage.[60]

Aleqa Taye links two quite different explanations of the origin of the name based on etymology and tradition. Both may have some validity. The twelve Gurage dialects are basically Semitic, but they vary more widely from each other than dialects within the major Semitic languages of Ethiopia. They all have a Sidama substratum. Physically the Gurage closely resemble neighboring Sidama peoples. They also display great religious variety, being divided among Orthodox Christians, Muslims and animists with, in more recent times, both Catholic and Evangelical Christians. They have a rich oral culture and depend on cattle raising and intensive gardening, specializing, like many other southwestern peoples, in cultivation of the false banana, *ensete edulis,* as a major food source. When they edged tenuously into written history, they were already regarded as loyal to the north Ethiopian empire. Emperor Bakaffa directed his campaign against Adal from the Gurage area, a fertile region directly south of the upper Awash river that only became part of Shoa in the time of Emperor Menelik II. Before the Oromo migrations, the Gurage appear to have occupied a much more extensive area to the west of their traditional homeland around the central Rift Valley lakes.[61]

The Zay, who speak a Gurage dialect, survived into modern times on islands in Lake Zway, where they retreated to escape the Oromo in the sixteenth century. Before the Oromo migrations, their ancestors may have been a segment of the population of medieval Dawaro. Their traditions hold that their ancestors originally came from Tigray and Manz. The Zway island churches and monasteries were established in the thirteenth or fourteenth century. The Book of Saints preserved in the monastery church of Debra Tseyon Maryam on the island now known by the Oromo name Tullu Guddo ("Big

[60] *Ye-It'yop'ya Hizb Tarih,* ed. by Grover Hudson and Tekeste Negash, Uppsala University, 1987, p. 88-9, originally published in Addis Ababa, 1922.

[61] They have attracted considerable attention from anthropologists and linguists with the result that they are among the most studied of Ethiopian peoples: William A. Shack, *The Gurage, a People of the Ensete Culture,* Oxford University Press, 1966; W.A. Shack and Habte-Mariam Marcos, *Gods and Heroes,* Oxford University Press, 1974; Gebreyesus Hailemariam, *The Gurage and their Culture,* Vantage Press, New York, 1991. The Polish-born American scholar Wolf Leslau devoted much of his life to the study of the Gurage dialects, publishing the *Etymological Dictionary of Gurage,* Harrassowitz, Wiesbaden, 1979, in three massive volumes.

Island") is one of Ethiopia's finest illuminated medieval manuscripts. There is evidence that the Zay, who developed a self-contained way of life based on intensive terraced agriculture, rational livestock raising, fishing, and weaving, may have occupied islands in Lake Langano and Shala, and perhaps as distant as Lake Wonchi above Ambo, until modern times. Those on Zway remained tenaciously Christian even though they were isolated from contact with the north until Menelik II conquered the region in the 1880s.[62]

Harar, a Semitic-speaking city state and a citadel of Islamic belief and scholarship, has been surrounded by an Oromo-populated countryside since the end of the sixteenth century. The survival of its Semitic population is puzzling, for Harar seems to have been of minor importance until the time it became the capital of the Adal sultanate a few decades before. Its language links it firmly with the north. Aleqa Taye summarized traditions of its origin:

> The people who live within the walls of Harar ... came from Hamasien. During the time of Emperor Dawit [1382-1413] there was in Hamasien a strong and valiant man ... [whose sons] migrated to Hararge and settled there. After a long period, when the Gallas would not let them live in peace, they defeated the Gallas. [...] They built a strong stone wall around their land and put five gates in it. With the passage of much time their language, which was Tigrinya, changed and became another. Even today, however, it closely resembles Tigrinya. When earlier the Ethiopian kingdom was not weak, they paid tribute to and were ruled by the Ethiopian state, but later they were ruled by the Turkish kingdom.[63]

Not only linguistically but also culturally, Harar has affinities to the Gurage region, especially Lake Zway. Handicrafts and interiors of Zay houses show resemblances to those of Harar, though handicrafts were developed to a far higher degree in the walled city state. Basketry in Harar became an art form. As on the Zway islands, weavers were prominent among craftsmen in Harar. A development parallel to that of the Christian empire when the capital became established in Gondar occurred in Harar after Emir Nur surrounded it with strong walls: the Muslim empire of Adal contracted during the seventeenth and eighteenth centuries. The walls kept out the Oromo and Somalis, except for trading purposes when they had to surrender their

---

[62] I did research on Zay history and culture, visiting all of the Zway islands as well as Zay communities on the shore, when I lived in Ethiopia in the early 1970s. My attention was first directed to this people by the great German ethnographer Eike Haberland's account of the Zay in his *Galla Sudathiopiens*, Kohlhammer, Stuttgart, 1963, pp. 647-77. I have published several articles on these people, the most recent being "Lake Zway – Southern Christian Outpost and Depository of Medieval Ethiopian Art" in *Proceedings of the First International Conference on the History of Ethiopian Art*, Pindar Press, London, 1989, pp. 30-40.

[63] Aleqa Taye, *op.cit.*, pp. 93-5.

weapons on passing through the city gates. The Oromo who migrated into the rich plateau country around the city soon settled and became good farmers. Gradually they accepted Islam. Feeling safe behind their walls, the rulers of Harar ceased attacking the highlands and concentrated on trade. They maintained close relations with regional rulers to the east and south. Both traders and rulers had regular contact with Yemen and the Arabian Peninsula through Zeila and Berbera. Harar developed its own currency. The agriculturally rich area around Harar produced grain, many kinds of fruit and vegetables, spices, coffee, and chat. The last two items became major exports along with dyes and ostrich feathers. Harar was a major market for slaves form the Ethiopian southwest.

Harar became a center of Islamic religious study and training with influence radiating far into southern Ethiopia. The principal buildings within the city were the Grand Mosque and the emir's palace, where the emirs were reported to have amassed quantities of silver, gold, ivory and arms. There were several religious shrines in the city: e.g. the impressive compound around the tomb of Sheikh Abadir next to the walls on the southern side and the Awliya at the tomb of Sheikh Abdal outside the walls. A goodly number of foreigners lived in Harar, but most were Arabs, Persians, Turks, Armenians and Greeks who accepted Islam. Argobba traders from the Shoan highlands were important participants in cross-desert trade and some settled also in Harar. Europeans who reached Harar were imprisoned and killed. A great air of mystery grew up around the city which only began to be lifted after Sir Richard Burton spent ten days there in 1853 and later published his *First Footsteps in East Africa*.[64]

The Southwest. Even in Aksumite times traders from the north seem to have penetrated into the lush, fertile and ethnically complex southwest. This is the region where one of the most characteristic products of Ethiopia originated: coffee. It still grows wild in the inter-mediate-level forests of the region. There were other forest products to be traded as well as minerals, ivory, horn, skins and civet. The late Aksumite ruler Dagna Jan allegedly sent a military expedition to Enarya.[65] The region was thickly populated. It was a major supplier of the slave trade whose origins are very old. Both before and after the invasion of Ahmad Gragn, Ethiopian rulers undertook expeditions to Damot and Gafat, both then located south of the Blue Nile in what would later become Wollega. When the Oromo began to pour northward in the latter half of the sixteenth century, the inhabitants

[64] Republished by Dover Books, New York, 1987.

[65] Pankhurst, *Borderlands*, p. 434.

116 Layers of Time

of these two regions were pushed northward, and settled across the Nile in Gojjam, where the term Damot became attached to a fertile highland area. The inhabitants of Damot were originally of Sidama stock, but appear to have been assimilated into the Amhara majority in Gojjam.

Farther south, all the way to the lower Omo valley, the region seems from ancient times to have been divided into rather small tribal areas, some of which evolved into long-lasting-kingdoms with complex social structures and hereditary ruling families. These included Enarya, Wolayta and Hadiya, which had relations with the north and were subject to Christian influence. Oromo migrants took over some, but many Sidama groups and languages survived.[66] In the Gibe region the Oromo established several sizable states which developed important trade relations with the Christian kingdom. These states became subject to strong Islamic influence in the seventeenth and eighteenth centuries.[67] By the end of the nineteenth century they had all been conquered and absorbed into the rejuvenated Christian empire.

Shoa/Manz. The name of Shoa, the political and cultural center of modern Ethiopia, appears to have had its origin in an area in the lowlands directly to the east of the Shoan Plateau that was dominated by Muslim traders from the ninth to the twelfth centuries. The Italian historian Enrico Cerulli called it the Sultanate of Shoa, but it seems to have become, or always to have been, part of the Sultanate of Ifat. Highland Shoa, where northern Christian migrants may have begun to settle after the decline of Aksum, was an outlying part of the large

---

[66] Italians pioneered research in southwestern Ethiopia. The area has been popular with ethnographers from many countries since the end of World War II. Several monumental works were published by the German Frobenius Institute based on many years of fieldwork: Haberland, *Galla Südäthiopiens*; A.E. Jensen (ed.), *Altvölker Südäthiopiens*, Kohlhammer, Stuttgart, 1959; Helmut Straube, *Westkuschitische Völker Südäthiopiens*, Kohlhammer, Stuttgart, 1963. Other important studies of groups in this area, all of which include efforts to reconstruct history on the basis of tradition include: Jack Stauder, *The Majangir*, Cambridge University Press, 1971; C.R. Hallpike, *The Konso of Ethiopia*, Oxford, Clarendon Press, 1972; Uri Almagor, *Pastoral Partners: Affinity and Bond Partnership among the Dassanetch of SW Ethiopia*, Manchester University Press, 1978; Ulrich Braukämper, *Geschichte der Hadiya Süd-Äthiopiens*, Steiner, Wiesbaden, 1980; Werner Lange, *History of the Southern Gonga*, Steiner, Wiesbaden, 1982; there are many others and an enormous body of article literature.

[67] Mordechai Abir, *Ethiopia, the Era of the Princes*, Longmans, London, 1968, Chapter IV, "The emergence of the Galla of the Southwest". A recent study of the spread of ox-plow agriculture in Ethiopia includes an informative reconstruction of the history of one of the small Gibe monarchies: "The Plow in the Forest: Agriculture, Population, and Maize Monoculture in Gera" in James C. McCann, *People of the Plow: An Agricultural History of Ethiopia, 1800-1990*, University of Wisconsin Press, Madison, 1995, pp. 147-90.

pagan kingdom of Damot (centered to the west, south of the Blue Nile) until the thirteenth century. Important religious leaders, e.g. Iyasus Mo'a and Tekle Haymanot, cooperated with princes who established the dynasty claiming Solomonic legitimacy initiated by Yekuno Amlak. The great evangelizing emperors of the Middle Ages, Amde Tseyon, Sayfa Arad, and Zara Yakob, consolidated Christianization of the region through military conquest and vigorous evangelization. As Christian communities expanded, Shoa became the southern center of the Christian Empire. Zara Yakob built a royal residence at Debre Berhan and spent the last fourteen years of his reign there. As late as 1520 the Emperor Lebna Dengel met Portuguese missions at his camp near Mt. Yerer to the southeast of present-day Addis Ababa.[68]

The conquests of Ahmad Gragn and the subsequent Oromo migrations resulted in the fragmentation and Oromization of Shoa. Gragn, however, did not penetrate into the highest regions of the northern Shoan plateau, in particular Manz. It remained solidly Christian and Amhara. Here, toward the end of the seventeenth century a Manze chief called Nagasi who claimed Solomonic descent through his mother began to expand his holdings. In alliance with the Walasma of Ifat, he reconquered areas taken by the Oromo and founded a dynasty. He was received in Gondar by Iyasu I but died there in 1703 of smallpox before he could be invested with the title of *Meridazmach*.[69] Nagasi's son Sebastie (Sebastyonos) shifted his seat to Ifat and his successors during the eighteenth century continually expanded their territory on the plateau and along the escarpment. The family adopted the same system used by the Gondarine emperors of incarcerating all brothers of a new ruler when he ascended the throne. Thus internecine strife was avoided and the dynasty gained steadily in strength.

Amha Yesus conquered the Ankober region and made Ankober his seat. He recolonized the more southerly Shoan district of Minjar with Christian Amhara. He kept his distance from the declining imperial court in Gondar, using the Wollo Oromo to the north as a buffer. In 1771 he traveled to Gondar and was received by Emperor Tekle Haymanot II more as an ally than as a subordinate. He died in 1775 after a thirty-year reign and was succeeded by his son, Asfa Wossen. Though from this time onward strategically situated Ankober remained the capital of the Shoan kingdom, the ruling group never

[68] Taddesse Tamrat, *Church and State*, pp. 119-25, 156-61, 274.

[69] Originally meaning "Commander of the Reserve Army", this title was unique to Shoa, whose rulers henceforth claimed or bore it. Haile Selassie's heir, Crown Prince Asfa Wossen, was the last to do so, though he served for decades as the titular governor of Wollo while Ras Mesfin Sileshi held the governorship of Shoa.

forgot their origins in Manz. The warrior traditions of Manz became a major component of Amhara imperial tradition.[70] The rest of the story of Shoa's rise to a dominant position in Ethiopia belongs in the two subsequent chapters.[71]

[70] Levine, *Wax and Gold*, pp. 28-38.

[71] Asfa-Wossen Asserate, *Die Geschichte von Sawa, 1700-1865*, Steiner, Wiesbaden, 1980, pp. 22-31.

5

THE EMPIRE FROM ATROPHY
TO REVIVAL

THE ERA OF THE PRINCES AND TEWODROS II

The era of the Princes

From many points of view, Ethiopia of 1800 was a weak state with serious internal problems and little visible cohesion. It was not, however, like many other areas of Africa, the home of a mere conglomeration of ... tribes. The many centuries of settled agricultural life in the Ethiopian highlands, the long history of the Ethiopian monarchy and the Christian Church in the area had weakened tribal structures in favour of a more regionally organized society. The politically and culturally dominating element in the region as a whole was the Christian and Semitic-speaking highland population who cultivated much of the plateau from the hinterland of Massawa roughly to the big bends of the Abbay and the Awash...[1]

The Era of the Princes began with the death of Iyasu II in 1755 and lasted until the crowning of Tewodros II in 1855. By formal count there were twenty-eight reigns during this century, but several of the men who held the crown were deposed and restored; one, Tekla Giyorgis, was put on the throne at least four times. Gondar remained the capital and regional chiefs became king-makers, often vying with each other for the opportunity to control the affairs of the empire, but most of the time to seek advantage for themselves. None, however, aimed to separate from Ethiopia. The idea of the Ethiopian Empire remained intact with its traditions of faithfulness to Christianity and the legacy of Aksum. Arcane religious controversies shook the church, but Oromo Muslims who at times played a prominent role in imperial politics did not think in terms of converting the country to Islam; instead they themselves more often than not embraced Christianity.

Europeans developed ever greater curiosity about Ethiopia during this period. Explorers, missionaries of several persuasions, traders, and official emissaries visited the country with increasing frequency. Trade revived, firearms came in in increasing quantities, but Ethiopia – like most of Africa – was still outside the range of the sustained expansionist interest of colonial powers. This was

---

[1] Sven Rubenson, *The Survival of Ethiopian Independence*, Heinemann, London, 1976, pp 31-2.

fortunate, for during this period of internal disarray the country did not have to fend off invasion. Ottoman power in the Red Sea had long since withered, but Egypt – which became the first major external threat – was already picking away at the edges of the Ethiopian area as a result of the expansionist policies of Muhammad Ali, the Albanian-origin pasha who had freed himself from Ottoman control.

The Era of the Princes was actually the time when a basis was laid for the survival of Ethiopian independence. This process of overcoming challenges from beyond the country's borders was successfully completed only with the victory at Adwa in 1896. Independent Ethiopia survived because its two most important component regions gained steadily in strength during the period of the near collapse of the Gondarine monarchy: Tigray and Shoa. Begemder under the Yejju dynasty preserved the imperial mystique in Gondar, but it became increasingly hollow. Most twentieth-century historians have interpreted the evolution of modern Ethiopia almost exclusively in terms of Amhara dominance. This is questionable, for during this crucial period the northern Amhara were almost continually divided and at odds with each other. Shoa was Ethiopia's most stable and dynamic region in the nineteenth century. Shoa expanded under a succession of vigorous Amhara rulers, but they, like Shoa itself, had a strong strain of Oromo blood and the Shoan line was eventually further enriched by the absorption of other non-Amhara elements from the south. Shoa's dynamism may be attributable in part to its amalgam of ethnic groups with varying traditions. The Amhara of the more northerly regions – western Wollo, Gojjam, and Begemder – contributed much less creative energy to the process which enabled Ethiopia to triumph over its would-be colonizers during the final decades of the nineteenth century. Close entanglement in the futile politicking of the old capital absorbed too much of the talent and time of the northern Amhara and northern Oromo lords and, consequently, their role in Ethiopia after the first two decades of the twentieth century became regressive and marginal.

The decline of Gondar gave the most historically conscious region of the Empire, the one with the deepest claim on its most hallowed traditions – Tigray – the opportunity to assert itself and generate the political skill and force to play a major role in resisting foreign encroachment and in supporting the restoration of imperial momentum. Stimulated by challenge from beyond their borders, the Tigrayans made a major contribution to the revival of Ethiopian political momentum during the last third of the nineteenth century. It was not accidental that the decisive Battle of Adwa was fought in Tigray. But the impetus toward moving boldly into the modern world was weaker in Tigray than in Shoa. The social conservatism of the Tigrayans left them trailing the Shoans. They played only a minor role in the survival of the Empire during its second great crisis following the death of Menelik II. During most of the twentieth century, Tigray remained a political, economic and social backwater, at times alienated from the mainstream of Ethiopian life. Only in the final two decades of the century did it come to play a creative role in liberating the country from the disaster of Mengistu Haile Maryam's misguided dictatorship. At the end of the twentieth century Tigray moved into the forefront of Ethiopian political and economic development, overcoming a long legacy of stagnation. But to make this observation is to jump far ahead. There is much ground to cover before we approach the present.

The Era of the Princes is also known as the "Era of the Judges" because of its resemblance to the Old Testament time when "there was no king in Israel: every man did that which was right in his own eyes". For Ethiopia the second half of this formulation could better be phrased "every leader did what he thought advantageous to him and his region." To attempt to recount all the rivalries and intrigues, shifts of loyalty, marriage alliances, skirmishes and battles of this period would lead the story into by-ways of secondary importance to the final outcome. To give an impression of the period, a sketch of some of the principal protagonists and their major moves will suffice.

Ras Mikael Sehul, long-lived ruler of Tigray, gained dominance over his region by acquiring weapons from the Turks in Massawa and strengthened his position in Gondar by helping Emperor Iyasu II maintain his authority during the final years of his reign. About the time of Iyasu's death, Mikael married one of his sons to Dowager Empress Mentuab's daughter and then himself married another daughter of Mentuab, Aster, greatly enhancing his own position. He was about seventy at this time. He resented the expansion of Oromo influence under Iy'oas, pushed him from the throne and had him killed, then did the same with the successor he himself had chosen, Bakaffa's brother, Yohannes II. He then set Iyasu's fifteen-year-old son on the throne as Tekla Haymanot II. Ras Mikael, Empress Mentuab, and her daughter Aster were dominant personalities when James Bruce arrived in Gondar in 1770. He included vivid portraits of them in his account of Ethiopia. Mikael's final years were troubled, for he was challenged and defeated by a combination of Amhara and Oromo lords. He returned to Tigray, where he retained power and died of old age in Tembien near (or perhaps over, according to some sources) the age of ninety about 1780. Tekla Haymanot II had abdicated and died in 1777.

Following the defeat of Mikael Sehul, the Yejju dynasty became the real power in Gondar, reducing the poverty-stricken emperors to puppets. The Yejju dynasty had its origin in northern Wollo[2], founded in the last quarter of the eighteenth century by a strong chief named Ali Gwangul, who became known as Ras Ali I. Originally Oromos who had converted to Islam, these men, like so many Oromos who moved into the northern highlands, tended to become Christianized and Amharized. Ras Ali ruled the provinces of Amhara and Begemder, and died in 1788. Six members of his family followed him as *ras*. Yejju power reached its peak during the reign of his nephew, Ras Gugsa Mersu, (1803-25), who founded Debre Tabor and used it as his administrative center. The next major Yejju ruler was Ras Ali II Alula, grandson of Gugsa through his son Alula. He was elected by a council of the clan in 1831 when he was thirteen years old. His widowed mother Menen[3] dominated the regency council until he came of age and retained strong influence afterward. He married Hirut, the daughter of Wube, lord of Semien and Tigray, who nevertheless tried to unseat him in 1842.

In Tigray Ras Wolde Selassie of Enderta who had his seat in Cheleqot south of Makelle was, in effect, Ras Mikael's successor. Like Mikael, he had acquired firearms through cooperative dealings with the Turks on the coast and by the turn of the century dominated most of the Tigrayan highlands, extending his authority into the eastern lowlands as well. He was the first regional ruler to have close contact with Europeans and had hopes of gaining British support as a result of the Valentia/Salt visits. The young Englishman Pearce who spent more than a decade as his aide kept a detailed diary describing campaigns against the Oromo and rivals in Tigray and Gondar (See above, p. 109). Wolde Selassie was strongly opposed to the Amhara-Oromo elements who were the power behind the wobbly throne on which nominal rulers in Gondar succeeded each other in quick succession.

After a period of confusion following Wolde Selassie's death in 1816, Sebagadis Woldu of Agame, of Saho (Irob) origin, who had become a close ally of Wolde Selassie in his final years, emerged dominant by 1822. Ottoman influence in Massawa had become residual as Muhammad Ali extended Egyptian control in the Red Sea. Tigrayan rulers found it comfortable to deal with the Turks, but the

[2] Wollo, major sections of which were known as Angot and Amhara Saynt in medieval times, took the name of the principal Oromo tribe that penetrated into this region and established themselves there. It became and has remained Ethiopia's most ethnically and religiously varied province.

[3] Known as *Itege* (Empress) Menen after her marriage to Emperor Yohannes III in 1840. She is another of the formidable women in Ethiopian history. See C. Prouty and E. Rosenfeld, *Historical Dictionary of Ethiopia and Eritrea*, Scarecrow Press, Metuchen, NJ, 1994, p. 222.

Egyptians were another matter, for the Egyptian conquest of Sudan in 1820 caused worry about Ethiopia's northern border regions. Sebagadis felt the need to overcome Ethiopia's isolation from Europe and sought British support to gain control of Massawa, the best route through which firearms could be imported.[4] Britain, however, was not interested in a permanent foothold in Ethiopia. Sebagadis welcomed European missionaries, gained a reputation as a champion of Christianity, and succeeded in building a kind of coalition among the rulers of Gojjam, Lasta and Semien against the leading Yejju lord, Ras Marye Gugsa of Begemder. Ras Marye successively defeated each of these princes and isolated Sebagadis. Leading predominantly Oromo contingents from Wollo and Begemder, and supported by Wube of Semien and Goshu of Gojjam, Marye crossed the Takazze into Tigray with cavalry and defeated Sebagadis's much better armed force at the Battle of Debre Abbay on 14 February 1831. Marye was killed and Sebagadis surrendered to Wube. Wube handed him over to the Oromos who killed him in retaliation for Marye's death. The Oromos ravaged Tigray but eventually withdrew and left Wube in charge.

Wube Haile Maryam of Semien is one of the most fascinating figures of this era. He was born about 1800, son of a powerful regional chief, and came to power in 1826 on the death of his father. He extended his rule over Tigray after Sebagadis's death and continued the practice of welcoming Europeans and seeking European support. He became the most powerful lord of the north, allied himself with the ruler of Gojjam, Biru Goshu, but was defeated in the Battle of Debre Tabor on 7 February 1842 in a contest with Ras Ali Alula, now the Yejju ruler of Begemder. As he was celebrating his victory, Wube was captured by men loyal to Ras Ali and henceforth allied himself with him. Returning to Tigray, Wube had to deal with rising Egyptian power along his northern and eastern borders.

Troops of the Naib of Arkiko invaded Hamasien in 1843. A sizable Egyptian force invaded Habab in 1844. Wube countered with a campaign toward Kassala in the west and an attack on Massawa and sought support from both the British and French. The concerns of most of these men, like Wube himself, revolved around trade, especially firearms.[5] Wube continued to be deeply involved in defense of his

---

[4] Rubenson, *op.cit.*, pp. 58-68.

[5] More than any other Ethiopian chief during this period, Wube was involved in complex relations with Europeans. These included emissaries, consuls, missionaries and traders. Some of these men originally came to Ethiopia privately and later took on tasks for their governments. Rubenson, *op.cit.* makes by far the most comprehensive effort of any modern historian to describe their activities and judge their impact.

territories against Egypt and gained the sympathy of a variety of
Europeans who were active in both Tigray and Gondar at this time.

British consul Plowden, who had been in Ethiopia earlier but
arrived in an official capacity in Gondar in 1848, was one of Wube's
strongest supporters. He encouraged him to maintain his alliance
with Ras Ali against Kassa Hailu, the future Tewodros II, who had
gained victory after victory over rival chiefs in 1852 and early 1853 and
then faced the forces of Ali, Biru Aligaz of Yejju and Wube in the
Battle of Ayshal on 29 June 1853. While Ali fled, Wube eventually
made peace with Kassa and was allowed to return to Tigray in return
for releasing Abuna Selama, whom he had in custody. Wube's overwhelming ambition was to become emperor himself. He prepared
the church at Derasge in Semien for his coronation, but was defeated
there by Kassa on 9 February 1855. Kassa was crowned two days later as
Tewodros II. Wube was imprisoned at Magdala, but released from
chains in February 1860 when Tewodros married his daughter
Tirunesh. He continued to be kept in prison and died there in 1867.

Developments in the Ethiopian Orthodox Church complicated
internal political conflict during the first half of the nineteenth century in both the northern regions and in Shoa. Doctrinal disputes
about the nature of Christ led to factions supporting various regional
rulers. The *abuns* from Alexandria were unable to cope with the situation, and when an *abun* died, political rivalries resulted in delayed
arrival of his replacement. The position was vacant between 1803 and
1816 and again from 1830 to 1841. During these times the senior
Ethiopian bishops, the *echeges*, attempted to maintain religious peace
but usually became embroiled in arcane religious debates themselves.
Abuna Selama, who arrived from Egypt in 1841, became a prominent
figure in the politics of the time. "One of the most controversial
figures of the nineteenth century, a proud, difficult, and very young
man"[6], he was in his early 20s and had received part of his education
from the British Church Missionary Society in Cairo, where he met
the missionary Krapf. He was sympathetic to Protestants and hostile
to Catholics. He allied himself with Wube but after Ras Ali's victory at
Debre Tabor he went to Gondar. As a foreigner he had difficulty finding his way through the complexities of Ethiopian regional politics:

[He was] condemned ... to the role of an intriguer, falling back on his popular
mystique and charisma, his power of withholding ordination and of issuing
limited anathemas, in return for temporary political alliances. Until the advent of Tewodros, no politician was to offer him consistent, effective support.[7]

[6] Donald Crummey, *Priests and Politicians: Protestant and Catholic Missions in Orthodox Ethiopia, 1830-1868*, Oxford, Clarendon Press, 1971, p. 85.

[7] *Ibid.*, p. 86.

Missionaries

In the late sixteenth and early seventeenth century the Portuguese Jesuits had attempted to persuade the Emperors to place the Ethiopian Orthodox Church under Rome. When European churches became interested in Ethiopia in the mid-nineteenth century, their aims were more differentiated and the possibility of achieving rapid results by converting the Emperor was absent because Emperors changed in quick succession and had little authority. Catholics still sought subordination to Rome but their most successful missionaries showed tolerance for Ethiopian practices and strove for adaptation. As a consequence they succeeded in establishing small Ethiopian-rite Catholic communities that have survived to the present day. Protestant missionaries, on the other hand, hoped to create church organizations independent of the Orthodox hierarchy which would be in control of their indigenous congregations. Some of their missionaries condemned the high regard Ethiopians accorded to the Virgin, to icons, and to fasts and other formalistic practices. They tried to convince Ethiopians that Scripture alone should be the basis of religious observance and individual behavior. Consequently, even when they were cautious, they fell into disfavor and had to abandon their efforts again and again. It was not until the beginning of the twentieth century that Protestants created a church that put down permanent roots.[8]

Most nineteenth century Ethiopian rulers were less interested in the missionaries' religious aims than in the potential they offered for gaining foreign support and arms, and bringing in artisans with skills. Some of the missionaries were not above pretending to far greater influence than they had with their home governments. If missionaries pressed Ethiopian religious authorities too hard and intervened in religious quarrels among Orthodox church factions, they became a nuisance to rulers. Some enjoyed playing politics and became deeply embroiled in the contests and rivalries of the time. Lack of appreciation of Ethiopian attitudes and sensitivities caused others to stumble into awkward situations. Attitudes among Ethiopians had changed

[8] The Mekane Yesus church was the result of the efforts of the Swedish Evangelical Mission which began work among the Kunama in the Sudan border region in 1866. It expanded its activities into Eritrea and by the end of the century developed a strong interest in the Oromo of the southwest, especially Wollega, where incorporation of the region by Menelik created conditions favorable to missionary effort. Completion of translation of the Bible into Oromifa by the Oromo activist, Onesimus Nesib, in 1899 was a landmark in the process of establishment of this church, which had considerable difficulties until the third decade of the 20th century, but has grown strong in Wollega and has expanded in southwestern Ethiopia ever since. See Gustav Aren, *op.cit.*; also Brian L. Fargher, *The Origins of the New Churches Movement in Southern Ethiopia, 1927-1944*, Brill, Leiden, 1996.

since the seventeenth century when the Jesuits had been expelled. The doctrinal controversies of Orthodox churchmen during the Era of the Princes prompted curiosity among both political and church leaders about the messages of the missionaries and the help that Europeans might provide to improve conditions in Ethiopia. This help was always assumed to be greater than it proved to be.

Rulers sometimes tried to divert the missionaries to work among the Oromo, the Shankalla, the Falashas or Muslims. For some of the missionaries conversion of the Oromo was appealing, but most concentrated on the old Christian regions of the north and center. The London Society for Promoting Christianity Amongst the Jews took a special interest in Falashas. Some Ethiopian rulers found this prospect appealing but preferred that Falashas be converted to Orthodoxy instead of Protestantism. Several converted German Jews became active in Ethiopia at mid-century.

Initial Protestant efforts were sponsored by the Church Missionary Society (CMS) in London which combined Swiss and German evangelizing interests with British. It sent Samuel Gobat and Christian Kugler along with a German carpenter named Aichinger to Ethiopia in 1830. In spite of a warm welcome from Sebagadis, they found themselves in a politically confused situation. Kugler was accidentally killed and Sebagadis died the next year. Gobat returned to London and came back in 1834, being joined by Charles Isenberg in 1835. Gobat advocated adjusting to indigenous customs as much as possible; Isenberg was an impatient Protestant purist. Their relationship with Wube, who had difficulty establishing full authority over Tigray, was equivocal, though initially he protected them from expulsion. The Orthodox clergy at Adwa, where they established themselves, were hostile. Gobat, in ill health, left at the end of the year. The Rev. Charles Blumhardt arrived in early 1837 and the Rev. J.L. Krapf at the end of that year. By early 1838 clerical opposition to the missionaries had reached the point where Wube told them he could no longer protect them and they all departed. Krapf then made a determined attempt to establish a mission in Shoa but met frustration there too (see below). In spite of his disappointment, Gobat retained a strong interest in Ethiopia and after several years in Malta became Anglican Bishop of Jerusalem in 1846. When Tewodros became emperor in 1855, he was instrumental in inaugurating new missionary endeavors in Ethiopia.

Just before the CMS missionaries departed, two French adventurers, Antoine and Arnaud d'Abbadie, and a young Lazarist priest from Syria, Father Giuseppe Sapeto, arrived in Adwa. Sapeto developed close relations with the Adwa clergy, judged the situation favorable to Catholic missionary endeavor, and arranged for the Propaganda

Fide in Rome to appoint an Apostolic Prefect to Ethiopia. Father Justin de Jacobis arrived in October 1839 to establish a mission in Tigray. Antoine d'Abbadie penetrated to the Gibe River region in 1843. Remnants of Christian settlements from medieval times in this thickly populated pagan region caught his interest. Encouraged by a Belgian diplomat active in Gojjam, Blondeel, he asked Rome to send a Capuchin mission. Four missionaries headed by Bishop Guglielmo Massaja arrived to take up the task at the end of 1846. Massaja remained active there until 1863, then went to Europe, but when he came back Menelik forbade him to return to the southwest. He remained in Shoa until expelled at the order of Yohannes IV in 1879.

Both De Jacobis and Massaja became involved in French and Italian (then Sardinian) efforts to expand influence in Ethiopia and both helped foster closer commercial relations with France and Italy. De Jacobis attempted to gain support for Tigrayan leaders opposed to Tewodros, but was unsuccessful. He died of a stroke in 1860. His legacy was the Catholic Saho[9] community in northeastern Tigray around Alitena and Catholics in Akele Guzay in Eritrea. De Jacobis maintained the Ge'ez rite, while the Capuchins favored Latin. A colleague of Massaja, Father Taurin, was eventually permitted by Menelik to establish a mission station in Harar.

In retrospect it is difficult to demonstrate that European missionaries had more than marginal influence on politics and society in Ethiopia in the 19th century. In a modest way, they created awareness of the possibilities of technological progress. In religion the dialogue some of them maintained with the Ethiopian clergy had some influence on opening up minds. Politically they suffered disaster with the fall of Tewodros, though it would be unjust to argue that they brought it on themselves. They left an enormous body of reports and memoirs which shed light on conditions in many parts of the country and on important personalities as well as the activities of European officials and private adventurers.[10]

The rise of Shoa

Shoa was an exception to the extreme disorder that plagued northern Ethiopia during the Era of the Princes. King Asfa Wossen[11]

[9] Saho are also known as Irob.

[10] Aren's and Crummey's comprehensive studies, already cited, are by far the best sources of information and judgment about missionary activity. Both have extensive bibliographies.

[11] Though in retrospect usually termed king, he was never given the title *negus* but was content with the traditional Shoan title *meridazmach*, generally considered a notch below *negus* in rank.

during his long reign (1775-1808) continued the policies of his father Amha Yesus: non-participation in the quarrels of the north and outward expansion while at the same time acknowledging the nominal supremacy of the Gondarine emperors and maintenance of the Ethiopian idea. He expanded into Efrata and Geshe, Antsiokia and Gedem, then annexed the old Amhara regions of Morat and Merhabete. Oromos in the area where Addis Ababa would later be built recognized his authority and the whole region enjoyed peace. The chronicler Atme reported: "Under Asfa Wossen a small group of five or six Amhara could travel without danger from Bulga to Debre Libanos, taking the shortest route through the Galla area.[12]"

Asfa Wossen introduced tax reforms and established a viceroy in each district. These measures provoked rebellions which he suppressed. His son Wossen Seged then rebelled out of fear that his father would favor his younger brother as successor. He was apprehended and imprisoned, but his father forgave him and named him his successor.

Wossen Seged continued his father's policy of territorial expansion. First adding territory in the southwest, Wossen Seged developed the ambition to become the unifier of the empire and added more territory northward toward Wollo. He undertook an energetic campaign of church-building and restoration of sites that had been damaged during the Oromo migrations. He restored the Church of the Trinity in Debre Berhan as well as the Church of the Virgin in Debre Libanos. He built a new church in Sala Dingay. At the same time he treated his Muslim and non-Christian Oromo subjects with moderation, solidifying control over the northern, predominantly Oromo region of Shoa Meda. Nevertheless the Orthodox priesthood and some Amhara chiefs resented his policy of religious toleration, plotted against him and had him assassinated by a slave in 1813. Thereupon Oromo groups rose and sacked Debre Berhan. But this disorder did not last long.

A younger son of Wossen Seged, Sahle Selassie, overcame his older brother Bakure, gained the support of his father's most loyal followers as well as some of the Oromo chiefs, and emerged as the new ruler of Shoa, first as *ras*, then as *negus*. Eighteen when he took power, he had a highly successful thirty-four-year reign. Sahle Selassie undertook frequent campaigns in the Awash lowlands, subjugated Oromos and Argobbas, established his authority in Selale and Muger, and campaigned south of the Awash in territory inhabited by the Karayu, Arsi and Macha Oromo as well as Gurage. His predecessors had begun to import European weapons from the coast. He acquired

---

[12] Asfa Wossen Asserate, *op. cit.*, p. 31.

more through trade reaching as far as Gondar and Tigray and these served him well in dealing with the Oromos. However it was not only by force of arms that Sahle Selassie expanded his territory. Oromos tended to be highly factionalized. He played tribal groups against each other, steadily increasing his control. Southward conquests gave Sahle Selassie access to a greatly increased supply of ivory, coffee, gold, civet and slaves. He established fortified trading posts as far south as Soddo and Aymallal in Gurageland and planned an expedition to Lake Zway which never materialized. Feeling confident of the security of his holdings, in 1830 Sahle Selassie built a new camp outside Debre Berhan on the open plateau which developed into a town called Angolala. Ankober, however, remained his capital, with a population perhaps as great as 25,000.

Trade had become important to Shoa and the British and French were keen to expand it. For the first time since the 16th century, Europeans again began coming to Shoa. The first were the missionaries Isenberg and Krapf in 1837. Krapf advised the king to seek arms from the British in India. The French chemist Rochet d'Hericourt arrived in 1839 and returned to France the next year, promising to persuade the French government to send Shoa arms and modern technology. Krapf's recommendations to London led to the dispatch of a large official British mission to Shoa in 1841-3 headed by Major W. Cornwallis Harris. Harris was welcomed by the king, and spent the better part of a year and a half in Ankober and Angolala. He accompanied Sahle Selassie on campaigns in both the lowlands and highlands. Krapf, Rochet d'Hericourt and Harris all became involved in complex intrigues for Sahle Selassie's favor which resulted in a formal treaty between Shoa and Britain.[13] Krapf's interest in a mission to the Oromo never materialized. He left Shoa for Egypt in March 1842 intending to return. When he arrived at Tajura in November

---

[13] Rubenson, *op.cit.*, esp. pp. 144-71, provides detailed description and analysis of all this negotiating, scheming and diplomatic by-play. He concludes that these and other attempts by Europeans to establish close relations with Ethiopia were motivated more by the ambitions of individuals than European governments' policies. Sahle Selassie, like most of his contemporaries, was interested primarily in firearms and military technology that would enable him to gain greater influence over his rivals. The text of the treaty which Harris negotiated is available in Rubenson (ed.), *Acta Aethiopica*, Vol. I: *Correspondence and Treaties, 1800-1854*, pp. 59-60, with an inset copy of the ornamented original in both languages. This volume and its successor, *Acta Aethiopica*, Vol. II: *Tewodros and his Contemporaries, 1855-68*, both published by Addis Ababa University in conjunction, respectively, with Northwestern (USA) and Lund (Sweden) University Presses encompass a total of 440 documents in English translation and the original language relevant to the history of the first two-thirds of the nineteenth century. This detailed treasure-trove has only begun to be exploited by Ethiopian and foreign historians.

the Sultan confronted him with a letter from Sahle Selassie which
demonstrated that he had been ordered to keep the missionaries
from returning.

A great body of letters, reports, memoirs and travel accounts
resulted from the activities of Europeans in Ethiopia in the nineteenth century. Among the most valuable is Harris's three-volume
report of his mission, published immediately after his return to
England. Pompous in style, his account is nevertheless rich in details
of life in Shoa at the residence of the monarch, experiences on campaigns and tours in the countryside. On an outing in the Termaber
range the party was welcomed in the house of an official by a royal
princess married to a regional chief:

[We] were received ... and entertained according to the perfection of
Abyssinian etiquette. [...] Fat, fair, and forty, [the princess] seated in a gloomy
recess upon an *alga* [couch] ... put a few preliminary questions touching the
number of wives possessed by each of the party, and appeared highly to
approve of the matrimonial code that limited the number to one. [...] The
host, who was either unable or unwilling to answer my interrogatories
respecting his own country, edified himself ... by subjecting his ... guests to a
lucid catechism; and like the Arab Bedouin who formed his estimate
of the poverty of Europe by the fact of its producing neither dates nor
camels ... conceived a passing indifferent idea of Great Britain from the
discovery that it boasted no mules. "Have you *mashela* [millet] and *daboo*
[bread] and *tullah* [beer] in your country?" he inquired. [...] "Oh, you have
all these, well, and have you oxen and sheep, and horses and mules?" –
"How, no mules?" he shouted in derision, while the slaves tittered and ... the
princess laughed outright: "Why what a miserable country yours must
be!"[14]

Harris made acute general observations:

Abyssinia, as she now is, presents the most singular compound of vanity, meek-
ness, and ferocity – of devotion, superstition, and ignorance. But, compared
with other nations of Africa, she unquestionably holds a high station. She
is superior in arts and agriculture, in laws, in religion, and social condition,
to all the benighted children of the sun. [...] There is, perhaps, no portion of
the whole continent to which European civilisation might be applied with
better ultimate results; and although now dwindled into an ordinary kingdom, Habesh, under proper government and proper influence, might
promote the amelioration of all the surrounding people, whilst she resumed
her original position as the first of the African monarchies.[15]

Harris's instructions were to gather commercial information and
undertake as much scientific exploration as possible. He was also
told to look into the slave trade. Like most Englishmen of his time,

[14] Harris, *op.cit.*, vol. II, pp. 319-20.

[15] *Ibid.*, vol. III, pp. 184-5.

he was opposed to slavery in principle, but he was discriminating in his judgment of the institution in Ethiopia:

[Slavery] is in fact little more than servitude. The newly captured become soon reconciled to their lot and condition, their previous domestic life having too often been one of actual bondage. [...] From the governor to the humblest peasant, every house in Shoa possesses slaves of both sexes in proportion to the wealth of the proprietor; and in so far as an opinion may be formed upon appearances, their condition, with occasional, but rare, exceptions is one of comfort and ease. Mild in its character, their bondage is tinctured with none of the horrors of West Indian slavery. [...] Slavery amongst the Galla tribes is cradled and nursed in the unceasing intestine feuds of that savage and disorganized people; but the circumstances attending its existence in Gurague, although resting upon the same basis, are something different in character. Since the period that the heathen inroads first cut off that Christian country from the ancient Ethiopic empire ... it has been thrown into a position of peculiar misfortune, and would gladly seek repose by placing itself again under the protection of...Sahela Selassie; but ... he has not chosen to extend either his visits or his authority beyond the frontier village of Aimellele. [...] To accomplish the freedom of Africa, were it practicable to do so, before her sons shall have become qualified to use their liberty for the advantage of society, would be to confer, not a boon, but a curse. To put down the foreign slave trade, without first devising honest occupation for a dense, idle, and mischievous population, would seal the death-warrant of every captive who ... is preserved as saleable booty.[16]

After the departure of the Harris mission, Sahle Selassie declined in health. He tried to abdicate but was prevented from doing so by his closest advisors. His second son Seifu Selassie was actually his favorite, but he designated his first son, Haile Malekot, heir and had Seifu Selassie swear that he would not challenge his brother. Seifu was sent to Merhabete as governor. Sahle Selassie called Oromo chiefs to a council in Angolala and had them swear subservience to his successor. He proclaimed Haile Malekot king shortly before he died in Debre Berhan in 1847.

Sahle Selassie was the greatest of the Shoan rulers before his grandson Menelik whom he is said to have named in hope that he would prove as great as the legendary Menelik I, son of King Solomon by the Queen of Sheba.[17] It was a foresighted move, for Menelik was only three years old when his grandfather died. It is difficult to characterize Sahle Selassie as a modernizer. Though never more than a Shoan king, he was a vigorous traditional ruler of the mold of the great medieval emperors. His priorities were to extend his

---

[16] *Ibid.*, vol. III, pp. 308-37, *passim.*

[17] Harold Marcus, *The Life and Times of Menelik II: Ethiopia 1844-1913*, Oxford, Clarendon Press, 1975, p. 16.

territory and consolidate his power. He had a keen sense of history, but he also had the wisdom to understand the folly of overextending himself by attempting to play imperial politics. His son as successor was not so wise.

In spite of the precautions his father had taken, Haile Malekot, who was about twenty-two on becoming king, had to face continual rebellions and disorder during his short reign. The Abichu Oromo rose up, attempted to retake Tegulet and marched on Ankober. Haile Malekot was able to save the capital with his father's firearms, faithful soldiers, and the help of some loyal Oromos. It took more than a year to subdue peoples along the southern Shoan borders. Haile Malekot attempted to gain Ras Ali's support but relations were strained until 1849. He sought arms and money from the British to no avail.[18] After the Battle of Ayshal, Ras Ali fled to the Tulama Oromo and was rescued by Haile Malekot, who let him return to Yejju. This angered Kassa Hailu (the future Tewodros II), who had advanced into Wollo after his coronation in Derasge in 1855. The confused and now sick Shoan king made an alliance with the Wollo chiefs but was deserted by his brother Seifu Selassie, who retreated to Manz and then to Tegulet. Oromos rebelled again and burned Angolala. Increasingly beleaguered, Haile Malekot burned Debre Berhan to keep provisions there from falling into Tewodros' hands. He died at Ankober, probably of malaria, in November 1855, barely thirty years old. A group of Shoan chiefs escaped to Bulga and Minjar taking the eleven-year-old Menelik with them. These Shoans were defeated by Tewodros's commander, Ras Ingeda of Gojjam, in a final battle in Bulga. They were required to bring Menelik to Tewodros, who entered Ankober in February 1856 and received the submission of the local clergy and officials. Tewodros appointed Haile Mikael, Sahle Selassie's third son by a concubine, *Meridazmach* of Shoa. Seifu Selassie, on the other hand, continued to resist Tewodros until his death in 1860.

Haile Malekot had fathered Menelik at the age of 18 with a palace servant girl named Ejjigayehu whom he is said to have married after the boy, originally named Sahle Maryam, was born. There are other conflicting accounts of Menelik's maternal ancestry, but whatever it may have been, the boy enjoyed a respected position in the royal household and was given a traditional church education.[19] When Tewodros took Menelik back to his court, he treated him as a royal prince and continued his education in the same manner as that of his own son Mengesha. He was eventually given Tewodros's daughter, Alitash, as wife and the rank of *dejazmach.*

---

[18] Rubenson, *op.cit.*, pp. 164-5 recounts details of this futile effort.

[19] Marcus, *op. cit.*, pp, 16-18.

Tewodros II: from victory to disaster

The first Tewodros reigned briefly at the beginning of the fifteenth century. In the late eighteenth century James Bruce observed:

There must have been something very brilliant that happened under this prince, for though the reign is so short, it is before all others the most favourite epoch in Abyssinia. It is even confidently believed, that he is to rise again, and reign in Abyssinia for a thousand years, and in this period all war is to cease and everyone, in fulness, to enjoy happiness, plenty, and peace.[20]

This prophecy was incorporated in the *Fikkare Iyesus*, a popular apocryphal religious treatise. During the troubled times of the Era of the Princes it encouraged hopeful thinking. The population longed for a leader who would bring peace. Kassa Hailu had apparently convinced himself that he was the fulfillment of the prophecy when he chose Tewodros as his throne name in 1855. His reign made a mockery of it. Nevertheless during the mid-twentieth century he became the most popular of all Ethiopian rulers. Young Ethiopians saw him as a harbinger of modernism. Novelists and playwrights glorified him. Intellectuals named their sons after him. They judged him by the ideals he represented rather than by his behavior or accomplishments.[21] There are aspects of parallelism between the careers of Mengistu Haile Maryam and Tewodros II. Both were great champions of Ethiopian unity and territorial integrity. Both plunged the country into rebellion, war and dissolution as drastic as anything it had seen in the preceding century. When he provoked a British expeditionary force that came to topple him, Tewodros at least had the courage to commit suicide, admitting complete failure. Mengistu during his final period in power hinted several times at following Tewodros's precedent but ended up fleeing, leaving his closest associates in the lurch, and the country in dismal condition.

[20] Bruce, *op.cit.*, II, p. 64.

[21] Fortunately in recent years there has been an effort by some Ethiopian scholars to evaluate Tewodros more objectively. See e.g. Shiferaw Bekele, "Kassa and Kassa: the State of Their Historiography" in *Kasa and Kasa: Papers on the Lives, Times and Images of Tewodros II and Yohannes IV (1855-1889)*, IES, AAU, 1990, pp. 289-404. Shifferaw goes so far as to question the validity of the notion that Tewodros was a modernizer in any sense other than his desire to dominate a centralized state. He points out that Tewodros did not effectively delegate authority, established no lasting institutions, had little respect for the rule of law, was intolerant of minority views and rights, and unwilling to tolerate dissent or appreciate the value of advice from counsellors. Thus Tewodros's legacy is a poor basis for creating a modern open society. This critique seems valid to me. The intensity of Tewodros's self-assurance and religious zeal had a greater resemblance to the arrogance and fanatic dedication to "socialism" displayed by Mengistu Haile Mariam than to the humane approach to leadership and governance characteristic of Yohannes IV, Menelik II and Haile Selassie I.

The best proof of Tewodros's humble origin is the fact that he became increasingly sensitive about it as his hold on power weakened. Only late in his reign did he make strong but doubtful claims of Solomonic descent. Born sometime between 1818 and 1820, he was the son of the governor of the border region of Qwara west of Lake Tana. His father may have died when Kassa was a child for his mother, a woman called Attitegeb from the district of Emfraz, brought up her son in Gondar where she is alleged to have sold the wormkiller *kosso* in the market. (Kassa was later derisively called son of a *kosso*-seller.) He was sent for schooling to a monastery between Gondar and Lake Tana but after it was destroyed in civil war he fled to Qwara and apparently continued religious schooling there. He joined his elder half-brother Kinfu Hailu and as a youth participated in his campaigns, gaining valuable military experience and a reputation for strength and bravery. After Kinfu was killed, Kassa joined Dejazmach Biru of Gojjam and then withdrew to Qwara where he spent his twenties as chief of a *shifta* (outlaw) band plundering caravans, attacking Shankalla villages and gathering livestock, grain and slaves. His friend and chronicler Zeneb describes him during this period as something of a Robin Hood, popular with local people because of his generosity.[22]

By 1845 Kassa had a large following and was "too successful to be ignored and too strong to be subdued".[23] Ras Ali's mother *Itege* Menen offered him the Ras's daughter Tewabech in marriage and confirmed him as ruler of Qwara. His relationship with Tewabech became close but his subordination to Menen was temporary. In the next three years Kassa gained control over the large area Kinfu had originally ruled, expanded his army, and strengthened his standing among all rivals in the region. It is quite possible that he now had his eye on the throne. But he was headstrong: he mounted an attack on Egyptian forces in Sudan beyond Metemma, advanced to Debarki 100 miles east of Sennar, was defeated, and had to retreat. Returning to his own area, he captured men who had rebelled in his absence and reportedly had their hands and feet cut off – an early example of the kind of cruelty that became common during the final years of his reign as emperor. Ras Ali summoned him to Debre Tabor in 1849, Kassa

---

[22] Three chronicles deal with Tewodros II's life and activities. They differ in many details. Rather than attempting to reconcile these, this account is based primarily on work Sven Rubenson did in his *King of Kings*, cited above. Taddesse Tamrat relates a different tradition of Tewodros's origin in "The *Kosso*-Vendor Mother: A new Tradition of Origin" in Taddesse Beyene *et al.* (eds), *Kasa and Kasa: Papers on the Lives, Times and Images of Tewodros II and Yohannes IV*, IES, AAU, Addis Ababa, 1990, pp. 117-25.

[23] Darrell Bates, *The Abyssinian Difficulty*, Oxford University Press, 1979, p. 13. Of the many books to have been written about the Napier Expedition, this is the most informative.

refused and Ali declared war, but neither could defeat the other. They reconciled and Kassa joined Ali and Goshu campaigning in Gojjam. He spent the years 1850-1 in Agawmeder. Differences developed and Ras Ali sent an army against him in 1852. Kassa withdrew to Qwara to prepare for the struggle that would bring him to the throne.

In the 26 months between November 1852 and February 1855, in four major battles[24], Kassa defeated all the major leaders who had arisen in northeast Ethiopia during the previous twenty-five years, became King of Kings Tewodros II, and consciously set about changing the course of Ethiopian history. The Era of the Princes was at an end, but a time of severe testing lay ahead. Crowned by Abuna Selama in the church of Derasge Maryam on 11 February 1855, Tewodros proclaimed his intention of unifying and revitalizing his country:

Tewodros perceived as did none of his predecessors ... that the political anarchy, moral laxity, and technological backwardness of his people threatened national survival. The reforms he announced, the policies he tried to implement, the very singlemindedness and perseverance with which he tackled the problems, indicate that he aimed at nothing less than a national revival combined with the transformation of his country into a modern state.[25]

But the newly crowned emperor's energy, ambition and intemperate nature plunged him into continual internal conflict. Understanding little about international relations, he was obsessed with the danger he believed Ottoman Turkey represented for Christianity.[26] He was puzzled by the fact that Britain and France came to the aid of Turkey against Russia in the Crimean War. He had better reason to fear the threat of an expanding Egypt to Ethiopia's territorial integrity, of which he had already had experience. In spite of his close friendship with British Consul Walter Plowden and Scottish adventurer John Bell[27], whom he made his *Liqemaquas* (personal aide and *alter ego*), he became increasingly frustrated by Britain's failure to respond to his overtures for closer relations. The year before Derasge, Tewodros

[24] Ras Goshu of Gojjam was defeated at Gur Amba on 27 November 1852; several important vassals of Ras Ali at Gorgora Bichin on 12 April 1853; Ras Ali and allies at Ayshal on 29 June 1853; and Ras Ali and Dejazmach Wube at Derasge on 9 February 1855.

[25] Rubenson, *Survival*, p. 269.

[26] He had no way of knowing that the Ottoman Empire had long been regarded as the "Sick Man of Europe", protected by Britain and France against Russia and Austria.

[27] Bell had adopted local dress and customs, married the daughter of a noble, acquired land and fathered several children. He introduced Tewodros to Shakespeare's plays which had great fascination for him.

had effected a reconciliation with Abuna Selama, endorsed him as
the arbiter of all religious disputes, and confirmed his marriage to
Tewabech by having him give Holy Communion to them together.
He saw missionaries, particularly the Protestants, as a potential for
constructive influence on the Ethiopian church, but his primary
interest was in their capacity as artisans, teachers, and intermediaries
to foreign governments.

Tewodros began his reign by leading his army into Wollo and Shoa.
While he was occupied there, rebellions broke out in Gojjam and
Gondar itself was captured by nephews of Wube. They soon withdrew
but one of them, Agaw Neguse, later became a continual problem for
Tewodros in Tigray, for he gained the support of France and the
Lazarists. From the beginning of his reign, Tewodros was almost
continually on campaigns. He tried to introduce military reforms,
forming regiments made up of men from different regions rather
than leaving military organization to regional chiefs. He aimed to have
a salaried officer corps. He forbade soldiers to plunder and was
severe in disciplining those who out of old habit did. But he accomplished little. The need to maintain a large army led him into conflict
with the church, for he was constantly in need of resources to support
the army and implement his plans to make governors and judges
salaried officials. He gained the cooperation of Abuna Selama in his
program for moral regeneration of the church, but he soon provoked
clerical opposition by proposing reductions in the numbers of clergy,
limiting each church's land to enough to support only two priests and
three deacons while surplus land was to be given to farmers who paid
taxes. He postponed these measures for four years but attempted to
implement them in 1860, turning the clergy into enemies.

Agaw Neguse consolidated control in Tigray, protected the Lazarists
and sought support from France. Neguse was ready to embrace
Catholicism. But the French were cautious and wary of Britain, and
the French consul in Ethiopia considered Neguse too weak to with-
stand a determined attack by Tewodros. The Catholic missionary
Massaja meanwhile arranged negotiation of a commercial treaty with
Sardinia. Little of value came of it or of Neguse's overtures to France,
but British Consul Plowden was assassinated in January 1860 seemingly at Neguse's instigation. He was given a huge funeral in Gondar.
About the same time Bell was also killed. It took some time for
Plowden's replacement Cameron to arrive. In December 1860
Tewodros entered Tigray and within a month Neguse was dead. The
Catholic missionaries suffered less than they expected. Tewodros
was still able to display the tolerant side of his nature, forbidding
proselytization but extending to Catholics the same kind of religious
freedom Muslims and Falashas enjoyed.

Relations with Abuna Selama soured. The fact that Selama was Egyptian, like all Ethiopian Patriarchs, made Tewodros suspicious of him and a visit of the Egyptian Coptic Patriarch complicated matters. After several serious disagreements, Tewodros imprisoned Selama on Magdala in 1864 where he died three years later. After the *abun* was banished, Tewodros ordered his troops to punish the recalcitrant priests of Gondar. They burned most of its churches and seized all their valuables and manuscripts which were added to the imperial treasury.

Even before Derasge, Samuel Gobat in Jerusalem had begun encouraging renewed Protestant initiative in Ethiopia. Several new missionaries arrived in 1855 and 1856. They were welcomed by Abuna Selama, and included a sizable group of Swiss and German artisans. Most of the new men were enthusiastic supporters of Tewodros's plans for national renewal which was to combine Christian education with training in modern skills. But after Tewabech fell ill and died in April 1858, Tewodros's reforming zeal waned. He became more concerned with self-preservation, suffered violent outbursts of temper, let slave-trading resume and took several concubines. In 1860 he directed the missionaries to settle at Gafat near his headquarters at Debre Tabor where they were allowed to teach and hold religious services but their main job was to establish an arms industry. They were given Muslims, captured Oromos and Falasha artisans as laborers. As Tewodros steadily lost ground to rebels, he pressed the missionaries to repair muskets, produce gunpowder, cast cannon and mortars, and make carriages to transport them. Relations between Tewodros and the missionary artisans at Gafat became so warm that some began to believe that he was accepting their beliefs.

The London Society for Promoting Christianity among the Jews had become interested in Ethiopia again too and sent a converted German Jew, Henry Stern, to set up a mission in 1860. Tewodros disappointed Stern by insisting that converted Falashas be baptized into Ethiopian Orthodoxy. Stern knew that contributors to the Society would not be pleased with this requirement, but he set up a station at Jenda near Gondar and recruited Martin Flad and his wife from Gafat to head it. The Flads were happy to escape industrial activity and turn to preaching and teaching. Stern then returned to England to explain what he had done and raise more money. He published his *Wanderings among the Falashas* in London in 1862 and returned to Ethiopia. The next year Stern clashed with Tewodros who had been shown a translated passage in the book which referred to his mother's low status as a *kosso* seller. Stern and another missionary were put in chains. Meanwhile Tewodros had become increasingly angered by the lack of reply to a letter he had sent Queen Victoria in October 1862.[28] When Consul Cameron attempted to gain Stern's release and explain the delay in reply to the letter, he too was imprisoned.

In May 1864 the Foreign Office finally replied with a letter signed by Queen Victoria. A special emissary, Hormuzd Rassam, First Secretary of the British Indian Agency in Aden, was sent to seek release of the consul and the missionaries. Rassam was a Nestorian Christian born in Mosul in northern Iraq. Tewodros delayed granting Rassam permission to proceed beyond Massawa for more than 15 months. Finally departing from Massawa in October 1865 and travelling via Metemma with a sizable party, Rassam arrived at Tewodros's camp on 28 January 1866. The next day, after he had read Victoria's letter in translation, Tewodros told Rassam he would release the prisoners on condition they be taken immediately out of Ethiopia. But the original three had been moved to Magdala along with five more missionaries and several other Europeans, 18 persons in all, of whom only four were British subjects. Meanwhile the Rassam party camped in comfort near Lake Tana and Tewodros sent them 5,000 thalers "to spend any way you like except in a way unpleasing to God". He let the whole Gafat missionary/artisan group come to the Rassam party's camp to greet them.

The Magdala prisoners finally arrived at Lake Tana on 12 March, but it took another month before they were ready to depart. When Rassam and his party went to bid Tewodros farewell, they found themselves accused of misdeeds and put in chains. Tewodros had apparently decided some time before that he should try to exploit the hostages to gain more British support. In the back of his mind, he hoped to persuade Britain to help him attack Egypt. He had become desperate. He had lost control of all but the territory between Tana, Debre Tabor and Magdala. The rest of the country had deserted him. He sent a message to Rassam on 17 April.

God's creature and slave, the son of David and of Solomon, King of Kings Tewodros. May this letter reach the servant of the Queen of England: What I require from you ... is that you should send me a cannon-maker, a gunsmith, an iron smelter, a sapper, and a gunner. By the power of God, let all these craftsmen come together with their equipment so that they may return after instructing me...[29]

---

[28] Considering the state of the world in the 1860s and the many problems the British Foreign Office had to contend with, it is hardly surprising that Tewodros's letter and requests for aid forwarded through Cameron did not receive rapid attention. The letter was in Amharic and was sent to Germany for translation. For the text, see Rubenson, *Acta Aethiopica*, pp. 197-201.

[29] Rubenson, *Acta Ethiopia* II, p. 298.

London did not learn that Rassam's mission had gone awry until 24 June when a message came from Cairo. The Jenda missionary, Martin Flad, persuaded Tewodros to let him go to London as his emissary to the Queen. He carried a longer list of items Tewodros wanted than the one given to Rassam. Meanwhile Tewodros had become utterly capricious, at times insanely vicious, in his behavior. On 24 June 1866 he gave a grand feast to celebrate the Queen's birthday. A few days later he had the whole group of foreigners sent to Magdala. When this news reached London, attitudes in the government hardened and so did public opinion. After more than a year of futile efforts to reach some sort of compromise with Tewodros, Queen Victoria announced the decision to send a military expedition in a speech to the country on 21 August 1867.[30]

Colonel Merewether, the Government of India's Resident at Aden, with the help of the Swiss Werner Munzinger, who had been looking after British interests in Massawa since 1865, had begun gathering information in February 1867 about routes an expeditionary force could use. London decided that the Indian Army was best suited for the task and its commanding general, Sir Robert Napier, was directed to plan and organize the force needed.[31] An enormous amount of careful work, as well as some controversy, went into putting the expedition together and arranging its transport.[32] An advance party reached Zula (ancient Adulis) at the end of October. The main force embarked in December and Napier arrived in Zula on 7 January 1868.

At Gafat more than a dozen Europeans and family members had remained at work for Tewodros. When Flad returned with confirmation that Queen Victoria had decided on military measures if the captives were not immediately released, Tewodros decided to move the Gafat Europeans and their gear to Magdala, but before setting out on the long trek in the rainy season he ordered them to manufacture a supremely powerful weapon. He provided thousands of laborers and came frequently to observe progress. By the end of summer they had successfully cast the giant mortar which the elated Tewodros christened Sevastopol. He saw it as his salvation. He destroyed his

---

[30] Percy Arnold in *Prelude to Magdala: Emperor Theodore of Ethiopia and British Diplomacy*, Bellew, London, 1991, provides extensive background on Tewodros' confrontation with Britain.

[31] Like many Ethiopian leaders, Napier had begun his career at an early age, entering the East India Company's military college at the age of 14 and being commissioned in the Bengal Engineers at the age of 16. He had a distinguished record fighting in the Sikh and China wars, and was aged 57 in 1867.

[32] For background on the organization of the expedition and some of the questions which arose, see Darrell Bates, *op.cit.*, as well as Frederick Myatt, *The March to Magdala: The Abyssinian War of 1868*, Leo Cooper, London, 1970.

Debre Tabor camp and on 9 October set out on the arduous journey
to Magdala with 5,000 soldiers and several times as many camp
followers. He brought along the Gafat Europeans and their families
and several hundred Ethiopian prisoners and hostages. At a rate
sometimes less than a mile a day with Sevastopol and other heavy
guns and supplies requiring superhuman exertions, the expedition
was still far from its destination when Tewodros learned of the British
landing. By word of mouth information of both approaching parties
reached the hostages at Magdala at Christmas. While Napier had
400 miles to cover, Tewodros had about 50. As Napier's force was
negotiating the formidable gorge of the Zhita river, Tewodros learned
that other enemies were also converging: Wagshum Gobeze from
the north, Oromos from Wollo and Menelik from Shoa.[33]

Napier had to traverse a route to Magdala at least as rugged and
difficult as Tewodros, but the British had the advantage of the latest
European technology backed by an efficient logistics system.[34] There
were vast numbers of mules and donkeys, even forty-four elephants,
but most effective was a rail line equipped with six steam locomotives
quickly laid across the first part of the flat Samhar. Great effort was
expended in improving the trail up the escarpment to Senafe.
Napier personally inspected every stage of the work. Crossing Tigray
he gained the cooperation of Dejazmach Kassa Mercha, a descendant
of Sebagadis, who had gained ascendancy in the province only a short
time before but was still wary of his brother-in-law to the south,
Wagshum[35] Gobeze. Gobeze tolerated the expedition's passage
through his territory but showed no warmth toward it. These chiefs
were suspicious of Napier's insistence that Britain had no purpose
but release of the hostages. If that were really the case, they feared
that once they were released the British might leave Tewodros in
charge of a sizable force which could be used against them. If either
Napier or Tewodros ever seriously considered this kind of outcome,
the subsequent course of events made it impossible.

By 18 March Tewodros was camped on a plain below Magdala and
had brought along enough supplies to last for a six-month siege. To
confound his domestic enemies, many of whom were bitter rivals
of each other, Tewodros let rumors spread that the British were really
coming to aid him in putting down internal opposition. He deployed
his forces skillfully. He told them, "Be not afraid of these English

[33] See the next chapter on Menelik's escape from Magdala.

[34] Napier's insistence on paying for everything he needed instead of following
the old Ethiopian custom of demanding animals, services, food and supplies from
the local population greatly facilitated his movement.

[35] Traditional title of the ruler of the mountainous region of Wag, directly south
of Tembien in Tigray.

soldiers [for] in the name of God I shall conquer." He had the chains removed from most of the European captives. As the British force neared Magdala, messengers carried letters back and forth between Napier and Tewodros. On 3 April Napier wrote him:

By command of the Queen of England I am approaching Magdala with my army, in order to recover from your hands Envoy Rassam, Consul Cameron ... and the other Europeans now in your Majesty's power. I request your Majesty to send them to my camp, as soon as it is sufficiently near to admit of their coming to safety.

When by 9 April there was no reply, Napier, who had deployed his forces around the great natural fortress, prepared to attack the next day, Good Friday.[36] By afternoon of that day Tewodros's artillery had begun to fire on the advancing British, but most of the shot was only balls of stone, and one of the largest cannons burst its barrel when fired and provoked Tewodros into a fit of anger. It had taken more than 500 men to haul Sevastopol up the steep slope, but it was never fired. When the soldiers of both sides finally faced each other, the modern breech-loading Snider rifles of the British proved vastly superior to the muzzle-loading muskets of the Ethiopians. Sikhs still used muzzle-loaders but when they failed to halt attacking Ethiopians, the Sikhs drove them back with bayonets. After a difficult night for both sides, Tewodros sent Napier a mournful message on 11 April which indicated he was resigned to defeat:

In the name of the Father, and of the Son, and of the Holy Ghost, one God in Trinity and Unity, Kassa who believes in Christ. [...] Believing that I had power, I brought all Christians to the land of the heathen. [...] When I used to tell my countrymen, "Submit to taxation and discipline," they refused and quarreled with me. But you have defeated me through men obedient to discipline. The people who loved me and followed me fled, abandoning me, because they were afraid of a single bullet. When you attacked them, I was not among the people who fled. Alas, believing myself to be a great man, I kept on fighting with worthless artillery. [...] If God had allowed me, I planned to rule all; if God prevented me, [I planned] to die. [...] You people who passed last night rejoicing, may God not make you like me, let alone my Ethiopian enemies. I had thought of marching to Jerusalem and driving out the Turks. He who has subjected men will not in turn be subjected by other men.[37]

The next day, Easter, Tewodros attempted to commit suicide, but failed, and then sent Napier another message which seemed to offer

---

[36] It was later learned that Napier's message had not been delivered because no man could be found who was willing to risk the Emperor's wrath when he read it. Finally a woman gave the message to Tewodros on 10 April. He refused to read it, saying "It can go back to its master ... it would not change my mind."

[37] Rubenson, *Acta Aethiopica, II*, pp. 354-5.

a truce in return for release of the hostages.[38] The captives, released the day before, had reached the British lines, but Tewodros himself refused to surrender. Napier decided on an assault. Withdrawing into the inner area of the fortress, Tewodros came out in a final dramatic gesture, challenging Napier to single combat. It was not accepted. Tewodros went back. The final assault began at 3 p.m. on 13 April. Before sundown the King of Kings was dead by his own hand. The pistol at his side bore an inscription from Queen Victoria: "To Theodorus, Emperor of Abyssinia, as a slight token of her gratitude for his kindness to her servant Plowden, 1864."

Long before he killed himself Tewodros's hopes for a revivified Ethiopia had been shattered by his excessive zeal, his arrogance, and his readiness to resort to violence. If the British had not pursued him to the top of Magdala, his own countrymen would surely have unseated him within months. His end was nevertheless a tragedy for the country. If he had had a reasonably organized government and a small corps of capable administrators, he would have had a chance of implementing parts of his idealistic program of reform and renewal. In his ideals, he was woefully ahead of his time. In his methods of putting them into effect, he was still a medieval monarch. He left a country as torn and rudderless as he had found it when he was crowned at Derasge thirteen years before.

General Napier made no effort to influence the course of events following the defeat of Tewodros. He saw that Tewodros was buried and burned Magdala. The troops were allowed to plunder and auctions were subsequently held to distribute booty and souvenirs.[39] Napier's only priority was to get the expedition back to the coast. It departed on 19 April. Kassa Mercha was helpful during the crossing of Tigray, and by 10 June 1868 the entire party had all embarked.

[38] Text in *Ibid.* pp. 356-7.

[39] The most important booty was the huge hoard of well over 1,000 Ge'ez and Amharic manuscripts Tewodros had assembled. Of these, 350 which were judged most valuable were selected by the expedition's archaeologist for the British Museum. They have served as the basis of valuable scholarship on Ethiopia ever since. Many others were taken by individual officers and soldiers. Of these 40-50 are known to have found their way into other libraries in England and Europe. Those that remained were disposed of in Ethiopia, several dozen being given to the Church of Cheleqot Selassie in Tigray. See Rita Pankhurst, "The Magdala Library of Tewodros" in *Kasa and Kasa* pp. 223-30. Napier took the emperor's crown and royal seal and presented them to Queen Victoria. In 1925 King George V personally returned the crown to the future Haile Selassie I on his visit to England. Tewodros's wife Tirunesh and his son Alemayehu were also taken along by Napier. Tirunesh died en route and was buried with honors at Cheleqot Selassie. Alemayehu was brought to England and became the ward of Queen Victoria. He was sent to Cheltenham College and then to Sandhurst, but became sick and died at nineteen and was buried at Windsor Castle.

Shortly thereafter Britain closed its consulate at Massawa. For a colonial power it was uncommon behavior. Ethiopia was left to sort itself out. Weakened and confused as it was, the country fortunately demonstrated the capacity to do so.

The first historian of the Napier expedition concluded his account with an observation that represented both a judgment and a hope:

The future destiny of Abyssinia will depend much on the rise of some man with strong will and great ability, a Theodore without his fanaticism and mad devilish pride, who will have the power to consolidate all the Christian highlanders into one people. The experiment of dividing the country into separate principalities has been tried ever since the disruption of the old monarchy, and has failed. Interminable feuds and civil wars have been the result.[40]

He was right. But it turned out to be not one, but two men who had the wisdom to tolerate each other much of the time – and when they came to the brink of conflict, to compromise – and who determined the destiny of the country for the rest of the century.

[40] C.R. Markham, *A History of the Abyssinian Expedition*, London, 1869, pp. 389-90, as cited by Zewde Gebre Selassie, *op.cit.*, p. 15.

6

YOHANNES IV AND MENELIK II

THE EMPIRE RESTORED, EXPANDED, AND DEFENDED

Menelik, King of Shoa

The escape from Magdala of Dejazmach Menelik and some of his friends in July 1865 was one of many factors that contributed to the deterioration of Tewodros's situation. During his imprisonment, Menelik had managed to maintain contact with the world outside and had planned his escape route in advance. Troops of the Oromo Queen Worqitu of Wollo, hostile to Tewodros, met the fugitives at the border of her domains and helped them on to Shoa. In revenge Tewodros had the queen's son and more than two dozen other Oromo prisoners hacked to death and twelve Amhara notables from Wollo beaten to death with bamboo rods.[1]

When Menelik got back to Ankober, he concentrated on building up support and stopping factional infighting. He forbade religious debate and declared all cults free to practice. Priests who encouraged religious controversy were threatened with execution. Menelik discovered that a certain Bezabih, whom Tewodros had put in charge in Shoa in 1859, had declared himself Shoan monarch and had tried to persuade Queen Worqitu to support him. Menelik gathered supporters, confronted Bezabih, gave him an opportunity to make submission but discovered he was still plotting against him. He called a council which condemned the plotter to death and confirmed Menelik as King of Shoa, ninth in direct line from Negasi. By 1866 Menelik had reestablished order in Shoa and built up a strong army. He moved troops toward Magdala in November 1867, but withdrew without attacking. Following a discussion with Massaja about the prospects of the Napier expedition (Massaja thought they would succeed), he prepared a new expedition at Worailu in March 1868 in which Queen Worqitu was expected to cooperate, but allegedly had to call it off because his men wanted to spend Easter at home. He sent Napier a message from Ankober:

[...]I sent you one of my servants with this letter to make acquaintance with you. Far from being the enemy of the Queen of England, I am her friend. Before, I had intended to liberate the captives and come very near to Magdala, but as the business seemed impossible, and my army had no more provisions, I returned to my country. Now I am far off and I have no

[1] Marcus, *op.cit.*, pp. 24-5.

hesitation ... to help you, and want in no wise to trouble you. As to my friendship to the Queen, it is not a matter of today. I had sent to London and have received a friendly answer; perhaps you have read it. May God give you full welfare.[2]

It is likely that Easter was only an excuse. Menelik saw no purpose in becoming directly involved in the final act of the drama at Magdala. He was uncertain about British intentions and unsure of his ability to overcome rivals. He wanted, however, to be seen favorably by the British, for he was already interested in the imperial throne and had termed himself *negusa negast* (king of kings) in correspondence. Witnessing Tewodros firsthand had been a valuable education in how *not* to rule and how *not* to deal with foreigners. In his message to Napier he was displaying, at the age of twenty-four, the keen appreciation of the complexity of both domestic and foreign interrelationships that characterized his entire subsequent life. He was not impulsive. He knew how to practice patience. He knew he had strong rivals in Wagshum Gobeze and Kassa Mercha and possibly in other regional chiefs as well. But he also knew he had advantages in Shoa that were not going to disappear. Menelik was also by far the youngest of the three major claimants to the throne. All three had a better claim of Solomonic descent than Tewodros.[3]

Wagshum Gobeze moved first. Born in 1836, he had gone into hiding after Tewodros had his father hanged in 1858. He returned to Lasta in 1865, took over an army his mother and her second husband had built up, and moved into Tigray, where he defeated Tewodros's deputy, Tiso Gobeze, and married Kassa Mercha's sister Dinkinesh. With an army that had grown to 60,000 by the time of the battle at Magdala, Gobeze moved soon after to proclaim himself Emperor Tekla Giyorgis. There was no *abun* to crown him, so he had the *echege* perform a coronation ceremony in August 1868 on the plain of Zebit in Lasta where his father had been hanged. He had Abuna Selama's body brought from Magdala for reburial in the Church of St. Gabriel in Gondar and restored other Gondar churches. He resented Kassa Mercha's moves to consolidate his position in Tigray following the British withdrawal, tried to persuade Menelik to join him in challenging Kassa, but was put off. In June 1871 he crossed the Takazze into Tigray and but was soundly defeated by Kassa in a battle near Adwa on 11 July and taken prisoner. He died the next year.

Kassa Mercha aspired to the imperial throne but was cautious and referred to himself merely as Head of the Nobles of Ethiopia. At their

---

[2] *Acta Aethiopica II*, p. 353.

[3] Technically the most logical successor was Yohannes III who had been briefly on the throne at the beginning of the 1840s and was still living in Aksum. He seems, however, to have been forgotten.

meeting at Senafe on 25 May 1868, Napier turned over to him a
battery of mountain guns, enough muskets to arm a regiment, and a
large quantity of ammunition. In 1869 Kassa hired the Scot John
Kirkham, formerly Adjutant to General Charles Gordon (later killed
at Khartoum), as trainer for his army. Thus he was well prepared to
overcome Gobeze's far larger force at Adwa. Kassa had used the short
reign of Tekla Giyorgis to bolster his position in Tigray, especially in
the northernmost highland province, Hamasien. He could prove
descent from all the principal Tigrayan noblemen of the preceding
century. His credentials as an Ethiopian patriot were impeccable.
He was deeply attached to the Orthodox Church and soon after the
British left set about negotiating with the Egyptians to procure a
new *abun*. He paid $20,000 for Abuna Atnatewos who arrived in June
1869. Kassa still had plenty of problems to face when he was crowned
Yohannes IV on 12 January 1872 at the age of forty-one. He was the
first emperor to be crowned at Aksum since Fasilidas in 1632. 3,000
priests took part in the ceremony. He had taken a vow on recovering
from an illness some years before that he would never wreak vengeance on enemies or amass a personal fortune. It was a welcome
departure from Tewodros's violence.

Menelik and Yohannes IV: competition and accommodation

Ethiopia was fortunate in the 1870s and 1880s in having two vigorous,
farsighted rulers, one in the north and one in the south. While
Menelik expanded southward and extended trade routes, Yohannes
protected the country's northern marches against Egypt, Italy and
disorder in Sudan. In the center of the country the two were competi-
tors and were sometimes motivated by a desire to disadvantage the
other, but each time they clashed, they realized the folly of unbridled
competition and compromised for the benefit of the country. They
worked together to bring about religious peace among the Orthodox
and to contain the zeal of missionaries and foreign adventurers.

In his time, Tewodros had known almost nothing of the real world
beyond Ethiopia's borders. Except for some Egyptian incursions in
the north, he had no foreign dangers to contend with. Yohannes IV
faced real threats. Both he and Menelik realized the necessity of
engaging in diplomacy to defend the country. Muhammed Ali's
grandson Ismail became ruler of Egypt in 1863, took the title of
Khedive[4] the next year, and continued the policy of vigorous southward expansion. The Sultan ceded Suakin and Massawa to him in

---

[4] In effect Viceroy of the Ottoman Sultan, though only nominally subject to
Constantinople.

Above Slaves were a major export from Ethiopia during the 19th century.
Below Sahle Selassie, King of Shoa, receiving gifts from the Harris Expedition
at Ankober, 1841 (from Harris, *The Highlands of Ethiopia*, London, 1844).

Above The Church of St Michael at Ankober where the Shoan kings are buried (both etchings are from J.M. Bernatz, *The Highlands of Shoa*, London, 1852). *Below* Drawing from the *Illustrated London News* of the fortress of Magdala being fired by the Napier Expedition on 17 April 1868 after the suicide of Emperor Tewodros.

Left Kassa Mercha was crowned Emperor Yohannes IV in January 1872 and reigned until 1889 when he fell fighting the Sudanese in the Battle of Metemma. *Below* Emperor Menelik II and Empress Taitu Betul. This energetic and devoted royal pair dominated Ethiopia during the 1890s and the first years of the 20th century.

Above Enda Giyorgis, Adwa, the church where Emperor Menelik II and his *rases* prayed on the morning of their great victory on 1 March 1896 (photograph taken during the centenary celebrations on the same date in 1996). *Below left* Ras Tasfari and Princess Menen Asfaw at the time of their marriage on 3 August 1911. *Below right* Haile Selassie at Bath, England, in 1937. He wrote his autobiography, *My Life and Ethiopia's Progress*, during this time.

1867. The Suez Canal opened in 1869, and Ismail, eager to expand down the coast, found himself competing with France and Italy. An Italian company had purchased Assab in 1869 and the French followed by gaining a foothold in Tajura and Obock. Egypt took control of Harar in 1875. Ismail continued to consolidate control over Sudan all the way to Equatoria, constructing roads and railways and improving navigation on the Nile. The Swiss Munzinger who had lived many years as a trader in Keren knew the north Tigrayan border region well. He entered Egyptian service in 1872, was given the rank of Pasha and made governor of Eastern Sudan. Most of the people inhabiting the Sudan-Ethiopian border region had been converted to Islam in previous centuries, but the region around the old town of Keren, also called Bogos or Senhit, had Orthodox survivors as well as communities of Catholics and Protestants, the result of missionary activity.

Egyptian troops moved into Bogos a few months after Yohannes was crowned and subsequently occupied Mensa and Ghinda. Yohannes sent Kirkham to appeal to the powers of Europe to press Egypt to withdraw. They were reluctant to get involved. Europeans considered a rapidly modernizing Egypt more important than an Ethiopia that was still largely an economic and political question mark. Britain showed a bit more concern, but Queen Victoria wrote Yohannes that it was her impression the Khedive was only pursuing bandits. A series of moves including an effort by Munzinger to get Menelik to attack Yohannes ensued while Yohannes was occupied pacifying Begemder and Gojjam.

Overestimating internal strains in Ethiopia, the Khedive decided on a military offensive against Yohannes. He sent a Danish officer in his service, Soren Arendrup, to Massawa to lead an expedition into the highlands. Arendrup moved quickly into Hamasien *en route* to Adwa. Yohannes declared war on 23 October 1875. The Egyptians hoped to subvert rulers in Begemder and Gojjam as well as for Menelik to isolate Yohannes, but decided not to wait and attacked Yohannes's army at Gundet on the Mareb in mid-November. The encounter ended in disaster and Yohannes gained an enormous booty in arms. Arendrup was killed. At almost the same time Munzinger was killed on an expedition into the Danakil country. The Khedive tried to suppress news of the disaster and decided on rapid revenge. He prepared an expedition in which Americans in Egyptian service held important positions. It sailed from Suez on 5 December 1875 and included nine American officers.[5]

[5] From 1869 onward the Khedive had hired a total of forty-eight former Union and Confederate officers on five-year contracts to modernize his army. The US Government played no role in this undertaking. These officers were involved in most of the important Egyptian campaigns of the time and some saw service in

Yohannes was not motivated by vindictiveness. He made an unsuccessful attempt to negotiate with the Khedive while assembling a
large army in Enderta. A new Egyptian army moved from Massawa
to the plain of Gura at the end of January 1876. The Egyptians persuaded a few local chiefs to defect, but most of the north Ethiopian
rases rallied to Yohannes. The battle was fought between 7-9 March
1876. With heavy losses on both sides, the Egyptians were badly
defeated thanks to the strong leadership of *Shaleqa* (major) Alula, a
man of modest origin from Tembien to whom Yohannes entrusted
leadership of his army. The Khedive again attempted to suppress
news of the extent of the disaster and sent reinforcements to Massawa
to support his conditions for peace: return of arms and prisoners and
free trade. When Yohannes released the prisoners, the Egyptians
pressed for concessions and maneuvered to neutralize Hamasien
as a barrier to their holdings farther north. After a summer of futile
efforts to reach an agreement with the Egyptians, Yohannes broke off
relations and ordered his troops into Hamasien. On 9 October 1876
he raised Alula to *ras* and appointed him ruler over Hamasien and
Serae.

Ras Alula henceforth became the emperor's most valuable and
loyal lieutenant in the Mareb Mellash – the region north of the Mareb
river, which became the boundary between Tigray and the future
Eritrea.[6] While the Egyptians were reluctant to recognize the full consequences of their defeat, their ambitions in Ethiopia had been dealt
a mortal blow. Khedive Ismail was deposed in 1879 and repla- ced by a
young and inexperienced successor. The country was near bankruptcy
and its army disaffected. Adventurism in Ethiopia had weakened the
Turco-Egyptian administration in Sudan and a grass-roots religious
rebellion led by Mohammed Ahmad ibn al-Sayid Abdallah broke out
in 1881. Claiming to be a descendant of the Prophet, he proclaimed
himself the Mahdi, agent of Allah with a mission to restore righteousness to the evil world. There is some similarity between the Mahdi
and Tewodros II in their self-assurance and intensity of belief in
their mission. The Mahdi's followers, also called the Ansar, were
more fanatically loyal than Tewodros's soldiers. Concerned about its
lifeline to India, Britain occupied Egypt in September 1882.

---

remote parts of Sudan. There are several published accounts of experiences of
which the most informative is Colonel William M. Dye, *Moslem Egypt and Christian
Abyssinia or, Military Service under the Khedive, in his provinces and beyond their
Borders, as experienced by the American Staff*, New York, 1880, republished by Negro
Universities Press, New York, 1968.

[6] See Haggai Erlich, *Ras Alula, a Political Biography: Ethiopia and Eritrea 1875-
1897*, Red Sea Press, Lawrenceville, NJ, 1996; also by the same author: *Ethiopia
and the Middle East*, pp. 53-82.

Neither Yohannes nor Menelik was able to enjoy quiet times in the 1870s. Fortunately both were men in their prime and served by able aides and officials. Menelik was eager to extend Shoan influence over Wollo, Begemder and Gojjam. Returning from Gojjam in 1877, he had to contend with a plot hatched by a charming courtesan many years his senior, Bafena, whom he had taken as consort shortly after returning to Ankober from Magdala. She had previously been married to five other men and had several children. She encouraged Menelik to challenge Yohannes in Wollo. In league with disgruntled Shoan nobles she decided to try to put one of her sons on the throne. In Menelik's absence in Gojjam her accomplices occupied Ankober in April 1877 and Bafena proclaimed herself regent. The plotters accused Menelik of being too much under the influence of Massaja. Even after he returned, it took Menelik some time to recognize how treacherous Bafena had been. He did not neutralize her and the plotters until early 1878.

At this point Yohannes moved from Begemder toward Shoa in league with Mohammed Ali of Wollo. Yohannes reached Manz and Menelik readied his forces for battle. War between the two seemed imminent when Yohannes reached Sala Dingay, a short distance north of Ankober. A council of Shoan nobles was called at Liche. Menelik's uncle Ras Darge[7] was again influential, as he had been in dealing with Bafena's plotters. Yohannes's army had been strengthened by 20,000 men supplied by Ras Adal of Gojjam and was better armed than Menelik's. A truce was declared and negotiations began. Menelik was permitted to remain dominant in Wollo provided he built churches and Christianized Muslims. In return he agreed to pay a heavy annual tribute to Yohannes. Menelik made submission at Yohannes's camp at Dembaro on 20 March 1878 in an elaborate ceremony. He carried a stone on his neck to meet the emperor while *azmaris* sang: "A road that is perilous is far – one has to climb and then descend." Yohannes was generous, had Menelik sit beside him, offered to crown him Negus of Shoa, and the next day had him formally review the imperial army, which included troops of Ras Adal and Mohammed Ali. After further festivities Menelik was crowned King of Shoa on 26 March on a throne only slightly lower than that of Yohannes.[8]

Yohannes and Menelik were both eager to see religious controversy among the Orthodox settled, for Islam, encouraged by Muslim

---

[7] Fourth son of Sahle Selassie, later famous as the conqueror of Arsi, he remained an important – and often moderating – influence on Menelik until his death in 1900.

[8] The crowning was the first time a Shoan monarch had been so confirmed by an Ethiopian emperor.

traders and the Muslims of Wollo, was spreading around the periphery of the country. At Dembaro Menelik seems to have agreed to ban all missionaries, including the now seventy-two-year-old Massaja, whom Yohannes ordered out of Ethiopia the next year, and concentrate on reviving the Orthodox church. Yohannes called a religious conference at Borumeda in Wollo in the summer of 1878 to settle the still seething doctrinal debates. Dozens of senior clergymen came from Shoa, Tigray and Gojjam. In the debates, the *Sost Lidet* (Three Birth) concept popular in Shoa was condemned and the *Kara Haymanot* or *Qebat* (Two Birth or Unctionist) doctrine was proclaimed by Yohannes as the only valid position in the presence of Menelik and Ras Adal of Gojjam. Christians, Muslims and pagans were given two, three and five years respectively to conform. Muslim officials were given three months to renounce either their positions or their religion, pagan officials were to accept Christianity immediately. The most notable convert was Mohammed Ali of Wollo who was baptized Mikael and made a *ras*.

Menelik returned to Shoa and undertook mass conversions of Muslims and Oromos. Yohannes made similar conversion efforts in Wollo. He opened negotiations with the Patriarch of Alexandria in June 1881 for a new *abun* and three additional bishops and enjoyed quick success. Abuna Petros with bishops Matewos, Marqos and Luqas were escorted to Ethiopia by the Naib of Arkiko in the fall of the year. Petros was assigned to Tigray, Marqos to Begemder and Semien, Matewos to Shoa, and Luqas to Gojjam and Kaffa. All four were empowered to consecrate Ethiopian clergy, thus greatly simplifying the operations of the Ethiopian church.

With his relationship with Yohannes regularized, Menelik returned to Shoa and concentrated on expansion southward. During the next ten years he more than tripled Shoan – and there-by Ethiopian – territory in the south. While the eastern Gurage – the Christian Kestane – were absorbed into Shoa in the mid-1870s with little resistance, the Western Gurage, more under Islamic influence, were subdued only after heavy fighting. Tension arose in the Gibe region. Rulers of Gojjam had been expanding into the southwest since mid-century. When Ras Adal was crowned King Tekla Haymanot in January 1881, Yohannes confirmed him as ruler of Gojjam and Kaffa. When Menelik sent his Oromo general, Ras Gobena, to gain submission of the Gibe kingdoms, he found Tekla Haymanot's deputy, Ras Dereso, already there. Their clash escalated to a major battle between forces of the two leaders at Embabo in Wollega in June 1882. Menelik took the Gojjami king prisoner. Yohannes had the two come to Borumeda to work out a compromise. He took Agawmeder from Gojjam and Wollo from Shoa and put them under direct imperial rule. Menelik was required to give Ras Alula the arms he had captured. A marriage was arranged between Yohannes' son Araya and Menelik's daughter Zewditu and Araya was appointed governor of Wollo.

Yohannes then suggested Menelik marry Taitu Betul, daughter of an aristocratic Semien family whose two brothers had been prisoners with Menelik at Magdala.[9] Abuna Matewos presided over the wedding in the Church of Medhane Alem in Ankober at Easter 1883. Taitu was in her early 30s and had already been married several times. She was bright, energetic, patriotic, a devout Christian and unusually well educated for the time. The marriage was a most fortunate step, for Taitu as empress became a true partner for the rest of Menelik's long life.[10]

Ras Gobena had advised the principal chief in the rich territories that became Wollega, Moroda Bakure, to avoid taking sides in the quarrel between Shoa and Gojjam. In 1884 Moroda brought tribute to Menelik and was made a dejazmach. The region produced gold as well as a surplus of agricultural produce and was declared a *madbet* – a source of food for the royal court. But Menelik was cautious about moving too rapidly to absorb it, for some of the Oromo tribes were rebellious. Menelik was also concerned that Ras Gobena, much his elder and an Oromo himself, might have designs on the region as an independent power base. No serious tension arose, however, and Ras Gobena was kept busy defending western Wollega against Mahdist incursions from Sudan in the last part of the 1880s. Like several other regions of the southwest, full incorporation of Wollega did not occur until the next decade.[11]

Ras Darge led a campaign into Arsi in 1886. Menelik launched it with a proclamation to his soldiers:

Let your horses and mules eat and become fat, prepare flour, red pepper, salt, and other provisions and let all be found here at Entoto the day of Abo, after the eighth of Easter. Whoever does not heed my words will be punished with confiscation of all his goods.[12]

The Oromo of Arsi put up fierce resistance, but were brutally subdued by Ras Darge, who was appointed governor after the Battle of

[9] Menelik had broken off relations with Bafena and banished her to a village.

[10] Chris Prouty, *Empress Taytu and Menelik II, Ethiopia 1883-1910*, Ravens Educational & Development Services, London, 1986.

[11] For background on the history of this entire region see Alessandro Triulzi, *Salt, Gold and Legitimacy: Prelude to the History of a No-Man's Land, Bela Shangul, Wallagga, Ethiopia (ca. 1800-1898)*, University of Naples, 1981.

[12] Cited in Marcus, *op.cit.*, p. 65. Abo is a popular name for Abuna Gebre Manfas Qiddus, a semi-mythical Egyptian saint reputed to have lived for several hundred years atop Mount Zuqualla.

Azule in September 1886. The region soon became a dependable source of agricultural wealth and revenue. A by-product of this campaign was the liberation of the islanders of Lake Zway, an old Christian population, which Menelik undertook personally that same year. Menelik consciously extended his borders to include all the territories that had formed part of the medieval empire of Amde Tseyon. Armed camps – *ketemas* – were established in the newly conquered regions and became towns. Officers and settlers were rewarded with land where they set up farms that were worked with local tenants. These northern colonists, called *neftanya* (lit. rifleman) formed an elite that introduced Christianity, the Amharic language and northern concepts of administration. Where indigenous elites offered little resistance or cooperated with the Shoan conquerors, they were sometimes co-opted into the *neftanya* system and became landholders with tenants themselves.[13]

The subjugation of Arsi was a prelude to Menelik's final great conquest as King of Shoa: that of Harar. Britain had Egyptian forces withdraw in May 1885 and members of the Adare ruling dynasty took charge. Menelik made no secret of his intention to take the city and so informed King Umberto of Italy. He wanted to protect trade routes to the coast and keep Harar from being taken over by a European power, but he was also conscious of the immense political and emotional significance of incorporating the city which had so long been a menace to the Christian highlands into the empire. He moved confidently and systematically, fighting a final battle against Harari forces at Chelenqo on 6 January 1887. He turned Hararge, which included vast stretches of the Ogaden whose borders were still undefined, over to his cousin, Dejazmach Makonnen Wolde Mikael, who was soon promoted to *ras*. Large numbers of highland Christians came to Harar to settle as the new ruling class. The new arrivals developed a strong sense of attachment to their new home. There was no resistance from the native Adare population, for they benefitted from the commercial expansion stable Ethiopian rule brought.

In between campaigns, Menelik found time to become more active in relations with Europeans. In April 1879 he engaged a young Swiss engineer, Alfred Ilg, as adviser. Ilg remained with Menelik for the next twenty-nine years. In the early 1880s Menelik welcomed French and Italian offers to expand trade through the Red Sea ports they had acquired. Menelik wanted dependable sources of arms and ammunition, for in this respect he was still inferior to Yohannes. Two years of negotiations led to the signing of a treaty with the Italian

[13] Situations varied from region to region, as demonstrated by a series of excellent studies by Donald Donham and Wendy James (eds), *The Southern Marches of Imperial Ethiopia*, Cambridge University Press, 1986.

explorer Antonelli at Ankober in 1883. It provided for regular relations with Italy and trade concessions through Assab. Under Egyptian rule, Harar's trade had already expanded and the city became a major transit point for products of the Ethiopian south, above all slaves, who were transported to the French Red Sea port of Obock, mostly destined for Arab countries.[14] The trade was highly profitable. Menelik was always in need of money, so he encouraged all aspects of trade, including that in slaves, though he discreetly avoided identification with it. In early 1884 a French warship brought a new French Resident to Obock, Leonce Lagarde. Lagarde and another Frenchman, Leon Chefneux, became major players in the trade and politics of the Horn of Africa during the next two decades.

It is not surprising that the political disorder of the first three-quarters of the nineteenth century delayed Ethiopian economic development. The population lived off subsistence agriculture and livestock raising. When harvests were good, the demands of contending armies could be met without impoverishing the peasantry, but subsistence agriculture seldom produced significant surpluses and the combination of heavy military demands and poor rainfall caused outbreaks of animal and human disease and regional famines. All the way back to Aksum, livestock raiding had been a way of accumulating wealth. Even in the 1880s Menelik sent large expeditions into Arsi to raid Oromo herds. Though Ethiopia was widely thought to be rich in resources and Europeans were constantly enticed by prospects of trade, till the end of the century the market for imports was limited to arms and luxury goods desired by the aristocracy. Of the three major caravan routes: from the northwest through Adwa to Massawa; westward from Metemma and Gambela through Sudan; and from Shoa and areas to the north across the lowlands to Red Sea and Indian Ocean ports, the last became the most important in the 1880s. Shoan conquests in the south and southwest brought peace and greatly increased production of traditional products such as coffee, civet, ivory, honey, ostrich feathers, furs and hides.

There were many barriers to trade besides problems of transportation. Local rulers exacted tribute at numerous toll stations. In wartime thievery was common. Even with expansion of the use of the Maria Theresa dollar, barter remained widespread and salt bars remained in use as the equivalent of fractional coinage. Agreements with Europeans as navigation in the Red Sea increased after the opening of the Suez Canal encouraged action by Ethiopian rulers to facilitate trade.

The establishment of Addis Ababa as capital of Shoa in 1886 was of both political and economic significance. Traditions held that

[14] See Pankhurst, *Economic History of Ethiopia, 1800-1935,* pp. 73-134.

medieval emperors had had camps on Entoto, the mountain range
north of the city. Menelik found Entoto secure and convenient as a
base for campaigning in the south and west and visited ruins north of
Entoto in 1879 which were reputedly the remains of a medieval town.
A large unfinished rock church on the southern slope of Entoto,
Yekka Mikael, provided proof that Christians had been settled in the
area before Gragn's invasion and the Oromo migrations. In 1883
Taitu started construction of a church dedicated to the Virgin Mary
on Entoto. The next year Menelik endowed a second Entoto church
dedicated to the Angel Raguel. The 2 km. of terrain between the two
churches became, in effect, the capital by the mid-1880s, but the site
at 10,000 feet was cold and difficult to supply with water, food and
fuel. The hot springs at Filwoha in the valley south of the mountain
attracted the imperial party in the rainy season and Taytu had a house
built near them in 1886. This came to be regarded as the founding of
the city of Addis Ababa, the New Flower.[15] In 1887 Menelik allocated
land to all his *rases* and officials and began construction in earnest.
The process accelerated after Menelik became emperor in 1889,
though a fire destroyed his own palace in 1892 and it had to be rebuilt. After the Battle of Adwa the capital attracted foreign legations
and both commercial and private building steadily increased. The
introduction of the blue gum eucalyptus into Ethiopia at this time
eventually solved the fuel problem. By the mid-twentieth century
the eucalyptus had turned Addis Ababa into a city that appeared to
rise out of a forest against the background of the Entoto range, also
covered with eucalyptus.

The challenge of Italy

Italy became a unified state only in 1871. As heirs of the Roman
Empire, Italians were eager to take their place as equals among other
European powers. Since the Middle Ages Italian traders, missionaries, craftsmen and artists had been travelling to Ethiopia and living
there for long periods. Like other European countries, Italy had many
men interested in exploring remote regions. The Horn of Africa
attracted the members of the newly organized Italian Geographical
Society. The region also attracted Italians eager to acquire colonies,
which were believed to be a prerequisite for attaining the status of a
modern nation.

[15]Menelik's chronicler Guebre Selassie describes the founding of the city in
de tail. Pankhurst's *Economic History of Ethiopia 1800-1935*, pp. 694-717, contains
a good summary. Mengistu Haile Mariam who, as his rule degenerated into disarray, became increasingly eager to place himself in the mainstream of Ethiopian
history, enthusiastically supported celebrations of the 100th anniversary in
1986. The proceedings of an international symposium held in November 1986

Britain was sympathetic to newly unified Italy. Britain had acquired Aden in 1838 and developed it into a key naval station on the route to India. The Somali coast opposite Aden was judged necessary for its defense and as a source of supplies, so Britain proclaimed a protectorate over it in 1884 without defining the interior limits of the protected area. But the rapid withdrawal of the Napier expedition in 1868 revealed a reluctance to acquire territory along the Red Sea. British activists who advocated a permanent presence in the region did not gain support in London. Britain's intervention in Egypt and subsequent involvement in Sudan reinforced conservative attitudes toward the Ethiopian region. In the 1880s leaders in London and Cairo were agreed on priorities: first, a strong position in Egypt, second, unhindered navigation in the Red Sea, and third, stability in the Ethiopian region. This led Britain to favour Italian presence in the area.

On the other hand, few British officials sympathized with the more far-reaching aspirations of Italian empire-builders. The Foreign Office feared that Italian aggressiveness could drive Yohannes IV into an anti-Egyptian and anti-European alliance with the Mahdi which would threaten Egypt's own stability. Egypt's position in Sudan deteriorated steadily in 1883. A British-led force was wiped out by Mahdists in Kordofan in November. As a consequence, Britain persuaded the Egyptians to abandon Sudan entirely. General Charles Gordon was sent to Khartoum to take charge of the withdrawal.[16] The British emissary Wylde arrived in Massawa at the end of 1883 and found the city in panic. He worked out arrangements with Ras Alula for resumption of caravan trade from the highlands. One of the Americans in Egyptian service, Mason Bey, was made governor of Massawa in early 1884. Planning for a British mission to mediate a settlement between Yohannes and Egypt proceeded over the objections of Gordon.

Vice-Admiral William Hewett, Governor of Suakin in charge of Red Sea operations, was chosen to head the mission. He brought a gift of rifles and guns to Adwa. He worked out a draft agreement with Ras Alula which Yohannes accepted on 3 June 1884. Ethiopia gained free transit through Massawa of all goods, including arms and ammunition. Yohannes agreed to facilitate withdrawal through his territory

---

published by the city council in 1987 contain informative essays by Ethiopian and foreign scholars.

[16] The situation in Sudan soon deteriorated further. Gordon was killed when the Mahdists captured Khartoum in 1885. Though the Mahdi himself died soon after, his successor, the Khalifa Abdullahi, continued to expand the movement. The rebellion was not put down until 1899, by which time the correlation of forces in the region had changed radically.

of Egyptian garrisons in eastern Sudan. Bogos was recognized as
Ethiopian and reoccupied in September 1884. It took a year of major
military operations by Yohannes and Ras Alula, however, for Ethiopian forces to accomplish the rescue of besieged Egyptian garrisons
along the frontier. They met bitter Mahdist resistance, completing
the process only when Alula defeated Mahdist forces at the Battle of
Kufit on 23 September 1885.

Ethiopian elation at success with the Hewett mission was short-
lived. Yohannes and Alula had briefly hoped that free trade through
Massawa would eventually lead to restoration of Ethiopian control.
In mid-February 1885 the Italian flag was raised alongside the
Egyptian banner at the port, and Italian Admiral Caimi proclaimed
an Italo-Egyptian condominium.[17] Britain had secretly acquiesced
in the Italian move. During the next few months, the Italians took
over the administration of the area as Britain withdrew the Egyptian
forces. Then the Italians started to push inland. Italy had been
encouraged by the General Act of Berlin, signed on 26 February
1885 which, in effect, provided for cooperative division by the
powers of Europe of the "coasts of the African continent" though,
from a strictly legal viewpoint, the entire coast was still under Ottoman suzerainty.

Yohannes was distracted by a revolt in Wollo in November 1885
which Menelik helped him put down. The task took until February
1886, when Yohannes appointed Ras Mikael governor of Wollo in
place of his son Araya, whom he transferred to Begemder. Returning
to Tigray in March, the emperor received a British emissary and sent
a message to Queen Victoria on 19 April 1886:

As for our friendship with the Italians, until now we had no enmity, but they
have taken my land when I did not take theirs, so I should like to know how
to make friends with them. I pray your Majesty will advise me when I receive
your reply and I will tell you what I can do.[18]

Yohannes still desired to work out a *modus vivendi* with the Italians,
just as Menelik did when he signed the Treaty of Wichale two years
later. Both underestimated Italian zeal for an empire. Alula was more
skeptical of Italian intentions than Yohannes and tension rose
between the two. While Yohannes was in Wollo, a Mahdist force
seized Dembea in January, advanced as far as Chilga, and burnt the
monastery of Mahbere Selassie. Negus Tekla Haymanot organized a
large army, and undertook a successful counteroffensive against

---

[17] Sensing an opportunity, France entered into negotiations with Ras Alula who
was willing to consider turning over Zula in return for a quantity of arms. But
when presented with a treaty confirming this arrangement, Yohannes rejected it.
[18] As cited in Zewde, *Yohannes IV*, p. 201.

Metemma[19] in January 1887. Meanwhile the Italians continued to probe southward along the coast as well as inland and clashes with Ras Alula's soldiers became increasingly frequent. Finally on 25 January 1887 Alula led an attack on the fort the Italians had established at Sahati and was repulsed. Far from feeling defeated, on the following day at Wadi Dogali, Alula ambushed an Italian battalion on its way to reinforce Sahati and practically wiped it out. Haggai Erlich, Alula's biographer, concludes:

The Battle of Dogali was undoubtedly one of the most important events in the history of Ethiopia in the late 19th century. The open enmity it created between the emperor and the Italians assisted the rise of Shoa's hegemony...[20]

Yohannes was in Makelle at the time of the battle. When Alula requested his permission to continue to the coast and eject the Italians from Massawa, he is reported to have received a message chiding him: "Who gave you permission to go and make a war there? Those soldiers are not yours but mine; I shall cut off your hand."[21]

Alula contained his disappointment, stayed in contact with the Italians about release of hostages, and was summoned to Makelle in late March where Yohannes promised reinforcements in case the Italians attacked but forbade offensive operations. Dogali damaged Italy's prestige in Europe and brought calls for revenge in Italy itself, which alarmed the emperor, even though Italian forces had been pulled back to the coast. A well-armed punitive expedition was organized in Italy in the summer of 1887 and sent to Massawa. Alula worsened his situation by trying to enforce a total blockade against trade through Massawa and thereby angered the Muslim traders of the whole region who began to sympathize with Italy. He also took measures against French and Italian Catholic missionaries and native Catholics in Serae and Akele Guzay whom he feared were pro-Italian.

Britain, fearing a full-scale war, sent a young diplomat, Gerald Portal, consul in Cairo, to try to persuade Yohannes to apologize to

[19] Called Qallabat by the Sudanese and referred to by both names in records of the period.

[20] Erlich, *Ras Alula*, p. 106. Mengistu Haile Mariam chose the 100th anniversary of the Battle of Dogali as an occasion for reaffirming Ethiopia's age-old sovereignty over Eritrea, with commemorative events in both Addis Ababa and at Dogali in January 1987, where a monument topped by a red star was erected. Proceedings of a gathering of scholars in Addis Ababa were subsequently published as *The Centenary of Dogali*, IES, Addis Ababa, 1988. Mengistu's increasingly violent efforts to bring Eritrea to heel by military force so alienated the Eritrean population that it gave full support to the EPLF's demand for separation from Ethiopia. When I crossed the battlefield in 1996, I could detect no trace of the monument.

[21] As cited in Erlich, *Ras Alula*, p. 110.

Italy for "the unjust attack" at Dogali and get him to remove Alula as governor of the Mareb Mellash. Portal's meeting with Alula at Asmara on 11 November 1887 confirmed his conviction that the Ras was committed to war with Italy. When he finally reached Yohannes's camp at Lake Ashangi on 7 December 1887, he found Yohannes as firm as Alula. He told Portal: "I did not give them Massowah; England gave it to the Italians, but I will not give them an inch of land. If they cannot live there without Sahati, let them go." Portal went on to try to persuade Yohannes to assign Alula elsewhere, with equal lack of success: "Ras Alula did no wrong; the Italians came into the province under his governorship and he fought them, just as you would fight the Abyssinians if they came into England."[22]

Thus in the end the emperor had accepted Alula's view of the Italians, but the outlook was ominous. While Portal was in Tigray a 20,000-strong Italian expeditionary force landed in Massawa. By early January 1888 two brigades had moved up to Dogali. Yohannes n obi lized the country for war. He was not entirely sure of Menelik's loyalty, but kept him informed of Italian actions and ordered Menelik to guard Wollo and Begemder while Ras Mikael brought 25,000 Oromo cavalry to Tigray and other *rases* mobilized their troops. Alarming news came a few days later: the Mahdists had had their revenge against Negus Tekle Haymanot. They defeated his army at Sar Weha in Dembea and moved on to sack Gondar. Yohannes was faced with war on two difficult fronts as well as the prospect of domestic defections. While Alula made futile preparations to meet the new Italian advance, Yohannes abandoned the fight against the Italians at the end of March. Alula withdrew his troops from the lowlands to Asmara in early April. On 23 April 1888 Alula slipped out of Asmara, leaving it undefended, but the Italians did not immediately move up. Alula withdrew to Adwa.[23]

---

[22] As cited in Erlich, *Ras Alula*, p. 116. Portal's mission was a failure; he published a colorful account of it 1892, when he had become consul-general in Zanzibar: *My Mission to Abyssinia*, London, 1892, reprinted by Negro Universities Press, New York, 1969.

[23] A curious episode during this period was the Russian attempt to establish a "New Moscow" at the coastal town of Sagallo on the Bay of Tajura. It was the work of a Cossack adventurer, N.I. Ashinov, who had gained the support of the Russian Orthodox Church. The Tsar's government had only a lukewarm commitment to the venture. The French had already established a protectorate over the area and removed the 175 Russian settlers in February 1889 shortly after they arrived. Russia had been a minor participant in exploration in the Horn since mid-century. It established a more significant presence during Menelik's early years as emperor. See "Russians in the Horn" in Paul B. Henze, *The Horn of Africa from War to Peace*, Macmillan, London, 1991, pp. 65-89.

Meanwhile Menelik, who had been too late to prevent the sacking of Gondar, joined Tekle Haymanot in an agreement to cooperate against the weakened Yohannes. The increasingly beset emperor experienced a further blow of fate in June 1888 when his son and heir, Ras Araya Selassie, who had been gathering a large army for Begemder, died of smallpox in Makelle. To punish Menelik and Tekle Haymanot, Yohannes crossed the Blue Nile into Gojjam in early August and was joined the next month by Ras Alula leading a Tigrayan army. "The angry Tigrayans led by a frustrated emperor"[24] devastated Damot, fueling Amhara resentment. While this was going on, chiefs in Tigray, feeling abandoned, made contact with both the Italians and the British in Aden and took matters into their own hands. Dejazmach Dabbab Araya, governor of Akele Guzay, took over Alula's capital, Asmara, on 9 February. Three days earlier an Italian expeditionary force had entered Keren. Italy was poised to take the entire Mareb Mellash when the time became ripe.

The end of Yohannes IV

Historical memory is long in the Horn of Africa: "Warfare against the Abyssinians aroused some repugnance among Sudanese Muslims because a tradition ascribed to the Prophet excepted them from the *jihad* on account of the asylum granted by the Negus to the Prophet's companions."[25] The Mahdists had not originally seen the Ethiopians as their prime enemies, but they felt themselves released from the Prophet's injunction when Yohannes persisted in fighting them to liberate the Egyptian garrisons they had besieged. Yohannes had remained faithful to the commitments he made to Britain in the Hewett treaty in 1883 to facilitate removal of the Egyptian garrisons in the Ethio-Sudanese border regions. The emperor's personal antipathy to Islam and desire to see the Mahdist rebellion contained must also have carried weight in his decision to give priority to the war against the Mahdists over defense against Italian encroachment.

Though Ethiopia was on the verge of a disastrous civil war after Yohannes and Alula ravaged Gojjam and threatened to proceed to Shoa to do the same, Yohannes fortunately had second thoughts. Menelik had aroused the Shoan population to resist and appealed to Italy for support. Italy sent him arms. Yohannes was reluctant to challenge Menelik and instead concentrated on preparing an offensive against Metemma. Alula was reportedly less than enthusiastic

[24] Erlich, *Ras Alula*, p. 130.

[25] P.M. Holt, *The Mahdist State of the Sudan, 1881-1898,* Oxford University Press, 1970, p. 150.

about the undertaking, or at least the tactics to be employed, but he joined the operation along with Yohannes's second son, Ras Mengesha, and his nephew Ras Haile Mariam Gugsa, son of his elder brother. An imperial army estimated at 100,000 reached Metemma at the end of February 1889.

The battle began on 9 March 1889 against 60-70,000 Mahdists in well entrenched positions. The fighting initially went well for the Ethiopians. The right wing under Mengesha was successful in pushing the Mahdists back, though Alula suffered minor wounds. On the left wing Haile Mariam was killed and confusion ensued. Yohannes moved up to bolster Mengesha. He took three bullet hits and had to be carried to his tent in the rear. Seeing their leader badly wounded, Ethiopian troops broke and ran and the Mahdists regrouped. That evening the mortally wounded Yohannes declared Mengesha his successor and enjoined Alula to look out for him. He died the next morning. Three days later his corpse was captured in a battle on the Atbara river by a pursuing Mahdist detachment and several nobles and priests accompanying it were killed. The emperor's head was severed and sent to Omdurman.

Deserted by their troops, Mengesha and Alula retreated northward to Semien and then to Tembien, which they reached in early April. Tigray was in disarray. Famine had broken out the previous year; human and livestock diseases were spreading. Chiefs were fighting among themselves. While some resisted pressure from the Italians, others sought to make their peace with them. Though Alula urged Mengesha to proclaim himself emperor, he refused, realizing that unless he could gain unequivocal support as ruler of all Tigray he could not make a serious bid for the throne. No one in Tigray offered serious opposition to Menelik's claim to be the logical successor to Yohannes.

Emperor Menelik II and the Powers

Given the importance of the Treaty of Wichale in the first years of the reign of Menelik II, it will be useful to describe the main points of Menelik's relations with Italy as King of Shoa.

When he became emperor, Menelik's contacts with Italy had a history of almost a decade and a half. An expedition of the Italian Geographical Society to Shoa in 1876 headed by Marquis Orazio Antinori opened the first stage. The mission did have serious scientific purposes, but it was impossible in nineteenth-century Africa to separate exploration from colonial expansion. Menelik needed arms. He granted the Italian explorers a research station at Let Marefia near Ankober in return for a promise of weapons.

In 1879 Pietro Antonelli arrived in Shoa as an explorer, travelled extensively, and was joined by Antinori in 1880 in proposing the opening of a trade route through Assab. In March 1881 Antonelli signed a contract with Menelik to deliver 2,000 rifles and left for Italy. There he found Foreign Ministry support. He came back empowered to negotiate a treaty of friendship and commerce with Menelik.[26] It was signed in Ankober on 21 May 1883, granted concessions to the Italians for ten years, and specified favorable trade conditions. For the next six years Antonelli served as Italy's official representative in Shoa and cultivated Shoan nobles.

News of the Italian occupation of Massawa in 1885 alarmed Menelik but Antonelli assuaged his fears by offering an agreement that promised no annexation of Ethiopian territory and delivery of 5,000 rifles within six months. It was signed on 20 October 1887. Menelik, however, resisted being drawn directly into the Italian struggle with Yohannes and Alula. But he never lost suspicion of Italian motives. He delayed accepting a draft treaty Antonelli proposed in September 1888.

Menelik received word of Yohannes's death on 25 March 1889.

Knowing little of the actual situation in Tigray, and fearing that the Italians might encourage a challenger to him, he decided to accept Antonelli's treaty because it referred to him as heir to the Ethiopian throne. The treaty was signed at a ceremony at Menelik's camp at Wichale in northern Wollo on 2 May 1889. Neither party seems to have realized at the time that it would become a major bone of contention, though Antonelli could hardly have failed to know that there were differences between the Italian and Amharic versions of Article XVII. The Amharic text gave Menelik *the option* of using Italy's good offices for contacts with other countries. The Italian version *obligated* Menelik to make all such contacts *through* Italy, thus making Ethiopia an Italian protectorate.[27]

Italy had officially occupied Keren on 2 June 1889 and Asmara on 10 August, as permitted by the Wichale treaty. In late August 1889 Antonelli took an Ethiopian mission headed by Dejazmach Makonnen to Rome to receive the ratification of the treaty and buy arms. Italian Prime Minister Crispi took advantage of the opportunity to extend Italy's gains by another duplicitous move. He arranged to have a

[26] On the way back to Shoa he negotiated a treaty with the Sultan of Aussa to facilitate trade from Assab through Afar territory, eliminating Tajura and Zeila.

[27] A palace clerk, Atme, who later became an important chronicler of the period, was apparently the first to notice the disparity between the Amharic and Italian versions of Article XVII of the treaty Menelik had signed at Wichale. When it was first called to his attention, Menelik, confident of his own position, dismissed it as a mere translation problem. He soon realized better.

supplementary convention signed on 1 October 1889 which provided that the boundaries of Italy's territory would be demarcated in accordance with "effective possession". The Amharic version had used the simple term *zare* – meaning that the boundaries would be those applicable "as of today". On Makonnen's return to Ethiopia, when it was found that the Italians were using the "effective possession" clause to justify title to further territories they were occupying, Menelik became alarmed. The Italians refused to alter the phrase and persisted in taking over most of Hamasien and Akele Guzay and all of Serae. After the Rome meeting Crispi had notified the European powers that Menelik had agreed "to avail himself of the [Italian Government] for all negotiations of affairs which he might have with other powers or governments", without citing Article XVII. This, too, was deceptive, and it led to three years of diplomatic debate and argument among the European powers and between Italy and Ethiopia, culminating in Menelik's abrogation of the entire Treaty of Wichale in February 1893 when he declared:

It is with much dishonesty that [the King of Italy], pretending friendship, has desired to seize my country. Because God gave the crown and the power that I should protect the land of my forefathers, I terminate and nullify this treaty. I have not, however, nullified my friendship. Know that I desire no other treaty than this. My kingdom is an independent kingdom and I seek no one's protection.[28]

On 3 November 1889 Patriarch Matewos crowned Menelik emperor at the Church of Entoto Mariam and two days later Taitu was crowned empress. The new city of Addis Ababa had become the capital of the country. The feasts held for these occasions were kept modest because of famine that was most severe in the north but also affected many other parts of the country. The peasantry suffered most severely, for they lost most of their livestock, including plow oxen. Grain and meat prices rose. Rudimentary government machinery was unable to do much to alleviate the situation. Menelik and Taitu urged the population to pray and, when little improvement occurred, admonished people for not praying hard enough, but they brought in oxen from the south and sent them to Tigray. The famine and epidemics finally eased in 1892 but their effects were felt for years afterward.

To demonstrate that he had not accepted the Italian version of Article XVII of the Treaty of Wichale, Menelik sent letters directly to European heads of state informing them of his accession. In December he sent them a circular letter complaining about the ban on arms to Africa the European powers had agreed upon.

---

[28] As cited in Rubenson, *Survival,* p. 394.

On 1 January 1890 Italy proclaimed Colonia Eritrea, its Red Sea Colony, incorporating all the territories it had occupied in northern Ethiopia as well as the coast from north of Massawa down to French-controlled territory around the Gulf of Tajura. During the next three years Tigray remained in an unsettled state and an area of continual contest between the Italians, the Tigrayan princes, and Menelik.

European powers watched closely the development of Menelik's relations with Italy and sought advantages for themselves. French Resident Lagarde abandoned Obock for Djibouti in 1892. Lagarde wanted good relations with Ethiopia and made two visits to Menelik with the approval of Paris. France saw itself as a competitor to Italy in the Horn of Africa and, like Britain, also felt a need to defend its sea route into the Indian Ocean. Menelik proposed construction of a railway from Djibouti to Addis Ababa. A French company was formed in 1896 and construction started the next year. Djibouti grew rapidly and had 10,000 inhabitants by the end of the century. Its hinterland was sparsely populated by nomadic Afars, but it attracted people from Ethiopia and Somaliland. France signed a treaty guaranteeing Ethiopia a trade outlet through Djibouti. The newly founded city profited not only from legal trade, but from smuggling of arms and ammunition. Tajura continued to export slaves originating in south-western Ethiopia for sale in Arabian and Persian markets, but the town soon declined, as did the slave trade. The Indian Ocean coast of Africa from Cape Guardafui southward was unclaimed by Europeans until Italy began negotiations in 1885 with local rulers all the way to Zanzibar whose sultan had exercised loose sovereignty over Brava, Merca and Mogadishu. In 1889 Italy gained British concurrence to declare a protectorate over the entire Somali coast north of Kismayu and set up a chartered company to administer her new colony from Mogadishu. Interior boundaries remained undefined.

The major European powers wavered in the controversies of the early 1890s over the nature of Italy's relationship to Ethiopia, but two on the periphery were entirely consistent. Turkey refused to acknowledge Italian communications relating to Ethiopia at all, insisting that its own sovereignty over the Red Sea coastal region had been violated – though it was, of course, powerless to do anything about it. Early the next century it would be compelled to cede some of its possessions in the Mediterranean to expansionist Italy.

Russia consistently refused to attribute any validity to Italian aspirations in Ethiopia. A Russian officer who had served in Central Asia, V.F. Mashkov, led a delegation to Ethiopia in October 1889 which was warmly received by Menelik as "military representatives of my brother, the Negus of Muscovy." Discussions on arms followed. Mashkov returned to Russia and was decorated by the Tsar. He came back to

Ethiopia early in 1891 under the sponsorship of the Imperial Russian Geographical Society. His party included an Orthodox priest. The reason was no doubt political, but the fact that both countries were Orthodox encouraged favorable attitudes on both sides. Mashkov brought a gift of rifles and stayed until mid-1892, surveying commercial prospects, accepting requests for more military assistance, and meeting with the Patriarch. French officials in Ethiopia provided assistance. The foreign ministry in St. Petersburg tried to assuage Italian worries by insisting that Russia had no political aims. In contrast to Ashinov's earlier misadventure, Mashkov's missions marked the beginning of a coherent Russian approach to Menelik.

Mashkov brought back a message from Menelik to the Tsar asking for diplomatic support to counter Italian intrigues in Tigray. Menelik told the Tsar he would punish the Italians "in the same way as their brothers [were punished] at Dogali". At the same time Ras Makonnen wrote to the Russian Minister of War:

We have not found among the Europeans who have become our neighbors any who desire our welfare and independence but those who want to deprive us of them. The West Europeans in their desire for new land have encircled us; in groups they have crossed our borders to deprive us of our independence, and are causing us trouble.[...] Now we have heard and understand that there is no Orthodox kingdom except Moscow.[29]

Mashkov was followed by another Russian officer, A.V. Eliseev, who had first gone to Sudan in 1893 disguised as an Arab to assess the Mahdists' chances, which he judged not good. He led a new "scientific" expedition to Ethiopia in early 1895 and brought another batch of weapons. Ras Makonnen welcomed him in Harar and explained that Menelik desired rapid expansion of relations and wanted to send an Ethiopian mission to Russia. Eliseev returned immediately and had no difficulty persuading Tsar Nicholas II to welcome an Ethiopian mission. Menelik sent several trusted associates and an Orthodox priest. Captain Leontiev and Father Efrem, who had come with Eliseev, escorted the Ethiopians to St. Petersburg. In the process Leontiev became a "colonel" and "brother to the Tsar" and Father Efrem became a "bishop".[30] The party landed in Odessa and made

[29] As cited in Rubenson, *Survival,* p. 396.

[30] "Leontiev ... was a 34-year-old lieutenant in a reserve regiment ... [He] had been expelled from his regiment for not honoring his gambling losses. He was well known as a scrounger and a cheat who had pawned his sister's patrimony to pay some of his debts. On the basis of his travels to India and Persia he had managed to insinuate himself into the Moscow Geographical Society, even though during those travels he had indulged in more shady dealings." Prouty, *Menelik and Taytu,* p. 121. An astonishingly bold and irrepressible confidence man, Leontiev was involved in a colorful series of episodes connected with Ethiopia for the remainder of the century, many of which Prouty describes subsequently in her book.

triumphal progress through Kharkov and Moscow to the capital. They were treated like royalty, taken to arms factories and military maneuvers, feasted and lionized by the press, and presented to high officials including Tsar Nicholas who, with his new wife Alexandra, kissed the gold cross presented by the Ethiopian "bishop". The Russians assured the Ethiopians that they would never recognize an Italian protectorate over Ethiopia. The mission returned by way of Constan-tinople and Jerusalem to Djibouti, where Ras Makonnen met them. The Russians appear to have sent no further large quantities of arms to Menelik, but the success of this mission must have contributed to Menelik's resolve to bring the conflict with Italy to a head.

After Menelik abrogated the Treaty of Wichale, the Italians sent an emissary, Traversi, with two million cartridges which Menelik bought and paid for, but Traversi had no success in persuading Menelik to reverse his decision. In fact he became increasingly angered by reports of Italian subversion of Tigrayan chiefs. This problem was largely brought under control the next year. Following Negus Tekle Haymanot, who had come to Addis Ababa to declare his loyalty to Menelik in February, Ras Mengesha arrived in the capital with a retinue of 6,000 at the beginning of June 1894 to receive pardon for his independent dealings with the Italians in 1891-2. He was accompanied by Rases Alula, Hagos, and Wolde Mikael, the other three senior Tigrayan leaders of the time. They marched to Menelik's new palace preceded by priests carrying a *tabot* from Aksum. Menelik received them wearing a crown. Each of the four *rases* carried a rock on his shoulder. They prostrated themselves, Menelik forgave them, salutes were fired, and the priests brought their cross for all to kiss.

No wonder the Italians had no success when another mission arrived two weeks later. Crispi had appointed Antonelli Undersecretary of State for Colonies in the Foreign Ministry. He did not want to see almost two decades of hard work lost. While both sides readied their forces, the Italians tried to persuade Menelik to cede the entire province of Tigray as a price for avoiding confrontation. Tough-minded Taitu supported every move Menelik made to prepare for confrontation with the Italians.

While they continued to try to foment dissension in Tigray, the Italians had their own difficulties in Eritrea. Eritrea had also been affected by cattle disease, locusts, drought and famine. For many Eritreans, expropriations of land to make way for Italian colonists was the last straw. These actions led an originally pro-Italian chief, Dejazmach Bahta Hagos of Akele Guzay, to lead a revolt in 1894. He claimed to be supported by Ras Mengesha. Bahta was killed on

17 December by a force led by Major Toselli. Mengesha seems to have had little to do with Bahta's rebellion, for he was in the Inticho area at the time, but General Baratieri, fearing Tigrayan attack, ordered Mengesha to disperse his forces. Baratieri crossed the Mareb on 28 December and marched to Adwa, chased Mengesha into Tembien, and then withdrew back into Eritrea. Mengesha moved into Eritrea himself, as far as Coatit, but was badly defeated at Senafe in early 1895. All this was a foretaste of the sparring that intensified during the following year and led to the confrontation at Adwa.

Famine and the resultant economic decline in the north had drawn attention to the resources of the rich, newly conquered south and the desirability of extending imperial control over parts of it that had resisted conquest. Though preoccupied with the Italian challenge in the north, Menelik took time out for a campaign in Wolayta in late 1894. Accompanied by several of his most loyal generals, and supported by Abba Jifar II of Jimma, he mounted a brutal assault against King Tona's army, finally wounded the king and brought him as prisoner to Addis Ababa early in 1895. Most of the southwest was now in Ethiopian hands.

There was a good deal of European diplomatic maneuvering as a prelude to the confrontation at Adwa early the next year, but with the possible exception of his involvement with the Russians, it had little effect on Menelik's decisions and none on the outcome of the battle. Menelik issued a mobilization proclamation, in effect a declaration of war, on 17 September 1895:

Assemble the army, beat the drum. God in his bounty has struck down my enemies and enlarged my empire and preserved me to this day. [...] Enemies have come who would ruin our country and change our religion. They have passed beyond the sea that God gave us for our frontier. I, aware that herds were decimated and people were exhausted, did not wish to do anything [about it] until now. These enemies have advanced, burrowing into the country like moles. With God's help I will get rid of them. [...] You who are strong, give me your strength, and you who are weak, help me by prayer. If you refuse to follow me, look out! . [...]I shall not fail to punish you. [...] Men of Shoa, await me at Worailu and may you be there by the middle of Teqemt [end of October].[31]

The emperor and empress and their armies began the great trek northward in the second week of October 1895. Other contingents moved northward at the same time. By mid-November up to 100,000 men had gathered at Worailu and were ready to move on to Tigray.

---

[31] As cited from Prouty, *Taytu and Menelik,* pp. 133-4; see also Rubenson, *Survival,* p. 401.

The prelude and the Battle of Adwa

After he was defeated at Senafe by Baratieri at the beginning of 1895, Ras Mengesha collected troops in the Hawzien area for an attack on Adigrat, but Baratieri preempted him by occupying Adigrat at the end of March. Baratieri moved on to Adwa on 2 April, but budgetary stringency in Rome forced him to evacuate Adwa soon after. He went to Rome and secured more money, returned to Adigrat on 3 October, and pushed Mengesha back again. He issued a proclamation annexing Tigray to Eritrea, moved on to Makelle and started fortifying the old church of Enda Yesus on a spur above the town. Meanwhile leaders in every region were responding to Menelik's call to arms. Ethiopians had never been more single-minded. The Italians were utterly wrong in their assessment of the situation they faced:

Menelik is weak, uncertain, and in the hands of his wife. Everyone is sick of his long rule and awaits with resignation the arrival from Jerusalem of a European who will bring peace to the country. To the ignorant Ethiopians all Europeans come from Jerusalem. Public opinion is prepared for the downfall of Menelik. At the first blow the empire will fall to pieces.[32]

Two major engagements preceded the Battle of Adwa. Both were clear Ethiopian victories and cost the Italians heavy losses, but they drew no lessons from them. Before the final confrontation began, Menelik gave the Italians two final opportunities to reconsider. At the end of October 1895 he sent Ras Makonnen to Zeila to relay an offer of peace talks. The offer was not taken seriously. By the end of November the Ras had brought his largely Oromo army up to the formidable position of Amba Alagi in southern Tigray. There he confronted Major Toselli with 2,000 Italians augmented by Eritreans and contingents of Tigrayan chiefs who for various reasons had joined Italy, perhaps 5,000 troops in all. He sent the same offer to Baratieri through Toselli's telegraph line. While Baratieri requested instructions from Rome, Toselli haughtily told Makonnen to withdraw his troops to Lake Ashangi. Eventually Baratieri advised Toselli to arrange a meeting, but it was too late.

Makonnen had been joined by Ras Mengesha Yohannes and Ras Wole Betul, Taytu's brother, and their armies. His forces totalled about 30,000 men. On the morning of 7 December an Ethiopian reconnaissance party clashed with an Italian lookout post. In no time a major battle was under way. In six hours Toselli lost more than 2,000 men and was himself killed. General Arimondi who arrived at just that point to reinforce Toselli was barely able to extract himself from the melee and retreated with 400 survivors to Makelle. In a single day Italy had lost almost a quarter of the military strength of its Eritrean

[32] As cited by Prouty, *Taytu and Menelik*, p. 119.

colony. Since the fort at Makelle was not yet complete, Arimondi left the wounded with the garrison and retreated all the way up to the pass at Edaga Hamus, south of Adigrat. Though they, too, had sustained heavy losses, the victory at Amba Alagi boosted Ethiopian confidence.

In early December Menelik told the French journalist, Mondon-Vidailhet:

I find ... that the Italians are impossible to deal with. Power is with God. But from now on, no one will try to appease the Italians. I have endured all this until now so that the European powers would know how I have been attacked and not believe me to be the evildoer. This war does not worry me.[...] As for [the Italians], all the people of Europe who see how worried they are will laugh at them.[33]

Italy sought British approval to mount a flank attack on Harar through Zeila, but Britain refused. Menelik knew he had the sympathy of the Russians, but French sympathy had more impact. Two French officers accompanied his army and France continued to let arms flow into Ethiopia through Djibouti.

While Ras Makonnen moved his forces up to Makelle, Menelik and Taytu led their huge army (followed by perhaps 25,000 women and servants)[34] up the escarpment at Alamata and across the plateau to Lake Ashangi, arriving on 19 December. Negus Tekle Haymanot brought 5,000 Gojjamis into the imperial camp on 24 December. Armies from Quara, Begemder and Dembea were also converging on Lake Ashangi and those from Semien were on their way to Makelle. The imperial army moved north and was joined to Ras Makonnen's at Makelle on 6 January.

While Italian journalists filed sensational reports about the "45-day siege of Makelle" where their brave countrymen were holding out against "war-crazed black barbarians",[35] Makonnen established contact with the Italian commander and gave him the opportunity to retreat peacefully to Adigrat. He refused to consider the offer without permission from Baratieri. The Ethiopians cut off the fort's water supply. The fifteen-day siege came to an end on 21 January when the Italians surrendered and the Ethiopian flag was raised over Enda Yesus. To the objections of many of his Tigrayan chiefs, Menelik let the survivors leave with their arms and go back to Adigrat. He hoped the Italians could be persuaded to abandon the campaign entirely,

---

[33] As cited by Rubenson, *Survival*, p. 402.

[34] Women still served as the logistics service of an Ethiopian army, carrying supplies, preparing food and drink, tending sick and wounded, repairing clothing, and helping men manage pack animals.

[35] Prouty, *op.cit. Taytu and Menelik*, p. 144.

but Baratieri refused to recognize the weakness of his position or the strength of the forces Menelik had brought up against him.

Menelik's concentration on arms in previous years now served him well. Most of his troops were equipped with rifles and had adequate ammunition, as well as artillery and machineguns. The Italians estimated that they were faced with over 50,000 well-armed men plus a number of traditionally armed warriors. Baratieri had abut 9,000 Italians, including officers, and 11,000 Eritreans. Both armies, however, had a logistics problem, for local resources were scarce. Menelik's terms for peace talks were Italian withdrawal to the frontier defined by the Treaty of Wichale. Crispi ordered Baratieri to hold out for most of Tigray. Crispi secretly reappointed General Antonio Baldissera Eritrean governor but Baratieri was not to be told of his removal until Baldissera arrived. He left Italy on 23 February and was on his way to Adwa when the battle was fought.

Menelik decided against attacking the Italians at Adigrat and marched west to the plateau east of Adwa. The landscape, studded with extinct volcanos, many of them with picturesque churches, is one of the most dramatic in Ethiopia. No better stage could have been chosen for a major battle. Menelik's move drew the already overextended Italians much deeper into Tigray, for Baratieri feared Menelik intended to invade Eritrea from Adwa and followed him, fortifying a series of new positions to the east of the area where the Ethiopians were deployed. In addition to his 20,000 well-armed soldiers, Baratieri had fifty-two cannons. He had no prospect of receiving reinforcements. There is no evidence that Baratieri knew that he had been relieved of command as he prepared to enter battle. He called a meeting of his four generals – Arimondi, Ellena, Dabormida, and Albertone – on 28 February, told them their provisions would run out in four days, and asked whether they wished to attack or fall back to Asmara. They were all opposed to retreat. Baratieri decided to rely on surprise, tighter discipline, and concerted action to make up for his deficiency in manpower. He issued a battle order at 9 p.m. on 29 February (it was a leap year).

Menelik had nearly 100,000 men deployed on the rolling ground between the mountains, probably three quarters of them with rifles, but he had less artillery than his opponents. His army was hungry and so were the Italians. He and Taitu had pitched their camp with Ras Makonnen at the ancient Monastery of Abba Gerima, founded by one of the Nine Syrian Saints. At 4 a.m. on 1 March the imperial couple and the principal *rases* took Holy Communion at the Church of Enda Giyorgis on a ridge above Adwa and prayed to St. George. With considerable confusion the Italians had deployed during the night and at dawn one of General Albertone's patrols drew Ethiopian fire. The battle began.

For the Italians, almost everything went wrong. A faulty map, poor reconnaissance, communications failures and misunderstood orders left Baratieri with only half his forces where he expected them to be. Some of the Ethiopian commanders had gone to Aksum during the night to attend religious services and pick up food for their men, but the Ethiopian troops were impatient for the fight and confident of their strength. Taitu organized the women to bring jugs of water to them as they beat back the Italians and Eritrean auxiliaries. Some of the Eritreans joined their Ethiopian brothers in the course of the fighting. Italian commanders lost contact with each other. Each soldier fought where he stood. It nevertheless took the troops of four Ethiopian commanders – about 25,000 men – to break the Italian center. Shortly after noon Baratieri began preparing to retreat. The retreat turned into a rout, though skirmishes continued until late afternoon. Torrential rain ended the day.

The Italians lost about 7,000 dead, 1,500 wounded, and 3,000 prisoners. The Ethiopians may have had 6,000 killed and as many as 8,000 wounded. Though the Ethiopian casualties exceeded those of the Italians in absolute numbers, Baratieri's army had been completely annihilated while Menelik's was intact as a fighting force and gained thousands of rifles and a great deal of equipment from the fleeing Italians. The Italians lost all their artillery.

The tenuous Italian telegraph lines brought news of the disaster to Italy and the world almost immediately. The *New York Herald Tribune,* starting 3 March, headlined the story: "Italian Defeat in Abyssinia, after a Desperate Struggle they are Finally Vanquished by Overwhelming Odds". During the next few days the headlines continued: "Crushing Defeat for Italian Arms. Crispi Resigns. Whole Battalions Slain. An Irreparable Disaster. Signor Crispi's Effigy Burned in Rome and other Popular Demonstrations Take Place", "Russia Pro-Abyssinian. Sympathy in St. Petersburg not on the Side of the Italian Invaders".

Baratieri was accused of abandoning his troops: "Baratieri's Offense. Said to have left the Field while his Troops were Fighting. Ten Thousand Lost". He was later tried for this offense.

Italy was shaken by political crisis and popular demonstrations. Adventurism in Africa had never been universally popular: "Determined to Resign. Italian Cabinet Takes a Final Decision - Demonstrations in the Principal Cities. Frenzy in Milan. Italy Like Pandemonium. Abyssinian Reverse Provokes a Paroxysm of Rage in Rome".

In the weeks that followed attention continued to be focussed on the aftermath of the Adwa defeat: "Menelik Applicant for the Red

Cross. Attack Begun on Kassala. Dervishes Attempt to Take the Italian Post".[36]

As a preliminary to discussion of armistice terms, Ras Makonnen invited an Italian intermediary, Major Salsa, to stand beside him on 7 March while 80,000 victorious troops marched across the battlefield' in review. Then the major was taken to Menelik and learned that the emperor would conclude peace if Italy would abandon Adigrat, publicly renounce its claim to a protectorate over Ethiopia, withdraw to the border between Tigray and Eritrea agreed on at Wichale, and permit free trade between Ethiopia and Eritrea. Baldissera, who had meanwhile arrived, accepted these terms on condition that Menelik agree not to accept protection from any other European power. At this Italian arrogance, Menelik broke off talks and withdrew his original offer.

He distributed some of the 2,000 Italian prisoners among the *rases* and sent the rest to Addis Ababa where those with skills were assigned to useful work. He also ordered the captured arms and other booty taken to the capital. Then he and the empress set out for a triumphal trip to Shoa, spending two months along the way. The country had never been as unified before, even though Eritrea remained under Italian control. Menelik and Taitu were greeted by salvos fired by prisoners manning the captured cannons when they entered the capital on 22 May 1896.[37]

Menelik's triumphal decade

The ten years following Menelik's return to the capital from Adwa were a time of ceaseless activity, a greater degree of respite from disorder and war than the country had ever known, and progress in many directions. Addis Ababa expanded rapidly. It still resembled a huge camp more than a city, consisting of great expanses of traditional thatched houses interspersed with larger buildings, and occasional churches. Provincial chiefs built compounds and their

---

[36] Cited from newspaper files of the Library of Congress.

[37] The preceding account of the prelude and Battle of Adwa has been drawn from several sources, the most complete, colorful, and well referenced of which is in Prouty's *Taytu and Menelik*, pp. 138-86. It also reflects my tours of the battlefield in 1995 and 1996 in the company of Ethiopian specialists and participation in the conference and related events commemorating the 100th anniversary of the battle in Addis Ababa and Adwa in February-March 1996. In visits to churches in Tigray, Wag, Lasta, and Gaynt in recent years I have found numerous representations of the battle which were painted in the decade following the victory. They demonstrate how news of the victory over the invading Italians, brought back to the remotest regions of the country by men who fought at Adwa, fed the pride of Ethiopians.

own smaller *gibbis* at prominent sites on the foothills of Entoto. The imperial palace rose on a prominent hill above the Filwoha springs. New structures were added to its large compound where thousands of servants were employed. The palace gates and inner areas were always alive with officials, visitors from the provinces, petitioners, diplomats, businessmen and clergymen. Vast amounts of food were prepared daily and thousands of retainers and visitors were regularly fed in the palace's huge dining hall. The widely separated sections of the sprawling capital were connected by rocky trails and paths that gradually turned into roads. The lower classes walked or rode donkeys. Donkeys carried wood and loads of grain. Better-class citizens rode mules and horses. Chiefs, important clergymen and foreign ambassadors moved about accompanied by colorful retinues of attendants and retainers. The city required large quantities of food and firewood. A large market developed on the western side and smaller local markets attracted sellers and tradesmen on particular days of the week. Eucalyptus, introduced from Australia a few years before, was beginning to give the city an overlay of greenness and spread its pungent scent through the thin cool air.

Menelik's first business on returning to the capital was the peace treaty with Italy and settling the prisoner problem.

Italy recognized "absolutely and without reserve the independence of the Ethiopian Empire" in the Treaty of Addis Ababa signed on 26 October 1896 and at the same time a convention on repatriation of prisoners of war was agreed upon. By mid-1897 over 1,700 had been sent home or to Eritrea.

The European powers moved rapidly to adjust relations with Ethiopia. In March 1897 a French mission under Leonce Lagarde signed a treaty granting Ethiopia most of the desert lowlands the French had originally considered part of their Somaliland protectorate. Menelik granted Lagarde the title "Duke of Entoto". The treaty reduced French territory to the immediate hinterland of Djibouti, designated Djibouti Ethiopia's official outlet to the sea, and provided that arms for Ethiopia would transit Djibouti duty-free. In return Menelik signed a secret agreement promising Ethiopian support for French efforts to gain a foothold on the White Nile. A year and a half later it would lead to the famous Fashoda crisis, but Menelik had not made himself a French tool. He knew France wanted to preempt Britain by gaining a west-east corridor across Africa. Britain was aiming at a Cape-to-Cairo corridor, and to complete it had to defeat the Mahdist rebellion in Sudan. Menelik played all his cards with skill and held control of the game. He let trade resume through Metemma and Gedaref but was cautious about entanglement with the increasingly beleaguered Mahdists to whom he showed sympathy but he let no arms pass to them. Britain had stepped up its operations against the Mahdists immediately after Adwa.

The ink had barely dried on the treaties with France when Sir James Rennell Rodd, a senior British official in Egypt, was given a ceremonial welcome in Addis Ababa on 29 April 1897. He came to regularize relations with Menelik in respect both to Sudan and Britain's Somaliland Protectorate. Menelik readily agreed to give no aid to the Mahdists and assured the British he would permit no Sudanese territory to be occupied by another power. Discussion of Somaliland was more difficult. When the treaty with Britain was signed on 14 May 1897, the task of defining the border was left up to Rennel Rodd and Ras Makonnen in Harar. Rennell Rodd eventually persuaded Makonnen to abandon the Ethiopian claim that possession of Harar entitled them to all the territory between Harar and the sea. A provisional boundary was agreed upon on 4 June in Harar.

Having regularized relations with the three major European powers, Menelik turned his attention to the southwest. The Kingdom of Kaffa had continued to resist Ethiopian domination. Menelik had Ras Wolde Giyorgis organize a strong army for a campaign against it. With the help of neighboring provincial rulers, including Abba Jifar II of Jimma, Kaffan forces were defeated and Gaki Sherocho, the King, pursued and brought in silver chains to Addis Ababa. Ras Wolde Giyorgis was named governor of Kaffa. He marched south into Borana and brought the Ethiopian frontier to the north end of Lake Rudolf (now Turkana). With the Mahdist state collapsing, Menelik sent Ras Makonnen to push the Wollega frontier westward with the help of Dejazmach Gebre-Egziabeher (Kumsa Moroda before his baptism). By a combination of military pressure and astute diplomacy, Beni-Shangul and Asosa were brought under Ethiopian control. Omdurman fell to General Kitchener at the beginning of September 1899 and the Mahdists were finished.

Tigray remained troublesome. Ras Alula had clashed with Ras Hagos in early 1897, killed him but then died of his own wounds. Menelik's settlement with Italy which left the northernmost Tigrayan highlands under Italian rule was resented by many Tigrayans, but Tigrayan nobles were quarreling with each other and a few were still dickering with the Italians. Menelik was unhappy that Ras Mengesha Yohannes was not collecting taxes due the central government. Mengesha resented Menelik's failure to elevate him to Negus. He rebelled in 1898. Menelik mobilized a large army and marched north, joined by Ras Makonnen, whom he named governor of Tigray in addition to Harar. In February 1899 Mengesha surrendered to Menelik at Dessie, was taken to Addis Ababa and sent to prison at Ankober, where he died in 1906. Makonnen spent the next year trying to pacify Tigray and was then replaced by Ras Wole. Menelik divided Tigray into separate areas under local chiefs. In 1901 Negus Tekle Haymanot of Gojjam died. Menelik applied a Tigray-type solution there and divided the kingdom into three parts among the sons of the Negus.

Meanwhile Menelik had used various stratagems to keep the French from free-wheeling in the southwest. As British forces under General Kitchener were advancing toward Khartoum in 1898, he finally decided to permit two Frenchmen to accompany Dejazmach Tessema's army on an expedition to the White Nile.[38] Three Russians – Col. L.R. Artamonov and two Cossacks – accompanied the expedition too. Tessema advanced along the Baro river to a point not far from its confluence with the White Nile but his troops were affected by heat and sickness in the lowlands. A small party of Ethiopians moved ahead to the great river and placed their flag on the right bank. The exhausted Frenchmen had to let Artamonov and one of the Cossacks swim across the Nile and raise the French flag on the opposite shore. But the potential gains of this daring advance were never realized. Artamonov and the Ethiopians withdrew. They had failed to establish communication with a French party known to be approaching the area. Under Marchand, it was advancing toward Fashoda, where the French were confronted by Kitchener on 19 September 1898 and had to back down. Their dream of a corridor across Africa was over.

Several Russians, enjoying Menelik's good will, were active in Ethiopia during this period, but they were not universally backed in St. Petersburg. The irrepressible Nikolai Leontiev had missed the battle of Adwa but busied himself as a self-appointed Ethiopian emissary to Italy, the Pope, the Tsar and various other European dignitaries, and then returned to Ethiopia in the spring of 1897. Menelik granted him an ill-defined territory in the far southwest to develop. He organized "shareholders" in Europe, angered Ras Wolde Giyorgis and Ras Tessema by his maneuvers in the area, but with the support of Alfred Ilg remained in Ethiopia for several years, continually busy with new schemes. A new Russian minister, P.M. Vlasov, arrived in September 1898 with orders to take charge of the Russians in Ethiopia. He had difficulty getting control of Leontiev, but several other Russian officers were more amenable to accepting Vlasov's guidance.

---

[38] Tessema, later Ras, who died in 1926, was the father of Dejazmach Kebbede Tessema, patriot hero in whose house the communist dictator Mengistu Haile Mariam grew up. According to a version of Mengistu's parentage current in Addis Ababa in the 1980s, his mother was the natural daughter of Kebbede Tessema by a servant girl. If so, Mengistu's lineage was more distinguished than generally believed. Dejazmach Kebbede Tessema died in 1986 and was given an elaborate funeral which Mengistu, who was otherwise never seen in church, attended. He was buried in an impressive tomb in front of Trinity Cathedral in Addis Ababa.

Captain A.R. Bulatovich constructed a series of forts in the far south-west which earned him praise from Menelik. In the diplomatic excitement and confusion which followed the Fashoda crisis, Tsar Nicholas would have liked to support the French more strongly. He even concentrated troops in the Caucasus as a potential threat against the British in the Near East. But when the French backed down, the Russians also shifted to a conciliatory posture. Menelik was not really eager to gain a foothold on the White Nile. For him it was an outside chance. Ethiopia had no historic claims or ethnic ties there. Menelik lost nothing of importance when the undertaking failed. The episode marked the high point in Russian ambitions in Ethiopia.[39]

However, Russia's desire to acquire a port on the Red Sea had not died with the embarrassing fiasco of Ashinov's colony at New Moscow. With the Eritrean coast firmly in Italian control, Russia focussed on the Afar Sultanate of Raheita, adjacent to the French protectorate on the Bay of Tajura. Eliseev had visited Raheita in 1895. Leontiev and Artamonov made contact with the Sultan of Raheita in 1898, and Vlasov sent a naval ensign, Babichev, who had come with the Russian Red Cross mission in 1896. Babichev became involved in a private deal with Leontiev which angered the Italians. Vlasov ordered Babichev back to Russia. He resigned, married an Ethiopian wife, and spent the rest of his life in Ethiopia, dying in Addis Ababa in 1955 at the age of 84.[40]

The French, too, were disturbed by Russian maneuvers on the coast and decided on a countermove. In late 1898 they offered to help Russia establish a coaling station on the Bay of Tajura without actually ceding any territory. The commitment was never implemented. Events in the Persian Gulf aroused common European fears of Russian ambitions in the Indian Ocean. By the time Russia got into war with Japan in 1904, the French-Russian friendship had cooled so far that France remained neutral in the conflict and denied the Russian navy use of Djibouti.

Meanwhile Menelik continued his skillful defense of Ethiopia's interests. He signed a treaty with Britain in 1902 in which he gave up all claim to the east bank of the White Nile and in return gave the British a veto over any plan to dam or divert Nile headwaters in Ethiopian territory. This was an easily affordable concession, for Menelik must have been more aware than the European powers that diversion

[39] Several detailed accounts of the Fashoda crisis have appeared in recent years. None of them gives adequate attention to the Russian involvement. The most recent account shares this shortcoming but is otherwise comprehensive: David L. Lewis, *The Race to Fashoda*, Weidenfeld & Nicolson, London, 1987.

[40] Prouty, *op.cit.*, pp. 197-8.

of Nile waters was a theoretical threat. The investment necessary to regulate – let alone divert – the massive flow of the Blue Nile or any Nile tributaries in Ethiopian territory was then – as it remains today – far beyond the capacity of Ethiopia to muster.[41]

Trade and diplomatic relations with America

Trade expanded rapidly after Adwa. By the end of the century, the United States, with no other interest in Ethiopia, had become its major trade partner. Complete trade statistics are difficult to assemble because both American exports to and imports from Ethiopia passed through European firms based in Djibouti, Berbera and Aden and trade through Massawa was often not listed as trade with Ethiopia. So statistics we possess must be seen as minimal, which makes them even more impressive. During the period 1897-8, one-seventh of all textiles imported through Djibouti consisted of American cotton cloth, termed *merikani*. In 1901 the US was the sixth largest importer of Eritrean goods exported through Massawa. In 1902 the US bought $820,443 worth of Ethiopian coffee. Total Ethiopian foreign trade (imports and exports) amounted to $2,316,000 in 1902 and the American share was $1,389,000 – 59 per cent. Of this $579,000 was accounted for by *merikani* exports to Ethiopia, $675,000 by imports to the US of Ethiopian hides and skins and $135,000 by coffee imports. In 1905-6 *merikani* accounted for half of all Ethiopia's recorded cotton imports.[42] An English traveller who visited Ethiopia during this period wrote: "The Americans practically monopolize the two chief branches of trade...the importation of grey shirting and the export of skins and hides."[43]

In 1900 the American Consul-General in Marseille, Robert P. Skinner, wrote President McKinley recommending that diplomatic relations be opened with Ethiopia:

... in order to procure exact information for American exporters and manu-facturers ... and more particularly to safeguard an important existing com-merce which has created itself in spite of American indifference ... [and] without the presence of an American citizen or the advantage of official contact.[44]

[41] The Ethiopian Blue Nile and the Takazze/Atbara together normally supply up to four-fifths of Nile water that reaches Egypt. Threats by Ethiopian rulers to block the flow of the Nile and fears in Egypt that this could actually come to pass have a long and colorful history. See Elisabeth-Dorothea Hecht, "Ethiopia Threat-ens to Block the Nile", *Azania* (Journal of the British Institute in Eastern Africa), Nairobi, 1988.

[42] Statistics are from David Shinn, "A Survey of American-Ethiopian Relations prior to the Italian Occupation of Ethiopia", *Ethiopia Observer*, V. XIV. 4, 1971.

[43] P.H.G. Powell-Cotton, *A Sporting Trip through Abyssinia*, London, 1902.

[44] Robert P. Skinner, *Abyssinia of Today*, London/New York, 1906, p. ix.

It took three years for Washington to act on Skinner's recommendation. In the summer of 1903 he was commissioned by President Theodore Roosevelt, who had a keen interest in Africa, to go to Ethiopia and negotiate a commercial treaty. Skinner's party left New York on 8 October 1903, boarded the USS *Machias* in Naples and sailed on to Beirut, where they were joined by an escort of nineteen Marines and six sailors, making a total party of thirty. They proceeded down the Red Sea to Djibouti, landing on 17 November. The mission caused a modest flurry of diplomatic excitement in European capitals. A London newspaper speculated on its possible strategic purpose, concluding that: "the establishment of a *point d'appui* on the Abyssinian coast is not to be left out of consideration". Skinner was amused and noted that Ethiopia no longer had a coast and was "as effectually hemmed in from the sea as Switzerland". Throughout the course of the mission he combined humor, keen powers of observation and dedication to commercial purposes, commenting on arrival in Djibouti on "the shiny black Somali children, whose nakedness was not encouraging to my desire to find a market for American sheetings".

Skinner had already learned a good deal about Ethiopia by the time he arrived in Djibouti. He saw Djibouti as the key to Ethiopia's commercial future, for with the completion of the first segment of the Franco-Ethiopian Railway to Diredawa earlier that year, it became an important entrepot for Ethiopian trade. With the "expected development of Ethiopia", Djibouti was destined to become "the focal point of its contact with the modern world," Skinner observed, continuing in classic American gung-ho spirit:

Indeed, it was this expectation, and the partial completion of the railroad, that took me to Africa. Hitherto, trade in general, and American trade in particular, had drifted to Aden, thence across to any one of half a dozen ports, where camels took it up, and plodded into the interior. The railroad meant evolution and revolution; it was time for a watchful people like ours to be up and doing.[45]

From Djibouti Skinner's party traveled by rail to Diredawa and made a detour to Harar to call on Ras Makonnen, who put his new palace at their disposal and brought out jars of "the native champagne" (*tej*) with which they drank to the health of President Roosevelt and Emperor Menelik.[46] Back in Diredawa there were delays getting their caravan organized for the journey to Addis Ababa and adventures with hostile Afar tribesmen once they were under way. They reached the outskirts of Addis Ababa on 18 December, having taken almost three weeks to cover 275 miles, and were welcomed by a party

[45] Skinner, *op.cit.*, p. 6.

[46] Skinner did not record whether he met the Ras's eleven-year-old son, Tafari, the future Haile Selassie.

headed by the Frenchman Léon Chefneux, now Menelik's foreign affairs adviser. They entered the capital with an escort of 3,000 men and went directly to Menelik's palace, where he welcomed them in the presence of a vast crowd: "As we left the *aderash* ... cannon roared out twenty-one guns and the band of the native musicians played Hail Columbia and then the Marseillaise." Skinner noted that the Emperor's band had been provided with instruments by "a Russian political prospector, Count Leontieff".

The Skinner mission remained in Addis Ababa only nine days, but learned an immense amount about Menelik's empire. Menelik was then in his prime. Skinner was impressed by his curiosity for everything modern, his keen appreciation of the intricacies of international politics and his skillful use of both foreign and native advisers. He concluded that Chefneux and Ilg, both long in Ethiopia, were key figures in the country. Always looking to the future, Skinner expected that completion of the railway to Addis Ababa would speed development and give impetus to expanded trade. Anticipating the flood of Ethiopian students that would begin study in the US half a century later, Skinner suggested to Menelik that he should consider sending young Ethiopians to American schools and colleges. Menelik replied: "Yes, that will come; our young men must be educated. We have much to do. We are a very primitive people."

The "Treaty to Regulate Commercial Relations between the U.S. and the King of Ethiopia" which Skinner negotiated was formally signed and Menelik's seal affixed to it the afternoon of the mission's last day in the capital, 27 December 1903. Its term was ten years.[47] As a farewell gift Menelik gave Skinner two matched 8-foot elephant tusks and a pair of young lions for President Roosevelt and presented decorations to each member of the mission.[48]

Skinner judged his mission highly successful. His final report stated:

Probably for the first time in the modern history of Ethiopia has a foreign mission visited the country upon an errand of peace and amity, bringing no vexed questions of territorial integrity or national honor to decide and neither asking nor granting anything to which both sides could not accede.[49]

He reviewed the activities of each foreign mission in Ethiopia, concluding with the Russians:

[47] Ratification procedures were completed in August 1904. The treaty continued in force until 1914 when it was replaced by a second treaty signed in Addis Ababa on 27 June 1914.

[48] One of the lions died on the way to Diredawa. The other eventually reached Washington and was placed in the National Zoo.

[49] Skinner, *op. cit.*, p. 6

We come now to the most interesting mission in Ethiopia, because it is the least comprehensible by the ordinary rules of interest which govern international relations. Our Russian friends have no apparent stake in Ethiopia ... There is no Russian trade ... and there are no Russian frontiers nearer than Turkestan. Yet the Russian mission presided over by the accomplished M. Leschine includes a hospital and a dispensary ...

It is said that some very strong sympathy exists between the Russian and Ethiopian churches ... Europeans are somewhat skeptical, however ... regarding the religious bond as one which unites these two peoples diplomatically. If Ethiopia possessed a coastline, it would be exceedingly easy to assume that Russia hoped sooner or later to obtain a Red Sea port ... The real inwardness of Russian diplomatic effort in Ethiopia is a never-ending source of conversation in the empire and many ingenious theories are spun regarding it. Probably ... the amateur in politics misses the true cause in order to spin out theories which only the next forty years or perhaps century can demonstrate ... Ethiopia being a Christian power, now important, and ruled by wise men, it is a safe policy for Russia ... to maintain cordial relations with this power. May not the mysteries of diplomacy, here as elsewhere, consist largely in the fact that there are no mysteries?[50]

Skinner did not know that he was observing Russia's diplomatic mission in Addis Ababa at the end of an era. On the other side of the world Russia was about to enter a war that was going to have consequences even more far-reaching than the defeat at Adwa had for Italy. Russian interest in Ethiopia, already slackening, declined precipitously. The Russian hospital closed in 1906. There were no further special missions in either direction and no more Russian military activity in Ethiopia.

Skinner's high hopes for a steady expansion of US trade with Ethiopia did not materialize, but trade continued at a modest level. The US Government did little to foster trade and nothing to encourage broader relations in other respects, though a consul or vice-consul was on post in Addis Ababa most of the time between 1906 and 1913. After that the British legation looked after American interests.

The Singer Sewing Machine Company established a branch in Addis Ababa in 1909 and engaged agents in provincial towns. Skinner may not have known of him, but the Adwa victory had inspired a Black US citizen, William Henry Ellis, a successful Southern cotton planter, to come in 1899 and obtain a concession from Menelik to establish a cotton plantation which is said to have prospered. A few American Blacks followed in the early part of the century. Most came with unrealistic expectations, had difficulty establishing themselves in the distinctive cultural milieu of Ethiopia, and most failed in their undertakings. A few other Americans came to Ethiopia during this period. A geologist, Arthur Donaldson Smith, had led an expedition

[50] Ibid., pp. 96-7.

through Somaliland, southern Ethiopia and Kenya in 1894-5 and published a book.[51] An American named MacMillan who explored the area northwest of Lake Rudolf in 1903 was later murdered in the Danakil. Emperor Menelik sent a regiment of troops to catch the murderer who was brought to Addis Ababa and publicly hanged. Two more generations were to pass before any more than a handful of Americans developed awareness of Ethiopia.

Before summarizing Menelik's final years, let us pause for a more comprehensive evaluation of the significance of the Battle of Adwa.

The Significance of Adwa

The confrontation between Italy and Ethiopia at Adwa was a fundamental turning point in Ethiopian history. In comparison, Dogali was a skirmish. To realize its significance, one only has to ask: What would the subsequent history of Ethiopia and the Horn of Africa have been if Italy had been victorious? Within less than a decade as the nineteenth century turned into the twentieth, the Western world was shocked by two defeats of major European powers. Italy, a newly unified state consciously striving to revive the glory of the Roman Empire, was defeated by an African country that until then had been regarded as a relic of the past. Eight years later Japan, a small island kingdom on the edge of Asia which had been jolted out of medieval isolation less than half a century before, defeated Russia, the largest contiguous state in the world.

Though apparent to very few historians at the time, these defeats were the beginning of the decline of Europe as the center of world politics. Looking back a century later, that is clear. But all historical processes consist of strands of development that twist and cross and sometimes even reverse direction.[52] The internal consequences for

[51] *Through Unknown African Countries: The First Expedition from Somalia to Lake Rudolf,* London, 1897.

[52] Russia's defeat by Japan had far-reaching domestic consequences – the Tsar's empire was shaken by revolts and disturbances that led to democratizing political reforms. Imperial authority was so weakened, however, that Russia could not weather the strains generated by World War I. After an ordeal of acute disorder, the empire was reconstituted as the oppressive Soviet Union.

For Japan the consequences of victory were twofold and interconnected. The country was accepted as a new world power and acclaimed by other Asians as a model for modernization. It joined the victors in World War I. The confident ruling classes of Japan rapidly accelerated evolution toward European levels of modernization. The longer-term political consequences of Japan's rise to world power status were, however, much less positive. Authoritarianism became consolidated. Overconfident nationalism drove Japan less than three decades later into military adventurism first in China and then against the United States, Britain, and France. Japanese leaders allied themselves with Nazism and Fascism with ultimately disastrous results.

Italy of the defeat at Adwa may have been a contributing factor to the rise of fascism in the 1920s. The urge to create a new Roman Empire remained alive and was exploited by Mussolini after he seized power. By the beginning of the 1930s avenging the defeat at Adwa was widely accepted as a national objective. The result was the 1935 invasion of Ethiopia and the evanescent glory of Africa Orientale Italiana.

In Ethiopia, victory at Adwa consolidated Menelik II's position. His compromise on Eritrea caused resentment in Tigray, but Menelik could afford this inconvenience because Tigray had been decisively overshadowed by the rising power of Shoa. Shoa had advanced steadily to primacy after the collapse of Tewodros. By letting Italy retain Eritrea Menelik gained a stable northern frontier and freed himself to capitalize on the status gained at Adwa by consolidating Ethiopia's borders on the east, south and west. Ethiopia was no longer a relic of the past. The powers recognized it as a state to be treated as an equal.

What if Menelik had followed the victory at Adwa with a campaign to expel the Italians from their brief tenure in Eritrea? Could he have succeeded in regaining control of at least the Tigrinya-speaking highlands in expelling the Italians from Massawa, from Assab? Perhaps. He could equally well have overextended himself and squandered everything that was gained at Adwa. Other Ethiopian regional leaders might not have been willing to support a further offensive in the north. Resources might have proved inadequate. Britain or France might have intervened to prevent further Italian humiliation. On balance, Menelik's decision to make a clear-cut peace with Italy seems not only prudent but most advantageous from the viewpoint of overall Ethiopian interests. A campaign to eject Italy from Eritrea would have absorbed so much of Menelik's energy that he would not have had time to strengthen his administration and advance the modernization of the country.

The Adwa victory had a strong impact in Europe. In Italy the Crispi government fell. Italy's reputation for being less than a fully effective military power persisted into the twentieth century. Britain, whose pragmatic sympathies for Italian designs on Ethiopia had prevailed until the Adwa victory, rapidly revised its calculations. Britain established an embassy in Addis Ababa in 1896 and the Rennel Rodd mission regularized relations to the advantage of Ethiopia, enabling Menelik to consolidate control over the Ogaden, though the British Somaliland border remained unsettled until 1907. Confident of Ethiopian benevolent neutrality, Britain was able to move decisively to deal with the Mahdists in Sudan.

France had helped Menelik get arms through its Red Sea ports at Tajura, Obock and then Djibouti. Plans for a railway from Djibouti to Diredawa had been made before Adwa and were rapidly implemented afterwards. The railroad reached Diredawa in 1903. France was eager to consolidate its relationship with Menelik for larger political purposes as well. It hoped to gain his collaboration in securing a foothold on the White Nile. On this Menelik gave the French and their Russian colleagues encouragement, but avoided overcommitment. He invested no significant resources in the adventure that culminated at Fashoda in the summer of 1898 and thus lost nothing when the French effort failed.[53]

Russian Slavophiles and military adventurers eager to develop Ethiopia as an ally against the Ottoman Empire made abortive efforts to gain a foothold in the Horn after Adwa. The Tsarist Government was more skilful in the years immediately preceding Adwa, sending arms and advisers to Menelik. Menelik saw Russia as his best foreign friend. Russian military advisers may have had more impact on the tactics which Menelik employed in defeating the Italians than has generally been acknowledged. Following the victory, Menelik entrusted missions to Russians, welcomed more Russian arms, and agreed to construction and staffing of a Russian hospital in Addis Ababa, the first European aid project of its kind. Russia remained influential in Ethiopia into the first years of the twentieth century, but Menelik, at the peak of his performance in the classic role of balancing foreign relationships to Ethiopia's advantage, was not about to make the country a vassal of any European power.

Secure on the imperial throne against internal challengers and enjoying international respect after Adwa, Menelik expanded the country's new capital and welcomed foreign traders and specialists. Ethiopia entered a period of economic expansion. The United States, which had no political ambitions in East Africa and where the political consequences of the Battle of Adwa were exciting only to a small minority of African-American intellectuals (but of little interest to anyone else) was, nevertheless, interested in trade and a few years later, out of this motivation, established relations with Ethiopia.

What if Ethiopia had been defeated by Italy at Adwa? There might now be no Ethiopia at all – only a historical memory. Some twentieth-century deconstructionists have argued that Ethiopia never actually existed except as the modern invention of an oppressive elite.[54] The

---

[53] Fashoda, to judge by the number of books it has inspired, has proved more appealing to historians than the Battle of Adwa, which has yet to be thoroughly described and analyzed as the historic battle it was.

[54] Prominent among the deconstructionists have been emotional supporters of the Eritrean struggle against the Derg. Few of them have much grounding in history. It is incongruous for these people to claim that Eritrea is a state with deep historic roots when it only came into being as a colony in 1890, while condemning Ethiopia, one of the most ancient polities in the world, as artificial and without historical validity.

ifs of history are infinitely debatable, but some portion of the Ethiopian idea, though perhaps not the state in the form in which we have
known it in the twentieth century, would probably still exist. Ethiopia,
after all, had survived from the time of the Greeks and the Romans,
though it was often more a geographical concept than a polity. The
legacy of Aksum survived through the Middle Ages. After the 4th
century Christianity became an essential component of the Ethiopian sense of nationhood and gave impetus to southward expansion.
If the memory of far more short-lived and nebulous empires in Africa,
such as Mali, Ghana, and Zimbabwe, remained alive to be revived as
names of new states in the mid-twentieth century, some notion of
Ethiopia as a geographical expression or a cultural concept is likely
to have survived defeat at Adwa.

If Italy had been able to follow up on victory at Adwa, kill or capture
Menelik, and gain control of more territory south of Tigray, it might
have consolidated its conquests, including Eritrea, into the kind of
colony Antonelli and Crispi aspired to acquire in the Treaty of
Wichale. It might even have called it Ethiopia. It is doubtful, however,
that even with victory at Adwa, Italy would have had a free hand to do
as it wished in the region. Britain, France and perhaps even Russia,
would have moved to limit Italian gains. Italians had had their eyes on
Harar before Menelik's conquest. So had the French. And Britain,
who saw its protectorate over Somaliland as essential to maintenance
of its hold on Aden as a key station on its route to India, might have
intervened to prevent permanent French or Italian domination of
Hararge and the Ogaden.

If Menelik had been defeated but survived, he might have withdrawn into Shoa and remained independent there. He might have
had trouble holding onto Gojjam or Wollo, let alone Begemder. He
would have had difficulty consolidating control of all the conquests
he had made in the south during the 1880s. Britain, expanding its
position in Kenya and Uganda, might have moved up into southern
Ethiopia, even into Shoa itself. But Britain, as was repeatedly evident
in the decades before Adwa, had never developed a desire to move
permanently into Ethiopia, which did not bear directly on maintenance of the lifeline to India. Neither, later, did it relate to Britain's
determination to maintain control of Egypt, as Sudan did. So it is
likely that Britain would have confined her actions to adjusting to
Ethiopian defeat and efforts to prevent rival powers from having
such a free hand in arranging the wreckage of Menelik's empire that
they might endanger major British interests in the wider region:
Aden, Sudan, Kenya and Uganda.

The cost of Russia's commitment to Menelik was insignificant
compared to the Soviet Union's investment in Ethiopia in the 1980s.

Menelik's defeat would have been a disappointment primarily for the Russian activists on the scene. Their position in St. Petersburg was always weaker than the impression they gave of it in Ethiopia. Ethiopia ranked very low among the concerns of the Tsar.

In contrast to sixty million at the end of the twentieth century, the population of the entire modern territory of Ethiopia can have been no more than five million, probably less, at the end of the 19th. Famines and disease had taken a heavy toll in the north before Adwa, but Menelik and his regional leaders had little difficulty mobilizing formidable manpower. Sheer numbers, combined with modern weapons, enabled the Ethiopians to overwhelm the overextended Italian forces. Italian victory at Adwa would have had little impact on the overall population situation. Territory over which Italy would have been able to establish control would have retained substantial population and little migration of people is likely to have taken place. What was left of Ethiopia would continue to be relatively populous. People would have gone on speaking their native languages. For official purposes, Amharic had long been dominant over Tigrinya. Ethiopians would have continued to adhere to the Orthodox Church and some to other traditional religious faiths, including Islam. The social structure of the population and basic characteristics of Ethiopian life would not have been significantly altered.

But whatever territorial arrangements might have been made, the process of political and psychological consolidation of Ethiopia which had been advanced under Yohannes IV, and had already gained further momentum under Menelik, would have been reversed by defeat at Adwa. The Italians would have lacked the manpower to establish an administrative system down to the local level. They would have relied on regional leaders as they did in Eritrea and after 1935 had to do in Ethiopia. Thus the power of regional potentates in Ethiopia would have been greatly enhanced and rivalry between them would have delayed, probably for generations, the development of strong central government. All aspects of the processes of administrative consolidation and incipient modernization that accelerated under Menelik when he returned victorious from Adwa would have been delayed until much later in the twentieth century. As slowly as Ethiopia developed during the first decades of the twentieth century, the process would have been far slower if the confrontation at Adwa had resulted in an Italian victory.

Ethiopian defeat at Adwa would have had a negative impact on the economy of the whole Horn. Traditional trade, including slave trade, would have continued, but the economic development of the Ethiopian center and south that began after Menelik's conquests would have stalled. The Franco-Ethiopian railway would not have been

built. Culturally, Ethiopia's development would have been inhibited
by defeat at Adwa. Literacy and education would have developed
even more slowly than they did and contacts with the outer world
which Menelik encouraged would have been delayed. In short,
Ethiopia would have resembled the rest of Africa – terrain for
European colonialists to play out their own rivalries and apply their
own priorities. Even if Italy had been able to take over the whole
of Ethiopia, it would not have increased its influence among the
European powers. Italian victory at Adwa would not have changed
the course of European politics. World War I would probably have
occurred and had the same outcome. Italy could never have generated the resources to transform part or all of Ethiopia into a profitable
modern state. The task was beyond her. And, inevitably, Italy would
have been forced to disband her colonial empire even if it had
emerged intact from World War II.

So whatever the fate of the territory that constitutes Ethiopia today
might have been if Menelik had been defeated at Adwa, it would in
all likelihood have evolved into independence as the rest of Africa
did during the second half of the twentieth century. Whatever state
or states might have emerged would be less solidly based in history
and less influential internationally than modern Ethiopia. Though
the ultimate effect of the victory at Adwa was almost dissipated by
the disarray into which Ethiopia fell with the illness and death of
Menelik, the international stature which Ethiopia won at Adwa helped
it survive. Independent Ethiopia encouraged hopes among Africans
for eventual liberation from colonialism. It became a symbol for Blacks
in America and the Caribbean. Adwa enabled Haile Selassie to play a
constructive role in African decolonialization after World War II and
to gain recognition of Ethiopia as a responsible state. Since the fall of
Mengistu Haile Mariam, the same process has resumed.

Menelik's Final Years

By the time he turned 60 in 1904 the strains of an extraordinarily
active life and the effects of syphilis contracted in his youth began to
take their toll on the old emperor. Joseph Vitalien, a dark Frenchman
from the Caribbean island of Guadeloupe, became Menelik's doctor
in 1904. He urged him to cut down on eating and drinking, but
predicted he could expect to live many years longer. Nothing serious
troubled the continually active emperor until after Ras Makonnen
suddenly sickened and died in March 1906. Menelik was deeply
affected and spent three days in deep mourning. Taitu, on the other
hand, who had never liked Makonnen, was relieved.[55] The Ras had

[55] Prouty, *op.cit.*, p. 281.

named his fourteen-year old son Tafari as his heir, but Taitu had his older brother Yilma, born of a concubine, appointed governor of Harar while Tafari, who held the rank of Dejazmach, was named titular governor of Selale and kept in the palace where he became acquainted with the grandson Menelik soon named as heir, Lij Iyasu Mikael.

A few weeks later, while he was inspecting a construction project at Entoto Maryam, Menelik had a fainting spell which seems to have been a mild stroke. Word of it got out and the diplomatic community became alarmed because by this time Taitu had acquired a reputation among Europeans for disliking foreigners and trying to limit their influence. Nevertheless Menelik participated fully in the ceremonies and talks connected with the visit of the Eritrean governor, Ferdinando Martini, who had arrived in the capital in June 1906 after a journey of almost two months with an enormous escort including 10,000 soldiers of the three Tigrayan *rases*, Araya, Gebre Selassie and Seyum Mengesha. During the seven weeks Martini stayed in Addis Ababa, the Tripartite Pact between Italy, France and Britain was signed in London, settling most of the diplomatic issues relating to Ethiopia at the time.[56] Ethiopia and Italy had already agreed in 1902 on the Mareb river as the Eritrean boundary.

At a reception for his 63rd birthday in 1907, Menelik did not look well. He had suffered an obvious stroke shortly before. But he was not disabled and was strong enough to engage in hard negotiations on the new railroad with a French envoy. In October 1907 he announced the appointment of a European-style cabinet, though it did not meet until July 1908. Taitu showed increasing signs of worry about her husband's health and her own status if he died. Nevertheless, the pace of life in Addis Ababa had gained so much momentum that any basic change in the way the government operated was difficult. There was a steady flow of Ethiopian and foreign visitors, development projects progressed, the telephone made it possible for Menelik to talk to provincial governors almost daily. At the end of 1907 Taitu opened her own hotel, the first in the capital, and the first motor car arrived over land from Djibouti.

In May 1908 Menelik set out on a mule trip to Selale and suffered a stroke again. He was incapacitated for three weeks before returning to the capital and from this time onward Taitu guarded him jealously. New doctors were consulted, various treatments were tried, occasionally Menelik rallied and even took decisions on issues relating to the extension of the railroad to Addis Ababa and beyond, on

---

[56] It validated all the previous agreements signed by any two of the three European powers and confirmed the commitment of all not to interfere in Ethiopian internal affairs.

appointments of officials, and concerned himself with new troubles in Tigray. But for all practical purposes Taitu became the ruler of the country.[57] She generated a good deal of strain. In the summer of 1909, under somewhat confusing circumstances, the faltering Menelik named his grandson Lij Iyasu heir to the throne.[58] By the end of 1909 Menelik's condition had deteriorated to the point where he was expected to die at any time. The long process of Menelik's demise marked what, in effect, was the beginning of the confused, brief reign of Emperor Lij Iyasu and, more importantly, the rise to prominence of the man who was to dominate the next sixty years of Ethiopia's history – Ras Tafari Makonnen who became Emperor Haile Selassie I.

[57] Prouty provides a detailed description of the decline of Menelik into total incapacity: *op.cit.,* pp. 280-321.

[58] Born in 1896, Iyasu was the son of Ras Mikael (originally Mohammed Ali) of Wollo by Shoarega, a daughter of Menelik by an early liaison.

7

THE RISE OF HAILE SELASSIE

TIME OF TROUBLES, REGENT, EMPEROR, EXILE

For over half a century the man who became known as Haile Selassie I dominated Ethiopian life. He ranks as one of the outstanding world leaders of the twentieth century. He was castigated during the communist/Derg era as the incarnation of backwardness and greed, but the new government that came to power in 1991 permitted a re habilitation of his reputation. His remains were dug up from a cellar in the Grand Palace where he had been secretly buried in late August 1975 when Mengistu Haile Mariam had him strangled barely a year after he had been hauled off from his palace in a Volkswagen and imprisoned. Now, at the end of the twentieth century, the visitor to Ethiopia sees his photograph everywhere: in shop windows and bars, on automobile bumper stickers, on T-shirts. A political party, Moa Anbasa, advocates restoration of the monarchy but is hampered by the fact that there is no descendant of the last Lion of Judah credible as a contender for power.[1]

Like all great leaders, Tafari Makonnen – the name by which he was first known – was a man of many facets who inspired envy, love, awe, hatred and admiration. He had both virtues and shortcomings in good measure. Profoundly aware of his country's past, he devoted his life to leading it to a more progressive and productive future. He faced enormous obstacles and overcame most of them. The great British Ethiopianist, Edward Ullendorff, wrote appropriately of him: "For two thirds of his life all the problems Haile Sellassie had to face arose from the fact that he was in advance of his time."[2]

Haile Selassie's personality and record will continue to be studied in Ethiopia and abroad for decades to come.[3] I will advance a further

[1] Severely disabled Crown Prince Asfa Wossen, living in London in exile, had himself declared Emperor Amha Selassie in 1988, but was not taken seriously by any but a few people in his immediate entourage. He moved to Washington the next year and died there in 1996. His remains were returned to Ethiopia for burial.

[2] Edward Ullendorff, translator's preface to *The Autobiography of Emperor Haile Sellassie I, "My Life and Ethiopia's Progress", 1892-1937*, Oxford University Press, 1976, p. xiii.

[3] A good beginning has been made by Harold Marcus in his *Haile Sellassie I, the Formative Years, 1892-1936*, University of California Press, 1987. A comprehensive biography was published in France soon after his death: Gontran de Juniac, *Le dernier Roi des Rois*, Plon, Paris, 1979. A recent Italian evaluation of the last Ethiopian emperor is also noteworthy: Angelo Del Boca, *Il Negus. Vita e Morte dell'Ultimo Re dei Re*, Editori Laterza, Rome, 1995.

assessment of the last Emperor of the Solomonic line at the end of this book. Let us now look at his rise and early activity.

Tafari's early years

There was nothing preordained about Tafari Makonnen's rise to the throne. He was tangential to the line of succession to Menelik when he came into the world at Ejersa Goro near Harar on 23 July 1892. He was the tenth[4] and last child born to his mother, Yeshimabet Ali, daughter of a minor, originally Muslim, nobleman from Wollo. Noted for her beauty, she had married Makonnen Wolde Mikael, son of a daughter of King Sahle Selassie of Shoa, in 1876 in a binding Christian ceremony when Makonnen was twenty-four.[5] He had already fathered a son, Yilma, by an earlier liaison. A cousin of Menelik, Makonnen was a close friend and devoted follower from the time Menelik returned to Shoa from Magdala in 1866. When he conquered Harar in 1887, Menelik appointed Makonnen its governor. Yeshimabet died when Tafari was two. Makonnen had the boy placed in the household of a relative, Fitwrari Haile Selassie Abayneh, and raised with the Fitwrari's young son, Imru Haile Selassie. The two cousins remained close friends all their lives. Though Makonnen (who was soon elevated to the rank of *ras*) was often away for long periods, he took a keen interest in the education and training of his attractive young son:

... the Ras's personality – a good mix of shrewdness, gentility, sophistication, and political acumen – provided the boy with an apt role model. From his father [he] learned to hide his tenacity of spirit and ambition behind diffidence, deference, and gentle grace. Makonnen taught his scion to respect learning, especially the modern education seeping into Ethiopia. The Ras recognized that the country had to change with the times, or fall prey to imperialism. He was determined that his son would learn the new lore and become one of Ethiopia's agents of modernization.[6]

Tafari's Western education was entrusted to the French missionary Andre Jarosseau (known in Ethiopia as Abba Endreas), but for three years he also attended a traditional Orthodox school, learning Ge'ez and religious traditions. Large numbers of Shoans settled in Harar after the conquest. The city's commerce expanded and visitors from

---

[4] Of the ten, only Tafari survived into adulthood; he was christened Haile Selassie but did not use the name until he was crowned emperor in 1930.

[5] Makonnen's father, Wolde Mikael, was a nobleman from eastern Tigray. Haile Selassie's ancestry thus included Tigrayan, Oromo and Amhara antecedents, the three principal ethnic strains of Ethiopia, and Muslims as well as Christians, the two principal religions.

[6] Marcus, *Haile Sellasie I*, p. 3.

the outside world were frequent. Many paid their respects at Ras Makonnen's court. From these associations the growing boy learned about the variety and complexity of the world. Harar itself, with its Muslim traditions and ancient Semitic language, was the center of a region that included several different peoples: Oromos, Somalis and Afars, with Amharas and other highlanders as the ruling class. Thus Tafari from his earliest years became aware of the ethnic and religious complexity of Ethiopia itself. To give him experience in leadership and government, in 1905, when he reached 13, Makonnen made him *dejazmach* and appointed him governor of the region of Garamulata near Harar.

The next year Makonnen fell ill at Kulubi while on a journey to Addis Ababa. His condition worsening and sensing death, he wrote Menelik consigning Tafari to his care. Tafari was summoned to his father's bedside the day before he died on 21 March 1906. He had hopes of succeeding his father, but Menelik felt he needed a mature man in charge of Harar. Under the influence of Empress Taitu, he appointed Tafari's older half-brother Yilma, who had been married to the empress's niece. When Dejazmach Tafari went to Addis Ababa to attend his father's *tezkar*,[7] Menelik insisted he stay as a palace page and gave him two successive appointments as titular governor of small Shoan regions. He was given another, Orthodox, baptism by palace priests to assure conservative clergymen that he had not absorbed Roman Catholicism from the missionaries who had played an important role in his education.

Tafari remained in Addis Ababa for two years, attending Menelik's new palace school where he associated with other young nobles, including his cousin, Lij Iyasu, and had frequent opportunities to observe activities at the court. Life in rapidly expanding Addis Ababa extended Tafari's horizons and attendance at court gave him a continuing education in statecraft. Yilma's tenure as governor of Harar was brief. He died in October 1907. Tafari would like to have taken his place, but Menelik was still not ready to appoint him to Harar. He sent his loyal lieutenant, Dejazmach Balcha Safo[8], while Tafari was assigned to part of Balcha's previous governorship in Sidamo. He remained there for a year, profited from the learning

[7] Commemoration ceremony 40 days after a death.

[8] Balcha ranks as one of the most unusual figures among the hundreds of extraordinary personalities in recent Ethiopian history. Born humbly about 1862 and found castrated on a battlefield in Gurageland, he came to Menelik's notice. He took pity on him, brought him to Addis Ababa and educated him. Balcha showed talent as a soldier, fought with distinction in Wolamo and at Adwa and became one of Menelik's most reliable officers. Though he opposed Lij Iyasu, his relationship with Tafari Makonnen was never easy, as episodes recounted subsequently will demonstrate.

experience, then arranged to return to Addis Ababa to find that Menelik's condition had deteriorated.

Time of troubles

Concern mounted steadily in the capital during the first weeks of 1910. Had Menelik actually died? Was Taitu keeping his passing secret? If he was still alive, was there any hope he might recover? Rumors multiplied. French and British diplomats tried to influence developments to keep the succession from falling to Taitu. A broad group of Shoan *rases*, *dejazmaches* and other notables, with the concurrence of Abuna Matewos, worked out a plan to remove Taitu from power. They met in the house of Fitwrari Habte Giyorgis, Minister of War. Menelik had degenerated into complete mental incompetence. Learning of the plot against her, Taitu deployed loyal troops to defend the palace, but on 21 March 1910 Ras Tessema joined the conspirators in a swift move. The next day Taitu was forced to agree that in future she would confine herself to care of the disabled emperor and avoid interfering in governmental processes. Ras Tessema was declared regent, backed by a regency council dominated by Shoans. Lij Iyasu, then fourteen, was respected as heir but was not expected to govern.

Balcha as governor of Harar "had a well-merited reputation for ruthlessness, brutality and avarice, and was hated and feared by his subjects".[9] He alienated the merchants with measures restricting commerce and overtaxed the peasants. He was recalled to the capital. The logical candidate to succeed him and restore civic and commercial tranquility was Tafari. Taitu had approved his appointment. Ras Tessema and Fitwrari Habte Giyorgis supported it. While other pending appointments were cancelled, Tafari's assignment to Harar survived the coup against Taitu. Tafari had quietly and effectively cultivated support among senior figures, many of whom already had reservations about Iyasu. The respect in which Ras Makonnen had been held as well as Tafari's discreet behind-the-scenes lobbying worked in his favor. He had been careful to avoid direct involvement in the coup against Taitu. Ras Tessema was determined to exercise his authority as regent in keeping with Menelik's decision on the succession. There were rumors of tension between Tafari and Iyasu. The Ras brought both before Abuna Matewos and had them swear that neither would scheme against the other. This delicate matter having for the time being been settled, Tafari set out to take over his post:

[9] Wilfred Thesiger, *The Life of My Choice*, Collins, London, 1987, p. 25.

I took leave of the great men of rank to whom it is proper to say good-bye by going to each of their houses. Although it was a very delicate time for taking leave of Empress Taitu, I felt that my conscience would reproach me if I went without saying good-bye; hence I went to the Palace, took my leave, and set out on my journey.[10]

When he entered Harar on 12 May 1910 he was not yet eighteen. He was welcomed by the inhabitants as one of their own. He lost little time instituting tax and other reforms that pleased the population.

On 11 April 1911 Ras Tessema died. His body was immediately taken to Debre Libanos and his death was not announced for two days. Lij Iyasu appealed to the regency council to become regent himself. He was eager to act as emperor. In effect, his confused and hectic reign, which lasted five years, began at this point. Menelik, however, refused to die. He lingered almost to the end of 1913, so Iyasu remained only heir, not emperor. Menelik is believed to have expired during the night of 12-13 December, but his death did not become common knowledge until the middle of January 1914.[11] Meanwhile the government had fallen into disarray and provincial lords, especially in the north, had taken advantage of the confusion in the capital. Had it not been for the consolidation that had occurred in the country in the ten years following the victory at Adwa and the steps Menelik had taken to create an effective governmental structure, Ethiopia might have fallen apart. It was fortunate that the European powers who threatened Ethiopian survival in the late nineteenth century had checkmated each other and no longer sought to expand territorially. In fact, in the spirit of the Tripartite Treaty of 1906,[12] their legations in the capital cooperated in encouraging order and moderation among contenders for power and influence.

On 3 August 1911 Tafari married Menen Asfaw, grand daughter of Ras Mikael of Wollo and, therefore, niece of Lij Iyasu. Politically the marriage was evidence of Tafari's desire to strengthen his

[10] *Autobiography*, p. 35.

[11] Priests at Entoto Raguel still show visitors the "Menelik cave", a series of rock-cut chambers (perhaps originally a medieval rock church) in a cliff near the modern church where his body is said to have been kept until his daughter, the new Empress Zawditu, had a mausoleum built for him in the 1920s on the slope east of the Grand Palace. After Menelik's death Taitu retired to a small residence beside Entoto Maryam, lived a religious life, and died there on 11 February 1918. Her body too was transferred to the new mausoleum and Zawditu herself was buried there when she died in 1930. When Haile Selassie's bones were disinterred from under his office in the Grand Palace in 1992, they were temporarily placed in this same mausoleum. As of this writing they remain to be reburied in the tomb he had prepared for himself in Trinity Cathedral.

[12] For background on the treaty see Harold G. Marcus, "A Preliminary History of the Tripartite Treaty of December 13, 1906", *JES*, July 1964, pp. 21-40.

relationship with both Lij Iyasu and his father, but the marriage was sanctified in a church ceremony and seems to have been based on genuine affection.[13]

Lij Iyasu's efforts to assert himself as ruler of Ethiopia lasted from his fifteenth to his twentieth year. He had grown up to be a strong, handsome young man with an outgoing personality. He was brave, but also headstrong and impulsive. The fact that his father was a convert from Islam aroused suspicion among the Christian establishment. Though baptized an Orthodox Christian himself, Iyasu could not have helped knowing that his father's Muslim ancestry would inspire Shoan mistrust, compounded by suspicions that Ras Mikael might be aspiring to dominate Ethiopia through his son. He gave no weight to these considerations; in fact, he seems deliberately to have antagonized the Shoan establishment. He lacked the diplomatic skill and the refined sense of discretion that came naturally to Tafari. In spite of the oaths Ras Tessema had made the two potential rivals swear, Iyasu became bolder after Menelik's death in intervening in Tafari's territory. Meanwhile he had taken on several opportunistic advisers who commanded little popular respect. In spite of his youth, he became notorious as a womanizer and for long periods paid little attention to affairs of state.

The modern Ethiopian historian Bahru Zewde calls the reign of Iyasu "the most enigmatic in Ethiopian history",[14] but attributes a concept of Ethiopian nationhood to him that transcended religious and ethnic differences. During most of Haile Selassie's long tenure as ruler of Ethiopia Lij Iyasu was practically an "unperson". If he was referred to at all, it was almost invariably in extremely negative terms. Photographs of him were rare and a chronicle of his reign by Aleqa Gebre-Egziabeher Elias remained unpublished.[15] Lack of information generated curiosity. In more recent years a new generation of Western-trained Ethiopian historians has begun to seek a more balanced understanding of his personality and activity. The process is far from finished. While an objective assessment of Iyasu's dramatic performance on the Ethiopian historical stage is desirable,

---

[13] Menen, at least two year's Tafari's senior, was an attractive young lady and the two became cooperative partners. The marriage produced six children and endured over fifty years, until the Empress died on 22 February 1962.

[14] *History of Modern Ethiopia*, p. 121.

[15] A translation of one version of this work was published in Germany in 1994: Reidulf K. Molvaer (ed.), *Prowess, Piety and Politics, the Chronicle of Abeto Iyasu and Empress Zewditu of Ethiopia, 1909-1930*. A manuscript in the Ethiopian National Library was used as the basis for a monograph in Amharic by Gobeze Taffete, *Abba Tena Iyasu*, published with an introduction by Jacques Bureau as Bulletin no. 6 of the Maison des Etudes Éthiopiennes, Addis Ababa, 1996.

the fairest conclusion that can be reached on the basis of present knowledge may be to credit him with good intentions but condemn him for intemperate, inept, and in the end, disastrous performance. He gave his critics and enemies more than ample basis for accusing him of undermining Christianity in favor of Islam and abetting the disintegration of imperial authority.

While he became notorious for escapades in Addis Ababa which often ended in shoot-outs with police or palace guards, he disappeared from the capital for long periods into the countryside, married at least four wives, had numerous other liaisons and fathered several children. He dismissed and appointed senior officials with little concern for suitability and with the deliberate aim of humiliating many of Menelik's appointees. He had his father crowned negus of Wollo and Tigray in a great ceremony in Dessie. He encouraged him to plan a campaign to liberate Eritrea from the Italians which never began. He had little understanding of Ethiopia's position in the world and let himself be drawn into intrigues in favor of Germany and Turkey after World War I broke out.[16] He sent a caravan of arms and ammunition to the perennial Somali rebel, Sayid Mohammed Abdille Hassan, the "Mad Mullah" of Somaliland, an action which made little sense in terms of Ethiopia's own interests. These actions alarmed the European powers who feared moves against their own neighboring colonial possessions. Their representatives in the capital encouraged the Shoan leaders to act to forestall the chaos Iyasu's actions were likely to cause.

Iyasu deprived Tafari of his financial base in Harar by giving authority to collect revenues in the region to a Syrian adventurer, Ydlibi. On 13 August 1916 he officially removed Tafari (who had been in Addis Ababa since May) from the governorship of Harar and assigned him to Kaffa while he sent Ydlibi to Gambela, then an important outlet for Ethiopian trade. "The net effect of Iyasu's appointment policy was to create a number of disgruntled persons who were ready to come together to overthrow him."[17] The transfer of Tafari seems to have been the last straw for the Shoan aristocracy and probably for Tafari himself as well. Menelik's reign had not only made Shoa the most dynamic region in the country, it had also consolidated Shoan political dominance over Ethiopia. Shoans had extended their influence from their own province to Harar and throughout the south while the northern regions of the country – Tigray most of all – had been disturbed by chronic rivalries among

[16] The extent to which Iyasu was actually the object of serious efforts by Germany and Turkey to lure Ethiopia to the side of the Central Powers in 1915-16 remains to be clarified. Ottoman archives may eventually shed light on this question.

[17] Bahru Zewde, *op.cit.*, p. 125.

regional chiefs and had lost influence at the center. The Shoan elite could not be expected to let their dominance be dissipated. The reassertion of Shoan leadership which was now to occur was to last for almost sixty years.[18]

The Shoan aristocrats assembled in the palace on 27 September 1916, the Feast of the Finding of the True Cross (Maskal), and in the presence of the *abun* and the *echege* a proclamation deposing Iyasu was read.[19] The action already had the concurrence of Tafari and Minister of War Fitwrari Habte Giyorgis Dinagde. Iyasu, who was in Harar, was accused of treason and apostasy and excommunicated by Abuna Matewos.[20] Menelik's daughter Zewditu was designated Empress, arrived in the capital on 30 September, and was proclaimed sovereign on 2 October. Tafari was elevated to *ras* and declared heir.[21]

Iyasu had reason to expect these developments and remained in Harar. Orders from Addis Ababa for his arrest were misdirected and never carried out. He assembled troops and sent them marching toward the capital, but they were met half way at Mieso by an army led by half a dozen Shoan notables and driven back. Harar fell into disorder. On 9 October a column commanded by Balcha reached Harar. They looted the city and killed several hundred Muslim inhabitants. Iyasu withdrew toward Jijiga and then into the Afar lowlands. In Dessie, Negus Mikael, shocked at the rapid turn of events, was at first unsure how to react. The delay settled his son's fate.

[18] Shoan predominance and Amhara domination were not the same thing. The Haile Selassie era has often been characterized as a period of Amhara rule. In actuality the core Amhara regions – Gojjam, Begemder, and Wollo – provided only a small proportion of the leading officials in the imperial government and were at least as neglected as Tigray in allocation of developmental resources during the entire period. See Christopher Clapham, *Haile Selassie's Government*, Longmans, London, 1969, pp. 75-82. The table on p. 77 of this work shows that during the period 1942-66 Shoans occupied 62 per cent of the senior posts in the imperial administration. Eritreans, with 14 per cent, took second place. While Amhara culture and the Amharic language prevailed in Shoa, many of the Shoans were assimilated Oromo, Gurage, or of mixed ethnic background. Some Harari Muslims also came to occupy prominent posts in the central government.

[19] Text in Haile Selassie's *Autobiography*, pp. 48-50.

[20] Though Iyasu had a strong leaning toward Islam, there is no firm evidence that he actually converted.

[21] Some sources indicate he was designated regent at the same time by a smaller group of supporters. His citation of the aristocrats' declaration in his autobiography states, "We have appointed Dejazmach Tafari ... Crown Prince, with the rank of Ras, and Regent of the Empire" (p.50), but as late as 1925 one of the men who had joined in the 1916 coup, *Ligaba* Beyene Wondimagagnehu, organized a conspiracy against him, claiming that Tafari had usurped the status of regent. The conspiracy failed and Beyene was imprisoned in Harar. Bahru, *op.cit.*, p. 129.

In mid-October Mikael led an army approaching 80,000 across the Shoan frontier. At Tora Mesk, 130 km. northeast of Addis Ababa, part of his force annihilated the Shoan army defending Ankober and moved on to occupy the old Shoan capital. The Shoan commander, Ras Lulseged, was killed. The contest now hung in the balance. Fitwrari Habte Giyorgis was meanwhile rushing northward with a large force and Tafari left the capital with another contingent on 19 October. For nearly a week, as more Shoans and southerners joined the Shoan force, the two armies probed each others' positions. By the time the Shoans engaged Mikael's forces at Sagale on the morning of 27 October, Habte Giyorgis had about 120,000 men under his command.

Sagale was Ethiopia's greatest battle since Adwa. It was hard fought, but Mikael's artillery was put out of action by the Shoans and his machine-gunners ran out of ammunition. He made a belated attempt to have the Archbishop of Wollo offer a truce, but it was too late. By mid-afternoon the Shoans mounted a final attack, forcing the Negus into a trap and taking him prisoner. His camp and supplies were captured intact. His troops fled in disorder, but those who pledged loyalty to the new Empress were permitted to return home unharmed. Total casualties, heavier among the Wollo troops than the Shoans, probably reached 10,000. Fitwrari Habte-Giyorgis and Ras Tafari, both unscathed, led the victorious troops back to Addis Ababa.

Lij Iyasu had reached Ankober with a few thousand loyal followers the very morning of the Battle of Sagale. He withdrew quickly back into the desert, following caravan tracks to Dessie, and arrived there on 8 November. He offered Italy concessions in Tigray in return for support and tried to get the chiefs of the north to back him, but to no avail. The Shoans occupied Dessie on 10 December. Iyasu fled to Magdala, managed to elude capture and roamed as a fugitive through the north for the next five years. He was permitted for a time to stay in southern Tigray by Ras Seyum. When Tafari finally decided in 1920 to undertake a campaign to capture him, he had the support of most of the northern chiefs and the help of Ras Hailu of Gojjam. In January 1921 Ras Gugsa and Lij Desta Damtew surprised Iyasu in a small church in Tembien, took him prisoner, and brought him to Amba Alagi. On 21 May Ras Gugsa formally delivered him into Tafari's custody in Dessie. Tafari included a crisp summary of the occasion in his autobiography:

Ras Seyum was also summoned. We took away from him the governorship of Adwa as punishment for sending off Lij Iyasu without arresting him and gave the governorship to Dejazmach Gebre Selassie. To Ras Gugsa we gave an additional governorship, on top of his previous one, for capturing and bringing in Lij Iyasu. We made a number of adjustments in promotions and demotions and gave leave to Ras Hailu to return to Gojjam. We went back to Addis Ababa and got there on [19 July 1921]. We dispatched Lij Iyasu to Selale, to Fiche, and arranged that he should reside there guarded by Our faithful Ras Kassa.[22]

To go back to November 1916: the victory at Sagale validated the decisions taken the month before by the Shoan establishment. Ras Tafari and Fitwrari Habte Giyorgis entered the jubilant capital on 2 November and a victory parade was held at Janhoy Meda the next day. The then six-year-old son of British Minister Wilfred Thesiger, who later became the famous African explorer of the same name, recalled the occasion in his memoirs seventy years later:

Early that morning my father and mother, with Brian and me, preceded by the Legation escort with their red and white pennoned lances, rode down the wide lane between Balcha's troops to the royal pavilion. The war drums throbbed, a muffled, far-carrying, never-ceasing sound that thrilled me to the core; the five-foot trumpets brayed. Above the lines of waiting troops a host of banners fluttered in the breeze.[23]

Soon after, the elder Thesiger described the occasion in a long letter to his mother in England:

Huge tents, open fronted, had been put up and the Empress came in state with all her ladies ... and took her place on the throne.[...] About 10:30 a.m. the army began to march past. First came the minstrels, yelling war songs.[...] The advance guard of men on mules and horses came up in regular lines but as soon as they got near they dashed up at full gallop, shouting and brandishing their weapons, each man shrieking out how many men he had killed.[...] Men and horses were decorated with green, yellow and red silks and shields covered with gold and silverwork; and round the horses' necks were hung the bloodstained cloaks and trophies of the men each rider had killed.[...] Each big chief was preceded by some twenty slaves on mules banging away on kettle drums, with war horns and huge flutes blaring away.[...] Ras Tafari's army came in and he received a great ovation. The Abuna ... rode on a mule with his throne carried before him. After him came more chiefs and then banners and icons of the two principal churches which had sent their Arks to be present at the battle.[...] Then Negus Mikael was brought in. He came on foot and in chains, an old, fine-looking man dressed in the usual black silk cloak with a white cloth wound round his head, stern and very dignified, to bow before the Empress before being led away. One felt sorry for him; he had fought like a man, leading the charge of his troops, for a worthless son who had not even the courage to risk death in supporting the father who had thrown away everything for his sake...[24]

[22] *Autobiography*, p. 62.

[23] Thesiger, *Life*, p. 54. Young Thesiger had been born in Addis Ababa in 1910, the year his father arrived to take charge of Britain's legation.

[24] Ibid., pp. 54-5. The elder Thesiger headed the British Legation in Addis Ababa until 1919 but died in January 1920 of a heart attack shortly after returning to England.

Lij Iyasu had never been crowned. No time was lost in arranging a ceremony for Empress Zewditu. Tens of thousands of people, including official representatives of the European powers, assembled in the lavishly decorated capital on 11 February 1917 for imposing ceremonies. It was the first crowning of an empress as sole ruler since the legendary Queen of Sheba. She delivered her coronation address with Tafari standing behind her right shoulder. She pledged to safeguard her people "without being unjust and without making the poor suffer, respecting the great as my fathers and the small as my brothers".[25]

Ras Tafari and Empress Zewditu

Bahru Zewde has observed that "Zewditu's sole qualification for the throne was her birth as the daughter of Menelik – her supreme attraction to the nobility [was] her political innocuousness."[26] Though not much more than half her age, Tafari was already well grounded in Ethiopian politics. Deeply religious Zewditu had neither political experience nor ambition but took her role as symbolic head of state seriously and consented to divorce her fourth husband (Taitu's nephew), Ras Gugsa Wole of Begemder, a step the Shoan establishment considered necessary to prevent political scheming by him or his relatives.

Subsequent history would show that Tafari was undoubtedly the best choice for regent – and *de facto* ruler – the Shoan aristocrats could have made. He was eager to exercise authority and capable of it. He could not, however, have been elevated to the throne. Patience was his greatest virtue. There were still too many men among Ethiopian leaders whose ideal was a predictable, unintrusive central government that preserved traditional privileges and showed deference to regional potentates. Tafari knew this, but he also knew that the country had to progress and modernize or fall victim to outside forces. He showed deference to Zewditu, kept her informed of his actions, but took the reins of administration into his own hands. He took charge of military and civil appointments, judicial matters, and foreign relations. Officials and chiefs who sought to by-pass Tafari and gain favors from Zewditu found themselves quietly blocked by Tafari's vigilance.[27] He relied on his loyal cousin, Ras Kassa, whom

[25] As cited in Marcus, *HSI* , p. 26.

[26] *Op. cit.,* p. 128.

[27] He included in his *Autobiography* a chapter entitled "About men who were an obstacle to the work of government by coming between Queen Zawditu and myself", but provided no names and few details.

he appointed governor of Shoa, to back him when necessary and carefully cultivated a relationship with War Minister Habte Giyorgis, though the two were of quite opposite temperament in respect to reform and relations with Europe. In spite of periodic strains, the relationship lasted until Habte Giyorgis's death in 1926. He put his cousin Imru into the important governorship of Harar, but made few other early appointments.

Tafari had difficulty maintaining good relations with Dejazmach Balcha whom he skillfully frustrated when Balcha tried to organize a plot against him in 1920. Tafari was neither frightened nor deterred by opposition, but he was invariably cautious about the way he dealt with it. During his first year and a half in power he gradually won more and more influential men to his side. To foreign diplomats in Addis Ababa at the time he appeared weak. Several of them sent home dispatches predicting that his efforts to expand his authority and set the country on a progressive path would end in failure. The Italians, who never lost hope that Ethiopia might somehow be turned into their protectorate, completing Italian domination of the whole Horn of Africa, were foremost among the pessimists. Italians in Eritrea found it impossible to resist the temptation to dabble in intrigue in Tigray, where descendants of Yohannes IV kept competing with each other for dominance: "Practically all prominent Tigrayans throughout the period starting with the fall of Yohannes, at one stage or another, joined hands with the Italians against their emperors or against their local Tigrayan rivals."[28]

Tafari took advantage of dissatisfaction among the soldiery in 1918 to arrange the abolition of the Council of Ministers inherited from the Menelik era. Habte Giyorgis, Tafari and Zewditu cooperated in this action which was taken in the name of the Empress and represented an initial success in Tafari's plan to modernize the central administration. Ethiopia was severely hit by the great worldwide influenza epidemic during the latter months of 1918. Tafari himself was severely stricken. As much as 20 per cent of Addis Ababa's population is estimated to have died and mortality was heavy in other parts of the country.[29]

Tafari and the outside world

Tafari toyed with the idea of entering World War I on the Allied side, but received no encouragement from the French or British who, with Italy, still maintained an arms embargo against Ethiopia

---

[28] Haggai Erlich: *Ethiopia and the Challenge of Independence*, Lynne Rienner, Boulder, CO, 1986, p. 136.

[29] Marcus, *HSI*, pp. 36-7.

on the justification that it would prevent the destabilization of the country. Many traditional leaders were less enthusiastic than he was about the victory of the powers – Britain, France, and especially Italy – who in the past had threatened Ethiopian independence. Neverthe- less in 1919 Tafari arranged for delegations of notables to travel to Europe to congratulate the victors. These delegations did not result in the establishment of diplomatic relations: Ethiopia did not begin to maintain permanent diplomatic posts abroad until the late 1920s.

At the end of World War I the horizons of the great majority of Ethiopians were still narrow. Except for awareness of Jerusalem and Egypt, they seldom extended beyond the boundaries of the country itself, and often not far beyond their particular region. Menelik had dealt skillfully with foreign powers and for the most part defended Ethiopia's interests with diplomacy, only resorting to force when other methods were ineffective. But few leading Ethiopians cared about World War I or the debates about international order that followed it. On the other hand, Tafari's education and early experiences in Harar had instilled in him a deep awareness of the outer world. He understood the value of Menelik's skillful management of foreign relations. He also appreciated Ethiopia's precarious uniqueness in an African continent almost wholly colonized by Europeans. The concept of collective security which lay at the basis of the new League of Nations brought into being at the end of World War I had a strong appeal to him.

With Lij Iyasu captured and imprisoned, with a workable *modus vivendi* established with Zewditu, with progress toward a more modern governmental system, and with improved communications and increasing prosperity throughout the country, Tafari had time by the early 1920s to concern himself with foreign relations. These, of course, were linked in various ways to domestic considerations. Arms were needed to ensure internal stability. Britain and France were gradually persuaded, over Italian objections, to lift restrictions on their importation. Britain's desire to gain Ethiopian permission to build a barrage on Lake Tana to control the flow of the Blue Nile into Sudan moderated her stance. Tafari exploited the issue of entry into the League of Nations to commit both progressive and conservative elements in the country to support modernization and reform:

We asked them to let us know their present thoughts, lest we should experi- ence difficulties in the League if we failed to improve our governmental procedures, once we had entered. [...] The nobles and ministers declared unanimously that it was impossible to effect major improvements within one year but that it was their wish to improve the entire work of government year by year in slow stages, and therefore it was right for us to enter the League...[30]

[30] *Autobiography*, p. 77.

But slavery still existed in Ethiopia, resting on ancient practices and attitudes. There were objections from many quarters in Europe that Ethiopia was unfit to be a League member. In England the century-old anti-slavery movement was critical both of conditions in Ethiopia and slave traffic to Arabia, but the Foreign Office adopted a more pragmatic stance. Some Italian officials saw the issue as a way to frustrate Ethiopia from gaining international respectability. Tafari always understood that slavery for both moral and economic reasons was incompatible with modernization. The principle was clear – but as with most of the other reforms he aimed at – he knew that implementation would be a complex process. He issued an edict restricting slave-trading in 1918 and took several steps to enforce it. He worked to persuade southern landlords of the advantages of turning slaves into tenants to increase agricultural production. In August 1923 Tafari sent a delegation to assure the League Assembly that "association with the League would permit this Christian government ... to govern its people in peace and tranquility, and to develop its country under prosperous conditions", and promised that Ethiopia would keep the League fully informed of its progress in abolishing slavery. He issued an edict banning the slave trade on the eve of the League conference. In the final League debate the support of Britain and France was crucial. Ethiopia became a League of Nations member by unanimous vote on 28 September 1923.

Early in 1924 Tafari began planning a journey to Europe.[31] The idea of such a visit

> ... was a strange thing for all the princes and nobles and the army; they had great difficulty over this matter. We gave instructions to have the princes and nobles convened in a great assembly. In the end they all accepted the matter with pleasure, because We had convinced them that by Our ... extending our friendship with the governments of Europe, We were causing people to meet in trade and in work and getting to know each other as a sign of friendship ... and this would induce them to come and visit our country.[32]

To ease his reception in Europe he issued two edicts: on gradual emancipation of slaves on 31 March and on weapons control on 9 April 1924. He put Habte Giyorgis in charge of the government and left Addis Ababa by rail for Djibouti with a large party on 16 April.[33] A ship took them up the Red Sea to the Suez Canal from where they proceeded to Jerusalem by train. There they observed Easter and

[31] He had only left the country once before on a brief trip to Aden in 1922. There the Royal Air Force put on a display for him and he had his first ride in an airplane.

[32] *Autobiography*, p. 83.

[33] Many senior nobles accompanied him, among them: Ras Hailu, Ras Seyum, Dejazmach Nadew, Dejazmach Gebre Selassie, Dejazmach Haile Selassie Abayneh, Blattengeta Heruy Wolde Selassie and Lij Makonnen Indalkachew.

visited all the holy places. Tafari reached an agreement with the Greek Patriarch on improvements in access to Deir-es-Sultan, the Ethiopian chapel at the Holy Sepulcher. During the next three months the party visited Cairo, France, Italy, Belgium, Luxemburg, Switzerland, Sweden, Great Britain and Greece, inspecting schools, hospitals, factories, and churches. They were received by kings, presidents, foreign ministers and other dignitaries. The colorfully dressed Ethiopians attracted attention everywhere from the press and public. For them it was an enormous educational experience, so much so that when the exiled emperor wrote his memoirs a decade and a half later he devoted over forty pages to the details of the great journey.[34]

Tafari and his party were received in triumph when they returned to Addis Ababa on 4 September 1924. He had had more than sightseeing in mind for this trip but returned with a major strategic objective barely advanced. He had hoped to obtain an outlet to the sea at Zeila, Djibouti or Assab from his European colonial neighbors. Neither Britain, France nor Italy was prepared to give Ethiopia extra-territorial privileges in any of these ports, though the Italians proposed an elaborate ninety-nine-year agreement on Assab involving construction of roads and railways that would have given them the economic stranglehold on the country they got a few years later by invading. Discussions in London about a Lake Tana concession produced no result and Britain remained opposed to complete lifting of arms limitations. In May 1925 French support finally helped Ethiopia prevail in a League conference on arms control to get all restrictions on arms imports lifted. Tafari eventually took the Lake Tana barrage proposal into his own hands and in 1928 dispatched Dr. Worqeneh Martin[35] to the US to engage the White Engineering Company to make a feasibility study.

Reform and opposition

In Chapter 12 of his autobiography Tafari lists thirty-two reform initiatives taken during the years 1916-35 to advance modernization and

---

[34] *Autobiography*, pp. 81-123. For both serious and amusing highlights of the trip, see Marcus, *HSI*, pp. 60-77.

[35] The life of this man rivals the most improbable ancient Ethiopian legends. As an abandoned child of three he was picked up at Magdala and taken to India by two British officers, Charles Chamberlain and Colonel Martin, christened Charles Martin, and educated. He graduated from Lahore Medical College in 1882, and later went to Scotland for further studies which he finished in 1890. He was then appointed to Burma as a medical officer. He knew he was of Ethiopian origin. In 1896, on hearing of the Italian invasion, he decided to return to his native land, arrived in Addis Ababa in 1898, and began to treat patients. He had to operate

development and "allow foreign civilization to enter Ethiopia".[36] Many
of these were initiated before the European journey. They included
abolition of such medieval practices as cutting off the hands and feet
of criminals, chaining felons and debtors to those who had been
victimized by them, and outlawing the traditional ritualistic system
of determining guilt, *lebasha.*[37]

He established a military training school in 1919 and began the
process of creating a modern army to avoid dependence on regional
lords' levies, but it was far from complete when the Italians invaded in
1935. In the wake of the Russian Revolution several dozen Tsarist
exile Russians found their way to employment in Ethiopia, and during the later 1920s and early 1930s many Europeans and Americans
were engaged as technicians, advisors and teachers. The European
trip increased the Regent's confidence that reform could be accelerated. He had no doubt that modern education was the key to progress.
Menelik's school (opened in 1908) which Tafari had attended could
not handle the growing demand among youth. Over traditional
opposition he opened a high school named after himself Tafari
Makonnen, in 1925 and in 1926 launched an education tax of six per
cent on all imports and exports. He began to send promising young
men to Europe and America for higher education. By 1924, twenty-
five young Ethiopians were studying abroad and dozens more followed during the next decade, including a few women.[38] Tafari
imported two printing presses from Europe. One began publishing
the weekly newspaper, *Berhanena Selam* (Light and Peace) in 1924.[39]

Two of the most influential traditionalists, Fitawrari Habte Giyorgis
and Abuna Matewos, passed from the scene in December 1926.

---

through an interpreter. Eventually his grandmother identified him by scars on
his left arm and right leg and he learned that his mother had died a few days after
his disappearance and his father had not long survived. He remained in British
service, returning for a long period to Burma, till 1919 when he returned permanently to Ethiopia. He learned Amharic, played an important role in establishment of Tafari Makonnen High School and was later appointed by Ras Tafari
Ethiopian Minister to London. Several of his descendants became prominent in
Ethiopia later in the twentieth century.

[36] *Autobiography,* pp. 65-76.

[37] This entailed giving a boy a hallucinatory potion and then turning him loose
to identify the guilty party, which often led to punishment of totally innocent
persons. The system also lent itself to corruption. Tafari promulgated a modern
criminal code in 1930.

[38] They also included a number of young Eritreans, for the Italian administration
in Eritrea restricted education to the elementary level and Eritreans seeking
education came to Ethiopia. One of these, Lorenzo Taezaz, later became prominent as Haile Selassie's secretary.

[39] For a detailed account of early printing in Addis Ababa see R. Pankhurst, *Economic
History, 1800-1935,* pp. 676-84.

Younger progressive men became more prominent as associates of Tafari and were appointed to influential positions. They included Blattengeta Heruy Wolde Selassie, an early editor of *Berhanena Selam*, afterward mayor of Addis Ababa and Foreign Minister in the mid-1930s. Another was Heruy's close friend, Lij Takele Wolde Hawariat, who eventually became *Afenegus*,[40] and who introduced Tafari to the three Habtewold brothers who later became prominent in Ethiopian political life. Tafari put Nasibu Zamanuel, a Catholic convert educated by missionaries and a speaker of French and Italian in charge of the security of the capital in 1926 and later assigned him to the War Ministry. There were many others.

From the mid-1920s onward Tafari was less cautious in dealing with conservative opponents. As a rule, he refrained from moving against uncooperative chiefs in the provinces until he was sure of his position in the capital. Dejazmach Balcha again challenged him in 1927, but the old warrior found himself outwitted and deprived of both his soldiery and his lucrative governorship of Sidamo.[41] The head of the palace guard who was originally a Menelik appointee, Abba Weqaw Biru, resented the Treaty of Friendship Tafari signed with Italy on 2 August 1928 and became convinced he was defending Zewditu against preemption of her prerogatives. He mutinied at the beginning of September, made an abortive attempt to imprison Tafari, and then barricaded himself in Menelik's mausoleum. The Empress persuaded him to surrender. He was tried and given a death sentence, later commuted to imprisonment.[42]

Abba Weqaw's action backfired badly, for it caused tension in the capital that spurred Tafari's entourage to demand his coronation as *negus*. Ras Kassa supported the move and Zewditu acquiesced on 22 September. His coronation was delayed until representatives could come from Eritrea, Somaliland and Djibouti. Tafari was crowned by Zewditu on 6 October 1928. Since no regional lord had held the title since Negus Mikael had been defeated, Tafari's title was not linked to a region. He now became "King of Ethiopia, Heir to the Throne and Regent Plenipotentiary".

The coronation annoyed Ras Hailu in Gojjam. He felt entitled to the title of his father, Negus Tekla Haymanot. Tafari made no move against him, left him to enjoy his autonomy and his wealth, but refused to consider raising him in rank. Zewditu's former husband,

---

[40] "Mouth of the King", i.e. Chief Justice.

[41] The episode is recounted in Christine Sandford, *Ethiopia under Haile Selassie*, J.M. Dent, London, 1946, p. 34. Balcha retired to a monastery but came out to fight the Italians and was killed near Addis Ababa in 1937.

[42] This account is based on Bahru Zewde, *op. cit.*, pp. 134-5, Sandford, *op.cit.*, p. 35, and *Autobiography*, pp. 153ff.

Ras Gugsa Wole of Begemder, had been embittered, isolated, and out of the mainstream of developments in the country ever since he had been forced to divorce the Empress more than a decade before. Deeply conservative, he resented everything Tafari did and bad-mouthed him repeatedly. His resentments were exploited by the Italians in Eritrea and he was encouraged to resist Tafari by Ras Hailu and Ras Seyum of Tigray. Locusts and drought affected many parts of the north in 1928 and disorders broke out. Tafari ordered Gugsa to meet him in Worailu to assist in reassertion of the central government's authority. Gugsa refused. Zewditu wrote urging him to cooperate. He continued to refuse. Tafari sent an army led by his new Minister of War, Dejazmach Mulugeta Yigezu, and used his new aircraft to bomb and drop leaflets. Gugsa died on the battlefield at Anchem on 31 March 1930. Zewditu lay deathly ill of typhoid complicated by diabetes in her palace in Addis Ababa, relying on prayer for recovery. On 2 April, shortly after priests doused her with holy water, she fell into a coma and died in the early afternoon with Tafari at her bedside. The next morning the Crown Council proclaimed Ras Tafari emperor.[43]

Emperor Haile Selassie I

Patience, a sense of mission, energy, statesmanship and a favorable concatenation of circumstances had brought Ras Tafari Makonnen to the Solomonic throne. He attributed his good fortune to God's will, but throughout his life he relied on a conviction that God helps those who help themselves. Reverting to his baptismal name, Haile Selassie ("Power of the Trinity"), upon coronation, he saw the con-solidation of his authority as an opportunity to accelerate and extend his efforts to bring the country to a higher level of civilization. But he was also determined to savor his elevation and impress the country and the world with his power and determination. He postponed his coronation for seven months to make it a grander occasion than any in previous Ethiopian history. He scheduled it for early November 1930, a time when Ethiopia normally enjoys splendid weather. He sent invitations to emperors, kings and presidents throughout the world. Addis Ababa underwent months of cleaning, painting and polishing. A striking statue of Emperor Menelik II on horseback was raised in front of St. George's Cathedral. Magnificent vestments were sewn, and

We arranged ... golden headgear for Rases who had been appointed by virtue of hard work and services, while for the Crown Prince and princes of

[43] No substantiation has ever been found of the allegation that Tafari had Zewditu poisoned to clear his path to the throne.

royal descent We had made a pearl-studded ... coronet smaller than a crown
but excelling the golden headgear in size and in beauty of workmanship;
for the ladies of Our family and the wives of princes, golden diadems, smaller
than those for princes, and corresponding to their rank. For military commanders ... vestments and headgear were made of lion's manes that were
interlaced with gold and embroidered with velvet.[...] Gold medals were
manufactured in large quantities on which effigies of Myself and Empress ...
which were ... given as souvenirs to foreign guests...[44]

No emperors or kings came for the lavish and colorful festivities but
all who had been invited sent high-level representatives who were
sometimes accompanied by large parties. King George V sent his
third son the Duke of Gloucester, and King Victor Emmanuel sent
the Prince of Udine. During the 1920s Ethiopia had been visited by
increasing numbers of travellers, adventurers and researchers, but
never before had so many foreigners come to the capital at once.
These included dozens of journalists, among them the budding
English novelist Evelyn Waugh, twenty-seven at the time, who subsequently immortalized the experience in two books, one fiction and
one journalism.[45]

Addis Ababa was a different place in 1930 from what it had been at
the time Tafari became regent. Though with a permanent population of more than 50,000 by 1916, it was then still more a sprawling
camp than a city. By 1930 it had doubled in population. The Austra-
lian blue gum eucalyptus, introduced in the 1890s, had transformed
the capital into a city of green and also solved the firewood problem.
Schools, hospitals, churches, a mosque and many commercial
establishments had been built. The imposing station, terminus of
the railway line from Djibouti which had reached the capital in 1917,
was completed in 1929. Foreign legations had added new buildings
to their compounds, as had most of the nobles who maintained
residences in the capital. The city had become the commercial hub
of Ethiopia, thanks to the railway and the expansion of the market
economy. Motorcars had increased markedly. On Saturdays tens of
thousands of peasants from the surrounding area brought produce
to the city's great market. People from all parts of Ethiopia were
migrating to the capital, for there was a steady demand for labor.
Gurages and Oromos supplied much of it, officials were predominantly Amharas, and Tigrayans engaged in commerce and crafts.
Enormous crowds gathered for the coronation festivities.

Bahru Zewde comments that "it was to be the major historical
achievement of Hayla-Sellase that he finally succeeded in realizing

[44] *Autobiography*, p. 174.
[45] *Black Mischief*, first published in 1932 and reissued numerous times since;
and *When the Going Was Good*, Duckworth, London, 1946, and subsequently; both
have been republished in numerous paperback editions by Penguin and others.

the unitary state of which Tewodros had dreamt."[46] A constitution was an important part of the newly crowned Emperor's plan for the future. He had earlier attempted to persuade Zewditu to authorize a constitution, but "there were complex circumstances involved" and the initiative had been blocked by "some of the great nobles".[47] There was no popular demand for a constitution; in fact, the Emperor had to expend considerable effort to persuade the great nobles to accept the idea. He set up a commission to examine foreign constitutions, consult knowledgeable foreigners, and get the opinions of the senior nobles and ministers. He gave his Minister of Finance, Bejirond Tekle Hawariat, the task of organizing the process. With the exception of Ras Imru, the nobles argued for a decentralized system of government and a solid definition of their privileges. Haile Selassie was determined to lay the legal basis for the centralized system he was eager to reinforce. The document Tekle Hawariat drafted consisted of 55 articles.[48]

It confirmed the Emperor's divine right to rule by making "the person of the Emperor ... sacred, His dignity inviolate, and His power incontestable", confirmed his right "of His own free will", to issue laws for his people, and provided for the succession "perpetually in the line of His Majesty Haile Selassie ... whose lineage continues unbroken from the dynasty of Menelik I, son of King Solomon and the Queen of Sheba". It provided for the establishment of a bicameral parliament, a senate appointed from the nobility by the emperor and a chamber of deputies to be elected indirectly on the basis of property qualifications. No law approved by the parliament could go into effect until promulgated by the Emperor. It is evident that this extremely restrictive constitution was in part intended to impress foreign countries, but Haile Selassie went to great length in his memoirs to justify it as the beginning of an educational process.[49] Developments during the remainder of the twentieth century have offered little basis for arguing that Ethiopia at this stage of development was ready for any degree of popular participatory democracy.

Haile Selassie ceremonially signed the constitution on 16 July 1931 and it was in turn signed by senior notables. On 3 November 1931, the anniversary of his coronation, the Emperor opened the new parliament. He chose men of humble background as president and vice-president of the Senate, a foretaste of what would be a major characteristic of his technique of governing for the rest of his life:

[46] *Op. cit.*, p. 140.

[47] *Autobiography*, p. 178.

[48] Clapham, *HSI's Government*, pp. 34-6.

[49] *Autobiography*, pp. 180-201.

keeping the influence of the traditional nobility limited by elevating
educated young men whose status and loyalty would be dependent
only on himself. At the same time he was always careful to avoid bruis-
ing the sense of pride of the traditional elite and avoided gratuitous
provocation or disparagement.

Ras Hailu of Gojjam, however, went too far. The Emperor's intelligence was good. He knew that Hailu had become unpopular with the
peasantry in Gojjam, for he had taxed too heavily, accumulated too
much wealth, and alienated the clergy.[50] So he did not permit him to
depart from the capital after the constitution ceremonies. In April
1932 Hailu found himself facing charges leveled against him in
the Emperor's court. Haile Selassie fined him heavily, took away his
customs and taxing privileges as well as his governing authority over
half of Gojjam, and kept him in the capital. The recalcitrant *ras* attempted to negotiate independently with Britain and America about
the Lake Tana project and became implicated in an ill-thought out
scheme to enable Lij Iyasu to escape.[51] This brought his arrest and
another trial on 27 June 1932 at which he was sentenced to death,
commuted to imprisonment and confiscation of all his wealth. Ras
Imru was made governor of Gojjam and gained a reputation for
enlightened rule, though the province remained potentially troublesome.

In return for peaceful submission, Menelik had guaranteed
Jimma autonomy in 1882 under Sultan Abba Jifar. When the old man
became senile and his grandson, Abba Jobir, attempted to escape
Addis Ababa's control, Haile Selassie sent military forces against him
and brought him to the capital. Jimma's autonomy thus came to an
end.[52] The two rases of Tigray, Seyum and Gugsa Araya, were cooperative, but to be sure of their loyalty, Haile Selassie arranged marriage
alliances. Ras Gugsa Araya was married to the Emperor's niece;
his son, Haile Selassie Gugsa, to the Emperor's daughter, Zenebeworq;
and Crown Prince Asfa Wossen to Woleta-Israel, Ras Seyum's
daughter.

By appointing Ras Kassa to Begemder, Haile Selassie practically
completed his program for placing loyal supporters in provincial

---

[50] Major R.E. Cheesman's *Lake Tana and the Blue Nile*, Cass, London, 1968, provides much information about Ras Hailu and life in Gojjam during the period
1925-34 when the author was British Consul for Northwest Abyssinia in Dangila.

[51] The captive prince did escape during Ras Kassa's absence from Fiche and fled to
Gojjam where he was captured by government forces, taken to Garamulata in
Hararge, and reincarcerated.

[52] For a detailed study of this kingdom, see Herbert S. Lewis, *A Galla Monarchy,
Jimma Abba Jifar, Ethiopia, 1830-1932*, University of Wisconsin Press, Madison,
1965.

posts. Only one old traditionalist, Dejazmach Ayalew Biru of Semien, remained at the time Italy invaded.[53]

Economic development

The confused period of Menelik's decline and Lij Iyasu's troubled reign had only a limited effect on the country's economic development, for momentum generated after the Battle of Adwa continued and accelerated steadily after 1916. Northern trade routes declined, but the newly incorporated provinces of the south developed rapidly. Djibouti quickly became Ethiopia's main outlet to the sea, eclipsing Berbera, Zeila and Assab after completion of the railway in 1917. The railway also consolidated a process already under way: Addis Ababa became the commercial center of the country as well as its political capital. In the west Gambela became a major outlet for trade with Sudan, which Britain was eager to encourage. Coffee became the country's principal export. It has been ever since. Britain established consulates at Harar, Mega, Gore and Dangila, while Italy set up consulates in Adwa, Gondar and Dessie. Trade was mostly in the hands of foreigners, including Greeks, Armenians, Arabs and Indians. Greeks established groceries, bakeries, flour mills, and were especially prominent in the liquor trade. They also worked as carpenters and tailors. Arabs, primarily Yemenis, were often itinerant traders in remote parts of the countryside. Indians dealt in textiles, carpets and small manufactures. Armenians established jewelry shops, machine shops, and engaged in manufacturing of furniture, saddlery and metalwork.

European entrepreneurs established general trading companies, often first as branches of firms based in Aden, which engaged in both import and export. Enterprising Ethiopians gradually became involved in the economy, but their activities were still overshadowed by expatriates in the period before the Italian invasion. The Bank of Abyssinia was originally set up in 1905 with backing of the National Bank of Egypt. Its first banknotes issued in 1915 gained almost no acceptance – people continued to prefer the Maria Teresa dollar. In 1931 Haile Selassie had the government buy out the Bank of Abyssinia and reestablish it as the Bank of Ethiopia. Both Ethiopia's financial system and its economy were still in an underdeveloped state when Italy invaded.

---

[53] Clapham, *HSI's Government*, p. 18. Dejazmach Ayalew Biru had fought with Ras Imru in Shire against the Italians and, though later proclaimed Governor of Gondar by the Italians, he joined the Patriots and participated in the final attack on the city in November 1941. Greenfield, *op.cit.*, p. 260.

While in the south a few commercial agricultural undertakings
had been established and employed hired labor, the great majority of
the Ethiopian population[54] lived as subsistence farmers in traditional
fashion. Land tenure systems varied from one region to another, with
communal systems of redistribution prevalent in the north and
tenancy amounting to serfdom in the south. As many as 300,000
Ethiopians are thought to have still lived in some form of slavery in
1935, though trade in slaves had for the most part been stopped.[55]
Pastoralists predominated in lowland regions, many living in a
manner little changed from ancient times.[56] In the forested country
in the west and southwest bordering Sudan and Kenya remote tribes
still lived a Neolithic life.

Addis Ababa experienced a further spurt of growth during the
early 1930s. The modern Parliament Building with clock tower, was
inaugurated in 1934. The last major building to be erected before
the Italian invasion was the Emperor's palace, *Genetta Leul* (Prince's
Paradise), completed in the last eight months of that year.[57]

Eritrea under Italy

By the 1930s the majority of Eritreans had grown up in a colonial political
and economic system which was markedly different from the rest of
Ethiopia. Throughout the colonial period Ethiopia was treated [by the
Italians] as the hinterland of Eritrea. The Eritreans were better clothed,
enjoyed a greater consumption of goods, and had access to a way of life
considered superior ... to ... that enjoyed by their Ethiopian counterparts. [...]
Eritrea with its urban centres, its considerable wage-earning population
combined with an increased purchasing power, was considered more
developed ... than the rest of Ethiopia. [...] The main aim of the Italians
in concentrating on the material well-being of Eritreans was, no doubt, to

[54] There were no censuses. Estimates of the country's total population in the
early 1930s vary between six and ten million. While birthrates remained high,
there had been little improvement in health or longevity during the first decades of the twentieth century. Infant mortality remained high.

[55] As late as 1972, when I travelled to his home country in Gojjam with novelist
Abbe Gubegna, I saw him welcomed in his father's house by a tall old black man
who embraced his knees and kissed his feet for several minutes. Embarrassed,
Abbe explained that the man had been a slave who, though long since freed, had
remained attached to the family.

[56] An account of a perilous journey across the Afar lowlands to the Eritrean coast
at the end of the 1920s, L.M. Nesbitt's *Desert and Forest*, Jonathan Cape, London,
1934, provides a vivid picture of the unchanged life of this region. It is one of the
greatest classics of Ethiopian travel.

[57] It is now the main administration building of Addis Ababa University, having
been donated to the newly established university by Haile Selassie after the
abortive coup of 1960.

gain and mobilize support within Eritrea for their planned invasion of Ethiopia.[58]

Italian leaders were proud of their *colonia primogenita* and initially looked upon it as a region to be settled by Italian peasants, producing raw materials, and relieving the mother country of population pressure. The Bahta Hagos rebellion of December 1894, protesting against the confiscation of land for settlers, brought this approach into question even before the defeat at Adwa forced a revision of Crispi's plans for conquest of Ethiopia. Ferdinando Martini, Governor of Eritrea during the decade 1897-1907, put an end to grandiose settlement plans and inaugurated a moderate approach designed to encourage peaceful development with minimal disruption of the existing social structure. Henceforth Italy relied on traditional Eritrean elites: "The privileges of ruling castes were virtually left untouched.[...] The Eritrean chief was a spokesman of the colonial state."[59]

Because of the peace and stability that colonial rule brought, the Eritrean rural elite probably had more power and influence than they had had under Ethiopian rule. Hereditary leaders administered the peasantry and collected taxes, being officially sanctioned to take five per cent at each step upward as the tribute went to the administration in Asmara.

From 1908 onward the development of a colonial army supplying manpower for consolidation of Italian control of Somalia and conquest and pacification of Libya became a priority objective. Six thousand Eritreans had been recruited and trained by 1910, 10,000 by 1914. By 1925 over 60,000 Eritreans were serving in the Colonial Army. The drain of manpower resulted in a labor shortage in the colony as development of infrastructure gained momentum. Migrant laborers from Tigray were welcomed. Many brought their families and settled permanently in Eritrea. Government schools were introduced in 1911 to train a limited number of low-level civil servants, clerks and workers who needed elementary skills; but, like the Belgians in the Congo, the Italians permitted no middle-level or higher education. Barely 1,500 students were enrolled annually in government schools by the early 1930s. A few Eritreans were able to obtain limited further education from the Catholic and Swedish missions.[60] While Italy encouraged the spread of Catholicism (with

[58] Tekeste Negash, "Italian Colonialism in Eritrea, 1882-1941", Ph.D. diss., Uppsala University, Sweden, 1987, pp. 154-6. The summary which follows reflects the conclusions of this study, for it is the most comprehensive and objective available on the subject in English.

[59] *Ibid.*, p. 152.

[60] One of the most significant products of early Swedish-mission education was a Tigrayan born near Adwa in 1886, Gebrehiwot Baykedagn, who became an impor-

little success), it feared that the educational activities of Swedish missionaries encouraged Ethiopian nationalism and expelled the Swedish mission in 1932. Young Eritreans with intellectual inclinations found their way to Ethiopia for education and often stayed there. There were no native-language newspapers or magazines. No organizations were permitted that could foster the development of a native intellectual class.

Italy's routine racist practices did not originally differ markedly from those of other European colonial powers. White supremacy was taken for granted. Wages for native workers were kept six to eight times lower than those of Italians and most Eritreans were confined to menial employment. Efforts to curb *madamismo* – marriage and/or cohabitation between Italians and native women – were never very successful, with the result that by the 1930s a sizable mixed-race group had resulted. Many of these were initially permitted to acquire Italian citizenship, but as Fascist racial doctrine became entrenched in the 1930s, they were reclassified as African and suffered discrimination.

Eritrea's total population was estimated at slightly below 200,000 when Italy proclaimed the colony in 1890. Seven censuses carried out between 1905 and 1939 recorded a steady growth of population. Highland Tigrinya-speakers accounted for 35 per cent of the population in 1905. By 1939 their proportion had risen to 54 per cent of a total that had increased more than threefold in fifty years.[61] In contrast to the Christian Tigrinya-speaking highlanders who formed a regionally compact group, the other indigenous groups in Eritrea, mostly Muslim and pastoralist (except for the Baria and Kunama, animist agriculturalists), were scattered around the western, northern, and eastern periphery of the colony. Of these the Tigre,

---

tant theorist of modernization. He went to Europe to continue his education and returned from Germany with a medical mission that came to treat the declining Menelik. He had been exiled by Empress Taitu, but now joined Ras Tafari's supporters. Though he died in 1917, Ras Tafari encouraged collection of his writings which were one of the first publications of the Berhanena Selam press in 1924. Reissued again in Amharic in Ethiopia in 1960, they have been translated into English by Tenkir Bonger (ed.) as *The State and Economy of Early 20th Century Ethiopia*, Karnak House, London, 1995.

[61] Tekeste Negash, *op.cit.*, pp. 127ff., 159-61. The Tigrinya-speaking increase can be explained in part by inflow from neighboring Tigray. Almost all highlanders were Orthodox Christians and residually Ethiopian in sentiment. Only 8,000 Orthodox Christians were converted to Catholicism during the existence of the Italian colony. Until 1929, when the Italian administration arranged for the Coptic Patriarch in Cairo to exempt Eritrea from the jurisdiction of the Ethiopian Orthodox Church, highland Christians recognized the Ethiopian Patriarch and Eritrean monasteries considered themselves subordinate to the Ethiopian religious hierarchy. Eritrean monasteries sent representatives to the coronation of Haile Selassie in 1930.

speaking a Semitic language, were the most numerous. The Bilen, an Agau enclave around Keren, included both Catholics and a sizable number of Protestant Christians converted by Swedish missionaries. Population pressure in the Tigrinya-speaking highlands resulted in land shortage and outflow of settlers into more thinly populated lowland areas. This provoked occasional Muslim resentment. The Italian administration officially observed a policy of complete equality between Islam and Christianity. Muslims were administered through local leaders in the same way as Christians. During the 1930s Mussolini adopted a pro-Arab and pro-Muslim stance.[62] Italy instituted measures favoring Islam during the occupation of Ethiopia. These had little direct effect in Eritrea, however.

Eritrea was always a deficit area from the viewpoint of budget, trade and investment. The colony attracted little private Italian capital and that usually came in only under highly concessionary arrangements. Revenue collected in Eritrea rarely covered as much as a third of the colony's budget. Exports, which always lagged behind imports in value, included large quantities of coffee re-exported from Yemen and in certain years a substantial proportion of goods from northern Ethiopia. The most important Eritrean-origin export, in both quantity and value, was salt. The overwhelming proportion of Eritrean imports came from Italy. Cotton goods, other textiles and yarn predominated. As the comparative well-being of the population increased during the 1920s, demand for elementary consumer goods rose sharply. During the 1920s Ethiopian imports through Massawa and Assab were also significant, but fell sharply in the 1930s. Italy permitted goods to move freely across the Ethiopian border.[63]

Telephone and telegraph lines were systematically extended to most parts of the colony. Characteristically, the Italians concentrated on roads. Ethiopian rulers thought roads only made it easy for invaders, so had neglected improving tracks and trails. The Italians undertook an energetic road-building program into all parts of the territory. Even before the colony was officially proclaimed, a narrow-gauge railroad inland from Massawa was started in 1887. A spectacular engineering feat, it was completed to Asmara in 1911, extended to Keren in 1922, and on to Agordat by 1930 with expectations of extension to Kassala across the Sudanese border, which did not materialize.

Asmara was a tiny village around a church when Ras Alula chose it as his seat in 1877. After Italy made it the colony's capital, it grew

[62] Erlich, *Ethiopia and the Middle East*, pp. 96-8.

[63] Pankhurst, *Economic History*, pp. 371-92; Tekeste Negash, *op.cit.*, pp. 37-43, 153-4.

rapidly and had a population nearing 9,000 by 1905. It was laid out as a compact Italian town, in contrast to the vast sprawl of Addis Ababa, but did not reach 20,000 until the early 1930s. The 1931 census counted 15,732 "natives" and 3,057 Europeans in Asmara. After 1932, as Mussolini began preparing for the invasion of Ethiopia, more than 50,000 Italian laborers were brought to Eritrea. By 1939 Asmara had over 100,000 people, more than half of whom were Italians. The Italian influx generated no significant resistance among Eritreans, for it brought vastly expanded opportunities for employment. Italian colonial policy had never envisioned a permanent, separate Eritrea. There was no pretense of even limited power-sharing with the indigenous population. Haile Selassie's coronation and his commitment to modernization and reform nevertheless excited many highland Christians in Eritrea and aroused concern among more far-sighted Italians. Governor Zoli wrote in 1930: "Since we have not even benefited from the modest degree of evolution which existed in the local institutions, we now find ourselves in a condition of inferiority in respect to the population of Ethiopia."[64]

For concerned Eritreans, Ethiopia acted as a safety valve: they could migrate there if they became sufficiently alienated from the colonial regime. The great majority of Tigrinya-speaking highlanders thought of themselves as Ethiopians from a cultural and religious viewpoint, but they were not actively politicized. Their concerns were local and limited. Muslims in Eritrea, on the other hand, though equally oriented toward local concerns, did not share the same feelings toward Ethiopia. Neither of these sets of attitudes was sufficiently strong to affect Italy's plans for conquest of all of Ethiopia. They would become politically operative only after Italian defeat when British occupation permitted and encouraged a politicization of Eritrean society.

Mussolini prepares to absorb Ethiopia[65]

Ras Tafari received a genuinely warm welcome when he visited Italy in 1924 and met with Mussolini, with whom he was impressed. But

[64] Tekeste Negash, *op.cit.*, p. 130.

[65] Italian writing and scholarship on Ethiopia and the Horn of Africa is enormous and since the end of World War II often extremely frank and informative. The brief sections which follow will draw upon only a small portion of it. Particularly noteworthy is the three-volume history of Angelo Del Boca, *Gli Italiani in Africa Orientale*, originally totalling more than 2,300 pages, published by Mondadori between 1976 and 1982 and reissued by Editori Laterza in 1992: *La Conquista dell'Impero*, *Dall'Unita alla Marcia su Roma*, and *La Caduta dell'Impero*. The same author's *La Guerra d'Abissinia, 1935-1941*, Feltrinelli, Milan, 1965 (published in English as *The Ethiopian War, 1935-1941* by the University of Chicago Press,

he was wary of falling into dependence on Italy and rejected the Italian offer of a ninety-nine-year lease for a free port in Assab in return for sweeping economic concessions. He may have believed that Italy's commitment in the Treaty of Peace and Friendship signed on 2 August 1928 guaranteed Ethiopia's security within the framework of the League of Nations system. He apparently felt it was a chance worth taking, but he remained wary. The annex to this treaty providing for a highway from Assab to Dessie was never implemented.

It is clear that many Italians longed to avenge the defeat at Adwa in 1896. Mussolini correctly assumed he could whip up popular enthusiasm for an effort to take over Ethiopia. For many years the Italian military had systematically gathered intelligence that would be useful in invasion. Fascist propaganda began to berate Ethiopia as a primitive country where slavery still flourished. Preparations for a logistic build-up in Eritrea began in 1932. Mussolini wanted a quick, easy war to bolster Italian pride and demonstrate how fascism was making the country a factor to be reckoned with in the world. He resolved to move against Ethiopia as soon as he could find a pretext for mobilization. The long Ogaden frontier had never been clearly demarcated, and Italy had for several years sent military patrols into territory the Ethiopians regarded as theirs. When in December 1934 an Ethiopian patrol clashed with a party of Italian troops at an obscure cluster of wells called Walwal, Mussolini claimed an Ethiopian provocation.

No matter that Ethiopian casualties at Walwal were three times those of the Italians, Mussolini made shrill demands for apologies and reparations. Though his commander in Eritrea, Emilio De Bono, wrote him on 13 February 1935 "at present the *Nagusa nagast* is ordering too many prayers and fasts to give us reason to think that he wishes to attack us",[66] he had already ordered the mobilization of two divisions and in the weeks that followed gave instructions for elaborate preparations in Eritrea and Italian Somaliland for invasion. Italy was seized with a nationalistic frenzy which drowned out voices of caution and fears of failure, as soldiers, equipment and ships were readied for a massive movement to East Africa. By the end of May, in merely four months, the number of Italians in Asmara had quadrupled as soldiers and laborers arrived and set to work on an unprecedented building program.

Clear-sighted politicians out of office, such as Winston Churchill, and hundreds of later twentieth-century historians would see Italy's

---

1969) remains the best short history of the war. His *I gas di Mussolini*, Editori Riuniti, Rome, 1996, documents Italy's use of poison gas during the 1935-6 invasion.

[66] As cited in Del Boca, *The Ethiopian War*, p. 21.

invasion of Ethiopia as the beginning of World War II, the great
contest between the dictators and the democracies. There was little
vision in Europe in 1935. Haile Selassie appealed to the League of
Nations for help and went to considerable lengths to be conciliatory
toward Italy. Little help came, for both France and Britain were ready
to resign themselves to Italy's aggression. A process of diplomatic
to-and-fro began in Europe that lasted until autumn.[67]

Determined action could have deterred Mussolini, who had no
allies, not yet having forged an alliance with Hitler. Public opinion in
Germany and even in Japan was not sympathetic to Italy. If Britain had
closed the Suez Canal, how could Italy have sent men and material to
East Africa? Fear of war deterred England and France from decisive
action. The crisis was the beginning of a test of the collective security
system on which the League of Nations was based. Ethiopia's increasingly anguished appeals for League of Nations action produced
only endless palaver. Haile Selassie's sincere desire to have the crisis
settled by international action (rather than go to war) combined with
French and British equivocation gave Mussolini good reason to
believe Ethiopia might be a pushover.

The Italian invasion[68]

Mussolini announced to the world on 2 October 1935, "We have
been patient with Ethiopia for forty years; now our patience is
exhausted." General De Bono was given orders to attack across the
Mareb the next morning with his 100,000-man army. Its three
columns made rapid progress. Adigrat fell on 5 October. Adwa was
brutally bombarded and then occupied on 6 October. Toselli,
Arimondi and Dabormida who were killed at the Battle of Adwa in
1896 were thus "avenged" as was the entire defeat suffered by Italy

[67] This has resulted in an enormous body of scholarly writing which will not be
summarized here because it belongs more to the history of Europe than to that
of Ethiopia. The most comprehensive and succinct works are two books by George
Baer, *The Coming of the Italo-Ethiopian War*, Cambridge University Press, 1967, and
Italy, Ethiopia, and the League of Nations, Stanford University Press, 1976.

[68] In addition to Angelo Del Boca's, there are many other accounts of the Italo
Ethiopian War, both journalistic and scholarly, e.g. Ladislas Farago, *Abyssinia on
the Eve*, Putnam, London, 1935; G.L. Steer, *Caesar in Abyssinia*, Hodder & Stough-
ton, London, 1936; G.L. Steer, *Sealed and Delivered*, London, 1942; A.J. Barker,
The Civilizing Mission, Dial Press, New York, 1968; James Dugan and Lawrence
Lafore, *Days of Emperor and Clown*, Doubleday, New York, 1973; Thomas M.
Coffey, *Lion by the Tail*, Viking Press, New York, 1974; Anthony Mockler, *Haile
Selassie's War*, Oxford University Press, 1984. Haile Selassie devoted the last
third of his *Autobiography* to a frank description of the Italian invasion and the
Ethiopians' attempt to defend themselves: pp. 212-312. The section which fol-
lows is based primarily on these sources, but draws on others as well.

there. On 11 October Dejazmach Haile Selassie Gugsa, the ruler of eastern Tigray, already in Italian pay, defected with more than 1,000 men. On 8 November Makelle fell. But few soldiers had been killed on either side. Most of Tigray was occupied peacefully. Three days after Makelle was captured Mussolini ordered De Bono to march on to Amba Alagi. De Bono objected that the position was of only historical significance and tactically risky. Mussolini was impatient. He replaced De Bono with Pietro Badoglio who he believed would follow orders and move ahead more rapidly.[69] Under Badoglio's direction, the invasion soon degenerated "into a bloody affair of wanton and brutal destruction".[70]

Haile Selassie had his most loyal *rases* rush tens of thousands of hastily armed troops north to mount a counteroffensive. He himself left the capital for Dessie on 28 November 1935. Rases Imru, Seyum, Kassa and Mulugeta reached southern Tigray with separate armies by the end of the year. Their operations were poorly coordinated. Troops fought bravely but were badly defeated at the great natural fortress of Amba Aradom southwest of Cheleqot in mid-February by artillery and air bombardment. Mulugeta was killed and the remnants of his 50,000-man army took heavy punishment from the air as they fled southward. Badoglio then concentrated on the armies of Kassa and Seyum around Worqamba in Tembien. A ferocious Ethiopian counterattack at the end of February shocked the Italians but their vastly superior arms enabled them to recover quickly and prevail. They ended up decimating the Ethiopians, killed great numbers, and forced the rest to flee.

In Shire Ras Imru actually advanced to the Eritrean border and hoped to retake Aksum and Adwa. Badoglio used aerial bombardment, artillery and gas on Imru's troops. They came primarily from Gojjam and Semien where chiefs were already unenthusiastic about fighting. By early March Ras Imru was forced to attempt an orderly retreat across the Takazze. Italian pilots machine-gunned them mercilessly as they forded the river. Ten thousand made the crossing, but as a fighting force the army disintegrated. Imru later recalled:

It had been my intention to carry on a guerrilla war in the mountains ... of Tsellemti and Semien, but when I told Dejazmach Ayelu Biru [of Semien] ... he would have nothing to do with it. [...] Day by day my ranks thinned out; many were killed in the course of air attacks, many deserted. When at last I reached Dashan, all that remained of my army was my personal bodyguard of 300 men.[71]

[69] Mussolini preserved De Bono's honor by promoting him to marshall. De Bono remained loyal and published a stirring account of the entire Italian campaign in 1936, translated as *Anno XIII - the Conquest of an Empire*, Cressey, London, 1937.

[70] Del Boca, *op.cit.*, p. 54.

[71] Cited from Del Boca, *op.cit.*, p. 156, from an interview with Ras Imru in the 1960s.

Meanwhile General Rodolfo Graziani, moving out of Italian Somaliland, faced two comparatively well organized Ethiopian armies garrisoning the Ogaden and Bale. They were led by Ras Desta Damtew and Ras Nasibu Zamanuel[72] and totalled perhaps 80,000 men. Hoping to outflank the Italians and penetrate Somaliland, Ras Desta made a bold march eastward across the Ogaden. Though he had been blocked by stubborn Ethiopian resistance at Qorahe in November, Graziani massed a well equipped force at Dolo. Badoglio ordered Graziani to remain on the defensive, but the eager general gained permission from Mussolini to make a limited attack and took advantage of the fact that Ras Desta had overextended himself. The Ethiopians had been weakened by sickness and thirst in the desert and found themselves under Italian air bombardment and showered with gas. They were hopelessly defeated in a three-day battle at Ganale Doria in the second week of January. Graziani pursued their remnants 400 miles eastward to Negelle Borana, cutting the main road to Kenya. Thus victory in the north had been matched by victory in the south. Harar and the railroad link to Djibouti, however, remained in Ethiopian hands.

The final, decisive battle in the north took place near Maichew in southern Tigray on the last day of March 1936. Harassed by continual air attacks, Haile Selassie had moved from Dessie to Korem in February where he received firsthand reports of the disasters in Tembien and Shire. After the collapse of Ras Imru's forces, he decided to lead the Imperial Bodyguard in an offensive against the advancing Italians. It was a dramatic but futile gesture. His enemy, Badoglio, later wrote:

The negus was drawn to it, not so much by the will to attack as by the advice of his chiefs, the dignitaries of the empire, and even by the empress herself, all of whom, in accordance with the Ethiopian tradition, now saw a possible solution of the conflict only in a great battle directed by the emperor in person.[73]

Joined by remnants of the armies that had been defeated farther north, the young soldiers of the Bodyguard fought bravely under incessant air bombardment and gas attacks but had to retreat. The Italians pursued them beyond Lake Ashangi to Korem. The White Russian Colonel Konovaloff, the Emperor's aide who accompanied him through the battle and its aftermath, later described the massacre near the lake:

The wide valley ... lay level under the blazing African sun. To its side the blue surface of the lake was lightly ruffled by the breeze. Along the road the

---

[72] Governors respectively of Sidamo and Hararge.

[73] Badoglio, as cited from his memoirs in Del Boca *op.cit.*, p. 163.

weary people dragged themselves, scattering for a moment in panic or massing together in groups. Four, six, eight bombs burst one after the other. [...] Here is another aeroplane which seems to be choosing its victims as it flies just over their heads. One explosion ... then another which raises a jet of earth clods, sand and stones. People are hit this time. [...] I turn around and see someone dying on the ground. [...] Fear pushes the survivors upon their road without attending to the wretch that cannot follow them, for he has lost his legs. At the same moment our allies the Azebu Galla fire on us from the hilltops where their village lies. When they see stragglers, they kill them and strip the bleeding bodies of rifles, cartridges and clothes. [...] Before us there is a corner of hell which none of us can avoid. On one side of the road is the lake, on the other are the mountains. The pass is narrow and the human flood finds it hard to press forward and through. [...] At last we are near the caves of Korem which will shelter us from the Azebu bullets and the aeroplanes.[74]

The defeated Emperor and a diminished set of followers made their way southward on caravan tracks through Lasta. At Muja the exhausted but still uncowed Lion of Judah decided to make a pilgrimage to Lalibela. Arriving there on 12 April at dusk, he went into the largest of the rock churches, Medhane Alem, and remained, praying, without food or drink, for two full days. His strength restored, he rejoined the main party on 15 April and learned that Crown Prince Asfa Wossen had abandoned Dessie the day before. A week later Badoglio transferred his headquarters there and prepared for the advance on Addis Ababa. Meanwhile the Emperor and his party followed trails across the gorges of the Nile tributaries to Ras Kassa's seat at Fiche in Shoa, reaching it on 28 April. From there he took fifty dignitaries with him to Addis Ababa by car. The capital was in chaos. Badoglio's victorious men were making steady progress southward against waning resistance through Debre Sina, up Termaber, and onto the Shoan plateau.

Back home, Haile Selassie considered moving the capital to Harar which was still in Ethiopian hands, thought briefly of joining Ras Imru to launch guerrilla resistance in Gojjam, then told the British and French ambassadors he had decided to stand and defend Addis Ababa. In the morning of 1 May what was left of the Crown Council, including Rases Kassa and Getachew, Foreign Minister Heruy, and Lorenzo Taezaz, met in Menelik's palace. They were more aware of the disintegration of Ethiopian resistance than the Emperor and unanimously advised him to depart for Geneva to appeal to the world. That afternoon he ordered Ras Imru as his viceroy to move the

[74] Cited in Steer, *Caesar in Abyssinia*, pp. 321-3. The same area was the scene of heavy fighting as the Derg attempted to stem the advance of the TPLF guerrilla forces in 1990. In February 1999 a disabled Soviet tank still stood stuck at the edge of the road on the very top of the pass Konovaloff described.

government to Gore in Illubabor and prepared to leave. Before dawn on 2 May he boarded a train for Djibouti with the imperial family and several dozen nobles and officers. On 4 May the group boarded the British warship *Enterprise* and sailed up the Red Sea. On 5 May Badoglio's forces, in the wake of a violent thunderstorm, made a triumphal entry into Addis Ababa.

Some Ethiopians who remained behind would later accuse Haile Selassie of abandoning the country in cowardly fashion. Emotionally understandable as the accusation was, it showed little appreciation of politics and history. If he had stayed he might have been killed and, as a defeated fugitive in an occupied country, he would have been condemned to ineffectiveness. He quickly sensed that the best way to continue the struggle was to appeal to the world and inspire resistance from abroad. It was a long shot, and no one could anticipate the ultimate outcome in May 1936, but in the end the Lion of Judah did prevail. The decision to go into exile paid off. It involved the kind of faith and luck Haile Selassie enjoyed until the last year of his life.

Europe, America, and the Ethiopian crisis

In spite of his persistent efforts to get the League of Nations to condemn and stem the Italian onslaught, Haile Selassie's reliance on collective security proved illusory. Geneva was the scene of endless talk but little came of it. After Italy's all-out assault on Ethiopia began, the League voted on 18 November 1935 for import and export sanctions against Italy. They had no real effect. An oil embargo might have. Mussolini feared an oil embargo and encouraged Britain and France to believe that he might unleash a general war if it were imposed. None of the ensuing negotiations and debates about sanctions and embargoes helped Ethiopia.

When the *Enterprise* reached the Suez Canal, Haile Selassie disembarked and proceeded by train to Jerusalem, as he had done 12 years before. He left his family and much of his entourage there and sailed on the British warship *Capetown* from Haifa on 23 May. It brought him to Gibraltar where he boarded a commercial vessel for Southhampton. He was warmly welcomed in London, for the brutality of Mussolini's assault on Ethiopia had angered the British public and many citizens' groups supporting Ethiopia had formed.

On 30 June 1936 the exiled Emperor travelled from England to Geneva and appeared before the League Assembly. Italian journalists who harassed him were ejected before he began a long speech in Amharic that was then translated into French and English.[75] His eloquence won him applause from the Assembly and worldwide sympathy, but not much else. As Haile Selassie spoke, Mussolini had

---

[75] Text in *Autobiography*, pp. 299-312.

King Victor Emmanuel III proclaimed Emperor of Ethiopia. The *Times* commented the next day, "For the little good it can do him now, Haile Selassie has and will hold a high place in history."

The United States was not a member of the League, but President Franklin Roosevelt followed the crisis with sympathy for Ethiopia and, as in England, Italian brutality provoked condemnation from many segments of American society, especially African-Americans. Nevertheless there was no basis for direct American action:

Although the US maintained one of the eight foreign legations in the Ethiopian capital ... Americans had little interest in the ancient and proud Christian empire. Missionary and philanthropic activities engaged most of the hundred or so American citizens living in the country ... Annual trade between Ethiopia and the US amounted to less than half a million dollars.[76]

When the crisis began, the foreign policy of the United States was isolationist and the mood of the American public even more so. Haile Selassie had pressed steadily for American support. As early as November 1934 he explained to American chargé d'affaires W. Perry George that

... we worked very hard to secure American diplomatic representation in Ethiopia. We cherish our relations with the United States, understanding that their friendly character is undisturbed by any political aims in this part of the world, and realizing our great need for politically disinterested cooperation in our economic development.[77]

If Britain and France had taken a stronger stand, Roosevelt would have been supportive. When the invasion began in earnest, reporting from Europe and Africa aroused the American public. Sympathy for Ethiopia was expressed in editorials, resolutions of church and labor organizations, Black organizations, Jewish groups, international affairs associations and in letters to newspapers, congressmen and the White House. Many Italian-American groups, some Catholic organizations, and a few businessmen eager to profit from sales to Italy were exceptions. Isolationists in the Senate forced the Administration to ban exports narrowly classified as war materials, but nothing else, to both Ethiopia and Italy. Thus, while the United States sold no arms to either party, exports of food, fiber and petroleum products to Italy increased sharply. Ethiopia lacked the means of either buying or receiving such products.

Blacks, Protestants and peace groups organized an American Committee on the Ethiopian Crisis. Italy persuaded a hundred leading Italian Americans to form a United Italy Association, but the result was counterproductive. Tension between African- and

---

[76] Brice Harris, Jr., *The United States and the Italo-Ethiopian Crisis*, Stanford University Press, 1964, p. 30.

[77] *Ibid.*, p. 31.

Italian-Americans rose and riots erupted in cities where both lived in adjacent neighborhoods.[78]

In June 1936 the State Department terminated the Italian-American Treaty of Commerce and Navigation of 1871 and refused to receive a new Italian ambassador who arrived with credentials from "the King of Italy and Emperor of Ethiopia".

Before the Italo-Ethiopian crisis, the U.S. had considered Mussolini not so much a dictator as a strong leader seeking to bring order and prosperity to an impoverished country. After 1935 ... Mussolini appeared to Americans not only as an autocrat but as one who had planned and perpetrated overt aggression.[79]

But whatever President Roosevelt or concerned Americans might have wished, the United States could not avoid playing a secondary role to the European powers in the Italo-Ethiopian crisis. Even if the Congress had permitted the Administration more freedom of action, a more energetic policy could have accomplished almost nothing in face of European hesitancy and prevarication. US exports helped Italy but were not decisive for her military operations in Ethiopia.[80]

European public opinion – including that in Germany and Russia – remained sympathetic to Ethiopia but had little effect on governments' behavior. All the major European powers recognized the Italian conquest. In the world at large, only the United States, Mexico, New Zealand and the Soviet Union withheld recognition of Africa Orientale Italiana. Leaders of the democracies failed to anticipate the consequences of their indulgence of Italian aggression. Mussolini soon allied himself with Hitler, and both of them with Japan. Hitler had occupied the Rhineland while Mussolini was preparing his assault on Ethiopia. He followed by destroying Austria and Czechoslovakia. Like Britain and France, Stalin let him get away with it but then turned around and joined the Nazi leader in unleashing World War II. Mussolini delayed joining the totalitarian alliance until June 1940. It turned out to be a fateful – and fortunate – decision for Ethiopia.

[78] Dugan and Lafore, *op.cit.*, pp. 190-1.

[79] Harris, *op. cit*, p. 144.

[80] The events of the mid-1930s created an awareness of Ethiopia and sympathy for the country in the United States that benefitted Ethiopia after World War II. The "special relationship" formalized in the treaties of 1953 was more than a case of self-serving strategic cohabitation. For most Americans the social, economic and educational dimensions of the relationship outweighed military considerations. During the Derg-induced famine of 1984-6 many older Americans recalled their sympathy for Ethiopia at the time of the Italian invasion, and reacted with a readiness to help.

Africa Orientale Italiana (AOI)

Mussolini's empire in Africa lasted exactly five years, only a moment in the broad sweep of history. The Italian colonies, Eritrea and Somaliland, were merged into Ethiopia, making the entire Horn of Africa Italian except for the enclaves of French and British Somaliland. Mussolini hoped eventually to absorb them as well but was unable to develop a pretext. Eritrea was enlarged to include Tigray and the Somali-inhabited Ogaden was merged with Somaliland. The rest of Ethiopia was divided into four regions, each with an Italian governor: Amhara (the entire northwest), Galla-Sidama (the entire southwest), Harar (Hararge plus the southern Afar region, Arsi and northern Bale, but minus the Ogaden and southern Bale) and Shoa, including Addis Ababa. The map, however, is deceptive, for Italy never occupied all of Ethiopia. Vast areas remained outside Italian control and in others the degree of Italian control fluctuated.

Eager as he was to conquer Ethiopia, Mussolini had done almost nothing to prepare coherent plans for administering it. While Italy had gathered military intelligence over many years and engaged in subversion among Ethiopian chiefs, it lacked economic and socio-logical data on which even a straightforward program of systematic exploitation of the country's population and resources could be based:

Italian colonial policy in Ethiopia was not coherent ... Fascist colonization was racist, nationalistic, authoritarian, sterile, and founded on economic exploitation.[...] [It was] archaic and paternalistic.[...] It adopted the old colonial concept of sacrificing the colony to the interest of the metropolis. The Fascist occupation of Ethiopia repeated what the European powers had done in Africa without scruples in the 18th and 19th centuries, but the West was now no longer willing to tolerate [such behavior]. In Italy there was no dialogue between the country and the government on colonialism.[81]

Mussolini dreamed of settling millions of Italians in the fertile high-lands of Ethiopia who would supply the motherland with unlimited quantities of food and raw materials. But when the excitement of conquest was past, he showed little interest in the country's economic development: "As an outlet for emigration, Ethiopia was a total fail-ure."[82] Preparations for the invasion had created a great demand for Italian labor in East Africa. At the end of 1936 there were 146,000 Italian workers in the East African "Empire". By June 1939 their numbers had dropped to 23,000 and over 6,000 Italians in Addis Ababa were estimated to be unemployed. Some lived in squalor. No

[81] Alberto Sbacchi, *Ethiopia under Mussolini: Fascism and the Colonial Experience*, Zed Books, London, 1985, pp. 234-5.

[82] Haile Mariam Larebo, *The Building of an Empire: Italian Land Policy and Practice in Ethiopia, 1935-41*, Clarendon Press, Oxford, 1994.

more than 400 peasants were settled on the land and barely a third of these brought families. 54,296 non-military Italians in all capacities were counted in Ethiopia in 1940. Far from relieving demographic pressure in Italy, Ethiopia was a heavy burden.[83]

Commercially and industrially Italian performance in Ethiopia turned out to be a repetition of the experience of Eritrea writ large. Italy's imports from all her colonies in 1938 were little more than 2 per cent of her total imports. Self-sufficiency in food and raw materials remained a distant dream. In 1938 the value of Italian exports to AOI was twenty times that of imports. AOI required enormous budgetary subsidies. Though Italian investors were reluctant to put large amounts of capital into commercial farming in Ethiopia, some were attracted. Ethiopians were usually ejected from land allocated to Italians and then employed as day laborers. Italian occupation was too brief to permit development of rational policies for coordinating settler and native production. Italians did, however, make Ethiopians aware of improved techniques of agriculture and forestry and introduced new crops: oilseed, cotton, sugar, and new fruits and vegetables. Small-scale Italian entrepreneurs set up agricultural-and raw-material-based industries: coffee-washing and roasting establishments, oil mills, sawmills, flour mills, bakeries and a textile mill in Diredawa. While many Italians who remained in Ethiopia after 1941 established viable plantations and enterprises, practically none of the projects undertaken during the occupation survived the collapse of Italian rule.

As guerrilla operations by indigenous forces intensified, Italian control was confined largely to major towns and the highways between them. This resulted in two kinds of construction which became lasting contributions to Ethiopian development: first, a great many administrative and commercial buildings in cities and towns, usually in solid, austere Fascist style; and second, extensive road-building, which began as soon as fighting stopped. The initial priority was to meet military needs and facilitate control, but the economic significance of improved transport arteries was important for the future. During the Italian occupation more than 4,000 km. of good highways were built, equipped with strong bridges and good drainage arrangements. When Italy entered the war on the Axis side in 1940, these made it easier for British Commonwealth forces to conduct the offensives that brought AOI to an end.

Fascist doctrine consigned Ethiopians to a lower status as human beings but basic Italian humanitarianism and *dolce vita* habits led, as in Eritrea, to *madamismo* which neither the military nor the civil

[83] The data are all from Haile Mariam Larebo, *op.cit.*, as are those in the following paragraph.

authorities were ever able to control. While resentment of official racist policies was strong among Ethiopians, every gradation of attitude and relationship developed from pragmatic collaboration, cooperation and even friendship between individual Italians and Ethiopians to hostility and resistance, both passive and active.

"Italian administration was characterized by top-heavy bureaucracy and corruption."[84] Marshal Badoglio held the title of Viceroy until he returned to Italy on 22 May 1936. He was replaced by General Graziani, a poor choice as a pacifier and administrator because he was short-tempered and inclined to violence. Nevertheless Graziani attempted to implement policies designed to co-opt Muslims and Oromos as supporters of Italy. He also capitalized on the resentments of some of the traditional nobles against Haile Selassie and the Shoans. Ras Hailu was his favorite[85], Abba Jobir of Jimma another. Both facilitated Italian penetration of the west and southwest.[86] Ras Seyum submitted to the Italians after they occupied Addis Ababa.

Resistance during the first year of the occupation was essentially a continuation of the war. On 28 July 1936 Ras Kassa's sons Aberra and Asfa Wossen led several thousand men in an attack on Addis Ababa. They infiltrated parts of the city but were beaten back by the Italian garrison. They attacked again the next day and were beaten back again. Graziani suspected the Archbishop of Dessie, Abuna Petros, was behind the attack and had him shot the same afternoon. He declared all resisting Ethiopians "bandits" and ordered that they be shot on capture. Mussolini approved his harsh actions, but directed that the policy be kept secret.

Ras Imru, who had difficulty organizing resistance in the west, surrendered in early December 1936, but was not executed. Ras Desta Damtew, son-in-law of Haile Selassie, remained in the southeast with 10,000 men mounting attacks on Italian installations and convoys. In December 1936 Graziani offered to spare his life if he surrendered. Desta doubted the general's sincerity in light of the fact that his cousins, Ras Kassa's sons, had recently been caught and executed. He entered into negotiations but refused to submit. Graziani moved his headquarters to Yirgalem to mount a massive offensive backed by

[84] Bahru, *op.cit.*, p. 162.

[85] Suspecting Ras Hailu's leaning toward Italy, Haile Selassie had initially taken him with him as a semi-prisoner when he left Addis Ababa on 5 May 1936. He released Hailu, however, when the train reached Diredawa.

[86] To these and a dozen other cooperative aristocrats the Italians paid monthly salaries (list in Sbacchi, *op.cit.*, p. 137), but reaped little in the way of positive gains. Large numbers of Ethiopian nobles and chiefs whose loyalty was suspect were confined in Eritrea or sent to Italy and detained.

air power to scatter Desta's troops. 1,600 of them who surrendered were summarily executed by firing squads. Villages that had been friendly to Desta were burned to the ground and women and children shot, but Desta escaped to Butajira in Gurageland. Here he was finally captured and executed in February 1937.[87]

Graziani's vindictive behavior and Fascist racial policy provoked indignation among many Ethiopians, but he kept seeking cooperation – on Italian terms – with the population. On 19 February 1937, to celebrate the birth of the Prince of Naples, Graziani invited a large number of Ethiopian dignitaries to the palace and announced distribution of two Maria Theresa dollars to each of 3,000 poor people. As the distribution began at noon, two Eritreans who had mingled with the crowd, Mogus Asgedom and Abraha Deboch, threw seven hand grenades at Graziani and his entourage as they stood on the palace steps. Three Italian soldiers were killed, fifty Italians and Ethiopians were injured, and Graziani fell pierced by more than 300 splinters. Bleeding profusely, he was rushed to hospital. Chaos ensued as police and soldiers, fearing a general uprising, fired indiscriminately into the crowd. Large numbers of innocent bystanders were executed on a neighboring field as suspected accomplices. For the next three days the Italians, led by the notorious Blackshirts, went on a rampage of murder and arson throughout the capital.

The two Eritreans escaped through a side door of the palace, reached Debre Libanos and then attempted to join the Patriot forces of Abebe Aregai and Mesfin Sileshi. They were refused because they were Eritreans. Attempting to go to Sudan, they were shot by peasants near Metemma, but no one claimed the reward the Italians offered for them and their demise has never been explained. In the aftermath 350 chiefs were exiled to Italy and several thousand Ethiopians were sent to penal colonies in Eritrea and Somalia. By the end of 1937 more than 5,000 people had been executed for alleged crimes related to the attempt on Graziani. Among them were practically all the young educated Ethiopians the Italians could lay their hands on and all the officers and cadets of the Holeta Military Academy. Graziani went on to have hermits, soothsayers and travelling minstrels rounded up and killed. He was convinced that high church officials knew of the plot and that monks at Debre Libanos had helped the perpetrators hatch it.[88] He initiated investigations, but they were still inconclusive when the impatient Graziani ordered executions and destruction of the famous old monastery, Debre Libanos, the most eminent in Shoa. On 21 May 1937, 297 monks and 23 other

---

[87] Sbacchi, *op.cit.*, pp 186-9.

[88] Mogus had sent his wife to Debre Libanos beforehand. She was said to have Patriot relatives.

individuals suspected of complicity were shot. Over 100 deacons and students were first sent to Debre Berhan and later shot there. Several hundred additional monks were sent to concentration camps.[89] Added to the execution of Abuna Petros, the Italian atrocities at Debre Libanos solidified resistance in the Ethiopian Orthodox Church.

The Italians undertook many other terrorist actions during this period. The "civilizing mission" had reached its nadir. The events of 1937 marked a watershed in the Italian occupation. Mussolini finally removed Graziani in November 1938 and replaced him with a cultured and humane man, the Duke of Aosta. The Duke took no pleasure in violence or repression, but a year of slaughter had had an irreversible effect. From 1937 onward Patriot operations expanded and their ranks increased. Violence and reprisals fed resistance. Support for them was widespread among all ethnic and religious groups. Mussolini ordered far-reaching repressive measures.

Taking up permanent residence at Bath in England, Haile Selassie kept informed of developments in the homeland as best he could. Officially, Britain paid little attention to him. Some officials considered the Ethiopians' presence an embarrassment. There was a widespread impression in the world at large, which Mussolini encouraged, that Africa Orientale Italiana would become a permanent feature of the map. The Patriots operating in the mountains and gorges of the Ethiopian highlands, like the exiled Emperor, had little reason to expect the situation to change for the better soon, but neither the Emperor nor the Patriots gave up hope.

Resistance

No region of Ethiopia was entirely under Italian control – manifestations of resistance occurred throughout the country. The guerrilla warriors who formed bands to undertake operations against the Italians were concentrated in the northern provinces where Amharas formed the majority of the population. Known as Patriots (Amh. *Arbaññyoch*) these fighters became legendary during the Italian occupation and have remained so ever since. The Patriots were able to maintain almost total control of several mountainous areas where Italian forces could only penetrate temporarily but could never predominate. These included the Rift Valley escarpment northeast of the capital from Minjar through the Ankober-Termaber region to southern Wollo; northern Shoa; eastern Gojjam from Bichena north to the region of Mount Choke; western Wollo; eastern Begemder, especially Belesa and Gaynt; and the Semien.

[89] Sbacchi, *op.cit.*, pp. 189-97; Del Boca, *op.cit.*, pp. 221-6.

Patriot activity took many forms: attacks on convoys, attacks on police forces and small garrisons; destruction of Italian supply dumps and warehouses; threats and attacks against Italian settlers and Italian commercial farms; occasional daring raids into provincial towns. Patriots became increasingly better armed during the final years of the occupation, for they captured continually greater quantities of Italian weapons and ammunition. Patriot forces included women as well as men. Women were particularly effective as spies and informers, but both sexes were active within the Italian administrative and economic structure. Ostensibly collaborating with the occupiers, they supplied valuable intelligence to guerrilla fighters. Some guerrilla leaders also became adept at ploys to buy time and lure the authorities into complacency by pretending to be ready to negotiate submission. Ras Abebe Aregay, the great Shoan resistance leader, used this tactic skillfully.[90]

Haile Selassie was never able to find a way of coordinating Patriot operations from abroad. Patriot groups lacked means of communicating with each other, or with sympathizers and supporters abroad, except by written word and messenger. While all Patriots were united in antipathy toward the Italian occupiers, the antipathy did not automatically create trust or inspire cooperation. Nor did it produce agreement on the ultimate aims of the resistance and the nature of the government desired once the Italians were driven out. Most Patriot leaders were parochial in their loyalties and aims. Some were interested only in strengthening their standing in their own regions. Rivalries developed among leaders and groups. These were sometimes cleverly exploited by Italian authorities. In Gojjam, for example, two grandsons of Negus Tekle-Haymanot were bitter rivals. A small group of exiles in Sudan developed republican ideas but had no significant effect on the Patriot movement as a whole.[91]

[90] Bahru Zewde, *op.cit.*, pp. 172-3.

[91] *Ibid.*, pp. 174-6.

8

ETHIOPIA IN THE MODERN WORLD

HAILE SELASSIE FROM TRIUMPH TO TRAGEDY

Liberation

When Mussolini declared war on Britain and France on 10 June 1940, Britain moved quickly to punish him where he was most vulnerable – his African Empire. For a brief period, it was Britain that was punished, but less than a year later Africa Orientale Italiana was under British occupation, Ethiopia had been liberated, and Haile Selassie was back on his throne.

It was not superiority in manpower which enabled British Commonwealth forces to prevail in 1941. The Italians had far more manpower in East Africa than Britain: 84,000 men, 7,000 officers, and a locally recruited colonial army of 200,000.[1] British Commonwealth forces were scraped together from many sources: Sudan, India, Kenya, South Africa[2], Northern Rhodesia, Australia, as well as British regiments that had come directly from fighting in Egypt and a few men from other Middle Eastern locations. Advancing from three directions they overcame Italian regulars and native levies. Not all of the latter remained loyal to Italy. The support – and welcome – British Commonwealth troops received from Ethiopian Patriot forces was essential to their success. But success was not preordained and could never have been taken for granted. There were frustrations and complications. The major portion of Africa Orientale Italiana was actually overrun in just four months.

From life as an obscure exile in Bath, Haile Selassie suddenly returned to the center of a major historical drama. He arrived in Khartoum on 24 June 1940, having been flown via Malta, Cairo and Wadi-Halfa on orders of Winston Churchill, who overruled the objections of the British governor-general and colonial service officers in Sudan who did not want to have an Emperor on their hands. Some of them considered it a mistake for Britain to sponsor his return to Ethiopia. Controversies among British generals and diplomats kept

---

[1] Del Boca, *op.cit.*, p. 256.

[2] The fact that South African troops accounted for an important portion of Commonwealth forces was seldom acknowledged until after apartheid came to an end. The official South African history of these campaigns, with photographs and detailed maps, is the most authoritative source available on them: Neil Orpen, *East African and Abyssinian Campaigns*, Purnell, Capetown, 1968.

the Emperor marking time until almost the end of the year. But the Italians, too, lost valuable time. Instead of a major attack into Sudan – which they had the strength to undertake – they contented themselves with crossing the frontier in early July and briefly occupying Kassala, Metemma and Kurmuk. There was no follow-up. In August the Italians took the offensive against British Somaliland and quickly dealt Britain an embarrassing defeat, occupying the entire Protectorate, but it made little difference in the overall scheme of things. British Somaliland was briefly incorporated into the Italian Governorate of Harar.

Elated at this easy victory, Mussolini then ordered Marshal Rodolfo Graziani (who had left Ethiopia in 1937) to lead an invading force into Egypt from Libya with the aim, Mussolini hoped, of pursuing British forces to Cairo, but Graziani failed to advance. In early December the British Middle East Commander General Sir Archibald Wavell attacked Graziani's forces at Sidi Barrani and sent them reeling back deep into Cyrenaica. Meanwhile British officers in Sudan had been engaged in pin-prick operations against the Ethiopian border and had been sending weapons and ammunition across the border to Patriot bands in Ethiopia. For months Colonel Daniel Sandford and other British officers had gone deep into Partisan-held territory to boost morale, assess strength, and promise British aid. But no one had come up with a comprehensive operational plan. Haile Selassie was intensely frustrated. He knew there were arguments among the British about his role, or whether he should have any role at all.

At the end of October the newly appointed British War Minister Anthony Eden and General Wavell flew to Khartoum to find out why so little was happening. Churchill was eager to see Italy decisively defeated in Africa. Intelligence on the situation inside the country was clear on the fact that Patriot resistance was steadily growing, but it was also clear that the Patriots' operations lacked the focus of clear leadership. Churchill was convinced that only the presence of Haile Selassie could remedy the situation. So was Eden. Action followed quickly after he and Wavell flew back to Cairo. Serious planning for an offensive into Ethiopia began. Major Orde Wingate was sent from Cairo to Khartoum to work with the Emperor organizing an invasion force.

Wingate was well chosen for the role and enthusiastic about the task. Haile Selassie appreciated his dynamism. Wingate quickly developed a plan for gaining maximum effect from the Patriots: ten operational groups, each consisting of a British officer, five British non-commissioned officers, and 200 Ethiopians recruited from refugees in Sudan would be organized. "Fast moving, lightly but well-equipped, they would open up Gojjam ahead of the Emperor and spread the rebellion ... by setting the Patriots an example."[3] On 20 November Wingate, accompanied by an Ethiopian aide, Makonnen Desta, landed at an improvised airstrip at Sakala (the source of the Blue Nile in the very center of Gojjam) and met Sandford who briefed him on the Partisans' situation in the region. The Italians held very little territory, but the Patriots were rent by rivalries. Sandford was optimistic that the promise of determined British action would have a positive effect and promised that 5,000 mules could be gathered to meet the Emperor's force when it arrived at the top of the escarpment.

Wingate returned to Khartoum and began to whip what was christened Gideon Force into shape. In early December he flew to Cairo to see Wavell. With adequate supplies and air support he promised that there would be little need for regular troops: "Give me a small fighting force of first-class men and from the core of Ethiopia I will eat into the Italian apple and turn it so rotten that it will drop into our hands."[4]

The Italians knew there were British officers in Gojjam and developed a plan to entice chiefs loyal to Italy to intrigue against Partisan leaders. On 11 December they brought Ras Hailu back, hoping he would inspire resistance against Haile Selassie's return.[5] It was a clever move and temporarily successful. Some Patriot leaders submitted, but the majority of the guerrilla fighters did not. Haile Selassie was alarmed. He was eager to move. He wrote Churchill complaining of delay. Churchill sent a directive to Eden on 30 December:

[...]I am strongly in favor of Haile Selassie entering Ethiopia. Whatever differences there may be between the various Ethiopian tribes, there can be no doubt that the return of the Emperor will be taken as a proof that the revolt has greatly increased, and will be linked up with our victories in Libya.[6]

Stepping on many toes and devoting himself day and night to the task, Wingate spared no effort to ready Gideon Force for action. It crossed into Ethiopia at Omedla on 20 January 1941. Haile Selassie was in the vanguard, accompanied by his most loyal associates.[7]

[3] Mockler, *op.cit.*, p. 285.

[4] Mockler, *op.cit.*, p. 292.

[5] After release at Diredawa in May 1936, Hailu remained in Addis Ababa during the Italian occupation and sought contacts with the conquerors. Graziani as viceroy had found Hailu a useful collaborator, but the Duke of Aosta had kept him at a distance. Neither had permitted him to return to Gojjam.

[6] Mockler, *op.cit.*, p. 312.

[7] The distinguished historian W.E.D. Allen, who served as a captain in Gideon Force, published a firsthand account of the experience two years later: *Guerrilla*

Banderachin (Our Fighters), a leaflet developed to support the campaign, was prepared under the direction of journalist George Steer at Roseires in Sudan. It was air-dropped over Gojjam as Gideon Force marched in and carried Haile Selassie's notification of his return.

On January 20 His Majesty the Emperor Haile Selassie, accompanied by the Crown Prince and the Duke of Harar, by the *Echege*, Ras Kassa, Dejazmach Makonnen Indalkachew, Dejazmach Adefrisu, by his delegate to the League of Nations Lorenzo Taezaz, and by his principal secretary Ato Wolde Giorgis, by the Chief of his Imperial Guard Kenyazmach Mokria, by two powerful Ethiopian and English armies equipped with war material superior to the Italian, crossed the frontier of the Sudan and Ethiopia. [...] Therefore we rejoice in the tender mercies of our God and of Jesus Christ and we give thanks before the Divine Throne.[8]

"Two powerful ... armies" was an immense exaggeration. The emperor's party of a few dozen had to camp for a week along the Dinder river while Wingate moved ahead with two trucks on almost impassable tracks to scout out a way to get up the escarpment and meet Sandford at Mount Belaya. Gideon Force assembled there on 6 February. Mockler describes it as

... a motley collection of men and beasts. A few hundred Ethiopian refugees ... plus a bevy of impoverished nobles who had spent the last five years ... in Jerusalem, were balanced by a few hundred Sudanese soldiers with their amateurish British officers. A little group of Kenya settlers, five Australians, a handful of Jews, and several eager young cavalry subalterns from the regiments stationed in Palestine added more to its confusion than to its effectiveness. The fighting force was totally outnumbered by the thousands of hired camelmen with their dead and dying animals. There was hardly a professional army officer in the force, Wingate apart.[9]

Sandford was waiting, but without mules, for they proved hard to find. Gideon Force had to rely on camels for transport. At the same time, small troop detachments were crossing the Sudan frontier into Ethiopia all the way south to the Kenya border with the aim of keeping the Italians off balance and encouraging Patriot action. Commonwealth forces led by General Alan Cunningham advanced from Kenya into Italian Somaliland at the end of January and occupied Mogadishu on 25 February. To the north General William Platt, the overall Commander of British and Allied Forces in Sudan,

---

War in Abyssinia, Penguin Books, 1943. Others who later became famous as writers also took part in the campaign, notably Laurens van der Post and Wilfrid Thesiger, who described it briefly in *Life*, pp. 323-54.

[8] As cited in Mockler, *op.cit.*, p. 316.

[9] *Ibid.*, p. 338.

set out toward Kassala the same day Gideon Force crossed the frontier. Kassala was easily occupied, for the Italians had abandoned it two days before and Platt's army moved on toward Agordat. During the last half of February Wingate led Gideon Force up onto the Gojjam plateau, occupied Injibara, which had been abandoned by the Italians, and moved on to lay siege to Bure. The Royal Air Force helped by bombing Italian strongpoints around Bure. It took hard fighting to overcome Italian resistance, but Bure was occupied and Dembacha taken against more Italian opposition. The advance opened the road to Debre Marqos. The Emperor established himself at Bure.

Italian General Guglielmo Nasi, Vice Governor-General and in command of the Italian western sector, decided to make Gondar the center of resistance and put Ras Seyum, who had been brought back from detention in Italy, in charge of Tigray. Even though he was not entirely sure of Seyum's loyalty, he hoped he could keep the Tigrayans from assisting the British. Ras Hailu in Gojjam meanwhile would frustrate Wingate's hopes of rallying Patriot forces to the Emperor. In an attempt to neutralize Ras Hailu, Wingate, with a small party of Sudanese, made a daring dash across the center of Gojjam to the edge of Mount Choke where the Ras was camped with 6,000 followers. The Ras consented to talk, but refused to cooperate. Instead he moved half his men down into Debre Marqos to reinforce the Italian garrison. Meanwhile other Patriot leaders were rallying to support the Emperor. Wingate's operational groups gathered Patriots around them as far north as the Semien. Wingate hoped to gain control of the approach to the Shafartak crossing of the Blue Nile, which would open the way to Addis Ababa. Though Gideon Force had been stretched almost to its limits, it had never turned back. Wingate's response to a difficult situation was to attack. He was helped by distant developments.

On 26 March Italian forces evacuated Keren after giving General Platt's army a hard fight, clearing the way to Asmara.[10] Asmara surrendered on 1 April.[11] Bad news was coming in from the south and east as well. A British force from Aden landed at Berbera on 16 March, took Jijiga the next day, Hargeisa on 24 March and Harar on the 27th. Italian morale was sinking. More irregulars joined the Patriots and more Italian colonial troops deserted. On 3 April several thousand Italians withdrew from Debre Marqos toward the south, leaving Ras Hailu in charge. The Emperor and his entourage moved up to the edge of the town. The Ras was unwilling to risk action against a

[10] Barker, *op.cit.*, recounts this campaign in detail.

[11] The next day Ras Seyum arrived in Asmara and offered his services to the British, recalling the good relations his grandfather, Yohannes IV, had enjoyed with Britain.

Haile Selassie backed by the British, but held off two days before submitting. He rendered a last service to the Italians: he arranged for maverick guerrilla leader Belay Zelleke to help the Italians cross into Shoa at Shafartak and then destroy the bridge. It was frustrating to Wingate but the Italians gained little from it. On 6 April the Emperor entered Debre Marqos in triumph and his old enemy made a formal act of submission to him. Hailu was, in effect, a prisoner but was treated with comparative leniency by Haile Selassie.[12] The same day General Cunningham occupied Addis Ababa. He ordered Wingate to keep the Emperor in Debre Marqos out of fear that his immediate return would unleash Ethiopian reprisals against the 40,000 Italians living in the capital. Haile Selassie was suspicious at the delay but conducted himself with characteristic patience. Churchill sent orders a few days later that the Emperor should be allowed to return to Addis Ababa as soon as possible. On 27 April with Cunningham's concurrence he set out for the capital.

He was escorted by Wingate and his closest associates in Gideon Force and took Ras Hailu along. Each day, as April turned into May, good news reached the party: Dessie surrendered to the South Africans, Sekota fell to Patriots, Italian resistance was overcome at Bahr Dar. Reaching Fiche, the party prayed for Ras Kassa's sons, executed by the Italians in 1937, and Ras Kassa visited their graves. The group then proceeded to devastated Debre Libanos, where memorial services were held for the monks and deacons killed on Graziani's orders four years before. On 5 May 1941 the Emperor and his entourage crossed Mount Entoto and descended into the capital. Ras Abebe Aregay's Patriots lined the route, looking like savages with their long hair hanging to their shoulders. General Cunningham and an honor guard greeted the Emperor on a rostrum before the Grand Palace. Speaking to the crowd before him, the Emperor appealed to all Ethiopians to refrain from reprisals against the Italians and to behave like Christians.

There was still difficult fighting in the north. The Duke of Aosta was kept under siege at Amba Alagi by South African and Indian contingents of General Platt's army. He finally surrendered on 18 May. He was taken to Nairobi and hospitalized, where he died of tuberculosis early the next year.[13] In the region north and east of Lake Tana some Italian units held out during the summer rains. In

---

[12] It seems that Haile Selassie may have asked the British to intern Hailu in Sudan, though this did not occur (Mockler, *op.cit.*, p. 375). He was subsequently kept under house arrest in Addis Ababa and died in 1951.

[13] He goes down in history as a humane figure to whom Haile Selassie paid tribute, saying "Il a bien administre mon peuple." Del Boca, *op.cit.*, p. 262.

Gondar General Nasi put up stubborn resistance but was repeatedly attacked and forced to surrender at the end of November.[14]

Ethiopia, Britain, and the United States

Britain regarded all of Italian Africa as occupied enemy territory. Haile Selassie considered Ethiopia liberated and himself restored to full power and appealed to Churchill to have this status confirmed. A comprehensive Anglo-Ethiopian agreement signed on 31 January 1942 acknowledged Ethiopia to be "a free and independent state", but reserved many British privileges and deferred territorial issues.[15] Nevertheless, during the next two years frictions continued between the restored imperial government and British authorities. The inconsistent way in which democracies almost invariably perform when confronting tactical decisions of far-reaching import sometimes left Ethiopians with the impression that Britain's actual priority was to advance its long-term territorial interests.

Some British officials favored adding Somali-inhabited Ethiopian territories to a Greater Somalia, eventually to emerge as an independent country. The private views of British officials on Eritrea stretched across a full spectrum from return to Ethiopia to partition with the lowlands being added to Sudan. In subsequent years, regional partisans of special interests, journalists and a few historians have scanned the historical record and used portions of it to demonstrate that Britain (and eventually the United States) was high-handed and unprincipled in dealing with all these issues. Evidence of some sort can be found to support almost any emotional interpretation. There were, unfortunately, no easy solutions for any or all of the problems Ethiopia, Britain and the US faced. Developments far beyond the Horn of Africa made it inevitable that Britain would have to limit its commitments in Ethiopia, which it formalized with a new agreement in 1944, and welcome greater US involvement.[16]

[14] Del Boca, *La caduta dell'Impero*, pp. 515-29. This book, the second volume of the author's trilogy *Gli Italiani in Africa Orientale*, provides an enormous amount of detail on the final phase of the Italian occupation of Ethiopia (as well as Eritrea and Somalia) unavailable from other sources.

[15] The text is given in Lord Rennell of Rodd, *British Military Administration of Occupied Territories in Africa, 1941-1947*, HMSO, London, 1948, pp. 539-58.

[16] The most extensive available examination of this period utilizing declassified official records is Harold Marcus, *Ethiopia, Great Britain, and the United States, 1941-1974*, University of California Press, Berkeley, 1983. The book provides a selection of documentary material otherwise not easily available, but gives undue weight to field reporting and the opinions of lower-level officials who did not necessarily reflect policy judgments in London and Washington. Thus it fails to substantiate its thesis that Britain and the US crassly exploited a greedy, opportunistic, self-seeking or gullible Haile Selassie for shortsighted purposes.

Though Haile Selassie made no secret of his desire to have Eritrea ultimately restored to Ethiopian sovereignty, Britain administered the former Italian colony entirely separately from Ethiopia. Ports, highways, the railway, power, industry and a willing labor force made it immediately attractive for support of military operations in the Middle East and Persian Gulf. After Hitler attacked the Soviet Union, Allied bases in Eritrea facilitated the flow of American equipment and supplies to the Soviet Union via Iran under the official United States Lend-Lease Program. By August 1942 over 3,000 US soldiers and civilians were stationed in Eritrea, and they had hired more than 13,000 local employees. A US consulate was opened in Asmara, preceding the reopening of an American legation in Addis Ababa by nearly a year.

Haile Selassie welcomed the American presence as a counterbalance to the British. He wrote President Roosevelt to assure him that Ethiopia would do everything in its power to assist the allied war effort. Though the Emperor had been discouraged from making a visit to the US while he was in exile, Roosevelt took this opportunity to make amends and sent a warm reply:

It is a source of much satisfaction to me and to the people of the United States that your country, which fought so courageously against a ruthless enemy, has regained its independence and self-government. The steadfast friendship of the American people and their sympathy with you in your period of trial will continue to be manifested during the days of reconstruction now facing your country.[17]

The American consul in Asmara urged a technical aid program for Ethiopia and pointed out that the experience could be valuable for the United States when the time came for rebuilding countries that would later be freed in Europe. Haile Selassie sent Yilma Deressa, a graduate of the London School of Economics and one of his most promising young technocrats, to Washington to discuss the scope of such a program. Ethiopia was ruled eligible for assistance under the US Lend-Lease Program and a mutual aid agreement was signed on 9 August 1943. The Foreign Economic Administration lost no time in sending a mission to Addis Ababa.

As early as July 1943 a memorandum prepared by the staff of the Secretary of State advised him: "It is our opinion that a fairly strong case could be made in support of the Ethiopian contention that Eritrea, or a part of it, should be incorporated into Ethiopia."[18]

In September of the following year at Quebec, Roosevelt gave Churchill a memorandum to the same effect. A few months later

---

[17] As cited in Marcus, *op. cit.*; the letter was dated 4 August 1942.

[18] Marcus, *op. cit.*, p. 20.

Haile Selassie had his first meeting with an American president. On his way back from Yalta Roosevelt suggested the Emperor come to meet him in Egypt. The meeting took place on 13 February 1945 aboard the USS_*Quincy* in the Great Bitter Lake, lasted an hour, and was described by the American Minister as "especially cordial and agreeable".

Haile Selassie left memoranda with the President dealing with six topics of fundamental interest to Ethiopia. They had been prepared by American advisor John Spencer, who had originally been engaged by the Ethiopian Government on the eve of the Italian invasion.[19] These priority concerns included Ethiopia's desire to play a role in drafting the United Nations charter and participate in the peace conference with the Axis powers; requests for support for rapid return of the Ogaden by Britain and for concessions by France that would give Ethiopia greater control over the Franco-Ethiopian Railway; an explanation of Ethiopia's urgent need of financing for additional arms, transport and communications equipment; and, last but not least, Ethiopia's need for access to the sea, which meant control of Eritrea. To the President's query Haile Selassie replied that Djibouti was the best port because of the railway but that Ethiopia's basic interests would eventually require ports in Eritrea.[20]

Imperial consolidation

The Emperor lost no time on return in rapidly organizing his court and appointing officials. British advisers helped him lay the ground-work for a national army so that he would no longer be dependent on the armies of regional lords. They also helped organize a modern police force. He recalled Parliament and had legislation passed on provincial administration, the church and the financial system. He launched the *Negarit Gazeta* in 1942 to provide for systematic publication of laws and decrees. Peace and order were established throughout most of the country more rapidly than either the British or the Ethiopians had expected. The Italian occupation had strength-ened the position of the central government in respect to regional

---

[19] Born in Iowa in 1907, Spencer was fresh from study of international law in Paris when he was hired. After US Navy service during World War II, he returned to Ethiopian employ and served as an advisor to the Foreign Ministry until 1960. He played a major role in arranging the Eritrean settlement to Ethiopia's advantage. His memoirs are a valuable source for the period during which he remained in Ethiopia (up to 1960) but less reliable for the period after: John H. Spencer, *Ethiopia at Bay, a Personal Account of the Haile Sellassie Years*, Reference Publications, Inc., Algonac, MI, 1984.

[20] *Ibid.*, pp. 159-60.

lords. Provincial boundaries were systematized into 12 large units. In the north these corresponded for the most part to traditional kingdoms: Tigray, Begemder, Gojjam and Shoa. Wollo was greatly enlarged by inclusion of Wag, Lasta, Amhara Saynt, Yejju and the desert extending to the Eritrean border.

As insurance against resurgence of regional divisiveness, some traditional rulers of small regions that had enjoyed separate status until the Italian invasion were brought to Addis Ababa. Wagshum Wossen, for example, was later made ambassador to Greece and never returned to his ancient principality. In the south and southwest many small units which were originally conquered and administered separately were combined into large units: Sidamo, Gamu Gofa, Kaffa, Wollega, Illubabor. In the east, the immense province of Harar originally included Bale which was established as a separate province in 1960, making 13.

As his closest associates Haile Selassie returned to dependence on many of the same men who had held high positions before the Italian invasion, many of whom had been with him in exile. No Ethiopians had received higher education under the Italians and many had been killed, so there were few new men to choose from. Makonnen Indalkachew became Interior Minister and then Prime Minister when the post was created in 1943. He remained in that post until 1957. The Prime Ministry, along with the Council of Ministers and the Crown Council, was less influential than the Ministry of the Pen, the personal secretariat of the Emperor. Its head, who carried the traditional title *Tsahafe Taezaz*, was Wolde Giyorgis Wolde Yohannes, a Shoan who had been Haile Selassie's secretary before the Italian invasion and went into exile with him. Extremely close to the Emperor, Wolde Giyorgis was the dominant political figure of the era until he fell from favor and was sent to Arsi as governor in 1955. As Clapham observed, "Not least among the Emperor's achievements was the way in which he caused the resentment both of the nobility and of frustrated reformers to be directed against Wolde Giyorgis rather than himself, thus remaining detached from policies for which he was essentially responsible."[21]

Secure in his conviction that modernization would now proceed, Haile Selassie was less concerned about the rapidity of reform than about consolidating his own power and creating a government structure amenable to control and manipulation. He was mindful to prevent any concentration of authority that could challenge his own preeminence. Thus he became a master at *shumshir* – the rotation of individuals from one position to another in both the capital and in

---

[21] *Op.cit.*, p. 22.

the provinces. Loyal officials were frequently moved from one position to another.[22]

The Patriots were a problem. Though formally respectful of authority, Ethiopians have always been ready to think for themselves. Many Patriots had little understanding of the rationale that led Haile Selassie to go into exile in 1936. While resisting the Italians they made their own decisions independently. Some resented the fact that the Emperor on return forgave the Italians and showed leniency to Ethiopians who had collaborated with them. Haile Selassie, aware of these attitudes, wished to prevent Patriot dissidence from coalescing into a political force. He gave some of them modest appointments in the capital, removing them from their local surroundings. Others were given appointments in other regions. Some Patriot leaders were given positions in the territorial army that was created to supplement the regular armed forces. Ras Abebe Aregay was one of the few Patriot leaders to receive a major post (Minister of War) and remain basically loyal to Haile Selassie. After putting down the Weyane rebellion, he remained Governor of Tigray until 1947, returned to Addis Ababa as Minister of War for two more years and then served as Minister of Interior till 1955 and Minister of Defense till 1960.

Takele Wolde Hawariat was briefly Governor of Shoa, but fell out with Haile Selassie over organization of the government and the role of parliament. He was removed in March 1942, arrested and imprisoned. He never forgave the Emperor for leaving in May 1936, though Haile Selassie was eager to bring him back into his inner circle. He released him from prison in 1945 and appointed him deputy to Wolde Giyorgis, but Takele was soon caught in another plot and imprisoned again till 1954. The emperor released him once again, made him Vice Minister of Interior and then *Afenegus*, but in 1961 he was re-jailed once more for plotting.[23]

---

[22] Lorenzo Taezaz was made Foreign Minister, then Minister of Posts and President of the Senate and finally sent to Moscow as ambassador in 1943 because of differences with Wolde Giyorgis. Yilma Deressa, the only Ethiopian with foreign training in economics, served as Finance Minister for eight years and Minister of Commerce for four and was then sent to Washington as ambassador. Ras Kassa's only surviving son Asrate and Mesfin Sileshi rotated through a succession of provincial governorships. The three Habtewold brothers occupied several important positions: Makonnen first as Minister of Agriculture and soon also Minister of Commerce (1942-9), Aklilu as Vice Minister of the Pen until 1943 and then Minister of Foreign Affairs for the next 15 years. The youngest brother, Akaleworq, was made Minister of Education and assistant to Wolde Giyorgis.

[23] An inveterate schemer, he was unable to live quietly and nursed a permanent grudge against Haile Selassie. In November 1969 he mined a bridge on the road to Sebata over which Haile Selassie travelled on weekends. The scheme backfired, he barricaded himself in his house, and was killed in a shoot-out with the

Belay Zelleke was given the Governorship of Bichena, his home district in Gojjam, but, wishing to minimize the likelihood of trouble in this difficult province, Haile Selassie offered him a southern governorship with the rank of *ras*. He rejected the offer, denounced the Emperor for having left the country in 1936, and rebelled against both Addis Ababa and Debre Marqos, where Hailu Belaw, a grandson of Negus Tekle Haymanot, had been made Governor of Gojjam. In January 1943, with the help of Hailu Belaw, a military expedition was sent against him. It took three months of fighting to force his surrender. He was brought to Addis Ababa, where he soon became involved in a plot to depose the Emperor with Mamo Hailu, a son of Ras Hailu. Both were hanged.

Sweden was invited to advise on reconstitution of the Imperial Bodyguard, the elite element of the regular armed forces. It was headed by the Oromo General Mulugeta Bulli until 1955, after which he was made Chief of Staff of the Armed Forces. Security and domestic intelligence were of great interest to the Emperor. A Public Security Department was established under the Ministry of the Interior, but it had too many routine responsibilities to deal with sensitive matters, so General Mulugeta chose Col. Worqeneh Gebeyehu, a Gondare Bodyguard officer who had fought with distinction in Korea, as Chief of Security. The two were instrumental in creating the Imperial Private Cabinet in 1959 which rapidly became influential as the Emperor's national security staff. Its creation illustrated another important characteristic of Haile Selassie's style of ruling. He not only practiced *shumshir*, shifting officials with some frequency; he also checked and balanced important centers of power and influence in his increasingly complex government by creating alternate and competing bureaucracies. The Private Cabinet acted as a check on ministers and on the Prime Minister himself.

The "disposal" of Eritrea

After Eritrea fell to Britain in 1941 it was governed by a military administration. It was a province without politics, but not for long.[24] The natural evolution toward political modernization that Italian colonial policy had blocked set in quickly. British military rule was mild. A large Italian community remained and was well treated. The complex of military installations at Asmara and port facilities at Massawa provided employment opportunities and good income for

security forces. See numerous references in Greenfield, *op.cit.*, and Bahru Zewde, *op.cit.*, pp. 210-11.

[24] Stephen H. Longrigg, *A Short History of Eritrea*, Clarendon Press, Oxford, 1945.

workers. There was no friction between the local population and Allied military personnel. British military administrators placed no obstacles in the way of politicization of Eritrean society; in fact they encouraged it. Labor unions formed, a press was established[25] and independent institutions and associations of many kinds came into being. Educational opportunities expanded. Wartime prosperity encouraged Eritreans' expectations of rapid economic development, for a good deal of new industry was established to serve Allied wartime needs. When the war came to an end in 1945, however, Eritrea began to experience an economic slump that exacerbated political, social and religious tensions. Britain developed no plan for the colony's future British officials were divided on what the future of Eritrea should be.

Negotiations on the peace treaty with Italy entailed difficult discussions on how her colonies were to be dealt with. Haile Selassie intervened strongly in the process to support Ethiopia's claim to Eritrea.[26] Italy surrendered all claim to Eritrea in the 1947 peace treaty and a commission consisting of representatives of the Four Allied Powers[27] was charged with arranging the future of the colony "in accordance with the wishes of its inhabitants". This was more easily said than done. The Tigrinya-speaking Orthodox Christians of the highlands had never stopped regarding themselves as Ethiopians during the half century of the Italian colony's existence. A majority of them favored reunion with Ethiopia. Muslim lowlanders, divided ethnically, felt little inclination toward Ethiopia, though a few favored a form of union that guaranteed their interests. Many Muslims favored partition and amalgamation of the northern and western regions with Sudan. Smaller groups advocated a continued British mandate, independence or even restoration of Italian rule. The four-power commission was unable to reach any agreement and turned the problem over to the United Nations in 1948.[28]

[25] The distinguished British Ethiopianist Professor Edward Ullendorff in *The Two Zions: Reminiscences of Jerusalem and Ethiopia*, Oxford University Press, 1988, pp. 165-175, describes establishment and operation of the Eritrean press during the early period of British military administration, in which he served. The popular *Nai Ertra Semunawi Gazeta* (Eritrean Weekly News) in Tigrinya had an important influence on modernization and standardization of this widely spoken but literarily underdeveloped language.

[26] These efforts are well chronicled in Margery Perham, *The Government of Ethiopia*, Faber & Faber, London, 1969, pp. 479-501.

[27] Britain, the United States, France and the Soviet Union.

[28] The Soviet Union had sought trusteeships over both Libya and Eritrea. Its oppressive approach to Eastern Europe and expansionist efforts in the Middle East kept the allied powers from giving serious consideration to its requests. Had "disposal" of Eritrea come onto the international agenda in the 1960s, it would

The UN appointed a five-man commission[29] which was charged with determining the amount of support for each proposed solution and judging its economic viability. Both Ethiopia and Italy were subsidizing political factions favoring their interests. The commission's members had to contend with their own substantial differences and pressures from many directions, both inside and outside Eritrea. During the latter part of 1949 violence broke out:

Fighting between the Christian villagers of the Hamasain and Serai and the Moslem Bani Amir reached a new and ugly ferocity. Fighting broke out once more between the Kunama and their ... neighbours ... of the Gash-Setit lowlands, and ... between the Moslem Saho and their Christian neighbours in the Akelli Guzai. On the Plateau itself the sturdy Moslem minority in the Serai clashed with the Christian majority.[...] The small, feeble Moslem minority in the Hamasain ... was terrorized into silence. On the northern flanks of the Plateau occasional clashes occurred between the villagers of the Hamasain and the Tigre[30] clans of the coastal plain. The only parts of Eritrea to which the conflagration did not spread were the ... remote extremities – the Northern Highlands and the Danakil Lowlands.[31]

The UN commission finally came to Eritrea in early 1950 and spent nearly two months conducting enquiries, but much of its activity was poorly organized and members clashed with each other. It ended up making two separate reports and three sets of proposals.

When it came to consider the Commission's report in September 1950, the (UN) General Assembly was no better informed as to what the inhabitants of Eritrea wanted, or the truth about Eritrea's economy, than it had been two years earlier.[32]

The outbreak of the Korean War in June 1950 underscored the importance of communications facilities in Eritrea which had come completely under American control. Haile Selassie's offer of Ethiopian battalions to fight with UN forces in Korea gave the US

---

most likely have been set up as an independent country, as so many insignificant and less developed colonial remnants in Africa were during that time, but at the beginning of the 1950s independence was regarded as a distant prospect for most African colonies.

[29] Made up somewhat incongruously of representatives from Burma, Guatemala, Norway, Pakistan and South Africa.

[30] The Tigre are a mostly Muslim, pastoralist, lowland people who speak a Semitic language not mutually intelligible with that of the Tigrinya-speaking highlanders.

[31] G.K.N. Trevaskis, *Eritrea a Colony in Transition, 1941-52*, Oxford University Press, 1960, p. 109. This book, by a high British official who served in Eritrea during most of the time covered, is the most comprehensive account available of the period.

[32] Trevaskis, *op.cit.*, p. 101.

government assurance that American interests in Eritrea would be protected by Ethiopia. The United States was instrumental in securing a resolution approved by a vote of 46-10 in the General Assembly on 2 December 1950 that established Eritrea as "an autonomous unit federated with Ethiopia under the sovereignty of the Ethiopian Crown". It provided for a federal government with responsibility for defense, foreign affairs, finance, foreign and interstate commerce, and external and interstate transportation and communications. It prescribed an autonomous Eritrean government with legislative, executive and judicial powers, and responsibility for all matters not vested in the federal government, including police, taxes and budgeting. An Eritrean assembly was to be democratically elected and an administration organized no later than 15 September 1952. A Bolivian, Eduardo Anze Matienzo, was appointed on 14 December 1950 as UN commissioner to draft an Eritrean constitution .

Disorders continued in Eritrea after the UN decision as factions vied for advantage, banditry persisted, men who had been deposed during the Italian and British administrations sought to recover their positions, and the economy remained stagnant. Anze Matienzo delayed his work until British officials took strong measures to reduce violence. He began consultations in July 1951 and complicated his task by adopting a high profile with meetings, press conferences and debates throughout the territory. The process tended to magnify and harden differences between political parties and factions. Strongest and best organized were the Unionists, supported by Ethiopia and the Orthodox Church. They reflected the Ethiopian desire that federation in practice become merely a veneer over full Ethiopian control. As a gesture to its acceptance of the principle of federation, the Independence Bloc changed its name to Democratic Bloc. The Moslem League of the Western Province had difficulty forging a unified position, but most of its members were eager to keep Ethiopian links as nebulous as possible. The small Liberal Unionist Party, supported by Britain, was probably the only group that was committed to a genuine federal system.

In spite of all the divisions in Eritrean society the notion of federation of a small politically and economically more advanced but highly factionalized territory with a far larger but backward and autocratically governed Ethiopia seemed incongruous at the time. Haile Selassie and the Ethiopian ruling classes would have preferred outright annexation, but membership in the UN and the close relationship with the US ruled this out. So Ethiopia argued that the Emperor should be empowered to appoint an Eritrean governor general who would have the powers of a viceroy, appointing all high officials and with veto power over legislation. The Unionists shared this view and advocated a single-chamber assembly. The Democratic Bloc advocated two chambers that would check and balance each other. The Moslem League wanted two regional assemblies which would partition the territory into Muslim and Christian halves, each federated separately with Ethiopia. There were lesser arguments over the status of half-castes, language, flag and symbols.

Anze Matienzo departed in November 1951 to prepare his constitution. It provided for a Governor General appointed by the Emperor with the function of reading a speech from the throne and promulgating legislation and a single-chamber assembly empowered to elect its own President. Executive power was vested in a Chief Executive elected by the assembly who appointed heads of government departments and judges. A civil service commission was in charge of other appointments.

Preparations for elections for an assembly to approve the constitution began in January 1952. In Asmara and Massawa the vote was direct by secret ballot. In other areas village and clan groups elected delegates to regional electoral colleges which, in turn, elected representatives by secret ballot. The electoral process was completed by the end of March 1952. In the cities 88 per cent of registered voters participated. In rural areas participation was almost 100 per cent. When the votes were counted, the 68 seats were neatly divided between Christian and Moslem candidates: the Unionists won 32, the Democratic Bloc 18 and the Moslem League 15. Two minor parties and an independent won the remaining three.

When the Assembly convened, the Unionist representatives approved the constitution without demur. The Moslem League joined them while the Democratic Bloc abstained. Rather than have new elections, the Assembly transformed itself into the legislative body provided for in the constitution, which continued to be called by the same name. In the following months all but 348 of the 2,217 foreigners who staffed the British Military Administration were replaced by Eritreans. Eritreans were appointed as provincial governors and heads of departments, legal formalities and property transfers were arranged, and Haile Selassie signed the Federal Act on 11 September 1952.

On the evening of 15 September the Union Jack was lowered in Asmara and the Ethiopian tricolor raised. Eritrea became "an autonomous state federated with Ethiopia". Trevaskis concluded his account of the transition, written in Aden, where he had been transferred, with these prescient observations:

The [Ethiopian] temptation to subject Eritrea firmly under her own control will always be great. Should she try to do so, she will risk Eritrean discontent and eventual revolt, which, with foreign sympathy and support, might well disrupt both Eritrea and Ethiopia itself. [...] The future of the

Federation, and indeed of the whole group of young countries in Northeast Africa, is likely to be affected by the course that Ethiopia takes. She has acquired a great responsibility.[33]

Formalization of the American relationship

The warmth that characterized the meeting between President Roosevelt and Haile Selassie in February 1945 was not rapidly transformed into a close relationship. Ethiopia was only one of a score of countries in which America had comparable interests. Creation of the UN fed euphoria about the postwar world. Defeat of Germany and Japan resulted in rapid dismantling of much of the American strength that had been mobilized to defeat them. American military and economic aid programs and information and intelligence services had all been improvised during the war and the prevailing inclination in Washington in 1945 was to disband them. But during the ensuing years persistent Soviet aggressiveness and refusal to cooperate in restoration of representative governments in Eastern Europe or in settling disputes in other parts of the world soon compelled the United States to face harsh reality.

With what in retrospect appears remarkable speed and sense of purpose, the US Government was reorganized during the late 1940s to meet new responsibilities: a National Security Council and intelligence system were created; the three armed services were unified in a single Department of Defense; a professional foreign aid organization was set up to implement the Marshall Plan; and Congress created new committees, subcommittees and staffs to carry out the necessary legislative and review functions. Crises did not wait for the ideal structure required to deal with them but came in quick succession: Iranian Azerbaijan in 1946; Greece and Turkey, resulting in the proclamation of the Truman Doctrine in 1947; the Berlin Blockade in 1948; Chinese communist victory in 1949; and finally the Korean War in June 1950.

In the face of such momentous developments, it is not surprising that the US Government gave little coordinated attention to Ethiopia. Nevertheless, Britain's transfer of responsibility for Greece and Turkey to the United States provided a foretaste of the future in the Horn of Africa. From 1944 onward Britain gradually conceded her predominant position in Ethiopia to the United States and reduced her financial assistance. Ethiopian trade with America soon outstripped trade with Britain. It was obvious to Ethiopians that the US offered greater promise of economic development assistance and

[33] Trevaskis, *op.cit.*, p. 131.

private investment. The American Embassy in Addis Ababa replaced the British Embassy as the focus of Ethiopian attention.

The first American activity to be formalized was a private commercial one in which the US Government had little involvement. The Emperor was convinced that a good air service was the best way to overcome Ethiopia's difficult terrain. Ethiopian Airlines (EAL) was established in 1946 with the assistance of Transworld Airlines and the Boeing Corporation. During its first years of operation, the airline was dependent on American pilots and technicians and concentrated on domestic service. Airstrips were built in parts of the country that were otherwise accessible only over foot and donkey trails. EAL helped Haile Selassie forge a sense of national unity and aided development of outlying regions. Gradually expanding into international routes selected for their economic importance rather than political symbolism, but stressing African services, EAL matured during the 1960s into one of the most reliable and profitable airlines in the Third World.[34],

Britain was too deeply committed in Eritrea and Somaliland to extricate herself quickly and did not yet anticipate withdrawal from Aden and the Gulf or from Sudan. The Allied peace treaty with Italy concluded in 1947 returned Somalia to Italian trusteeship with the obligation to prepare it for independence. Britain finally returned the entire Ogaden to Ethiopia in 1954 over strong objections from some of her own subjects.[35] By this time Britain had decided that its Somaliland Protectorate would best be amalgamated with the former Italian colony to form an independent state. The United States took only incidental interest in Somali developments.

The United States provided $800,000 in economic assistance to Ethiopia during the years 1946-8 and the US Export-Import bank granted a $2.7 million loan for improvement of ground transportation. $1.3 million in economic assistance was provided during the period 1949-52.[36] A new Treaty of Friendship and Economic

[34] EAL was managed and fully staffed by Ethiopian personnel by the time it celebrated its 25th anniversary in 1971. It survived the confusion of the early post-revolutionary years, preserved its autonomy and maintained profits by adding unique cross-Africa services to frequent schedules to Europe and the Middle East and extensive domestic passenger and cargo flights. The *Economist* highlighted EAL in a late 1980s series on successful enterprises in seemingly hopeless economies: "In Search of Excellence, the Hard Way", 31 December 1987. To celebrate its 40th Anniversary the management of EAL published a detailed history, *Bringing Africa Together*, EAL, Addis Ababa, 1988.

[35] See John Drysdale, *The Somali Dispute*, Pall Mall Press, London, 1964, and the Earl of Lytton, *The Stolen Desert: A Study of Uhuru in Northeast Africa*, Macdonald, London, 1966.

[36] These and subsequent such statistics are taken from the US Agency for International Development publication, *US Overseas Loans and Grants and Assistance*

Relations was negotiated in 1951. US military activities in Eritrea fed several million dollars annually into the Eritrean economy. With implementation of the federation in 1952, this income directly benefited the Ethiopian balance of payments.

Ethiopia and the United States signed a preliminary military assistance agreement in June 1952. During late 1952 and early 1953 two treaties were negotiated: one covering use of military facilities in Ethiopia, the other provision of military assistance to the Ethiopian armed forces. Both were signed in Washington on 22 May 1953.[37] The US obtained unlimited access to its military installations by surface, sea and air, and overflight privileges over all of Ethiopia. The treaties were valid for a period of twenty-five years, but they fell short of being a mutual defense pact.[38]

The 1953 treaties nevertheless marked the beginning of a close and warm relationship that both parties found beneficial for the next two decades involving a steady flow of American military and economic aid, the presence of sizable (but far from huge)[39] military and economic aid missions and a wide range of auxiliary relationships: training of Ethiopian military personnel in the United States, projects of several US educational institutions in Ethiopia, a major Peace Corps program during the 1960s, private philanthropic programs and a modest amount of American business investment.[40]

---

from International Organizations, Obligations and Loan Authorizations, 1 July 1945 - 30 September 1981, Washington, DC, 1982.

[37] Texts are available in US Department of State, *Treaties in Force...on 1 January 1975*, USGPO, Washington, 1975.

[38] The adverse international political consequences that John Spencer believed eventually resulted from these treaties are debatable. For his rather convoluted argumentation see *op. cit.*, pp. 261-79.

[39] US military personnel in Ethiopia never exceeded 5,000 and never included combat troops. The great majority were communications technicians stationed at Kagnew Station in Asmara. During the early 1960s, the US Army Map Service was invited to prepare accurate maps of the entire country. Its American complement averaged 100 technicians who worked closely with the Imperial Mapping and Geography Institute. They finished their work in 1971. The 1:250,000 maps that resulted were used by Ethiopian, Cuban and Soviet forces after 1974. The US Navy maintained a small tropical medical research team in Ethiopia until 1977.

[40] During the period 1953-61 Ethiopia received $84.4 million in US economic assistance, $9.4 million in Export-Import Bank loans and $63 million in military assistance grants. A pattern was set that persisted through 1977: economic aid always exceeded military aid. American personnel in Ethiopia carrying out economic assistance programs always outnumbered military assistance personnel. Military aid was kept at a level that limited Ethiopia's armed manpower to 50,000 and discouraged acquisition of military equipment beyond Ethiopia's realistic needs or ability to maintain. From its very beginning the US military assistance program was strictly geared to conservative estimates of Ethiopia's internal

The American military presence in Ethiopia was concentrated in Eritrea. It caused no frictions and benefited both Eritrea and Ethiopia in many ways. When dissidence and insurgency developed in Eritrea after Ethiopia terminated the federation arrangement, American activities remained practically immune from criticism or attack. Americans did not attempt to intervene in, or influence Addis Ababa's management of the Eritrean relationship. Could matters have evolved differently if it had? There are too many if's to make even a speculative answer easy. Developments in Eritrea during the 1960s will be treated separately below. In several respects they predetermined Ethiopia's own history during the final quarter of the twentieth century. The same may be said of the region immediately to the south, Tigray. It became a serious problem for the restored Emperor well before he became preoccupied with Eritrea.

The Weyane rebellion

In spite of Italy's long interest in the region, Tigray experienced relatively little development during the Italian occupation. Amalgamation with Eritrea gave Tigrayans the opportunity to migrate easily but many men who went north to work left their families in their home villages. Loyalty to the Orthodox church remained strong. Most of the population remained illiterate, for educational opportunities were few and far between. Many chiefs who had originally collaborated with the Italians began to shift allegiance in the late 1930s and some joined the Patriots during the final period of the Italian occupation. After defeating the Italians in 1941, British Commonwealth forces occupied Tigray as well as Eritrea. Some British military officers favored retaining the administrative connection with Eritrea, but the issue was settled with the restoration of Ethiopian sovereignty within the boundaries of the country as of 1935.

Haile Selassie sought not only to reassert the authority of the central government in the provinces, but to extend it and thus complete the process of centralization he had begun before the Italian invasion. Control of Tigray was high on his agenda.[41] He appointed new officials and sent troops under central government command. Traditional forms of tribute were abolished and a new tax system was introduced. Though publicized as a guarantee of land tenure, imperial taxation met resistance from the greater part of the

---

security requirements and its ability to meet limited international security obligations. This approach contrasted sharply to that of the Soviet Union in Somalia and Sudan.

[41] Perham, *op.cit.*, pp. 343-52, 356-8.

peasantry. Few peasants had paid taxes during the occupation when much of the province had been out of effective Italian control. Bands of Patriots, locally recruited Italian auxiliaries, troops loyal to local leaders and bandits had all roamed the region and compelled the population to support them when they had it in their power.

Tigrayan peasants could probably have been won to the Emperor's new system only by an efficient and rational bureaucracy. The officials and military commanders appointed from Addis Ababa were inefficient and rapacious. A local poem of the time expressed prevailing attitudes:

> *Woe, woe, woe – death unto the officials of today*
> *Who abuse their authority for a kilo of grain,*
> *And destroy documents for the gift of a goat –*
> *The emperor is not aware of these scandals,*
> *But surely he has sent hyenas to all places.*[42]

Some Tigrayan chiefs who wanted to remain as autonomous as possible encouraged peasant resistance. British military authorities failed to realize the complexity of political relationships in Tigray and encouraged local leaders to assert themselves to enhance security. Trouble developed first in southeastern Tigray among the Raya, Azebu and Wejerat, peripheral Oromo-related peoples with a long history of resistance to all authority and complex relations with the Tigrinya-speaking elite. In a clash in January 1942 at Kobbo three British officers and several Ethiopian soldiers trying to force tax payments were killed. Planes were sent to bomb the area with little effect. It took 30,000 soldiers from the south, all regarded by the Tigrayans as Shoans, from April to July 1942 to subdue the rebellious tribesmen. Large tracts of country were devastated and severe fines in both livestock and money were imposed on the defeated Raya and Azebu. These punitive measures had no effect on the rest of Tigray. Security worsened and tax arrears accumulated.

Addis Ababa responded with force and sent in more troops. A large force failed in an attack on the Wejerat in May 1943 and its commander was captured and humiliated. Open resistance soon broke out all over eastern Tigray under the slogan, "There is no government – let's organize and govern ourselves." Local assemblies sent representatives to a *shengo* which elected leaders and set up a

[42] Cited by Gebru Tareke, "Rural Protest in Ethiopia, 1941-1970: A Study of Three Rebellions", Ph.D. diss. Syracuse University, NY, 1977, p. 147. Many of the details which follow are taken from this important study based on British and Ethiopian documentary sources and interviews carried out in Tigray and elsewhere in Ethiopia in the 1970s. With changes and additions this dissertation was published as *Ethiopia: Power and Protest, Peasant Revolts in the Twentieth Century*, Cambridge University Press, 1991.

command structure. Authority crystallized around Haile Mariam
Redda, a young man of peasant origin who had been a *shifta* (outlaw/
bandit)[43] during the Italian occupation. The Italians coopted him
and in 1938 put him in charge of his native parish, Dandiera, in
Enderta. Removed from that position after the Italian defeat in 1941
he sought reinstatement in Addis Ababa but was rebuffed. Returning
home, he went back to being an outlaw and won support among local
people by protecting them from corrupt officials. Haile Mariam's
program was conservative:

> He accused the Shoan Amhara aristocracy of having impoverished Tigray
> and ... of setting the Tigrayan nobility against each other. He attacked them
> for [calling] Tigrayans ... unpatriotic and less nationalist than the Amhara
> while they sold the latter's lands to foreign powers – presumably a reference
> to Eritrea. He dismissed the emperor as a coward who had betrayed the
> country and was thus unfit to rule. He ... accused him of being an agent of
> the Catholic church. [...] He vowed to liberate Tigray from Shoan Amhara
> hegemony if the central government failed to respond to the call of the
> rebels and reform itself.[44]

Many of Haile Mariam's commanders were traditional Tigrayan chiefs.
The rebels were well armed, for the Italians had distributed large
quantities of weapons to Tigrayan peasants during their occupation.
Haile Mariam established his headquarters at Wokro. He had the
support of the Orthodox clergy and condemned Catholics, Protestants, and officials who smoked and wore long pants. Elected officials
were required to take an oath administered by a priest. Haile Mariam
had a natural gift for delegating authority and inspiring cooperation.
He used the rainy season of 1943 to organize his forces. After
celebrating the Ethiopian New Year on 12 September, the rebels
went on the offensive. Their first victory was an attack on a besieged
government garrison at Quiha, a key highway junction south of
Wokro. From there they moved westward, 20,000 strong, to Enda
Yesus, the fort overlooking Makelle. They captured it and then took
Makelle. Central government officials fled. Haile Mariam issued a
proclamation to the inhabitants of Makelle declaring:

> *Our governor is Jesus Christ*
> *And our flag that of Ethiopia*
> *Our religion is that of Yohannes IV*
> *People of Tigray, follow the motto of Weyane.*[45]

[43] This widely used term in Ethiopia can have positive as well as negative connotations; some *shifta* are seen as Robin Hoods.

[44] Gebru Tareke, *op.cit.*, pp. 185-6.

[45] The term *Weyane* comes from a traditional Tigrayan game. It connoted resistance and a sense of unity. Gebru Tareke, *ibid.*,p. 217.

By 20 September the successful Weyane turned south to face an army the Emperor had sent under the command of Minister of War Ras Abebe Aregay which had arrived at Korem on 17 September. The Ras was accompanied by a small contingent of British officers and specialists. Raya, Azebu and Wejerat blocked them. Fighting centered on Amba Alagi, the scene of bloody battles in 1936 when the Italians invaded and when they were finally defeated in 1941. The Weyane outnumbered government troops, but their advantage in numbers was offset by artillery and British air power and the struggle dragged on inconclusively. Interviewed in 1974, Haile Mariam maintained the Weyane could have won by exhausting their opponents had it not been for artillery and air attacks. A British officer observed at the time:

The bombing was accurate and inflicted considerable casualties which had their effect in undermining the rebel determination. Quite apart from the actual casualties inflicted, however, after one or two attacks the appearance of the aircraft alone was sufficient to cause concentrations of tribesmen to disperse. Ground troops were thus enabled to move forward and occupy key places without opposition.[46]

In the second week of October, Ras Abebe began a systematic march northward, taking Quiha and Makelle on 14 October, and capturing the rebel headquarters at Wokro on 17 October. Haile Selassie subsequently appointed Ras Abebe governor of Tigray and charged him with the pacification of the province. The pacification was brutal. Ten Weyane leaders who were caught were sent to Shoa and imprisoned at Debre Berhan. Haile Mariam himself did not surrender until 1946. He was exiled to Illubabor and then to Gamu Gofa for twenty years.[47]

The Weyane rebellion was motivated primarily by Tigrayan pride and particularism; separatism played no part. Haile Mariam was not an ideologue or a conscious ethnic nationalist. The Tigrayan rebels considered themselves as good Ethiopians and Christians as the Shoans whose domination they resented. Muslim Tigrayans took part in the Weyane struggle. The rebels did not question the existing social structure, because traditional Tigrayan patterns of land ownership and generational interrelationships provided for adjustment up and down the social scale.[48] Loyalties were to local communities, traditional leaders and leading families. Such loyalties gave the rebellion great strength as it gathered force but made the

---

[46] British after-action report cited in Gebru Tareke, *op.cit.*, p. 196.

[47] In 1975, the Derg appointed him head of the militia in Tigray.

[48] Dan F. Bauer, "Land, Leadership, and Legitimacy among the Inderta Tigray of Ethiopia", Ph.D. diss. University of Rochester, NY, 1973.

movement brittle when the rebels met sustained resistance and frustration. Thus spectacular victories were followed by quick and devastating defeat. The Weyane rebellion drew on no outside inspiration, either material or ideological. It was in large part because of prompt and effective British support to Haile Selassie's forces that it was so quickly put down.

The next major rebellion the Emperor had to deal with – in Bale – was different in all respects, but before we come to it, let us review the process by which Haile Selassie reestablished his authority and his emergence as an African and world leader.

The Constitution of 1955

Several factors made a new constitution desirable, including accommodation of the Eritrean federation, shortcomings and omissions in the 1931 constitution, the increasing complexity of government, and the need to adjust to the requirements of modernization and of a constantly expanding central administration. Several years of meticulous work went into the revision which was overseen by the Crown Council under its chairman, the senior Shoan noble, Ras Kassa Darge. Respected by the Church and the nobility and a participant in the 1931 constitutional process, Ras Kassa had the complete confidence of the Emperor who took a keen interest in the project. Like the 1931 constitution, Haile Selassie saw it as part of an educational process but was reluctant to surrender any of his own authority. The new constitution was more than twice the length of its predecessor. It was defined as applicable to all territory under the Ethiopian Crown. Thus it took precedence over the more liberal constitution of Eritrea, but the Federation was not mentioned. The draft was written primarily by American advisor John Spencer in English and then translated into Amharic. It went through a lengthy process of review and revision before it was approved by Parliament and promulgated by Haile Selassie on the silver jubilee of his coronation in November 1955.

The constitution reaffirmed the Emperor's descent from Solomon and Sheba and confirmed his primacy in all important respects: appointment of officials, control of the armed forces and of foreign relations, and oversight of the judicial system. It went into detail on provisions for the succession and a regency in case of incapacity of the Emperor. Parliament was given the power to approve treaties, but the Emperor was empowered to dissolve Parliament. Parliament consisted of a Chamber of Deputies elected every four years and a Senate appointed by the Emperor, but it was given much broader powers than in 1931. These, however, were all subject to conditions which enabled the Emperor to prevail in case of serious controversy. Laws, for example, had to be approved by both chambers, but the Emperor was authorized to issue decrees in times of emergency or parliamentary recess. Such decrees would have to be rejected by both chambers to be reversed.

Chapter III, "Rights and Duties of the People", granted all citizens freedom of religion, speech and assembly, and direct petition of the Emperor. It specified that "no one ... may be deprived of life, liberty or property without due process of law", but conditioned these rights on "respect for the rights and freedoms of others and the requirements of public order and the general welfare" which were to be elaborated in legislation.

Executive authority was vested in the Emperor. The "Ministers of the Empire" derived their authority from him, as did the Council of Ministers and the Crown Council, which was formally established as an advisory body to the Emperor. The distinction between judicial and administrative authority was ill defined. While universal adult suffrage was introduced for election of deputies, property qualifications were maintained for candidates. Political parties were not authorized. The Ethiopian Orthodox Church was defined as the state church and its organization and administration made subject to secular law. The church retained autonomy only in matters of monastic life and spiritual affairs.

The new constitution thus created the framework of a more modern governmental system but left many of its provisions more theoretical than actual. There was no widespread popular demand for accelerated reform and modernization in Ethiopia at this time. There was, in fact, very little understanding among the people of governmental processes independent of the judgments of traditional leaders or appointed officials. In the years that followed, parliament met and debated, often at great length, and produced useful legislation. Important new legislation nevertheless almost always depended on the initiative of the Emperor himself. When the Emperor failed to take a position, Parliament proved incapable of dealing with controversial issues, such as land reform.

The Bodyguard Coup of 1960

By the end of the 1950s both the capital and the provinces were experiencing a burst of development. A trickle of people from the countryside into Addis Ababa and provincial capitals had become a steady flow. Young men were returning from study abroad and taking low-to-medium-level positions in government. The presence of an increasing number of foreigners – aid workers, technical advisors, diplomats, teachers, graduate students and businessmen – resulted in interactions that steadily broadened Ethiopians' awareness of the world. The 1955 constitution reflected a compromise between those who recognized the inevitability of change and the traditional elite's reluctant recognition of the necessity of accommodating to the modern era. The constitution initially dampened both fears and expectations of sharp change, but the departure of Wolde Giyorgis from the capital left the Emperor maneuvering between several ambitious ministers and cliques around them: Makonnen Habtewold, Ras Abebe Aregay, Ras Andargachew Masai, and General Mulugeta Bulli (Ras Kassa had died in 1956). Politics were dominated by traditional habits of intrigue. Absent were the provincial pressures that Haile Selassie had to contend with both before and after the Italian invasion – his goal of centralization of authority had essentially been attained. But some of the western-educated young men tended to be frustrated.

Among them were the Neway brothers, Germame and Mengistu, born in a family of Manze origin. Mengistu, the elder, had been a Holeta cadet before the Italian invasion and during exile in Sudan sympathized with the short-lived Black Lion movement. After the Liberation he moved up rapidly in the Imperial Bodyguard, was promoted to Brigadier General in 1956 and made its commander. Germame, eight years younger, was the more serious and intense of the two. He did so well in HSI Secondary School at the end of the 1940s that he was one of five graduates sent to the United States under the sponsorship of Crown Prince Asfa Wossen. While at the University of Wisconsin, he was elected president of the Ethiopian Students' Association in North America (ESUNA). He came to the notice of Ras Imru, by then Ethiopian Ambassador in Washington, and after receiving his bachelor's degree at Wisconsin, transferred to Columbia, where he wrote a dissertation on Kenya for his master's degree. On return to Ethiopia in 1954 he was assigned to the Ministry of Interior and sent as an administrator first to Wolayta and then to Jijiga. He became deeply concerned about Ethiopia's backwardness and the need to speed up modernization. He influenced his brother and persuaded him to act.

They created a clandestine Council of the Revolution in 1960 and began planning but, fearing that word of their intentions had filtered out, they rushed a coup attempt with little advance organization when Haile Selassie departed on a trip to Brazil. Having failed to draw in the army, but in cooperation with Col. Worqeneh Gebeyehu, Head of Security in the Emperor's Private Cabinet, they took the Crown Prince into custody and occupied the central bank, the radio station, and the Ministry of Finance in the night of 13 December 1960. They arrested several ministers and dignitaries without a shot. They proclaimed their purpose to be overcoming the country's backwardness and accelerating change. The evening of 14 December they announced a new government with Asfa Wossen as constitutional monarch, Ras Imru as Prime Minister, and Mulugeta Bulli as Chief of the Armed Forces. They refrained from directly denouncing Haile Selassie. The coup was neither pro-leftist nor anti-American. They promised to build new schools and factories and increase agricultural production. They pledged to honor all international commitments and promised soldiers a salary increase.

They underestimated the traditional aristocracy, the church, the army and air force, the population of the capital and the Emperor himself. Only "automatic radicals" among students manifested sympathy with the coup[49], but events transpired too fast for any of them to act. Ras Asrate, Patriarch Basileos and the military commanders organized a counteroffensive. Units from outlying garrisons and planes from Debre Zeit rushed to the capital. Though the Crown Prince made (he later maintained he was forced) a broadcast approving the coup on 15 December, it quickly crumbled under the attack by the army and the air force which began that evening and continued into 16 December. Haile Selassie, rushing from Brazil across Africa, arrived in Asmara the same evening. The revolt ended the next day as the rebels machine-gunned the ministers and other hostages they held in the Genetta Leul palace as it was stormed by the army. Among the 18 killed were Ras Abebe, Makonnen Habtewold, Mulugeta Bulli and Ras Seyum.

The Neway brothers and Colonel Worqeneh fled. When the colonel was found hiding under a bridge by an army patrol the next day, he emptied his carbine at them, then pulled his pistol and put it to his mouth, shouting that he was emulating Emperor Tewodros. The next day Haile Selassie returned to the capital to a tumultuous welcome. Fleeing first to the forests of Entoto, the Neway brothers and a few followers made their way south during the following week but were reported to the police by peasants near Mount Zuqualla. In the ensuing skirmish Girmame was killed, Mengistu severely wounded and taken captive. Like Colonel Worqeneh's the week before, Girmame's body was hung up for a day before St. George's Cathedral, where crowds gathered. There was no public sympathy for the rebels. Haile Selassie addressed the public over the radio:

You all know how much We trusted and how much authority We reposed in those few who have risen against Us. We educated them. We gave them authority. We did this in order that they might improve the education, the

[49] The phrase is Clapham's; see *HSI's Government*, pp. 24-6.

health and the standard of living of Our people. We confided to them the implementation of some of the many plans We have formulated for the advancement of Our nation. And now our trust has been betrayed. [...] We cannot reward [those who crushed the rebellion]. [...] Almighty God, who elected Us to lead Our people, will reward them. [...] The judgment of God is upon [the rebels]; wherever they go they will never escape it.[50]

Aftermath of the coup: education

Was the 1960 coup the harbinger of the revolution of 1974? Only in a very general sense, if at all. It was a premature manifestation of the generalized discontent that developed among politicized students and Marxist intellectuals during the next thirteen years, but this was only one of the currents of opinion during the time and not the predominant one. Though Haile Selassie felt betrayed, he seemed more puzzled than angry. Perhaps from experiences with his own sons, he was tolerant of the waywardness of youth. He did not consider students capable of plotting a revolution. Fatherly persuasion would convince them to work conscientiously for modernization. Far from reducing his faith in education at home and abroad, he renewed his commitment to it by giving full support to plans for combining existing colleges into a full-scale university and donated Genetta Leul – the palace and grounds that had figured in the attempt to overthrow him – to it.[51]

Literacy in Ethiopia in 1941 had probably not exceeded five per cent, primarily resulting from the work of traditional church schools. Education stagnated during the Italian occupation, though knowledge of elementary Italian spread. In spite of his own preference for French, Haile Selassie decided on his return that English, likely to develop further as a world language, would be the second official language of the country. He returned from exile with his faith in education as a prerequisite for progress undiminished. There was a need for trained men in every branch of government. Young men began to be sent abroad for training in increasing numbers before the end of the 1940s. Expansion of primary and secondary education was at first slow. There was an acute shortage of teachers. Foreign governments and individuals as well as missionaries were invited to help expand secondary education. To rebuild his favorite secondary school, Tafari Makonnen, the Emperor invited a group of Canadian Jesuits led by Dr Lucien Matte, to start the job in 1945. It was quickly

---

[50] Greenfield, *op.cit.*, p. 433. Greenfield was sympathetic to it. He devotes the last quarter of his history to the coup and its aftermath, pp. 337-452, with a great deal of otherwise unreported detail.

[51] He had moved into the Jubilee Palace built to celebrate the 25th anniversary of his coronation in 1955.

brought into operation. In 1950 Haile Selassie asked Dr Matte to organize a two-year college. It became the University College of Addis Ababa, beginning operation in 1951. During the next two years an affiliation with the University of London was arranged.

During the remainder of the 1950s, with the help of foreign governments and advisers of several nationalities, five more colleges were established. Under USAID funding, the University of Oklahoma first set up an agricultural school at Jimma in 1953 and then opened an agricultural college at Alemaya near Harar in 1956. A public health college sponsored by UN agencies and USAID was opened at Gondar in 1954. In the same year the Swedish government founded a building technology institute in Addis Ababa. The two-year engineering college that began operation in Addis Ababa in 1952 was intended to be a faculty of Haile Selassie I University (HSIU) for which planning had already begun.[52]

Once in being, HSIU expanded rapidly and was generously supported by USAID, private American foundations and several European governments and institutions. By 1970 it had nearly 5,000 students and a teaching staff of 460, of whom 212 were expatriates from 15 different countries. Teaching was in English and nearly two thirds of the expatriates were Americans or Britons.[53] Well trained young Ethiopians were joining the university's faculties at an increasing rate. While secondary-school graduates could gain a good undergraduate education in Ethiopia, those who wished to specialize or return to teach had to go abroad for advanced degrees. By the end of the 1960s thousands of Ethiopians were studying abroad, primarily in America and Europe, but some also in the Middle East and, especially, in India. A few went to the Soviet Union and Eastern Europe. In Eritrea a group of Catholic sisters organized a private university which was eventually absorbed into the state system.

Primary and secondary education at first expanded slowly, especially in the provinces, but received an enormous boost in the early 1960s when President Kennedy agreed to have the largest Peace Corps contingent in the world assigned to Ethiopia. There were over 900 volunteers, mostly teaching in secondary schools, by the middle of the decade. During the same period, Sweden undertook a massive school building program and primary and secondary education spread rapidly throughout the country, sometimes with local communities raising funds to supplement the central government's budgetary allocations. Ethiopian teacher training institutes could not satisfy

[52] Teshome G. Wagaw, *The Development of Higher Education and Social Change, an Ethiopian Experience*, Michigan State University Press, East Lansing, MI, 1990.

[53] *Ibid.*, pp. 134-6.

the demand for teachers, so the government hired several hundred Indians, Sri-Lankans and Filipinos to teach in secondary schools. It is not uncommon today to meet middle-aged Ethiopians who speak English with a distinct Indian accent.

Aftermath of the coup: government and foreign affairs

Soon after suppressing the coup, Haile Selassie reorganized the government with Aklilu Habtewold as Prime Minister[54] and gave him and other ministers greater leeway in governing. He encouraged assignment of more university graduates to the government. He sometimes seemed more open to criticism. He showed his appreciation of the armed forces by raising their pay. But he also gave less attention to domestic affairs and devoted more time to foreign affairs, making a place for himself in the Pan-African movement and championing decolonization. He personally supervised the erection of Africa Hall and arrangements for the African Heads of State Conference in May 1963 which resulted in establishment of the Organization of African Unity (OAU). Not to be overshadowed by many of the new personalities on the African scene – Nkrumah, Sekou Toure, Kenyatta, Nyerere – he continued to take a leading role in Pan-African politics. He made Addis Ababa the capital of Africa. Hundreds of African diplomats have ever since been prominent in the life of the capital.

He had already discovered the pleasures of foreign travel in the 1950s. He hosted frequent visits by foreign dignitaries and took a personal interest in negotiations for development assistance agreements of many kinds. Aside from the fact that the Soviet Union was among the few countries that had refused to recognize the Italian conquest of Ethiopia, Haile Selassie had little basis for interest in it, but the Soviets maintained an embassy and an information office in Addis Ababa. *Pravda* had sneered at him in the early 1950s as "not the Lion of Judah but the jackal of American imperialism",[55] but Nikita Khrushchev's audacious approach to foreign affairs brought an invitation to visit Moscow and he went in the summer of 1959. There Haile Selassie was warmly received and awarded one of the highest Soviet military orders as well as an academic degree. Gifts, including an IL-14 airplane, were lavished on him and he was sent home with a long-term $100-million credit. Ethiopia needed an oil refinery, so the Russians bundled up one which had been seized from Romania

---

[54] He remained in that position until early 1974.

[55] Cited by Sergius Jakobson in "The Soviet Union and Ethiopia", *Review of Politics*, July 1954, p. 334.

in 1944 and set up in Baku, where after long use it was redundant to
Soviet needs, and shipped it to Ethiopia.[56]

The good fighting record of the three Imperial Bodyguard battalions that had been sent in succession to Korea during the early
1950s was a source of pride to the Emperor. Participation in this UN-
sponsored undertaking reinforced his long-standing commitment
to the concept of collective security and interest in UN affairs. In
addition to Britain and the United States, Sweden, Norway, India,
Belgium and Israel were invited to send advisers and provide training for the Ethiopian military. In the early 1960s Ethiopia provided
peace-keeping troops for the Congo. Haile Selassie made his first
trip to the United States in 1956 and went again twice in 1963, the
second time to attend President's Kennedy's funeral. He went again
in 1967 and 1969, visiting other countries en route. Among foreign
visitors were Queen Elizabeth and Prince Philip, who made a state
visit in 1966.

The legacy of the coup

Among students and intellectuals until the end of the 1960s revolutionary thinking was a minor, not major current. Desire for personal
betterment and a guarantee of steady, prestigious government
employment was always stronger. As secondary schools throughout
the country graduated larger classes, demand for higher education
exceeded enrolment possibilities at HSIU and other institutions.
Among students competition for good grades was keen because a
good record increased chances of study abroad. Educated young
men became common in government departments and overshadowed traditionalists. As Ethiopian society became steadily more open
and more complex in the 1960s, the 1960 coup was discussed more
as an episode than as a watershed event.

Haile Selassie's vanity was bolstered by his successes in Africa and
on the wider world scene. His deep-rooted habit of balancing
supporters of reform and speedier progress against traditionalists
persisted. Nevertheless frustrations and pressures were building up:
for more educational opportunities, for more rapid development, for
land reform, for wider opportunities for freedom of expression, for
recognition and use of languages other than Amharic, for recognition of ethnic and religious diversity. Haile Selassie was reluctant to
recognize these as serious. He adamantly opposed development of
political parties. Without legitimate outlets for debate and interplay
of ideas, students and intellectuals resorted to leaflets, clandestine

[56] It was set up at Assab and went into operation in 1967.

meetings and conspiracy. In this atmosphere genuinely subversive
forces – indigenous and foreign – found opportunities to build tensions and foment clashes. With seldom anything but naive good
intentions Peace Corps teachers added to this ferment.

Haile Selassie seemed not greatly affected by the death of
Empress Menen after a long illness in February 1962. His favorite
son, Makonnen, Duke of Harar, had been killed in an automobile
accident in 1957, leaving five children. He occupied himself with
them and was close to his elder daughter Tenagneworq and her
various offspring. His relationship to the Crown Prince after the 1960
coup remained cool. It was restored by mid-decade but lacked warmth.
There was little evidence that the Emperor felt lonely after the
Empress's death. If he did, he dealt with the problem by remaining
continually active. Nevertheless, as he approached his eightieth birthday, the pace of development in the country began to escape his
ability to manage and manipulate politics with the sureness of two
decades before. He delayed decisions and appointments. But there
was nothing in the gradual changes that were occurring in Haile
Selassie's relationship to the awesome responsibilities he insisted on
retaining that made the revolution of 1974, and in particular the
course it took, inevitable.

Christopher Clapham's observations in 1968 when he completed
his definitive study of Haile Selassie's government, often cited above,
were prescient:

One comes away not so much with the impression of development as of
stagnation: despite changes the *ancien regime* is still basically with us; and the
various reforms have not yet got down to essentials. The new conditions
which will presumably follow Haile Selassie's death, and which are now
rather apprehensively awaited, will no doubt prove to have been latent
in the present situation. [...] The abiding impression is ... of an era slowly
reaching its end.[57]

Insurgency in Bale

After suppression of the Weyane rebellion, eastern Tigray remained
sullenly peaceful under Ras Abebe Aregay. The western half of the
province had not been much affected. In 1947 Ras Abebe was
replaced as governor by Ras Seyum who, however, was required to stay
in the capital most of the time. He handled regional appointments
in his native province skillfully and Tigray remained at peace. It was
not favored with development projects however, nor was there a great
deal of urban growth. The peasantry remained deeply traditional.
When Ras Seyum was killed in December 1960, the Emperor

[57] *Op.cit,* p. 26.

appointed his son Mengesha in his place, thus keeping Tigray in the hands of descendants of Yohannes IV. Mengesha and his wife Aida Desta, the Emperor's granddaughter,[58] established themselves in the castle in Makelle and worked hard to develop the limited resources of this environmentally degraded region. For the last two decades of his rule, Tigray confronted Haile Selassie with no serious problems. The southeastern province of Bale, separated from Hararge in 1960, was a different matter.

There were local grievances in Bale, but a serious insurgency would never have developed had it not been stoked from beyond Ethiopia's borders. Bale was the country's second largest province in area, but the most thinly populated.[59] Three-quarters of Bale's inhabitants were Oromo, living in its forested northern highlands where Ethiopia's second highest mountain, Batu, rises to 14,360 feet. The vast central and southern regions of Bale are sparsely inhabited savannas that slope gradually to the Somali border. This area has for at least three or four centuries provided grazing for Somali nomads. The highlands of Bale may have been the original home of the Oromo, but for several generations, perhaps longer, Somalis had been advancing westward through lowland Bale into Sidamo, where they occasionally clashed violently with Borana Oromo.

Though the river valleys of the Ogaden[60] have a good potential for irrigation, there was little cultivation. The Ethiopian government and foreign aid donors initiated modest agricultural development projects in the 1960s. In Somalia, the lower Webe Shebelle valley was opened to agriculture during the Italian colonial period. The Somali Youth League (SYL) founded after British occupation in 1943 first articulated territorial claims to the Ogaden. Britain returned the major portion of the Ogaden to Ethiopian administration in 1948 but kept the Haud, the area directly south of then British Somaliland, until 1954. Thus it took thirteen years for Ethiopia to regain the entire area

[58] Aida was the daughter of Haile Selassie's oldest daughter, Tenagneworq by Ras Desta Damtew. Her marriage with Mengesha united the Tigrayan and Shoan royal lines.

[59] Some estimates in the 1960s put its population below 200,000. No estimates were larger than one million – for an area the size of England. For a summary of estimates and impressions of Bale in the early 1970s, see my *Ethiopian Journeys*, pp. 213-35.

[60] The Ogaden encompasses the entire lowland area of Hararge and Bale. It has always been a geographic expression rather than an administrative region. The name comes from the Somali clan that forms the major portion of its population. It is semi-desert, though traversed by several rivers that rise on the eastern plateau and seasonally carry a large volume of water into Somalia. The Webe Shebelle and Ganale are the most important.

it had held since the colonial boundary arrangements negotiated during the early twentieth century.[61]

But Ethiopian control remained tenuous. The region had few roads and few settlements. Many names on the map were only weekly market sites or wells with no permanent inhabitants. Lack of readily exploitable resources gave the region low priority for economic development. While lowland Somalis were primarily nomadic camel and goat herders, highland Oromos herded cattle and some were cultivators. As the Addis Ababa government resumed control of the area, friction developed between Oromo peasants and Amhara officials who sought to impose taxes and exact services. The arrival of Amhara settlers caused further strain as local grazing and land rights were arbitrarily abrogated. Northern Bale had vast expanses of open land to which the central government claimed title by right of conquest at the end of the nineteenth century. Retired soldiers were prominent among the settlers attracted to the province by land grants.

Local resentments accumulated. In contrast to the Christian settlers, the indigenous population was almost entirely, though somewhat nominally, Muslim.[62] In spite of local tensions and grievances, serious insurgency would have been unlikely if Somalia had not become independent in 1960.[63] Grievances among the Oromo in Bale did not fuel separatism, and circumstances in Bale did not differ greatly from those elsewhere in southern Ethiopia. The reason similar grievances did not result in rebellions and insurgency in other southern Ethiopian provinces was that it was not in the interest of a neighboring country to organize, finance and arm insurgents.

A group calling itself the United Liberation of Western Somalia was set up in Mogadishu at independence. It included all of Hararge, Arsi, Bale and southern Sidamo in its definition of Western Somalia. This organization evolved into the Ogaden Liberation Front that announced its existence in 1963. The new Somali government gave asylum to disaffected Somalis and Oromos from Ethiopian territory. Radio broadcasts from Mogadishu encouraged dissidents to look to Somalia for support. Soon Somalia's agents were infiltrating Ethiopian territory and smuggling in arms. Revolt first broke out in an ethnic Somali area, Elkere, in 1963. Rebel groups then formed in

[61] S. Pierre Petrides, *The Boundary Question between Ethiopia and Somalia*, People's Publishing House, New Delhi, 1983.

[62] Muslim influence in the area extends back 1,000 years, but many pre-Muslim practices have survived and been absorbed into local Islam. Ethiopia's most popular Muslim pilgrimage site, the tomb of Sheikh Hussein, is located on the Webe Shebelle in northern Bale.

[63] The new Somali government was strongly irredentist, openly claiming territory in Kenya, Ethiopia, and Djibouti.

each subprovince, often under the leadership of local notables. A general offensive began in 1964, with attacks on police stations in Oromo regions.

Addis Ababa moved to stem peasant discontent by announcing liberalized arrangements for reclaiming confiscated lands and settling tax arrears, but bureaucratic delays created new grievances between peasants and authorities. The Somalis had meanwhile trained a cadre of insurgent leaders, foremost among them an Oromo named Waqo Gutu, who was given the rank of general. Subprovincial leaders were designated colonels. By early 1965 the whole region was in a state of high tension as a result of rebel attacks on police stations and government offices and harassment of road traffic. Several settlements and road junctions fell to the insurgents. Government forces were thrown off balance. In March 1966 the governor of Ganale subprovince and a sizable entourage were ambushed and killed.

Addis Ababa declared martial law in Bale and in the neighboring Borana region of Sidamo in December 1966. Ethiopia accused Mogadishu of fomenting the rebellion. To reduce the potential for conflict between Somalis and Oromos, Mogadishu encouraged the insurgents to emphasize Islam as a common denominator and depicted their struggle as a jihad against Christian Amhara domination. Ethiopia could not keep insurgents from moving in and out of Somalia because control of so long and distant a border was beyond the capabilities of the armed forces. By this time, Somalia had acquired mortars, land mines, bazookas, and light artillery, as well as a wide range of light weapons – largely from the Soviet Union – and had little other need for them, so most of them were sent to the rebels in Ethiopia.

Demands in Eritrea for Ethiopia's manpower were growing. In Bale Addis Ababa had to mobilize units of the Territorial Army and recruit local militia among Christian settlers. A Christian Oromo General, Jagama Kello, was put in charge of a determined effort to defeat the Bale insurgency. In the face of more coherent Ethiopian military operations, the guerrillas became more professional, too, avoiding pitched battles and attacks on well-defended positions, and turning to hit-and-run raids. They achieved their maximum effectiveness, with 12 - 15,000 fighters, in early 1969.

Several factors helped Addis Ababa turn the situation around. During late 1968 Ethiopia's air force began bombing rebel strongholds and livestock concentrations. A British army engineers unit flew in to build a bridge across the Ganale River, greatly facilitating the mobility of Ethiopian forces. Most important was a lessening of support from Somalia, for Prime Minister Mohammed Ibrahim Egal on coming to power decided it was unwise to challenge Ethiopia and

Kenya and neglect his own country's development. The effect of this policy change was not immediately apparent because the insurgents had been so generously supplied that they were able to maintain momentum even with a slowing of Mogadishu's logistical support. The Ethiopian administration in Bale began an effort to divide the rebels from the population by cracking down on corruption and moving energetically to deal with peasant grievances. Both carrot and stick had effect, for aerial bombardment struck terror into peasants supporting the insurgents and encouraged disengagement from them.

When rebels began to surrender at the end of 1969, the insurgency quickly lost momentum. Somali Chief of Staff General Mohammed Siad Barre's military coup in Mogadishu in October 1969 further weakened Mogadishu's support for the insurgency in Ethiopia, for he too chose to concentrate on internal priorities. Ironic as this may be in view of Siad Barre's adventurism a few years later, it demonstrates how quickly the direction of the tide of history can change in the Horn of Africa. By February 1970 the Ethiopians had surrounded General Waqo Gutu who retained barely 200 armed men under his command, in Arana, an isolated area south of Mount Batu. He surrendered. He and his fighters were pardoned on condition that they return to a peaceful life. Haile Selassie subsequently granted Waqo Gutu a title and a commission in the Ethiopian army.[64]

The Emperor appointed General Jagama Kello governor of Bale and several other Oromos and Somalis to other positions. The pacification of the province and of most of the Ogaden was complete by 1971.[65] Although a few guerrillas may have remained at large in isolated areas during the next year or two, they did not challenge the government.[66] Addis Ababa resumed small-scale land grants for settlement of Ethiopian soldiers and made modest efforts at economic development. Somali adventurism in the Ogaden had been contained, but the Somalis had not learned their lesson.

[64] The preceding account of the Bale insurgency is based both on Gebru Tareke, *op.cit.*, pp. 227-317, 481-4, and on personal knowledge gained during my service at the American Embassy in Addis Ababa, 1969-72.

[65] Compromise and conciliation as a conclusion to conflict are more characteristic of this part of Africa than fighting to the finish and humiliation of those who concede defeat. As previous chapters show, Ethiopian history provides many examples. There is also a parallel between the termination of the insurgency in Bale in 1970 and the manner in which Nimeiry settled the southern Sudanese rebellion two years later.

[66] I trekked on horseback into the region around Mt. Batu in early summer 1972 over a route that had been used by insurgents less than three years earlier.Memories of rebel activities were alive among local Oromo, but conditions were entirely peaceful; see *Ethiopian Journeys*, pp.221-4.

As the Bale insurgency was easing, a diffuse rebellion broke out in Gojjam over a new rural tax system Addis Ababa introduced in 1967. By 1968 large parts of the province were out of government control as protesters attacked government offices, police stations, and tax assessors who tried to collect arrears that in some cases extended back two decades. Investigators were sent from the capital, but negotiations dragged on. The fact that Eritrea and Bale occupied most available military manpower, made sending in troops difficult, so the air force was sent to bomb recalcitrant villages that were centers of resistance. Concessions by Addis Ababa finally brought the rebellion to an end in May 1969.[67]

Intellectual life, literature and art in the 1960s

Rebellions in Bale, Eritrea and Gojjam notwithstanding, Ethiopia probably enjoyed a greater degree of peace in a greater portion of its territory in the 1960s than at any previous period in its history. Air service and new roads made much of the country accessible to officials, technicians, researchers and tourists. Tourism developed steadily during this time, skillfully promoted by EAL and the Ethiopian Tourism Organization (ETO). The Historic Route which linked Bahr Dar (the point of access to the island monasteries of Lake Tana and the falls of the Blue Nile), Lalibela, Gondar, Aksum, Makelle and Asmara, attracted continually increasing numbers of visitors. A Peace Corps volunteer took on the task of producing the first English-language guidebook to the country.[68] Other Peace Corps volunteers, as well as missionaries and development specialists from many countries who lived in remote areas developed knowledge and understanding of Ethiopia's many cultures. Some returned as anthropologists and historians and produced reports, articles, books, recordings of folktales, oral history and music – activities which young, educated Ethiopians soon emulated.

HSIU developed with surprising speed. By the end of the 1960s it had a thriving law school, an engineering school, an Institute of Development Studies and all the departments of a major American or European university, and granted degrees in arts, sciences and law. Richard Pankhurst, son of the famous Suffragette and tireless advocate of Ethiopian freedom, Sylvia Pankhurst, founded the Institute of Ethiopian Studies (IES) at HSIU in 1962.[69] He was joined

[67] Gebru Tareke discusses the Gojjam tax rebellion at length in *op.cit.*, pp. 160-93.

[68] Joel Rasmussen, *Welcome to Ethiopia*, ETO, Addis Ababa, 1969.

[69] By the end of the 1960s he had published two monumental volumes on Ethiopian economic history as well as dozens of articles and began a remarkable career

by Stanislaw Chojnacki, an exile Pole who came to Ethiopia by way
of Canada to teach at the University College, moved to HSIU when it
was founded and within a year, created a first-class ethnographic
museum and founded the most important collection of religious art
and manuscripts in the country. Pankhurst, Chojnacki and several
other expatriates at the university produced the first issue of the
important *Journal of Ethiopian Studies (JES)* in January 1963 which,
appearing twice a year until the Derg era, published the research of
young Ethiopians returning from abroad, as well as the work of
foreign scholars, in history, anthropology, linguistics, sociology and
contemporary issues. In 1966 HSIU hosted the Third International
Ethiopian Studies Conference (IESC), with participants from more
than a dozen countries. Its *Proceedings* were subsequently issued in
three volumes by HSIU Press, which also published textbooks and
more than a dozen major works of scholarship during the decade.

The 1966 IESC in Addis Ababa symbolized a decisive watershed
in the field of scholarship on Ethiopia. Study of the country had
begun in Europe with the work of Job Ludolf in the 17th century. For
the next 250 years all research and publishing on Ethiopia occurred
in Europe. In the mid-twentieth century it began to shift to Ethiopia
itself. With the 1966 conference, the first to be held in Ethiopia,
Addis Ababa became the focal point of scholarship on the country.
Almost all the American, European and Israeli scholars cited in
footnotes in this and preceding chapters worked in Ethiopia in the
1960s and many taught at HSIU, some for several years.

Though Ethiopia has had a history of literacy dating from
pre-Aksumite times, writing was confined to inscriptions, chronicles
and religious treatises until the 19th century and was almost all in
Ge'ez.[70] Emperor Tewodros was the first to have his chronicles written in Amharic, the language of the court and army since medieval
times. The country's first newspaper *Aymero* (Wisdom or Knowledge)
was printed on a press ordered by Menelik in 1906. The first Amharic
novel, *Tobbiya,* by Afewerk Gebre-Yesus, was printed in Rome in 1908,
and the first Amharic drama, *Yewarewoch Komediya* (Comedy of the

in scholarship on Ethiopia, as citations in previous chapters demonstrate. Sylvia
Pankhurst started the *New Times and Ethiopia News* in London in 1936, and
turned it into a popular quarterly, the *Ethiopia Observer,* when she moved to
Ethiopia in 1956. Before coming to Ethiopia she published the fruits of her
intensive study of the country in a massive book, *Ethiopia, a Cultural History,*
Lalibela House, London, 1955. She died in 1960 and is buried in front of Trinity
Cathedral in Addis Ababa. Several biographers have been attracted to her life
history in recent years, e.g. Patricia W. Romero, *Sylvia Pankhurst: Portrait of a
Radical,* Yale University Press, New Haven, CT, 1990. Richard Pankhurst contin-
ued editing *Ethiopia Observer* to the end of the Imperial period.

[70] Chronicles were written in Arabic in Harar.

Animals), was reputedly written during Lij Iyasu's brief reign by Tekle Hawariat Tekle Maryam, a protege of Ras Makonnen who had been educated in Russia and Europe.[71] During the decade and a half before the Italian invasion, educated Ethiopians began to write fiction, as well as history, travel, and didactic and moral literature. The most active writer in this period was the politically prominent Heruy Wolde Selassie, called by Molvaer "the Father of Amharic Literature".[72] Haile Selassie's memoirs, already extensively cited, are in themselves a significant contribution to Amharic literature.

After the Liberation, Ethiopians began writing in many genres, a sizable reading public developed, and both writers and readers multiplied throughout the 1960s.[73] Many prominent political figures published extensively: Wolde Giyorgis Wolde Yohannes, Makonnen Indalkachew, Ras Imru and Haddis Alemayehu. Some writers specialized in poetry and plays: e.g. Mengistu Lemma and Tsegaye Gebre Medhin.

Abbe Gubenya wrote historical novels that were eagerly read by young people, and was so popular in the 1960s that he was characterized as "Ethiopia's only writer who almost made a living from his books". Abbe, educated in church schools in Gojjam, was steeped in Ethiopian tradition but also adopted many progressive views. His novel *Aliwelledim* (I refuse to be born) has as its main character a fetus who does not want to come into the world of current Ethiopia because it has so many shortcomings. Haile Selassie had the novel suppressed and sent Abbe into three years of exile in Illubabor.[74] Many writers of the period also translated foreign writers, including Shakespeare, whose plays in translation became popular with large audiences.

Art also experienced a great efflorescence in the 1950s and 1960s. Until the beginning of the 20th century, all painting in Ethiopia had been religious – i.e. devotional or didactic – though wall paintings in churches often included court and battle scenes and representations of emperors and nobles. Stylized portraits of donors who paid for the paintings often provide information about prominent regional personalities. About the turn of the century, travellers and foreigners resident in Ethiopia started to buy and collect non-religious painting which created a whole new market for traditional artists. Ever since, in addition to religious themes, they have been painting battle scenes,

[71] Reidulf K. Molvaer, *Black Lions*, pp. xiii-xiv.

[72] *Op.cit.*, pp. 1-27.

[73] Reidulf K. Molvaer, *Tradition and Change in Ethiopia, Social and cultural life as reflected in Amharic fictional literature, ca. 1930-1974*, Brill, Leiden, 1980; Thomas Kane, *Ethiopian Literature in Amharic*, Harrassowitz, Wiesbaden, 1975.

[74] Molvaer, *op.cit.*, p. 181.

court scenes, aspects of daily life, portraits and hunting scenes. Some of these have been of high quality. Ethiopians soon followed foreigners in collecting such paintings. After the liberation more and more popular painters went to work. The works of many of them have been the subject of several European exhibitions and high-quality publications in recent years.[75]

When Ethiopians began travelling abroad in the 1920s, their numbers included a few painters who became exposed to European art. After the Liberation more Ethiopian artists went abroad to study and European and American artists also began to come to Ethiopia. An art school was founded in Addis Ababa in 1957. During the 1960s the Addis Ababa art scene was lively, with frequent exhibitions and sales in galleries; painters such as Skunder Boghassian, Gebre Christos Desta and Goshu Worku emerged as serious exponents of trends in modern art. The most famous artist of the period who enjoyed imperial patronage was Afewerk Tekle who was given commissions for major public projects, such as windows in the new church at Debre Libanos and in Africa Hall. Most creative Ethiopian artists to some degree imitated and adapted Western trends and techniques but many were also concerned to include Ethiopian themes in their work.[76] Debates about how to reconcile features of Ethiopian culture with modern trends, along with concern with "Africanness" in art became lively and have continued ever since.

Addis Ababa's population passed the half million mark in the early 1960s and continued to grow rapidly. By the end of the decade, the central area of the city had taken its present form with many impressive modern buildings: city hall, the imaginative Commercial Bank, the National Theater, several hospitals, new university buildings, the Wabi Shebelle Hotel and many commercial buildings. The Addis Ababa Hilton, completed in 1969, became the modern social center of the city as soon as it opened. A new airport was built at Bole on the southeastern edge of the city. As more people came into the capital from the countryside, the extensive areas of simple housing where the great majority of people lived – villages in the midst of urban development – expanded in all directions but particularly

[75] E.g. the exhibitions organized by Girma Fisseha of the Staatliches Museum für Völkerkunde in Munich, and published in *Mensch und Geschichte in Aethiopiens Volksmalerei*, Pinguin-Verlag, Innsbruck/Frankfurt am Main, 1985, and *Aethiopien in der volkstümlichen Malerei*, Institut für Auslandsbeziehungen, Stuttgart 1993.

[76] Most successful in this respect has been a painter educated at art school, Zerihun Yetmgeta, who came into his own only during the Derg period. During the time of the Derg, though some prominent artists fled abroad, the art scene in Addis Ababa remained lively, for the Derg was too beleaguered to have time to attempt to impose socialist realism in painting. Socialist realism and related communist themes likewise had only limited influence on creative writers.

to the west and south. Along Debre Zeit Road, the main route out of
the city to the south, industrial and commercial development continued at a steady pace.

A quarter century of economic development

Upon Liberation in 1941 the currency situation in Ethiopia was
chaotic. Four currencies besides the Italian lira were circulating: the
Maria Theresa dollar (MTD), the East African shilling, the Indian
rupee, and the Egyptian pound. The British military administration
declared all but the lira legal tender. Haile Selassie proclaimed the
establishment of the State Bank of Ethiopia (SBE) on 26 August
1942 with a capital of 1 million MTD. Britain opposed it and the
disagreement was not resolved until 1943.[77] A new national currency,
the Ethiopian dollar (birr), was launched in July 1945 linked to gold
and set at 40.25 US cents. The Ethiopian dollar was well received, but
the MTD continued in circulation in the countryside for several years
in spite of government efforts to curtail its use. The SBE gradually
took on the functions of a central bank while continuing to function
as a commercial bank. In 1963 SBE was replaced by the National Bank
of Ethiopia, with the functions of a central bank, and the newly founded
Commercial Bank of Ethiopia. Special-purpose banks were also
created in the 1950s and early 1960s: a Development Bank, an Investment Bank and a Home Ownership and Savings Bank. The banking
sector continued to develop effectively and contributed to the
economic stability of the country.[78] A high degree of economic
momentum did not, however, develop till the 1960s.

As a result of Italian occupation Ethiopia gained a high-quality,
expanded highway system, a good deal of urban construction and
civic improvements, and the establishment of a few small industries,
electricity generating plants, waterworks and the like. But there was
little systematic development of skill and talent to serve the economy.
This confronted liberated Ethiopia with a serious problem in 1941,
and Haile Selassie's appeal to individual Italians to remain and
help develop the country was an effort to ease it. Economic needs also
played a role in Ethiopia's desire to regain Eritrea. After 1952 Eritrea
made a contribution to Ethiopia's economy greatly out of proportion
to its population and area, not only because it possessed almost half

[77] Its original Canadian governor was replaced by an American in 1943. It remained under American management until 1949.
[78] Befekadu Degefe, "The Development of Money, Monetary Institutions, and
Monetary Policy, 1941-75" in Shifferaw Bekele (ed.), *An Economic History of
Ethiopia*, vol. I: *The Imperial Era*, Codesria, Oxford, 1995, pp. 232-76.

the industrial and service capacity of the country, but because it was also a reservoir of trained manpower.

In the 1940s agriculture did not loom large in thinking about economic development in Ethiopia. Concern for the development of industry took priority. There were hopes that the country would prove to have exploitable mineral wealth. Before much development could take place, however, it was clear that infrastructure had to be given high priority: transport, communications and electric power. Initially the Imperial Highway Authority concentrated on maintenance of roads built or improved during the Italian occupation. In the 1950s it started building new roads.

A ten-year industrial plan was formulated in 1944. Foreign capital was encouraged and development aid sought from many friendly countries as well as the World Bank, the UN and other international agencies. Foreign specialists were widely employed and helped draw up the first Five Year Plan, which went into effect in 1956 and emphasised infrastructure development. Industry was stressed in the second Five Year Plan, which extended from 1962 to 1967. Even before the five-year plan system became a permanent feature of Ethiopian development efforts, several important institutions had been established: Ethiopian Airlines, the Imperial Highway Authority, the Power and Light Authority, the Telecommunications Board and the Central Statistical Office. It was only in the 1960s that it became possible to use aggregated statistics to measure Ethiopian development.

By 1967 Ethiopia's Gross Domestic Product (GDP) had increased approximately 50 per cent over the level of 1961. Allowing for inflation, estimated at slightly more than 2 per cent per year, average annual growth during the period was about 5 per cent. Per capita GDP reached $60 with an estimated population of twenty-four million. Population was estimated to be increasing at 2 per cent per year, but since no census had been taken, all population statistics were based on small samples and extrapolations. Modern manufacturing increased rapidly, growing at an average rate of 17.6 per cent per year between 1961-7. In spite of substantial increases in production by expanding commercial farms, which were being encouraged but accounted for only an extremely small proportion of cultivated land, agriculture was expanding at a much slower rate than the rest of the economy, averaging about 2 per cent growth per year. Food production was no more than keeping up with population growth and could not, without major expansion of productivity, provide for increased consumption by the population, let alone supply the needs of agro-industry or provide large increases in commodity exports.

Though expenditures on medical and health services increased at 12.1 per cent per year during 1961-7, the base had been so low and the needs so great that initial progress merely served to emphasize the enormous needs yet to be faced. The same was true in education, where a revolution of rising expectations was already under way. About 530,000 students were attending primary and secondary schools in the 1967-8 school year. Nearly 2,000 Ethiopian students were studying abroad in 1967. Public education outlays increased at an average annual rate of 16.3 per cent during the decade of the 1960s, substantially above the level for Africa as a whole. Nevertheless, in spite of expanding adult literacy campaigns, literacy among the population as a whole was estimated to be no greater than 10 per cent by 1970.[79]

External economic aid appeared large in absolute terms and rose steadily during the 1950s and 1960s. It was, on the whole, well used. Ethiopia had no spectacular misconceived development projects. In view of the country's large population, per capita aid was nevertheless very low in comparison with most of the rest of Africa – an average of $13.80 per capita during the entire decade of the 1960s in contrast to $56.90 for Kenya and $90 for Somalia! The size of external economic assistance had little relationship to the efficiency of its use. It is quite likely that it was being used more efficiently in Ethiopia than in Kenya, for example, for while Ethiopia grew at half Kenya's rate in the 1960s, on a per capita basis it received only a quarter as much aid as its southern neighbor. Direct foreign investment in Ethiopia was not large, but some projects were notably successful, especially the great sugar estates in the Awash valley developed with Dutch capital in the 1950s. They came into production in the 1960s and the country became self-sufficient in sugar. Commercial cotton growing to supply expanding textile mills also increased rapidly with both foreign capital and local resources being invested.

The composition of Ethiopia's exports remained what they had traditionally been: predominantly coffee, hides and skins, and other elementary agricultural products. Coffee exports expanded from 21,000 tons in 1950 to 63,000 tons in 1963, worth approx. $43 million, and rose to over 90,000 tons in the early 1970s with earnings approaching $200 million in a period of high world coffee prices.

By the time the third Five-Year Plan was being drawn up in 1967, deepened realization of the importance of agriculture to Ethiopia's

---

[79] Data in the preceding paragraphs is derived largely from "Basic Data on the Economy of Ethiopia" prepared by the US Embassy, Addis Ababa and issued by the US Department of Commerce, August 1973; Irving Kaplan (ed.), *Area Handbook for Ethiopia*, USGPO, Washington, DC, 1971; and Imperial Ethiopian Government, *Third Five Year Development Plan, 1961-1965 EC (1968-73)*, Addis Ababa, 1968.

economic and social development had set in. The large traditional subsistence sector combined with the modern agricultural sector continued to occupy more than 90 per cent of the country's population. Unless agriculture could be made more productive, market access expanded, and elementary processing of agricultural produce improved, the country could never hope to develop a foundation for sustained modernization and improvement of living standards. Both foreign specialists and the now substantial group of young, educated Ethiopian technocrats agreed on the seriousness of the problem. Within both groups, however, there were increasingly divergent opinions as to how to tackle the task. Official policy favored development of commercial agriculture for export: agricultural machinery imports almost quadrupled between 1962 and 1966; fertilizer imports increased almost ten times between 1962 and 1965. Large increases in coffee production and export were achieved by improved collection and processing methods. The 1967 Arab-Israeli war disrupted plans for large-scale export of fruits and vegetables from Eritrea via the Suez Canal, but prospects for increased trade with parts of the Middle East appeared good.

Nevertheless, agriculture as a whole was seriously undercapitalized. It accounted for only a small proportion of total governmental development expenditure. Foreign donors took the initiative in drawing up pilot development projects, some on a very large scale, such as the Swedish-supported Chilalo Agricultural Development Unit (CADU) in Arsi. Intense controversy gradually developed among development specialists and foreign aid donors about land reform. The advice the Ethiopian government received on land reform from foreign specialists was often contradictory. Political, economic and social considerations were not clearly differentiated. The great bulk of the Ethiopian peasantry remained, as far as could be determined, largely indifferent to the land reform debate.[80]

Except in selected commodities and in commercial agriculture, productivity increased slowly in Ethiopia. The country as a whole did not benefit markedly from the Green Revolution which was then beginning to have a major impact in many parts of the world. Prob-

---

[80] There is a large, high-quality literature on agricultural development in Ethiopia by both Ethiopians and foreigners. Especially useful is a summary by Dessalegn Rahmato, "Peasant Agriculture under the Old Regime" in Shifferaw Bekele (ed.), *op.cit.*, pp. 143-93. Other significant works include Siegfried Pausewang, *Peasants, Land and Society: A Social History of Land Reform in Ethiopia*, Weltforum Verlag, Munich, 1983; John M. Cohen, *Integrated Rural Development, the Ethiopian Experience and the Debate*, Scandinavian Africa Institute Uppsala, 1987; Mesfin Wolde Mariam, *Rural Vulnerability to Famine in Ethiopia, 1958-1977*, Vikas, New Delhi, 1984; and S. Pausewang *et al.* (eds), *Ethiopia, Rural Development Options*, Zed, London, 1990.

lems of erosion, overpopulation, and addiction to primitive methods of cultivation, especially in the northern highlands, were diagnosed, but corrective programs were barely set in motion by the time severe famine conditions developed in 1973.[81]

Critics of Ethiopia's slow pace of development – both domestic and foreign – frequently singled out military expenditures as a major inhibiting factor. Actually the proportion of the Ethiopian budget devoted to military outlays was on the same level as the average for Africa as a whole and far below that of Ethiopia's neighbours, Sudan and Somalia.[82]

According to World Bank statistics, Ethiopia's per capita GDP was reckoned at $126 in 1974. During the period 1960-74 energy consumption increased in Ethiopia at an annual rate of 22.7 per cent, but only a small percentage of the country's vast hydroelectric potential had been tapped. Ethiopian trade was very close to being in balance throughout this period. Ethiopia's imports exceeded exports in value by only 5 per cent in 1974. 118,000 tons of cereals were imported in this year, of which 59,000 were donated for alleviation of famine conditions. Ethiopia's outstanding and disbursed foreign indebtedness in 1970 stood at $169 million and represented only 9.5 per cent of GDP. Debt service required only 1.2 per cent of GDP and 11.2 per cent of the value of exports of goods and services. Ethiopia's extremely low debt service ratio enabled her to weather the period of petroleum price increases more easily than most Third World countries. As of 1974, military expenditures absorbed 3.8 per cent of GDP and 20.2 per cent of the national budget. Men under arms totalled only 45,000.

Nevertheless, in the political uncertainty that developed in 1973 and early 1974, the petroleum price increases that came in the wake of the war in the Middle East had an unsettling psychological effect. Ethiopians were already becoming concerned with economic stagnation and the inability of the government to formulate long-term economic policies that would ensure self-sustained growth.

The end of the Eritrean Federation

The Eritrean-Ethiopian Federation never became functional as a political entity. Haile Selassie and most Ethiopians felt no deep commitment to the spirit or the details of the arrangement crafted

---

[81] Mesfin Wolde Mariam pointed out in 1972 that Ethiopia was already tending to become a net importer of food: *An Introductory Geography of Ethiopia*, HSIU Press, Addis Ababa, 1972, p. 127.

[82] "Arms and their Social and Economic Effect" in Henze, *Horn of Africa*, pp. 95-132.

by the UN.[83] The UN, as such, took no interest in the status of the federation after it was proclaimed. No federal institutions were established on the Ethiopian side and Eritrea's autonomy was systematically eroded during the next ten years. An opportunity for modernization of Ethiopia's own political structure was thus lost, to be regained forty years later and only after immense suffering and bloodshed on both sides of the Mareb.[84]

It is surprising that the pretense of federation was maintained as long as it was. Haile Selassie's desire to retain international respectability was part of the reason.[85] Within weeks of the federation being proclaimed, press freedom and party activities were curtailed. The largely ceremonial position of Governor-General in the constitution was translated into *Enderassie* in Amharic (Viceroy) and the first man the Emperor chose to fill it, his son-in-law *Bitwoded* Andargchew Masai, was disinclined to confine himself to ceremonial tasks. In 1952 the Assembly had elected the head of the Unionist Party, Dejazmach Tedla Bairu, Chief Executive. He resigned in August 1955. Haile Selassie appointed him Ambassador to Sweden, but he later defected. The *Enderassie* replaced him with his own deputy, an advocate of complete integration into Ethiopia. Carefully managed elections in September 1956 produced a more pliant Assembly, but its Muslim president, Idris Mohammed Adem, resigned in 1957, went to Cairo and joined Wolde-Ab Wolde-Mariam, a Protestant Christian who had originally edited the British-sponsored *Nai Ertra Semunawi Gazeta*, and then headed the Eritrean trade unions and the small Liberal Progressive Party.[86] Ibrahim Sultan, former head of the Democratic Bloc, was also there. They eventually joined the Eritrean Liberation Movement (ELM) which had had a very modest beginning in Port

[83] Haggai Erlich, "The Eritrean Autonomy, 1952-1962: Its Failure and Its Contribution to Further Escalation" in Y. Dinstein (ed.), *Models of Autonomy*, Transaction Press, New York, 1981. The same essay is included in the same author's *Ethiopia and the Challenge of Independence*, pp. 213-24.

[84] The most complete study of the federation experience is Tekeste Negash, *Eritrea and Ethiopia, the Federal Experience*, Scandinavian Africa Institute, Uppsala, 1997.

[85] No pressure was brought to bear on Ethiopia to live up to the commitments it had made to the UN by the countries who had devised the federation arrangement. The United States enjoyed full cooperation from the authorities in Asmara and activities at Kagnew Station expanded steadily during the 1950s as a high degree of East-West tension persisted, so it had no incentive to concern itself with operation of the federation.

[86] He finally returned to Eritrea in 1991 where I met him in early 1992. He was honored by the EPLF as the founding father of independent Eritrea. He died in Asmara in 1995 at the age of 90.

Sudan in 1958, where the Sudan Communist Party helped five young Eritrean exiles organize it.[87]

In December 1958 the Assembly abolished the Eritrean flag. The next year Ethiopian law was introduced, and in May 1960 the Assembly changed the name of the government to "Eritrean Administration under Haile Selassie, Emperor of Ethiopia". The vote of the Assembly abolishing itself on 14 November 1962 surprised no one. Eritrea became Ethiopia's 14th province, governed like all the rest.

It is useful, however, to see these developments in the regional and international context of the time. Pan-Arabism and Islamic assertiveness had been on the rise for several years and Nasserist revolutionary fervor was sweeping the Middle East. The Soviet Union was increasingly supportive of all radical Arab movements. Some Arabs claimed Eritrea was an Arab country, and similarly for Somalia. When Somalia became independent in July 1960, it adopted a five-star flag. Two stars represented the former British and Italian colonies that made up the new country. The other three stars symbolized Somalia's claim on Djibouti and all Somali-inhabited territory in Ethiopia and Kenya. With Eritrean exiles gravitating to Cairo and other Arab capitals (they were also welcomed in Mogadishu) and broadcasting rebellion, it was not surprising that Ethiopia felt threatened. The failed 1960 coup strengthened the Emperor's determination to act decisively to preserve his power. In September 1961 Muslims in western Eritrea clashed with Ethiopian forces and eventually declared themselves to be the Eritrean Liberation Front (ELF).[88] The next year directly across the Red Sea a radical revolution flared up in Yemen and Nasser sent an Egyptian expeditionary force to support it. Though worried, Haile Selassie took comfort from the fact that Ethiopia itself was calm and his international prestige remained high. Nasser and the Soviets avoided denouncing him or challenging him directly. For the time being, the abolition of what had become a totally fictional federative arrangement in Eritrea enhanced rather than detracted from the Emperor's standing in the world.

After 1941 Eritreans had become active throughout Ethiopia as businessmen, officials, teachers and traders, and the process

---

[87] Ruth Iyob, *The Eritrean Struggle for Independence: Domination, resistance, nationalism, 1941-1993*, Cambridge University Press, 1995, pp. 99-100. This useful book provides an immense amount of detail on Eritrean exile personalities and their complex interrelationships but has relatively little information on developments in Eritrea itself during the period.

[88] The independent Eritrean government that came into being with the defeat of the Derg celebrates this episode as the official beginning of the 30-year fight for independence.

accelerated during the federation period and continued after the federation ended. More economically developed than the rest of the country, Eritrea continued to attract investment and foreign aid. The enterprising Italian and half-caste population as well as the majority of highland Christians were pro-Ethiopian. US military installations continued to contribute substantially to the Eritrean economy. Eritrea remained peaceful through the mid-1960s and more prosperous than the rest of Ethiopia.

Dejazmach Asrate Kassa was appointed *Enderassie* in Eritrea in 1964, replacing General Abiye Abebe.[89] After Ras Kassa's death in 1957 Asrate Kassa had taken his father's place as one of Haile Selassie's closest confidants in Addis Ababa.[90] He had held several important governorships and had played an important role in restoration of the Emperor's authority after the coup of 1960. He was also a close friend and supporter of Crown Prince Asfa Wossen whom he wished to see succeed his father on the throne. Contrary to conventional radical "wisdom" in Ethiopia at the time, Asrate seems genuinely to have had no desire to succeed Haile Selassie himself.[91] Asrate was strongly disliked by Prime Minister Aklilu Habtewold because of his close relationship to the Emperor. Aklilu was glad to see him removed from the capital and "exiled" to Asmara. Well aware of their mutual dislike, the Emperor, on giving Aklilu authority to appoint ministers in 1966, raised Asrate to Ras. Rebel activities were already becoming more serious.

Taking up his new responsibilities energetically, Asrate appointed Tigrinya-speaking Eritreans to most major offices and brought them together periodically as an advisory council. He continued the use of Amharic, however, for educational and official purposes. His rivalry

[89] The Emperor gave him the title *Yigermawi Negusa Negast Enderassie ba Eretra* (Viceroy of His Imperial Majesty in Eritrea), though he was called Governor-General in English. Ras Mengesha Seyum in Tigray carried the same title which gave these two senior scions of the royal houses of Shoa and Tigray higher rank than other provincial governors.

[90] Ras Kassa's claim to the throne was actually stronger than Haile Selassie's but he never aspired to it and from the time of the regency onward had given crucial support to Haile Selassie at every important juncture. The same proved true of his only surviving son, Asrate.

[91] This judgment is based on personal acquaintance and frequent contact with Asrate Kassa in the period 1969-73 when I found him deeply concerned about the country's future, keenly aware of the need for accelerated modernization of the political structure and of a far less conservative cast of mind than radical students and intellectuals maintained at the time. He regarded Aklilu as the primary reactionary influence on the Emperor. Given his importance in the final decades of the Imperial Era in Ethiopia, a serious biography of Asrate Kassa would be an important contribution to Ethiopian history.

with Aklilu led to two major problems: control of Eritrean revenues and control of the Army.

The Ethiopian armed forces in Eritrea were...inefficient, brutal, and corrupt. Their activities lacked planning and coordination. Furthermore, the army was led by generals and colonels who considered military power the only proper way to deal with the Eritrean problem. Whenever the army was given a free hand in the province, the result was a bloody escalation and the crystallization and strengthening of anti-Ethiopian emotions among Eritreans, Christian and Muslim alike.[92]

To counter the negative influence of the army, Asrate set up two groups under his direct control and financed from the Eritrean budget: a commando force made up mostly of Christian Eritreans and trained by Israelis; and an Eritrean security service, which benefited from both Israeli and American support. He maintained close relations with American officials in Eritrea. As rebellion in Eritrea grew, Addis Ababa failed to develop a coherent policy to deal with it. Traditional habits of intrigue resulted in conflicting instructions to Asmara. A coordinating committee Asrate established in 1967 brought little improvement. Neither did the Emperor's periodic visits to the province when every official reported separately to him and he sometimes gave them conflicting advice. Asrate repeatedly encouraged discreet dialogue with rebel elements in hope of gaining support for reconciliation on the basis of Christian highland solidarity. He had the support of his neighbor in Tigray, Ras Mengesha, in these efforts. Actual rebel strength was not great, and much of Eritrea remained unaffected by their activities. To attain greater impact, they turned to sabotage and assassination. Mounting violence gave Aklilu justification for encouraging the army to take harsher action.[93]

Eritrean politicians and intellectuals who went into exile had some sympathy but little following at home. Despite efforts to represent themselves as a united group, Eritreans in exile were continually rent by tensions and rivalries. These were reflected in competition among fighters in the field. When radical Arabs and various Soviet proxies began to provide arms, rebels had more to work with. In the late 1960s they carried off several hijackings of Ethiopian Airlines flights. They were among the first to engage in systematic air piracy and may have been encouraged to do so by Cubans, who, along with communist Chinese and Syrians, began taking young Eritreans for

[92] Erlich, *The Struggle over Eritrea, 1962-1978: War and Revolution in the Horn of Africa*, Hoover Institution Press, Stanford, CA, 1983, p. 39.

[93] *Ibid.*, pp. 36-42, has a perceptive summary of this period based to a considerable extent on background information gained from Israeli sources.

guerrilla training. Isaias Afewerki and Ramadan Mohammed Nur went to China during this period.

The economic stagnation that set in after the closing of the Suez Canal in 1967 dampened economic expansion and created a larger pool of unemployed young men for insurgents to draw from. Nevertheless the great majority of Eritreans during this period remained oriented toward Ethiopia, where many found employment because they had the advantage of skills and training. At the end of the 1960s 3-400,000 Eritreans lived and worked in other parts of Ethiopia as technicians, teachers, officials, lawyers and businessmen. Eritreans occupied 19 per cent of senior positions in the central government, second only to Shoans, during the period 1941-66.[94]

Rivalries did not prevent insurgents from gradually expanding their operations on the ground – they encouraged them, in fact, to engage in more violence. By 1968 they were fighting pitched battles against Ethiopian military forces and carrying out spectacular acts of sabotage and urban terrorism. Israeli advisers had difficulty countering the tendency of Ethiopian commanders to use brutal search and interrogation methods, tactics which drove civilians to seek protection from the rebels. Officers and enlisted men were primarily from central and southern Ethiopia. Still no more than half of the imperial regime's 45,000-man army was ever deployed in Eritrea.[95] US military installations were never attacked and the US, as a matter of policy, stayed very much in the background of Ethiopian efforts to cope with the insurgency.

On the advice of Aklilu and his military chiefs and contrary to Asrate's desire, Haile Selassie considered declaring martial law in Eritrea in early 1970, but Asrate dissuaded him. The Emperor nevertheless authorized a major military offensive. In response in April Isaias Afewerki assassinated two judges in Asmara. This caused Haile Selassie to authorize his commanding general, Teshome Irgetu, to act without consulting Asrate in advance. Asrate departed for London and left his Eritrean deputy, Tesfa-Yohannes Berhe in charge. Tesfa-Yohannes was even easier to ignore by the general, who embarked on an intensive "pacification" campaign punishing villages judged to be rebel safe havens. Meanwhile Isaias and Ramadan Mohammed Nur drew together a stronger guerrilla organization with fighters who had returned from training in Syria and China: the Popular Liberation Forces (PLF).[96] On 21 November 1970 the PLF

[94] Clapham, *op.cit.*, p. 77.

[95] Ethiopia's armed forces were all volunteer. Few young Eritreans found the prospect of military service attractive.

[96] Rivalries among rebels in the field as well as with and among leaders abroad during this period defy simplification. See Ruth Iyob, *op.cit.*, pp. 113-17.

succeeded in ambushing General Teshome and killing him. This was the last straw for the Aklilu forces in Addis Ababa. They persuaded the Emperor to remove Asrate, declare martial law in Eritrea, and appoint General Debebe Haile Mariam military governor.

While Qaddafy embraced the Eritrean cause after he came to power in 1969 and Syria kept up support for the insurgents, funneling in supplies from Soviet-related sources, Moscow stayed in the background. There is reason to believe that the Soviets shifted their expectations in the early 1970s to longer-range goals, preferring that Eritrean insurgency, should it eventually succeed, result in the establishment of a Marxist state rather than an Eritrea where Muslim influence could predominate. Eritrean movements kept fragmenting and regrouping. Prospects for a quick outcome of the Eritrean struggle were receding when the Marxist Eritrean Popular Liberation Front (EPLF) was formally proclaimed in February 1972. The Soviets must have welcomed it, but they avoided open endorsement. They had plenty of surrogates to work through.

Ethiopia's international position at the beginning of the 1970s

The pace of history in the Horn of Africa accelerated in the early 1970s. Sudan changed course sharply after its communist party tried to overthrow Jaafar Nimeiry in July 1971.[97] He survived by the skin of his teeth, concluded that the Russians had abetted the coup, and abandoned his pro-Moscow orientation. Haile Selassie was relieved. 1971 was a watershed year for Ethiopia too, though changes in political orientation were less obvious. US Vice-President Agnew arrived in Addis Ababa early in July on a mission that seemed puzzlingly routine at the time. His real purpose – not revealed even to senior officers at the American Embassy – was to tell Haile Selassie that the United States was preparing to recognize Communist China. He advised the Emperor to do what he wished to advance Ethiopia's interests. Subsequent events provided an example of the energy and statesmanship of which the old Lion of Judah was still capable as he neared 80. In October 1971 he took a delegation of his most trusted advisers and several senior aristocrats to Beijing, met with Mao Zedong and Zhou-Enlai, and came back with agreements that both countries immediately began to implement. In return for establishing diplomatic relations, Mao promised to cease support for Eritrean insurgents and inaugurate an economic aid program for Ethiopia, including construction of an east-west highway across the center of the country.

---

[97] Moscow had welcomed Nimeiry when he seized power in a coup in May 1969 and, though he was not a communist, the Sudan Communist Party at first supported him enthusiastically.

About the same time Nimeiry asked Haile Selassie to mediate a
settlement of his fifteen-year-old war with Sudanese southerners. The
Sudanese president was ready to give the south autonomy and
integrate rebel fighters into his armed forces. In return he agreed to
restrict Eritrean insurgent use of Sudanese supply lines. Completing
the bargain, Haile Selassie promised Nimeiry that he would no longer
permit Ethiopian territory to be used to support movements challenging his government.[98] The southern Sudanese rebellion formally
came to an end in March 1972 with the signing of a set of agreements
in Addis Ababa. Nimeiry and Haile Selassie were able to settle these
problems speedily and without outside help because they accepted
each other's assurances of good faith, calculating that the links each
country had with outside powers would not take priority over its own
interests. Ethiopian-Sudanese strains, then as later, were a function
of external factors. Neither country had serious economic, political
or territorial claims against the other.

Americans and Europeans welcomed Ethiopian-Sudanese reconciliation and reduction in the intensity of the insurgency in Eritrea
which both Sudanese and Chinese reduction of support for the rebels
brought about. During this same period the United States quietly
decided to reduce operations at its Kagnew Communications Station
in Asmara in anticipation of complete withdrawal by 1978, but Ethiopia was not officially informed.[99] Leftist harassment of the US Peace
Corps in 1969-70, and the abrupt withdrawal of most Peace Corps
volunteers from provincial secondary schools, added impetus to a US
effort to reduce its direct role in development activity and shift more
responsibility to international organizations. The US military assistance group was gradually reduced from 125 officers and men to 75.
The US Army Mapping Mission had finished its work in 1972 and
gone home. Though American advisers were assigned to Ethiopian
military units at training bases, the United States continued to avoid
involvement in counter-insurgency operations in Eritrea, leaving
this task to Israelis. Overall, US-Ethiopian relations remained close

[98] Less than two years before, Ethiopia had delivered Israeli-supplied arms to
the Sudanese Ansar to support their revolt centered on Aba Island. For several
years large quantities of arms from Israel and other Western sources had been
reaching the southern Sudanese through Ethiopia. Southern fighters were
using Ethiopian territory as a safe-haven and their leaders enjoyed hospitality
in Addis Ababa.

[99] The decision was based entirely on technical considerations. The US Diplomatic Telecommunications Service, based at Kagnew and serving US embassies
throughout Africa and the Indian Ocean region, began to be replaced by direct
satellite communications in 1971. Military communications also shifted to satellite during this period. Other technical advances had made Kagnew largely
redundant for communications intelligence collection.

and friendly, as the Nixon Administration's advance notice on the shift in China policy demonstrates. US commercial investment and tourism were expanding. Americans were playing a leading role in higher education and American foundations were an increasingly important source of funding for programs in Ethiopia and for Ethiopians studying abroad, the majority of whom preferred to go to the United States. Only Ethiopian students who could not gain entrance to schools in Europe or America went to the Soviet Union or Eastern Europe.

Moscow must have been unhappy, but showed no overt displeasure at Ethiopia's establishing relations with Beijing. Several other African countries, the Yemens, Dhofar and elsewhere in the Arab world looked more promising to the Kremlin than Eritrea. In the Horn itself, Somalia loomed large in Soviet plans for the future.

Having defeated the Somali-backed Bale-Ogaden insurgency and established a close relationship during the 1960s with Somalia's elected leaders, Haile Selassie was alarmed when Siad Barre seized power in October 1969 and turned abruptly toward Moscow. He regarded Soviet arms pouring into Somalia as a much greater danger to Ethiopia than rebellion in Eritrea. Ethiopia's relations with Somalia remained uneasy in the early 1970s. The Emperor went to Washington in May 1973 and asked for $450 million to modernize his armed forces to meet the Somali threat.[100] It was not a good time for a Washington visit, for the Nixon Administration had become enmeshed in the Watergate scandal and the problem of withdrawal from Vietnam, but he came back with a promise of $200 million over the next several years to include M-60 tanks, F5-E fighter-bombers and Swift patrol boats useful for intercepting clandestine infiltrators along the Eritrean coast. The advanced aircraft would probably not have been promised without the Emperor's personal appeal to President Nixon.[101]

[100] This was Haile Selassie's last visit to the United States. He prided himself on having had a personal relationship with every American president from Roosevelt to Nixon.

[101] Though they were not delivered until 1976, these American fighter-bombers helped save the Derg when the Somalis attacked the next year. They enabled Ethiopia to cripple Somalia's Soviet-supplied air force and delay the Somali advance in the summer of 1977.

9

REVOLUTION, WAR, AND "SOCIALISM"
THE FIRST DECADE OF THE DERG

Prelude to Revolution

Haile Selassie celebrated his eightieth birthday in August 1972. There were ceremonies and parades, diplomats brought congratulations, and delegations from the provinces brought gifts. At night the streets of the capital were bright with colored lights. Even on the university campus student radicals who had criticized the Emperor as an out-dated reactionary and called for Marxist revolution remained subdued. A majority of Ethiopians, had they been polled at this time, would probably have admitted some concern about the future, for the birthday festivities underscored the Emperor's mortality. But there was little expectation of violence or abrupt change. The constitution provided for orderly succession. When he succeeded to the throne, Crown Prince Asfa Wossen was expected to introduce a more open society and a more liberal political system. People wanted faster economic progress and broadened educational opportunity. They expected that processes already under way would bring all these things. Only a few intellectuals and radical student organizations abroad advocated total replacement of the existing political and economic system but showed little understanding of what that would mean. Most Ethiopians thought in terms of personalities, not ideology, and out of long habit still looked to Haile Selassie as the initiator of change, the source of status and privilege, and the arbiter of demands for resources and attention among competing groups.

Fate conspired in 1973 to confront the aging Emperor with a plethora of problems simultaneously. It was a disquieting year for Ethiopia. In January the Crown Prince suffered a stroke and was flown to London for treatment. Ras Asrate Kassa, appointed by the Emperor to rejuvenate the Crown Council in July 1971 and oversee an orderly succession, accompanied him at the Emperor's order. At Easter, Haile Selassie proclaimed the Crown Prince's eldest son, twenty-year-old Zara Yakob, next in succession after his father, but it was too late to dampen increasing concern about the continuity of the monarchy. Famine developed in Wollo. The government first tried to ignore it, then to minimize its extent and discourage reporting. Eventually foreign reporters dramatized it. Intellectuals and officials were embarrassed and angered by government prevarication. Ethiopia's break in relations with Israel under Arab and African pressure after the Yom Kippur War in October 1973 raised doubts about Haile Selassie's ability to manipulate an increasingly complex international situation. Even more psychologically subtle in its impact but profoundly unsettling was the spreading fear among the Ethiopian elite that the US was falling into internal disarray and might no longer be a reliable source of support.[1]

Petroleum price increases were the immediate cause of crisis in early 1974. Taxi drivers struck. Soldiers in the south and in Eritrea demanded more pay. Labor unions became restive, students debated and demonstrated.[2] Suddenly a lethargic government was confronted with civilian and military demands from all sides. On 28 February the Emperor dismissed Aklilu Habte-Wold, who had been Prime Minister since 1961, and appointed a progressive aristocrat, Indalkachew Makonnen, in his place. The population rejoiced in the expectation that the long expected transition to a more open political system would go smoothly and a liberalized government would be in place before Haile Selassie departed from the scene. Journalists started writing freely and political groupings began to form. There was no violence. Prospects for peaceful change in Ethiopia looked good.

Abbe Gubenya, the country's most popular novelist, had come to the United States in the fall of 1973 for a year at the Iowa Writers' Seminar and spent the Christmas holidays with me in Washington.[3] He was uneasy about Ethiopia, for he had been close to the Crown Prince and had high expectations that he would lead the way to a liberalized constitutional monarchy. He went back to Iowa depressed about Asfa Wossen's slow recovery in London. As the revolution got under way, Abbe began telephoning three or four times a week from

[1] Fears were compounded when US Ambassador E. Ross Adair left his post in January 1974 because of declining health. He was not replaced and a weak embassy staff was hard put to maintain effective contact with Ethiopian officialdom during the fast-moving changes in the months that followed.

[2] The Confederation of Ethiopian Labor Unions (CELU) carried out a brief general strike, centering on union issues, in early March. During the same period, intense student and intellectual agitation developed against the Educational Sector Review, a comprehensive scheme for revision of priorities in education worked out in the early 1970s by Ethiopian educational authorities in cooperation with Western donors. It proposed broadening access to education with priority for vocational training and decreased emphasis, with a proportionate reduction in budgets, for secondary and elite liberal arts education. The Ethiopian educational system was producing more lawyers than engineers or doctors. The shift in emphasis was logical, but it alarmed intellectuals. Spurred on by radicals, they provoked so much commotion that implementation of the review was suspended.

[3] For background on Abbe, see Molvaer, *Black Lions*, pp. 181-4.

Iowa, often late at night, for news from home. He found it more and
more encouraging. One night at the end of May I picked up the
phone and heard Abbe's voice: "I can stand it no longer. I can do no
work here. I have decided to fly back home tomorrow. How proud I
am of my country! All that change and no blood! I must be part of it!"[4]

Ferment turns into revolution

Seen in retrospect, in spite of the apparent confusion of events, the
undermining of imperial authority in Ethiopia was systematic and
efficient. Whether there was a guiding hand behind it remains an
open question. In February 1974 a group of lower-level officers including Majors Atnafu Abate and Alemzewd Tessema organized an
armed forces coordinating committee. The committee, which was
soon called the Derg (a hitherto seldom used word derived from the
ancient church language, Ge'ez) went through several transforma-
tions before its consolidation in June, when it appealed to military
units in all parts of the country to send delegates to the capital. Lower
grade officers or enlisted men were usually chosen. Major Mengistu
Haile Mariam came from Harar and, along with Atnafu Abate who
had preceded him, quickly became a dominant Derg figure. From
the beginning the Derg was secretive about both its membership
and method of operation. It aimed to exercise power without taking
over the government. Clandestinity served the Derg well, for no one
knew how much high-level support it had, what factions existed within
it, or what foreign support it might be able to draw upon. No competing civilian leadership emerged. Senior military officers simply stood
by. Popular attitudes toward the Derg were equivocal: fear, doubt,
expectation and trust all mingled together.

At Derg request many men who held important positions in the
imperial regime delivered themselves voluntarily into detention in
June and July on the promise that their alleged misdemeanors and
financial irregularities would be systematically investigated and
fairly judged.[5] Others were arrested, including Prime Minister Indalkachew, who was replaced on 22 July by Mikael Imru, son of Ras Imru,

---

[4] Abbe became disillusioned with the course of the revolution in 1975 and 1976,
stopped writing, took to drink, and died on 7 February 1980 as a result of injuries
in a bar-room brawl. He was forty-five years old at the time.

[5] These included the President of the Crown Council, Ras Asrate Kassa, who had
returned from London at the end of 1973, supported the appointment of Indalkachew, but was unable to stabilize the course of events. David Hamilton, British
commander of the Naval College at Massawa during Asrate's tenure as *Enderassie*
in Eritrea, happened to return to Ethiopia in February 1974 and spent considerable time with him in connection with a research project on which he was working. He reported: "[Asrate] saw that the situation was not one of mere unrest, but

the popular liberal aristocrat and cousin of the Emperor. By this time Haile Selassie seems to have been numbed by the rapidity of changes that were taking place. The country's traditional leadership – both the established aristocracy and the young technocrats whom the Emperor had raised to positions of responsibility and influence – offered the Derg little challenge as it grew bolder. Potential opposition was neutralized, co-opted or circumvented. The Derg acted under the slogan *Ityopya Tikdem,* which meant "Ethiopia First" and carried no specific political implications except a vague sense of nationalism.

A comprehensive analysis of events during Ethiopia's summer of revolution is still not possible.[6] No outside influences on revolutionary actions became visible. In spite of the past close relationship, the US stood aside as Haile Selassie's authority eroded. So did European countries who had long been supportive. None of the low-and medium-level Ethiopian military men who joined the Derg were well-known to US military missions or foreign embassies. US, European and international economic aid and advisory groups went about their business as usual. In Washington during these very weeks the Watergate crisis reached its culmination and President Nixon resigned. No one had time for Ethiopia. In spite of Haile Selassie's prestige and the high priority Ethiopia had long enjoyed in US policy, there was no US effort to influence the course of events in Addis Ababa. No other Western country tried to do so.

Where were the Russians? Less diverted by crises at home than the Americans, considerable numbers of them were present, as usual, in the Soviet Embassy in Addis Ababa, but they stayed very much in the background. If some of the junior military men who played a role

---

of incipient revolution. The events then taking place were valid and almost predictable reactions to widely based popular dissatisfactions and demands which he understood and in large measure shared. They were events ... that he had been expecting. They were events that he knew foretold deep and permanent changes."

In April 1974 Asrate was sent by Haile Selassie to represent him at the funeral of President Pompidou in Paris. His son Asfa Wossen, studying in Germany, urged him not to return to Ethiopia. He refused, saying "How can I leave the Old Man alone after all those years? Don't forget that I owe him everything and will not desert him when he needs me most. The people of Ethiopia have a right to know by whom they were governed for the last 50 years and I have nothing to hide." Asrate kept a detailed diary during the period which is in the possession of his son who intends eventually to publish it. (The above information all derives from a private communication from Asfa Wossen Asserate, May 1998.)

[6] The best single description by foreign eyewitnesses to most of the events of the period 1974-7 is the book of David and Marina Ottaway, *Ethiopia, Empire in Revolution,* Africana/Holmes & Meier, New York, 1978. Memoirs of Ethiopians, investigations and trials undertaken by the new government after 1991, as well as memoirs key surviving Derg members may write, may eventually provide much greater insight into the events of 1974 and subsequent years.

in the formation of the Derg had been recruited by KGB or GRU officers in preceding years and were under Soviet guidance as they forged this secretive military junta into an instrument of power and took charge of the revolution, the undertaking was accomplished with exemplary discretion.[7]

On 9 July 1974 the Derg announced that a revised constitution was being drafted and would soon be presented to parliament for approval. It was published on 10 August but was never adopted and played no further role in the revolutionary process, which aimed at destruction – rather than reform – of imperial authority and neutralization of all elements supporting it. (Ethiopia remained without a new constitution until 1987.) Step by step the Emperor became the target of a vilification campaign. He was formally accused in August of devising a cover-up of the famine in Wollo. He was alleged to have sent enormous quantities of money abroad. When Abune Tewoflos, Patriarch of the Ethiopian Orthodox Church, endorsed the revolution at the end of August, it was apparent that the Emperor's fate was sealed. He was arrested and taken from his palace in a Volkswagen on 12 September, Ethiopian New Year's Day.[8]

---

[7] The Russians may have been applying the lessons learned in Sudan a few years before when they hurriedly embraced Nimeiry only to find themselves in the cold when the Sudanese communists tried to topple him. In 1974, soon after Mengistu consolidated his position by killing Aman Andom and proclaimed "Ethiopian socialism", the Russians began a discreet effort to gain leverage on the Ethiopian revolutionary process by inviting the Derg to send members to Moscow for political training. Several men who later became prominent went, e.g. Goshu Wolde and Alemu Abebe. Starting in 1975, the Russians supplied propaganda to Ethiopian media, prompted East European countries to offer assistance of many kinds and sent delegations which tempted Ethiopians with the prospect of large-scale military assistance. Information provided by the late Getachew Kibret, who was a senior foreign ministry official in Addis Ababa during the early period of the revolution and defected in 1985 from the position of Ethiopian Ambassador to France, has provided strong substantiation for the hypothesis that uncertainties or disagreements among the Russians over how to maintain Soviet equities in Somalia led them to improvise and compromise in Ethiopia, but always with the aim of extending their influence and leverage over Ethiopia while retaining a strong position in Somalia. This judgment has been substantiated by Soviet and East German documents released in the early 1990s which I and others analyzed in the *Bulletin of the Cold War International History Project*, Wilson Center, Smithsonian Institution, Washington, DC, 1996.

[8] Derg fear of popular reaction against abolition of the monarchy led it to declare Crown Prince Asfa Wossen, incapacitated in London, "King of Ethiopia". Revolutionary Ethiopia thus technically remained a monarchy until March 1975 when the Derg declared that the Crown Prince's "failure" to return from London and assume his throne had brought the Solomonic Dynasty to an end. Haile Selassie was murdered by suffocation in September 1975.

The Derg and Eritrea

Eritrea was bound to test the political skill of any new Ethiopian government. It was the most important political challenge the Derg faced on taking full power. More than any other single factor, Eritrea determined the Derg's fate. Eritrea owes the independence that was formally confirmed in May 1993 not only to the lengthy armed struggle of Eritrean guerrilla fighters and the sacrifices of its people, but to the Derg – and specifically to Mengistu Haile Mariam – for the decision taken in the fall of 1974 to bring the region to heel by force. The manner in which the Derg dealt with the Eritrean problem, more than any other single aspect of its performance, also predetermined its own fate.

Armed insurgency in Eritrea was thirteen years old in the summer of 1974. Prospects for a peaceful solution were better than at any time in the preceding decade. The Marxist Eritrean Popular Liberation Front (EPLF) was formally proclaimed in February 1972 as a "unified" competitor to the Revolutionary Command of the older, largely Muslim, Eritrean Liberation Front (ELF-RC).[9] All Eritrean movements lacked cohesive leadership and were susceptible to fragmentation, for they were coalitions of disparate elements and reflected the diversity of Eritrea's population. The Marxists included many young men from families who had been converted to Protestantism in the nineteenth century. Competitive politicking among Eritrean exile leaders and the propaganda they broadcast from various Arab capitals magnified the impression of the size of the insurgency. Fighters of all factions probably numbered no more than 2,000 at the beginning of the 1970s. In effect, the situation in early 1974 boiled down to a stubborn but unimaginative Addis Ababa government trying to subdue fractious coalitions of insurgents sustained in part by an input of foreign money and supplies. Neither side was doing well. Neither side had leaders with the breadth of vision to attempt to escape from a vicious cycle of violence. The population felt victimized by both sides, but most Eritrean highland Christians remained committed to the Ethiopian state.

During 1972 and 1973, Ethiopian military forces extended their control over all major Eritrean towns and highways. The Eritrean

[9] The long struggle of the Eritreans eventually produced an enormous literature, most of it more adulatory and self-congratulatory than analytical. Erlich, *Struggle Over Eritrea, 1962-1978*, remains the most comprehensive and balanced account of the early activities of the Eritrean guerrilla movements. Chapter 5, "The Eritrean Revolution", pp. 104-45, in John Markakis's *National and Class Conflict in the Horn of Africa*, provides valuable additional detail. Detail and background information unavailable from other sources, as well as some alternate interpretations of events and motivations, can be found in Iyob, *Eritrean Struggle*.

economy experienced a modest revival. The provincial government organized an impressive commercial exposition that ran for several weeks in Asmara in the spring and summer of 1972. Politically the situation remained stalemated. Though Chinese assistance for the insurgents ceased and Sudanese supply lines contracted, Qaddafy's support and supplies funneled in from Syria and South Yemen from Soviet and East European sources helped sustain the rebellion. Cuba continued to train Eritrean fighters and conduct anti-Ethiopian propaganda.

When the Derg deposed Haile Selassie, it needed an acting head of state. No Derg member was prominent enough to step into this role. A reputable general of Eritrean origin, Aman Andom, was chosen. In fighting against Somali-backed insurgents in the Ogaden in the 1960s, Aman had made a name for himself as both a good commander and a champion of the common soldier. On Derg recommendation, Haile Selassie appointed him Chief of Staff of the Armed Forces in early July 1974. Before the end of the month he became Minister of Defense. He was a logical choice for head of state when the Derg deposed the Emperor a few weeks later. During the spring and summer of 1974 expectations of a negotiated settlement had grown in Eritrea, for the population was eager for peace and wanted to take advantage of the economic opportunities made possible by reopening of the Suez Canal. The situation looked propitious.

Unfortunately, factional rivalry among Eritreans in exile had spread into Eritrea, where Tigrinya-speaking Christians, newly recruited into the Marxist EPLF, began an assassination campaign against people regarded as collaborators with Addis Ababa. Several prominent Muslims were killed. Muslim-Christian political relations have always been sensitive in Eritrea. Violence worked against compromise among the insurgents. During his weeks as Minister of Defense, Aman devoted much of his time to his home province. He returned from a trip there on 9 September to present a 19-point plan for settling the insurgency calling, *inter alia*, for:

> ... general reform of the administrative system, removal of all obstacles which had impeded social progress ... amnesty of political prisoners in Eritrea, return of exiles and their resettlement, promotion of foreign investments ... lifting the state of emergency, punishing officials guilty of misconduct in Eritrea ... [and] safeguarding Ethiopian unity.[10]

Aman hoped to persuade Christians in the EPLF to cooperate with the government against the predominantly Muslim ELF.[11] He had a

---

[10] As cited in Erlich, *Struggle*, p. 49.

[11] A decade later the tactics of the Addis Ababa government were exactly the opposite. Mengistu's regime began an effort to win the collaboration of ELF

Above left Haile Selassie in Beijing, October 1971, where he negotiated an opening to China with Mao Zedong. *Above right* Painting of Mengistu Haile Mariam as head of the Workers Party of Ethiopia. The painter has emphasized his "African", as opposed to Semitic/Ethiopian features. *Below* Revolution Square, Addis Ababa, 1980. Formerly and after 1991 again called Maskal (Holy Cross) Square.

Above Kiros from Tigray and Ali from Wollo at the Kishe resettlement site in Kaffa, 1987. The Derg deliberately mixed families of different religious and ethinc backgrounds in these sites. Most resettlement sites dissolved as the Derg collapsed. *Below* Derg soldiers expelled from Eritrea making their way back through Tigray, July 1991.

The Lenin Statue (*above left*) donated by Moscow in 1984 to mark the founding of the Workers' Party of Ethiopia had only a brief "life". A young artist, Anteneh, painted the crowd pulling it down at the end of May 1991 (*above right*). It was dumped at the edge of the city (*below*).

Above right Bullet-riddled portrait of Mengistu at the entrance of an Army camp in Debre Berhan, June 1991. *Above right* The classical Arab architecture of Massawa was severely damaged by Derg bombing after the city's capture by the EPLE in early 1990, but has been largely restored. *Below* An Oromo farmer in Arsi with his 12 children, 1989.

broad concept of Eritrean-Ethiopian reconciliation and had Christian Eritreans appointed as both governor-general of the province and chief of police. The population of Asmara showed strong support for Aman's program. This aroused Major Mengistu to mobilize the Derg against him. Eritrean exile politicians rejected Aman's proposals. Thus Mengistu and Eritrean exiles collaborated, in effect, to block progress toward an Eritrean settlement. The Derg appointed General Teferi Banti, an Oromo hard-liner, military commander in Eritrea. Like Prime Minister Aklilu three years earlier, Mengistu encouraged the army commander in Eritrea to pursue all the rebels vigorously. ELF-RC leader Osman Salih Sabbe issued a call from Beirut for intensified offensive action by the rebels. EPLF forces on the ground could not afford to be less militant. All major actors concerned with Eritrea succumbed to the fatal illusion that they could impose their will by force. So the tragedy was doomed to continue for the better part of the next two decades.

On 23 November 1974 Mengistu sent troops to Aman's house in Addis Ababa to arrest him. In the ensuing firefight, Aman was killed. That night 59 former imperial officials were summarily shot. All had surrendered or been arrested during the previous summer and were being held for investigation. Thus, in a single night the Ethiopian revolution turned bloody. Blood never ceased to flow for the next 17 years. Mengistu's uncompromising approach not only hardened the Eritrean insurgents' will to resist. It drove the Eritrean populace into a more negative position toward Ethiopia than had ever occurred in imperial times. Shocked by Aman's violent death and no longer obligated by his 1971 agreement with Haile Selassie, Sudanese President Nimeiry soon let increased aid flow to the Eritrean insurgents through Sudanese territory.[12] As the Ethiopian revolution took a pro-Soviet turn, Nimeiry permitted several Ethiopian resistance groups to build up military forces in Sudan. By 1976, he was convinced that Mengistu and Qaddafy were collaborating in an effort to oust him and gave even greater support to the Eritreans.

Though Mengistu was already dominant in the Derg, he did not assume the position of head of state. Perhaps there was sufficient

---

exiles in Sudan and ELF sympathizers among Muslims in Eritrea to build up internal Eritrean opposition to the EPLF. The effort was given intellectual support in the form of a lengthy, cleverly written but grotesquely argued book: Tesfatsion Medhanie, *Eritrea, Dynamics of a National Question*, Gruener, Amsterdam, 1986. Notwithstanding its Dutch publisher, the book was printed in the United States. Its actual sponsorship has never come to light. It attempted to demonstrate, *inter alia*, that the EPLF was created and supported by the United States!

[12] I published a more extensive account of these developments in *Rebels and Separatists in Ethiopia, Regional Resistance to a Marxist Regime*, RAND R-3347-USDP, Santa Monica, CA, December 1985.

opposition in the Derg to make this inadvisable. Perhaps he preferred to remain officially behind the scenes. Both he and the workings
of the Derg remained mysterious.[13] With Aman gone General Teferi
was made head of state.

The proclamation of "Ethiopian Socialism"

On 20 December 1974, less than a month after the killings that shocked
the country, Mengistu proclaimed "Ethiopian Socialism".[14] In implementation of the concept, nationalization of all banks and insurance
companies was announced on 1 January 1975. On 3 February 1975,
seventy-nine industrial and commercial companies (many foreign-
owned) were nationalized and the state took a controlling interest in
twenty-nine others. On 4 March 1975 all rural land was nationalized
in the framework of a sweeping "land reform", soon followed by
"urban land reform". This meant that the government took over all
rental property not occupied by owners. Addis Ababa University and
high schools were closed and 50,000 students were dispatched to the
countryside on a *zemecha* (campaign) to help the farmers establish
peasant associations. Most of the men who formed the traditional

[13] Even after he emerged into the open as Ethiopia's strongman, many aspects of
Mengistu's background were never clarified. A biography of him remains to be
written. He was born in 1937. He is known to have grown up in the household of
Dejazmach Kebbede Tessema, a minor noble and one-time Governor of Gojjam.
Mengistu's mother was a servant in Kebbede Tessema's household. In spite of
rumors that the Dejazmach was actually his father, his mother is said to have
married a soldier of Konso origin. This man, Haile Mariam, was occasionally seen
in Addis Ababa in the 1980s. Mengistu is reported to have been a problem
teenager, being expelled from high school and arrested for public misbehavior.
He was eventually enrolled in the army by the Dejazmach. In military service he
attended the Holeta training school rather than the more prestigious Harar
Academy. In the early 1970s he spent a few months in the United States on an
artillery course. Experience of racial discrimination was given as an explanation
of his strong anti-American attitude, but no specific evidence of incidents has
come to light. He was serving in Harar under General Nega Tegegn in early 1974
and was sent as a delegate to the incipient Derg because the general considered
him a trouble-maker and wanted to get rid of him. During the 1980s Mengistu
appears to have let aspects of his background be distorted to give himself greater
importance. Toward the end of the 1980s, when he appeared eager to identify
himself with Emperor Tewodros, rumors circulated that he actually had aristocratic blood and could trace his ancestry to earlier emperors. When as an American emissary I met him in September 1977 in his office in the Menelik Palace, I
was struck at how much darker he was than his portrait on the wall behind him.
The fact that he was more Negroid than the average Ethiopian highlander gave
him an inferiority complex.
[14] The Derg's formal title was Provisional Military Administrative Committee
(PMAC). After the proclamation of "Ethiopian Socialism" the Derg redesignated
itself as The Provisional Military Government of Socialist Ethiopia (PMGSE).

structure of authority in the countryside revolted or fled. These included large numbers of northerners whose ancestors had settled in the south after Menelik's reconquests in the late 19th century. In less than four months, the Derg had shattered most of the lines of authority that had bound imperial Ethiopia together. The bloodshed unleashed in Eritrea and Addis Ababa soon engulfed the entire country.

Dispatch of students generated acute political ferment in the countryside. The notion that the revolution resulted from an upwelling of peasant discontent was one of several myths that were spread by the Derg in an attempt to give itself greater legitimacy.[15] In actuality, most of rural Ethiopia was peaceful during 1974. The revolution was initially an urban phenomenon. But the Derg's increasingly pro-Marxist ideologues realized they needed a massbase, i.e. a proletariat. There were too few Ethiopian industrial workers – barely 100,000 in a population then approaching forty million – to provide it. The effort to politicize the countryside in 1975 and turn the peasantry into supporters of the revolution was deliberate and not illogical, but it began to miscarry from a very early stage. Anti-Derg resistance movements mushroomed.

Like the violent thunderstorms that pursue each other across the Ethiopian highlands during the annual great rains, the revolutionary process, once begun, gathered inexorable momentum. After four months the great rains come to an end. It took four years for the revolutionary storms to begin to abate. Each new "reform" brought others in its wake and generated controversy and resistance not only among the "broad masses", in whose name the Derg claimed to rule, but within the Derg itself. Its exact membership was always a subject of speculation and never announced. During 1975-7 it was periodically wracked by violent shoot-outs that sometimes ended with bodies being carried out of the meeting room. Its membership was estimated to have fallen from an initial 130 to perhaps seventy-five by early 1977.

Eritrea was the cause of some of this controversy but the speed and nature of the "reform" process also played a role. Repeated offensives in Eritrea led to steady loss of ground during 1975 and 1976. General Teferi Banti survived as head of state until early February 1977 when he and seven others, including one Mengistu loyalist, were killed in the most violent Derg meeting to date. After this episode Mengistu moved into the open as Derg chairman. Soviet Ambassador Ratanov came to congratulate him personally and Fidel Castro sent a warm message.

---

[15] Fred Halliday and Maxine Molyneux, among others, attempted to give scholarly respectability to this notion in their *Ethiopian Revolution*, Verso, London, 1981.

The Ethiopian Democratic Union (EDU), an amalgam of pro-Western civilians and northern aristocrats as well as a few senior military officers, advocated replacement of the Derg with a liberal democratic government. The group gained popular following in Gondar and Tigray but had few overt supporters in the capital. Its head, Ras Mengesha Seyum, a grandson of Yohannes IV married to a granddaughter of Haile Selassie, had been a progressive governor of Tigray since 1960. Two generals, Iyasu Mengesha, a Christian Eritrean, and Nega Tegegn, who had commanded the Third Army in Harar, were prominent in the leadership. General Nega served briefly as governor of Gondar under the Derg.[16]

The Tigray People's Liberation Front (TPLF) was founded by a small group of Addis Ababa University students who fled to Tigray in 1975. They considered themselves inspired by Marxism and initially received very modest support from like-minded Eritreans. In spite of close ethnic affinity, they were in no way dependent upon the Eritreans. Tigrayan peasants were alienated by Derg land and labor policies and offered a fertile field for development of a grass-roots insurgency. Men from this environmentally degraded and overpopulated province had long migrated annually as seasonal laborers to other parts of the country. In its "socialist" zeal, the Derg forbade labor migration as capitalist exploitation, thus providing the TPLF with ready recruits. Though rent by rivalries among leaders, competition with the EPRP and disagreements with the Eritreans, the TPLF gradually developed close rapport with the rural population in somewhat the same way the Chinese Communists had done in the 1930s and 1940s.[17]

One of the more remarkable aspects of TPLF evolution and one that contrasts sharply with a doctrinaire Marxist approach, was the group's approach to religion. Tigrayan Christians and Muslims are both among the most traditional adherents of their respective faiths in Ethiopia. Both communities are conscious of their ancient origins. Christians were alarmed by the Derg's animosity to religion. Tigrayan Muslims, who were predominantly weavers, craftsmen and traders, were alienated by Derg restrictions. Young TPLF activists refrained from offending religious sensitivities and imposed no restrictions

[16] The EDU built up military forces in Sudan and captured substantial territory along the northwestern border in the winter of 1977-8, but was unable to hold it. It maintained a presence in Khartoum for several years and a small underground network inside Ethiopia but had little effect. Eventually it succumbed to disagreements among its leaders.

[17] In contrast to the Eritrean struggle, that of the Tigrayans has produced very little literature. The only comprehensive account that has so far appeared is John Young, *Peasant Revolution in Ethiopia, the Tigray People's Liberation Front, 1975-91*, Cambridge University Press, 1997.

on Muslim occupations. They were soon able to enlist the support of the clergy, some of whom became active fighters. The TPLF's close relationship with the clergy reassured the population that the organization had their basic interests at heart.[18] John Young concludes his discussion of the TPLF approach to religion with the following observations:

With its doctrinaire fixation on the establishment of a Marxist state in Ethiopia, the Derg proved incapable of understanding the peasants' religious attachments. Like its attacks on the educated youth in the towns, the Derg's assault on the Church and mosque and their rural representatives was a major cause of peasant estrangement. While the Derg's insensitive approach to the values and institutions of the peasants cannot alone account for the TPLF's accomplishments in the countryside, it is inconceivable that the TPLF could have succeeded in gaining the support of the peasants if the Derg had not first infuriated them by [attacking] religion. The TPLF worked within and through the religiously overlaid society of Tigray, demonstrated great sensitivity to the peasants' religious sensitivities...[19]

The Ethiopian Peoples' Revolutionary Party (EPRP) came into the open in Addis Ababa in August 1975.[20] It was Marxist but anti-military and rapidly attracted a large following of ill-disciplined intellectuals, students and junior government officials. The eagerness of EPRP activists to claim the right to lead the revolution soon put them at odds with dominant Derg elements. Their relations with the EPLF, the TPLF and MEISON also came to entail a great deal of rivalry and competition.

Meanwhile the Derg had moved to organize a political party of its own. General Teferi announced in September 1975 that a political party would soon be formed and a Politburo was quietly established to

[18] When I came back to Addis Ababa in 1993 and described to Meles Zenawi a visit I had just made to his former cave headquarters near Hagere Selam in Tembien, he recalled evening meetings with elders and priests of nearby villages in which TPLF plans and aims were discussed. Support for the TPLF was so strong in the area that the Derg was never able to pinpoint the location of the cave complex from which the guerrillas led the final phase of the offensive that toppled Mengistu.

[19] *Op.cit.*, p. 178.

[20] This party was an outgrowth of the shadowy Ethiopian Peoples' Revolutionary Movement (EPRM) a radical grouping that appeared in the late 1960s among Ethiopian students in Europe and the United States. Haile Selassie's security services had evidence that the Soviets regarded it as an embryonic communist party and used it as a channel for supporting student agitation in Ethiopia after several Soviet and East European operatives working with students were expelled in 1968 and 1969. Under guise of literacy campaigns, student welfare and other worthy causes, Ethiopian student organizations in Europe and North America sent money to Ethiopia to support student agitation at Addis Ababa University and in secondary schools.

create it. This Politburo was headed by a French-educated Oromo Marxist, Haile Fida, who had recently returned from exile. He set up the All-Ethiopia Socialist Movement, abbreviated MEISON, which also established cells in the provinces. Ideologues of the EPRP and MEISON, both espousing Marxism, quickly found themselves at odds, though both for a while seemed to enjoy the favor of the Provisional Office of Mass Organization Affairs (POMOA) set up by the Derg in early 1976. Divisions within the Derg came to a head in July 1976 when the head of its Political Affairs Committee, Captain Sisay Habte, was arrested and executed. His deputy and successor, Senay Likie[21], set up another organization, Wez Ader (Proletarian League), and about the same time other Derg elements created Abyot Seded (Revolutionary Wildfire), which aimed at controlling the *kebeles*, Cuban-style neighborhood associations established to mobilize and control the urban population in support of revolutionary objectives. Arms were distributed on a large scale to *kebeles* and peasant associations and political murders and executions became routine.

But what were the revolutionary objectives? All these groups claimed to be Marxists, like the EPLF and the TPLF whose control of the countryside in the north steadily expanded, but shared Marxism did not promote harmony. Understanding of Marxism was very elementary. It appears that the Russians (and some of their East European proxies) during the entire period from mid-1975 to mid-1978 were encouraging competition among radical groups to see which might best qualify to serve as a true Marxist-Leninist Vanguard Party (MLVP) – an organizational device which Soviet ideologues during this expansive period believed applicable to all Third World situations. As much as Mengistu desired a close Soviet relationship and exerted himself to be attractive to them, the Russians seem to have been far from convinced that he represented the kind of leader they preferred in Ethiopia.[22]

But a problem that affected all these parties, Derg-favored and otherwise, was absence of a legitimate arena in which they could compete – no parliament, no independent mass media, no informal milieu where positions could be debated and theories tested, no

---

[21] Senay was among those killed in early February 1977.

[22] This and subsequent discussion of developments in the early stages of the Ethiopian revolution draws on several extensive analyses which I published in the 1980s, *inter alia* "Communism and Ethiopia" in *Problems of Communism*, May-June 1981; *Russians in the Horn: Opportunism and the Long View*, European American Institute for Security Research Paper No. 5, Marina del Rey, CA, 1983; a three-part series in *Encounter* between June and October 1986: "Behind the Ethiopian Famine: Anatomy of a Revolution"; and *The Ethiopian Revolution: Mythology and History*, RAND P-7568, 1989.

prospect of elections. Consequently they quickly resorted to violence which kept infecting the Derg itself. On 20 April 1976 Mengistu proclaimed a "National Democratic Revolution" which he claimed would quickly create the prerequisites for "scientific socialism" and establishment of a "people's democratic republic" with guarantees of "national self-determination" – all reflecting popular Soviet jargon. The proclamation had no effect on the mounting disorder in the capital and the countryside.

Moscow's dilemma

The priority which Moscow gave to consolidation of its position in Somalia was undoubtedly a major cause of uncertainty in its approach to revolutionary Ethiopia.[23] The Soviet Union and Somalia signed a Treaty of Friendship and Cooperation in July 1974. Moscow delivered Mogadishu $300 million worth of arms during the next three years. In October 1970, on the first anniversary of his taking power, Siad had proclaimed "Somali Socialism" and speedily proceeded to build a society and economy modeled on Soviet-style Marxism-Leninism.[24] Soviet generosity with arms was not matched by economic support. By the mid-1970s, Somalia's efforts to generate momentum toward modernization and economic development were bringing the country into the same kind of stagnation that set in in Ethiopia a few years later. As difficulties mounted, Siad shifted from emphasizing economic and social development to agitation for uniting all Somali-inhabited territories. Watching the mounting political turmoil in Ethiopia and noting that the Derg's military forces were hopelessly bogged down in Eritrea, Siad began planning invasion.

The Western Somali Liberation Front (WSLF), which had continued a tenuous existence since the late 1960s, was newly "founded" in 1975.[25] In 1976 the Somali Abo Liberation Front (SALF) announced

---

[23] During the early stages of the Ethiopian revolution, fear of provoking the United States must also have played a role in Moscow's overtly reserved approach.

[24] Devising a term for socialism in the Somali language required ingenuity. *Hanti-wadaag*, which means "cattle sharing", i.e. "wealth sharing", was chosen. The term alarmed nomads who feared their herds would be seized by the government. In Amharic the term adopted for socialism was less provocative: *hibretesebawinet*, a compound made up of "union" and "humanism".

[25] I.M. Lewis, "The Western Somali Liberation Front and the Legacy of Sheikh Hussein of Bale" in Joseph Tubiana (ed.), *Modern Ethiopia from the Accession of Menelik II to the Present*, Balkema, Rotterdam, 1980, pp. 409-15. For a more detailed and somewhat different description of these events see John Markakis, *National and Class Conflict in the Horn of Africa*, pp. 222ff. Like so many other aspects of recent Horn history, a definitive account remains to be written if, indeed, it ever can be.

its formation. It purportedly represented Oromo aspirations for separation from Ethiopia and incorporation into Greater Somalia. Agents of these two fronts were active in the Ogaden and Bale by the end 1976. By this time southern Ethiopia, though free of the kind of major insurgencies that had taken hold in the north, had also been engulfed in the political ferment generated by rival political movements in the capital. The two Somali fronts began to infiltrate arms into southeastern Ethiopia during the winter of 1976-7. Supplies were being stockpiled in Somalia to support a major offensive.

Strong pro-Somali feelings among Oromos were rare, for the two peoples have more often been rivals for grazing areas than friends. However, Oromo grievances of many kinds had accumulated against the Derg. Though the Mogadishu regime was in both theory and practice at least as socialist as the Derg, the two Somali fronts stressed nationalism without bothering about detailed economic and social programs for the future. As political ferment increased in Ethiopia and confidence in the Derg's ability to maintain its hold on power in outlying regions waned, some Oromos in the southeastern highlands were ready to hedge bets on the future by cooperating with Somali-supported infiltrators.

Siad's original plan may have been to build up insurgency gradually through the two fronts. As the political situation in Ethiopia deteriorated and worldwide concern about killings and oppression mounted, Siad sensed an opportunity to strike a decisive blow. By the time the Russians brought Fidel Castro onto the scene in March 1977, they must have had a very good idea of Siad's plans; they may even have encouraged them. There were over 4,000 Soviet advisers in Somalia by this time, serving with the armed forces down to the battalion level and engaged in every aspect of the operations of the greatly expanded Somali National Security Service. Castro's efforts to bring all the contending elements in the Horn and South Arabia together into a federation in which the People's Democratic Republic of Yemen, Djibouti (about to be launched into independence by France), Eritrea and the Ogaden would have separate status along with Somalia and a truncated Ethiopia was too reminiscent of Mussolini's *Africa Orientale Italiana* to appeal to Ethiopians. Somalis and Eritrean guerrillas had other objections. Castro returned home by way of East Berlin with the Great Star of Somalia, which Siad pinned on him, and the complaint that all the leaders in the Horn were more nationalist than socialist.

In June 1977 Somali guerrillas cut the Addis Ababa-Djibouti railway, actually and symbolically one of Ethiopia's lifelines.[26] In July

[26] The Assab-Kombolcha-Addis Ababa highway route was carrying more traffic at the time. Curiously the Somalis made no attempt to disrupt it.

a full-scale Somali invasion began with regular Somali troops thinly disguised as WSLF fighters in the vanguard. Most of the Ethiopian army was in Eritrea. Lightly held Ethiopian positions in the Ogaden fell in quick succession. Soviet aid since the mid-1960s had enabled Somalia to expand its armed forces, based on a population no more than an eighth that of Ethiopia, to the point where in manpower alone they were half the size of Ethiopia's. In quantity of aircraft, tanks, and several other types of equipment, Somalia had gained equality with Ethiopia. Ethiopia's forces were still armed with American equipment even though, as the crisis with Somalia intensified, Mengistu had all but broken relations with the United States.

The United States and the Derg

The Ethiopian Revolution produced many myths. Among the most pervasive were that the Derg was driven into the arms of the Russians by US hostility and refusal to supply arms, and that President Carter encouraged Somalia to attack Ethiopia. Neither has any validity. In spite of the long, friendly relationship with Haile Selassie, the United States accepted his deposition without disruption of relations. There was regret but no rancor. The same was true of the killing of 59 former high officials in November 1974, most of whom had been personally known to US officials and American residents. A distinct coolness toward Americans and American values and principles was obvious on the part of the Derg from the beginning. By the end of 1974, Ethiopian newspapers were full of Soviet-supplied anti-American material. In early 1975 a Derg group which included three of Mengistu's closest associates – Fikre Selassie Wogderes, Addis Tedla and Legesse Asfaw – had gone to the Soviet Union for political training.

The US military aid program continued into 1977 and elite Ethiopian Air Force pilots were sent to the United States to learn to fly the Northrop F5-E fighter-bombers promised to Haile Selassie in 1973. Despite misgivings about Derg offensives in Eritrea, US military assistance was increased and Ethiopia was permitted to buy an additional $100 million worth of military supplies from the well supplied treasury the Derg inherited from Haile Selassie.[27] While Ethiopian media praised the Soviets and vilified the United States, Ethiopians officials argued continually for increased American support to meet the growing Somali threat – the result of a steady and massive inflow of Soviet arms. Considering the atmosphere of the time, the United States was remarkably responsive.

[27] One third in current dollar value of all US military assistance given to Ethiopia over the twenty-five-year period 1953-77 was supplied during the first three years after the 1974 revolution.

Mengistu, however, was playing for high stakes. He wanted a full military relationship with Moscow and made this clear on several occasions during 1976. The Soviets exploited his eagerness skill-fully. Their highest immediate priority was to get the United States out of Ethiopia, but they had never forgotten the lesson they learned in 1950 at the time of the Korean War: an apparently passive United States can shift suddenly and put decisive effort into defending in-terests for which, a short time before, it displayed little concern. Krem-lin leaders were cautious. They watched Angola become a contentious issue in US politics in 1976. They could not be sure about Ethiopia. It was best to wait for the outcome of the US presidential election of 1976. When the Democrats, who had been conciliatory on Angola, won in November 1976, Moscow lost little time moving. Mengistu was invited secretly to Moscow and a military aid agreement was signed on 14 December 1976. It became apparent a few months later that full implementation was conditioned on the Derg's severing its American military link. If anyone in Moscow at this time warned that the eventual cost of military support of Mengistu could become astronomical, the warning has never come to light. Brezhnev and his cronies nursed the fatal illusion that Ethiopia, and with it hegemony over the whole Horn, could be bought cheaply.

The US fighter-bombers promised to Haile Selassie in 1973 were ready for delivery in the spring of 1976, and the question arose in Washington: should they be turned over to Ethiopia as promised? After considerable debate, Henry Kissinger took the lead and decided they should. Shortly afterward, word of a Derg plan for a shocking "final solution" in Eritrea reached Washington. The geno-cidal scheme involved a march by peasant militia recruited in the south who would kill or drive out all Eritreans and be offered the opportunity to settle the region themselves. Kissinger sent an ultima-tum to Mengistu: stop the peasant militia march or the planes will not be delivered. Mengistu denied the existence of the plan and the march did not materialize. A squadron of F5-Es arrived in Ethiopia in July.

Rising concern about violence in Ethiopia led to US Senate hear-ings in August during which a wide range of American pundits on Ethiopia agonized over developments there but reluctantly recom-mended continuation of a US military relationship with restrictions. A huge shipment of ammunition was held back to keep it from being used in Eritrea.

During the final weeks of the Ford Administration in 1976, the draft annual worldwide human rights report was completed in the State Department. It was reviewed and released shortly after the Carter Administration took office. It condemned Derg-sanctioned violence in Ethiopia. But the time had passed when withholding of US military or economic aid could be used as a lever for pressuring Mengistu into more rational and moderate behavior. With the Moscow agreement of December under his belt, the human rights report gave him just the pretext he needed to terminate the American military relationship. When the United States officially informed Ethiopia of the decision to close Kagnew Station by the end of the year[28], he feigned outrage and in April and May 1977 in two ultimata designed to inflict maximum humiliation ordered the immediate closing of all US military facilities, research activities and USIS libraries, leaving only a severely reduced embassy staff and AID mission.[29]

When Mengistu and leading Derg members arrived in Moscow in the first week of May 1977, they were welcomed at the airport by high-ranking generals, and senior Brezhnev aides participated in the talks which ended in an agreement for full Soviet military support. At a formal dinner, President Podgorny praised Mengistu warmly but avoided clear political endorsement of the Derg and made no comments about the United States. Mengistu, flush with satisfaction at joining the Communist Bloc, replied in fulsome Marxist-Leninist jargon and denounced all groups opposing him: "The guardian, coordinator and leader of these groups, is the sworn enemy of oppressed peoples – imperialism, especially American imperialism."[30]

During early 1977 Washington began receiving confidential messages through private intermediaries from Somali President

[28] It had gradually been reduced since 1972 to the point where only a few dozen men remained. Ethiopian military leaders were by that time well aware it was scheduled for closing.

[29] Nearly three months before this sequence of events Mengistu had again given vent to his obsessive animus against the United States. Following the Derg shoot-out from which he emerged as full chairman, he gave an interview to a Cuban journalist, Miguel Roa. Roa gave him a lead: "The Ethiopian government has accused the USA and the CIA in regard to what happened on 3 February..." to which Mengistu replied: "I confirm it. I cite in this regard the so-called Spencer report presented by the CIA to the American Congress after the fall of the Emperor in which it is recommended that the US should maintain with Ethiopia the same close ties that existed with the earlier fascist and feudal regime. All in order to control the situation and neutralize the revolutionary trend that was making progress. To put this plan into operation, the Americans chose two courses. On the one hand, they encourage foreign support for the Eritrean separatists fighting against us. At the same time they support the counterrevolutionary forces, either in the capital to create an atmosphere propitious for a coup, or in the northern provinces where the old aristocracy sends armed bands to shoot soldier and peasant. The wave of political assassinations which has recently developed is also part of this strategy." Cited from *La Repubblica* (Rome), 4 March 1977. Former private American advisor John Spencer's testimony before the US Senate in August 1976 was actually remarkably indulgent of the PMGSE.

[30] Cited from a cable from the American Embassy in Moscow, 5 May 1977.

Siad. The theme: Somalia could be detached from its close relationship with Moscow for a price. Saudi Arabia was reported ready to underwrite a break by putting up money for a huge economic development program.[31] By June it was apparent that Siad's price had nothing to do with economic development. He wanted backing for an attack on Ethiopia. President Carter received Siad's ambassador in the Oval Office on 17 June 1977. Ambassador Addou brought an urgent message from Siad who claimed that Ethiopia, with Soviet backing, was preparing to invade Somalia. Would the United States provide immediate military aid? US intelligence indicated that reality was exactly the opposite of what Siad alleged. Well briefed, Carter told Addou that if Somalia were actually attacked the US would be sympathetic and would consider defensive aid but stressed that his information did not substantiate Siad's fears.[32] As the Somali invasion of Ethiopia gained momentum, Carter adopted a policy of aiding neither combatant.

The Ethio-Somali War and Soviet intervention

By August 1977 the Somalis were in control of large parts of southeastern Ethiopia. The distinction between guerrillas and Somali regulars became blurred and disappeared. In the south, the Somalis advanced beyond Somali-populated territories into Oromo-populated highlands. Here Siad expected the SALF to draw Oromos into supporting Mogadishu. Some Oromos wavered briefly, but most rallied to Ethiopia. In the east, on the third anniversary of the Ethiopian Revolution, 12 September 1977, Mengistu suffered his most serious defeat. Jijiga, key to the route up the eastern plateau, fell. With it the Ethiopians lost a new American-supplied battle-management radar that had only recently gone into operation at the Karamara Pass. But American fighter-bombers obliterated Somalia's Soviet-supplied MIGs and the Somalis were unable to capture Harar. Moscow arranged to have a South Yemeni regiment with artillery flown over to bolster Mengistu's forces.

During early September both Soviet and US official missions came to Addis Ababa to size up the situation. I headed the latter. Mengistu had dampened anti-American rhetoric. Ethiopian officers and

[31] The possibility had appeal for members of the Carter team who calculated that by detaching a client state from Moscow, they could overcome Senate scepticism about a conciliatory disarmament agreement with the USSR, a high priority for US liberals at the time.

[32] The ambassador reported this meeting to Siad in much more positive terms than Carter's response justified. Siad was eager to believe that he had inveigled a naive US president into a commitment.

officials made personal appeals for delivery of spare parts and equipment that had been in the pipeline when Mengistu abruptly terminated the US military relationship that spring. Mengistu made no formal request for such action, let alone for resumption of military aid. He was betting on a Soviet rescue effort. I reported to President Carter that Ethiopia was likely to rally, rather than disintegrate, but recommended no reversal of what had become a US arms embargo against both belligerents. The United States could not abet Somali aggression while Mengistu's actions had made it impossible for the United States to resume aid to Ethiopia.

By this time there were perhaps 100 Cubans in Ethiopia training hastily recruited militia, but very few Russians. Moscow delayed making a commitment. Hesitation may have been provoked in part by Derg political infighting which aroused doubts about Mengistu's ability to maintain his position. EPRP activists were challenging him. Mengistu may also have become suspicious of MEISON organizer Haile Fida, for there is some reason to believe that Haile was regarded by some Soviets as an alternative civilian leader to Mengistu. He fell out with the Derg, fled Addis Ababa over Entoto and reached Chancho, where he was captured and killed.

Soviet military shipments continued to arrive in Somalia through August 1977. Siad flew to Moscow at the end of August to try to persuade the Russians to refrain from supporting Ethiopia, which he argued was on the verge of collapse. The Russians equivocated. Siad could not. He had to follow upon his initial successes or risk a fatal loss of momentum. He was bolstered by airlifted deliveries of arms from Egypt and Iran. He pressed on into Oromo territories in the highlands of Bale, Arsi and Sidamo, laid siege to Harar, and came close to surrounding Diredawa. This was all that was needed to consolidate the great upwelling of national feeling that gripped Ethiopians throughout the country. The Derg was seen defending Mother Ethiopia. *Ityopya Tikdem* took on meaning. Like Stalin after the Nazi invasion in June 1941, Mengistu suspended revolutionary reforms, dampened Marxist rhetoric, and made speeches full of references to history and tradition. He invited Christian and Muslim religious dignitaries to join him on the podium on public occasions.

Several divisions of newly recruited militia swelled Ethiopia's forces while Somalia's manpower was stretched to its limits. Mengistu flew to Cuba and Moscow at the end of October. Raul Castro flew to Moscow in early November, accompanied by the same Cuban generals who later figured prominently in the campaign in Ethiopia. Somewhere in this sequence of visits, the Soviet decision to commit massive numbers of Cubans, a greatly expanded Russian advisory group, and enormous quantities of Soviet arms and equipment to

Ethiopia was made. Moscow made no move to break relations with
Somalia even when Siad permitted mobs to attack departing Russians and Cubans. On 13 November Siad finally expelled all remaining Soviet advisers but retained diplomatic relations. General Petrov,
who became the senior Soviet commander in Ethiopia, arrived in
Addis Ababa on 17 November.

These momentous developments generated serious strain in the
Derg itself. On 13 November 1977 Mengistu announced that "a revolutionary step had been taken" against his deputy, Lieutenant
Colonel Atnafu Abate, the previous day. He was said to have "placed
the interests of Ethiopia above the interests of socialism". A more
detailed bill of particulars accused Atnafu of "providing solace" to
counterrevolutionaries, of fear of politicization and arming the
masses, of failure to believe in "the ideology of the working class" and
of "making constant contacts with internal and external enemies of
the Revolution, including CIA agents". Just what Atnafu's real crimes
were remains a mystery. Was he opposed to the massive influx of
Soviets and Cubans? Had he plotted against Mengistu? The next
day the assassination of another Derg member "by counterrevolutionaries while returning to his home" was publicized. Since the
killing of General Teferi and seven other Derg members the previous February, nothing so drastic had happened. Other high-level
acts of violence that occurred at the time were only admitted later.
In June 1978, Ethiopian media revealed that there had been nine
assassination attempts against Mengistu during the preceding year,
four of them in September 1977.

In the last week of November a massive airlift of Cuban troops
and supplies from the Soviet Union began. The aim was to expel the
Somalis from all Ethiopian territory. Airlifts and sea deliveries that
followed during December and continued into early 1978 brought
in 18,000 Cuban soldiers and equipment for them. They took the
lead in driving the Somalis back from the Ogaden. Soviet and
Cuban generals directed operations. By the end of January 1978,
the Somalis were everywhere on the run. Cubans and Ethiopians
relieved the siege of Harar and Diredawa on 12 February and
declared the eastern highlands wholly liberated on 5 March. On
9 March Siad announced the withdrawal of all Somali regular forces
from Ethiopian territory (he had never officially admitted they
were there!), but pledged moral support to the struggle of his two
"liberation" fronts. All the main roads and population centers of
the Ogaden were quickly reoccupied by Ethiopian forces with close
Cuban support.

A large portion of the Ogaden Somali population fled to Somalia
with the retreating Somali army. WSLF guerrilla operations contin-

ued for the next two years, at times reaching a high level of intensity. They were hampered by lack of a popular base, so Siad again infiltrated disguised Somali regulars. Continued SALF operations were confined primarily to hit-and-run tactics. Most Oromos remained loyal to Ethiopia.

The struggle in Eritrea

Eritrean rebels gained ground steadily during 1976, though rivalry among factions grew and new splinter groups appeared. There were three axes of tension: between exiles and guerrillas in the field; between fighters in various regions of Eritrea along ethnic and religious lines; and between leaders in exile abroad. It is difficult to summarize the situation because at any given time there were uncertainties about the true strength of sub-factions and individual leaders' hold over their followers. The Derg announced a nine-point program for settlement in Eritrea in May 1976. Rivalry among Eritrean factions deterred all of them from considering compromise with the Derg. The EPLF's "National Democratic Program" proclaimed in January 1977 contained more hard-line Marxism than the Derg's. Both the Soviet relationship and Eritrea may have been among the contentious issues that provoked the Derg shoot-out in February 1977. As the Somali offensive began in the summer of 1977, Eritrean insurgents captured the important towns of Keren and Decamere, but military success heightened factional competition.[33]

The fact that Eritrean insurgents of various factions were able during the remainder of 1977 to expand the area under their control while factional struggle intensified was due to diversion of Ethiopian manpower to fight the Somalis. By the end of 1977, only five per cent of Eritrea remained under Derg control. Massawa was under siege, Asmara was preparing for assault, and the Ethiopian lifeline to the south was under attack. But the competing and mutually hostile insurgent organizations could not agree on a plan for consolidating victory:

On the threshold of victory ... young leaders ... lost their chance to implement their goals. They had pushed aside older leaders in exile, but their radicalism prevented them from benefiting from what was fundamentally a pro-Eritrean process in the region. [...] The neighboring Red Sea Arab states [now] conceived an independent, radical Eritrea as a great threat to their interests. Thus the stronger the EPLF became, the more isolated it became.[34]

[33] Two hundred ELF-RC fighters were killed in factional fighting in July and the EPLF arrested hundreds of its members for opposing its National Democratic Program.

[34] Erlich, *Struggle*, p. 95.

Nimeiry encouraged the Eritreans to unify at a meeting in Khartoum in March 1978, but his initiative was unsuccessful. Meanwhile, with the aid of Soviet air and naval bombardment which inflicted heavy damage, Derg forces relieved the siege of Massawa. Transferring manpower from the south and benefitting from vast amounts of Soviet weaponry, advice and air support, Mengistu was able to regain control of major Eritrean cities and communications routes by the end of the summer of 1978 by mounting a Russian-style, massive, slow-moving offensive.

Consolidation of the Soviet relationship

The Russians gave Mengistu full support in Eritrea, but deployed no significant manpower there. The Cubans stayed in the background, demonstrating some sense of principle, for they had originally trained and supported many of the Eritrean insurgent leaders. There were pragmatic advantages for the Russians in Cuban inaction, for by refraining from engagement in Eritrea, Cuba extended Soviet options for a shift in tactics. Moscow kept hoping for almost a decade to persuade the Marxist EPLF and the Marxist Derg to compose their differences and collaborate in laying the groundwork for a Marxist Horn federation.[35] In Addis Ababa, Cubans and Soviets collaborated in an effort to coerce Mengistu into broadening his political base and setting about the business of building a Marxist party.

Though they had rescued him from defeat at the hands of the Somalis, the Russians remained equivocal about Mengistu as a chosen instrument in Ethiopia. A narrow and stubborn military man backed by a contracting military junta, Mengistu had weak credentials as an ideological communist. Leaders who came out of the military in Sudan and Somalia – Nimeiry and Siad Barre – had turned out to be hard for Moscow to control, just as Nasser had. There was a strong case for seeking a civilian leader with a good grasp of ideology who could base his control on a tightly organized party.

Negade Gobeze, a crafty Marxist intellectual who had been a close associate of Haile Fida, was judged to be the man. He was brought back from exile in Europe by the Cubans in May 1978 and smuggled into Ethiopia on a South Yemeni passport. At this very moment Mengistu was visiting Havana to thank Castro for the help he had provided in defeating Somalia. Castro tried to persuade him that Negade was the ideal choice to "help organize a proletarian party". Mengistu was unconvinced. When he returned he found himself

[35] The East German and Italian Communist Parties were enlisted in this effort. They hosted repeated meetings well into the 1980s, but none came close to bringing the Derg and the EPLF together.

confronted with a *fait accompli.* He insisted Negade depart forthwith.
In retaliation he expelled most of the Cuban embassy in June and
sent the South Yemeni chargé back to Aden. A few weeks later he
ordered the Soviet ambassador out, along with several members of his
embassy staff. Mengistu boldly demonstrated he was in charge and
Moscow acquiesced, though it has never become clear how, exactly,
Moscow saved face.[36] Castro came to Addis Ababa to celebrate the
fourth anniversary of the Ethiopian revolution in September 1978.
Mengistu was invited to Moscow for the anniversary of the October
Revolution in early November and signed a Treaty of Friendship and
Cooperation. A new Soviet ambassador, an experienced party man,
arrived. Ethiopia was firmly in the Soviet bloc, and on Mengistu's
terms.

Mengistu promised Moscow he would set up a Marxist party, but
he was in no hurry. Meanwhile he flattered Moscow by imitating
Soviet practice in numerous other ways. Media regularly referred to
him as "The Communist Leader" and his photograph appeared at
the top of the front page of most newspapers in the same prominent
position as Haile Selassie's had – handing out awards, visiting development sites, praising model students. Blue uniforms became the
order of the day for officials who called each other comrade (*guad* in
Amharic). Visitors coming into Addis Ababa from Bole International
Airport passed huge signs urging "Proletarians of the World, Unite!"
and assuring travellers that "The Victory of Socialism is Inevitable!"
Giant paintings of Marx, Engels and Lenin were put up in Revolution Square and stylized portraits of the communist trinity, along
with Mengistu's photograph, decorated government buildings in
the countryside. The Soviet hammer-and-sickle fluttered beside the
red-green-yellow national banner throughout the capital and the
countryside.

In the wake of the victory over Somalia and in light of the liberaliza-
tion of life, including religion, that Mengistu had permitted during
the crisis, hope had spread in the population that he might soften
many of the more odious features of "Ethiopian Socialism". The hope
was vain. East German advisers moved into the security ministry and
built it up into a Stasi-style instrument of oppression. Mengistu saw
no need to compromise with any of the parties that had competed
for influence during the previous two years. The Red Terror he unleashed in 1977 raged into the first months of 1978 and resulted
in mass slaughters of all suspected EPRP and MEISON supporters,
round-ups of Tigrayans and Eritreans, and killings of other suspected
"enemies of the revolution". Signs proclaiming "Let Red Terror be

[36] This astonishing sequence of events may be ascribable to lack of coordination,
or even disagreement, between different elements of the Soviet power structure.

Intensified" appeared throughout the capital. Remnants of the EPRP fled to the northern countryside.

Mengistu was not confident the Russians might not use the party they wanted him to form to build up an alternate leader. On 18 December 1979 he finally announced formation of the Commission for Organizing the Party of the Workers of Ethiopia (COPWE). It was given the former British colonial-style parliament building in the center of Addis Ababa as a headquarters. The clock tower was painted deep red and the iron gates were ornamented with the hammer and sickle, but the symbolism was no measure of COPWE's importance. It had little to do. The Russians displayed outward official enthusiasm for COPWE, all the time pressing for its rapid transformation into a full-fledged Marxist-Leninist vanguard party.

Mengistu delayed for almost five years. The core of COPWE was little more than a truncated Derg. With the addition of more military officers, civil servants and a few opportunist intellectuals and technocrats, it finally became the Workers' Party of Ethiopia (WPE) on 11 September 1984 during festivities which featured a glittering array of guests from Moscow and the entire socialist world. Andropov had died the previous spring and Chernenko was too ill to come, so Politburo hardliner Gregory Romanov shared top billing with East German leader Erich Honecker. Leading communists from Cuba, Vietnam and North Korea shared places of honor with Nyerere, Kaunda, Mugabe and other African celebrities. In the months preceding the proclamation of the party all other governmental activity gave way to construction of a great congress hall, quarters for dignitaries, statues of Marx and Lenin and a huge monument, topped with a lighted red star, to the revolution itself. North Koreans oversaw the construction of triumphal arches, obelisks and bill boards all over the capital. Provincial towns were also adorned. To demonstrate to his guests his loathing of private enterprise, Mengistu had all commercial signs removed in the capital's business districts. Government buildings were all topped, Soviet-style, with slogans in huge red letters. Slum areas were blocked from view by miles of painted tin fences.

Rigidly applied socialist economic policies brought rapid deterioration across the entire spectrum of the Ethiopian economy. Per capita cereal production fell from 172 to 146 kg. during the decade 1974-84. During the same period exports declined 67 per cent. The military share of the national budget rose from 49.2 per cent in 1974 to 59.1 per cent in 1984. By 1984 petroleum imports were absorbing 47.5 per cent of export earnings. Foreign currency reserves fell from $221 million in 1979 to $67 million in 1984. The Soviet Union continued to pour in military supplies and equipment to sustain Mengistu's relentless campaigns against northern insurgents, but Soviet economic assistance was paltry. Economic support from Western donors and international organizations had declined sharply.

Signs of famine in several parts of Ethiopia were multiplying in 1982 and 1983. By the spring of 1984, it was clear that Ethiopia was going to experience a major food shortage. Drought was a contributing factor, but not the major cause.[37] The Derg's sweeping and hastily executed land reform of early 1975, which was actually land nationalization, initially resulted in expanded agricultural production, for farmers in the south, where tenancy had previously been the rule, did come to think that they really owned the land, planted more, and took better care of their crops. By 1980, however, Derg measures aimed at pressing the country's peasantry – between 85-90 per cent of the population – into various forms of collective agriculture were discouraging private farmers from making improvements in their land. Compulsory pricing and delivery systems acted as disincentives for surplus production for sale. In the national budget, state farms were given priority in all categories of agricultural services and investment. Erosion-control and water-conservation programs were neglected, especially in the north, where much of the population was openly hostile to the Derg.

As signs of famine began to appear in these regions, many Derg officials found it convenient to do nothing. Inaction appealed to Mengistu for he thought hungry people might be less eager to support expanding guerrilla movements. Besides he needed to concentrate on preparations for celebrating the 10th anniversary of the revolution and the proclamation of a Marxist-Leninist vanguard party. According to the authoritative and dramatic account of Dawit Wolde Giorgis who was in charge of the Relief and Rehabilitation Commission (RRC) at the time, and in late 1985 sought asylum in the US, at least $100 million was spent on preparations for the festivities of September 1984.[38]

---

[37] During this same period nearby Kenya experienced drought and crop failures more widespread and intense than Ethiopia. The Nairobi government took timely preventive action by importing grain. Kenyan officials set up efficient distribution networks through local authorities. Stricken populations did not have to flee and be gathered in camps. Few people died and when rains came again rural areas recovered quickly. The world hardly knew that Kenya had a problem. The Ethiopian famine was publicized worldwide and gave the country a negative image that persisted into the 1990s. I summarized the Kenyan situation in contrast to that in Ethiopia in the second of my three-part series, "Behind the Ethiopian Famine, Anatomy of a Revolution", *Encounter*, July-August 1986.

[38] Dawit Wolde Giorgis, *Red Tears: War, Famine and Revolution in Ethiopia*, Red Sea Press, Trenton, NJ, 1988.

10

THE END OF THE DERG

THE VICTORY OF THE NORTHERN
GUERRILLA MOVEMENTS[1]

The Great Famine and its Consequences

Days after the festive proclamation of the Ethiopian Workers' Party, films of starving peasants, abandoned homesteads and dying livestock began to be aired on television in Europe and the US. The Derg was forced to admit that a serious crisis existed. Its first response was to accuse Western relief organizations and governments of negligence in providing aid. These were the very groups that, in collaboration with conscientious Ethiopian officials, had been doing their best to call attention to, and forestall, the developing crisis for many months previously while Mengistu and his colleagues ignored it. Reluctantly, Mengistu had to order his government into action. Operations of the Relief and Rehabilitation Commission were expanded. The Ethiopian Orthodox Church and other religious groups organized relief operations in conjunction with religious and secular aid groups from abroad. By the end of the year rural areas long inaccessible to foreigners were opened up to relief workers. Mengistu was never able to close them off again.

The Derg at times harassed and hampered relief operations and accused relief organizations of supporting insurgents. Providers of relief insisted that starving populations, whether in areas controlled

[1] Though no longer a government official, I remained closely involved in Ethiopian affairs during the period covered by this chapter as a Resident Consultant at the RAND Corporation Washington office. I visited Ethiopia in early 1980, was twice in Ethiopia in 1984 and during each of the years between 1987 and 1991 I made visits of several weeks to Ethiopia and always travelled extensively. I was in continual contact with American and many foreign officials concerned with Ethiopia as well as with many Derg officials, Ethiopian scholars and private individuals. I also developed relations with representatives of the guerrilla movements, including their leaders, met frequently with members of relief organizations, and with both Ethiopian exile leaders and Ethiopian diplomats abroad, many of whom were out of sympathy with the Derg. This chapter is based primarily on my own recollections and notes and reports made at the time. Quotations from statements and speeches are from FBIS and official documents. References to and dates of conversations are from my own records. For more extensive background information on the evolution of the Derg, the most comprehensive and objective academic assessment that has appeared is to be recommended: Christopher Clapham, *Transformation and Continuity in Revolutionary Ethiopia*, Cambridge University Press, 1988.

by the government or by insurgents, were entitled to food and medicines. They refused to let themselves become instruments of the Derg's aim to starve out populations opposed to the Derg. Mengistu continued for some time to attack Western governments for slowness in sending assistance. He asked nothing from the Soviet Union. Of East European countries only Poland rose to the opportunity. Looking back, it is easy to see that the Great Famine was the beginning of the end of the Derg. It exposed Mengistu as dishonest, brutal and unprincipled to the world as well as to his own people, but for a few weeks hope rose among both Ethiopians and foreigners that under the pressure of the crisis Mengistu might ease his pursuit of war in the north and moderate his Stalinist extremism.

As after the repulsion of the Somali invasion, this hope was in vain. Mengistu had no desire to give his socialism a human face. Instead he seized on the famine to expand two socialist programs that had hitherto only been a matter of experimentation: resettlement and villagization. If populations sympathetic to northern insurgents could not be starved to death, they could at least be moved to remote areas of the south and west, as Stalin had moved Crimean Tatars, Volga Germans and several Caucasian nationalities to Central Asia at the end of World War II. Mengistu flew out to identify resettlement sites in thinly populated lowland areas. Hundreds of thousands of people from Tigray and Wollo, fewer from other parts of the north and center of the country and almost none from Eritrea were hauled off to them. The Russians, who provided only token amounts of food and medical supplies to alleviate famine, provided trucks and planes to transport "settlers". There was a pretense of voluntarism, but Derg operatives soon resorted to drastic methods: e.g. surrounding busy market places and loading people onto trucks. Families were divided. The resettlement sites were poorly prepared. Destitute "settlers" found themselves dumped in unfamiliar, malarial terrain. Tens of thousands died.

The United States and most European governments judged the resettlement campaign inhumane and economically wasteful and refused to provide support for it. Private relief organizations varied in their attitudes. Italy, on the other hand, decided to make a major investment in the largest of all the resettlement projects at Pawe in the Gojjam Metekel to which 125,000 people were transported. Many died and the site became a target of harassment by EPRP remnants operating in the area. In spite of heavy investment of Italian money and man power over several years, it remained an unsuccessful experiment.

In all over 800,000 persons were taken to nearly a dozen resettlement sites during 1985 and early 1986. I visited many of these sites in 1987 and 1988. All had serious problems. None was financially viable. The only crop produced in most of them was corn (maize) which Ethiopian highlanders seldom eat and which could not be transported profitably to ports for export. The sites were administered like concentration camps by party officials on short-term assignment. Many of the men fled from them and joined guerrilla units, leaving women and children behind.[2]

Comparatively, resettlement affected only a small portion of the country's people. Far more Ethiopians had their lives disrupted by villagization – probably 12-15 million people in all parts of the country under Derg control. The aim was to move rapidly to a Soviet-style collective farm system. Arrangements were ingeniously contrived to make people accept full collectivization, pooling poultry and animals and cultivating land communally. Peasants were forced to tear down their houses and carry them to large artificial settlements laid out in grid pattern with tiny garden plots and little provision for livestock. Farmers often had to travel great distances to reach their fields but were not allowed to remain outside the new villages overnight. Most villages were permitted neither churches nor mosques. Promised facilities such as wells, schools and clinics seldom materialized. The villages made it easier for officials to collect quotas of grain and other produce, to organize work parties and propaganda sessions,

[2] Observations I made after a visit on 16 March 1987 to the Kishe resettlement site in Kaffa, by no means one of the most depressing, sum up the character of these undertakings:
As we said our farewells, looking at this group in their blue party uniforms and tan bush suits, all with new wristwatches and good leather shoes, some wearing the shiny chrome-rimmed glasses that seem to be a ubiquitous status symbol among party people, I was struck by the contrast between them and the settlers whom they were sent to "serve". They all looked as if they had had a shower in the last day or two and had shaved this morning. None of the settlers did. They mirrored the spirit of "Ethiopian Socialism". It is imposed from above and the broad masses have no choice but to be its "beneficiaries". The system is at least as paternalistic and much more coercive and intrusive than the imperial system it replaced. Kishe is operated as a state fief. Everything goes from the top down. We heard nothing of self-government, no plan for devolution of authority to the settlers. The Derg's aim is obviously to turn the resettlement areas into vast Soviet-style state farms. This is, thank God, an impossible goal and the party men on the spot know it. They know how difficult it is simply to hold these areas together and bring them to the point of producing a reasonable share of the food they need. They know how dependent they are on foreign charities such as the Jesuit Relief Service, Oxfam, and Irish Concern. There has always been a good case for resettlement in Ethiopia. The country's long history is the story of settlers moving southward, introducing new crops, farming techniques, and other features of early North Ethiopian civilization, including Christianity. There is a sound rationale now for encouraging some people to leave overpopulated, environmentally degraded regions beset by drought and famine. If the Derg had gone at resettlement in a more humane way, it would have had some chance of success.

indoctrinate children and nip dissidence in the bud. There was resistance to both resettlement and villagization, but security controls kept it from coalescing into a widespread general movement. Instead people resisted passively until Derg control weakened.

Soviet reactions to Mengistu's frenzied efforts to turn the country into a model of "developed socialism" were contradictory. From the early 1980s onward Soviet ambassadors in Addis Ababa were all party officials with service in non-Russian Soviet republics. They saw Ethiopia as an extension of the Soviet Empire itself and they encouraged Mengistu to mould the WPE into a replica of the CPSU. There is no evidence that Mengistu got cautionary advice from Moscow to slow his pace. Weapons and ammunition kept pouring in to support military campaigns in the north. Chernenko had died and Gorbachev was new on the Moscow scene. But the GOSPLAN advisory group in Addis Ababa was close enough to the situation to see trouble ahead. It produced a lengthy critique of the Ethiopian economy in September 1985 with modest recommendations for change of policies. In English (Russians had to use English in Ethiopia), the report was first kept tightly under wraps but it eventually circulated widely in the Addis Ababa bureaucracy and copies found their way to Western embassies.[3] If Mengistu had wanted to moderate his dogmatic approach, he could have taken advantage of this report. Instead he ignored it, preferring to curry the favor of Moscow conservatives by pressing forward along Stalinist lines.

The culmination of this course was proclamation on the 13th anniversary of the revolution in 1987 of the "People's Democratic Republic of Ethiopia" (PDRE) in ceremonies even more lavish than those for the founding of the Workers' Party three years before. CPSU Central Committee member Lev Zaykov, appointed by Gorbachev only a week before as Moscow party chief to replace Boris Yeltsin, headed the Soviet delegation. He shared the limelight with veteran East European satraps Erich Honecker and Todor Zhivkov. Zaykov had warm words of praise for Mengistu and brought a painting of Red Square as a gift, but he also set tongues wagging in Addis Ababa by reminding his audience in his speech that it was not wise to rush too fast into communism and important to pay attention to the "objective conditions" of the economy. This was interpreted as a Gorbachevian slap on Mengistu's wrist, but that was all.

The revolution unravelling

Like the WPE before it, the PDRE was the last example of its kind to be established in the world and its three and a half years of life were

[3] I obtained a copy in Ethiopia in 1987 and published both the text and an analysis: *Ethiopia: Crisis of a Marxist Economy*, RAND, Santa Monica, CA, April 1989.

brief and bitter, though the communist oligarchs who came to help Mengistu celebrate his "People's Democracy" fell into the dustbin of history even sooner than he did. Greater and greater numbers of Ethiopians now realized that they were not doomed to a communist future. Resistance and rebellion spread in most parts of the country. It became increasingly clear that collapse would come not from the agitation of exiles abroad, but from the efforts of opponents inside the country.

Mengistu forbade Ethiopian media to use the terms *glasnost* and *perestroika.* In effect, he was defying Gorbachev, who was rumored to have no fondness for him. But Gorbachev had no time for Ethiopia. He was preoccupied with opponents in his own party. So he let communist conservatives and military men in Moscow go on sending military aid to Ethiopia at the rate of almost $1 billion dollars a year for the next three years. Perhaps it was the shock of having three Soviet "advisors" captured by the EPLF when they overran Afabet, taking 20,000 Ethiopian prisoners along with vast quantities of equipment, that eventually gave Gorbachev the opportunity to tell Mengistu that military aid would cease in 1990. But this is to get ahead of the story of Mengistu's long, agonizing collapse. Several other factors played a role in the process.

Mengistu's most effective opponents, the guerrilla movements in Eritrea and Tigray, began to undergo a decisive evolution in the mid 1980s.[4] For a decade and a half these movements had espoused Marxism-Leninism and issued programs envisioning implementation of communist-style societies. Until the mid-1980s some among the guerrilla leaders, particularly in the EPLF, hoped to persuade the Russians to abandon Mengistu and shift support to them. The EPLF was uncompromisingly separatist; the TPLF was isolationist and for a long time equivocal about the survival of the Ethiopian state. There was a continual process of debate within the organization on ultimate aims. Until the late 1980s the TPLF and the EPLF held each other at arm's length and avoided coordinating operations. In spite of its lack of extensive foreign contacts or significant support from abroad, the TPLF, after the emergence of Meles Zenawi as leader in

---

[4] Accounts of the EPLF appeared frequently in the 1980s. They provide vivid descriptions of the harsh conditions its fighters endured and the remarkable lengths to which they went to achieve a high degree of self-sufficiency. Almost none of these accounts, however, contain information about the political and ideological struggles that took place during these years, sometimes accompanied by violence. The TPLF also experienced dissension and occasional violence, but less than the EPLF. One of the few firsthand journalistic accounts was that of Dieter Beisel, *Reise ins Land der Rebellen,* Rowohlt Verlag, Hamburg, 1989. Young's *Peasant Revolution,* is the only comprehensive study of the TPLF to appear to date.

1989, came to realize that the collapse of communism in Eastern Europe and the decline of the Soviet Union made it desirable to develop links to the West. Isaias Afewerki was slower to reconcile himself to the desirability of abandoning Marxism-Leninism and recognizing the realities of world politics.

By the end of the decade both movements had not only achieved spectacular military victories on the ground against Mengistu's armies; they had developed a comprehensive political strategy for defeating the Derg by abandoning most aspects of dogmatic socialism and conceding the advantages of a mixed economy, multi-party democracy and an open society. Both began to work to develop close ties to the US. The TPLF committed itself to preservation of the Ethiopian state by raising the Ethiopian People's Democratic Movement (EPDM) to the level of a partner in the Ethiopian Popular Revolutionary Democratic Front (EPRDF). The EPDM was a satellite Amhara front founded in 1980. For several years it had a tenuous existence in the provinces south of Tigray. As an umbrella organization still dominated by the TPLF, the EPRDF provided the banner under which the final phase of the anti-Derg struggle was waged as it was expanded by the addition of other guerrilla groups.

Thus, by the beginning of 1990 several trends and events had set the stage for the final phase of the fight against the Derg and the end of Mengistu's long, bloody effort to bring Eritrea to heel by force of arms. These included, not necessarily in order of importance (for all these factors interacted with each other) the following:

–The great EPLF victory at Afabet in northern Eritrea in March 1988, already mentioned. EPLF confidence in its ability to liberate the entire province was boosted. It captured large amounts of ammunition and equipment which were put to good use in subsequent operations.

–The defeat of Mengistu's armed forces by the TPLF, with the support of EPLF armor, near the western Tigrayan town of Enda Selassie in February/March 1989. It was followed by the withdrawal of all Derg forces from Tigray and abandonment of all but the south-eastern corner of the province by the Derg. The value of close coordination between the TPLF and the EPLF was demonstrated to both movements. The Derg was now deprived of a land connection with Eritrea. The TPLF had meanwhile consolidated support among the Tigrayan population and its army was free to move southward. As EPRDF forces advanced, applying the same moderate principles of home rule developed in Tigray, they were welcomed by the Amhara peasantry. In territories they took over, people were freed of the threat of resettlement and villagization. They could engage in crafts, trade, private business and service activities as they wished.

–Spurred by the defeat at Enda Selassie, senior military officers mounted a coup in Addis Ababa on 16 May 1989 as Mengistu flew off to East Berlin to seek arms from Erich Honecker. The coup was poorly planned and hastily implemented, though supported by substantial elements in the Northern Command headquarters in Asmara. Mengistu flew back and ordered widespread arrests by his still loyal security chief, Tesfaye Wolde Selassie. These arrests inhibited further active plotting in the depleted and demoralized Derg officer corps. But henceforth commanders and men fought against the advancing rebels with less and less conviction and the rate of desertion and surrender among the rank and file, made up mostly of reluctant southern conscripts, increased.

–In early February 1990 the EPLF captured the Eritrean port of Massawa, cutting the sea link to Mengistu's armies in Asmara and central Eritrea. Mengistu sent his air force to bombard the port and damaged it severely. From this time onward, Derg soldiers in Eritrea and a civilian population totalling more than 1 million, had to be supplied by air.

–As communist regimes began to collapse in Eastern Europe and *glasnost* and *perestroika* in the Soviet Union brought open criticism of the rigidities of Mengistu's rule from Russian journalists and academicians,[5] expectations of change rose in Ethiopia and undermined the confidence of WPE members. Mengistu, however, kept temporizing on economic reform and persisted in throwing tens of thousands of new, hastily trained conscripts against the northern insurgents. Soviet arms deliveries totaled almost $1 billion in 1989 but fell to $300 million in 1990. Increasing quantities of these arms fell into the hands of the guerrilla forces as Derg armies suffered successive defeats.

–In the spring of 1989 former US President Carter began a private effort to mediate between the EPLF and the Derg. At the end of the year the Italian foreign ministry invited TPLF and Derg representatives to Rome in a parallel effort to get mediation under way. Both these undertakings proved fruitless. Mengistu refused to consider even token concessions. The guerrilla leaders saw no need to accommodate him when their forces were continuing to advance. But the talks deepened their relations with the United States and European countries and became a prelude to discreet but direct US Government involvement in the final weeks of the collapse of Mengistu's rule.

---

[5] Unusually sharp in its criticism was an article by Galina Krylova, apparently acting as a front for her husband Aleksandr and a group of friends: "The National-Democratic Revolution in the Light of New Political Thinking (the Example of Ethiopia)" in *Narody Afriki i Azii*, 1/1989. I translated and analyzed this article in *Glasnost about Building Socialism in Ethiopia: Analysis of a Critical Soviet Article*, RAND, Santa Monica, CA, 1990.

–Many parts of Ethiopia and most of Eritrea continued to be threatened by famine. While extensive international relief operations, which Derg officials usually tolerated but sometimes tried to block, averted mass starvation, the food situation remained precarious in many parts of the country. The overall condition of the Ethiopian economy continued to deteriorate during 1989 and 1990. Exports during EC 1982 (1989-90) fell to $375 million, less than half the country's severely curtailed import bill. Coffee earnings reached an all-time low for the Derg period of $175 million. The free market value of the Ethiopian birr fell to more than double the official rate. To a continually greater extent, the economy went underground, depriving the government of badly needed revenue.

–Somalia degenerated into chaos during 1989 to the point where most Western countries curtailed their assistance programs and embassies drastically reduced their staffs. In late 1990 remaining American and other foreign diplomatic personnel were evacuated by helicopter from Mogadishu. The deterioration of Somalia raised the specter of a much greater catastrophe in Ethiopia which Americans and Europeans were eager to avoid.

A surprising Israeli initiative

During 1989, originally in great secrecy, Israel established relations with Mengistu's government and agreed to supply both military and economic assistance as well as military advisors. Both sides in this Devil's pact had naive expectations. Mengistu and his close Derg associates hoped that the indirect aid Israel would be able to arrange could compensate for loss of Soviet military assistance that they had been told would soon be terminated. Naive Israeli hawks believed they could wean Mengistu from communism and exploit his resentment of what he seemed to believe was major Arab backing for the EPLF and TPLF to transform Ethiopia into an Israeli ally against the Arabs. These same hawks promised Mengistu that they could manipulate the Jewish lobby in the US to transform American hostility to Mengistu's regime into support for it. Israeli architects of this alliance misjudged both the situation in Ethiopia as well as American intelligence capabilities and political processes.

The arrangement could not be kept secret. The presence of an Israeli mission in Addis Ababa, at first clandestine, became rapidly known. By the end of 1989 both northern guerrilla movements reported detecting Israeli advisers in Ethiopian army field units. Weapons deliveries, including arms covertly supplied from Chile and Argentina, began to arrive in Ethiopia. Israel began a concerted effort to persuade the United States to modify its stance toward the

Derg, ostensibly to facilitate emigration of Ethiopian Jews. The Israeli lobbying campaign in behalf of Mengistu peaked in early 1990 with the February visit of a senior Israeli Foreign Ministry official to Washington. He failed to gain understanding from any significant Jewish organization or leader or from any member of the Jewish Lobby in the US Congress.

In April 1990 an Ethiopian delegation led by Kassa Kebbede,[6] Mengistu's putative half-brother and architect of the Israeli alliance, took a delegation to Washington and spent about six weeks of intensive lobbying among American Jews and US congressmen to gain their support for a deal with Mengistu. In return for reforms and a commitment to the West, Mengistu was allegedly ready to welcome US investment and would permit Falashas to emigrate freely to Israel. This mission achieved no results. Both official and private Americans, Jewish or otherwise, regarded Mengistu's regime as beyond salvation, though American Jews continued to have a strong interest in the welfare of Falashas.

Reform and aftermath – too little too late

After repeated rumors and postponements, Mengistu finally delivered a lengthy speech on 5 March 1990 to his *Shengo* (parliament) in which he reluctantly acknowledged that the world situation had changed and changes had become necessary in Ethiopia as well "to safeguard the country's unity and territorial integrity while ameliorating the economic and social malaise facing the population". Mengistu finally recognized the need for change because he knew that northern Amhara peasants had warmly welcomed advancing EPRDF forces. He knew too how alienated Oromo farmers in the south had become with his restrictive policies. He may also have hoped to gain support from exiled Ethiopians for continued efforts to defeat secession in Eritrea. The speech had been drafted in the Central Planning Commission where a number of young Ethiopians were keenly aware of the hopelessness of the country's economic situation and the changes that were taking place in the world.

The reforms Mengistu proclaimed were far-reaching. They included introduction of a mixed economy balancing state, cooperative and private ownership and management in industry, agriculture

---

[6] Kassa was Dejazmach Kebbede Tessema's legitimate son and about the same age as Mengistu. He, too, had had a raucous youth and had been sent to Israel to experience discipline and gain maturity by the Dejazmach about the same time Mengistu was sent to the army. He held various senior positions, including Consul General in Geneva accredited to the UN, during the Derg period. After the fall of the Derg, he managed to obtain asylum in the United States.

and commerce; abolition of compulsory deliveries of grain and other products to the Agricultural Marketing Corporation; a shift to voluntarism in cooperatives, villagization and resettlement programs; introduction of the principles of profitability and managerial autonomy in state industrial enterprises, trading agencies and state farms; a program to attract foreign investment and partnerships between Ethiopians and foreigners in all aspects of the economy; and, finally, replacement of the Workers' Party of Ethiopia by a new broad grouping designed to represent all elements in the population, to be called the Democratic Unity Party of Ethiopia (DUPE).

The speech was welcomed by the public. *Perestroika*, it appeared, had at last dawned in Ethiopia. For once regime-organized student demonstrations to endorse a speech of Mengistu reflected genuine enthusiasm. During the remainder of the year most of the agricultural cooperatives dissolved. Hundreds of private small-scale manufacturing, construction, trading and service enterprises were set up throughout the center and south of the country. By the end of 1990 large numbers of new hotels and restaurants were opening in Addis Ababa and provincial centers. Country towns "killed" (i.e. razed to the ground) during the villagization campaign were reconstructed and traditional country markets were operating again. Free to plant and harvest according to their own calculations of profit, and to trade in livestock and produce of all kinds, the rural population took advantage of good rains and produced a larger harvest than the country had seen in almost a decade. By the end of 1990 a large proportion of the collective villages on which party members had expended so much energy in the previous five years had dissolved as farmers returned to their original homesites. State farms, most of them never profitable in spite of massive subsidies, fell into crisis. Large numbers of people abandoned the resettlement sites in the western lowlands and returned to their original home areas.

But no sooner had he proclaimed them than it became apparent that Mengistu's commitment to the reforms he had announced was lukewarm. Regime bureaucrats and party cadres tried to slow changes in the countryside and create administrative obstacles to expansion of private enterprise. These tactics had only a temporary delaying effect, for the momentum generated in the population outstripped the capacity of regime bureaucrats to dampen it. The larger aspects of economic reform, however, lagged. State-run factories continued to limp along, hampered by shortage of parts and supplies that could only be obtained from abroad. The country's foreign exchange position continued to deteriorate. Foreign investors showed little interest. Ethiopians, including many government and party officials who desperately hoped that Mengistu could be turned into a committed reformer, gradually succumbed to disillusionment. The acronym of the "new party", DUPE, proved prophetic. The demoralized WPE limped along.

In the wake of the abortive coup of May 1989, Mengistu had arrested 176 senior military officers, including twenty-four generals. Interrogations and investigations continued for almost a year before the trial of the coup plotters began. Delay aroused widespread wishful thinking that Mengistu might show leniency and shift to a serious effort to end the civil war by negotiating with the TPLF and the EPLF. Among the military as well as in the population at large, the coup organizers evoked sympathy as Ethiopian patriots. When Mengistu announced reforms on 5 March 1990, expectations rose further, but were soon dashed. On 19 May 1990 the country was shocked at the announcement that the trials were finished and twelve of the generals had already been shot at Mengistu's order. I was in Cairo at the time at a conference on the Horn sponsored by the Egyptian Strategic Studies Institute. Ethiopians attending it wept. While the optimism generated by the reforms receded, the population continued to take advantage of them. Mengistu was powerless to reverse them.

In December 1990 I travelled through the south. In the Arsi and Shoan countryside it was now impossible to find some of the villages I had been taken by Derg escorts to "admire" a few years before. They had literally disappeared without a trace. People had pulled down their houses and returned to their original homesites. Everywhere happy farmers were reaping a bounteous harvest that they could keep or sell as they wished. Country towns were busy with trade and new small-scale industry; "killed" towns were being rebuilt. Back in Addis, Mengistu invited me to come to talk. I congratulated him on the success of his reforms. He winced, changed the subject and denounced the book I had just published, a copy of which he had beside him.[7] By this time Germany had been united and the countries of Eastern Europe were freeing themselves of Soviet control. Gorbachev had stopped deliveries of arms and ammunition to Ethiopia. The Soviet Union was in its death throes and communism was all but dead. Mengistu found it impossible to recognize the consequences for Ethiopia of these developments. He rambled on for four hours trying to convince me how constructive his intentions for Ethiopia were and how successful he could have been if only perfidious America had supported him.

Mengistu's behavior became steadily more contradictory and irrational during his final months. Government media kept claiming illusory victories against guerrilla forces and putting out tales of

[7] *The Horn of Africa, from War to Peace*, Macmillan, London, 1991.

alleged guerrilla atrocities. Throwing more and more young Ethiopians into the war in the north, Mengistu tried to discredit the guerrilla
movements as corrupt lackeys of Arab states. When Iraq invaded
Kuwait and the Gulf War followed, the Ethiopian Embassy in
Stockholm headed by a former Addis Ababa University professor,
Negussay Ayele, produced a series of forgeries aimed to create the
impression that the EPLF supported Iraq. The EPLF circulated the
forged documents and attributed them to the Derg. They ended up
discrediting Mengistu, and, of course Negussay. Mengistu instructed
his UN delegation to vote with the majority in condemning Iraq.

In contrast to Derg claims, the guerrillas' appraisals of their
military situation were realistic and showed a keen sense of the
relationship between military operations and ultimate political
objectives. For example, Berhane Gebre Christos, then TPLF
representative in Washington[8], gave me the following situation
report in early July 1990:

Despite regime claims that they have made important advances against us,
our military situation is good. During the past three weeks we have scored
important successes. We destroyed large regime forces in Merhabete and
hold Alem Ketema. We have made important advances in Manz. We control
Wollo as far south as Haiq. We have neutralized eastern Gojjam and could
take it if we felt a strong need, but we do not want to overextend ourselves.
We could take several major towns – Gondar, Bahr Dar, and Dessie – but we
do not want to invite regime bombing attacks against them.

We hold north Gondar to the Sudan border. The regime has repaired
the Nile bridge north of Bahr Dar but only for light traffic. They have
opened a road west of Lake Tana, but they cannot send much over it. They
continue to try to supply Gondar by boats across the lake. But their situation is deteriorating.

We are also operating east of the main north-south highway in Wollo and
we have penetrated as far into northern Shoa as Termaber. The regime
considered blowing up the Termaber tunnel, but thought better of the idea
because it would block the road for their own use. We are trying to avoid
needless destruction because we do not want to inherit a country that is
unnecessarily damaged. This is not the attitude of the regime. Before they
withdrew from Tigray last year, they destroyed all microwave relay installations. We are absolutely confident that we could now move down from
Selale and Merhabete and come over Entoto into Addis Ababa, but we do
not want to move on the capital until we have agreed with other opposition
movements on a provisional government.

The fighting spirit of government forces has hit rock bottom. We try to
take advantage of these attitudes by treating prisoners as leniently as we
can. We give them the same food we have ourselves. We do not take their
clothes or personal possessions away. Most of the soldiers sent against us
are southerners. Many have been told horrible things about the way we will

[8] He returned as Ambassador to the United States in 1992.

treat them. We want the population of the areas we move into to understand that we are bringing them freedom. We tell the peasants to do as they
please: to leave the villages and dissolve the peasant associations if they wish.
We discourage violence against party officials and peasant association
chairmen, though sometimes the peasants want to take measures against
them. We cannot always prevent them. We urge people to trade freely. We
tell people to open shops, restaurants, hotels, and provide services such as
vehicle repair. All these activities are private or cooperative. We do not try
to direct them.

We have even started giving land back to some of the churches and
monasteries and we are encouraging them ... to undertake welfare projects
for the people, provide food for those who need it, organize medical services if they can, and help with orphans and displaced people. We have
made some progress with other groups toward agreement on a transitional
government, but not enough.

Relations among guerrilla groups – positioning for victory

The leaders of both guerrilla organizations, Isaias Afewerki of the
EPLF and Meles Zenawi of the TPLF, had to resolve problems within
their organizations, and with each other, as the collapse of the Derg
neared. Though comment about the TPLF's past Marxist-Albanian
rhetoric in the international press[9] often failed to take into account
the remarkable evolution in political thinking that dominant TPLF/
EPRDF leaders had undergone by 1990, the organization still contained isolationists and Marxists with whom compromises had to
be struck. The first EPRDF Congress was held in Tigray during 17-21
January 1991. There was earnest debate about its program for the
future of Ethiopia. The program as published on 10 March contained
a contradictory combination of democratic principles and old-
fashioned Marxist rhetoric: it advocated a "People's Republic"
dominated by "workers and peasants" and spoke of punishing
"feudals" and "capitalists with foreign sponsorship". The TPLF/
EPRDF clandestine radio broadcasting from Sudan kept using
rhetoric that aroused concern among both Ethiopians and foreigners. Meles urged diplomats and journalists to "judge us by what
we do, not by what some of our people say".[10] Feeling confident in

[9] E.g. *The Economist*, which, surprisingly, has never shown much understanding of
Ethiopia, characterized the TPLF as consisting of "old communists" in its 9 March
1991 issue.

[10] The Derg attempted to capitalize on internal differences within the guerrilla
movements by putting out a forged version of the 10 March EPRDF program
which condemned the United States and promised to replace the PDRE by a
government true to the principles of genuine socialism. The EPRDF publicized
the forgery immediately to discredit the Derg version.

their leadership, Meles and his colleagues were more concerned about two practical issues: relations with the EPLF and relations with the Oromo Liberation Front (OLF). The two problems were interrelated and part of the broader and complex issue of the future of Ethiopia itself.

The EPLF was heir to a long history of factionalism among Eritrean resistance organizations. During the 1980s, under Isaias Aferwerki's forceful leadership, the EPLF gained clear predominance inside Eritrea and did most of the serious fighting against Derg forces, but the older Islamic-oriented Eritrean Liberation Front (ELF) was active among refugees in Sudan and had received support from Iraq and other Arab countries. The EPLF, though containing both Christians and Muslims among its leaders, was apprehensive of ELF influence among the Muslim half of the Eritrean population, especially if encouraged by Sudanese fundamentalists. Anti-Ethiopian feeling had originally been stronger among Eritrean Muslims than Christians, but Derg brutality in the long struggle pushed the majority of Eritreans, Muslims and Christians, toward separatism. No Western country, however, had come out in favor of Eritrean independence; neither had Moscow nor Beijing.

At heart Meles preferred that Eritrea remain within Ethiopia. Isaias argued that anti-Ethiopian feeling among Eritreans made compromise impossible. He intended to declare independence as soon as the Derg collapsed. This would have confronted the international community with a *fait accompli* and deprived the ELF of an issue. Meles hoped to forge as broad a coalition as possible as a basis for a transitional government in Addis Ababa. He wanted to avoid, or at least have time to minimize and neutralize, the strong opposition of Ethiopians in the center of the country to the loss of Eritrea. He wanted the EPLF to participate in the formation of the transitional government and offered the concession, in turn, of agreeing in advance to a referendum on independence at a future date. Isaias delayed accepting this formula until the Derg was on the verge of total collapse.

The OLF became an important but awkward element in this complex calculus because it had a divided leadership, no clear program and only a modest fighting record. It had confined its operations to harassing resettlement sites, kidnapping foreign relief workers and occasional hit-and-run strikes against Derg outposts until, with EPLF assistance, it captured Asosa on the Sudan border in February 1991. It lacked the strength to hold it. From 1989 onward, as it tried to coordinate field operations with the OLF, the TPLF found that there was little cohesion between its western and eastern wings. These were based on the mixed Christian-Muslim population of Wollega on the one hand and the very traditional Muslim peasants of Hararge on the other. The large Oromo population of the south-central Ethiopian provinces showed little interest in guerrilla warfare. They had to some degree been favored by the Derg in the 1970s, but had become alienated by villagization. In 1990 they were among the first beneficiaries of Mengistu's reforms. Some OLF leaders advocated the unrealistic notion of a separate "Oromia" somehow detached from the rest of the Ethiopian state, though on maps it sprawled across the center of it.

Unable to reach an agreement with the OLF on either military or political coordination, the TPLF formed the Oromo People's Democratic Organization (OPDO) in late 1989 as the third major component of the EPRDF. Initially weak, it attracted defectors from Derg units and gained supporters as the EPRDF pushed southward into Oromo-inhabited regions of Wollo and Shoa. As the collapse of the Derg approached, TPLF leaders could not be sure of the strength of the OLF or of the ability of the OPDO to eclipse it. They were also not sure that Mengistu might not succeed in maintaining resistance from redoubts in the south and attracting Oromo support. The most desirable course of action was to try to gain minimal OLF cooperation in the final phase of military operations and participation in the transitional government. Given these concerns, it was important for the EPRDF to avoid acquiescing in an Eritrean declaration of independence which OLF extremists could claim legitimized their demands.

At the end of January 1991 the EPRDF launched a campaign to liberate the northern Amhara regions, called "Operation Tewodros" after the emperor who had reunified the country in the nineteenth century and became a popular symbol for young liberal-minded Ethiopians during the 1960s (see Chapter 5). By early March Gondar and Bahr Dar had been taken over by the EPRDF and its fighters were moving southward through Gojjam to the Blue Nile. At the same time they began a southward advance in Wollo, approaching its capital, Dessie. EPLF forces had meanwhile advanced down the Eritrean coast to within thirty-five miles of Assab. At the end of March 1991 EPRDF forces crossed the Blue Nile at two points and secured the bridge at Shafartak undamaged. Derg forces put up only occasional resistance. The way lay open into northwest Shoa and Wollega and, indeed, to Addis Ababa itself. In early April the EPRDF took the capital of Wollega, Nekempte, and moved on to Gimbi – all Oromo-populated territory. Though apprehensive about relations with the OLF, the EPRDF avoided confrontation and reached a tentative agreement on cooperation in mid-April.

In early March 1991 the Afar Liberation Front (ALF) became an ally of the EPRDF without formally joining it. This move could have been troublesome for relations with the EPLF,[11] but cooperation between the TPLF and EPLF was now close enough to dampen suspicions. The TPLF agreed to recognize the original boundaries of Eritrea which the Derg had abolished in the late 1980s, dividing the province into several separate areas.

Indiscriminate Derg bombing of Massawa after the EPLF captured it in early 1990 deterred the EPLF from mounting an all-out offensive against Asmara, which could well have led the Derg to bomb that city and cause great loss of life. Instead, the EPLF kept the Eritrean capital under siege while UN-supervised food flights kept the population from starving. In spite of the near collapse of Derg forces in many areas, the EPRDF continued its cautious approach on the ground into early 1991, avoiding cities and taking only territory it was able to hold and administer.

United States involvement becomes decisive

British and Commonwealth (especially South African) military involvement was decisive in liberating Ethiopia from Italy in 1940-1. Ethiopian partisan forces ("Patriots") made an important contribution to the process but by themselves could not have done the job. The situation was different in the guerrilla contest with the Derg. The Derg, in spite of massive Soviet military support, was soundly defeated by the two northern insurgent movements. Exile Ethiopian groups abroad had little effect. The internal guerrilla movements ended up, in fact, benefitting more from Soviet arms and ammunition than the Derg itself because they captured massive amounts, including tanks and trucks, in the great battles of the late 1980s, and their fighting spirit remained high. I remember asking Isaias Afewerki in my first meeting with him, "Where do you get your supplies and equipment?" He replied with a smile: "From Moscow, delivered by the Ethiopian army." The EPLF and the TPLF occasionally acquired arms from other sources, but they did not need and did not ask for significant US or European military aid. The United States, however, had gradually established good contacts with both movements in Khartoum. These contacts helped provide the United States with accurate intelligence on their accomplishments and capabilities.

Neither the Reagan nor the Bush Administrations aspired to play a military role in Ethiopia, but the American, Canadian and most

[11] Except for the port of Assab, which attracted workers and officials from many parts of Ethiopia, the Eritrean panhandle was sparsely inhabited by Afars. In the late 1980s the Derg separated it from Eritrea and transferred it to an autonomous Assab region including eastern lowland portions of Tigray and Wollo. Some Afars joined the EPLF, but did not gain recognition as a separate ethnic element.

European governments contributed massive amounts of famine relief. This led to the establishment of numerous private groups in various parts of the country as well as a small USAID staff in the US Embassy in Addis in 1985. It was restricted by Mengistu to five officers. In 1983 Roberta Cohen, wife of American chargé d'affaires David Korn, had begun a modest effort to revive American cultural and exchange programs in Ethiopia for the US Information Agency (USIA). Starved for contact, Ethiopians responded enthusiastically. By the end of the decade, both USAID and USIA programs along with groups such as OXFAM, Save the Children and many church-sponsored organizations had become major features of the Ethiopian scene. They raised the morale of Derg opponents and developed widening contacts with Ethiopians at all levels of society. They were often more knowledgeable of conditions in remote areas than Derg officials. Famine continued to be a serious threat until the end of the Derg so, while Derg officials often harassed relief groups, they could do very little against them.

The major preoccupations of the United States and most of Europe at the end of the 1980s, however, were not Ethiopia but liberated Eastern Europe, the disintegrating Soviet Union and, finally, the Gulf War. In Washington only a few officials with a particular interest or special responsibility followed Ethiopian developments. Nevertheless the US Government had gradually become committed to efforts to mediate between the Derg and the EPLF, while Italy tried to get talks going between the TPLF and the Derg. Little came of these talks, but as the situation in Ethiopia became more critical, especially when guerrilla leaders were not only willing, but eager, to have US and European support, the mediation process provided a framework for direct involvement in the Derg's demise. The disastrous degeneration that occurred in Somalia in late 1990 and early 1991 served as an additional incentive for engagement in the Ethiopian crisis, for both Americans and Europeans were eager to avoid a vastly greater Somalia-type catastrophe in Ethiopia.

The successful outcome of the Gulf War increased the American propensity toward activism, but the United States might have become only hesitantly and ineffectively engaged in the Ethiopian denouement if it had not been for two crucial factors: the dedication and skill of three strategically placed US Government officials[12], and the

---

[12] These were Herman Cohen, Assistant Secretary for African Affairs, who kept contacts between Derg officials and guerrilla leaders from breaking off and at every crucial juncture prodded all parties to a commitment to limit violence; Robert Frasure, senior Africa officer in the National Security Council and former Deputy Chief of Mission in the US Embassy in Addis Ababa, who travelled tirelessly to Sudan, Addis Ababa and Europe to talk frankly both to insurgent leaders

Falasha issue. In the absence of the Falasha problem the three con-
cerned American diplomats might have been unable to gain enough
White House backing to perform a catalytic role. Thus the ill-advised
Israeli alliance with Mengistu, ironically, had a positive outcome.

In early 1990 Mengistu began to permit some Falashas to emigrate
to Israel, but procedures were cumbersome and the impression was
soon widespread among all interested parties that he was holding
back to get Israel to speed up arms deliveries. Israelis who had advised against the alliance when it was first being developed saw their
worst fears realized: Falashas were being traded for weapons used
to kill Ethiopian women and children as well as rebels resisting
Mengistu's tyranny. Neither party to the Israeli-Ethiopian partnership seems to have anticipated a mass movement by Falashas to Addis
Ababa in expectation of emigration. By the end of 1990 more than
20,000 had gathered in an improvised camp on the southeastern
edge of the capital and hundreds more were walking in weekly. They
were being cared for by international relief organizations. Only
a few were able to leave for Israel via Rome or Athens on regular
Ethiopian Airlines flights. Israelis were not always enthusiastic about
their coming, for the country was already under the strain of absorbing several hundred thousand Jews from the collapsing Soviet
Union. The prospect of many thousands of destitute Falashas, many
of whose claims to Jewishness were doubtful, generated demands for
careful screening, a job no one in Ethiopia was equipped to do well,
for most of the people claiming to be Jews had made their way to
Addis Ababa across battle lines. They had no documents. Their home
areas in the northeast were inaccessible from the capital. Mengistu's
efforts to defend the Israeli relationship only brought him deeper
into embarrassment. He placed much of the blame for the predicament on American Jews.[13]

---

and Mengistu; and Ambassador Robert Houdek, chargé d'affaires in Addis Ababa,
who steadily increased pressure on Mengistu to convince him of the hopelessness of his situation and the desirability of extricating himself in time to save his
life.

[13] For example, in an interview published in two parts in the *Jerusalem Post*, 9 and
11 November 1990. For once, Mengistu had a point, for there is little evidence
that he or others in the Derg had an animus against Jews or singled out Falashas
for harsher treatment than any other Ethiopian group hostile to Derg rule.
American, Canadian and international Jewish organizations assumed that any
Soviet-oriented communist regime would naturally be as anti-Jewish as the Soviet
Union itself. They publicized what many of them sincerely believed was Derg
persecution of Falashas and Falashas naturally took advantage of the opportunity
to gain foreign sponsorship. As conditions in northern Ethiopia deteriorated
and famine developed, many fled to Sudan from where a secret airlift to Israel,
eventually publicized as Operation Moses, was arranged by the United States in
the mid-1980s. When Israel undertook its ill-considered effort to back Mengistu,

As the Derg's grip deteriorated, fears mounted among Jews in the United States that Mengistu might take vengeful action against the Falashas or incite mobs to attack and disperse them. American Jewish delegations that came to Ethiopia to investigate were predisposed to be suspicious and were often ineptly handled by regime officials. American Jews, fearing an Ethiopian holocaust, alarmed the White House, which (preoccupied with the Gulf War) had little time for Ethiopia until the spring of 1991. The domestic implications of an Ethiopian holocaust were alarming for the Administration. President Bush sent Senator Rudi Boschwitz to Ethiopia at the end of April 1991 to appeal to Mengistu to let the Falashas emigrate to Israel and got qualified promises that they would not be harmed and would be allowed to leave.

Meanwhile US officials persuaded the EPRDF to concur in a mass airlift to Israel and to permit free movement of Falashas out of northern regions under TPLF and EPDM control. While EPRDF leaders shared widespread Ethiopian regret at losing an ancient component of the Ethiopian population, they saw the political advantage of settling a rancorous issue. The US and Israel collaborated in mounting an airlift in May and all but those whom Israel refused to recognize as Jews were flown out. Kassa Kebbede, Ethiopian architect of the Israeli alliance, was carried on a stretcher disguised as a desperately ill Falasha woman onto the last flight to leave the capital for Israel at the end of May. On the Saturday that Tesfaye Gebre Kidan's government lost control, Israeli officials deposited $35 million in the Ethiopian government's New York bank account as payment for release of the Falashas. If the money was intended for Mengistu or Kassa Kebbede, it was too late. With American recognition of assumption of governmental responsibility by the EPRDF, authority over the account passed to the new government over the weekend.

The Falasha issue had drawn President Bush's attention to Ethiopia at a particularly advantageous time. The cooperative stance of EPRDF leaders gained credit for them in Washington and helped ensure a good beginning for the new post-Derg Ethiopian-US relationship.[14] Israel was left to face the challenge of reestablishing relations

rescuing Falashas became a credible humanitarian cover. There is little evidence that this was originally the motivation of the undertaking.

[14] Until late April, however, both TPLF and EPLF leaders feared that the United States might try to effect a compromise that would leave Mengistu in power in return for his agreement to negotiate a truce with the guerrilla forces so that the Falashas could all be flown out. Therefore, they rejected proposals for a cease-fire. They also feared that Mengistu might attempt to make a last stand in Addis Ababa or elsewhere in the south. While holding off a direct attack on the capital, the EPRDF resolved to advance around it on both sides and consolidate control of the southern part of the country.

with the new Ethiopia – and Eritrea – along with the problem of absorbing more than 25,000 Falashas.[15]

The dog days of the Derg

As his doom became imminent, Mengistu alternated between vowing resistance to the end and hinting that he might follow Emperor Tewodros's example and commit suicide. The US aim was to effect a speedy departure for Mengistu and a bloodless transition to an interim administration. Americans shared Meles's view that postponement of an Eritrean declaration of independence was essential. Assistant Secretary Herman Cohen had brought mediation efforts into the open by inviting delegations from the Derg and the EPLF to come to Washington in late February 1991. These talks led to nothing more than an agreement to talk again in a few weeks, but they also served to clarify for both sides the choices that lay ahead and demonstrated US determination to do everything possible to make the transition in Ethiopia as rational and bloodless as possible. I talked to Isaias afterwards. He confirmed that he had accepted Meles's appeal for a cooperative stance:

"Nothing came of the negotiations. Addis Ababa is not serious. They were a waste of time. [Q: Will you join further talks?] Of course we are going to go on talking. We need to bring people together in Ethiopia. Mengistu's government hardly counts any more. It has no power to do what it claims it will do. We need to look forward to what comes afterward, so we are going to continue talking."[16]

Isaias was right, but Mengistu still refused to recognize his predicament. He tried to equate himself with Ethiopia. On 16 April 1991 he broadcast a long speech declaring the country's existence in jeopardy. Rambling incoherently through Ethiopian history, justifying the Derg's seizure of power as necessary to overcome backwardness, rationalizing the turn to the Soviet Union as forced upon him by the United States and blaming all his problems on foreign intrigue, he declared:

"I do not think that our country has ever been faced with such a problem as the one we now face. Although many are the times that traitors have come up against their country's and the people's weakness and brought about destruction, it was for the supremacy of one over the other, to gain central authority; it concerned minor nationality and religious conflicts within the umbrella of Ethiopian unity. But at no time in our country's history has our

[15] Israeli Ambassador Asher Naim remained in Addis Ababa during the collapse of the Derg and the arrival of the EPRDF and quickly established relations with the new government. Israel subsequently also established relations with Eritrea.

[16] My record of a conversation with Isaias on 11 March 1991.

country produced sell-outs of this magnitude. [The EPLF and the TPLF] are not organized through their own initiative but through the pressures of the country's enemies."

He offered no basis for negotiation. On 22 April he convened the *Shengo* in emergency session. It first called for establishment of a "peace forum" of all opposition forces to form "a transitional system", implement an immediate cease-fire, and a total amnesty. Then in contradiction to these conciliatory sounding objectives, he had the *Shengo* proclaim the general mobilization of

[...]all able-bodied youth 18 years old and above as well as farmers, government employees, workers in production and service sectors and all Ethiopians in general ... to safeguard the integrity of the motherland. [...] Displaced officials and employees of party, government and mass organizations in the crisis areas and those in neighboring areas, their health and age permitting, should immediately be trained to enable them to liberate areas. Government and party structures in the central and other areas should coordinate working relations between them optimally, in order to execute their duties effectively and efficiently. [...] The third emergency congress of the National Shengo strongly notifies all genuine Ethiopians that it is time to fight alongside the revolutionary army and the militia, on all fronts, to defend the country against the enemies' forceful imposition of their will.

Prospects for any of the actions decreed actually being taken were nil. The EPRDF broadcast on 25 April that it had captured Ambo, a short distance west of the capital. On 26 April Mengistu, clinging to all his titles,[17] announced the replacement of Vice President Fisseha Desta with former Defense Minister Tesfaye Gebre Kidan and elevation of Foreign Minister Tesfaye Dinka to the Prime Ministership. Alemu Abebe, one of the most notorious Derg hard-liners, was given the job of forming – incongruously – the supposedly broadly representative DUPE.

Like all Mengistu's other frenzied moves as his power evaporated, these shifts came too late to be effective. On 21 May he slipped out of the capital in a small plane that was ostensibly taking him to inspect military training camps in the south. To his surprise the pilot found himself ordered to fly across the Kenya border to Nairobi. From there Mengistu flew on to Harare, where Zimbabwe's President Mugabe, alone among African leaders, was ready to give him asylum.[18]

---

[17] "President of the People's Democratic Republic of Ethiopia, Secretary General of the Workers' Party of Ethiopia, and Commander-in-Chief of the Revolutionary Armed Forces."

[18] Mengistu's abdication, though unplanned in detail, was not accidental. Weeks before, American diplomats Houdek and Frasure had advised him he could hope to save his life only by stepping down and promised to facilitate his departure. In early May the United States suggested that the Zimbabwean foreign minister visit Addis Ababa to pin down final arrangements. He came the weekend before

Before he fled, Mengistu designated his recently appointed Vice President, Tesfaye Gebre Kidan, acting President. He abandoned the rest of his faithful cronies, taking no one but his family with him. The besieged Derg North Army – close to 200,000 men – surrendered in Asmara two days later. The same day citizens of Addis Ababa gathered to topple the statue of Lenin in a park on lower Menelik Avenue across from Africa Hall. Derg forces in the east and south of the country rapidly collapsed. EPRDF elements had no alternative but to move into most areas to fill the vacuum and were generally welcomed. They by-passed the capital to the east and reached Debre Zeit.

The Derg disintegrates and EPRDF forces enter the capital

With Mengistu gone, American officials accelerated efforts to effect an orderly transition. Assistant Secretary Cohen took advantage of a previously scheduled conference in London, which was planned as another step in continuing EPLF-Derg talks, to invite both EPLF and TPLF/EPRDF leaders as well as Prime Minister Tesfaye Dinka and a delegation of representatives of the rump Derg government to formalize a cease-fire. Isaias accepted a two-year postponement of a referendum on Eritrean independence as a precondition for this conference.[19] Meles agreed to hold his forces outside Addis Ababa. The OLF, now allied to but not part of the EPRDF, was invited to participate in the London conference to broaden it and draw OLF forces into the same framework of commitment to peace and cooperation as the two other insurgent fronts and the rump Derg government.

Mengistu fled. His visit was publicized as a routine exchange of views on South Africa.

[19] Several factors influenced Isaias's decision to postpone the independence referendum: (1) realization that major Western governments would in all likelihood refrain from recognizing Eritrean independence if it were declared unilaterally even with a hastily organized plebiscite, while recognition by radical Arab and Islamic countries would be counterproductive to Eritrea's longer-term interests; (2) lack of enthusiasm among other African countries for Eritrean independence because of the precedent it might set for separatist movements elsewhere in Africa; (3) a desire to have the referendum supervised and legitimized by the UN, inasmuch as the UN had sponsored federation of Eritrea with Ethiopia in 1952; (4) willingness to facilitate peaceful transition and stability in the rest of Ethiopia by cooperating with the EPRDF; and (5) recognition that the severely strained Eritrean population would need continuing emergency relief and that for full economic recovery Eritrea would have to cultivate cooperative relations with the major Western countries and international lending organizations, as well as with Ethiopia – objectives which defiance of the United States, other Western countries, and the UN could jeopardize.

By the time the London conference convened on 27 May, the EPRDF was announcing capture of the far southwestern cities of Jimma, Agaro and Gambela. Militarily Addis Ababa was completely surrounded and the situation in the capital was becoming critical. Derg authority had evaporated and army commanders were losing control of their troops. Prisoners in the capital's notorious Alem Bekagn prison liberated themselves. Bands of Derg soldiers were roaming the streets of Addis Ababa in disorder. An outbreak of looting appeared likely. Tesfaye Gebre Kidan telephoned Houdek at the American Embassy and declared: "It is all over. The army has fallen apart. I have instructed commanders to welcome in the *Weyane.*"[20] If chaos in Addis Ababa was to be avoided, Tesfaye realized that there was no alternative to permitting EPRDF forces to come in to maintain order. Houdek relayed his endorsement of this step to the London conference, Cohen and Frasure concurred, and Meles quickly agreed to instruct EPRDF forces to move into the city, which they did with minimal resistance and confusion on 28 May 1991. The population was relieved that bloodshed and wanton destruction had been avoided. Addis Ababa was not going to be a Mogadishu.

In London, Prime Minister Tesfaye Dinka and his delegation, refusing to recognize the altered situation at home, walked out of the US-hosted meeting. Tesfaye accused the US of duplicity, while a group of Ethiopian exile leaders in Washington descended on the State Department and denounced the US for having "given away" Eritrea to the EPLF, thereby destroying Ethiopian unity".[21]

The rebel movements become governments

The EPLF occupied Asmara as well as central and southernmost Eritrea during the final days of May with no significant resistance. It designated itself the Provisional Government of Eritrea as of 23 May 1991. From southern Eritrea and eastern Ethiopia, Derg army remnants fled across the border into Djibouti territory. Though *de jure* Eritrea remained part of the Ethiopian state until the proclamation of independence in May 1993, the fact that the EPLF administered it independently relieved the Transitional Government in Addis Ababa of a major burden and great expense.

[20] This term, stemming from the 1942-3 rebellion in Tigray, was originally used by TPLF fighters for themselves. Partly as a result of Mengistu's use of it as a term of derision, it came to be applied to all EPRDF guerrillas and regained positive connotations.

[21] These accusations ignored the fact that the United States never had the will or the power to "keep" Eritrea or to "give it away". Were it not for the persuasiveness of both Meles and US officials, Isaias might well have felt compelled to declare

In contrast to the well dressed and well shod Derg army, EPRDF fighters who were deployed throughout the great urban sprawl of Addis Ababa wore a mixture of uniforms and footgear that gave a superficial impression of improvisation and casualness. Armed young women who shared the same duties as men were common among the guerrilla soldiers. Appearances were misleading – EPRDF units proved to be remarkably well organized and led. They soon attracted the praise of citizens for their politeness, their discipline and their austere tastes and habits. In the capital and the area around it incidents of random looting, destruction and theft of property, or abuse of the population were rare.

In a final act of wanton destructiveness Derg remnants sparked the explosion of a huge ammunition dump in the southeastern part of the city on 3 June which cost more than 1,000 lives, rendered more than 10,000 people homeless, and ignited fires which caused immense property damage. But it was a last gasp. As Derg control disintegrated in the southern half of the country, there was a good deal of looting by deserting soldiers and random destruction by local inhabitants of WPE and government offices, warehouses, construction projects and even facilities in game parks. OLF units participated in some of this disorder, for they were less disciplined than those of the EPRDF.

Meles Zenawi arrived in Addis Ababa from London via Sudan on 1 June, immediately held a press conference and briefed the diplomatic corps on plans for restoration of law and order throughout the country and resumption of relief operations. He promised a new era of democracy and peace and pledged to convene a conference by 1 July which would create a transitional government that would rule till elections could be held. He addressed the nation over radio and TV the following evening, promising the formation of an interim government with the broadest possible representation of political groups, including exile organizations. He vowed to free Ethiopia from central planning and introduce free-market policies. He declared that detained Derg leaders and WPE officials would be given fair trials and decreed a temporary ban on public demonstrations and mass gatherings. Meles established his office in the old Menelik Palace, which had been used by Haile Selassie and by Mengistu until

---

Eritrean independence immediately, complicating his own situation as well as the immediate task of the EPRDF in taking control of the capital and the southern half of the country and the subsequent establishment of a new government. A sense of realistic statesmanship prevailed on the part of everyone who actually had power or influence. It was absent among exile leaders, most of whom had done little to alleviate the Eritrean problem in earlier years when some had the opportunity.

he moved into a new modern State Council building at the time of the formation of the WPE.[22]

Even before Meles's arrival, the surrender of twenty-eight former high Derg officials had been announced, as well as the surrender of the Eastern Army based in Harar. Several dozen senior military officers were placed in custody at Debre Zeit Air Base where the EPRDF, which had never possessed air power, took over the remainder of the Derg's Soviet-supplied air force. During the next two weeks thousands of WPE officials surrendered in the capital or were captured by the populace in the countryside. In some parts of the country WPE officials were killed when trying to escape or became victims of mob vengeance. More were collected in camps and put to work on reconstruction of roads and infrastructure. Several hundred senior WPE and government officials were interned in the comparative comfort of the Derg's High Party School in Addis Ababa. Acting President Tesfaye had sought asylum in the American Embassy but was turned down by Houdek. The Italian Ambassador gave him and three colleagues refuge. Contrary to Derg predictions and exile rumors, the red, yellow and green Ethiopian flag continued to fly throughout the country. Tigrinya did not replace Amharic as the official language.

As Meles and his colleagues took up the reins of government, they discovered that the treasury held only ninety-six million birr and the Derg had almost exhausted all the country's foreign exchange – only $3.6 million remained.[23] The country's fuel supplies were almost exhausted. A European Community consortium quickly created a $38 million credit to cover petroleum imports. New leaders showed a keen sense of priority in working to reestablish essential public services, leaving until later the cleanup of WPE iconography, triumphal arches and slogans that defaced the capital and provincial towns. The public took the initiative with portraits of Mengistu – most were immediately ripped, shot through or smeared with mud.

On arrival in Addis Ababa Meles assumed the position of Acting Head of State. On 6 June he announced formation of a Provisional

---

[22] A few months later, on 16 February 1992, the old Emperor's remains were uncovered in the basement of this palace, where he had been buried after Mengistu and his colleagues had him strangled at the end of September 1975. During this same period the remains of the fifty-nine officials of Haile Selassie's government who had been summarily shot on 23 November 1974 were exhumed from a mass grave in the grounds of Alem Bekagn prison and eventually reburied in a tasteful monumental tomb in the park beside Trinity Cathedral. The EPRDF began a systematic effort to expose mass graves of Derg victims in many parts of the country, publicized the discoveries in the media, and encouraged commemorative services.

[23] When the Derg ousted Haile Selassie in 1974, it fell heir to about $800 million in foreign exchange in the old Emperor's well managed treasury and the country had no debt arrears.

Government with Tamrat Layne, head of the EPDM, as prime minister. On the same day, agreement with the EPLF to make the port of Assab available for unrestricted Ethiopian use was announced. On 7 June Bole International Airport in Addis Ababa was reopened for regular traffic. A dusk-to-dawn curfew was enforced in Addis Ababa until the third week of July, when it gradually began to be reduced in length. On 18 June formal abolition of the WPE and all of its related organizations was decreed and restrictions were placed on activities of all former WPE members. At the same time the former Defence and Interior Ministries and the National Police were abolished. All remaining government departments were directed to continue operations.

On 26 June Meles announced that a National Conference to form a Transitional Government would convene, as promised, on 1 July. The EPLF had already announced its attendance and three Oromo groups declared their intention to take part along with the OLF. All Ethiopian exile organizations who abjured violence were invited to attend. About a dozen did. Peace and order were reported still fragile in parts of the south and especially in the region around Harar, but there was almost no organized resistance by Derg remnants. Mengistu's "People's Republic" had utterly disintegrated. For the most part, the country was undergoing as smooth a transition from Derg rule as could be expected at such an early date.

11

ETHIOPIA RESURGENT

ON THE THRESHOLD OF THE 21ST CENTURY

The defeat of Mengistu Haile Mariam and his infamous Derg by the EPRDF and the EPLF was a momentous development in Ethiopian history, as sharp and decisive a watershed as Menelik II's great victory at Adwa in 1896 or the defeat of the Italians and return of Haile Selassie in 1941. In spite of all the damage done during the country's 17-year experience of communist authoritarianism, it was in a better condition to recover in 1991 than it had been after the Napier Expedition defeated Tewodros in 1868. Mengistu was defeated by forces *inside the country* and, in the process, these forces developed leaders and movements capable of capitalizing on the inherent resilience of the population. They undertook a serious commitment to improve conditions of life in the country and prepare it for a better future. Recovery set in rapidly. This brief chapter, an epilogue, will describe major developments during the period of transition and recovery and attempt to place them in the broader context of Ethiopia's long history. Finally it will attempt to identify some of the challenges Ethiopia (and Eritrea) will face in the twenty-first century.

From the TGE to the FDRE and independent Eritrea[1]

The EPRDF led by the TPLF rapidly proved itself to be a competent governing group. Badly damaged as it was, few countries emerging from the collapse of communism were as fortunate in this respect as Ethiopia. Drawing a broad spectrum of organizations and individuals (including a few exiles) into the effort, leaders established a Transitional Government (TGE) in the first six weeks after entering Addis Ababa. They were unrealistic in their time-table for elections and completion of a new constitution, but ended up only a year behind the schedule originally envisioned for establishment of a constitutional government. They overestimated the capacity of the population and of political movements to understand and participate in party formation and electoral processes, but remained committed to

---

[1] I have discussed the subjects summarily reviewed in this section at much greater length in other places: e.g. the sections on Ethiopia in *Africa Contemporary Record*, vols. 23 and 24; in "Ethiopia: Post-Communist Transition and Adjustment to Eritrean Independence", *Problems of Post-Communism*, September-October 1995; and in "Democracy in Ethiopia, a Balance Sheet after Seven Years", *Journal of Democracy*, fall 1998.

the principles of democratic procedure.[2] EPRDF leaders were determined to reconstruct the country as a federal republic and chose
ethnic structuralism as the basis for administration – hoping as a
result to decentralize authority, giving ethnic groups and regions the
opportunity to develop politically, economically and culturally.

It is too early after eight years to declare the new arrangement an
unqualified success. It must pass the test of more time and of the
changes in leadership time is bound to bring. The constitution that
was drawn up in 1993, approved by a 547-member constituent assembly in December 1994, and implemented in elections to a 525-member
parliament in May and June 1995, led to the proclamation of the
Federal Democratic Republic of Ethiopia (FDRE) in August of that
year. The constitution meets all the criteria by which modern, democratic constitutions can be judged. The federal republic it created
consists of nine states authorized to manage a significant portion
of their own affairs. Some have done well, others less so. The arrangement will undoubtedly require adjustments in the future.

The fact that a majority of so-called opposition political parties
took little part in this process and boycotted voting reflects more
negatively on them than on the EPRDF leadership. The EPRDF
encouraged organization of parties immediately after it took power.
More than 100 parties and political movements emerged in Ethiopia
during the first year of the Transitional Government.[3] Most of them,
unfortunately, could not be taken seriously as parties at all. They
ranged from small followings of ambitious individuals to special-
interest lobbies and ethnic advocacy associations.[4] Dominant EPRDF
leaders hoped these parties would form coalitions and amalgamate
into a few serious parties capable of developing policy proposals
and engaging in constructive criticism of government operations.

[2] The first elections which took place in June 1992 were a confused experience,
but did result in creation of local governing bodies. They were evaluated by the
National Democratic Institute for International Affairs and the African-American
Institute, *An Evaluation of the June 21, 1992 Elections in Ethiopia*, Washington, DC,
1992, pp. 3-5.

[3] Their numbers were matched by an explosion of private publications. As early
as January 1992 the US Embassy reported the appearance of almost 100 private
newspapers and journals. Quantity was not matched by quality. Many collapsed
but have continually been replaced by others. In the latter half of the 1990s a
tendency toward more responsible journalism fortunately became evident.

[4] Unlike the experience of most ex-Soviet countries, including Russia itself, no
neo-communist movements formed in Ethiopia. The WPE was outlawed but former
members made no effort to resuscitate it with a party with a changed name, as
occurred so often in Eastern Europe and the former Soviet Union. Nor did the
WPE survive as an exile organization. Instead former WPE officials who were
successful in escaping abroad have tended to infiltrate anti-EPRDF exile groups.

Instead, with few exceptions, parties confined their activities to shrill criticism and demands for special consideration for their groups. As friendly foreign governments and NGOs became active in democracy-building programs, most opposition parties devoted most of their energies to lobbying them to pressure the EPRDF to accept them as governing partners. When such efforts did not succeed, they asserted themselves by refusing to participate in political or governing processes. Political rejectionism thus became an opposition habit.[5]

The EPRDF-led government did not allow itself to become distracted for long by opposition politics. The TGE was successful in accomplishing several important tasks. The nearly half-million-strong Derg army was demobilized and the soldiers returned to productive civilian life in the TGE's first year and a half.[6] Effective local administration was established throughout the country in 1993 and essentially peaceful conditions were restored everywhere except in eastern and western border regions where there was spillover of disorder in Somalia and Sudan and an inflow of refugees. On the other hand, refugees who had fled from Ethiopia during the Derg period returned and were resettled. Ethiopians were able to travel and live anywhere in the country.

Over 85 per cent of the population – those in rural areas – were freed to plant and sell their produce as they wished. Questions of land ownership, however, remained unresolved. TGE/FDRE performance in returning property confiscated by the Derg also left a good deal to be desired. Nevertheless, from 1994 onward economic expansion was rapid. Devaluation and a new system of periodic adjustment of exchange rates preserved the value of the currency. Ethiopia, as a result, did not experience the galloping inflation that every other ex-communist country had to endure, and the population benefitted.

Good weather during the early 1990s resulted in excellent harvests. By the second half of the decade Ethiopia was essentially feeding itself. Coffee production, Ethiopia's primary foreign exchange earner, reached new highs each year. Ethiopia's GDP

---

[5] A correspondent of the authoritative Swiss *Neue Zürcher Zeitung* reported as early as 24 February 1994: "There is little that is constructive from Ethiopia's opposition. The Ethiopian regime under Meles Zenawi displays autocratic tendencies. Whether this is working out to the disadvantage of the country and its people is for the time being an open question. Large parts of the opposition represent no alternative to the Transitional Government which, while it keeps all matters in its own hands, gets very good marks for its policies on a majority of issues."

[6] Establishing the degree of guilt of senior Derg officials and punishing them proved to be a more complicated task.

grew at an average rate of 6.9 per cent each year between 1992 and 1997. Budget allocations for education and health far outdistanced military and security expenditures.

EPRDF leaders quickly restored Ethiopia to a position of respectability in international organizations, including the Organization of African Unity. Ethiopia enjoys constructive and productive bilateral relations with Europe, the US, Japan and most of the rest of the world. Displaying a keen sense of international responsibility, President Meles Zenawi[7] expended valuable time and energy helping the international community bring warring Somali factions together in 1993-4. Responding to urgent international needs, as Haile Selassie did when he sent Ethiopian troops to Korea and the Congo in the 1960s, Meles sent contingents of the new National Army to help restore order in Rwanda in 1996. They received praise for their efficiency and effectiveness. Ethiopia has been in the forefront of international efforts to control drugs and terrorism.

True to the commitments made at the time of the collapse of the Derg, the EPRDF and the EPLF proceeded systematically toward Eritrean independence. Some Ethiopians strongly opposed the separation of Eritrea; most regretted it. EPRDF leaders knew they had no alternative. Exiles in America condemned the US Government for "permitting" it to happen – ignoring the fact that the US was powerless to stop it if it had been foolish enough to try. Eritreans had been driven to embrace separatism by the genocidal war Mengistu pursued against them for 17 years. When political opposition elements aroused students at Addis Ababa University to engage in violent demonstrations against the Eritrean independence referendum in January 1993, the TGE reacted strongly. Violence met violence. Demonstrators were arrested and the university was closed.[8] It was reopened at the beginning of April and the referendum in Eritrea, watched by hundreds of foreign observers, took place peacefully in the fourth week of April 1993.[9]

While Eritrean voters could only choose between being for or against independence – no intermediate alternatives were offered – the accuracy of the 99.8 per cent yes vote was not questioned by any international body. Eritrea became independent a month later on the second anniversary of the entry of the EPLF into Asmara in 1991.

[7] Prime Minister of the FDRE after August 1995.

[8] Most of the TPLF leaders had their first taste of politics at the university in Haile Selassie's final years. They understood how easily students can be exploited to serve politicians' purposes. They were determined to prevent the university from becoming a political hotbed.

[9] I was among them, serving with a team assigned to Om Hager on the Sudan border.

Agitation over Eritrea ceased in Ethiopia and legal and practical aspects of the separation were accomplished with good sense on both sides.

The evolution of Eritrea has been very different from that of Ethiopia, however. Politically Eritrea has evolved much more slowly and in a much more authoritarian direction than Ethiopia. The EPLF transformed itself into the Popular Front for Democracy and Justice (PFDJ) at the end of 1994 and a commission was appointed to draft a constitution. The commission engaged in elaborate study and consultation before producing a draft in 1996 which was then presented to the public for a lengthy discussion and review process and finally approved by referendum in 1997. It provided for a unitary state based on geographic regions into which the country was redivided in 1996. Eritrea's nine major ethnic groups, in contrast to Ethiopia's, were accorded no formal political recognition. As of the time of completion of this book, the constitution had not come into effect and the PFDJ had still not permitted other political parties to operate or independent newspapers to publish.[10]

Eritrea broke relations with Sudan in 1994 over activities of Sudanese religious extremists and incursions of Muslim Eritrean exiles from Sudanese territory. It became involved in a quarrel with Yemen over the Hanish islands soon after and subsequently quarreled with Djibouti. In spite of these problems with its other neighbors, relations with Ethiopia remained close and cooperative through 1997. Eritrea used Ethiopian currency until November 1997 when it replaced it with its own legal tender, the nakfa, initially valued at par with the Ethiopian birr. Ethiopia henceforth required that hard currency be used in trade.[11] Tensions which subsequently developed led Eritrea to send troops to occupy several Ethiopian border districts in May 1998. Clashes followed and were continuing at the time of completion of this book. No matter how this situation is eventually settled, the consequences are likely to prove far more fateful for Eritrea than for Ethiopia.

Looking backward

As previous chapters have demonstrated, periods in Ethiopia's long history when it was governed as a centralized state were rare. There

[10] Thus it avoided the political commotion and journalistic ferment that characterized Ethiopia after 1991. It also avoided international criticism for jailing journalists and oppressing politicians because none were permitted to operate.

[11] During the previous year two-thirds of Eritrea's external trade had been with Ethiopia: American Embassy in Asmara, "Eritrea's Economy: Challenging Structural Problems", 3 March 1998.

may have been times when Aksum was a tightly administered empire – we will probably always know too little to be sure – but however it was governed, it disintegrated after the eighth century. Only the Ethiopian idea remained alive. The idea had extraordinary vigor, for it persisted through changes of rulers and dynasties and in the face of violent foreign assault and foreign intrigue for hundreds of years. During this time Ethiopia, in effect, was a kind of federation. Some of this history is relevant to modern times.

Tewodros the first modern centralizer, was too limited in his knowledge of the world and too intemperate in his style of leadership to prevail. He brought a century of collapse of the state to an end, held up a vision of unity and progress, but provoked foreign intervention and his own destruction. Nevertheless he had aroused the country sufficiently that two purposeful successors – Yohannes IV and Menelik II – were able to reunite it. Yohannes's accomplishments in fending off pressures from Egypt and Sudan in the north were permanent gains for Ethiopia, but he lacked Menelik's much broader understanding of the country's situation in the world.

Menelik II's standing among Ethiopians and their rulers has remained high throughout the twentieth century. His reputation rests on more than Adwa, important as that battle and its aftermath were. Menelik understood that Ethiopia had to prepare itself to become part of the modern world and brought the country to the threshold of it. His accomplishments were substantial and for the most part lasting. His choice of successor was disastrous, but the consolidation he had effected and the confidence and pride he instilled in Ethiopians enabled the country to survive Lij Iyasu. Ras Tafari understood Menelik's strengths. As Haile Selassie he felt no need to disparage or disavow anything Menelik did or stood for to make himself look better. He knew he was building on foundations Menelik had laid.

To put Haile Selassie in perspective it is useful to compare him with twentieth-century leaders of other old countries undergoing the strains of modernization and development. He lacked Ataturk's impatience and zeal but, like the father of modern Turkey, he never wavered from his conviction of the value of Western civilization and held it up to his people as an ideal. Unlike Atatürk and the communist leaders, however, he saw value in religion and prided himself on a strong commitment to Christianity. He was skillful, at times even ruthless, in manipulating people and exercising power, but he took no satisfaction from cruelty or terror for its own sake, as Lenin did, and had little vindictiveness in his character. Unlike Stalin and Mao Zedong, he did not revel in enunciating dogma and doctrine. He did not see himself as a messiah. He did not try to beat his people into submission; as a reformer he was a gradualist. He created no concentration camps. Rivals, uncooperative regional magnates and obstreperous intellectuals were often exiled to remote regions, sometimes as governors with high local status, or sent abroad as ambassadors. He usually commuted death sentences pronounced for political crimes to prison terms, though there were notable exceptions during two periods: when he was challenged as he was re-consolidating his authority following the 1941 Liberation; and after the abortive coup of 1960.

During the last twenty years of his rule, the pace of development in Ethiopia outstripped Haile Selassie's capacity to anticipate the challenges accelerating change entailed. His paternalistic habits kept him from envisioning how the country might fare without him and preparing it for the challenges ahead. Accustomed to having ultimate decisions made by the Emperor, and to the Emperor's style of *shumshir* rule, the elite of the country lost the ability to think in terms of taking responsibility themselves. Haile Selassie must nevertheless be judged by the entire range of his accomplishments, not merely by his shortcomings as he reached advanced age. Menelik II laid the groundwork for the creation of modern Ethiopia. Haile Selassie carried the process much farther ahead than seemed possible in 1916 or 1936. It is sobering to reflect on what might have been Ethiopia's fate if Haile Selassie had never lived, or failed to prevail and never ruled.

Ethiopia was extremely unfortunate in having its leadership fall into the hands of Mengistu Haile Mariam. The country possessed many better men who could have led it effectively. Mengistu's stubbornness and willingness to resort to violence as the solution to any challenge cost the country dearly. His espousal of Stalinist communism revealed ignorance of the realities of the world. He surrounded himself with narrow-minded opportunists. In the end he abandoned them. The country's fortune changed when the Derg fell. Meles Zenawi, a highly intelligent, civilized man steeped in the old culture of Adwa, led his movement to victory with political skill and foresight, but he was not a dictator. He had thought deeply about the lessons of Ethiopian history and about the problems of leading and governing. The TPLF/EPRDF fought long and hard to oust the Derg. In spite of its determination to build a new democratic Ethiopia, it quickly shed its illusions about the simplicity of the task. Rival politicians showed less capacity than the EPRDF to adjust to realities. Opposition groups were naive in expecting fighters who had defeated the Derg – while many of their own members had contributed little but rhetoric to the anti-Derg struggle – to share responsibility for governing without demonstrating their ability to do so and without engaging in competition for popular support by participating in elections. Opposition politicians have been reluctant to apply determination and ingenuity to exploiting the channels the 1995 constitution offers for asserting themselves, preferring to generate foreign pressure against the EPRDF. There is still too little reason to believe that those currently active have drawn lessons from their mistakes.

Looking forward

EPRDF leaders were bold in devising a new administrative and political system in Ethiopia. They left some important issues undecided: above all, questions of land ownership. Serious questions remain about the working of an administrative system based on ethnic structuralism and decentralization. Will minority rights be respected and minorities protected? How will leaders of ethnic states be kept from creating self-perpetuating oligarchies? How will the federal government deal with corruption in state and regional governments? How will the federal government cope with state and regional governments that fail to perform effectively? The 1995 constitution does not provide formulas for dealing with these problems. It defines rights (to education, health care, environmental protection, e.g.) that no Ethiopian government will have the resources to put into effect for decades – how, gradually, will these be implemented? All these and other issues will have to be faced in the years ahead.

The 1995 constitution lays the foundations of a state ruled by law. Rule of law requires an efficient judicial system. Lack of sufficient talent to staff a nationwide court system has been a major problem since 1991. It can be remedied only by sustained corrective action.

Political parties have failed to coalesce into effective groups for developing policy positions and lack leaders who offer the promise of functioning effectively in a democratizing atmosphere. This failure has been one of the most disappointing features of post-Derg Ethiopia. It remains to be seen whether existing opposition movements abandon rejectionism and futile obstructionist tactics and evolve into constructive political instruments. A true democratic system requires competition and creative debate to operate effectively. If the opposition groups that have emerged in the 1990s fail to evolve, alternate political doctrine and leadership will have to emerge from within the governing group itself.

Leading Ethiopia into the twenty-first century will not be easy. The country's rapidly growing population can be a source of enormous strength if it can be educated, kept healthy, equipped with greater skills, and if the continually rising expectations of an increasing share of the population for a better life can be met. But sixty million Ethiopians are increasing at a rate of three per cent per year! As of the end of the twentieth century more than half of the country's young people still do not have the opportunity to get elementary schooling. Adult literacy does not exceed 30 per cent. Trends are positive but progress has been slow. Ways of accelerating it have to be found.

The country is on the verge of dependably feeding itself and has developed means of coping with harvest failures, so it may be relieved of future threats of famine. Rural development remains a high priority. There is still much underused and unused land that can be exploited for agriculture and livestock-raising. Irrigation development is in its infancy and could have a major impact on productivity of existing cultivated land. Post-Derg Ethiopia is making rapid progress in extending roads and communications. Both the opportunities and the needs are almost unlimited. One of the few positive – though unintended – consequences of Derg rule is the formation of Ethiopian emigrant communities in Europe, America and the Middle East. These people are invariably among the most energetic, reliable and talented of immigrants in their new countries. They provide proof of the enormous potential of Ethiopia's human resources. They also represent an asset for Ethiopia in its relations with the countries in which they have established themselves.

Ethiopia may be poor in mineral resources, but exploration is far from thorough. The same is true of oil and gas. There is no doubt about the country's hydro-power potential; less than three per cent is used.

Ethiopia's tradition of independence and self-government, its ability to produce effective leaders, its cultural pride and the population's deep-seated sense of history give it intangible advantages in facing the future. Ethnic diversity has never been a source of great weakness in Ethiopia. Neither has religion. Ethiopians have an inherent ability to interrelate as well as a proven capacity for energy and discipline. Their recovery from communism has been more rapid than almost anywhere else in the post-communist world. Ethiopia, when well led, has never found it difficult to maintain good relations with its neighbors and to participate responsibly in international affairs. On balance it appears better equipped to face the challenges of the twenty-first century than most comparable large African countries: Nigeria, Sudan, Congo, or even Egypt.

Ethiopia's relationship with Eritrea was not necessarily settled for all time by the referendum in 1993. Eritrea is an inherently weak state. It has a history of ethnic and religious tensions which have not been overcome. Its population barely exceeds that of Addis Ababa – somewhat over three million. Eritrea has a chronic food deficit. Unless it can find exploitable oil, gas or great quantities of other minerals in its territory or exploitable resources in its coastal waters, the country must rely on Ethiopia (or other countries in the region) for food and raw materials and, in turn, depend on its neighbors for markets for the output of its industry. Until 1998 two-thirds of Eritrea's trade was with Ethiopia. In the wake of the 1993 referendum Isaias Aferwerki spoke of the possibility of eventual confederation between Ethiopia and Eritrea in the distant future. He said:

"[...] Eritreans view strengthening the existing relations with Ethiopia a priority. The people of Ethiopia and Eritrea are very close. Our priority is to further strengthen the existing relationship with Ethiopia. [...] There is no need to lay down a formula on the issue of a confederation. We will do our utmost to develop devotion and fraternity among the people by avoiding boundary demarcations and limitations so that people can integrate easily."[12]

In spite of these sentiments, which were reciprocated by the EPRDF and prevailed through 1997, Eritrea provoked an armed confrontation with Ethiopia in May 1998 by occupying several Tigrayan border regions. War ensued. Almost 400,000 people were displaced. Taken by surprise, Ethiopia was unable to recapture part of its territory until early 1999. As of late 1999, Isaias Afewerki has refused to recognize the hopelessness of Eritrea's position and has frustrated international efforts to negotiate an end to the crisis. As long as he remains in power in Asmara, the outlook for a constructive future evolution of Eritrea is dim.

[12] FBIS-AFR-93-082, 30 April 1993.

BIBLIOGRAPHIC GUIDE TO
FURTHER READING

The historical, memoir, travel, and technical literature on Ethiopia is immense and continually growing. A complete bibliography would require a very thick volume. Included below are most of the major books cited in the text. Journal articles, pamphlets and monographs are not included. Many worthwhile books from my own collection not specifically referenced in the footnotes have been added. Books in languages other than English, German, French, Italian and Portuguese are not listed.

Among the most valuable sources for research on Ethiopia are the proceedings of the triennial International Ethiopian Studies Conferences (IESC), the most recent of which were held in East Lansing, Michigan in September 1994 and in Kyoto, Japan in December 1997. The former produced 2, 372 pages of papers published as *New Trends in Ethiopian Studies* (2 vols. Red Sea Press, No. 1994). The latter resulted in 2,345 pp. of papers published as *Ethiopia in Broader Perspective* (Shokado, Kyoto, 1997, 3 vols). The 14th IESC is scheduled to take place in Addis Ababa in November 2000. Many other volumes of conference proceedings have been published in Ethiopia and elsewhere during the past three decades. With only a few exceptions, these have not been listed below.

HISTORY AND CULTURE, GENERAL

Berhanou Abebe, *Historie de l'Éthiopie d'Axoum à la révolution*, Maisonneuve et Larose, Paris, 1998.

E. A. Wallis Budge, *History of Ethiopia: Nubia and Abyssinia*, Methuen, London, 1928.

David Buxton, *The Abyssinians*, Thames & Hudson, London, 1970.

Franz Amadeus Dombrowski, *Ethiopia's Access to the Sea*, E.J. Brill, Leiden, 1985.

Jean Doresse, *Ethiopia*, Elee, London, 1959.

———, *Historie Sommaire de la Corne Orientale d l'Afrique*, Geuthner, Paris, 1971.

Eike Haberland, *Untersuchungen zum Äthiopischem Königtum*, Wiesbaden, Fritz Steiner Verlag, 1965.

A. H. M. Jones & Elizabeth Monroe, *A History of Ethiopia*, Clarendon Press, Oxford, 1935.

Jules Leroy, *L'Éthiopie – Archéologie et Culture*, Deschede Brouwer, Bruges, 1973.

Donald N. Levine, *Greater Ethiopia*, Chicago University Press, 1974.

————, *Wax and Gold, Tradition and Innovation in Ethiopian Culture*, Chicago University Press, 1965.

Job Ludolphus, *A New History of Ethiopia*, SASOR, London, 1982.

Harold Marcus, *History of Ethiopia*, University of California Press, 1994.

Musée Royal d'Afrique Centrale, *Aethiopia, Peuples d'Éthiopie*, Tervuren (Belgium), 1996.

Thomas Ofcansky (ed.), *Ethiopia, a Country Study*, Library of Congress, Washington, DC, 1993.

Pero Pais, *Historia da Etiopia*, Livraria Civilização, Oporto, 1946, 3 vols.

Richard Pankhurst, *State and Land in Ethiopian History*, Addis Ababa, 1966.

———— (ed.), *The Ethiopian Chronicles*, Oxford Univeristy Press, 1967.

Sylvia Pankhurst, *Ethiopia, a Cultural History*, Lalibela, London, 1955.

C. Prouty and E. Rosenfeld, *Historical Dictionary of Ethiopia and Eritrea*, Scarecrow Press, Metuchen, NJ, 1994.

Piotr Scholz, *Orbis Aethiopicus. Studium in honorem Stanislaus Chojnacki*, Schuler, Albstadt (Germany), 1990, 2 vols.

Taye Gebre Maryam, *History of the People of Ethiopia*, trans. by Grover Hudson and Tekeste Negash, Uppsala University Press, 1987.

Edward Ullendorff, *The Ethiopians*, Oxford University Press, 1967.

Bahru Zewde, *A Short History of Ethiopia and the Horn*, Addis Ababa, 1998.

PALEONTOLOGY AND ANCIENT HISTORY

Kathryn Bard (ed.), *The Environmental History and Human Ecology of Northern Ethiopia*, Istituto Universitario Orientale, Naples, 1997.

Vimala Begley and Richard Daniel de Puma (eds), *Rome and India, the Ancient Sea Trade*, University of Wisconsin Press, Madison, WI, 1991.

Belaynesh Michael et al. (eds), *Dictionary of Ethiopian Biography*, Vol. I, Addis Ababa, 1975.

J. Theodore Bent, *The Sacred City of the Ethiopians*, Longmans, Green, London, 1893.

Stanley M. Burstein *Agatharchides of Cnidus on the Erythraean Sea*, Hakluyt Society, 1989.

Lionel Casson, *Periplus Maris Erythraei*, Princeton University Press, 1989.

J. D. Clark (ed.), *The Cambridge History of Africa*, Vol. I, Cambridge University Press, 1982.

A. J. Drewes, *Inscriptions de l'Éthiopie Antique*, E. J. Brill, Leiden, 1962.

Christopher Ehret & Merrick Poznansky, *The Archeological and Linguistic Reconstruction of African History,* University of California Press, 1982.

G. W. S. Huntingford, *The Periplus of the Erythraean Sea,* Hakluyt Society, 1980.

Otto Jaeger and Ivy Pearce, *Antiquities of North Ethiopia,* Brockhaus, Stuttgart, 1974.

Chris Johns, *Valley of Life: Africa's Great Rift,* Thomason-Grant, Charlottesville, VA, 1991.

Roger Joussaume (ed.), *Tiya, l'Éthiopie des Mégalithes,* UNESCO CNRS, Paris, 1995.

Donald C. Johanson and Maitland A. Edey, *Lucy, the Beginnings of Humankind,* Simon & Schuster, New York, 1981.

Yuri M. Kobishchanov, *Axum,* Pennsylvania State University Press, State College, PA, 1979.

Richard Leakey and Roger Lewin, *Origins Reconsidered,* Doubleday, New York, 1992.

John W. McCrindle, *The Commerce and Navigation of the Erythraean Sea...,* Philo Press, Amsterdam, 1982.

Stuart C. Munro-Hay, *Aksum, an African Civilization of Late Antiquity,* Edinburgh University Press, 1991.

———, *Excavations at Aksum,* British Institute in Eastern Africa, Nairobi, 1989.

National Research Council, *Lost Crops of Africa,* I: *Grains,* National Academy Press, Washington, DC, 1996.

James L. Newman, *The Peopling of Africa: a Geographic Interpretation,* Yale University Press, 1995.

Wendell Phillips, *Qataban and Sheba,* Johns Hopkins University Press, 1969.

David W. Phillipson, *Ancient Ethiopia,* British Museum Press, London, 1998.

———, *The Monuments of Aksum,* British Institute of Eastern Africa, London, 1997.

———, *The Later Prehistory of Eastern and Southern Africa,* Heinemann, London, 1977.

Sergew Hable Selassie, *Ancient and Medieval Ethiopian History to 1270,* Addis Ababa, 1972.

P. L. Shinnie, *Meroe, a Civilization of the Sudan,* Thames & Hudson, London, 1967.

Andrew B. Smith, *Pastoralism in Africa: Origins and Development Ecology,* Hurst, London, 1992.

Anthony Smith, *The Great Rift, Africa's Changing Valley*, BBC Books, London, 1998.

Philip Snow, *Star Raft, China's Encounter with Africa*, Weidenfeld & Nicolson, 1988.

Frank M. Snowdon, Jr., *Blacks in Antiquity, Ethiopians in the Greco-Roman Experience*, Harvard University Press, 1970.

F. Wendorf and R., Schild, *A Middle Stone Age Sequence from the Central Rift Valley, Ethiopia*, Polish Academy of Sciences, Warsaw, 1974.

HISTORY, MEDIEVAL

Mordechai Abir, *Ethiopia, the Era of the Princes*, Longmans, Green, London, 1968.

C. F. Beckingham and G.W.B. Huntingford, *Some Records of Ethiopia*, 1593-1646, Hakluyt Society, 1954.

Jean Doresse, *La vie quotidienne des Éthiopiens chrétiens aux XVII et XVIII siècles*, Hachette, Paris, 1972.

Franz Amadeus Dombrowski, *Tanasee 106. Eine Chronik der Herrscher Aethiopiens*, Franz Steiner, Wiesbaden, 1983.

William Foster (ed.), *The Red Sea and Adjacent Countries at the Close of the 17th Century*, Hakluyt Society, 1949.

G.W.B. Huntingford, *The Glorious Victories of Amda Tseyon, King of Ethiopia*, Clarendon Press, Oxford, 1965.

James S. Kirkham, *Men and Monuments on the East African Coast*, Praeger, New York, 1966.

David Matthew, *Ethiopia: The Study of a Polity, 1540-1935*, Eyre & Spottiswood, 1947.

Richard Pankhurst, *History of Ethiopian Towns from the Middle Ages to the Early Nineteenth Century*, Franz Steiner, Wiesbaden, 1982.

Richard Pankhurst (ed.) *Letters from Ethiopia's Rulers*, Oxford University Press, 1985.

Philip Caraman, *Lost Empire, the Story of the Jesuits in Ethiopia*, University of Notre Dame Press, 1985.

C. F. Rey, *The Romance of the Portuguese in Abyssinia*, Negro Universities Press, 1969.

Tadesse Tamrat, *Church and State in Ethiopia*, Clarendon Press, Oxford, 1972.

R. S. Whiteway, *The Portuguese Expedition to Abyssinia, 1541-43*, Hakluyt Society, 1902.

HISTORY, MODERN TO 1935

Absussamad H. Ahmad and Richard Pankhurst (eds), *Adwa: Victory Centenary Conference, 26 Feb-2 Mar 1996*, Addis Ababa, 1998.

Percy Arnold, *Prelude to Magdala,* Bellew, 1991.

Asfa Wossen Asserate, *Die Geschichte von Šawa, 1700-1865,* Steiner, 1980.

Bahru Zewde, *A History of Modern Ethiopia, 1855-1974,* James Currey, London, 1991.

Bairu Tafla, *Chronicle of Yohannes IV,* Franz Steiner, Wiesbaden, 1977.

————, *Ethiopia and Germany, Cultural, Political and Economic Relations, 1871-1936,* Franz Steiner, Wiesbaden, 1981.

Berhanou Abebe, *Évolution de la Propriété Foncière à Choa,* Geuthner, Paris, 1971.

Darrell Bates, *The Abyssinian Difficulty,* Oxford University Press, 1979.

Maurice de Coppet (ed.), *Guèbre Selassie. Chronique du règne de Ménélik II, roi des rois d'Éthiopie,* Paris, 1930-1, 2 vols.

Donald Crummey, *Priests and Politicians: Protestant and Catholic Missions in Orthodox Ethiopia, 1830-1868,* Clarendon Press, Oxford, 1971.

Angelo Del Boca, *Gli Italiani in Africa Orientale,* Mondadori, Rome, 1976-82, 3 vols.

Donald Donham and Wendy James (eds), *The Southern Marches of Imperial Ethiopia,* Cambridge University Press, 1986.

William M. Dye, *Moslem Egypt and Christian Abyssinia...,* Negro Universities Press, 1968.

Haggai Erlich, *Ethiopia and the Middle East,* Lynne Rienner, Boulder, CO, 1994.

————, *Ethiopia and the Challenge of Independence,* Lynne Rienner, Boulder, CO, 1986.

————, *Ras Alula, a Political Biography: Ethiopia and Eritrea 1875-1897,* Red Sea Press, Trenton, NJ, 1996.

Gabrehiwot Baykadagn, *The State and Economy in Early 20th Century Ethiopia,* Karnak House, London, 1995.

Robert L. Hess, *Ethiopia – the Modernization of Autocracy,* Cornell University Press, Ithaca, NY, 1970.

Czeslaw Jesman, *The Russians in Ethiopia: An Essay in Futility,* Chatto & Windus, London, 1958.

David L. Lewis, *The Race to Fashoda,* Weidenfeld & Nicolson, London, 1987.

Harold Marcus, *The Life and Times of Menelik II: Ethiopia 1844-1913,* Clarendon Press, Oxford, 1975.

C.R. Markham, *A History of the Abyssinian Expedition,* London, 1869.

James McCann, *From Poverty to Famine in Northeast Ethiopia,* University of Pennsylvania Press, Philadelphia, 1987.

Frederick Myatt, *The March to Magdala: the Abyssinian War of 1868,* Leo Cooper, London, 1970.

V.H. Norberg, *Swedes in Haile Selassie's Ethiopia, 1924-1952,* Uppsala University Press, 1957.

Richard Pankhurst, *Economic History of Ethiopia, 1800-1935,* Haile Selassie I University Press, Addis Ababa, 1968.

Kirsten Pedersen, *A History of the Ethiopian Community in the Holy Land from the time of Emperor Tewodros II to 1974,* Tantur, Jerusalem, 1983.

Gerald Portal, *My Mission to Abyssinia,* Negro Universities Press, 1969.

Chris Prouty, *Empress Taytu and Menelik II, Ethiopia 1883-1910,* Ravens Educational Services, London, 1986.

Felix Rosen, *Eine Deutsche Gesandtschaft in Abessinien,* Veit, Leipzig, 1907.

Alain Rouaud, *Casimir Mondon-Vidailhet,* Inalco, Paris, 1997.

Sven Rubenson, *King of Kings Tewodros of Ethiopia,* Oxford University Press, 1966.

———, *The Survival of Ethiopian Independence,* Heinemann, 1976.

———, (ed.), *Acta Aethiopica I: Correspondence and Treaties, 1800-1854,* Addis Ababa, 1987.

———, (ed.), *Acta Aethiopica II: Tewodros and his Contemporaries, 1855-68,* Addis Ababa, 1994.

Robert B. Skinner, *Abyssinia of Today,* Longmans, Green, London, 1906.

Tadesse Beyene et al. (eds.), *Kasa and Kasa...the Lives, Times and Images of Tewodros II and Yohannes IV (1855-1889),* Addis Ababa, 1990.

Teshale Tibebu, *The Making of Modern Ethiopia, 1896-1974,* Red Sea Press, Trenton, NJ, 1995.

Wondimneh Tilahun, *Egypt's Aspirations over Lake Tana and the Blue Nile,* Addis Ababa, 1979.

Ahmed Zekaria et al. (eds) *Proceedings of the International Symposium on the Centenary of Addis Ababa, November 1987,* Addis Ababa, 1988.

Carlo Zaghi, *I Russi in Etiopia,* Guida, Naples, 1972, 2 vols.

Zewde Gebre Sellassie, *Yohannes IV of Ethiopia, a Political Biography,* Clarendon Press, Oxford, 1975.

ITALIAN INVASION AND OCCUPATION

W.E.D. Allen, *Guerrilla War in Abyssinia,* Penguin, Harmondsworth, 1943.

George Baer, *The Coming of the Italo-Ethiopian War,* Cambridge University Press, 1967.

————, *Italy, Ethiopia, and the League of Nations,* Stanford University Press, 1976.

A.J. Barker, *The Civilizing Mission,* Dial, 1968.

Thomas M. Coffey, *Lion by the Tail,* Viking, 1974.

Angelo Del Boca, *The Ethiopian War, 1935-1941,* University of Chicago Press, 1965.

————, *I gas di Mussolini,* Editori Riuniti, Rome, 1996.

Emilio de Bono, *Anno XIII – the Conquest of an Empire,* Cressey, London 1937.

James Dugan and Lawrence Lafore, *Days of Emperor and Clown,* Doubleday, New York, 1973.

Ladislas Farago, *Abyssinia on the Eve,* Putnam, New York, 1935.

Brice Harris, Jr., *The United States and the Italo-Ethiopian Crisis,* Stanford University Press, 1964.

Haile Mariam Larebo, *The Building of an Empire: Italian Land Policy and Practice in Ethiopia, 1935-41,* Clarendon Press, Oxford, 1994.

Anthony Mockler, *Haile Selassie's War,* Oxford University Press, 1984.

Neil Orpen, *East African and Abyssinian Campaigns,* Cape Town, 1968.

Giuliano Procacci, *Il Socialismo Internazionale e la Guerra d'Etiopia,* Editori Riuniti, Rome, 1978.

Alberto Sbacchi, *Ethiopia under Mussolini: Fascism and the Colonial Experience,* Zed Books, London, 1985

G.L. Steer, *Caesar in Abyssinia,* Hodder & Stoughton, London, 1936.

————, *Sealed and Delivered,* Hodder & Stoughton, London, 1942.

HISTORY, MODERN – 1941-1974

Jacques Bureau, *Éthiopie, un drame impérial et rouge,* Ramsay, Paris, 1987.

David Talbot, *Contemporary Ethiopia,* Philosophical Library, New York, 1952.

Gebru Tareke, *Ethiopia: Power and Protest, Peasant Revolts in the Twentieth Century,* Cambridge University Press, 1991.

Patrick Gilkes, *The Dying Lion, Feudalism and Modernisation in Ethiopia,* St. Martin's Press, New York, 1975.

Richard Greenfield, *Ethiopia: A New Political History,* Pall Mall Press, London, 1965.

Harold Marcus, *Ethiopia, Great Britain and the United States, 1941-74,* University of California Press, Berkeley, 1983.

John Markakis, *Ethiopia – Anatomy of a Traditional Polity,* Clarendon Press, Oxford 1974.

Margery Perham, *The Government of Ethiopia,* Faber and Faber, London, 1969.

Pierre Petrides, *The Boundary Question between Ethiopia and Somalia,* New Delhi, 1983.

Lord Rennell of Rodd, *British Military Administration of Occupied Territories in Africa, 1941-47,* HMSO, London, 1948.

Christine Sandford, *Ethiopia under Haile Selassie,* London, J.M. Dent, 1946.

John Spencer, *Ethiopia at Bay, a Personal Account of the Haile Sellassie Years,* Reference Publications, Algonac, MI, 1984.

Teshome Wagaw, *An Ethiopian Experience – The Development of Higher Education and Social Change,* Michigan State University Press, East Lansing, 1990.

Edward Ullendorff, *The Two Zions: Reminiscences of Jerusalem and Ethiopia,* Oxford University Press, 1988.

HISTORY, POST-1974

Abebe Zegeye and Siegfried Pausewang (eds), *Ethiopia in Change,* British Academic Press, London, 1994.

Africa Watch, *Evil Days: Thirty Years of War and Famine in Ethiopia,* Human Rights Watch, New York, 1991.

Alemneh Dejene, *Environment, Famine and Politics in Ethiopia,* Lynne Rienner, Boulder, CO, 1990.

Andargachew Tiruneh, *The Ethiopian Revolution, 1974-1987,* Cambridge University Press, 1993.

Dieter Beisel, *Reise ins Land der Rebellen,* Rowohlt, Hamburg, 1989.

Christopher Clapham, *Transformation and Continuity in Revolutionary Ethiopia,* Cambridge University Press, 1988.

Jason Clay *et al., The Spoils of Famine: Ethiopian Famine Policy and Peasant Agriculture,* Cultural Survival, Cambridge, MA, 1988.

John M. Cohen & Peter H. Koehn, *Ethiopian Provincial and Municipal Government, Imperial Patterns and Post-revolutionary Changes,* Michigan State University Press, East Lansing, 1980.

Dawit Wolde Giorgis, *Red Tears: War, Famine and Revolution in Ethiopia,* Red Sea Press, Trenton, NJ, 1988.

Donald L. Donham, *Marxist Modern – an Ethnographic History of the Ethiopian Revolution,* University of California Press, Berkeley, 1999.

André Glucksman and Thierry Wolton, *Silence, on Tue,* Grasset, Paris, 1986.

Paul B. Henze, *The Horn of Africa from War to Peace,* Macmillan, London, 1991.

352   *Bibliographic Guide to Further Reading*

Kinfe Abraham, *Ethiopia, from Bullets to the Ballot Box,* Red Sea Press, Trenton, NJ, 1994.

Kurt Jansson et al., *The Ethiopian Famine,* Zed Press, London, 1987.

David Korn, *Ethiopia, the United States and the Soviet Union,* Croom Helm, London, 1986.

Jeffrey Lebebvre, *Arms for the Horn,* University of Pittsburgh Press, Pittsburgh, PA, 1991.

Réné Lefort, *Ethiopia – an Heretical Revolution?,* Zed Press, London, 1981.

John Markakis, *National and Class Conflict in the Horn of Africa,* Cambridge University Press, 1997.

Claudio Moffa, *La Rivoluzione Etiopica – Testi i Documenti,* Argalia, Urbino, 1980.

Fasil Nahum, *Constitution for a Nation of Nations, the Ethiopian Prospect,* Red Sea Press, Trenton, NJ, 1997.

David and Marina Ottaway, *Ethiopia, Empire in Revolution,* Holmes & Meier, New York, 1978.

Alula Panshurst, *Resettlement and Famine in Ethiopia,* Manchester University Press, 1992.

Robert G. Patman, *The Soviet Union and the Horn of Africa,* Cambridge University Press, 1990.

Teferra Haile Selassie, *The Ethiopian Revolution, 1974-1991,* Kegan Paul International, London, 1997.

Raúl Valdez Vivó, *Ethiopia's Revolution,* International Publishers, New York, 1977.

John Young, *Peasant Revolution in Ethiopia: The Tigray People's Liberation Front, 1975-91,* Cambridge University Press, 1997.

ERITREA

Amare Tekle (ed.), *Eritrea and Ethiopia, from Conflict to Cooperation,* Red Sea Press, Trenton, NJ, 1994.

A. J. Barker, *Eritrea 1941,* Faber & Faber, London, 1966.

Bereket Habte Selassie, *Eritrea and the United Nations,* Red Sea Press, Trenton, NJ, 1989.

Haggai Erlich, *The Struggle over Eritrea, 1962-1978,* Stanford University Press, 1983.

Ruth Iyob, *The Eritrean Struggle for Independence...1941-1993,* Cambridge University Press, 1995.

Jordan Gebre Medhin, *Peasants and Nationalism in Eritrea,* Red Sea Press, Trenton, NJ, 1989.

Stephen Longrigg, *A Short History of Eritrea*, Clarendon Press, Oxford, 1945.

Medhanie Tadesse, *The Eritrean-Ethiopian War, Retrospect and Prospects*, Addis Ababa, 1999.

Osman Saleh Sabby, *A History of Eritrea*, Dural Masirah, Beirut, 1974.

Sylvia Pankhurst, *Eritrea on the Eve*, New Times Books, Woodford Green, Essex, 1952.

Richard Sherman, *Eritrea: the Unfinished Revolution*, Praeger, New York, 1980.

Tekeste Negash, *Eritrea and Ethiopia, the Federal Experience*, Uppsala University Press, 1997.

———, *Italian Colonialism in Eritrea, 1882-1941*, Uppsala University Press, 1987.

G.K.N. Trevaskis, *Eritrea: a Colony in Transition, 1941-52*, Oxford University Press, 1960.

Ghada H. Talhami, *Suakin and Massawa under Egyptian Rule, 1865-1885*, University Press of America, Washington, DC, 1979.

Yemane Mesghenna, *Italian Colonialism, a Case Study of Eritrea, 1869-1934*, Lund, 1988.

TRAVEL AND MEMOIRS

R.P. Azais and R. Chambard, *Cinq Années de Recherches Archéologiques en Éthiopie*, Geuthner, Paris, 1931.

Alain Barer, *Rimbaud in Abyssinia*, Morrow, 1984.

James E. Baum, *Unknown Ethiopia, New Light on Darkest Abyssinia*, Grosset & Dunlap, 1935.

C.F. Beckingham and G.W.B. Huntingford (eds), *The Prester John of the Indies*, Hakluyt Society, 1961.

C.F. Beckingham (ed.), *The Itinerário of Jerónimo Lobo*, Hakluyt Society, 1984.

Melvin Bolton, *Ethiopian Wildlands*, Collins, Glasgow, 1976.

J.H. Arrowsmith Brown (ed.), *Prutky's Travels in Ethiopia and Other Countries*, Hakluyt Society, 1991.

James Bruce, *Travels to Discover the Source of the Nile in Years 1768-1773*, Edinburgh, 1890.

Richard Burton, *First Footsteps in East Africa: An Exploration of Harar*, Routledge and Kegan Paul, London, 1966.

Douglas Busk, *The Fountain of the Sun: Unfinished Journeys in Ethiopia and the Ruwenzori*, Max Parrish, London, 1957.

David Buxton, *Travels in Ethiopia,* Ernest Benn, London, 1949.

R. E. Cheesman, *Lake Tana and the Blue Nile,* 1936, repr. Frank Cass, London, 1968.

Lincoln de Castro, *Nella Terra dei Negus,* Fratelli Treves, Milan, 1915.

O.G.S. Crawford, *Ethiopian Itineraries, ca. 1400-1524,* Hakluyt Society, 1958.

Henry Darley, *Slaves and Ivory in Abyssinia,* Negro Universities Press, 1969.

Rosita Forbes, *From the Red Sea to the Blue Nile,* Macaulay, New York, 1935.

William Foster (ed.), *The Red Sea and Adjacent Countries at the Close of the 17th Century,* Hakluyt Society, 1949.

Samuel Gobat, *Journal of Three Years' Residence in Abyssinia,* Negro Universities Press, 1969.

Marcel Griaule, *Abyssinian Journey,* John Miles, London, 1935.

W. Cornwallis Harris, *The Highlands of Ethiopia,* 3 vols, Longmans, Green, London, 1844.

Paul B. Henze, *Ethiopian Journeys,* 1969-72, Ernest Benn, London, 1977.

C. W. Isenberg and J.L. Krapf, *Journals,* Frank Cass, London, 1968.

Charles Johnston, *Travels in Southern Abyssinia,* Gregg International, London, 1982, 2 vols.

Philip Marsden-Smedley, *A Far Country, Travels in Ethiopia,* Century, London, 1990.

Dervla Murphy, *In Ethiopia with a Mule,* John Murray, London, 1968.

L.M. Nesbitt, *Desert and Forest: Exploration of the Abyssinian Danakil,* Cape, London, 1934.

Thomas Pakenham, *The Mountains of Rasselas,* Weidenfeld & Nicolson, London, 1959, 1998.

Richard Pankhurst, *Travellers in Ethiopia,* Oxford University Press, 1965.

Mansfield Parkyns, *Life in Abyssinia,* Frank Cass, London, 1966.

Nathaniel Pearce, *Life and Adventures in Abyssinia,* 2 vols, SASOR, London, 1980.

Beatrice Playne, *St. George for Ethiopia,* Constable, London, 1954.

J. M. Reid, *Traveller Extraordinary: The Life of James Bruce of Kinnaird,* Norton, New York, 1968.

C. F. Rey, *The Real Abyssinia,* Seeley, London, 1935.

———, *In the Country of the Blue Nile,* Negro Universities Press, 1969.

Ernst Schrenzel, *Abessinien – Land ohne Hunger, Land ohne Zeit,* Gutenberg, Berlin, 1928.

Richard Snailham, *The Blue Nile Revealed,* Chatto & Windus, London, 1968.

Wilfred Thesiger, *The Life of My Choice,* HarperCollins, London 1987.

———, *Danakil Diary,* HarperCollins, London, 1996.

Viscount Valentia, *Voyages and Travels to India, Ceylon, the Red Sea, Abyssinia, and Egypt in 1802-1806,* London, 1809.

Evelyn Waugh, *When the Going was Good,* Penguin, Harmondsworth, 1946.

M.S. Wellby, *Twixt Sirdar and Menelik,* Harper, New York, 1901.

Augustus Wylde, *Modern Abyssinia,* Negro Universities Press, 1970.

ART AND ARCHITECTURE

Elizabeth Biasio, *The Hidden Reality: Three Contemporary Ethiopian Artists,* Zurich Ethnographic Museum, 1989.

Stanislaw Chojnacki, *Major Themes in Ethiopian Painting...from the 13th to the 19th Century,* Franz Steiner, Wiesbaden, 1983.

Girma Fisseha, *Mensch und Geschichte in Aethiopiens Volksmalerei,* Pinguin, Innsbruck, 1985.

Georg Gerster, *Churches in Rock,* Phaidon Press, London, 1970.

Roderick Grierson (ed.) *African Zion, the Sacred Art of Ethiopia,* Yale University Press, 1993.

Paul B. Henze (ed.) *Aspects of Ethiopian Art from Ancient Axum to the Twentieth Century,* JED Press, London, 1993.

Proceedings of the First International Conference on the History of Ethiopian Art, Pindar, London, 1989.

Richard Pankhurst, *The Life and Works of Afework Tekle,* Addis Ababa, 1987.

Richard Pankhurst and Leila Ingrams, *Ethiopia Engraved, an Illustrated Catalogue...from 1681 to 1900,* Kegan Paul, London, 1988.

Ruth Plant, *Architecture of the Tigre, Ethiopia,* Ravens, London, 1985.

Osvaldo Raineri, *Warrior Saints, Art and Legends of Ethiopia,* Ferrari Edizioni, 1996.

RELIGION

Ayala Tekla-Haymanot, *La Chiesa Etiopica,* Saggi i Esperienze, Rome, 1973.

Gustav Arén, *Evangelical Pioneers in Ethiopia: Origins of the Evangelical Church Mekane Yesus,* EFS Forlaget, Stockholm, 1978.

Aymro Wondimaganehu and Joachim Motovu (eds), *The Ethiopian Orthodox Church,* Addis Ababa, 1970.

Enrico Cerulli, *L'Islam di Ieri e di Oggi*, Instituto per l'Oriente, Rome, 1971.

Friedrich Heyer, *Die Kirche Äthiopiens*, De Gruyter, Berlin, 1971.

Ephraim Isaac, *Matshafa Berhan*, E.J. Brill, London, 1973.

David Kessler, *The Falashas: The Forgotten Jews of Ethiopia*, Holmes & Meier, New York, 1982.

Wolf Leslau, *Falasha Anthology*, Schocken, New York, 1951.

Yolande Mara, *The Church of Ethiopia*, Poligrafico, Asmara, 1972.

Stuart C. Munro-Hay, *Ethiopia and Alexandria, the Metropolitan Episcopacy of Ethiopia*, Nubica/Polish Academy of Sciences, Warsaw, 1997.

James Quirin, *The Evolution of the Ethiopian Jews, a History of the Beta Israel...to 1920*, University of Pennsylvania Press, Philadelphia, 1992.

Louis Rappoport, *Lost Jews, the Last of the Ethiopian Falashas*, Stein & Day, New York, 1982.

Kay Kaufman Shelemay, *Music, Ritual and Falasha History*, Michigan State University Press, East Lansing, 1986.

J. Spencer Trimingham, *Islam in Ethiopia*, Frank Cass, London, 1965.

———, *Christianity Among the Arabs in Pre-Islamic Times*, Longman, London, 1979.

Edward Ullendorff, *Ethiopia and the Bible*, Oxford University Press, 1968.

GEOGRAPHY, ECONOMY, AGRICULTURE:

Abdulhamid Bedri Kello, *Privatization and Public Enterprise in Ethiopia*, Addis Ababa, 1974.

John M. Cohen, *Integrated Rural Development*, Uppsala University Press, 1987.

Dejene Aredo and Mulat Demeke, *Ethiopian Agriculture: Problems of Transformation*, Addis Ababa, 1995.

Dessalegn Rahmato, *Famine and Survival Strategies*, Uppsala University Press, 1991.

Getachew Yoseph and Adulhamid Bedri Kello, *The Ethiopian Economy – Problems and Prospects*, Addis Ababa, 1994.

Pierre Gouin, *Earthquake History of Ethiopia and the Horn of Africa*. Development Research Center, Ottawa, 1979.

Fassil G. Kiros, *Challenging Rural Poverty*, Africa World Press, Trenton, NJ, 1985.

James C. McCann, *People of the Plow, an Agricultural History of Ethiopia, 1800-1990*, University of Wisconsin Press, Madison, 1995.

A.C. McEwen, *International Boundaries of East Africa*, Clarendon Press, 1971.

Mekonen Taddesse and Abdulhamid Bedri Kello, *The Ethiopian Economy, Problems of Adjustment*, Addis Ababa, 1994.

Mesfin Wolde Mariam, *Introductory Geography of Ethiopia*, Addis Ababa, 1972.

——, *Rural Vulnerability to Famine in Ethiopia 1958-1977*, Addis Ababa, 1984.

Marina Ottaway (ed.), *The Political Economy of Ethiopia*, Praeger, New York, 1990.

Richard Pankhurst, *An Introduction to the Economic History of Ethiopia*, Sidgwick & Jackson, London, 1961.

——, *Economic History of Ethiopia*, 1800-1935, Addis Ababa, 1968.

Edoardo Pollastri, *Dinamica dell'Economia in Etiopia*, Asmara University Press, 1968.

Siegfried Pausewang, *Peasants, Land and Society: A Social History of Land Reform in Ethiopia*, Weltforum, Munich, 1983.

Siegfried Pausewang *et al.* (eds), *Ethiopia: Rural Development Options*, Zed Press, London, 1990.

Shifferaw Bekele (ed.), *An Economic History of Ethiopia*, Vol. I: *the Imperial Era*, Codesira, Dakar, 1995.

Michael Stahl, *Ethiopia, Political Contradictions in Agricultural Development*, Uppsala University Press, 1974.

John Waterbury, *Hydropolitics of the Nile Valley*, Syracuse University Press, 1979.

LANGUAGE & DICTIONARIES

Lionel Bender et al. (eds) *Language in Ethiopia*, Oxford Univeristy Press, 1976.

Lionel Bender, *Nilo-Saharan Language Studies*, Michigan State University Press, East Lansing, n.d.

Lionel Bender (ed.), *The Non-Semitic Languages of Ethiopia*, Michigan State University Press, 1976.

Marcel Cohen, *Traité de la Langue Amharique*, Institut de l'Ethnologie, Paris, 1970.

J.C. Corbeil, *Amharic Visual Dictionary*, Stoddart, Toronto, 1986.

Gene Cragg, *Oromo Dictionary*, Michigan State University Press, East Lansing, 1982.

August Dillmann, *Grammatik der äthiopischen Sprache*, Akademische Verlagsanstalt, Graz, 1959.

E.C. Foot, *A Galla-English and English-Galla Dictionary*, Cambridge University Press, 1913.

Thomas L. Kane, *Amharic-English Dictionary*, Otto Harrassowitz, Wiesbaden, 1990, 2 vols.

Thomas Lambdin, *Introduction to Classical Ethiopic (Ge'ez)*, Harvard University Press, 1978.

Wolf Leslau, *Concise Dictionary of Amharic*, University of California Press, Berkeley, 1976.

———, *Etymological Dictionary of Gurage*, Otto Harrassowitz, Wiesbaden 1979, 3 vols.

John Main, *Tigrinya Grammar*, American Evangelical Mission, Ghinda, 1994.

N.M. Moreno, *Grammatica della Lingua Galla*, Mondadori, Milan, 1939.

Tilahun Gamta, *Oromo-English Dictionary*, Addis Ababa, 1989.

Edward Ullendorff, *An Amharic Chrestomathy*, Oxford University Press, 1965.

ETHNOGRAPHY, ETHNIC HISTORY

Uri Almagor, *Pastoral Partners...the Dassanetch of Ethiopia*, Manchester University Press, 1978.

Asmerom Legesse, *Gada, Three Approaches to the Study of African Society*, The Free Press, New York, 1973.

Dan F. Bauer, *Land, Leadership, and Legitimacy among the Inderta Tigray of Ethiopia*, Michigan State University Press, East Lansing, n.d.

Lionel Bender (ed.), *Peoples and Cultures of the Sudan-Ethiopian Borderlands*, Michigan State University Press, East Lansing, n.d.

Otto Bieber, *Gemeimnisvolles Kaffa*, Universum, Vienna, 1948.

Ulrich Braukämper, *Geschichte der Hadiya Süd-Äthiopiens*, Franz Steiner, Wiesbaden, 1980.

Donald L. Donham, *Work and Power in Maale, Ethiopia*, University of Michigan Press, Ann Arbor, 1985.

Katsuyoshi Fukui & John Markakis, *Ethinicity and Conflict in the Horn of Africa*, James Currey, London, 1994.

Frederick Gamst, *The Qemant, a Pagan-Hebraic Peasantry of Ethiopia*, Holt, Rinehart & Winston, New York, 1969.

Gebreyesus Hailemariam, *The Gurage and their Culture*, Vantage Press, 1991.

Elike Haberland, *Galla Südäthiopiens*, Kohlhammer, Stuttgart, 1963.

C. R. Hallpike, *The Konso of Ethiopia*, Clarendon Press, Oxford, 1972.

Mohammed Hassen, *The Oromo of Ethiopia: A History, 1570-1860*, Cambridge University Press, 1990.

Allan Hoben, *Land Tenure among the Amhara of Ethiopia,* University of Chicago Press, 1973.

G.W.B. Huntingford, *The Galla of Ethiopia – the Kingdoms of Kafa and Janjero,* International Africa Institute, London, 1955.

Wendy James, *'Kwanim Pa: the Making of the Uduk People,* Clarendon Press, Oxford, 1979.

A. E. Jensen, *Im Lande des Gada,* Strecker & Schroder, Stuttgart, 1936.

——— , *Altvölker Südäthiopiens,* Kohlhammer, Stuttgart, 1959.

Werner Lange, *History of the Southern Gonga,* Franz Steiner, Wiesbaden,1982.

Herbert S. Lewis, *A Galla Monarchy: Jimma Abba Jifar, 1830-1932,* Wisconsin University Press, Madison, 1965.

I.M. Lewis (ed.), *Nationalism and Self-Determination in the Horn of Africa,* Ithaca Press, London, 1983.

Brian Macermot, *Cult of the Sacred Spear, the Story of the Nuer Tribe in Ethiopia,* Robert Hale, London, 1972.

Melesse Getu, *Tsemako Women's Role and Status in Agro-Pastoral Production,* Addis Ababa, 1993.

Helen Pankhurst, *Gender, Development and Ethnicity,* Zed Press, London, 1992.

Richard Pankhurst, *The Ethiopian Borderlands,* Red Sea Press, Trenton, NJ, 1997.

Henry F. Stern, *The Falashas of Abyssinia,* Frank Cass, London, 1862.

William A. Shack, *The Gurage, a People of the Ensete Culture,* Oxford University Press, 1966.

——— , and Habtemariam Marcos, *Gods and Heros, Oral Traditions of the Gurage of Ethiopia,* Clarendon Press, 1974.

Jack Stauder, *The Majangir: Ecology and Society of a Southwestern Ethiopian People,* Cambridge University Press, 1971.

Volker Stitz, *Studien zur Kulturgeographie Zentraläthiopiens,* Dummlers, Bonn, 1974.

Helmut Straube, *Westkuschitische Völker Südäthiopiens,* Kohlhammer, Stuttgart, 1963.

Alessandro Triulzi, *Salt, Gold and Legitimacy: Prelude to the History of a No Man's Land, Bela Shangul, Wallagga, ca. 1800-1898,* Naples, 1981.

LITERATURE

Bereket Habte Selassie, *Ride the Whirlwind,* Red Sea Press, Trenton, NJ, 1993.

Philip Caputo, *Horn of Africa,* Holt, New York, 1980.

Daniachew Worku, *The Thirteenth Sun,* Heinemann, London, 1973.

Ignazio Guidi, *Storia della Litteratura Etiopica,* Istituto per l'Oriente, Rome, 1932.

Thomas L. Kane, *Ethiopian Literature in Amharic,* Otto Harrassowitz, Wiesbadan, 1975.

Thomas Keneally, *To Asmara,* Time Warner, New York, 1989.

Faye Levine, *Solomon and Sheba,* Marek, New York, 1980.

Reidulf K. Molvaer, *Black Lions – The Creative Lives of Modern Ethiopian Literary Giants,* Red Sea Press, Trenton, NJ, 1997.

Reidulf K. Molvaer, *Tradition and Change in Ethiopia as Reflected in Amharic Fictional Literature,* Otto Harrassowitz, 1975.

Edmund P. Murray, *Kulubi,* Crown, New York, 1973.

Sahle Selassie, *Shinega's Village,* University of California Press, Berkeley, 1966.

————, *The Afersata,* Heinemann, London, 1968.

————, *The Warrior King,* Heinemann, London, 1968.

————, *Firebrands,* Longman, London, 1979.

Claude Sumner, *An Anthology of Oromo Literature,* Addis Ababa, 1996.

Tadesse Adera and Jimale Ahmed, *Silence is not Golden, a Critical Anthology of Ethiopian Literature,* Red Sea Press, Trenton, NJ, 1995.

Yemane Deneke, *In the Mirror of Love,* Addis Ababa, 1990.

Evelyn Waugh, *Black Mischief,* Penguin, Harmondworth, 1938.

OTHER TOPICS

Dawit Abebe and Ahadu Ayehu, *Medicinal Plants and Enigmatic Health Practices in Northern Ethiopia,* Addis Ababa, 1993.

Ethiopian Airlines, *Bringing Africa Together,* Addis Ababa, 1988.

Dennis Bill, *The Coinage of Ethiopia, Eritrea and Italian Somalia,* New York, 1991.

Richard Pankhurst, *The Medical History of Ethiopia,* Red Sea Press, Trenton, NJ, 1990.

————, *A Social History of Ethiopia,* Addis Ababa, 1990.

Michael Powne, *Ethiopian Music,* Oxford University Press, 1968.

Geoffrey Tillotson and Brian Jenkins (eds), *Samuel Johnson's The Story of Rasselas, Prince of Abyssinia,* Oxford University Press, 1971.

Ahmed Zein and Helmut Kloos (eds), *The Ecology of Health and Disease in Ethiopia,* Addis Ababa, 1988.

INDEX

Abbreviations: B., Battle
Emp., Emperor
Empr. Empress
Gen., General
K., King
L., Lake
Pr., Prince
Q., Queen
R., River

Abba Filipos, 62n
Abba Gerima, 38, 169
Abba Jifar, Sultan, 166, 208
Abba Jifar II, 173
Abba Jobir, 208, 225
Abba Pantelewon, 38, 41
Abba Tekle Hawariat, 72
Abba Yohanni, 60
d'Abbadie brothers, 126ff
Abbay, 72
Abebe Aregay Ras, 228, 234, 239, 254-5, 260
Abbe Gubegna, 210n, 267, 283-4
Abiye Abebe, 276
Abreha Deboch, 226
Abreha, Gen., 33
Abreha, K., 33
Abu Bakr Mohamed, 83n, 86
Abuna Aregawi, 38, 60
Abuna Matewos, 191, 195, 203
Abuna Petros, 225
Abuna Selama (19th Cent.), 135ff
Abuna Selama Kesate Berhan, 33, 53
Abuna Yemata, 39
Adair, Ross, 283n
Adal, 66ff, 83ff
Adal, Ras, 149
Addis Ababa, 153ff, 171ff, 190ff, 206, 210, 234, 330-2,
Addis Tedla, 297
Adefa, 51
Aden, 201n

Adigrat, 167ff, 216
Adulis, 18, 21, 24, 28, 45
Adwa, B., 166-71, 180-5, 216, 339-40,
Aedisius, 32
Afabet, B., 313
Afar Depression, 1-2, 7
Afar Liberation Front (ALF), 322-3
Afars, 190, 210n
Afenegus, 204, 239
Afnin, 80
Africa, 258
Agatharchides, 17-19
Agaw (Agau), 16n, 47ff, 56ff, 73ff, 89, 111
Agaw Neguse, 136ff
Agawmeder, 111
Agnew, Spiro, 279
Agordat, 213
Agriculture, 9-14, 20-21, 91, 210, 270, 272, 307, 336, 342
Agula, 35
Ahmad Gragn, 76, 86ff
Aida Desta, 261
air force, air power, 219, 251, 255, 332
air travel, 201, 258, 265
Akele Guzay, 37, 127, 162ff
Aklilu Habtewold, 258, 276ff, 283
Aksum, 10, 17, 20-49, 69, 87, 95ff, 146, 339
Alem Bekagn, 320, 332

361

Alem Ketema, 319
Alemu Abebe, 328
Alemzewd Tessema, 284
Aleqa Gebre Egziabeher Elias, 193
Aleqa Taye Gebre Maryam, 53
Alexandria, 32-3, 44, 46, 52ff, 150
Ali Alula Ras, 123
Ali Gwangul, Pr., 122
Allen, W.E.D., 231n
Almeida, Manoel de, 97ff
Alula, Ras, 148ff, 173
Alvarez, Francisco, 22-3, 75ff, 108
Aman Andom, 288-9
Amba Alagi, 167ff, 196, 217
Amba Aradom, 217
Amba Gishen, 68
Ambo, 328
Amde Tseyon, Emp., 44, 63ff
Amde Tseyon II, Emp., 84n.
America, 208, 221, 235-7, 242-3,
  345-8 *See also* United States
Americans in Egyptian Service,
  147ff
Amha Yesus, K., 117
Amharas, 47, 101, 117, 120ff, 128ff,
  195, 217, 262, 316, 322
Amhara Saynt, 75ff, 238
Amharic, 77ff, 110, 259, 266
Anbasa Wudem, Emp., 49
Amchem, B., 205
Andargachew Masai Ras, 254, 274
Andrade, Lazaro de, 79
Andropov, Yuri, 306
Anfray, Francis, 21
Angola, 298
Ankober, 117ff, 144ff, 196, 227
Annesley, George, 109
Ansar, 148ff
Antinori, Orazio, 160-1
Antonelli, Pietro, 153ff, 161ff
Anze Matienzo, Eduardo, 243
Aphilas, 31
Arabs, Arabic, 59, 79, 90, 209, 275,
  277
Aramis, 1
Arendrup, S.A., 147
Argobba, 77-8, 115
Architecture, 34ff, 52, 96ff

Arkiko, 89, 123
Armah, Emp., 41
armed forces, 277
Armenia[ns], 62n, 209
Arsi, 151ff, 318
Art, 78ff, 267-8
Asfa Wossen Haile Selassie, Crown
  Pr., K., 188n, 208, 219, 254-5, 260,
  282-3, 276, 286n
Asfa Wossen, K. (Shoa), 117
Asfa Wossen Asserate, Pr., 118n,
  285n
Asrate Kassa Ras, 255, 276ff, 282,
  284-5
Ashama ibn Abjar, Emp., 41ff.
Ashangi, L., 218
Asmara, 36, 161ff, 213-15, 233, 255,
  289, 329
Assab, 202, 215, 259, 322, 333,
Asosa, 321
Aswan Dam, 3
Ataturk, Mustafa Kemal, 339
Athanasius, 32
Atnafu Abate, 284, 302
atrocities, 225-7
Atsbeha, K., 33
Atsbi, 27
Australopithecus afarensis, 1; afri-
  canus, 5; Ramidus, 5; Robustus,
  5;
Ayelew Biru, 209n, 217
Ayshal, B., 124
Awash R., 1, 7-8
Aymero, 266
Azais, R.P., 9
Azebu, 219, 249-51
Azezo, 96
Azule, B., 152

Bab el-Mandeb, 16, 19
Babichev, N., 175
Badlay ad-Din, Sultan, 70, 83
Badoglio, Pietro, Gen., 217, 225
Ba'eda Maryam, Emp., 72ff, 83
Bafena, 149
Bahr Dar, 319, 322
Bahr Negash, 71, 93
Bahrey, 91

Bahru, Zewde, 192
Bahta Hagos, 165-6, 211
Bakaffa, Emp., 104ff
Balcha, Safo, 190-1, 195ff, 204
Bale, 83ff., 238, 252, 260-5, 281
Bani al-Hamwiyya, 49
Bank of Abyssinia, 209
banking, 269
Baratieri, Oreste, Gen., 166ff
Bard, Kathryn, 26-7
barley, 11, 31
Barya, 46, 212
Bati del Wambara, 89
Batu, M., 261
Baybars, Sultan, 59
Begemder, 48, 123ff, 195n.
Beja, 33, 45
Belay Zelleke, 234, 240
Belgium, 202, 259
Bell, John, 135
Bent, J. Theodore, 24
Berbera, 83ff., 115, 233
Berhane Gebre Christos, 319-20
Berhanena Selam, 203
Bermudez, João, 92-3
Beseka, 9
Beta Israel, 53ff
Beyene Wondimagagnehu, 195n
Bible, 38, 55
Bichena, 240
Bicini, Gregorio, 79
Bilen, 111, 213
Biru Goshu, 123
Black Americans, 221-2
Black Lion Movement, 254
Bodyguard Coup, 253-60
Boeing Corporation, 246
Bogos, 147, 156
Borana, 92, 261
Brancaleon, Nicolo, 79
Brandt, Steven, 9
Brazil, 254-5
British Commonwealth Forces, 229, 323
British Institute in E. Africa, 9, 25, 35
Bruce, James, 23-4, 108-9
Brezhnev, Leonid, 299

Budge, E. Wallis, 58ff
Bugna, 50
Bure, 233
Burton, Richard, 115
Bush Administration, 323, 326
Butajira, 226
Buxton, David, 36
Byzantium, 40ff, 65n

CADU, 272
Cairo, 274-5
camels, 12
Candace, Q., 16n
Capuchins, 127ff
Carter, President Jimmy, x, 314
Carter Administration, 298-301
Castro, Fidel, 296
Castro, Raul, 301
Catholicism, 92ff, 120ff, 136, 190, 211
cattle, 13
CELU, 283
Central Asia, 32
Central Planning Commission, 316
Ceylon, 36-7
Chalcedon, 38
Chambard, Roger, 10
chat, 13n
Cheesman, R.E., 73n
Chefneux, Leon, 153ff, 178
Chelenqo, B., 152
Cheleqot, 122
Chernenko, Konstantin, 306
China, 22, 37, 277-9, 288
Chittick, Neville, 25
Choke, M., 227, 233
Christianity, Christianization, 22ff, 30ff, 44-82, 60ff, 72ff, 111
Chojnacki, Stanislaw, 79ff, 266
Churchill, Winston, 229ff, 236-7
CIA, 299
Clapham, Christopher, 54n, 195n, 238, 260
Clark, J. Desmond, 9, 13
Coffee, 12-13, 21, 209, 271, 336
Cohaito, 18n
Cohen, Herman, 324n
coins, 28ff, 44ff, 103, 15

Colonial Army, Italian, 211
communism, 100
constitution, 207, 252-3, 286, 335, 338, 341
Conti Rossini, 49
Copper, 21
COPWE, 306
coronation, 204-5, 212n.
coups, 253-60, 314, 318
da Covilhão, Pero, 83ff
Crispi, Francesco, 161, 165, 211
Crown Council, 235, 282
Crown Prince see Asfa Wossen
Council of Florence, 109
Cuba, 288, 296, 301ff
Cunningham, Alan, Gen., 232-4
currency, 269, 338
Cush, 55

Daga, 73
Dagna Jan, Pr., 47ff, 115
Dahlak Is., 45
Dakar, 83
Damot, 49, 65, 116-7
Damot/Diamat, 27
Dangila, 209
Dankaz, 94ff
Darge, Ras, 151ff
Dawaro, 70, 113
Dawit I, Emp., 64ff
Dawit Wolde Giorgis, 307
Debarwa, 89
De Bono, Emilio, Gen., 215-7
Debre Abbay, 68
Debre Asbo, 62
Debre Berhan, 72, 128ff, 227, 251
Debre Damo, 36, 38, 60ff, 88
Debre Bizen, 62n
Debre Libanos, 62, 69, 226-7
Debre Mitmaq, 69
Debre Marqos, 233, 240
Debre Tabor, 122, 124, 140
Debre Worq, 74ff
Debre Zeit, 329, 332
Decamere, 28, 302
Deir es-Sultan, 202
DelBoca, Angelo, 214n
Dembaro, 149

Dembea, 100ff
DUPE, 317-8, 328
Derasge, 135ff
Derg, 284-331
Dessie, 194, 196, 218
Desta Damtew, Ras, 218, 225-6
Dhofar, 281
Dhu Nuwas, K., 40
Dil Na'od, Emp., 48ff
Dima, 74ff.
Diredawa, 177, 302
Djibouti, 10, 11, 163ff, 176ff, 202, 218-9, 237, 275, 296-7, 330
Dogali, B., 157-8
donkeys, 14
Duke of Aosta, 234

early man, 4-10
East Germany, 306, 314
economic aid, 291
economy, 270-1, 306, 315, 337
Eden, Anthony, 230
EDU, 292
education, 211, 281
Egypt, Egyptians, 3-4, 11, 14-5, 23-4, 29, 52ff, 69ff, 100, 122ff, 146ff, 202, 274, 339
Ejersa Goro, 189
Elections, 244, 335n
Eleni, Q., 72ff, 84ff
elephants, 14, 16-8, 26, 28
ELF, 275, 289n
ELF-RC, 287ff
Eliseev, A.V., 164-5
Ella Amida, Emp., 32
Ella Amida II, Emp., 38
Ella Sahem, Emp., 41
Ellis, Wm. Henry, 179
ELM, 274
embargos, 220-1
emigrants, 342
Enarya, 103, 115-16
Enda Selassie, 313-14
Enderta, 122
Endubis, Emp., 31
enset, 12
Entoto, 154ff, 192n
EPDM, 313, 326

EPLF, 287ff, 303, 312ff, 337-8
EPRDF, 313-16, 343
EPRP, 293,, 301, 305, 338
Era of Princes, 119-24ff
Eritrea, xi, 11, 13-14, 17-21, 24, 39, 78-9, 87, 111, 112, 165ff, 210-14, 236-7, 240-5, 248, 257, 269ff, 273-9, 287-90, 303-4, 321, 329n, 330, 337-8, 342-3.
Eritrean invasion, 338, 343
Erlich, Haggai, 112n.
Erythraean Sea, 17n, 29
Ethiopian Airlines (EAL), 246, 277
Ethiopian Orthodox Church (EOC), 124ff, 227, 253, 293
Ethiopian Socialism, 290ff, 305
Ethio-Somali War, 300-3
ethnicity, 338, 341-2
Etissa, 61
Ewostatewos, 62n, 69
eucalyptus, 206
Europe, 201ff
European Community, 332
Europeans in Ethiopia, 70, 76ff, 107-10
exports, 271-3, 315
Ezana, Emp., 31ff

Falashas, 53ff, 67ff, 93, 137ff, 316, 324-5
Famine, 282, 286, 307-11, 315, 324, 342
Fasilidas, Emp., 97ff
Fashoda, 172, 174ff
Fattovich, Rodolfo, 9, 20n, 26-7
F5E Aircraft, 281, 297-8
Fiche, 219, 234
Fikre Selassie Wogderes, 297
Fisseha Desta, 328
Five-Year Plans, 270-1
France, 199-202, 216
Franciscans, 101
Frasure, Robert, 324n
Fremona, 94ff
forests, 14
France, 9, 9-10, 21, 24-6, 129ff, 136ff, 172ff
Frumentius, 32ff, 73

Funj Kingdom of Sennar, 137ff

Gadeb, 9
Gafat, 77-8, 138ff
Gaki Sherocho, K., 173
Galawdewos, Emp., 88-9, 93
da Gama, Christovao, 88
Gambela, 209, 230
Gamu Gofa, 238
Gaynt, 88
Ge'ez, 27, 31, 37, 47, 77ff
Gebre Christos Desta, 268
Gebre Egziabeher, 173
Gebre Hiwot Baykedagn, 211n
Gebre Maskal, Emp., 41, 47
Gebre Selassie, 196n, 201n
Gebru Tareke, 249n
Germany, 194
Germame Neway, 254
Gersem, Emp., 41
Getachew Kibret, 286n
Geology, 1-15
gesho, 13n
Getachew Haile, 56n
Getisemani, 74, 80
Gibe region, 150
Gideon Force, 231ff
Girma Fisseha, 268n
Gish Abbay, 96
goats, 13-14
Gobat, Samuel, 126ff
Gobedra, 9
Gobena, Ras, 150ff
Gobeze, Wagshum, 145ff
Gojjam, 65ff, 72ff, 103, 106, 136ff, 195n, 196, 204, 208, 217, 219, 228, 222-31ff, 265,
Gondar, 69, 100ff, 158-9, 319, 322
Gondarine era, 100-7
Gorbachev, Mikhail, 312, 318
Gore, 209
Gorgora, 96ff
Goshu Worqu, 268
GOSPLAN, 311
Graziani, Rodolfo, Gen., 218, 25-6, 230
Great Britain, 123ff, 148ff, 173ff, 199-202, 208-9, 216, 220, 227,

229-37, 240-5, 249-51, 261
Greeks, Greece, 17, 27ff, 37ff, 202, 209
Greenfield, Richard, 256n
Grierson, Roderick, 79n
Gudit, Q., 48, 53ff
guerrilla warfare, 224-8, 303-4, 311-15, 323-7,
Gugsa Wole, Ras, 196, 205, 208
Gulf War, 319, 324
Gumuz, 73
Gundet, B., 147
Gurage, 77-8, 83, 112-14, 129, 150, 206

Habashat, 33
Haberland, Eike, 114n, 116n
Habte Giyorgis Dinagde, 191, 195, 199, 201-4, 208, 225, 231ff, 240
Habtewold Brothers, 239
Hadar, 1
Haddis Alemayehu, 267
Hadhramaut, 19, 40ff
Hadiya, 65, 72, 116
Hagos, Ras, 173
Hahn, Wolfgang, 31n
Haile Fida, 294-301
Haile Malekot, K., 131ff
Haile Mariam Redda, 250-1
Haile Selassie, Emp., 73, 188, 228-81, 332n, 339-40
Haile Selassie Abayneh, 189
Haile Selassie Gugsa, 217
Hailu Belaw, 240
Hamasien, 87, 114, 123ff, 162ff
Hancock, Graham, 54n
Hanish Islands, 338
Haq ad-Din, Sultan, 67
Harar, 9, 77-8, 86ff, 114-15, 152, 189-90, 194-5, 209, 219, 238, 302, 333
Harbe, K., 51-3
Hargeisa, 233
Harris, W. Cornwallis, 129ff
HSIU, 257, 265-6
Hatsani Danael, 46
Haud, 261
Hayq, L., 48ff, 60ff, 87

Heruy Wolde Selassie , 201n, 204, 219, 267
Hewett, Wm., 155-6
Heyling, Peter, 99
highways, 269-70
Hilton Hotel, 269
Himyar, 19, 28, 40ff
Hitler, Adolf, 216, 222
Holeta, 226, 254
homo erectus, 5, 7
homo habilis, 5, 7
homo sapiens, 5
Honecker, Erich, 306, 311, 314
horses, 14
Houdek, Robert, 324n, 330, 332
hunting, 14-15

Ibn Haukal, 49
Ibrahim Sultan, 274
Idris Mohammed Adem, 274
IESCs, 266
Ifat, 59, 83ff, 117
Ilg, Alfred, 152ff, 178
Illubabor, 238, 267
Imperial Private Cabinet, 240
Imru Haile Selassie, Ras, 189, 209n, 217-20
incense, 15
Indalkachew Makonnen, 283-4
industry, 270-1
India, 202n, 209
Indian Ocean, 3, 17, 28
influenza, 199
Institute of Ethiopian Studies (IES), 265
iron, 21
irrigation, 21
Irob, 122, 127
Isaias Afewerki, 278, 320-1, 323, 327ff, 330n, 343
Isenberg, C.W., 129ff
Iskinder, Emp., 83-4
Islam, 42-3, 45, 83ff, 115-16, 193-4, 195n, 213, 262, 288
Ismael, Khedive, 146ff
Israel, 20, 53ff, 259, 277, 280, 315-16, 325-6, 327
Italian East Africa, 223-7

Italian invasion, 216-22
Italian-Americans, 221
Italy, 10, 25, 146ff, 154-9, 161ff,
   172ff, 199, 201-2, 209-28, 235,
   248-52, 269, 314
Iyasu, Lij, 187, 190, 197-200, 208,
   254-5, 267, 339
Iyasu I, Emp., 102ff
Iyasu II, Emp., 104ff
Iyasus Mo'a, 48ff, 60ff
Iyo'as, Emp., 106
ivory, 17-18

de Jacobis, Justin, 127ff
Jagama Kello, 263-4
Jarosseau, Andre, 189
Jerusalem, 52ff, 109, 126, 201, 220
Jesuits, 75ff, 92ff, 257-8
Jews, Judaism, 38, 40, 53ff, 72ff, 102,
   315-16, 325-6
Jijiga, 233, 254
Jimma, 330
judicial system, 341
Judith, Q., 48

Kaffa, 12n, 173, 238, 310n
Kagnew Station, 280, 299
Kaleb, Emp., 33, 39ff, 47, 54
Kassa Darge Ras, 198-9, 208, 217,
   219, 225, 234, 252-4, 276n
Kassa Hailu, 124ff, 133ff
Kassa Kebede, 326
Kassa Mercha, 140ff
Kassala, 9, 12, 46, 213, 230, 233
Kasu, 33
Kebbede Tessema, 290n.
Kebre Negast, 20, 53ff
Kennedy, President John F., 257,
   259
Kenya, 5, 7, 17, 271, 275, 307n
Keren, 111, 161, 213, 233, 303
Kestane, 150
Khartoum, 229
Kirkham, John, 146ff
Kishe, 310n
Kobbo, 249
Kobishchanov, Yuri, 25n
Koloe, 18n, 21, 27

Konovaloff, Col., 218
Korean War, 242, 245, 259
Korem, 218
Kosmas Indicopleustes, 29-30
Krapf, J.L., 129ff
Kubar (Kobar), 47
Kulubi, 190
Kunama, 212
Kumsa Moroda, 173
Kurmuk, 230
Kush, 16
Kyeneion, 18

Lagarde, Leonce, 153ff, 172
Lalibela, 36, 51ff, 219
land reform/tenure, 290ff, 336, 341
language(s), 27, 76ff
Lasta, 44ff, 50ff, 56ff, 106, 111, 238
Lazarists, 136
Leakey, Richard, 5n
League of Nations, 201, 216, 220-1
lebasha, 203
Lebna Dengel, 75ff, 84ff, 117
Legesse Asfaw, 297
Leontieff, Nikolai, 164ff, 174ff
Leslau, Wolf, 77, 113n
Leuke Kome, 29-30
Lewis, I.M., 295n
liberation, 229ff
literacy, 256, 266, 342
livestock, 12-14, 20
Littman, Enno, 24
Lobo, Geronimo, 97ff
London Conference, 330
Longriff, Stephen, 240n
Lorenzo Taezaz, 219, 239n
Lucy, 1, 4, 7
Ludolf, Job, 110, 266

Main, 19
Magdala, 138ff, 196
Mahdi[sts], 148ff, 173
Mahfuz, emir, 84-5
Mai Shum, 21
Makelle, 167ff, 217, 250
Makhzumi rulers, 83ff
Makonnen Habtewold, 254-5
Makonnen Indalkachew, 201n, 238,
   267

Makonnen Haile Selassie, Pr., 260
Makonnen Wolde Mikael, Ras, 152ff, 161, 167, 173ff, 185, 189
Mani, 22,
Manz, 116-18, 319
Mao Zedong, 279
Marcus, Harold, 235n
Mareb Mellash, 148
Maria Teresa Dollar, 209, 226
Mariam Tehot, 34
Marib, 28
Markakis, John, 287n
Martini, Fernando, 211
Marxism, 279, 287, 291ff, 303-5
Marye Gugsa, Ras, 123
Mashkov, V.F., 163-4
Massaja, Guglielmo, 127ff, 148ff
Massawa, 45, 65, 71, 88, 122ff, 138, 143, 146ff 161ff
Matara, 21, 25, 27, 32
Mateus the Armenian, 84
Matte, Lucien, 256-7
Mediterranean, 1-10, 15-18
Mega, 209
MEISON, 293ff, 301, 305
Meles Zenawi, xi, 312, 327ff, 329-33, 340
Melka Kontoure, 7-8
Mendes, Alfonso, 97ff
Menegesha Seyum, Ras, 261, 276n, 277, 292
Menegesha Yohannes, Ras, 166ff, 173
Menelik I, Emp., 20, 72, 207
Menelik II, Emp., 131ff, 144-87, 189-92, 339-40
Menen Asfaw, Empr., 192-3
Mengistu Haile Mariam, x, xi, 100, 133, 188, 284, 327-9, 334, 340
Mengistu Lemma, 267
Mengistu Neway, 254
Mentuab, Empr., 104ff
Merara Tekle Haymanot, Pr., 50
Merhabete, 319
Meroe, 16, 33
Meropius, 32
Mertule Mariam, 74ff
Mesfin Sileshi, 239n

Mesobe Worq, 50
Metekel, 73
Metemma, 134, 160, 230
Mexico, 222
Michels, Joseph W., 25n
Middle East, 11-12
Mikael of Wollo, Ras, 150ff, 192, 195-7
Mikael Imru, 284-5
Mikael Sehul, Pr., 106ff, 121ff
military aid, 247n, 247-8, 280
military expenditures, 273
military training, 203
millet, 12
Minas, Emp., 93
missionaries, 124-7, 265
"Mitochondrial Eve", 6
Minjar, 227
Mitraha, 104
Mogadishu, 232, 263-4, 275
Mogus Asgedom, 226
Mohammed (Prophet), 36, 42ff
Mohammed Abdille Hassan, 194
Mohammed Ali (Egypt), 122ff
Mohammed Ali (Wollo), 149ff
Molvaer, Reidulf, 267n
Mombasa, 99
Monumentum Adulitanum, 28-30
Moroda Bakure, 151
Moscow, 258
Motalami, 61
Mulugeta Bulli, 240, 254-5
Mulugeta Yigezu, 205
Munro-Hay, Stuart, 25ff
Munzinger, Werner, 139ff, 147
Muslims, 57ff, 63ff, 83ff, 102
Mussolini, Benito, 214-27, 230

Nagasi, 117
Nakuto La'ab, Emp., 51ff
Na'od, Emp., 84
Napata, 16
Napier, Robert, Gen., 139ff
Nasi, Guglielmo, Gen., 233-5
Nasibu Zamanuel, 204, 218
Nasser, Gamal Abdel, 275
National Conference, 333
nationalizations, 290

Nega Tegegn, Gen., 290n, 292
Negade Gobeze, 304-5
Negash, 43
Nekempte, 322
Nero, Roman Emp., 16n
Nesbitt, L.M., 210n
Neway Brothers, 254
New Zealand, 222
Nile, R., 2-3, 11-16, 26, 29, 45, 70ff, 174
Nimeiry, Jaafar, 279-80, 289, 304
Nine [Syrian] Saints, 38-39, 55
Nixon, President Richard, 280-1, 285
Noba, 33, 34
North Africa, 13
North Korea, 306
Norway, 259
Nubia, 16, 45
nug, 12
Nur ibn Mujahid, 89-90, 114-15

Obock, 153ff
Ogaden, 215, 218, 223, 237, 246, 261-4, 281, 296, 302
Olduvai Gorge, 5
OLF, 321-2, 329
Omedla, 231
Omo R., 7-8
OPDO, 322
opposition politicians, , 335-6, 340-1
Oreine, 18n
Oromos, 8n, 16n, 79, 90ff, 102, 106, 114-15, 119ff, 129ff, 190, 206, 261-65. 303, 321-22, 333
Osman Salih Sabbe, 289
Ottoman Empire, 85ff, 112
Ottoways, 285n
Ousanas, Emp., 31-2
Özdemir Pasha, 89

Pachomius, 39
painting, 79ff
Pais (Paez) Pero, 94ff
paleontology, 1
Pan-African politics, 258
Pan-Arabism, 275
Pankhurst, Richard, 55n, 265

parliament, 207, 237, 252-3, 310
Patriots, 227-8, 231-4, 239-40
Peace Corps, 257, 260, 265, 280
Pearce, Nathaniel, 109, 122
People's Republic, 311-12
Perham, Margery, 241n
Periplus of the Erythraean Sea, 17-19, 28
Persia, 28, 37, 45, 76
petroleum, 332
Petrov, Gen., 302
PFDJ, 338
Phillips, Wendell, 20n
Phillipson, David, 9, 24n, 25, 31n
Phoenicians, 16
Plowden, Walter, 124, 135
PMAC, 290n
Poland, 91, 309
politburo, 254
political parties, 259, 335ff
Poncet, Charles, 108
population size, 81, 210n, 212, 214, 270, 291, 341-2
Portal, Gerald, 157-8
Portugal, 84ff
press, 335
Prester John, 22, 70, 85ff
Protestants, 124ff
Prutky, Remedius, 108
Ptolemais Theron, 16
Ptolemys, 16
Punt, 15

Qaddafy, Muammar, 279, 289
Qataban, 19
qene, 47
Queen Elizabeth, 259
Queen Victoria, 137ff
Quiha, 250-51
Quirin, James, 56n
Qwara, 134ff

Raheita, 175
railways, 206, 213, 296-7
Ramadan Mohammed Nur, 278
Rapoport, Louis, 54n
Rassam, Hormuzd, 138ff
Raya, 249-51

Reagan, President Ronald, 323
Red Sea, 2-3, 15-17, 26-30, 45, 132ff
referendum, 337-8
reforms, 202ff, 290ff, 316-20, 340
refugees, 336
Relief & Rehabilition Commission
 (RRC), 308
resettlement, 309-10
revolution, 285ff
rhinoceros, 18
Rift Valley, 1-10
roads, 213
Rochet d'Hericourt, 129ff
rock art, 10
rock churches, 36
Roha, 51
Romania, 258
Romanov, Grigory, 306
Rombulo, Pietro, 70
Rome, 28, 32, 92ff, 109ff
Roosevelt, President Franklin D.
 221-2, 236-7, 245
Rubenson, Sven, 129n
Rufinus, 32-3, 40ff
Russia, 163ff, 174ff, 178-9
Rwanda, 337

Sa'ad-Din, Sultan, 67
Saba (Sheba), 19, 28, 40ff
Sagale, B., 196-7
Sahle Selassie, K., 128ff
Sakala, 96, 231
SALF, 295ff, 303
Salt, Henry, 23-4, 109ff
salt trade, 103
Samene, 29
sanctions, 220-1
Sandford, Daniel, 230
Sarsa Dengel, Emp., 94
Sasu, 30, 49
Saudi Arabia, 300
Sayfa Ar'ad, Emp., 64
Sazana, 33
scholarship, 266ff
Sebagadis Woldu, Pr., 122
Sebla Wangel, Q., 88
Sekota, 51
Sembrouthes, Emp., 28-9

Semien, 29, 93, 111, 123ff, 217, 233
Semitic languages, 16n
Senafe, 21, 140
Senate, 207
Senhit, 147
Serae, 162
Sergew Hable Selassie, 46
Sevastopol, 139ff
Seyum Menegesha, Ras, 196, 201n,
 208, 217, 233n, 254-5
Shafartak, 233-4
sheep, 13-14
Shelemay, Kay K., 54n
shengo, 316, 328
Shifferaw Bekele, 133n
Shihab ad-Din, Sultan, 90n
Shoa, 44, 58ff, 83ff, 116-18, 120ff,
 127ff, 136ff, 227-8
Siad Barre, Mohammed, 281, 299-
 300
Sidama peoples, 113
Sidamo, 190, 204, 238, 261, 263
Skinner, Robert, 176ff
Skunder Boghassian, 268
slavery, 15, 115, 131, 201, 210n
Solomon, K. in Jerusalem, 20
Solomonic Dynasty, 56ff, 111
Somali invasion, xi, 295ff, 300ff,
 325, 336
Somaliland, 10-11, 30, 173ff, 218,
 223
Somalis, 90-1, 190, 194, 232, 235,
 246, 261-5, 271-5, 281
Somali Youth League, 261
South Africa, 323
South Arabia, 16, 19-21, 26, 30,
 33ff., 44ff. *See also* Yemen
Southwestern peoples, 115-16,
 152n
Soviet army, 297ff
Soviet Union, xi, 222, 241n, 258-9,
 263-4, 275, 277-9, 285-6, 291ff,
 295-307, 311-12, 318, 323
Spencer, Diana, 80
Spencer, John, 237n, 247n
Steer, George, 232
stelae, 34ff
Stern, Henry, 137ff

students, 291, 293
Suakin, 89, 99, 146-7
Sudan, 16, 21, 33, 147ff, 155ff, 209, 229, 211n, 235, 273, 275, 279, 280n, 286n, 289, 336, 338
Sudan South[erners], 280
Suez Canal, 147, 216, 220, 279, 288
sugar estates, 271
Susenyos, Emp., 76, 95ff
Sweden, 13n, 125n, 211n, 212, 240, 257, 259, 272
Switzerland, 202
Syria, 37-8, 277

Ta'akha Mariam, 35
Tadesse Tamrat, xiii, 46ff, 62n
Tafari Makonnen, Pr., 10, 187-205, 339 *See also* Haile Selassie
Taggaiton, 29
Taitu Betul, Empr., 151ff, 162ff, 185ff, 191
Takazze, 29, 34, 217
Takele Wolde Hawariat, 204, 207, 239
Tamrat Layne, 333
Tana, L., 67ff, 72ff, 87ff, 202, 208, 319
Tana Cherqos, 73
Tanzania, 17
Tedla Bairu, 274
Teferi Banti, 289-1
teff, 12
Tegulet, 88
Tekondo, 21
Tekle Giyorgis, Emp., 145-46
Tekle Haymanot, St., 60ff
Tekeste Negash, 211n
Tembien, 196
Tenagneworq Haile Selassie, 260
Tesfa Yohannes Berhe, 278
Tesfaye Dinka, 328-9
Tesfaye Gebre Kidan, 326, 328-30
Tesfaye Wolde Selassie, 314
Teshome Irgetu, 278-9
Teshome, Wagaw, 257n
Tessema Ras, 191-3
Tewodros I, Emp., 68, 133
Tewodros II, Emp., 78, 124-43, 255, 339

Thesiger, Wilfred, 197
Tigre, 212-13, 242n
Tigray, 11, 15, 21, 25ff, 57, 65ff, 87, 93ff, 102ff, 112, 120ff, 160ff, 173ff, 194ff, 206-8, 216-17, 239, 248-52, 314ff, 320ff
Tigrinya, 77ff
Tobbiya, 266
Tora Mesk, B., 196
tourism, 265
TPLF, 292ff, 312, 333-4, 338
trade, 15-19, 20-1, 26ff, 45, 65, 73, 83ff, 103, 115, 119ff, 163ff, 172, 176-80, 209ff, 213, 221-22, 245
Transitional Government, 330, 334-38
Trevaskis, G.K.N., 242n, 244-5
Tripartite Pact, 186
Troglodytes, 17-19
Truman Doctrine, 245
Tsadkan, 38, 55
Tsegaye Gebre Medhin, 267
Turkey, Turks, 85ff, 122ff, 163, 194

Ullendorff, Edward, 55n, 56n, 63n, 188, 241n
Unionist Party, 243-4, 274
United Nations, 241ff, 257, 259, 270, 274, 329n
United States, 176-80, 259, 276, 280, 283, 285, 323-7, 330 *See also* America(ns)
USAID, 257, 299, 324

Vietnam, 281
villagization, 310-11, 318
Virgin Mary, 73
Vitalien, Joseph, 185-6
Vlasov, P.M., 174-5

Wafa Yesus, 74, 80
Wag, 44, 47, 51ff, 87, 111, 238
Wagshum Wossen, 238
Walasma Dynasty, 67ff, 83ff, 117
Walwal, 215
Waqo Gutu, 263-4
Watergate, 281
Waugh, Evelyn, 206
Wavell, Archibald, Gen., 230

Wayto, 73
Wazeba, Emp., 31
Webe Shebelle R., 261
Wejerat, 249-51
Weqaw Biru, 204
Weyane, 330
Weyane Rebellion, 239, 248-52
Weyna Dega, 48
wheat, 11, 31
White Engineering Co., 202
Wichale, 160ff
Wingate, Orde, Gen., 230
Wokro, 250
Wokro Meskale Christos, 51
Wolayta, 166, 254
Wolde-ab Wolde Mariam, 274
Wolde Giyorgis, Ras, 173
Wolde Giyorgis Wolde Yohannes, 238, 267
Wole Betul, Ras, 167ff
Woleta Israel Seyum, 208
Wollega, 115, 151ff, 321-2
Wollo, 93, 122ff, 136ff, 150ff, 194, 195n, 282, 286, 319, 322
Wolqayt, 46
Worqeneh, Gebeyehu, 240, 254
Worqeneh Martin, 202
World Bank, 270
World War I, 194-200
World War II, 216
Worqitu, Q., 145
Wossen Seged, K., 128
WPE, 306, 311, 317, 333, 335n
WSLF, 262ff, 295ff
Wube Haile Mariam, 133ff
Wudem Ar'ad, Emp., 60

Yared, 47
Ydlibi, 194
Yeha, 24-7
Yemen(is), 11, 13, 19-21, 33ff, 85ff, 209, 275, 296, 338
Yekuno Amlak, Emp., 57ff
Yejju, 238
Yejju Dynasty, 121ff
Yeshaq, Emp., 64
Yeshimabet Ali, 159
Yimrahana Christos, 51
Yilma Makonnen, 189-90
Yirgalem, 225
Yitbarek, K., 51ff
Yohannes IV, Emp., 144-60, 339

Zabid, 88
Za Dengel, Emp., 94
Zagwe Dynasty, 49ff, 77ff
Zara Yakob, P., 282
Zara Yakob, Emp., 44, 64ff
Zay, 113-14
Zaykov, Lev, 311
Zeila, 45, 65, 83ff, 115, 167-8, 202
Zena Marqos, 65ff
Zenebeworq, 208
Zerihun Yetmgeta, 268
Zewditu Menelik, Empr., 151, 195, 198-200, 205
Zhivkov, Todor, 311
Zhou Enlai, 279
Zimbabwe, 328
Zoskales, K., 18, 28
Zula, 139
Zuqualla, 8-9, 255
Zway, L., 2, 9, 64, 113-14, 152